Solemn Covenant

Solemn Covenant

The Mormon Polygamous Passage

B. CARMON HARDY

UNIVERSITY OF ILLINOIS PRESS
Urbana and Chicago

Library of Congress Cataloging-in-Publication Data

Hardy, B. Carmon.
    Solemn covenant : the Mormon polygamous passage / B. Carmon Hardy
    p. cm.
    Includes bibliographical references and index.
    ISBN 0–252–01833–8 (hard)
    1. Polygamy.   2. Church of Jesus Christ of Latter-day Saints—
Doctrines.   3. Mormon Church—Doctrines.   I. Title.
BX8641.H34   1992
261.8′358423′088283—dc20   91–7203
                                              CIP

To those courageous women and men who, responsive to their leaders and in defiance of a hostile nation, bent bodies and emotions to the assumed redemptive powers of "celestial marriage"—expectant souls whose trial-ridden lives have been too much forgotten by a later generation obedient to a different call.

How infinite are the possibilities of our nature when we reflect that these grave, unrebellious people, the waifs and findings of all lands, many of them dignified in apparel and culture, and steadily ascending in the scale of comfort and possessions, hold still with the tenacity of a moral purpose to the loose and spreading life of polygamy, preferring this fantastic reproduction like the Banyan's branches to the straight and peaceful unity of the European family.

—George Alfred Townsend, *The Mormon Trial at Salt Lake City* (New York: American News, 1871) 11.

Go ye, therefore, and do the work of Abraham; enter ye into my law and ye shall be saved. . . . Abraham received concubines, and they bore him children. . . . David also received many wives and concubines, and also Solomon and Moses my servants, as also many others of my servants, from the beginning of creation until this time; and in nothing did they sin save in those things which they received not of me.

—*D&C* 132:32, 37–38 (1843).

This manifestation of divine light unfolding the purposes of God in the exaltation of His obedient children, making plain the celestial or eternal order of marriage, with endless increase and the extension of the glory of the sons of God, is the most momentous and magnificent unfoldment of the plans, purposes and behests of the Almighty ever brought forth by the great seer of the nineteenth century.

—"Be Not Led Astray by Deceivers," *DN,* 13 Dec. 1879.

From these mountains is to roll the little stone that will bring to pass the purposes of the Almighty and settle this social question by a practical reform in the marriage system.

—Helen Mar Whitney, *Why We Practice Plural Marriage*. . . (Salt Lake City: Juvenile Instructor's Office, 1884), 53.

I hereby declare my intention to submit to . . . [laws forbidding plural marriage] and to use my influence with the members of the Church over which I preside to have them do likewise.

—President Wilford Woodruff, "Official Declaration" (1890).

[Apostle Cowley] told my dad that there was still a way to live polygamy and there were a few select people that he was able to choose to give this opportunity to.

—Elna Hart Palmer, interviewed by Leonard R. Grover, 2 Feb. 1980, p. 14, POHP.

Contents

Illustrations follow page 340.

Acknowledgments

Acknowledgment must be made of those who, in a variety of ways, contributed to the completion of this book. The extent of such debt is quite humbling. This is, above all, true in the case of Victor W. Jorgensen. Not only does the study draw extensively on Victor's research of many years but he participated directly in conceptualizing the book. The work could not have been assembled, and would not have taken its present form, without his contributions. His role was fully that of a collaborator. And, except for Victor's own decision, based on personal considerations, his name would have appeared alongside mine as coauthor of the volume. At the same time, I assume full responsibility for the final product. While every effort has been made to avoid errors and appropriate the subject with accuracy and respect, I alone am at fault if those goals have not been met.

Yet others, in ways often beyond their knowing, have helped by providing critiques and answers to queries. If this is true with all authors, it is more so in this case because of the enormous amount of research occurring in Mormon historical scholarship over the past two decades. While I have attempted, in both text and endnotes, to credit all from whom I have borrowed, it is necessary to specifically thank Thomas G. Alexander, Warren A. Beck, Lowell "Ben" Bennion, Klaus Hansen, Leo Lyman, Gary Shumway, David Whitaker, and Leila Zenderland for reading the manuscript, in whole or in part. The work has benefited immensely from their suggestions for its improvement.

Leonard J. Arrington and those associated with him during the years of his administration of the Historical Department of the Church of Jesus Christ of Latter-day Saints provided assistance of many kinds. Linda Haslam, James Kimball, and Ronald Watt of the Historical Department gave particular aid over many years of research in the church's archives. Ron Romig, Sarah Hallier, and Debbie Stroup of the Library and Archives of the Reorganized Church of Jesus Christ of Latter Day Saints were also generous with help during a visit to their facility. Donald Shaffer provided needed information concerning the Reorganized Church's policies on polygamous converts. Thomas G. Alexander and Jessie L. Embry of the Charles Redd Center for Western Studies at Brigham Young University kindly loaned numerous oral history interviews with Mormon polygamous family members.

Rulon Allred, Newell Bringhurst, Fred Collier, Jessie L. Embry, Rick Grunder, Richard Holzapfel, H. Grant Ivins, Stan Larsen, Shirley Stephenson, Samuel W. Taylor, James T. Thompson, and Guy C. Wilson, Jr., provided a rich sundry of insights over years of conversation and correspondence. Nancy Caudill of the California State University Library at Fullerton obtained countless necessary documents by inter-library loan. Without this valuable service the book could not have been completed. Kelly Donovan, of the Media Center at California State University, Fullerton, kindly gave additional help with the preparation of the tables, the graph, and the listing in Appendix II, all provided by Victor W. Jorgensen. Hiro Yasuda cheerfully gave of his time and expertise in connection with encoding the manuscript on computer, sparing the author untold grief and fits of profanation.

Elizabeth G. Dulany, associate director of the University of Illinois Press, is to be thanked for her early interest in the study and for agreeing to publish it. Cynthia Mitchell, assistant editor at the press, made invaluable suggestions for improving its style and format. Indeed, the University of Illinois Press, by its willingness to produce so many fine works on Mormon history, has made a large and enduring contribution to the remarkable quickening of scholarly examination into Latter-day Saint subjects generally. This study draws liberally on the findings of many of those publications.

Finally, I must recognize my wife, Kamillia M. Hardy. Her interest in the Mormon experience, as keen as my own and arising from a shared heritage in its colorful past, has made for wonderful and unending conversation. Her observations and thoughtful perspectives have unfailingly informed my own. I also acknowledge her patience in waiting for the volume's appearance through years of what seemed an endless gestation.

Again, of course, responsibility for the composition in all its parts is entirely my own.

Abbreviations

BYU	Brigham Young University
Church Archives	Archives and Historical Department, Church Offices Building, Church of Jesus Christ of Latter-day Saints, Salt Lake City, Utah
CHC	Brigham H. Roberts, *A Comprehensive History of the Church of Jesus Christ of Latter-day Saints, Century 1*, 6 vols. (Salt Lake City: Deseret News Press, 1930)
D&C	*The Doctrine and Covenants of the Church of Jesus Christ of Latter-Day Saints* (Salt Lake City: The Church of Jesus Christ of Latter-day Saints, 1982 ed., unless indicated otherwise)
Dialogue	*Dialogue: A Journal of Mormon Thought*
DN	*Deseret Evening News* (the official news organ of the church)
FGS	Family Group Sheet (a family reconstitution, usually by a descendant of the family, normally located in the Family History Library, Salt Lake City, Utah)
FHL	Family History Library, Church of Jesus Christ of Latter-day Saints, Salt Lake City, Utah
HC	*History of the Church of Jesus Christ of Latter-day Saints Period 1. History of Joseph Smith, the Prophet, by Himself*, 2d ed. rev.; 7 vols. (Salt Lake City, Utah: Deseret Book, 1973)
Ivins R of M	Typewritten record of marriages performed by Anthony W. Ivins in Mexico, 1897–1904 (an account of the origin of the record and its locations is provided below, 192n. 10)

JD	*Journal of Discourses by Brigham Young, President of the Church of Jesus Christ of Latter-day Saints, His Two Counsellors, the Twelve Apostles, and others . . . ,* 26 vols. (Liverpool: Franklin D. Richards et al., 1855–1886)
JH	Journal History of the Church of Jesus Christ of Latter-day Saints (multivolume compilation of letter and diary extracts, addresses, news clippings, and typescript accounts of events in the church's history from its beginning to the present, in the Church Historical Department, Church Offices Building, Salt Lake City, Utah)
JMH	*Journal of Mormon History*
Messages	James R. Clark, comp., *Messages of the First Presidency of the Church of Jesus Christ of Latter-day Saints, 1833–1964,* 6 vols. (Salt Lake City: Bookcraft, 1965–1975)
Mill. Star	*Latter-day Saints Millennial Star* ([Manchester]: The Church of Jesus Christ of Latter-day Saints in Great Britain, 1840–1970)
POHP	LDS Polygamy Oral History Project, Charles Redd Center for Western Studies, Brigham Young University, Provo, Utah
Proceedings	U.S. Congress, Senate, *Proceedings before the Committee on Privileges and Elections of the United States Senate in the Matter of the Protests against the Right of Hon. Reed Smoot, a Senator from the State of Utah, to Hold His Seat,* 59th Cong., 1st sess., Doc. no. 486, 4 vols. (Washington, D.C.: GPO, 1906)
RLDS	Reorganized Church of Jesus Christ of Latter Day Saints, as in RLDS Library and Archives, the Auditorium, Independence, Missouri
ROM	Record of Members, being listings by wards of church members, with varying degrees of information about member families, located both in the Library, Church Offices Building, and the Family History Library, Salt Lake City, Utah
SLT	*Salt Lake Tribune*
Trials	*The Trials for the Membership of John W. Taylor and Matthias F. Cowley* (n.p., n.d.) (excerpts from the official minutes of meetings held by the Quorum of Twelve Apostles in February, March, and May

1911, when inquiry was made into the views and polygamous activities of apostles John W. Taylor and Matthias F. Cowley. Because the transcription appears in a variety of formats and with differing pagination, specific page references are not used.)

UHi   Utah State Historical Society, Salt Lake City, Utah

UHQ   *Utah Historical Quarterly*

Introduction

This book is not, in any complete sense, a history of Mormon polyg-amy. There is, for example, no thorough inquiry into the plural mar-riages of the Prophet Joseph Smith. It does, however, describe the inception of the practice, reviewing the influences that contributed to its inspiration. Nor is there an examination of any breadth into the psychological dynamics of the polygamous arrangement. And, except to report the findings of others, the book does not attempt to statis-tically measure the number of Mormons who entered the practice before 1890. These, and other questions appropriate to any full ac-count of the subject, are touched only in passing. The challenge of that comprehensive labor is left to others.

This study began, more narrowly, as an attempt to explain the surprising number of high Mormon authorities who contracted plural unions after church president Wilford Woodruff declared he was at-tempting to bring the practice to an end with his famous Manifesto of 1890. The question arose in connection with an examination of the 1905 expulsion of John W. Taylor and Matthias F. Cowley from the Quorum of Twelve Apostles, a study undertaken by Victor W. Jorgensen and myself, published in the *Utah Historical Quarterly* in 1980. There, part of the evidence used to show that the two were excluded for political reasons also revealed that numbers of other apostles had taken new wives since 1890—the misdemeanor for which Taylor and Cowley were supposedly punished.[1] Contrary to what is commonly stated, President Wilford Woodruff's 1890 Manifesto did not mark the end of officially authorized polygamous marriages in the Mormon church. One is naturally led to ask why this should have occurred. Why would Mormon leaders encumber agreements allow-ing Utah to become a state, risking both their own and their church's

reputations by continuing to marry new plural wives—all the while
denying the fact to the world? To find the answer it was necessary to
retrace the history of Mormonism's best-known institution. This book
is a rehearsal of that exercise.

Not only did polygamy fill special Mormon needs from the beginning of its trial in the 1830s and 1840s, it also brought critical attacks
upon the church. It contributed to the social upheaval in Nauvoo,
Illinois, and became the signature by which Mormons were known to
the world after their removal to the Great Basin. Resistance to national pressures to abandon the practice was the chief reason for early
Mormon colonization in Mexico and Canada. Pretending to discontinue such performances, church leaders authorized new plural marriages within and outside the United States, both before and after
1890. Although it was never a way of life for the majority of Saints,
thousands experienced it firsthand, making it a departure of conspicuous proportions in Western family history.

Plurality of wives was not peculiar to the Mormons, but they gave
the practice a new and exalted status, considering it a prescription for
health, an antidote for immorality, and a key to history and government. Plural marriage, they believed, was a social law, a truth revealed
from heaven. It was for these reasons that they adhered to the practice
so long and with such determination. While eventually successful,
national opposition at first only sharpened Mormon defense of the
doctrine and perhaps prolonged its survival. This book follows the
thread of that survival as far as firm evidence will allow. In addition to
reflecting on the course of the polygamous ideal, including the consequences of dissimulation as a way of preserving it, this work also
describes Mormonism's astonishing transformation into a determined
advocate of the monogamous ethic.

While it is not a major concern of the study, some attention is given
to the rise of Mormon fundamentalism, emphasizing its usefulness as
a reliquary of nineteenth-century Latter-day Saint life. Mormons who
find in fundamentalist organizations a greater faithfulness to the doctrines and practices of the early church are the ideological descendants of adherents who, a century ago, feared those changes that have
become a part of twentieth-century Mormon belief. Conversely, reference will be made to the equivocation that attended others in their
relationship with gentile society and that, through time and trial, led
to the abandonment of polygamy and to those doctrinal formulations
accepted by orthodox Mormons today. All this—the attempt to live
and defend polygamy's domestic configuration, the national crusade
against it, divided efforts to secretly preserve it, and conformity to the

larger society's monogamous way—is what the book is about. It is a study of the rise and decline of an idea and of those sturdy acolytes who tried to preserve it.

Mormon polygamy naturally resists thematic confinement. Because it is descended from man's long and affluent interest in family, sex, and religion, the Saints drank from ancient springs. It is so branching and tantalizing in its implications that boundaries are difficult to draw. Plural marriage in Mormon society was so suffusive that a vigilant attention to my purposes was constantly required. In the midst of the anti-polygamy crusade, a Mormon correspondent to the church's official journalistic voice, the *Deseret News,* defiantly affirmed:

> The abandonment of polygamy, that is considered by some to be so easy of accomplishment, is more untenable even than fighting. However much the people might desire to do this, they could not without yielding every other principle, for it is the very key stone of our faith, and is so closely interwoven into everything that pertains to our religion, that to tear it asunder and cast it away would involve the entire structure.[2]

The statement spoke not only to the difficulty facing those who at that time sought to disentangle plurality from the skein of Mormon belief, but to the problem confronting historians who undertake the task today.

While enormous quantities of ink were expended on the subject in the last century, most writers on both sides were so partisan that one must read their materials with great caution. At the same time, observers like Richard Burton and Thomas B. H. Stenhouse wrote accounts of Mormon polygamy still essential to any researcher on the subject.[3] After the turn of the century, those writing on the Latter-day Saint past, Mormon and non-Mormon alike, seemed less interested in polygamy than in investigating topics like the influence of the frontier on Mormon institutions, political development, or Mormon village life.[4] Polygamy was not forgotten—there were, sometimes, chapter-length treatments of surprising insight[5]—but attention to the subject dramatically declined, especially in the post-Progressive era, from the prominence it enjoyed in the nineteenth century.

Since World War II, beginning with Fawn Brodie's biography of Joseph Smith, plural marriage has acquired renewed historical interest.[6] Brodie's naturalistic approach, combined with an engaging writing style, provoked considerable commentary, and her account of the Prophet Joseph Smith's plural marriages is still cited by students of the subject. Less than a decade later, Kimball Young's *Isn't One Wife*

Enough? appeared.[7] The work was based on extensive research, nearly all of which, unfortunately, was unreferenced in the book itself. The pseudonyms Young employed, however, are identified with a key to be read in his papers located in the Garrett Evangelical Theological Library in Evanston, Illinois—an aid of enormous help but one ignored by most researchers on Mormon polygamy. Two years after Kimball Young's production, Stanley Ivins, who immersed himself in Mormon historical materials of many kinds and had wanted since the 1930s to write a book-length treatment of plural marriage, published his "Notes on Mormon Polygamy."[8] Ivins's use of statistical data created new categories of questions that invited similar studies following the pattern of his investigation. There were also article-length inquiries such as that by Richard Poll which wove the Mormon question into the fabric of antebellum and reconstructionist federal politics.[9] Leonard J. Arrington's 1958 study of the church's material experience, including economic ramifications of plural family life, and Orma Linford's extended account in 1964 and 1965 of legal and juridical responses to the institution both remain enormously helpful resources.[10] And Gustive O. Larson's treatment of the anti-Mormon crusade, despite its strong political interpretation of developments, yet provides a detailed framework for understanding events of the time.[11]

The remarkable outpouring of Mormon historical scholarship dating from the early 1970s was largely commensurate with more liberal policies in the church's historical department and archives, due in great part to the leadership of Church Historian Leonard J. Arrington. Although official policies remained very cautious, significant new work on plurality began to appear. The studies of Lawrence Foster and Louis Kern, both published in 1981, examined the subject from the perspectives of anthropology and psychoanalytic interpretation, respectively. Their placement of Mormon marital experiment in a comparative framework, combined with interdisciplinary emphases, make them especially valuable.[12] The work of Lowell "Ben" Bennion and others, teasing from records not only a clearer understanding of the proportions of the polygamous experience but a more precise sense of its social patterns, is giving the subject long-awaited and helpful illumination.[13] Kenneth Cannon II's 1978 study dealing with continued polygamous cohabitation in the church and the article by Victor W. Jorgensen and me in 1980 on the Taylor-Cowley episode were followed in 1985 by the impressive (one might say daunting) account of post-Manifesto polygamy by D. Michael Quinn.[14]

The next year saw publication of Richard S. Van Wagoner's work, the first book-length overview of polygamy since that of Kimball Young; the heavily researched investigation by Edward Leo Lyman of negotiations leading to Utah statehood; and Thomas G. Alexander's superb account of the transformation of Mormonism into a twentieth-century church, including its abandonment of the practice of plural marriage.[15] One barely had time to finish these before the appearance of Jessie L. Embry's extensive inventory of life in the polygamous household based on hundreds of oral interviews conducted by her and others at the Charles Redd Center for Western History at Brigham Young University.[16] Clearly, if plural marriage suffered from scholarly inattention during the early twentieth century, compensatory efforts are energetically underway in its second half.

The present book, then, is part of a growing trend to restore and bring into clearer focus an American aberration of fascinating significance. Only by granting polygamy its full importance can one explain either gentile hostility aroused against it or Mormon reluctance to give it up. This work stands at odds with those who emphasize consensus as the controlling paradigm in nineteenth-century Mormon history.[17] Rather, it concurs with John Higham, who, writing in another context, said that by subordinating conflict to an "incantation" of common loyalties and triumphs, historical asymmetries disappear altogether.[18] Conscientious attention to charges traded in Mormonism's dispute with the nation over polygamy tells us not only why Saint and Gentile so fiercely quarreled but also much about the contending societies themselves. It helps us better understand, at once, the stubbornness of some in perpetuating the practice after its supposed abandonment and the speed with which others acceded to the nation's monogamous views. This inquiry is an examination of the Mormon-American experience from the perspective of its most fretful difference.

Most of the study is devoted to describing the transformation of Mormonism from a society that idealized polygamy to one that, with equal commitment, now exalts the traditional monogamous home. It was this phase of the Latter-day Saint past, with its internal adjustments and surreptitious attempts to preserve the practice, that first attracted this author's interest. This accounts for what may seem a disproportionate emphasis on the period from 1890 and beyond—the years of plurality's precipitous decline. It is a conscious bias, however, arising from more than the orientations of my own early encounters with the subject. Indeed, historians know that the demise of institutions and value systems is as fascinating as their birth. It is entirely a matter of perspective, or interpretation, whether one describes them as beginnings or as endings.

Some comment is necessary about the title chosen for this book, *Solemn Covenant*. It seemed appropriate because of the profound importance attached to the principle by the nineteenth-century church and because of the covenant-like nature imposed on plural relationships by Mormon theology and ritual. I am aware that the phrase was sometimes employed, especially in the later period of Mormonism's polygamous experience, to refer to plural alliances consummated without an official ceremony.[19] The phrase was never adopted in any formal way, however, and I have used the words because they so aptly communicate the book's chief-most theme—the commanding priority of the polygamous domestic ethic.[20]

An insistence on using *polygyny* as the correct term for what the Mormons professed has acquired some vogue with certain writers. This ignores the fact that there were instances in which polygamy literally describes the marital arrangements some Mormons consummated. But, more than this, I am partial to *polygamy* because so many of the Saints used the term themselves. Throughout the book, *polygamy, plurality, celestial marriage,* and *patriarchal marriage* are used synonymously to mean the marriage of multiple women to a single husband (including those few instances, just referred to, where some women were married to more than one man). This was the connotation given these terms by Mormons in the nineteenth century. When discussing the campaign against polygamy in the 1880s, and again at the time of the magazine crusade against Mormonism during the Progressive period, I will describe how the church altered the phrase *celestial marriage* to mean simply a union for eternity. *Polygamy* and *bigamy* are also used interchangeably to refer to the same illicit act, an approved duplication in legal reference since the eighteenth century.[21]

NOTES

1. Victor W. Jorgensen and B. Carmon Hardy, "The Taylor-Cowley Affair and the Watershed of Mormon History," *UHQ* 48 (Winter 1980): 4–36.

2. An Old Timer, "Expressions from the People," *DN,* 14 April 1885.

3. Richard F. Burton, *The City of the Saints and across the Rocky Mountains to California,* ed. Fawn Brodie (1861; New York: Alfred A. Knopf, 1963); Thomas B. H. Stenhouse, *The Rocky Mountain Saints: A Full and Complete History of the Mormons . . .* (New York: D. Appleton, 1873).

4. In addition to discussion of this in chap. 8, see the materials of Lowry Nelson employed in Carl Addington Dawson, *Group Settlement: Ethnic Communities in Western Canada*, vol. 7, *Canadian Frontiers of Settlement* (Toronto: Macmillan, 1936), 175–272; G. Homer Durham, "A Political Interpretation of Mormon History," *Pacific Historical Review* 13 (June 1944): 136–50; or the unrelieved Turnerian emphases of Milton R. Hunter in works like his *Brigham Young, the Colonizer* (Salt Lake City: Deseret News, 1940); and idem, *The Mormons and the American Frontier* (Salt Lake City: LDS Dept. of Education, 1940).

5. E.g., "Puritan Polygamy," in Morris Robert Werner, *Brigham Young* (New York: Harcourt, Brace, 1925), 280–320; or "Social Implications of Polygamy" in Nels Anderson, *Desert Saints: The Mormon Frontier in Utah* (Chicago: University of Chicago Press, 1942), 390–419.

6. Fawn M. Brodie, *No Man Knows My History: The Life of Joseph Smith, the Mormon Prophet* (New York: Alfred A. Knopf, 1946).

7. Kimball Young, *Isn't One Wife Enough?* (New York: Henry Holt, 1954).

8. Stanley S. Ivins, "Notes on Mormon Polygamy," *Western Humanities Review* 10 (Summer 1956): 229–39. The article was reprinted under the same title in *UHQ* 35 (Winter 1967): 309–21. Ivins's interest in writing a book on polygamy, one he said would probably never be completed, is found in Stanley Snow Ivins Diary, 1 Jan. 1935, Stanley Snow Ivins Collection, UHi.

9. Richard D. Poll, "The Mormon Question Enters National Politics, 1850–1856," *UHQ* 25 (Spring 1957): 117–31; idem, "The Political Reconstruction of Utah Territory, 1866–1890," *Pacific Historical Review* 27 (May 1958): 111–26.

10. Leonard J. Arrington, *Great Basin Kingdom: An Economic History of the Latter-day Saints, 1830–1900* (Cambridge, Mass.: Harvard University Press, 1958); Orma Linford, "The Mormons and the Law: The Polygamy Cases— Part 1," *Utah Law Review* 9 (Winter 1964): 308–70; and idem, "The Mormons and the Law: The Polygamy Cases—Part 2," ibid. 9 (Summer 1965): 543–91.

11. Gustive O. Larson, *The "Americanization" of Utah for Statehood* (San Marino, Calif.: Huntington Library, 1971).

12. Lawrence Foster, *Religion and Sexuality: Three American Communal Experiments of the Nineteenth Century* (New York: Oxford University Press, 1981); and Louis J. Kern, *An Ordered Love: Sex Roles and Sexuality in Victorian Utopias—the Shakers, the Mormons, and the Oneida Community* (Chapel Hill: University of North Carolina Press, 1981).

13. For reference to the work of Bennion and others, see below, chap. 1, n.113.

14. Kenneth L. Cannon II, "Beyond the Manifesto: Polygamous Cohabitation among LDS General Authorities after 1890," *UHQ* 46 (Winter 1978): 24–36. Also see the same author's "After the Manifesto: Mormon Polygamy, 1890–1906," *Sunstone* 8 (Jan.–April 1983): 27–35; Jorgensen and Hardy, "The Taylor-Cowley Affair"; D. Michael Quinn, "LDS Church Authority and New Plural Marriages, 1890–1904," *Dialogue* 18 (Spring 1985): 9–105.

15. Richard S. Van Wagoner, *Mormon Polygamy: A History* (Salt Lake City:

Signature Books, 1986); Edward Leo Lyman, *Political Deliverance: The Mormon Quest for Utah Statehood* (Urbana: University of Illinois Press, 1986); and Thomas G. Alexander, *Mormonism in Transition: A History of the Latter-day Saints, 1890–1930* (Urbana: University of Illinois Press, 1986).

16. Jessie L. Embry, *Mormon Polygamous Families: Life in the Principle* (Salt Lake City: University of Utah Press, 1987).

17. While this issue will receive attention at several points in the chapters that follow, I should indicate that the view that polygamy has been given too much weight in reconstructing Mormonism's past is long standing. See, e.g., Franklin D. Daines, "Separatism in Utah, 1847–1870," *Annual Report of the American Historical Association for the Year 1917* (Washington, D.C., 1920), 333. Later examples are Durham, "A Political Interpretation of Mormon History," 136 passim; all of Paul E. Reimann, *Plural Marriage Limited* (Salt Lake City: Utah Printing, 1974); James B. Allen and Glen M. Leonard, *The Story of the Latter-day Saints* (Salt Lake City: Deseret Book, 1976), 278; Leonard J. Arrington and Davis Bitton, *The Mormon Experience: A History of the Latter-day Saints* (New York: Alfred A. Knopf, 1979), 185.

18. John Higham, "The Cult of the 'American Consensus': Homogenizing Our History," *Commentary* 27 (Feb. 1959): 95.

19. Michael Quinn, for example, uses the term in this way in his "New Plural Marriages," 55–56; and idem, "Beyond the First Presidency: New Plural Marriages in the Church, 1890–1904" (Paper presented before the Sunstone Symposium, Salt Lake City, Utah, 25 Aug. 1990).

20. This was illustrated by Apostle Matthias F. Cowley, who in 1911 told how he always performed polygamous ceremonies only with great "solemnity," without disguise, and with prayer. *Trials.*

21. While the question of the proper use of *polygamy* was raised at the time of the Smoot investigations, in *Proceedings* 2:313–14, its interchangeability with *bigamy*, for legal purposes, has been affirmed again and again. See, e.g., William Blackstone, *Commentaries on the Laws of England*, 4 vols. (Oxford: Clarendon Press, 1765–69), 1:424; William Paley, *The Principles of Moral and Political Philosophy*, 2 vols., 9th rev. ed. (London: R. Faulder, 1793), 1:325; Joel Prentiss Bishop, *New Commentaries on Marriage, Divorce, and Separation as to the Law . . .* , 2 vols. (Chicago: T. H. Flood, 1891), 1:309; G. Keith Nedrow, "Polygamy and the Right to Marry: New Life for an Old Lifestyle," *Memphis State University Law Review* 11 (Spring 1981): 303.

Solemn Covenant

1

The Principle Commenced

In mid-August 1870, from the stand of the new Mormon Tabernacle in Salt Lake City, the yet-remembered Pratt-Newman debate occurred. The Methodist-Episcopal minister John Philip Newman, pastor of the recently completed Metropolitan Church in Washington, D.C., challenged Brigham Young to a debate on the scriptural correctness of plural marriage. Newman's musical voice and grand oratorical manner had lifted him to the level of one of North America's best-known religious spokesmen. He had also, this same year, been appointed chaplain of the United States Senate and was to become "court preacher" to President Grant, Vice President Colfax, Chief Justice Chase, and others.[1] Newman was determined to publicly demonstrate that, from a biblical point of view, Mormon plural marriage had no support. Brigham Young relinquished the task of facing Newman to Orson Pratt, the Mormon apostle and intellectual who, at the time, was the church's chief defender of "the principle."

The exchange was not a turning point in the struggle over polygamy, but it celebrated the contest, adding to an already conspicuous profile. "Never before, in the whole Christian era," said one observer, had polygamy been so elaborately and ably discussed between two divines, and certainly never was a religious debate "so extensively published and read."[2] Naturally, Mormons believed their point of view vindicated. As the same reporter remarked, the overwhelming majority were brought to see, even if against their wishes, that on scriptural grounds the Mormon practice was unassailable.[3] As another Saint put it, "Parson Newman came all the way from Washington to argue that point from the Bible but one of our wise men set him to rights."[4]

In their last volley, as part of his summation, Pratt trumpeted what would remain the Mormon position on polygamy throughout the balance of the century: "Here is the law of God; here is the command of the Most High, general in its nature, not limited, nor can it be proved to be so. There is no [biblical] law against it, but it stands as immovable as the Rock of Ages, and will stand when all things on the earth itself shall pass away."[5] The Saints were certain they had come into possession of the secrets of the Almighty. They had only to practice them. But how had the doctrine found its way into their councils? And, having heard the Word, where did it lead them?

To begin an answer, we must first recognize that polygamous marriage enjoyed support as a sort of underground, counterculture notion from at least the time of the Renaissance. As John Cairncross has shown, the Mormon experiment came at the end, rather than the beginning, of a series of efforts to implement the practice in Western society. The Münster Anabaptists, allowances granted by Luther and Melanchthon to Philip of Hesse, Milton's sympathies for the idea, and the resolution formulated at Nuremberg in 1650 permitting men to replenish losses of the Thirty Years' War by taking two wives are only the better remembered of numerous instances—Latin and Nordic, Catholic and Protestant alike.[6]

By 1730, a full century before Joseph Smith began thinking about it, polygamous advocacy was described as an epidemic.[7] The extent of such talk is chiefly known from treatises written to refute it: Patrick Delany's *Reflections upon Polygamy . . .* (1737) in Great Britain, for example, or Prémontval's *Monogamy; or, Unity in Marriage* (1751–52) on the continent.[8] Delany justified his refutation because, he said, polygamy had become "a doctrine daily defended in common conversation, and often in print, by a great variety of *plausible* arguments."[9] But it was Martin Madan who most thoroughly presented the case for men taking many women to wife. In his *Thelypthora* (1780), not only did he give the patriarchs of the Old Testament exemplary importance but he also claimed there was an absence of any censure of the practice by Christ and his disciples. The restoration of biblical polygamy, along with the Mosaic code, he said, would return discipline to the sexual informality of the age (by requiring, among other things, death for those guilty of adultery), correct a declining population, eliminate abortion, save innumerable women from ruin, and restore men to their rightful, patriarchal role.[10]

The period of the late eighteenth and early nineteenth centuries in American society was one of considerable sexual laxity. In addition to general attitudes of the age, raw, unsettled conditions in the New

West made for a further loosening of moral restraints. The "breezy freedom" Arthur Calhoun found characterizing marriage on the frontier included polygamous arrangements.[11] Plural relationships by the Cochranites, for example, while defended as necessary for raising up a holy race of men, seem chiefly to have been only the result of backwoods informality and lust.[12]

There were also utopian undertakings that, in their commitment to improve society, often seemed set on a disavowal of private property in all its forms, including marital exclusivity. From Ann Lee's followers with their unisexual god and millennial celibacy to Frances Wright and the generous, miscegenous activities urged at Nashoba, American ears were beset by proposals for experiment in male-female relations by a variety of criers.[13] An 1837 correspondent to the *Cleveland Liberalist* repeated the case for polygamy as the most likely method for redressing the excessive number of females. If first wives gave their permission, where was the harm, it was asked, in providing old maids and spinsters with husbands of their own? It would also lessen "ranging about" by men and so diminish prostitution.[14] Whether because of unsettling effects due to socioeconomic mobility or reform proclivities, the times were ablaze with sexual consideration.

As important as anything were Mormonism's own internal dynamics. Wherever inspirationist religion thrives, spiritual license is easily converted to other entitlements.[15] Early Mormonism displayed little of the closely bricked theological edifice it presents today. Many areas of ritual and belief were, if not inchoate, yet under construction. Private communications from Deity were adduced, letters were seen floating from heaven, and magical stones bequeathed special powers on their owners. There is something wonderfully telling about the practice of the prophet's father, Joseph Smith, Sr., who, when presiding at a meeting, would ask all to pray aloud at once, "and there would be as many different prayers as there were persons."[16] Part of what alienated the prophet's disciple Oliver Cowdery was that the church's leadership had "given loose to the enthusiastick."[17] It would be incorrect to classify early Mormonism as entirely antinomian or perfectionist, but the tendencies, rooted in an abundance of new revelation and the conviction that old things were passing away, were clearly present. We should naturally expect that such a pentecost would find an outlet for some of its fires in sexual behavior.

Inherited thought, life on the frontier, and enthusiastic religion do not by themselves, however, fully account for Mormon attitudes toward sex and marriage. A thoughtful search for naturalistic explanations in these matters is closely related to a concern with the origins of

Mormonism generally. And the unfailing tendency since World War II has been not only to broaden the causational network accounting for Mormon beginnings but to seek instruction from comparative and interdisciplinary studies.[18] Paralleling the shift in Jacksonian scholarship from political to social and economic emphases, recent historians focus on uncertainties of the age as especially formative. Early nineteenth-century America was overrun with economic striving, increased competition, and manifestos of sectionalist and individual interest. Religious contest was widespread. Political and sexual egalitarianism pulled at domestic accord. Many believed the traditional family was disintegrating. The disorder, some contend, was the greatest Americans ever have seen.[19] Individualism and pluralism, rapidly acquiring status as national principles, precipitated eager experiments with social restatement. The transformation of Romantic feeling, privacy, and domestic sentiment into the modern American family was, in many ways, an attempt to escape these splintering forces.[20]

Some of the most illuminating explorations of early Mormonism begin with a recognition of such insecurities. Gordon Wood emphasizes Mormon reaction to widespread religious disarray and social disjunction following the American Revolution.[21] Other scholars find in its primitivist-restorationist themes an anti-pluralist resolution.[22] Employing anthropological models, particularly Victor Turner's concepts of "liminality" and "communitas," Lawrence Foster portrays Mormon marital innovation as part of an attempted transition to a new and separate social order. While this had the appearance of license to some, it was, Foster contends, an attempt to formalize relationships in ways less vulnerable to fears of the day. Approaching the question psychoanalytically, Louis Kern points to tensions over reproductive, as opposed to erotic, employments of sex, particularly as they related to the role of women. When subsumed into more general concerns about rampant individualism and its threat to social harmony, the prescribed approach to sexual relationships that often characterized experiment in this area is more easily understood.[23]

Most contemporary scholarship dealing with early Mormon theology and social life explains their evolution as attempts at defining boundaries and exercising control. Responding to the pervasive sense of upheaval, Mormon programs of that time are best seen, in the words of one writer, as expressions of "status anxiety."[24] Students of recent decades give the birth of Mormon institutions a distinctly reflexive, if not conservative, cast. This does not mean that sexual concerns were of lesser interest. However real the preoccupation with order, there was also a sense of emancipation from older ways and the excitement of emotional validation. Even established denominations, as John L. Thomas and William G. McLoughlin observe, sometimes were swallowed up by the Romantic rush for feeling.[25] Latter-day Saints also responded to these challenges, as we will see, with affirmations of masculine preeminence and its reproductive power.

Notwithstanding the Book of Mormon had censured polygamy and concubinage, there is what Brigham H. Roberts long ago said was indisputable evidence that within a year of the book's publication Joseph Smith became convinced plural marriage was a correct principle. This may have resulted from prayerful inquiry by the young prophet while attempting a retranslation of the Bible. Polygamous practices by Old Testament patriarchs probably provoked the petition. Like Martin Madan before him, Joseph attached great importance to the instances of Abraham and others who, with divine sanction, had more wives than one. If Joseph was to restore the priesthood and learning of the ancients, their domestic arrangements could not be ignored.[26]

Near the same time, Joseph also approved intermarriage with Indian women. This was to be done at a future date, he said, to whiten the skins of Indian offspring and make them more "delightsome." The concept did not begin with the Mormons, but neither they nor other Anglo-Americans ever found it an attractive proposition. As one pamphleteer explained, opposing the idea less than a decade before it was embraced by the Mormon prophet, Indian maidens brought too much dirt and bear grease to the bargain to give it much appeal.[27] When later asked how Mormons who were already married were to fulfill such a directive, the prophet is supposed to have said it was to be done in the same way the ancient patriarchs enlarged their households, through polygamy.[28] Beyond the early date of the proposal, it is significant that Joseph looked upon plural marriage as a eugenic instrument.

There is evidence that during the 1830s Smith inaugurated the practice of taking plural wives in his own private life.[29] Although he shared his views on the subject with only a small number, some spoke and behaved too freely. Oliver Cowdery, one of the first of Joseph's disciples, earned the prophet's disapproval for intemperate zeal in the matter. If God's people desired the blessings He wished to bestow, they were not to run before they were sent.[30] Cowdery was not alone. The upheavals that distracted the church in Kirtland, Ohio, nearly to foundering involved, over and again, charges of immorality.

Some of this is known from hearings conducted by the church at the time.[31] It was also the subject of revelation, such as that in 1831 when Joseph was told that adulterers and adulteresses were among the Saints—some known, others yet to be discovered.[32] The prophet said the Mormon reputation was such that, on his way from Kirtland to Missouri, he was asked "a thousand times over and over again" if, among other things, Mormons took more wives than one.[33] Men remembered this early period as one when leaders sometimes behaved in ways that later made them blush. It is hardly surprising that when the Quorum of Twelve Apostles was organized Joseph warned that their greatest trial would be to resist temptations associated with the opposite sex.[34]

One of the things contributing to Mormon difficulty was the liberty taken in formalizing marriage and divorce without civil authority. In the heated atmosphere at Kirtland, it was inevitable that informal alliances would occasionally occur.[35] The leaders themselves, however, solemnized relationships without deputization from the state.[36] As others have suggested, these were less acts of defiance than attempts to resacralize matrimony. The growing incidence in American society of irregularity in marital relations, one non-Mormon commentator of the time said, was traceable to dissolute European theories that held marriage to be no more than a civil contract, subject to repeal whenever parties wished.[37] Beyond discomfort with secularization, the sense of withdrawal from an apostate world and belief that theirs was the authority of heaven allowed Mormons to view their own performances as quite sufficient.[38]

There was, even at this early stage, the idea that marriage was more than a terrestrial arrangement. In 1835 William W. Phelps said that the Saints would learn that men were destined to become archangels and that in heaven "man is neither without the woman, nor the woman without the man." And Parley P. Pratt said that in 1840 the prophet taught him that marital affections and family organization were eternal.[39] These sentiments likely arose from Romantic ideas that were displacing the traditional theocentric empyrean with an increasingly familiar and anthropocentric heaven. As McDannell and Lang have shown, Romantic writers, artists, and visionaries, drawing on a heritage including Milton and Swedenborg, portrayed heavenly inhabitants as men and women whose delights were but an exquisite, more intense version of their human counterparts. Family, sexuality, and the affections were the sacraments of a religion of love—one that was perpetuated in and found its most joyous fulfillment in the hereafter.[40]

Although we cannot be precisely certain at what point various ingredients appeared and were theologically incorporated. the emphasis on sealing couples together for eternity seems to have been one of the last and most mature developments in Joseph's thought. The Mormon concept of sealing and binding in both heaven and earth dates from 1831, but it seems not to have been connected with marriage until the 1840s. As we have seen, the earliest references to plural unions confine explanation to imitation of the ancient patriarchs and refinement of the native race. The idea had special appeal, however, and grew as an integrating element until, by the time Joseph formally dictated on the subject in Nauvoo, Illinois, it dominated nearly everything else.[41] From 1843 until the Saints ceased publicly arguing for it around the turn of the century, polygamy was insisted upon as a logical consequence, an "indissoluble" accompaniment of sealing, as in the case of a remarried widower, when all arose in the resurrection.[42]

It may be that the dynamics of "communitas," discussed by Foster, reached their most expressive phase in the Nauvoo period, especially during the last two years of Joseph's life. A recent study suggests that internal dissensions brought the leaders to crave rituals of assurance—very much the sort of thing involved in plural marriage, with its promises of silence, covenants, and eternal family ties.[43] The principle of sealing men and women together in units immune to change increasingly obsessed the prophet before his death. He preached upon and opened to view the concept of binding men to their ancestors and laid the foundations for living men to adopt one another, leading for a time to a kind of Mormon dynasticism.[44] Plural marriage was closely associated with and a part of this obsession. His secretary, William Clayton, said that during the last year of Joseph's life they were seldom together alone when the prophet did not talk about the subject.[45] As the prophet's nephew later expressed it, the Mormon founder "seemed irresistibly moved" to establish the sealing principle before he died, especially as it affected plural relationships. It became, he said in another context, "the very point-essence and culmination of [Joseph and his brother Hyrum's] . . . life-work and mission."[46]

That contemporary anxieties affected thinking on the subject is evident from a line in the 1831 revelation about marrying Indian women. After approving such unions, it adds: "for even now their [Indian] females are more virtuous than the gentiles."[47] This was further illustrated in a pamphlet apology of 1842 published by Joseph Smith's press in Nauvoo. Authored by Udney Hay Jacob, but undoubtedly reflecting the prophet's own thought, the writing stressed the disheveled condition of the family, the want of affection between many husbands and their spouses, and the loss of patriarchal authority in the home. Men were trampled not only by arrogant wives but by unruly children. Remedies, the piece argued, were to be found in a restoration of male prerogatives, easier divorce for women, and, of course, polygamy.[48]

Rather than helping, Jacob's publication only contributed to growing uneasiness among church members already disturbed by rumors of adultery and "spiritual wifery." Although Smith discontinued publication of the pamphlet, 1842 witnessed increasing outrage over sexual scandal expressed by voices both inside and outside the Mormon community.[49] A knave like John C. Bennett, befriended by the prophet and given civic and ecclesiastical honors, was especially embarrassing when found to have left a trail of sexual adventure through Nauvoo's female society—particularly since Smith had received a revelation in 1841 in which God was supposed to have said that He had "seen the work which he [Bennett] hath done, which I accept if he continue, and will crown him with blessings and great glory."[50] Neither did it help that, after being excommunicated from the church, Bennett published accounts accusing Joseph of sensational indulgences of his own.[51]

If more dramatic, the Bennett affair was far from singular. While the episode was unfolding in the spring of 1842, and for some months after, Nauvoo was convulsed with scandal. One woman told of having sexual relations with several men because she had been led to believe (incorrectly, she confessed) that the church's own leaders countenanced such things.[52] Numbers were brought before the church's councils and "cut off," others "forgiven on confession."[53] Church leaders sermonized against immorality, and ordinances were urged to suppress prostitution.[54] The Mormon capital acquired an unsavory reputation, deserved or not. Defections by members occurred because of it.[55] And inasmuch as Joseph was implicated in some of the indiscretions discovered, a rumor commenced circulating that he was a fallen prophet.[56]

What complicated the situation for Smith was that at least part of what was alleged was true. Not only he but others had embraced the principle of plural marriage and entered its practice.[57] This required that truth be sheltered and, sometimes, violated.[58] There was also the likely impression, as Irene Bates commented, that due to the rapidity with which many excommunicants were reaccepted into the church, their trials seemed only an exercise for appearances.[59] The situation with the Female Relief Society was especially problematic, not only because Joseph had secretly taken some of its leading members as plural wives but because the organization sought to be an implement for suppressing evils like bigamy and adultery, rumors of which were so abundant. And to complicate things further, the prophet's wife Emma, a staunch enemy of such things, was the organization's president.[60]

The problem of distinguishing between sexual interest and religious inspiration in the case of Joseph Smith and his associates is extraordinarily complex. Apart from rumors of his attraction to women, there is implication in Joseph's reported claim to have seen, long before he married them, all his wives in vision. And one need not be a psychoanalyst to recognize the symbolism in Joseph's claim that an angel appeared to him, sword drawn, commanding activity.[61] His advice to William Clayton that, so far as additional wives were concerned, Clayton had a right to all he could get, is also telling.[62] It is not unreasonable to look for the prophet's robust personality to have found some field for expression in relationships with the opposite sex. So far as others are concerned, it is significant that some admitted to personal intimations as to the doctrine's propriety even before Joseph taught them the principle.[63] And, despite insistence that accepting polygamy was a moral trial, one cannot help agreeing with Jan Shipps's observation that, quite soon enough, many came to resemble children suddenly told that eating candy was good for them.[64]

This notwithstanding, Joseph displayed an astonishingly principled commitment to the doctrine. He had to overcome opposition from his brother Hyrum and the reluctance of some of his disciples.[65] Reflecting years later on the conflicts and dangers brought by plural marriage, some church leaders were struck with the courage Joseph displayed in persisting with it.[66] And when one recalls a poignant encounter like that between William Law and Joseph in early 1844, it is difficult not to agree. Law, putting his arms about the prophet's neck, tearfully pleaded that he throw the entire business of plurality over. Joseph, also crying, replied that he could not, that God had commanded it, and he had no choice but to obey.[67]

Because of the commotions secret plural relationships created, Joseph was persuaded in mid-1843 to reduce the revelation on polygamy to writing. Although shown to Emma and others at the time in hopes they would be converted, the document was not made public until 1852 and was not formally included in the Mormon *Doctrine and Covenants* until 1876.[68] Twentieth-century Mormons associate the revelation quite exclusively with the principle of sealing, especially the sealing of monogamous couples for eternity—a tenet about which few, then or now, could become disturbed. Joseph's statement that the 1843 dictation was fixed in his mind from long familiarity cannot mean that it was entirely the same as his 1831 conveyance. All reference to the role of plural marriage as a means for ameliorating the Indian, for example, is absent. Nothing that we know concerning the 1831 statement refers to sealing and eternal family organization. Finally, the later document often alludes to the problems Joseph was currently experiencing with his wife Emma and could not, therefore, predate a period of more than one or two years previous to its issuance. It is clear that the 1843 revelation was a selective accumulation of the prophet's thought on the subject.[69]

That plurality of wives was the most important intent of the communication is clear from the reasons that led Joseph to dictate it. The opening lines expressly indicate that it was an answer to the prophet's inquiry as to why ancient men of God were justified in taking plural wives and concubines. Beyond this, there were the alarmed responses to its reading.[70] And one must take account of the language of the writing itself. Commencing with the examples of Abraham, Isaac, and Jacob, affirming the sealing authority of God's appointed and applying it to marriage for eternity, Joseph was instructed to "do the works of Abraham" and his wife Emma to accept them. The ancient patriarchs had taken wives and concubines "and it was accounted unto . . . [them] for righteousness . . . and they have entered into their exaltation . . . and sit upon thrones, and are not angels but are gods." More than this, the Lord stated that "those who have this law revealed unto them must obey the same."[71]

Whatever accounted for the prophet's decision to dictate on the matter, its portrait of the universe as a field for dominion by the patriarchal family had begun to take form. The capacity the message had for infecting the Mormon imagination is illustrated by the reminiscence of Joseph Holbrook. Farming near Nauvoo, Holbrook knew of Joseph's revelation on polygamy and wished to accept it but hesitated because he could not fully understand the reasons for it. One day, while working in the field, he was overcome with a vision. The heavens opened before him, he said, and he saw endless suns and planets moving in their orbits, vast systems waiting only to be filled and governed. This, a voice told him, was the reward to all eternity for those accepting the principle. Waking from the trance, he was yet cutting grain with his scythe, the rhythm of the task unbroken. But, he said, he never after doubted plurality, expecting its rewards, both for himself and his children, to be an endless exaltation.[72] Clearly, polygamy represented more to the Saints than only an opportunity to broaden their sexual experience. It was integral with their cosmology. So suffusive and grand a principle would not easily be laid aside.

Not all were favored, like Joseph Holbrook, with a presentiment of the doctrine's divinity. And much of the dissent dividing the church in the spring of 1844 dated from refusal to accept the revelation and the obligations enjoined by it.[73] Some of this arose from the sense of betrayal an associate like William Law could feel. Law had previously stood by Joseph, publicly denying rumors of church-sanctioned polygamy.[74] By the spring of 1844, however, the church's leadership was rent with ugliness and accusation. Not only did some refuse to accept the revelation on plural marriage, but charges of adultery and attempted seduction were traded. Violence was threatened. And, feeding on reports of scandal, the non-Mormon press made the most of it. Social structure in Nauvoo was becoming dangerously tangled.[75]

Then, while under indictment from a Carthage, Illinois, grand jury for adultery and polygamy but secure at home and among friends, Joseph was confronted with the publication by several disaffected members of the *Nauvoo Expositor*. Charging the Mormon leader with abuses of power and economic manipulations for private gain, the paper was primarily an attack on the personal morality of the leader and his brother Hyrum, including the revelation about and practice of polygamy. The seduction of young women, the ruination of innocent reputations, and the secrecy of sexual liaisons in the name of religion were all charged. Pleading for repentance by the brothers, asking that the old friendships and old orthodoxies be restored, the *Expositor*'s authors acknowledged the jeopardy they invited by their disclosures but hoped the venture, which promised future evidence in support of their allegations, would be protected by the freedoms of press and religion.[76]

Fearful of the paper's effect if it were permitted to continue, the city council held an extraordinary meeting with Joseph presiding, condemned the publication as a nuisance, and issued an order to wreck the press that printed it. Those responsible for the *Expositor* left town in fear, seeing to it that Joseph and others were charged in Carthage with instigating to riot and destruction of property. After some hesitation and considerable parleying involving Governor Thomas Ford, the prophet with several associates surrendered to authorities in Carthage to await trial. In the late afternoon of 27 June 1844, a mob of assassins with blackened faces stormed the jail, shot Joseph and Hyrum to death, and left John Taylor, one of their companions, terribly wounded.[77] In his account of the angel charging Joseph to move ahead with the principle, Joseph Lee Robinson said the messenger warned the prophet that he would be slain if he delayed with it.[78] An important reason for the murder of the Smiths, ironically, was their forwardness in following the angel's command.

This account admittedly ignores other developmental strains within the early church and other reasons, especially political and economic, for conflict encountered by the Mormon community. Like abolitionists' appropriation of southern slaveholders, criticisms of Mormon sexual thought masked deeper anxieties, especially concerns with power and social order.[79] Without discounting such possibilities, the intent here is only to underline polygamy as a large and significant ingredient. Its treatment has sometimes been given too little attention.[80] This, combined with the enrichments of other investigations, such as the influence of ideas about a literal kingdom of God, the impact of vigilante thinking, or the complicated role of economic interests, sometimes overshadows the disturbing effects of Latter-day Saint marital experiment.[81]

The Mormon trek to the Great Basin was expected to release the Saints from many of the restraints hampering them in Illinois. Looking ahead, Brigham Young said in early 1846, "I hope we will find a place, where no self-righteous neighbors can say that we are obnoxious to them."[82] And after crossing the Mississippi River, Apostle Lorenzo Snow rejoiced that they were free and could at last speak openly about things repressed.[83] These sentiments undoubtedly arose, in part, from anxieties associated with the law. Formally contracted bigamous unions not only contravened the Christian tradition but were illegal in every state to which the Saints had gathered—New York, Ohio, Missouri, and Illinois.[84]

Unfortunately, removal to less settled regions farther west did not dispose of the issue. The widening division between civil and ecclesiastical jurisdictions, begun centuries earlier, had not left the latter in exclusive possession of behavior considered immoral. With secularization of the marriage contract, adultery and polygamy were offenses forbidden not only by churches but by statute and common law. While the journey to the Salt Lake Valley traversed lands politically unorganized, the view of national legislators concerning them could be inferred from the Northwest Ordinance of 1787 and organic provisions for territories carved from the Louisiana Purchase of 1803, where the protective canopy of English common law was affirmed, prohibiting polygamy in what later became Indiana, Illinois, Missouri, and Iowa.[85] And, as will later be demonstrated, not only did bigamous contractions violate the laws of Mexico but, after Mormon settlements in the Great Basin were absorbed by the United States in 1848, the immunity of church members from traditional marital restraints soon became, as Michael W. Homer has shown, the subject of fierce debate. This, combined with national legislation and judicial rulings in following decades, eventually compelled Mormon obedience.[86] In other words, if circumstance and legal agility succeeded in saving most pluralists from the law during the three decades or so following their departure from Illinois, it was not for want of challenge and pointed argument. Even if one grants that during their sojourn across the plains no formal laws existed to prevent them from entering polygamous marriages, it was a brief respite. Contrary to those who contend Mormons were almost never outside the law, so far as plural marriage was concerned, it is probably closer to the fact to say they were seldom within it.[87]

It is doubtful, however, that at the commencement of their migration, the Mormon pioneers were greatly concerned with legal considerations. Rather, with no more than empty prairies and mountains before them, they were sometimes overtaken by such liberty that leaders had to upbraid them for what Wilford Woodruff, reporting a speech by Brigham Young, called their "horedoms."[88] The cramped, poverty-stricken circumstances at Winter Quarters, combined with the inevitable jar on feelings brought by a quickened pace in plural connections, may have precipitated an increased display of pentecostal gifts among women.[89] While it is necessary to distinguish between approved plural contractions and informal excesses on the trail, one cannot read accounts of these things without sensing that sometimes one ran into the other.[90] With all its hardship, there was unquestionably something of the air of emancipation Oscar Handlin discussed as infecting the emigrant experience generally.[91] The Saints' behavior on the way to the Rocky Mountains may have invited the rigor of the Mormon Reformation that swept their settlements in the mid-1850s.[92] Whatever occurred and however one explains it, the practice of plural marriage acquired added momentum among the migrants during their passage west.

The old debate over the intent of the pioneers, whether they were treasonous and secessionist or loyal American frontiersmen, with the correlative issue of how to interpret their kingdom-building activities—as defensive or imperial—is not only long standing but also involves their advocacy of polygamy.[93] The significance of Klaus Hansen's study of early Mormon political theory resides in the secular agenda it contemplated. The formulation of a literal political system to be set in place is less important than the assumptions on which it rested. Mormonism did not propose leaving the world so much as amending it. If millennialism coursed their thought, it did not diminish corrective employments expected of the elect before the event could dawn. The Saints were to be a guidon to others who, acknowledging their priority, would follow and find their places in an inspired temporal frame.[94] Whether in a Fabian or an engagement mood, the Saints always assumed complete victory would eventually be theirs. Terms like *revolution, reform,* and *regeneration,* referring to every aspect of life, including things familial, were used repeatedly to mean, in the words of George Q. Cannon, that they intended to establish *on earth* "a new order of society."[95]

With the public admission in 1852 that they were practicing polygamy, Mormons purposely called the world's attention to their revelation on celestial marriage. Although reports by disgruntled federal officials probably provoked the announcement, it was followed by a vigorous program of apologetics. Regular publications were commenced and lecture halls rented to set forth reasons for the Mormon system of marriage.[96] As David Whittaker has shown, throughout the years Mormonism embraced polygamy most arguments made for the practice are to be found, in embryo at least, in remarks made at the time of the 1852 declaration. This was especially true of Orson Pratt, who spoke in behalf of the practice at its public unveiling and, through his Washington, D.C., publication, the *Seer,* became the source to which defenders often turned when justification was needed.[97]

Not only Pratt but others spearheaded their defenses with insistence that, as a tenet of religion, plural marriage was protected by the United States Constitution. Brigham Young proudly stated he was a Green Mountain boy from Vermont, used to standing on his constitutional rights. He expected, he said, to claim those liberties "in spite of the poor, rotten, political curses" that pretended to enforce them.[98] It was an appropriate concern. The question as to whether plurality could be maintained in the face of unfriendly judicial decisions and hostile legislation, as earlier remarked, increasingly occupied the Saints and was eventually settled only after a period of intense strife.

For moral justification, Mormon spokesmen unfailingly rested their case, first and last, on the commandment God gave their prophet. Deity had spoken. And this was a formidable argument. Ann Eliza Young, who, after leaving Brigham Young, spent years lecturing against the practice, admitted that ignorant and educated alike were intimidated by the daunting effect that appeals to divine tuition carried.[99] Closely related to this was the authority provided by scripture, especially the examples of Old Testament patriarchs. Not only were God's truths unchanging, applicable in every dispensation, but a major theme of Mormon teachings was that they were restoring doctrines lost through the wickedness of men. "The whole Christian world, from Catholicism to the latest of her daughters," said Parley P. Pratt, had "trampled under foot the institutions of heaven, the holy practices of matrimony and family government," and Mormonism was seeking to restore them both in "theory and practice."[100]

Mormon belief in pre-mortal existence also played a part. Spirits by the millions needed to be clothed with flesh before continuing their progress through eternity. Those that were deserving required an appropriate earthly parentage. As Orson Pratt explained: "The Lord has not kept them in store for five or six thousand years past, and kept them waiting for their bodies all this time to send them among the Hottentots, the African negroes, the idolatrous Hindoos, or any other of the fallen nations that dwell upon the face of the earth."[101] Plural marriage would accommodate these legions while enlarging the church's ranks with men and women of character. God introduced the practice, Brigham Young said, to raise up a "royal priesthood."[102] And, as a plural wife of Apostle Moses Thatcher was later remembered to express it, the most choice and elect of all spirits were reserved for birth into polygamous households.[103] Additionally, those so multiplying their progeny would augment their own glory. Heber C. Kimball once boasted that he had "a good many wives and lots of young mustards." These, he calculated, in no more than a century would outnumber the population of the state of New York. And this, he said, was "doing the works of Abraham."[104]

There were also naturalistic claims made for polygamy. Most men world-wide, it was said, were polygamous, thus evincing nature's intent.[105] It was claimed that the number of females so exceeded males that polygamy was necessary to provide the surplus with husbands, homes, and children. Even if the sex ratio were equal at birth, it was held, war and other natural disasters, then believed to be increasing in the earth, assured a larger number of women by the time both sexes were of marriageable age. With the calamities foretold by the prophets, women were expected to flee to Zion, providing an abundance of wives for Mormon Abrahams and Jacobs. John Hanson Beadle wrote in 1870 that there was no quicker way to arouse a Saint's anger than to contend there was prosperity and calm outside Utah. And one was sure to be knocked down, he said, at the suggestion there were yet more men than women in the United States.[106]

Reasoning from nature was logical for the Mormons because of their belief in natural law and the essentially material basis of spiritual as well as terrestrial truths. The practical importance that polygamy carried for the Saints was in evidence from at least as early as their residence in Nauvoo. Benjamin F. Johnson remembered that Joseph Smith taught him that plural marriage was the only means by which prostitution could be eliminated. And Brigham Young said that a United States senator, commenting on Joseph's plural relationships, admitted that if the rest of the country did not adopt a similar system it would soon run to destruction through disease and shortened life spans.[107] Neither did Young forget Joseph's practical intentions with regard to the Indians. Shortly after arriving in the Salt Lake Valley, he said that he intended settling followers among the tribes to have children by them, thereby transforming them into "a white and delightsome people." When Mormon elders balked, Young said if someone would take his place as church president he would show them how to do it.[108]

In 1876 a new edition of the *Doctrine and Covenants* was issued containing Joseph Smith's 1843 revelation on sealing and plural marriage. While the 1852 public announcement had been reprinted a number of times, the 1876 publication constituted an important step, formally placing the principle in the Mormon canon of scripture. The superscript attached to the revelation was also significant. It read: "Revelation on the Eternity of the Marriage Covenant, including Plurality of Wives. . . ." Linkage of eternal marriage and the rite of plurality was clearly inferred. This wording was later changed, substituting "as also" for "including."[109] By placing the revelation in the *Doctrine and Covenants,* the church gave conspicuous recognition to polygamy at a time when it was under increasing attack. And the superscript that was chosen affirmed it as a tenet corporate with that of eternal or celestial family life.

The question of how many Mormons accepted the call and entered the principle has been debated for more than a century. After the Saints were established in the Mountain West and before the movement against polygamy became intense, Mormon authorities and their friends not infrequently indicated the number involved could have been 10 percent or more.[110] After the national crusade against them acquired teeth and Mormon leaders decided to mute their polygamous image, they began insisting that few of their number ever had more wives than one. By counting only polygamous husbands or using other devices, it was said that the number of pluralists amounted to no more than 2 or 3 percent of the church's membership.[111] Of course, critics of Mormonism sometimes exaggerated in the opposite direction.[112] Recent studies suggest that the number of Mormons living in polygamous families between 1850 and 1890, while varying from community to community and year to year, averaged between 20 and 30 percent. In some cases the proportion was higher. The practice was especially extensive with Mormon leaders, both locally and those presiding over the entire church. These calculations would indicate that, during the entire time the principle was practiced, the number of men, women, and children living in polygamous households amounted to tens of thousands. This was an awesome phalanx—one that confronted Western society with what was, perhaps, the most serious challenge to traditional family life in centuries.[113]

There can be little doubt that, for the majority of participants, plural family life was a large hardship, especially for women. It had the effect, said Joseph Lee Robinson, of nearly tearing "their heart strings out."[114] In 1860 Brigham Young told how he was often required to listen to accounts of sorrow associated with the institution that were, in his words, like "drinking a cup of wormwood."[115] We also know that divorce in such families was more extensive than heretofore believed and that at least some of the difficulty resulted from an absence of guidelines in such things as courtship and allocation of family resources.[116] Apostle Amasa M. Lyman recollected that the Saints were unprepared for plural family life and that it took some time to get used to it. But, he said, "we obeyed the best we knew how, and no doubt, made many crooked paths in our ignorance."[117] For this reason, Orson Pratt urged the Saints to do all they could to purge from their own and their children's memories knowledge of Christian marital tradition.[118] Monogamous expectations persisted, however. And this, combined with the example and urgings of the surrounding society, left an indelible print on the Mormon mind. When one adds to this the stress accruing from national campaigns against the practice, it is astonishing that Mormon plurality worked as well as it did.

Quite apart from leaders who, in the interest of policy, pleaded the superiority of the arrangement, some scholars have found Mormon polygamy not only to have been reasonably workable as a family system but to have offered distinct advantages. Women, for example, enjoyed a degree of independence exceeding that of their monogamous counterparts. There was also an unusual measure of social and affective reinforcement for children.[119] Whatever one's judgment of how polygamy worked, any review of the diaries and memoirs of those participating in it leaves one with a sense of extraordinary dedication.

The challenges of subsistence on the frontier, added to complications arising from life in plural households, confronted the faithful with severe trials. Some marriages did not survive. Those that did provide remarkable examples of nobility and self-denial.

Efforts by the twentieth-century church to gray its memory of polygamy, combined with those who emphasize that only a minority of church members ever entered the principle, portray plural marriage as incidental to the major thrust of the Latter-day Saint past. At the hands of such writers, the attempted cessation of the practice at the turn of the century also loses much of its significance as a transformation of pivotal importance in Mormon life.[120] While Mormon history is unquestionably amenable to a consensus interpretation, providing greater parallelism between the two centuries of its existence, much of what gave life among the Saints its distinctive character arose directly from things like plural marriage. George Q. Cannon once said it was a doctrine purposely revealed by God to bring His followers into conflict with the rest of the world and its established beliefs.[121] Church spokesmen were earnest in saying the revelation on polygamy constituted the most significant truth given by God to man; that it was the family order of heaven; that sealing authority and plural marriage were indissolubly bound together; that it would regenerate mankind, nurture a superior civilization, and eliminate sexual wickedness. Some believed that failure to implement the doctrine would delay the Second Coming of Christ. Thousands looked upon its practice as "the chief corner stone" of the work.[122]

Arguments for its importance, both spiritual and social, had to loom conspicuously in the minds of faithful Latter-day Saints. Need to practice the doctrine was intoned at every opportunity. Apart from sermons to adult congregations, children were told to emulate their polygamous leaders. At a gathering that included Eliza R. Snow and Zina D. H. J. Young in 1874, the audience was told that any wishing to see wives of the Prophet Joseph Smith then had an opportunity in the instances of those two women. They were then recommended to the young people as models. "The young girls could be like her [Eliza R. Snow], and the boys could become like Brother Brigham."[123]

To say that a majority of Mormons defied the church by abstaining is not enough. When the doctrine was carried out secretly, as at Nauvoo and after 1890, there was undoubtedly greater agreement between what was commonly believed and what was publicly professed. After their arrival in the Great Basin, however, when the principle was not only practiced openly but given the imprimatur of church leaders, assessing its impact on Mormon society requires more than simply tallying the number who actually practiced it. We must reckon with the conflict that surely attended a conscientious believer's hesitation. In 1883 Apostle Erastus Snow referred to those who, claiming to accept the principle, searched for excuses to escape it.[124] Addressing the same question, Orson Pratt said that, while he had encountered only a few who did not believe in the doctrine, the consciences of all should keep them from turning away from it. Not only was it commanded, with a penalty of damnation affixed to its rejection, but one could not, he said, rightfully call himself a Latter-day Saint without accepting and practicing polygamy.[125] President John Taylor publicly censured those who tried to find a way around it, saying that Mormon monogamists needed to look to the church's polygamists for direction.[126] With this kind of emphasis, reinforced by the hygienic arguments we will later see were adduced in its behalf, there had to be considerable self-examination, if not torment, by those who remained aloof. The man with one wife could not but notice that God chose His leaders most often from those who had two or more. We should not underestimate the power of the elite for establishing standards and creating expectations in any organization. In the authoritarian milieu of early Mormonism, theirs was an even greater influence.

The year preceding the Pratt-Newman debate witnessed completion of the transcontinental railroad, with ceremonies marking the event at Promontory, Utah. Although Mormons had favored the project, Brigham Young declaring that the locomotive would, at once, make the emigration of converts and the departure of apostates easier, it did more to hasten the demise of polygamy than the Reverend Newman and all his fellow spokesmen put together.[127] If it was an exaggeration for William Hepworth Dixon to say that "a railway train has done it all," he was not entirely incorrect.[128]

Edward W. Tullidge, a Mormon of vacillating faith but keen insight, saw this six months before the final spike was driven. Standing in Salt Lake City, watching the stringing of telegraph wires through the town, he told of remarking to a companion (who was himself): "Thank God Edward for that," he said. "Thank God, Edward, we are going into the days of telegraphs and railroads." Tullidge's imaginary respondent answered that, rather than a blessing, it meant only that the Gentile would sooner be upon them. Tullidge countered, however, that there could be no real threat from progress. What was more, "that which brings Washington nearer to us will bring us nearer to Washington." Then, again turning the argument, he repeated the fear that the railroad would soon bring "ten thousand Gentiles here to hurt us." But no, yet reflecting, he said: "Rather let ten thousand gentlemen come up to do us good."[129]

Tullidge's monologue, with its suspicion that those of contrary views might actually elevate Mormon society, betrayed an equivocal seam that would mark the Saints for decades to come.

NOTES

1. James R. Joy, "John Philip Newman," *Dictionary of American Biography,* ed. Dumas Malone, 10 vols. (New York: Charles Scribner's, 1927–36), 7:464–65.

2. Edward Wheelock Tullidge, *History of Salt Lake City* (Salt Lake City: Star Printing, 1886), 479.

3. Ibid., 479.

4. Margery W. Ward and George S. Tanner, eds., *A Fragment: The Autobiography of Mary Jane Mount Tanner* (Salt Lake City: Tanner Trust Fund and University of Utah Library, 1980), 168.

5. *The Bible and Polygamy: Does the Bible Sanction Polygamy? A Discussion between Professor Orson Pratt . . . and Rev. Doctor J. P. Newman . . .* (Salt Lake City: Deseret News, 1877), 56.

6. John Cairncross, *After Polygamy Was Made a Sin: The Social History of Christian Polygamy* (London: Routledge & Kegan Paul, 1974). For an account of Lutheranism's early struggle with the question, as well as a review of the Anabaptist experiment at Münster, approval of the practice after the Thirty Years' War, and treatment of the matter at the Council of Trent, see William Walker Rockwell, *Die Doppelehe Des Landgraffen Philipp Von Hessen* (Marburg: N. G. Elwert'sche Verlagsbuchhandlung, 1904), 6–19, 78–92, 155–22, 279–83, 308–9.

7. Cairncross, *After Polygamy Was Made a Sin,* 141.

8. [Patrick Delany], *Reflections upon Polygamy, and the Encouragement Given to That Practice in the Scriptures of the Old Testament . . .* (London: J. Roberts, 1737); André Pierre le Guay de Prémontval, *La monogamie; ou, l'unité dans le marriage . . . ,* 3 vols. (The Hague: P. van Cleef, 1751–52).

9. [Delany], *Reflections upon Polygamy,* 1.

10. [Martin Madan], *Thelypthora; or, A Treatise on Female Ruin . . . ,* 3 vols. (London: J. Dodsley, 1780–81). The best-known answer to Madan was James Cookson, *Thoughts on Polygamy, Suggested by the Dictates of Scripture, Nature, Reason, and Commonsense . . .* (Winchester: John Wilkes, 1782). But also see Richard Hill, *The Blessings of Polygamy Displayed, in an Affectionate Address to the Rev. Martin Madan . . .* (London: J. Matthews, 1781). William Paley devoted an entire chapter to refuting the practice in *The Principles of Moral and Political Philosophy,* 2 vols., 9th rev. ed. (London: R. Faulder, 1793), 1:319–25.

11. Outdated in other matters, Arthur W. Calhoun's work is quite accurate

in this regard. See his *A Social History of the American Family from Colonial Times to the Present,* 3 vols. (Cleveland, Ohio: Arthur H. Clark, 1917–19), 1:320, 2:35, 40 passim.

12. S. Bulfinch Emmons, *Philosophy of Popular Superstitions and the Effects of Credulity and Imagination upon the Moral, Social, and Intellectual Condition of the Human Race* (Boston: L. P. Crown, 1853), 92–94.

13. For general accounts of the socioreligious turbulence sweeping antebellum American society, see Alice Felt Tyler, *Freedom's Ferment: Phases of American Social History from the Colonial Period to the Outbreak of the Civil War* (1944; New York: Harper Torchbook, 1962); Whitney R. Cross, *The Burned-Over District: The Social and Intellectual History of Enthusiastic Religion in Western New York, 1800–1850* (1950; New York: Harper Torchbook, 1965); C. S. Griffin, *The Ferment of Reform, 1830–1860* (New York: Thomas Y. Crowell, 1967); and Ronald G. Walters, *American Reformers, 1815–1860* (New York: Hill & Wang, 1978). A recent review of relevant scholarship is provided in Lillian Wellman, "Crossing over Cross: Whitney Cross's *Burned-Over District* as Social History," *Reviews in American History* 17 (March 1989): 159–74.

14. "Enquirer," *Cleveland Liberalist* 1 (4 Feb. 1837): 164.

15. This was the observation of Ernest R. Sandeen, "John Humphrey Noyes as the New Adam," *Church History* 40 (March 1971): 87. Also see Judith Fryer, "American Eves in American Edens," *American Scholar* 44 (1974–75): 80.

16. The description of Joseph Smith, Sr.'s prayer habits was remembered in a sermon by Brigham Young. *JD* 6:42 (1857). It was the broad indulgence in gifts of the spirit by Mormons and Irvingites that constituted so much of the criticism made of both by Émile Guers throughout his *L'Irvingisme et le mormonisme: jugés par la Parole de Dieu* (Geneva: Emile Beroud, 1853).

17. Oliver Cowdery to Warren Cowdery and Lyman Cowdery, 4 Feb. 1838, Oliver Cowdery Letterbook, Henry E. Huntington Library, San Marino, Calif.

18. Two excellent essays that survey this tendency are Jan [JoAnn Barnett] Shipps, "The Prophet Puzzle: Suggestions Leading toward a More Comprehensive Interpretation of Joseph Smith," *JMH* 1 (1974): 3–20; and Thomas G. Alexander, "The Place of Joseph Smith in the Development of American Religion: A Historiographical Inquiry," ibid. 5 (1978): 3–17.

19. The author is especially indebted to the chapters "The Era of the Common Man," "The 'Copartnership of Marriage,'" and "Social Uses of Religion" in Rowland Berthoff, *An Unsettled People: Social Order and Disorder in American History* (New York: Harper & Row, 1971), 177–203, 204–17, 235–53. Also see Edward Pessen, *Jacksonian America: Society, Personality, and Politics,* rev. ed. (Homewood, Ill.: Dorsey, 1978), 77–100 passim; and Michael Feldberg, *The Turbulent Era: Riot and Disorder in Jacksonian America* (New York: Oxford University Press, 1980), 5–6 passim.

20. Regarding formative influences on the modern American family in the early and mid-nineteenth century, see John Lukacs's exploration of the idea

of "interiority" in his "Bourgeois Interior," *American Scholar* 39 (Autumn 1970): 616–30; Edward Shorter, *The Making of the Modern Family* (New York: Basic Books, 1975), 227–44; Carl N. Degler, "The Emergence of the Modern American Family," in his *At Odds: Women and the Family in America from the Revolution to the Present* (New York: Oxford University Press, 1980), 3–25; and Stephanie Coontz, *The Social Origins of Private Life: A History of American Families, 1600–1900* (London: Verso, 1988), 210–31.

21. Gordon S. Wood, "Evangelical America and Early Mormonism," *New York History* 61 (Oct. 1980): 358–86.

22. See "Soaring with the Gods: Early Mormons and the Eclipse of Religious Pluralism," in Richard T. Hughes and C. Leonard Allen, *Illusions of Innocence: Protestant Primitivism in America, 1630–1875* (Chicago: University of Chicago Press, 1988), 133–52; and the chapter "Social Disorder and the Resurrection of Communal Republicanism among the Mormons," in Kenneth H. Winn, *Exiles in a Land of Liberty: Mormons in America, 1830–1846* (Chapel Hill: University of North Carolina Press, 1989), 40–62. Also see Gordon Pollock, "In Search of Security: The Mormons and the Kingdom of God on Earth, 1830–1844" (Ph.D. diss., Queen's University, 1977). For Mormon primitivism, see Marvin S. Hill, "The Role of Christian Primitivism in the Origin and Development of the Mormon Kingdom" (Ph.D. diss., University of Chicago, 1968); the same author's discussion of the New York origins of the church's primitivist, anti-pluralist doctrines in "The Shaping of the Mormon Mind in New England and New York," *BYU Studies* 9 (Spring 1969): 351–72; and especially his *Quest for Refuge: The Mormon Flight from American Pluralism* (Salt Lake City: Signature Books, 1989).

23. Lawrence Foster, *Religion and Sexuality: Three American Communal Experiments of the Nineteenth Century* (New York: Oxford University Press, 1981), 3–18, 123–28, 226–47 passim; Louis Kern, *An Ordered Love: Sex Roles and Sexuality in Victorian Utopias—The Shakers, the Mormons, and the Oneida Community* (Chapel Hill: University of North Carolina Press, 1981), 137–204. Foster and Kern reviewed each other's books, especially as they related to Mormonism, in "Three Communities—Two Views," *Dialogue* 14 (Winter 1981): 204–12.

24. Geoffrey F. Spencer, "Anxious Saints: The Early Mormons, Social Reform, and Status Anxiety," *John Whitmer Historical Association Journal* 1 (1981): 43–53. Also see Mario De Pillis, "The Quest for Religious Authority and the Rise of Mormonism," *Dialogue* 1 (Spring 1966): 68–88; Marvin S. Hill, "Quest for Refuge: An Hypothesis as to the Social Origins and Nature of the Mormon Political Kingdom," *JMH* 2 (1975): 3–20; Peter Crawley, "The Passage of Mormon Primitivism," *Dialogue* 13 (Winter 1980): 26–37; and Klaus J. Hansen, *Mormonism and the American Experience* (Chicago: University of Chicago Press, 1981), 163–64. Michael Guy Bishop sees the church's best-known features, those relating to family life and vicarious work for departed ancestors, as rituals designed to secure the Saints against instability and death.

"The Celestial Family: Early Mormon Thought on Life and Death, 1830–1846" (Ph.D. diss., Southern Illinois University, 1981).

25. John L. Thomas, "Romantic Reform in America," *American Quarterly* 17 (Winter 1965): 656–81; William G. McLoughlin, *Revivals, Awakenings, and Reform: An Essay on Religion and Social Change in America, 1607–1977* (Chicago: University of Chicago Press, 1978), 112–40.

26. Disapproval of polygamy was expressed in the following passages from the Book of Mormon: Jacob 1:15, 2:23–35, 3:5; Mosiah 11:2, 4:14; Ether 10:5. Also see *D&C* 42:22 (1831), 49:16 (1831), and 101:4 (1835 ed.). For Brigham H. Roberts's statement, see his introduction to *HC* 5:xxix. More recent investigations into the origin of the doctrine under Joseph Smith, dating at least as early as 1831, can be found in Max H. Parkin, "The Nature and Cause of Internal and External Conflict of the Mormons in Ohio between 1830 and 1838" (M.A. thesis, BYU, 1966), 163–64; idem, "Kirtland, A Stronghold for the Kingdom," in *The Restoration Movement: Essays in Mormon History,* ed. F. Mark McKiernan, Alma R. Blair, and Paul M. Edwards (Lawrence, Kans.: Coronado, 1973), 72; Kenneth W. Godfrey, "The Coming of the Manifesto," *Dialogue* 5 (Autumn 1970): 11–12; Danel W. Bachman, "A Study of the Mormon Practice of Plural Marriage before the Death of Joseph Smith," (M.A. thesis, BYU, 1975), 56–58, 61–73; idem, "New Light on an Old Hypothesis: The Ohio Origins of the Revelation on Eternal Marriage," *JMH* 5 (1978): 19–32, in which the possibility of certain New Testament passages on marriage having precipitated Smith's inquiries is also explored. The entire early period of Joseph Smith's experimentation with plural marriage is reviewed in Richard S. Van Wagoner, *Mormon Polygamy: A History* (Salt Lake City: Signature Books, 1986), 1–25.

27. Thomas Cooper, *Strictures Addressed to James Madison on the Celebrated Report of William H. Crawford, Recommending the Intermarriage of Americans with the Indian Tribes* (Philadelphia: J. Harding, 1824), 1–13. A century before, William Byrd of Virgina had advocated "blanching" the Indian by intermarriage but admitted, for the same reasons given by Cooper, that such a plan required "a very strong appetite." William Byrd, *History of the Dividing Line betwixt Virginia and North Carolina Run in the Year of Our Lord 1728,* in *The Prose Works of William Byrd of Westover: Narratives of a Colonial Virginian,* ed. Louis B. Wright (Cambridge, Mass.: Harvard University Press, 1966), 218, 221–22. The perception of native Americans as degenerate, as worshippers of the devil, and "filthy" accounted for most of the programs launched to ameliorate them. See Roy Harvey Pearce, "'The Ruines of Mankind,'" *Journal of the History of Ideas* 13 (April 1952): 200–217; idem, *Savagism and Civilization: A Study of the Indian and the American Mind,* rev. ed. (Baltimore: Johns Hopkins University Press, 1965); and Francis Jennings, *The Invasion of America: Indians, Colonialism, and the Cant of Conquest* (New York: W. W. Norton, 1976), 15–16, 43–57.

28. For discussion of the 1831 revelation on marriage to Indian women, as

well as the prophet's later explanation to a follower that it was to be accomplished through polygamy, see Bachman, "A Study," 61–73; idem, "New Light," 22n.11; and Godfrey, "The Coming of the Manifesto," 11–12. Questions concerning William W. Phelps's recollections, the basis for Joseph's approval of *polygamous* intermarriage with the Indians, are explored in Van Wagoner, *Mormon Polygamy*, 3–4n.2. Also see Foster, *Religion and Sexuality,* 299n.29. A printed copy of the 1831 revelation is available in Fred C. Collier, comp., *Unpublished Revelations of the Prophets and Presidents of the Church of Jesus Christ of Latter-day Saints,* Vol. 1 (Salt Lake City: Collier's, 1979), pt. 10:57–58.

29. Benjamin Franklin Johnson to George F. Gibbs, 1903, pp. 9–10, Church Archives. Albeit, Oliver Cowdery's description of Smith's relationship with Fanny Alger as "a dirty, nasty, filthy affair" hardly qualifies as marriage. Oliver Cowdery to Warren Cowdery, 21 Jan. 1838, Oliver Cowdery Letterbook, Henry E. Huntington Library, San Marino, Calif. Also see Donald Q. Cannon and Lyndon W. Cook, eds., *Far West Record: Minutes of the Church of Jesus Christ of Latter-day Saints, 1830–1844* (Salt Lake City: Deseret Book, 1983), 167–68. For further discussion of Joseph's early marriages, see Fawn M. Brodie, *No Man Knows My History: The Life of Joseph Smith, the Mormon Prophet,* rev. ed. (New York: Alfred A. Knopf, 1971), 301–2; Parkin, "The Nature and Cause," 162–77; Bachman, "New Light," 28–32; James B. Allen and Glen M. Leonard, *The Story of the Latter-day Saints* (Salt Lake City: Deseret Book, 1976), 170–71.

30. "Chapters from the History of the Church," *Mill. Star* 39 (9 April 1872): 236. Also see the recollections of Brigham Young, as recorded in *Diary of Charles Lowell Walker,* ed. A. Karl Larson and Katherine Miles Larson, 2 vols. (Logan, Utah: Utah State University Press, 1980) 1:349, 26 July 1872; and Joseph F. Smith in *JD* 20:29 (1880). The most extensive accounts are in Parkin, "The Nature and Cause," 169–73; and Bachman, "A Study," 76–79. But cf. Foster, *Religion and Sexuality,* 300n.35.

31. In a perceptive essay on sexual attitudes in American society at the time, Professor Klaus Hansen questioned the significance of such concerns among Mormons prior to the death of Joseph Smith. His conclusion was partly based on a failure to locate more than a very few trials in which members were disciplined for sexual misconduct, as noted in the official *History of the Church.* See his *Mormonism and the American Experience,* 150–55. Not only is there question as to how many disputes involving sex were preserved in published Mormon accounts, a problem Hansen acknowledges, but there is the added consideration that such cases were sometimes masked by phrases like "unchristian conduct." There were also instances in which men and women were simply counseled or reproved or an accusation was heard, without formal disfellowshipping or excommunication. See, e.g., for the Kirtland and Missouri periods only, Lyndon W. Cook and Milton V. Backman, Jr., eds., *Kirtland Elders' Quorum Record, 1836–1841* (Provo, Utah: Grandin, 1985), 35, 49, 50–51, 55–56; *HC* 2:16, 139–40, 284–85, 442, 444, 511; *HC* 3:26, 31;

and Scott G. Kenney, ed., *Wilford Woodruff's Journal*, 9 vols. (Midvale, Utah: Signature Books, 1983–85), 1:94–95, 10 Sept. 1836.

32. *D&C* 63:14 (1831). Also see *D&C* 101:2, 6 (1831), and 101:4 (1835 ed.). It was the warning given by the prophet to William E. M'Lellin, in *D&C* 66:10 (1831), not to engage in adultery, "a temptation with which thou hast been troubled," that led William Alexander Linn, after reviewing Smith's own activities, to cynically ask, "Could religious bouffe go to greater lengths?" *The Story of the Mormons: From the Date of Their Origin to the Year 1901* (New York: Macmillan, 1902), 274.

33. Joseph Smith, in *Elders Journal* 1 (Nov. 1837): 28–29. Also see the various references contained in Stanley S. Ivins, "Some of the Comments on Mormon Marriage Customs Appearing in Print before 1852," unpublished compilation, box 11, fd. 9, Stanley Snow Ivins Collection, UHi.

34. See comments and recollections in *JD* 23:193 (Lorenzo Snow/1883); *JD* 4:170 (Heber C. Kimball/1857); *JD* 7:114 (George A. Smith/1858); *JD* 8:55 (Brigham Young/1860); the findings of Parkin, "The Nature and Cause," 166–73, 248–55; and Bachman, "A Study," 32, 75–86.

35. See, e.g., the case mentioned in *HC* 2:511.

36. *HC* 2:377; "History of Brigham Young," *Mill. Star* 27 (7 Jan. 1865): 6; and the case of Lydia Bailey and Newell Knight, discussed in Bachman, "New Light," 31–32.

37. Sereno Edward Dwight, *The Hebrew Wife; or, The Law of Marriage Examined in Relation to the Lawfulness of Polygamy and to the Extent of the Law of Incest* (New York: Leavitt, Lord; Boston: Crocker & Brewster, 1836), 54.

38. Foster, *Religion and Sexuality*, 135–36. Also see M. Guy Bishop, "Eternal Marriage in Early Mormon Marital Beliefs," *Historian* 53 (Nov. 1990): 77–88.

39. William Wines Phelps, "Letter No. 8," *Latter Day Saints' Messenger and Advocate* 1 (June 1835): 130; Parley Parker Pratt, *The Autobiography of Parley P. Pratt . . . Edited by His Son, Parley P. Pratt* (1874; Salt Lake City: Deseret Book, 1985), 259–60.

40. See the entire chapter "Love in the Heavenly Realm" in Colleen McDannell and Bernhard Lang, *Heaven: A History* (New Haven: Yale University Press, 1988), 228–75. These ideas also found agreement in Thomas Dick's description of the universe as filled with habitable globes and planets. See his *Philosophy of a Future State* (New York: R. Schoyer, 1831).

41. At least one woman later testified that the initial ceremony by which she was united to Joseph did not employ the language of a sealing formula. See the description of Emily D. Partridge Young in *The Reorganized Church of Jesus Christ of Latter Day Saints, Complainant. vs. The Church of Christ at Independence, Missouri . . . Complainant's Abstract* (Lamoni, Iowa: Herald Publishing House, 1893), 364. Nevertheless, testimony was given at the same time that plurality and sealing made their appearance together in Nauvoo and that *sealing*, as much or more than *plural marriage*, was the term used to connote a

polygamous union. See ibid., 386, 399, 406, 470. Van Wagoner provides a discussion, with examples, of the ways used and possible justifications employed by Joseph Smith when approaching women as plural partners. *Mormon Polygamy*, 27–46. Regarding the 1831 origin of the concept of sealing, see David John Buerger, "'The Fulness of the Priesthood': The Second Anointing in Latter-day Saint Theology and Practice," *Dialogue* 16 (Spring 1983): 12–16. The emergence of Mormon temple ordinances, including the use of sealing, is described in idem, "The Development of the Mormon Temple Endowment Ceremony," *Dialogue* 20 (Winter 1987): 34–76; and Andrew F. Ehat, "Joseph Smith's Introduction of Temple Ordinances and the 1844 Mormon Succession Question" (M.A. thesis, BYU, 1981), 52–65.

42. See, e.g., the reminiscence of Brigham Young's July 1843 discussion with a professor from a southern university in "Chapters from the History of the Church," *Mill. Star* 34 (19 March 1872): 181. Also see Pratt, *Seer* 1 (April 1853): 58; *JD* 3:125 (Heber C. Kimball/1855); *JD* 18:55 (Orson Pratt/1877); "Discourse by President Geo. Q. Cannon," *DN*, 12 Jan. 1884; "Discourse by Apostle George Teasdale," *DN*, 26 Jan. 1884; "Discourse by Elder Henry W. Naisbitt," *DN*, 28 March 1885. For the argument that sealing, rather than polygamy, was the definitive principle, see all of Bishop, "Eternal Marriage."

43. Kathryn M. Daynes, "Family Ties: Belief and Practice in Nauvoo," *John Whitmer Historical Association Journal* 8 (1988): 63–75.

44. See Joseph's sermons as reported in *HC* 6:183, 249–54. Also see the comments of Brigham H. Roberts in *HC* 5:xxviii-xxix. Jan Shipps pointed out that, in the last year or two of his life, Joseph relied increasingly on those men who accepted and were practicing the principle of plural marriage. See her "Mormons in Politics," 134–35. Both Quinn and Bishop have drawn attention to plurality's usefulness for cementing hierarchical networks. Dennis Michael Quinn, "The Mormon Hierarchy, 1832–1932: An American Elite" (Ph.D. diss., Yale University, 1976), 74–75; Bishop, "The Celestial Family," 23, 30. The best treatment of the practice of adoption is that of Gordon Irving, "The Law of Adoption: One Phase of the Development of the Mormon Concept of Salvation, 1830–1900," *BYU Studies* 14 (Spring 1974): 291–314. While the Quorum of the Anointed established by Joseph Smith in 1843 had other purposes, it may have reflected the need, Mason-like, to bind men and women together in units in which special ceremonies could be performed in confidence. For an account of the beginnings and history of such gatherings, see D. Michael Quinn, "Latter-day Saint Prayer Circles," *BYU Studies* 19 (Fall 1978): 79–105.

45. William Clayton's Testimony, 16 Feb. 1874, in Andrew Jenson, "Plural Marriage," *Historical Record* 6 (May 1887): 226.

46. Joseph F. Smith, as quoted by Brigham H. Roberts in *Outlines of Ecclesiastical History*, 2d ed. (Salt Lake City: George Q. Cannon & Sons, 1895), 431; and Joseph F. Smith to Joseph Smith III, 3 May 1889, P22, fd. 47, RLDS Library and Archives, Independence, Mo.

47. Collier, *Unpublished Revelations*, pt. 10:58.

48. Udney Hay Jacob, *An Extract from a Manuscript Entitled "The Peace Maker"; or, The Doctrines of the Millennium* (Nauvoo, Ill.: J. Smith, 1842). The pamphlet has been ably analyzed by Lawrence Foster, "A Little-Known Defense of Polygamy from the Mormon Press in 1842," *Dialogue* 9 (Winter 1974): 21–34. Also see Kenneth W. Godfrey, "A New Look at the Alleged Little-Known Discourse by Joseph Smith," *BYU Studies* 9 (Autumn 1968): 339–50.

49. Joseph's repudiation of the Jacob pamphlet is read in "Notice," *Times and Seasons* 4 (1 Dec. 1842): 32. The course of the difficulties that struck Nauvoo in 1842 has been told many times. See Brodie, *No Man Knows My History,* 297–322, 334–47; Kenneth W. Godfrey, "Causes of Mormon–Non-Mormon Conflict in Hancock County, Illinois, 1839–1846" (Ph.D. diss., BYU, 1967), 95–132; Bachman, "A Study," 218–60; Foster, *Religion and Sexuality,* 139–80; Hansen, *Mormonism and the American Experience,* 155–66; Ehat, "Joseph Smith's Introduction of Temple Ordinances," 46–96, 125–36 passim; Linda King Newell and Valeen Tippetts Avery, *Mormon Enigma: Emma Hale Smith, Prophet's Wife, "Elect Lady," Polygamy's Foe, 1804–1879* (Garden City, N.Y.: Doubleday, 1984), 95–182; and the always popular, slightly fictionalized account by Samuel W. Taylor, *Nightfall at Nauvoo* (New York: Macmillan, 1971), 112–35 passim.

50. *D&C* 124:17 (1841).

51. Case of Mrs. Catherine Warren, Minutes of the High Council of the Church of Jesus Christ of Latter-day Saints of Nauvoo, Hancock County, Illinois, from the 20th of May 1842 to the 19th February 1843, book 2, pp. 2–3, Church Archives, copy in private possession.

52. John C. Bennett, *The History of the Saints; or, An Exposé of Joe Smith and Mormonism* (Boston: Leland and Whiting, 1842). Documents associated with Bennett's excommunication, supporting the church's position, were collected in "John C. Bennett," *Times and Seasons* 3 (1 Aug. 1842): 868–78.

53. *HC* 5:18, 21. Also see the episode in which young George Q. Cannon denounced an employee in the church's Nauvoo printing shop for his immoral exploits. "George Q. Cannon," *Instructor* 79 (April 1944): 161.

54. *HC* 4:587, 5:8, 286; Kenney, *Wilford Woodruff's Journal,* 2:177, 27 and 28 May 1842.

55. See the cases discussed by Bachman, "A Study," 245–49. Not all who were offended on grounds of sexual impropriety remained away from the church. See, for example, the story of Rachel Grant as told by Ronald W. Walker in "Rachel R. Grant: The Continuing Legacy of the Feminine Ideal," *Dialogue* 15 (Autumn 1982): 108.

56. *HC* 5:123–24, 6:81. Also see Andrew F. Ehat, "'They Might Have Known That He Was Not a Fallen Prophet': The Nauvoo Journal of Joseph Fielding," *BYU Studies* 19 (Winter 1979): 133–66.

57. Due to Joseph Smith's ecclesiastical prominence and because he seems to have been more active in this way than others, numbers of scholars have attempted to identify as many of his wives as possible. See, e.g., Andrew

Jenson's compilation in "Plural Marriage"; Brodie, *No Man Knows My History,* 301–3, 434–65; Bachman, "A Study," 112–14, 333–36; Foster's discussion in *Religion and Sexuality,* 151–59, 308n.93; Newell and Avery, *Mormon Enigma,* 333n.51; the various lists and compilations of Stanley S. Ivins, in box 11, fd. 9, and box 12, fd. 1, Stanley Snow Ivins Collection, UHi; and the attempt to prepare a comprehensive list of both living and postmortem sealings in Thomas Milton Tinney, *The Royal Family of the Prophet Joseph Smith, Junior* (Salt Lake City: Tinney-Green(e) Family Organization, 1973). Regarding the plural contractions of others, see Brodie, *No Man Knows My History,* 303–4; Bachman, "A Study," 179–89; Lyndon W. Cook, "William Law, Nauvoo Dissenter," *BYU Studies* 22 (Winter 1982): 63; and Richard S. Van Wagoner, "Mormon Polyandry in Nauvoo," *Dialogue* 18 (Fall 1985): 67–83.

58. See the following: in *Times and Seasons,* letter to editor, 4 (15 March 1843): 143, "Notice," 5 (1 Feb. 1844): 423, Hyrum Smith to Richard Hewitt, 5 (15 March 1844): 474, "To the Elders Abroad," 5 (1 April 1844): 490–91; *HC* 4:582–83, 585–86; *HC* 5:36, 37, 40; *HC* 6:46, 411. Also see the acknowledgments and justifications provided by Joseph F. Smith, "Joseph the Seer's Plural Marriages," *DN,* 20 May 1886; idem, *Blood Atonement and the Origin of Plural Marriage: A Discussion* (Salt Lake City: Deseret News, 1905), 56, 57; and Brigham H. Roberts's editorial comment in *HC* 5:79. As Jan Shipps remarked, the shades and distinctions later adduced to justify the denials made in Nauvoo were not, significantly, defended at the time. JoAnn Barnett Shipps, "The Mormons in Politics: The First Hundred Years" (Ph.D. diss., University of Colorado, 1965), 99. For additional description of happenings in Nauvoo as they related to polygamy from the Bennett episode to the death of Joseph Smith, see Van Wagoner, *Mormon Polygamy,* 17–69; idem, "Mormon Polyandry in Nauvoo," 67–83; and the same author's "Sarah M. Pratt: The Shaping of an Apostate," *Dialogue* 19 (Summer 1986): 69–99.

59. Irene M. Bates, "William Smith, 1811–93: Problematic Patriarch," *Dialogue* 16 (Summer 1983): 19.

60. Newell and Avery, *Mormon Enigma,* 106–18. Additionally, see Linda King Newell, "Emma Hale Smith and the Polygamy Question," *John Whitmer Historical Association Journal* 4 (1984): 3–15; and James B. Allen, *Trials of Discipleship: The Story of William Clayton, a Mormon* (Urbana: University of Illinois Press, 1987), 96, 135–37, 193, 194.

61. For a gathering of accounts concerning the early behavior of Joseph Smith toward the opposite sex, see Van Wagoner, *Mormon Polygamy,* 4–7; and Brodie, *No Man Knows My History,* 181–82, 297. It was Joseph F. Smith who said that his uncle, the prophet, saw his wives in vision long before marrying them. "Funeral Services of Sister Elizabeth A. Whitney," *DN,* 17 Feb. 1882, and the correction, in Joseph F. Smith to the editor, *DN,* 18 Feb. 1882. For the angel story, see "History of Joseph Lee Robinson," bound typewritten manuscript, p. 13, Church Archives; Benjamin Franklin Johnson affidavit, 4 March 1870, in Jenson, "Plural Marriage," 222; Benjamin Franklin Johnson, *My Life's Review* (Independence, Mo.: Zion's Printing, 1947), 95–96; *JD* 20:28–29

(Joseph F. Smith/1880); and Lorenzo Snow, "Reminiscences of the Prophet," *DN,* 23 Dec. 1899.

62. Joseph Smith, quoted in William Clayton's Nauvoo Diary, Nov. 1842-Jan. 1846, 12 Aug. 1843, typewritten copy in private possession. In an 1874 statement Clayton used slightly different words but recollected the same advice. William Clayton's Testimony, 16 Feb. 1874, in Jenson, "Plural Marriage," 225. Heber C. Kimball once said that, if he remained faithful, he expected that when he went to heaven he would experience no deficit because of wives who refused to follow him. Rather, he looked to be summoned by the prophet Joseph Smith, who would tell him there were thousands of women in heaven and that Heber could take all he wanted. *JD* 4:209 (Heber C. Kimball/1857). The twentieth-century apostle Anthony W. Ivins, after marrying two Utah Mormons to women in Mexico, was reported to have been asked by his son if what he did was not approved by a revelation to the prophet Joseph Smith. Ivins supposedly answered: "He had to have a revelation, my boy, he had to!" Conversation with Heber Grant Ivins as reported by Mary Bennion Powell to Dr. George Stewart, 228-page transcript composed between 26 Jan. and 25 Feb. 1952, Henry E. Huntington Library, San Marino, Calif., pp. 183–84.

63. Anticipations are instanced in James B. Allen, *Trials of Discipleship,* 33; John Taylor to Lenora Cannon Taylor, 13 Feb. 1841, Letters and Extracts from the Journal of John Taylor, Church Archives; Brigham Young in *JD* 18:240–41(1877); George Q. Cannon in "Remarks Made by President George Q. Cannon," *DN,* 14 Nov. 1891; and Lorenzo Snow in "Discourse . . . ," *DN,* 3 June 1899.

64. Shipps, "The Mormons in Politics," 134. Exemplary statements asserting distaste for plural marriage when first revealed are *JD* 3:266, 5:208, 11:127 (Brigham Young/1855, 1857, 1865); *JD* 11:206–7 (Amasa M. Lyman/1866); *JD* 24:230–31 (John Taylor/1883); Charles W. Penrose, "Why We Practise Plural Marriage," *Mill. Star* 29 (14 Aug. 1867): 577–80; Orson F. Whitney, *"The Mormon Prophet's Tragedy"* (Salt Lake City: Deseret News, 1905), 35–36; and the account given in Elizabeth Wood Kane, *Twelve Mormon Homes Visited in Succession on a Journey through Utah to Arizona* (Salt Lake City: Tanner Trust Fund and University of Utah Library, 1974), 106. The story was told of James J. Strang, one of those claiming priority as a successor to Joseph Smith, that when confronted with the doctrine of polygamy while translating the *Book of the Law of the Lord,* he too rejected it, threw his materials on the floor in disgust, and refused to have more to do with it "until the Lord knocked it into him by main strength and awkwardness." L. D. Hickey testimony, *Reorganized Church vs. Church of Christ,* 409. The most complete account of Strang, in regard to polygamy, is John Quist, "Polygamy among James Strang and His Followers," *John Whitmer Historical Association Journal* 9 (1989): 31–48.

65. Accounts describing initial resistance by Hyrum Smith and others are *JD* 3:266, 5:208, 11:127 (Brigham Young/1855, 1857, 1865); *JD* 11:206–7

(Amasa M. Lyman/1866); *JD* 24:230–31 (John Taylor/1883); and Joseph F. Smith to Joseph Smith III, 3 May 1889, P22, fd. 47, RLDS Library and Archives.

66. Joseph F. Smith in *JD* 20:29 (1878); and George A. Smith's remarks as quoted by Brigham H. Roberts in his *Outlines of Ecclesiastical History*, 2d ed. (Salt Lake City: George Q. Cannon & Sons, 1895), 431.

67. Cook, "William Law," 66.

68. *D&C* 132 (1876 ed.). For accounts of circumstances attending dictation of the revelation, see William Clayton's Nauvoo Diary, 12 July 1843; Joseph C. Kingsbury's comments in *Reorganized Church vs. the Church of Christ*, 333, 336, 343; and the overviews provided by Brigham H. Roberts in *HC* 5:xxxii-xxxiv; Bachman, "New Light," 21–22; and Ehat, "Joseph Smith's Introduction of Temple Ordinances," 53–96.

69. *D&C* 132:1 (1843). The description of Hyrum, the prophet's brother, asking Joseph to dictate the 1843 revelation by using the Urim and Thummim, and Joseph's refusal, saying it was unnecessary on account of his knowing "the revelation perfectly from beginning to end," is in William Clayton affidavit, 16 Feb. 1874, Jenson, "Plural Marriage," 225. Danel W. Bachman provides a good comparison of the 1831 and 1843 documents in "New Light on an Old Hypothesis," 19–32.

70. The response by the prophet's wife Emma is described in Newell and Avery, *Mormon Enigma*, 151–56, and that of William Law in Cook, "William Law," 64–65. Also see the account of one Mormon woman who, while listening to Hyrum Smith read and explain the document, told him not to go any further, saying: "'I am full up to here,' drawing her hand across her throat." "Bishop S[amuel] A[mos] Woolley's Testimony," in Jenson, "Plural Marriage," 231. And there was the observation of Charlotte Haven, a nonmember visiting Nauvoo in the summer of 1843, that talk of the prophet's revelation made the rounds, men huddling on the streets to "whisper what they dare not speak aloud." "A Girl's Letters from Nauvoo," *Overland Monthly* 16 (Dec. 1890): 635–36.

71. *D&C* 132:3ff. (1843).

72. "The Life of Joseph Holbrook," 1:40, typewritten copy, Church Archives.

73. See, e.g., F. Mark McKiernan, *The Voice of One Crying in the Wilderness: Sidney Rigdon, Religious Reformer* (Lawrence, Kans.: Coronado, 1971), 133–35.

74. William Law, "Much Ado about Nothing," *Times and Seasons* 3 (1 July 1842): 831–32.

75. The course of conflict between Joseph and his accusers can be followed from inclusions constituting most of the last half of *HC*, vol. 6. There is also *CHC* 2:221–33; Brodie, *No Man Knows My History*, 367–79; Godfrey, "Causes of Mormon–Non-Mormon Conflict," 123–28; Donna Hill, *Joseph Smith: The First Mormon* (Garden City, N.Y.: Doubleday, 1977), 387–94; and Foster, *Religion and Sexuality*, 177–80. Examples of journalistic fun-making at the expense of the moral reputation of the Saints are "Mormon Matters,"

Warsaw Signal, 28 Feb. 1844; "Latest from Nauvoo," ibid., 27 March 1844; "Buckey's Lamentation for Want of More Wives," ibid., 24 April 1844. Also see Annette P. Hampshire, "Thomas Sharp and Anti-Mormon Sentiment in Illinois, 1842–1845," *Journal of the Illinois State Historical Society* 72 (May 1979): 82–100.

76. *Nauvoo Expositor* 1 (7 June 1844): 1–2.

77. In addition to *HC* 6:432–631 and *CHC* 2:221–87, there are good accounts of the entire affair, from the destruction of the *Expositor* to the murders of Joseph and Hyrum, in Brodie, *No Man Knows My History,* 367–95; Robert Bruce Flanders, *Nauvoo Kingdom on the Mississippi* (Urbana: University of Illinois Press, 1965), 306–11; Leonard J. Arrington and Davis Bitton, *The Mormon Experience: A History of the Latter-day Saints* (New York: Alfred A. Knopf, 1979), 77–82; Hill, *Joseph Smith,* 387–418; and Newell and Avery, *Mormon Enigma,* 169–98. There is no question but that the widespread use of vigilante methods contributed, on both sides, to the Mormon tragedy. Anyone who reads more than just those sections dealing with the Mormons in Governor Ford's history cannot but be struck with the extent to which such episodes plagued state officials generally. Thomas Ford, *A History of Illinois from Its Commencement as a State in 1818 to 1847* (Chicago: S. C. Griggs, 1854). Dallin H. Oaks's study of the destruction of the *Expositor* provides an analysis of the legal issues involved. "The Suppression of the *Nauvoo Expositor,*" *Utah Law Review* 9 (Autumn 1965): 862–903. Also see George R. Gayler, "The *Expositor* Affair: Prelude to the Downfall of Joseph Smith," *Northwest Missouri State College Studies* 25 (Feb. 1961): 3–15. The trial and acquittal of those involved in the assassinations, as well as an overview of immediate circumstances attending the murders of the Smith brothers, is provided in Dallin H. Oaks and Marvin S. Hill, *Carthage Conspiracy: The Trial of the Accused Assassins of Joseph Smith* (Urbana: University of Illinois Press, 1975).

78. "History of Joseph Lee Robinson," 13.

79. The best summary of this interpretation, as applied to the South, is Ronald G. Walters, "The Erotic South: Civilization and Sexuality in American Abolitionism," *American Quarterly* 25 (May 1973): 177–201. Danel Bachman is one who sees this as relevant for the Mormon experience. "A Study," 273–97.

80. I am not ignoring those who have pointed to Mormon sexual practices as an important reason for troubles at Nauvoo. See, e.g., *CHC* 2:93–110; Brodie, *No Man Knows My History,* 375–79; Foster, *Religion and Sexuality,* 124; Godfrey, "Causes of Mormon–Non-Mormon Conflict," 90–111; and Van Wagoner, *Mormon Polygamy,* 63–69. Many more, however, especially those close to official Mormon views, have tended to minimize polygamy's role in the Nauvoo period. As examples only, see the following, where page citations often illustrate a near absence of, rather than attention to, the topic: Joseph Fielding Smith, *Church History and Modern Revelation: A Course of Study for the Melchizedek Priesthood Quorums* (Salt Lake City: Deseret News, 1949), 169–97; idem, *Essentials in Church History . . . ,* rev. ed. (Salt Lake City: Deseret Book, 1971), 281–82, 291–302; William Edwin Berrett and Alma P. Burton, eds.,

Readings in L.D.S. Church History from Original Manuscripts, 3 vols. (Salt Lake City: Deseret Book, 1953–1958), 3:235–70, 465–88; Ivan J. Barrett, *Joseph Smith and the Restoration: A History of the Church to 1846* (Provo, Utah: BYU Press, 1973), 337–59, 531–57, 563–618; Gordon B. Hinckley, *Truth Restored: A Short History of the Church of Jesus Christ of Latter-day Saints* (Salt Lake City: Church of Jesus Christ of Latter-day Saints, 1979), 71–80. Paul E. Reimann argues that Joseph and the Saints were seldom, if ever, in violation of the law because plurality was a theological maxim only and before the westward migration little, if any, cohabitation occurred. See all of his *Plural Marriage Limited* (Salt Lake City: Utah Printing, 1974). Arrington and Bitton devote an entire essay to the subject of Mormon persecutions but provide little more than a paragraph on sexual practices as a causational issue. *The Mormon Experience,* 44–64. And see ibid., 69–82, for the comparatively small attention given the subject in the authors' description of troubles in Nauvoo. Also see Allen and Leonard, *The Story of the Latter-day Saints,* 170–71, 190–98. And there is Ronald K. Esplin's account of the prophet's need to remain alive until he had restored essential knowledge and ordinances. Although the article discusses temple work as a vital part of Smith's work in Nauvoo, plural marriage is nowhere specifically mentioned. "'God Will Protect Me until My Work Is Done,'" *Ensign* 19 (Aug. 1989): 16–21. Also see M. Guy Bishop, who argues that polygamy had little effect on family life for the majority of Mormons residing in Nauvoo. "Sex Roles, Marriage and Childrearing at Mormon Nauvoo," *Western Illinois Regional Studies* 11 (Fall 1988): 30–45.

81. For the kingdom of God idea, see Klaus J. Hansen, *Quest for Empire: The Political Kingdom of God and the Council of Fifty in Mormon History* (East Lansing: Michigan State University Press, 1967), 45–89. Regarding economic life in Nauvoo, nothing yet excells Flanders's *Nauvoo,* 114–78. And for violence as a part of the ethos of the time, see idem, "Dream and Nightmare: Nauvoo Revisited," in *Restoration Movement,* ed. McKiernan, Blair, and Edwards, 141–66.

82. Brigham Young, in *HC* 7:573.

83. "The Iowa Journal of Lorenzo Snow," ed. Maureen Ursenbach Beecher, *BYU Studies* 24 (Summer 1984): 265.

84. For New York, see "An Act to Restrain All Persons from Marrying, until Their Former Wives and Former Husbands Be Dead," *Laws of the State of New York,* 2 vols. (Albany: Charles R. and George Webster, 1802), ch. 24, 1:122–23 (1788); for Ohio, "An Act for the Punishment of Crimes," *Statutes of Ohio and of the Northwestern Territory, Adopted or Enacted from 1788 to 1833 . . . ,* ed. Salmon P. Chase (Cincinnati: Corey & Fairbank, 1835), ch. 830, sec. 7, p. 1724; for Missouri, "Crimes and Punishments," *Revised Statutes of the State of Missouri . . .* (St. Louis: Argus, 1835), art. 8, sec. 1–5, pp. 205–6; for Illinois, "Illinois Criminal Code," *Public and General Statute Laws of the State of Illinois . . .* (Chicago: Stephen F. Gale, 1839), div. 11, sec. 121–22, pp. 220–21 (1833).

85. "An Ordinance for the Government of the Territory of the United States Northwest of the River Ohio," art. 2, in *Documents of American History,*

ed. Henry Steele Commager (New York: Appleton-Century Crofts, 1958), no. 82, p. 130; "An Act Providing for the Government of the Territory of Missouri," sec. 14, *Laws of a Public and General Nature of the District of Louisiana, of the Territory of Louisiana, of the Territory of Missouri, and of the State of Missouri, up to the year 1824*, 2 vols. (Jefferson City, Mo.: W. Lusk and Son, 1842), 1:12.

86. Michael W. Homer, "The Judiciary and the Common Law in Utah Territory, 1850–61," *Dialogue* 21 (Spring 1988): 97–108. Other studies treating the quarrel are Thomas G. Alexander, "Federal Authority versus Polygamic Theocracy," ibid. 1 (Aug. 1966): 90–91; Gordon M. Bakken, "The English Common Law in the Rocky Mountain West," *Arizona and the West* 11 (Summer 1969): 110–11,121; Kenneth L. Cannon II, "'Mountain Common Law': The Extralegal Punishment of Seducers in Early Utah," *UHQ* 51 (Fall 1983): 308–27; Carol Cornwall Madsen, "Beyond the Limits: Religion, Women and the Law in Territorial Utah" (Paper delivered before the Western Association of Women's Historians, Henry E. Huntington Library and Art Gallery, San Marino, Calif., 14 April 1984), 3n.13.

87. The best example of one of this persuasion, arguing that even in Illinois no indictable offenses could be charged because the principle was embraced there without actual cohabitation, is Paul E. Reimann, *Plural Marriage Limited*, 21, 23–29 passim.

88. Brigham Young, quoted in *Wilford Woodruff's Journal*, ed. Kenney, 3:99–103, 20 Dec. 1846.

89. Maureen Ursenbach Beecher, "Women in Winter Quarters," *Sunstone* 8 (July-Aug. 1983): 11–19.

90. The inclination toward a general loosening commenced perhaps as much as a year before the Mormons left Nauvoo and continued into their early occupancy of Utah. Because this is sometimes disputed, see, as examples, the appropriations described in Minnie Jones Taylor, "History of Black River Falls," typewritten manuscript, p. 10, Wisconsin Historical Society, Madison, Wis.; and the references and comments in "Excerpts from a Journal or Sketch of the Life of Joel Hills Johnson (Brother to Benjamin F. Johnson)," bound, printed copy (n.p., n.d.), 8, 9–10, UHi; *HC* 7:352–54, 365, 366, 373, 597, 608 passim; Stanley B. Kimball, ed., *On the Potter's Wheel: The Diaries of Heber C. Kimball* (Salt Lake City: Signature Books in Association with Smith Research Associates, 1987), 119–20, 4 June 1845, 152, 27 Nov. 1845; the discussion in Richard Edmond Bennett, *Mormons at the Missouri, 1846–1852: "And Should We Die . . ."* (Norman: University of Oklahoma Press, 1987), 194–98; Juanita Brooks, ed., *On the Mormon Frontier: The Diary of Hosea Stout, 1844–1861*, 2 vols. (Salt Lake City: University of Utah Press, 1964), 1:67, 18 Sept. 1845, 73, 26 Sept. 1845, 81, 8 Oct. 1845, 267, 25–30 July 1847, 289, 28 and 30 Nov. 1847, 301, 2 and 5 Feb. 1848; Kenney, *Wilford Woodruff's Journal*, 3:71, 26 Aug. 1846, 75, 6 Sept. 1846, 80–81, 13 Sept. 1846, 128–30, 16 Feb. 1847, 247, 4 Aug. 1847, 297–99, 21 Dec. 1847; Charles Kelly, ed., *Journals of John D. Lee, 1846–47 and 1859* (Salt Lake City: University of Utah Press, 1984), 57, 9 Jan. 1847; Robert Glass Cleland and Juanita Brooks, eds., *A*

Mormon Chronicle: The Diaries of John D. Lee, 1848–1876, 2 vols. (San Marino, Calif.: The Huntington Library, 1955), 1:97–98, 3 March 1849, 118n.32, 2:463n.25; "History of Joseph Lee Robinson," 19; "Life Sketch of Jonathan Ellis Layne," typewritten manuscript, pp. 9–10, Church Archives; "Diary of Lorenzo Dow Young," *UHQ* 14 (Jan.–Oct. 1946): 160, 27 May 1847; William Clayton's Nauvoo Diary, 19 Oct. 1844; and *William Clayton's Journal: A Daily Record . . .* (Salt Lake City: Clayton Family Association and Deseret News, 1921), 191–94, 29 May 1847.

91. Oscar Handlin, *The Uprooted,* rev. ed. (Boston: Little, Brown, 1973), 270–71.

92. Brigham Young called for a reformation among the Saints as early as the autumn after their first arrival in the Salt Lake Valley. *HC* 7:619. See also Gustive 0. Larson, "The Mormon Reformation," *UHQ* 23 (Winter 1958): 45–63; Paul H. Peterson, "The Mormon Reformation of 1856–1857: The Rhetoric and the Reality," *JMH* 15 (1989): 59–87; and Eugene E. Campbell, *Establishing Zion: The Mormon Church in the American West, 1847–1869* (Salt Lake City: Signature Books, 1988), 181–200.

93. These questions have occupied historians since early in the century. See, e.g., the discussion in Thomas Cottam Romney, "The State of Deseret" (M.A. thesis, University of California at Berkeley, 1924), 129–37.

94. Klaus J. Hansen, *Quest for Empire.* Regarding the general revolutionary intent of Mormonism, see the same author's "Mormonism and American Culture: Some Tentative Hypotheses," in *Restoration Movement,* ed. McKiernan, Blair, and Edwards, 19–21; and *Mormonism and the American Experience,* 105. Cf. D. Michael Quinn, "The Council of Fifty and Its Members, 1844–1945," *BYU Studies* 20 (Winter 1980): 163–93.

95. George Q. Cannon, *JD* 22:367 (1881). Statements emphasizing nineteenth-century Mormonism's temporal, transforming intent are numerous. See, e.g., *HC* 4:610 (Joseph Smith/1842); *HC* 7:575 (Brigham Young/1846); *JD* 2:84 (Orson Hyde/1854); *JD* 2:190, 4:41, 13:273 (Brigham Young/1855, 1856, 1870); *JD* 9:360 (Daniel H. Wells/1862); *JD* 9:350, 10:148 (John Taylor/1862, 1863); *JD* 11:208 (Amasa M. Lyman/1866); *JD* 14:308–9 (Lorenzo Snow/1872); "Discourse by President John Taylor," *DN,* 7 March 1885; "The Spread of Liberal Principles," *Mill. Star* 18 (19 July 1856): 456–57; John Brown, "Progression versus Fogyism," ibid. 24 (12 April 1862): 225–27; John Morgan Diaries, 6 Oct. 1888, Church Archives—all of which amounted to little more than Brigham Young's terse comment: "The world is wrong and we have to right it." *JD* 10:222 (1863).

96. A history of the church's periodic publication of the 1843 revelation between the 1852 announcement and the mid-1860s was provided in "Plurality of Wives," *Mill. Star* 28 (28 April 1868): 257–61. Reasons accounting for the 1852 announcement are most thoroughly explored by David J. Whittaker in his "Early Mormon Pamphleteering" (Ph.D. diss., BYU, 1982), 321–33, and the same author's "The Bone in the Throat: Orson Pratt and the Public Announcement of Plural Marriage," *Western Historical Quarterly* 18 (July 1987): 293–314.

97. Whittaker, "Early Mormon Pamphleteering," 333–67; and the same author's "Early Mormon Polygamy Defences," *JMH* 11 (1984): 43–63.

98. Brigham Young, in *JD* 1:362 (1852). The constitutional argument was made repeatedly from 1852 until the end of the century. The following constitute only a fraction: Orson Pratt, "Celestial Marriage," *Seer* 1 (Dec. 1852): 12–14; idem, "Celestial Marriage," ibid. 1 (Feb. 1853): 30; *JD* 1:54, 138 (Orson Pratt/1852, 1853); *JD* 4:347 (Brigham Young/1857); *JD* 11:223 (John Taylor/1866); *JD* 26:14 (George Q. Cannon/1884); "The Constitution and the Anti-Polygamic Act," *Mill. Star* 28 (17 Feb. 1866): 97–101; "Plurality of Wives—Its Constitutionality," ibid. 28 (9 June 1866): 357–60.

99. "Letter from Mrs. Ann Eliza Young," *Anti-Polygamy Standard* 2 (May 1881): 9.

100. *JD* 1:308 (Parley P. Pratt/1853). Also see, as examples of appeals to scripture in behalf of plural marriage, all of Orson Spencer, *Patriarchal Order; or, Plurality of Wives!* . . . (Liverpool: S. W. Richards, 1853); "A Bird's-Eye Glance; or, Preface to the Law of Progression or Procreation," *DN*, 25 Dec. 1852; "Tabernacle . . . Sermon by Parley P. Pratt," *DN*, 19 Jan. 1854; "The Patriarchal Institution of Polygamy," *Mill. Star* 23 (30 March 1861): 204–5; "Presbyterians and Polygamy," *DN*, 7 Aug. 1879. On the need for consolidating the truths of former times, including plural marriage, in this dispensation, see Orson Pratt, "Christian Polygamy in the Sixteenth Century," *Seer* 1 (Dec. 1853): 182; *JD* 1:231–32 (John Taylor/1853); Alexander F. Macdonald, "A Marriage Law and Practice," *Mill. Star* 41 (28 April 1879): 258; "Remarks by Elder C[harles] W. Penrose," *DN*, 20 Sept. 1879. And for associating polygamy with "the eternal and unchangeable principles of morality, virtue and purity," see Parley Parker Pratt, *Autobiography*, 385; *JD* 1:347 (Jedediah M. Grant/1853); Benjamin Franklin Johnson, *A Glance at Scripture and Reason in Answer to an Attack through the Polynesian, upon the Saints for Polygamy* (San Francisco: Excelsior, 1854), 12.

101. *JD* 63 (Orson Pratt/1852). Also see Parley P. Pratt, *Key to the Science of Theology:* . . . (Liverpool: F. D. Richards, 1855), 163–64; *JD* 2:116–17 (Orson Hyde/1853); *JD* 5:92 (Heber C. Kimball/1857); Henry W. Naisbitt, "Body and Spirit," *Contributor* 3 (May 1882): 235.

102. *JD* 3:264 (Brigham Young/1855). Observers said that plurality was commonly urged as the best means to "build up the kingdom." William Chandless, *A Visit to Salt Lake: Being a Journey across the Plains and a Residence in the Mormon Settlements at Utah* (London: Smith, Elder and Co., 1857), 192; Thomas B. H. Stenhouse, *The Rocky Mountain Saints: A Full and Complete History of the Mormons* . . . (New York: D. Appleton, 1873), 500.

103. As told by Florence Ivins Hyde, interviewed by Victor W. Jorgensen, 18 Aug. 1972, transcript in private possession.

104. *JD* 5:20, 91 (Heber C. Kimball/1857, 1857); Orson Pratt, "Celestial Marriage," *Seer* 1 (April 1853): 60; Spencer, *Patriarchal Order*, 2; "Monogamic Problem," *Mormon* 3 (29 Aug. 1857): n.p.

105. Orson Pratt, "Celestial Marriage," *Seer* 1 (Jan. 1853): 11–12; *JD* 2:83 (Orson Hyde/1854); *JD* 14:43 (Brigham Young/1870); *JD* 23:296–97 (Eras-

tus Snow/1883); "Mormon Polygamy from a Philosophical Standpoint," *DN,* 15 Feb. 1881.

106. John Hanson Beadle, *Life in Utah; or, The Mysteries and Crimes of Mormonism . . .* (Philadelphia: National Publishing, 1870), 307–8. For nineteenth-century Mormon contentions regarding the sex ratio, see Orson Pratt, "Celestial Marriage," *Seer* 1 (April 1853): 58–59; Parley P. Pratt, *Key to the Science of Theology,* 166; "Disparity of Sex," *DN,* 5 Oct. 1854; *JD* 11:208 (Amasa M. Lyman/1866); "Population and Polygamy," *Mill. Star* 31 (10 July 1869): 443–44; "Matrimony and the Census," *DN,* 16 April 1881; "Superfluous Women," *DN,* 14 April 1883. But cf. Stanley S. Ivins, "Notes on Mormon Polygamy," *Western Humanities Review* 10 (Summer 1956): 236; Kimball Young, *Isn't One Wife Enough?* (New York: Henry Holt, 1954), 124; William Mulder, *Homeward to Zion: The Mormon Migration from Scandinavia* (Minneapolis: University of Minnesota Press, 1957), 108–9; and John A. Widtsoe, *Evidences and Reconciliations* (Salt Lake City: Murray & Gee, 1943), 307. For census summaries and graphs, see Wayne L. Wahlquist, "Age-Sex Characteristics," *Atlas of Utah* (Provo, Utah: Weber State College and BYU Press, 1981), 113; and the comments of Bruce L. Campbell and Eugene E. Campbell, "The Mormon Family," in *Ethnic Families in America: Patterns and Variations,* ed. Charles H. Mindel and Robert W. Habenstein (New York: Elsevier, 1976), 387–88. When it was to their advantage to emphasize how few Saints had entered polygamy, one of the proofs used by Mormons conversant with the facts was to show that, throughout the nineteenth century, more men than women resided in the territory. See the 1904 testimony of Charles W. Penrose in *Proceedings* 2:261.

107. Johnson, *My Life's Review,* 326–28; and Brigham Young in *JD* 6:281 (1852).

108. Brigham Young, in *Wilford Woodruff's Journals,* ed. Kenney, 5:240, 18 Nov. 1858. Also see ibid., 3:241, 28 July 1847, 5:98, 16 Sept. 1857; Brooks, *On the Mormon Frontier,* 2:516, 9 May 1854; John Nebeker, "Green River Company: Pioneer Camp of Israel," pp. 9–10, Church Archives; Cleland and Brooks, *A Mormon Chronicle,* 1:181, 15 Sept. 1858, 184, 8 Dec. 1858, 242, 10 March 1860, 327n.62.

109. Compare the superscript of *D&C* 132 (1876) with that of *D&C* 132 (1982).

110. Orson Pratt, in 1859, said the practice was "general" throughout the territory and that "a great many families . . . have practically embraced this doctrine." *JD* 6:350 (1859). George Q. Cannon repeatedly indicated that the number of men who had entered plurality was about one in ten. *JD* 17:337–38, 20:4 (1875, 1880); untitled, [New York] *Sun,* 8 Dec. 1879. For similar and higher estimates by Mormons and men considered fair in their treatment of the Saints, see "The Crusade—What Do They Want?" *Mill. Star* 37 (Jan. 1875): 51; "How to Fight 'Mormonism,'" *DN,* 16 Nov. 1880; Phil Robinson, *Sinners and Saints: A Tour across the States and round Them, with Three Months among the Mormons* (Boston: Roberts Brothers, 1883), 88; James W. Barclay, "A New View of Mormonism," *Nineteenth Century* 15 (Feb. 1884): 179.

111. E.g., "Epistle of the First Presidency," 4 April 1885, *Messages* 3:11. These low figures continued to be cited well into the present century. See "The Escheated Property," *SLT*, 20 Oct. 1891; *Proceedings* 1:108–9, 324–25 (Joseph F. Smith); Widtsoe, *Evidences and Reconciliations*, 85; Richard Vetterli, *Mormonism, Americanism and Politics* (Salt Lake City: Ensign, 1961), 483; Berrett and Burton, *Readings*, 3:122; Reimann, *Plural Marriage Limited*, 111–15.

112. "How Many in Polygamy?" *Anti-Polygamy Standard* 3 (Oct. 1882): 52; or the speech by Fred T. Dubois, *Cong. Rec.*, 50th Cong., 1st Sess., 1888, p. 19, pt. 8:7949–7950.

113. The best known of these studies are those of Lowell "Ben" Bennion, "Patterns of Polygamy across Mormon Country in 1880" (Paper delivered before the Mormon History Association, 11 May 1984, BYU, Provo, Utah); and "The Incidence of Mormon Polygamy in 1880: 'Dixie' versus Davis Stake," *JMH* 11 (1984): 27–42. Other inquiries that provide varying percentages for the number of Mormons practicing polygamy, all greater than traditional church estimates, are Stanley S. Ivins, "Notes on Mormon Polygamy," 230–32; James E. Smith and Phillip R. Kunz, "Polygyny and Fertility in Nineteenth-Century America," *Population Studies* 30 (Nov. 1976): 468–71; Dean L. May, "People on the Mormon Frontier: Kanab's Families of 1874," *Journal of Family History* 1 (1976): 172; Larry M. Logue, "A Time of Marriage: Monogamy and Polygamy in a Utah Town," *JMH* 11 (1984): 7–13; and the same author's *A Sermon in the Desert: Belief and Behavior in Early St. George, Utah* (Urbana: University of Illinois Press, 1988), 44–71. For evidence of the extensive nature of the practice among church leaders, see Quinn, "The Mormon Hierarchy," 59–62; and D. Gene Pace, "Wives of Nineteenth-Century Mormon Bishops: A Quantitative Analysis," *Journal of the West* 21 (April 1982): 49–57.

114. "History of Joseph Lee Robinson," 33.

115. *JD* 8:62–63 (Brigham Young/1860).

116. Regarding the incidence of divorce, see Eugene E. Campbell and Bruce L. Campbell, "Divorce among Mormon Polygamists: Extent and Explanations," *UHQ* 46 (Winter 1978): 4–23; and the examination of early divorce law and practice in Utah Territory by Richard I. Aaron, "Mormon Divorce and the Statute of 1852: Questions for Divorce in the 1980s," *Journal of Contemporary Law* 8 (1982): 5–45. There is also the recent survey of the disadvantaged experience of Mormon plural wives under Utah territorial laws in Carol Cornwall Madsen, "'At Their Peril': Utah Law and the Case of Plural Wives, 1850–1900," *Western Historical Quarterly* 21 (Nov. 1990): 425–43. Also see Foster, *Religion and Sexuality*, 216–20; Kern, *An Ordered Love*, 168–69, 196–98; and Phillip R. Kunz, "One Wife or Several? A Comparative Study of Late Nineteenth-Century Marriage in Utah," in *The Mormon People: Their Character and Traditions*, ed. Thomas G. Alexander (Provo, Utah: Brigham Young University Press, 1980), 53–71. The problem of "anomie" or normlessness as a reason for difficulty in Mormon polygamous life was referred to by James Edward Hulett, Jr., "The Social Role of the Mormon Polygamous

Male," *American Sociological Review* 8 (June 1943): 285 passim; Young, *Isn't One Wife Enough?* 209; Thomas F. O'Dea, *The Mormons* (Chicago: University of Chicago Press, 1957), 247; and Campbell and Campbell, "Divorce," 15–17, 21–22.

117. *JD* 11:206 (Amasa M. Lyman/1866). In this same regard, see the comments in "History of Joseph Lee Robinson," 33; and the story told by Mary Harker, interviewed by Leonard R. Grover, 31 Dec. 1979, p. 5, POHP. George P. Murdock, in his socioanthropological study of family practices, concluded that Mormon polygamy came to an end more from these difficulties than from pressures without. *Social Structure* (New York: Macmillan, 1960), 30.

118. Orson Pratt, "Celestial Marriage," *Seer* 1 (Nov. 1853): 173. Also see Pratt's comments in *JD* 12:92 (1867).

119. Young, *Isn't One Wife Enough?* 56–57, 256–60; Vicky Burgess Olson, "Family Structure and Dynamics in Early Utah Mormon Families, 1847–1885" (Ph.D. diss., Northwestern University, 1975), 117–19, 134–36; Foster, *Religion and Sexuality*, 211–16; Jessie L. Embry, *Mormon Polygamous Families: Life in the Principle* (Salt Lake City: University of Utah Press, 1987), 127–36, 151–73, 187–94.

120. See, e.g., Arrington and Bitton, *The Mormon Experience*, 185–205; and Grant Underwood, "Re-visioning Mormon History," *Pacific Historical Review* 55 (Aug. 1986): 403–26.

121. "Remarks Made by President George Q. Cannon," *DN*, 14 Nov. 1891.

122. *JD* 25:114–15 (Moses Thatcher/1884). Following are but a few of many statements contending for views like those described in the text: *JD* 4:254–55 (Daniel H. Wells/1857); *JD* 11:210 (Heber C. Kimball/1866); *JD* 11:354, 14:339, 20:352–53 (John Taylor/1867, 1872, 1880); *JD* 17:218–19 (Orson Pratt/1874); *JD* 25:21 (George Teasdale/1884); Charles W. Penrose, "Marriage," *Mill. Star* 30 (30 May 1868): 337–40; "Be Not Led Astray by Deceivers," *DN*, 13 Dec. 1879; "Expressions from the People," *DN*, 14 April 1885.

123. "Young Ladies Meeting," *Mill. Star* 36 (3 March 1874): 139.

124. *JD* 24:162 (Erastus Snow/1883).

125. *JD* 17:224–25 (Orson Pratt/1874).

126. "Discourse by President John Taylor," *DN*, 18 Oct. 1884.

127. *JD* 12:63 (Brigham Young/1867).

128. William Hepworth Dixon, *White Conquest*, 2 vols. (London: Chatto & Windus, 1876), 1:199.

129. Edward W. Tullidge, "The Era of Isolation," *Utah Magazine* 2 (Nov. 1868): 102–3.

2

Civilization Threatened: Mormon Polygamy under Siege

With all that was significant about the coming of the railroad to Utah, Mormon-American conflict began well before its arrival in 1869. Soon after the 1852 announcement, the question of Mormon polygamy became entangled with that of slavery, infecting it with the venom of the sectional dispute. As part of his defense for plurality, Orson Pratt argued that Utah citizens be treated like those of the South, where local institutions were left to local control.[1] Although Utah stood with the Union when war came, Brigham Young told Horace Greeley that he looked upon slavery as a divine institution, not to be abolished until "the curse pronounced on Ham" was removed.[2] Linkage was reinforced by non-Mormons who defended both institutions as approved by the scriptures. Contending that elevated society was dependent on them, Henry Charles Lea pleaded that Americans see the importance for every citizen having the liberty to possess "as many slaves as Abraham, and as many wives as Solomon."[3] Those friendly to Mormonism's "peculiar institution," however, were few. Plurality by the Saints rapidly acquired the reputation of a great social evil. And, like slavery, it became the object of a national crusade to destroy it.

Except for mutual interest in the right of regional populations to regulate themselves, there is little evidence of southern sympathy for polygamy. Mary Chesnut, writing in South Carolina in 1862, said there were "no negro marital relations, or the want of them, half so shocking as Mormonism."[4] Nevertheless, polygamists and slaveholders were thrown together in the minds of many Americans, including those debating in Congress. In 1854 Charles Sumner tied the Mormon with his "harem" to the southern slaver as a wicked company. And Gerrit Smith taunted Alexander Stephens on the floor of the

House of Representatives by asking if Stephens would like "dark-haired men" in Georgia to marry all the women they pleased, thus keeping "light-haired men" from having wives of their own.[5] The Republican party's well-known 1856 pledge to rid the country of "those twin relics of barbarism—polygamy and slavery" was an oath salted through with sexual implication.[6]

Arguments about Mormon polygamy, like the debate over slavery, traded heavily in theology. Immorality and violation of Christian tradition were charged against the Mormon practice in numerous British writings at the time.[7] It eventually earned condemnation by the Pope.[8] For many, even if "all the Abrahams and Solomons of the Old Testament" had practiced it, it was still a contrivance of the race of Cain and "no less devilish and damnable."[9] Some called it Buddhist and Mohammedan. Others expressed concerns of a more mundane character. It would, said many, result in a disproportionate number of female births.[10] Yet others complained that it was undemocratic and enslaved women. One congressman objected because Mormon pluralists would buy up more farms than their monogamist neighbors.[11] And, asked a female critic, how could any proper woman live with a man whose religion encouraged him to marry Indian squaws?[12] Hence the "spasm," the "paroxysm," and the "panic" Representative Daniel Gooch said was communicated to Congress by citizens anxious about the Saints.[13]

As menacing as anything were reports, most common in the early decades of the experiment, purporting to find evidence of physiological decline resulting from the activity. In the most memorable of such accounts, Mormonism was referred to as the "plague spot" of the Rocky Mountains, a place where one could see polygamous offspring degenerating into a new species: "the yellow, sunken, cadaverous visage; the greenish-colored eyes; the thick, protuberant lips; the low forehead . . . [all] constitute an appearance so characteristic of the new race, the production of polygamy, as to distinguish them at a glance."[14] That this was due to plural marriage was certain, it was held, because children by the polygamist's first wife were always well formed and strong. The dreaded consequences appeared only in the offspring of wives two, three, and four. But a few generations more, said Samuel Bowles, and Americans would witness, as the result of polygamy, a physical and mental decline beyond comprehension.[15] Mormons convicted for unlawful cohabitation in the mid-1880s, on their way to prison by train, found travelers surprised to discover they looked like other men.[16] A midwestern newspaper said Mormon president John Taylor resembled a "brute."[17]

Recapitulation of the sectional controversy occurs again and again in any charting of the nation's responses to Mormon polygamy. Allegations made by abolitionists concerning the moral decrepitude of the South and dangers threatened by miscegenous southern slaveholders, including the supposed expansive tendencies of their system, were turned against the Saints. "If it [polygamy] be tolerated as a local institution," said a critic of the 1850s, "it must be tolerated also as a national institution, and stamp its impress forever upon the national character."[18] After the war the bias surfaced in linkages contending that Mormonism, southern ignorance, and rum were "the Devil's Trinity."[19] A sense that family and morality were endangered and that providence was incensed underlaid comments by the Reverend George Whitfield Phillips of Plymouth Church in Massachusetts: "I do not think it strange when we recall the Divine method of dealing with great social wrongs, that this Mormon problem is laid at the doors of the American people." The nation must respond, he said, just as it did in expunging slavery, for "the whole question of the family is wrapped up in it."[20]

Bracketed with slaveholders as barbarians in the antebellum period, after the Civil War Utah polygamists were cast with blacks as animal and profligate. On the basis of contemporary theories that held an inverse relationship existed between health and sexual activity, blacks and Mormons were pointed to as evidence of disregard for nature's laws. Repeating Chief Justice Morrison R. Waite's association of polygamy with non-Western peoples, John A. McClernand of the Utah Commission referred to it as an "Asiatic and African pestilence," sure to stultify the nation's genius.[21] As Charles A. Cannon has described it, "the child of Mormon polygamy was simply a white negro."[22] Plurality cultivated a lustful nature, it was held, reducing both men and women to animal behavior. Polyandry was said always to accompany the polygamous involvements of men. Salt Lake City, it was charged, was little more than a common brothel, an infection likely to spread, weakening the physical and moral fiber of the nation.[23] Because of liberal divorce laws and the general image associated with polygamy, Utah Territory was looked upon in the nineteenth century much as Nevada is today.[24]

The danger presented an especially threatening countenance because Mormon polygamy emerged in the national consciousness just as monogamy was acquiring status not only as preferred but as a vital prerequisite of Western civilization. By mid-century, attention to romantic companionship and transformation of the home into an affective, sentimental nest was elevating monogamy to a near religion.[25]

Darwinian explanation gave support to the arrangement. Monogamous marriage was enshrined as an evolved form, one proved best
by time. The presumed superiority of Western culture was closely
related, it was believed, to its sexual ethic. Rigorous control of male
sensual impulse, conjugal duty, and childhood nurture by Christian
women were the community's best guarantors against social
disorder—a Victorian analogue for erotic informality. "Modern society reposes upon the monogamian family," said Lewis Henry Morgan. "The whole previous experience and progress of mankind culmi-
nated and crystallized in this pre-eminent institution."[26]

From the 1850s through the 1880s and beyond, the most persistent
criticism made of Mormon polygamous life was that its threat to monogamous restraints placed civilization in peril.[27] Representative Ferris Jacobs, Jr., told Congress that the Mormon question was nothing
less than Asia, with its polygamy, instability, and convulsions, versus
Europe and America, with their monogamy, liberty, and ordered society.[28] Monogamous marriage, said Representative Samuel S. Cox,
was the only sexual arrangement on earth that could be depended on
to ensure a continuation of the Western tradition.[29] Men allowed to
marry as many women as they pleased, said another critic, swept away
the "fence," exposing the rest to a storm of sensuality.[30]

Complementing monogamy's canalizing check on male sexual need
was the appropriation made of female nature. The apotheosization of
women as sexually undiverted called them to the tasks of balancing
male drive and providing the young with moral instruction. Regard
for their sphere as natural guardians of purity assured a respectful
social order.[31] Inasmuch as polygamy was believed to deprave women
as well as men, it confused Victorian domestic purpose. Virtuous
women regulating their homes through love and commitment were
what the nation craved. And these, said President Grover Cleveland,
were "not the cheerless, crushed, and unwomanly mothers of polygamy." Men strong in their devotion to hearths, children, and conjugal
fidelity were the stuff of patriots. And these, said Cleveland, were "not
the fathers of polygamous families."[32] Hubert Howe Bancroft, otherwise favorable to the Mormons, repeated the arguments against the
practice as having less to do with the Bible than with a higher morality, with civilization. Monogamy, he said, stood to polygamy as Greece
to China or England to India.[33]

It has been suggested that Victorian concern with the Mormon
system of marriage reflected uneasiness with itself.[34] Some have also
said that preoccupation with polygamy found its basis in the prurient
chambers of Victorian minds—that many protests were disingenuous

and reflected a fascination with Mormon sexual audacity. As Paul Wilbur Tappan put it a half century ago, the Mormons "had what the Gentiles secretly and unconsciously wanted."[35] There may have been something of this behind the outpouring of fiction and humor dealing with the institution.[36] Some of what was expressed, such as the remark by the Illinois congressman James Washington Singleton, spoke to human nature so realistically that even Mormons must have smiled. Singleton is reported to have recommended a full congressional surrender to Mormon wishes, requiring only that every husband live with all his wives in one house. If that were done, Singleton said, "none of them would look so fat and good-natured as my friend [George Q.] Cannon after six months of such a life."[37]

The most reasonable solution was to leave the issue to patience. As one writer put it, disgusting as it was to see several women stuck like burrs to a man's sleeve, the only remedy lay in teaching the people better.[38] Most who opposed polygamy, however, were unwilling to settle for the palliatives of either humor or time. Some urged quarantining the threat by subdividing Utah Territory, allocating political control to Gentile majorities in adjoining states. The Reverend Thomas DeWitt Talmage, referring to Utah as "the national stable," recommended troops be sent to Salt Lake City, the "salt plain Sodom of the New World," and guns of the greatest bore used to teach Mormons the seventh commandment. The Saints were particularly incensed at the suggestion of a Chicago journalist that the country could solve a double problem by shipping all its Negroes to Utah.[39]

The success of Senator Justin Morrill in obtaining passage in 1862 of an act to prohibit bigamy in territories under United States jurisdiction constituted the first major legislative move against the Mormons and their marriage system.[40] In speeches circulated to the public, he condemned the church's hierarchy for condoning both slavery and polygamy. The latter, he said, was animalistic, degrading to women, and, with its practice of easy divorce, a threat to the social order. He was especially outraged that the Saints would claim authority for what they were doing from the example of heaven.[41] The Morrill Act was, nevertheless, conspicuously ineffective. Not only were federal officials slow to enforce it but court jurisdictions in Utah were structured so that convictions for bigamy and adultery, dependent on local juries constituted of Mormons, were nearly impossible to obtain.[42] Bills were introduced into Congress during the 1860s and 1870s to strengthen the law or otherwise bridle what one gentile judge called Mormon "polygamic theocracy." However, only the Poland law of 1874, aimed at removing criminal jurisdiction from probate courts and enlarging the authority of federal appointees, succeeded in meeting approval from both houses.[43]

As Mormon spokesmen repeatedly insisted, the Morrill Act failed to distinguish between the crime of bigamy and "celestial marriage" as practiced by Latter-day Saints.[44] Western societies, with few exceptions, considered bigamists guilty of fraud against both the state and the yet-living first spouse. Both were deceived when one connived formal approval for a second conjugal union. It was to assist with the discovery of this and other irregularities that banns, use of witnesses, and the public register evolved. It was in this tradition, out of concern for plural unions performed by public magistrates, that the Morrill law was framed. Mormons frustrated the statute's assumptions in two ways: all partners in a plural arrangement were presumed to be both knowing and voluntary; and because their ceremonies were of a private, often secret nature, the state was never made a party to their solemnization. Sexual relations privately consummated apart from public approbation, like those of the Latter-day Saints, had historically been viewed as nothing more than adultery. But conviction here, as already suggested, was unlikely so long as Mormons constituted a strong majority of those sitting on juries. Added to this, the absence of any territorial law regulating matrimony, combined with a dearth of civic marriage records in Utah until the late 1880s, impoverished the evidentiary basis for prosecutions. Consequently, indictable infractions were difficult to find.[45]

The well-known *Reynolds* case of 1879 was expected by both sides to be a turning point. George Reynolds, a secretary to the Mormon First Presidency and husband of two wives, acceded to a request from his superiors in 1874 that he cooperate with prosecutors so that his case could be used to test the constitutionality of the Morrill statute. After the case spiraled through territorial tribunals, the United States Supreme Court unanimously upheld the law, sentencing Reynolds to prison and dashing the hopes of the Mormon community.[46] Until then, the Saints pursued the conflict, hoping for victories that would protect them in their practice and sometimes, as with the Englebrecht decision affecting the impaneling of juries, winning.[47] In the year the doctrine was publicly unveiled, Apostle Parley P. Pratt said that Latter-day Saints in good standing were expected to obey the laws of their country, whether they permitted one wife or sixteen.[48] After the *Reynolds* decision, however, even with the vagaries and caveats afflicting legal circumstances in Utah, the church was left to strategies of equivocation and, sometimes, outright defiance.

Reminding a tabernacle congregation that God had revealed the patriarchal order of marriage and commanded them to obey it or be damned, Wilford Woodruff asked: "Now, which shall we obey, God or Congress? For it is God and Congress for it." With a loud voice the assembly answered: "We will obey God."[49] At the time of the *Reynolds* case, the church's official public organ, the *Deseret News,* said it would be suicidal to give in and that Latter-day Saints would be no better than "knaves or noodles" to forfeit polygamous marriage because of the decision.[50] Most often, the church told members they were to choose and act for themselves—with the clear understanding that obedience to church doctrine was expected. In the spring of 1880, in churches throughout the territory, a sermon was read at the end of which members were asked to pledge that they "would stand by the Laws of God and take the consequences rather than obey the laws of man."[51] Mormons undoubtedly agreed with Dyer Daniel Lum, a socialistic admirer of the Saints, who reminded New England clergymen that, where moral issues were involved, Mormon polygamists had good precedent for disobedience.[52]

In that kind of atmosphere, it was inevitable that open clashes between Saint and Gentile would occur. This was illustrated during the spring of 1879 with John H. Miles. Following a procedure sometimes used to obfuscate polygamous arrangements, Miles married three women on the same day—Emily, Caroline, and Julia. Subsequently, due to confusion as to which of the wives had greatest seniority, Caroline became disaffected and took steps to have her husband arrested. Miles eventually won in court on grounds that, without independent proof of his marriage to the other women, Caroline must be presumed to be his only wife. As such, both statute and common law forbade the admissibility of her testimony against him. In the course of proceedings at the territorial level, however, Daniel H. Wells, a high Mormon official who had performed Miles's marriage in the Endowment House, refused to answer concerning oaths and costumes employed in the ceremony. Wells was held in contempt of court, fined and sentenced to two days' incarceration. The stubborn display by Wells and his journey to and from prison became a cause célèbre for the Saints.

At the end of his short confinement, Wells's return to Salt Lake City was made the occasion for a large parade. Some 10,000 Mormons joined in the procession. Another 15,000 lined the roads and streets, cheering his return. Critics later said that the American flag was trailed in the dust and that banners were held aloft declaring Mormon refusal to obey the law. Four hundred women marched with signs that read, "Women in favor of polygamy" and "We care less for the cut of our aprons than the loss of our rights." It is true these allegations were made by those unfriendly to the Mormon cause. But one Mormon responsible for making such placards admitted that his said, "When the laws of God and the laws of man are at variance, we will keep the laws of God."[53] The episode foretold a decade of bitter and sometimes violent dispute.

The Forty-seventh Congress of 1881–82 received hundreds of petitions insisting something be done about the Mormons. Even some of those dissenting from the extremes Congress was finally brought to enact thought polygamy a national threat.[54] George Q. Cannon, then serving as territorial delegate in Washington, D.C., said that feelings of animosity toward the Saints were greater than at any time in his memory. The result was the famous Edmunds Act, an amendment designed to strengthen the lame, twenty-year-old Morrill Act.[55] To understand innovations brought by the statute, we must recall difficulties associated with previous efforts to legally suppress polygamy. The Morrill Act addressed only formally solemnized multiple unions. Beyond the strict and traditional definition of bigamous offense contained in that law, there were attempts to use territorial enactments criminalizing adultery and "lewd and lascivious cohabitation" (the phrase Maurine Whipple imagined Apostle Erastus Snow to describe as "such a nasty mouthful"). But here, as in the widely publicized cases of Thomas Hawkins and Brigham Young, admissible evidence was almost impossible to obtain. To make sure further indictments were not brought under territorial acts, the relevant provisions were dropped for several years in subsequent compilations of Utah law.[56]

Seeking to avoid such difficulties, the Edmunds Act of 1882 amended the Morrill Act by enlarging the scope of criminality to include "unlawful cohabitation." In effect, the statute sought to reach the private unions involved in Mormon plural marriage by proscribing them with language traditionally used in connection with adultery. Beyond this, jurors were made subject to challenge on grounds of their practice of, or belief in, the doctrine; anyone cohabiting with more than one woman was disqualified from voting and holding public office; and a commission of five persons was established with quasi-judicial, legislative, and executive authorities. Aided by liberal judicial interpretations and an increase in the number of federal officials, prosecutions quickly mounted. As many at the time and since have observed, these reforms amounted to an application in Utah of coercive devices employed during Reconstruction in the South.[57]

By authority of the Utah Commission, public offices were vacated and polygamists barred from registering to vote. The oath used to screen offenders was particularly repugnant in that it required each man to swear he was innocent of cohabiting with more than one woman "in the marriage relation." The church was quick to emphasize the hypocrisy involved. Men keeping mistresses, prostitutes and their clients, fornicators, and seducers all were qualified under the oath to vote. But Latter-day Saints living with plural spouses "in the marriage relation," providing them with homes, supporting and educating their children, were singled out for disqualification.[58] Due to urging by church officials, non-polygamous Mormons went to the polls in ever larger numbers and the Supreme Court was brought to declare the test oath unconstitutional. But the same contest that saw the oath fall upheld the principle of disfranchisement and affirmed the constitutionality of other sections in the Edmunds Act. More than 12,000 Mormons were soon told they could not vote.[59]

Public hostility was nursed by groups such as the Women's National Anti-Polygamy Society, organized in Salt Lake City in 1878. The organization commenced publication of the *Anti-Polygamy Standard* in 1880, filling its pages with exaggeration and invective. Chapters were formed outside the territory, adding to the swell of complaint. The wife of Schuyler Colfax, vice president to Ulysses S. Grant, became a member. Non-Mormon religious denominations, especially those located in Utah, joined with the society, sometimes providing it with leadership. All were in tandem with the social purity movement of the day, transforming antebellum reform into a new abolitionism, using a variety of federations to strike at sexual and moral sin. Kimball Young only slightly exaggerated when he said that, between 1870 and 1920, Mormon polygamy rivaled prostitution and alcohol as a favored target by American reformers. Angry petitions were submitted to Congress asking for an amendment to the United States Constitution prohibiting polygamy everywhere in the United States. Although the attempt failed, efforts to pass such a measure were revived again and again, providing a cause around which opposition to Mormon polygamy clustered until well after the turn of the century.[60]

The Reorganized Church of Jesus Christ of Latter Day Saints, led since 1860 by the first prophet's son, Joseph III, also joined with those criticizing Utah Mormons for their erosion of the monogamous ethic. Joseph III adamantly insisted that his father had never engaged in plurality, that no children could be found as proof of such unions, and that his murder was not the result of polygamy. Anxious to disassociate themselves from "Brighamite" Mormonism, the Reorganized Church lectured and published extensively in behalf of its views.

Joseph III made four visits to Salt Lake City and surrounding communities before 1890 to argue that plurality was an invention of Brigham Young.[61] As the national campaign against polygamy acquired strength, the RLDS church found itself serendipitously provided with a vehicle for its own dearest causes. Both churches, their hierarchies spotted with men whose last names were Smith, scrambled to amass support for their respective claims. Paradoxically, by prompting Utah leaders to obtain affidavits and other evidence, RLDS badgering led only to the discovery of more proof for Joseph the prophet's plural relationships. Feelings of hostility between the denominational cousins, fueled by differences over the question, continued into the present century.[62]

More than anything, enforcement of the Edmunds Act turned Mormon columns. Rudger Clawson, one of the first to be indicted under the law, fought it through the courts, hoping to have it declared unconstitutional. When he failed, Apostle Francis M. Lyman said polygamists were seen to scatter and hide in a panic.[63] Even though Clawson was convicted for polygamy rather than unlawful cohabitation, the latter offense had the desired effect of snaring Saints by the hundreds. In the next half-dozen years, more than a thousand individuals were convicted for the crime and sent to prison. Local facilities filled up and those found guilty were sent wherever space was found, including as far away as Detroit, Michigan. Feelings ran so high that two Mormon missionaries were shot in Tennessee, and others horse-whipped and wounded. As part of the scrimmage in Utah, three shootings occurred there, including one fatality.[64]

The Mormon contention, expressed as early as the 1850s, was that the government had no more right to interfere with a man's marital relations than it did with "what he ate for breakfast."[65] Certainly the Mormon community did everything it could to bring attention to what they believed was a campaign of evil intent. Petitions signed by thousands of Mormon women objecting to laws barring them from the blessings of polygamous unions were sent to the nation's capitol; the great tabernacle stand was draped in mourning colors and funeral music played on the organ; flags were lowered to half-mast; and individuals walked about wearing black arm bands.[66] Perhaps the most singular of such gestures occurred at a special meeting of the twelve apostles held in early 1881. Charles C. Rich, near death, was carried to the gathering. Orson Pratt, also feeble, came as well. Then, after a special prayer in which particular government officials were named as among their oppressors, they all together washed their feet against such enemies. Wilford Woodruff, a participant in the ceremony, forgetting a similar ritual after the Saints' departure from Nauvoo, said, "It was truly a solmn [*sic*] scene and I presume to say it was the first thing of the Kind since the Creation of the world."[67] Surrender was clearly out of the question. The *Deseret News* said it would amount to apostasy if the church renounced the "New and Everlasting Covenant of marriage in its fullness." God would then reject the Saints as a people.[68]

Undeterred by Mormon stubbornness and anxious to give polygamy "a bold and manly lick," the second Edmunds law—the Edmunds-Tucker Act of 1887—pressured the Latter-day Saint community even more.[69] It provided that wives could be called to testify against their husbands; witnesses compelled to attend trials without benefit of subpoena; prosecutions for adultery permitted with or without complaint by spouses; enlarged powers given to federal officials in Utah; the church disincorporated and its properties, except for chapels and cemeteries, escheated to the United States. Female suffrage was abolished. And voters were required to swear to uphold the Edmunds Act of 1882, not even *advising* others to engage in unlawful cohabitation. The measure became law in 1887 and, when challenged, was upheld by the United States Supreme Court in 1890.[70] This statute, more than anything, is what led Orma Linford to allege that the antipolygamy crusade constituted the most intense campaign against any outlawed religious group in American history. Joy Wetzel summed it up best: "Though other eccentric religions suffered, none seems to have been more hated than Mormonism. Perhaps none was more feared either."[71]

But the Saints were ingenious at devising codes and resorts for deceiving federal marshals. The adventures of Mormon "cohabs" in their cat-and-mouse games with the deputies constitute a popular subject among polygamous descendants to the present day. Nothing was considered off-limits when it came to searches by government agents. Bedding was sifted for signs of cohabitation and the yet-uncompleted temple in Salt Lake City was combed for evidence. One polygamous bishop, hiding in the music department of a store, was crated up as an organ, the box labeled "Handle with Care" and shipped out. Another, caught at home by the deputies during a blizzard, left so precipitously that he forgot his trousers. Mormon folklore, however, holds that he soon found a pair of pants on a desert shrub, and three pair of warm socks, perfectly sized to his feet, fell from heaven.[72] The remarkable thing is that violence occurred as infrequently as it did. And it is to the Mormons' credit that, despite great hurt to themselves, no federal officers were seriously harmed during the entire struggle.[73]

Attempting to avoid discovery, men, women, and children were forced to prevaricate. Because of their studied ignorance, a judge in Arizona told one of the plural wives of Hans Adolph Thompson that hers was the smartest "don't know" family he ever encountered.[74] Utah's territorial governor, Arthur L. Thomas, said that the first requirement for catching a Mormon polygamist was to surround the house at night, then show skill as a runner and hurdler. If the accused were caught and brought to trial, however, one must expect every witness to be a perfect blank. Church members, he said, were known to deny events universally accepted as true.[75]

Persecution only hardened the Saints in their attitudes. Some of this was due to the natural psychological dynamics inherent in any scuffle. Mary Jane Mount Tanner, writing in the early 1880s, put it succinctly: "Aunt Cornelia says why do I defend poligamy [sic] so strongly I tell her because she attacts [sic] it."[76] Helen Mar Whitney said it was only natural that plurality, "being one of the greatest ideas ever advanced," should elicit great opposition.[77] Orson Pratt said conflict over the matter had the potential for becoming a "holy war."[78] Mormon leaders compared their predicament to that of the Israelites in Egypt or the early Christians in their difficulties with Rome.[79] Wilford Woodruff declared in 1873 that President Grant was like "Phario of Old," set on persecuting God's elect. One church leader told members that the recently sustained Morrill Act had been enacted purposely to make Mormons disobey God and that their predicament was the same as that of Daniel, who was placed between king and conscience.[80] Apostle Franklin D. Richards said passage of the Edmunds Act set apart those brethren "who believe in the Celestial Order of Marriage from those who do not and who are slow to practice it, and it seems to me that this is the Lord's preparation to bring those brethren to a higher platform."[81] Church members needed only to be faithful and God would fight their battle for them.[82] While monogamous inclinations among the Saints were never successfully smothered, the national campaign against them summoned both personal and collective resistence and resulted in more articulate defense of the principle.

When Apostle Lorenzo Snow was apprehended and placed on trial, the prosecuting attorney, Victor Bierbower, predicted that if Snow and others were found guilty and sent to prison church leaders would find it convenient to have a revelation setting aside the commandment on polygamy. Numbers of revelations were forthcoming—more, perhaps, than at any time since the death of Joseph Smith. But the messages invariably encouraged perseverance, spoke of the imminence of final things, and urged continued allegiance to the principle.[83] One communication affirmed that those to whom the law was given must obey it, that it was a requirement for life in the celestial kingdom.[84] In another the appointment of a new church authority was made contingent on his conforming to the law of plurality.[85] And in 1886 President John Taylor was told that the tenet would not be withdrawn, for it was an eternal principle. Too many, said the revelation, were negligent in obeying the commandment, and the only way to enter God's glory was by doing "the works of Abraham."[86] With a tabernacle audience intoning "amen" to his words, President John Taylor said in 1881 that God would put a hook in their oppressors' mouths and lead them away, while blessing and honoring Zion for its obedience to his holy law.[87]

Instruction by church authorities went beyond an acceptance of only the *doctrine* of plural marriage. Men were told they must actually engage in the practice. Only those willing to make the sacrifices involved in such a life-style, Joseph F. Smith said, were worthy of the highest glory.[88] George Q. Cannon informed an audience in St. George that he was reluctant to lift his hand to sustain any presiding officer who had not entered the principle. Church elders were told that having a dead woman sealed to them, or living "consecutive polygamy" by taking a new wife after a former one passed away, was not enough. One must live with more wives than one at the same time.[89] It was a requirement for membership in the revived School of the Prophets during the 1880s. There was, for example, question whether to admit Patriarch of the Church John Smith because he smoked and, though husband to two wives, spent all his time with only one.[90]

Church leaders—especially Mormon president John Taylor—were unyielding in their sermons. In his "coat collar" address he advised members to turn up their collars and tough out the storm, and in one of his last public appearances at the Tabernacle in 1885, he besought the church to stand absolutely firm. Joseph E. Robinson, though but a youth, related the dramatic effect the address had on him. As Robinson described it, guards were posted at the doors to the Tabernacle and only devout priesthood bearers were admitted. After recounting sufferings endured by the Saints, President Taylor turned to his two counselors and asked if they would stand by him. Both arose, moved to his side, and answered yes. He asked the Quorum of Apostles the same question. They arose and, with a single voice, said yes. He proceeded through all the leading priesthood quorums with the same result. Finally, he turned to the body of men in the Tabernacle and put the question to them. They rose to their feet and shouted yes. Taylor then declared that before losing wives, children, and possessions he would see their enemies damned in hell, "So help me, God." Robinson said it was the most dramatic moment of his life, that the Tabernacle thrilled and vibrated, and that chills ran through his body. Boy that he was, he said that he would have marched into the mouths of cannons had President Taylor asked it.[91]

Given such determination, it is not surprising that, before President Taylor's death in 1887, the church set in motion means for getting around the crusade and preserving the principle. Church properties were disbursed and transferred to avoid their escheatment. A more aggressive approach was taken in legal maneuvering. Money and energy were allocated to public relations and political influence.[92] The church also took a more subdued public stand on polygamy. Articles discussing the practice appeared less frequently in church publications. Reversing what had been said before, Joseph F. Smith testified that the practice was not binding on the Saints.[93] The public was repeatedly told that polygamous contractions were no longer occurring, that there were fewer bigamous marriages in Utah than in other states, and that the number living in polygamous households was not only small but "diminishing with wonderful rapidity."[94] In 1888 Wilford Woodruff told a subordinate that should a speaker raise the topic of plural marriage in general conference he should throw his hat at him.[95]

This did not mean that the leaders intended to let the principle die. Despite a debate among the apostles in the spring of 1882 over whether elders should continue to "live with but one wife under the same roof," the authorities disparaged any who advocated surrender. As late as 1887, the year of his death, President John Taylor continued to insist there could be no compromise, whatever the cost, so far as polygamy was concerned.[96] Under his direction expeditions were sent to find sites in northern Mexico and western Canada where polygamous families could settle, new plural unions could be performed, and the principle continued.[97] License to contract polygamous marriages was delegated to increasing numbers of individuals apart from the church president himself. On three separate occasions, while testifying in the Rudger Clawson case of 1884, President Taylor said the authority to perform plural marriages had been delegated to hundreds of men. At the same trial both George Q. Cannon and President

Taylor said that authority to seal couples in monogamy was the same as that for sealing them in polygamy.[98] Perpetuating the practice was assisted by the fact that, although the Endowment House as well as temples at St. George and Manti served as favored locations for couples wishing to be joined in plural relationships, it was always understood such ceremonies could be performed almost anywhere, in or out of doors.[99]

The conviction and imprisonment of hundreds of Mormons notwithstanding, plural marriages, both with and without the sealing ordinance, continued to be performed in private quarters and out-of-the-way locations. William Hendricks Roskelley's plural marriage to Agnes Wildman was solemnized by an individual hiding behind a blanket to conceal his identity. Women occasionally found it best to live with their parents or otherwise apart from their husbands after the marriage took place. James Douglas Harvey's plural wife stayed with her grandparents. When Harvey visited her, he dressed in female costume, hobbling to the residence in women's shoes.[100]

The proposed constitution of 1887 illustrates attempts to preserve polygamy while seeming to do the opposite. The document contained a self-executing provision punishing "bigamy and polygamy" as misdemeanors. It was hoped this, the first such clause in any of the six constitutions Utah had prepared, would persuade Congress to grant statehood to the territory. But the relevant section said nothing about unlawful cohabitation, rendering it as useless as the federal law of 1862.[101] Written comments from leaders to one another indicate that the provision was purposely worded to allow plural marriage to continue. As Franklin S. Richards, the church's attorney, explained to Joseph F. Smith, if the constitution were ratified, they could then "fix the penalties," administering them themselves, and so leave "cohabitation unrestricted."[102] Not surprisingly, the Utah Commission recommended against acceptance and Congress rejected it.[103]

An enactment by the legislature the next year, Utah's first marriage law, also avoided the phrase "unlawful cohabitation," forbidding only formal bigamy and prohibiting the performance of such contractions by anyone not authorized by the state. Since this enactment criminalized plurality in the traditional way, it was as ineffective an instrument as federal laws before the Edmunds Act.[104] But it was an attempt to persuade outsiders that Mormons were attempting to do *something* about polygamy and thereby, as Charles Walker said, "aid us in obtaining a State government."[105] And statehood, with its larger measure of local control (read Mormon control), the church itself having promised nothing, was looked upon as the means by which patriarchal marriage could be preserved. In the same column in which the proposed 1888 statute was printed, the *Deseret News* followed with an urgent plea that those Saints wishing to be saved in the highest degree of heaven remain faithful to all the commandments, however difficult they might be.[106]

An important step was taken, however, when the meaning of the phrase "celestial marriage" was modified. Although some basis exists for saying otherwise, evidence is on the side of an early equation of the term with church-solemnized, polygamous relationships.[107] The phrase referred to the plural households of the gods, a condition to which all Latter-day Saints should aspire.[108] When William Adams took a second wife in 1864, he said he had "entered into the Celestial Order of Marriage."[109] After the *Reynolds* case an article in the *Millennial Star* asserted, "Full well do they know that the Saints cannot give up plural, or rather the Celestial Order of Marriage without relinquishing their religion."[110] It was "celestial marriage," the First Presidency said in 1882, that the Edmunds Act sought to forbid.[111] In a revelation to President John Taylor, the superscript employed in the 1876 printing of Joseph Smith's 1843 revelation was repeated, giving divine sanction to language "including" the principle of plurality in the covenant of eternal marriage.[112] At a meeting of the School of the Prophets in 1883, Apostle Franklin D. Richards condemned the term *polygamy*, saying it was a Gentile word. Saints, he insisted, should better say "Patriarchal or Celestial marriage."[113] And children of polygamous parents have recalled that they were taught that not only were "celestial" and plural marriages the same thing but that those who refused to enter the principle would be disadvantaged in the world to come.[114]

Soon after passage of the Edmunds Act in 1882, an article in the *Deseret News* asserted that celestial marriage was not the same as plurality. Rather, Mormon authorities began saying that celestial marriage involved only a union for eternity and that this was what they taught their people. In his attempts to persuade Congress that Utah should be granted statehood, Franklin S. Richards insisted not only that plural marriage was permissive but that celestial marriage meant nothing more than being sealed to a single partner for eternity.[115] This shift, taken as one of several moves designed to lessen hostility toward the Saints, would be confirmed after the turn of the century when, again, the church labored with its public image.

All this persuades one to agree with Henry J. Wolfinger and Leo Lyman that, for the purpose of fixing on an axial time in the drama of Mormon transformation, our attention must be shifted backwards from 1890. The fact of hiding, of "underground" direction of church affairs in the 1880s, evinces Mormon intention to operate at two levels. These divided responses prefigured tactics employed for more than a quarter century. And one aspect of the strategy, Wolfinger and Lyman have demonstrated, was Mormon emphasis on the state or territory, rather than on the church, as the institution responsible for dealing with national agencies.[116] In other words, political agreements could occur only between the territory and the federal government. The church, as a private agency, could not bargain for the people of Utah. This was an important concept, and one emphasized by church spokesmen again and again in subsequent years. The attention given by Mormon fundamentalists in the twentieth century to the difference between church and priesthood as a way of disguising approved polygamy is but a declension of this earlier conceptual form.[117]

Given the willingness to engage in posturing of this sort, it is not surprising that leaders would consider temporarily abandoning the practice altogether. Apostle John Henry Smith told his cousin in 1888 that it was about the only thing left to try. He suggested renouncing the doctrine for five years. Then, after statehood was awarded, the Mormons could take it up again.[118] Leo Lyman's study makes it abundantly clear that, despite Wilford Woodruff's statement in 1888 that "the Lord never will give a revelation to abandon polygamy," the church continued its use of mollifying tactics to obtain statehood and so earn emancipation from federal control.[119] The seemingly contradictory nature of Mormon appearances led one Gentile to comment that public insistence on Mormon sincerity in ceasing the practice was matched only by Mormon sincerity in promising other audiences that they would never give it up.[120] Whether or not Brigham Young made the statement that the church would "pull the wool over the eyes of the American people and make them swallow Mormonism, polygamy and all," by the late 1880s that was the intention of a majority of high church authorities. As President John Taylor put it in 1887, the First Presidency had been united since before the death of Brigham Young on the proposition that there could be no compromise on plurality. Both belief in and practice of the principle must continue.[121]

Pressures of the anti-Mormon crusade also nourished millennial suppositions. The Saints had looked for the Second Coming of Christ as near at hand since the 1830s. The expectation was especially associated with the American Civil War, which, it was said, Joseph Smith foretold as early as 1832.[122] When the catastrophic consequences of the war, as set forth in the prophecy, did not occur, Mormons were loath to let the prediction go, believing that fighting would again break out and spread across the land. For years they seized upon events of national and world significance as signs that violence must soon erupt with redoubled fury. Missionaries and leaders found in each successive crisis the imminent fulfillment of Joseph's prophecy.[123] Early proposals for federal suppression of plural marriage were associated in the Mormon mind with expected destruction of the nation. During the Civil War Luke William Gallup told his non-Mormon aunt that the nation was old, bleeding, and dying. Disease and catastrophe were at the doors. Flight to Utah alone offered asylum.[124] Referring to anti-polygamy developments after the war, Brigham Young remarked: "Well, the faster it comes the sooner the end will be."[125]

After the *Reynolds* case L. John Nuttall confided in his journal that the cup of iniquity was surely full and that God must "shortly come out of his hiding place and vex the nation."[126] With passage of the 1882 law, things took an especially critical turn. And when the House of Representatives approved the Edmunds-Tucker Act in 1887, Wilford Woodruff said Congress had "turned the Last key that seals their Condemnation and lays the foundation for the overthrow & final destruction of the United States Government."[127] Events of the late 1880s seemed especially ominous because of a statement copied into Joseph Smith's journal by Willard Richards and included in the 1876 edition of the *Doctrine and Covenants*. Smith was quoted as saying that he had been shown that, if he lived to be eighty-five years of age, he would witness Christ's return. This pointed to the years 1890 and 1891.[128] Fig trees were leafing, and the hour was nigh.

Mormons also believed, with some reason, that by denying them the free exercise of their religion, all Americans were poorer. Considering the unhappiness attending traditional marriage, the Saints asked, why should they not be allowed to attempt an improvement? Was there no freedom even for experiment?[129] Recalling a prediction that the time would come when the United States Constitution would hang by a thread and that it would be the elders of the church that would save it, some leaders declared the time had arrived. George Q. Cannon said he was told from his youth up that it was the special destiny of the church to rescue the Constitution. By resisting assaults on plural marriage, the Saints saw themselves championing the liberties of all.[130]

The emphasis on plural family life as the primary goal of those responsible for the crusade has been questioned as ignoring a more important grievance—political control by the hierarchy and priest-hood. The role of the secret Council of Fifty and Latter-day Saint efforts to subordinate temporal to ecclesiastical authority are de-scribed as the crucial objects of the contest. Some suggest polygamy was but a Trojan horse, employed because of its sensational character to get at what was perceived as Mormon theocratic tyranny. The Saints themselves are said to have used plural marriage as a decoy, diverting attack from the more essential constitutional feature of their movement—the political kingdom of God. The struggle over polyg-amy, some say, concealed an agenda dearer to both sides.[131]

It is impossible to disagree that Mormonism's political hold at the territorial level was a major annoyance to Gentiles. Neither can one diminish the stubbornness of Mormon separatism, nor the puissant vision of earthly rule by men of God. Any understanding of Utah's mottled early history and delayed acceptance into the union would be seriously incomplete without such recognition. It is also true, how-ever, that polygamy and the church's theocratic pretensions were closely connected. Numbers said the two could not be separated, that political influence and plural marriage went together, that Mormon "polygamic theocracy" was of a piece.[132] It was increasingly apparent that to throttle polygamy required removal of the sheltering authority of the church in the legislature and the courts. As Franklin S. Richards told the leaders at the time he was working for statehood in the na-tion's capital, "the two great objections urged against our admission are polygamy and union of church and State or 'Mormon hier-archy.'"[133] As the Utah Commission explained in 1887, "The political history of the territory of Utah and the system of plural marriage are so closely interwoven that the one cannot be considered separate and apart from the other."[134]

Some Mormons agreed that the subject of plurality was being used to divert public attention. But, they said, it was rapacious Gentiles who manipulated the issue and who, carpetbagger-like, wished to displace the Saints to enrich themselves through territorial control.[135] More often yet, it was said this was part of a larger design—one that sought destruction of Mormonism altogether. John Thompson, speaking to Congress in the 1850s, referred to the Mormon tendency to portray opposition as "Gog and Magog . . . coming up against the Saints!"[136] Until past the Manifesto of 1890, a common response by church members to those opposing them was that ulterior motives were at work. John Taylor alleged that when President James Buchanan sent troops to Utah, "they had it all planned, and had our possessions apportioned, and had agreed who should have this establishment, that and the other."[137] After an encounter in the mid-1860s, in which he repeatedly threw gentile claim jumpers into the Jordan River, Charles Smith said it was for coveting Mormon property, "as they have always done."[138]

It was not polygamy, said many Saints, but the "milk in the Mormon coconut" that their enemies wanted.[139] And this, they said, had a familiar ring. The anti-polygamy movement was only an excuse for reenacting the dispossessions of Missouri and Illinois. With or without plural marriage, the Devil had been busy against them from the beginning. In 1887 President Taylor wrote that those behind the crusade wanted both Mormon liberty and Mormon treasure. Polygamy was but a pretext.[140] Observing that the Saints could not believe the Edmunds Act singly concerned with their marital behavior, that avarice was its real motive, Phil Robinson paraphrased Mormon attitudes by remarking, "The Gentiles . . . are hankering after the good things of Utah, and hope by one cry after another to persecute the Mormons out of them."[141]

If there was paranoia, there was also reason for what was believed, especially at the local level. In a review essay some years ago, Henry J. Wolfinger commented on the breadth of differences separating Mormons and Gentiles. To begin with, intense factionalism and one-party rule were common, as in most early territories. Added to this, Mormon-Gentile settlement patterns were not the same. Two school systems existed. Intense economic differences, as Leonard Arrington demonstrated, juxtaposed the camps. Governor Arthur L. Thomas, in 1889, said the situation reminded him of the rivalry between Christians and Saracens over possession of the Holy Land. Given these conditions, combined with agitation by local clergymen on the marriage question, Wolfinger's argument, that at the time polarization of its peoples was Utah's most striking feature, is persuasive.[142]

Without diminishing the importance of political considerations or the gulf of other differences separating Mormons from their neighbors, one cannot escape the insistent, near-myopic presence of polygamy in the perceptions of most non-Mormons at the time. It was not by accident that the overwhelming majority of federal laws and court cases involving Mormon-American relations were concerned with the Saints' marriage practices. Ambrose B. Carlton, a former member and chairman of the Utah Commission, wrote that to leave polygamy out of Mormon society would be like leaving the Prince of Denmark out of *Hamlet*. While acknowledging the sometimes fierce political concerns of Mormonism's local opponents, it was polygamy, he said, that had "attracted so much curiosity and brought upon the Mormons repres-

sive legislation by the United States Government."[143] Artists and writers found it the most popular theme they could choose when
caricaturing church leaders.[144] Anticipating the anti-polygamy crusade, one journalist asked in 1873 if "the home against the harem
might not prove as powerful a rallying call in the nineteenth century
as the Cross against the Crescent [had] in the twelfth."[145] And the
Reverend James David Gillilan, recalling Mormon-Protestant skir-
mishes of the 1880s, said it was not politics but "the sanctity of the
American Christian home" that actuated their cause.[146]

Mormon missionaries probably encountered the issue more often
than any other question about their faith. Joseph Marion Tanner,
visiting non-Mormon relatives in the East in the mid-1880s, wrote his
mother in Utah: "Of course poligamy [*sic*] is the great Monster. It is
everywhere abroad."[147] As early as the 1860s, a popular dictionary
defined the new religion, singly, as "a sect whose leading tenet or
practice is a plurality of wives."[148] And as late as 1905 there were non-
members from states who entered the practice on their own, expecting that they need only move to Utah to receive protection, inasmuch
as "the alpha and omega of Mormonism . . . was polygamy."[149] The
American attitude was overwhelmingly that of Senator John Tyler
Morgan: "Whenever you promote Mormonism you promote polygamy; whenever you promote the power of that church, you promote
polygamy. They are one and inseparable."[150] It was the Mormon
system of marriage, affirmed the *Chicago Evening Journal,* that was
"the especial curse and disgrace of this country."[151] For years, it was
remembered as what made Mormonism "a stench in the nostrils of the
Christian world."[152]

The reason for this noxious prominence was Mormonism's challenge to the accepted domestic way of life and the vital, dependent
connection this was believed to have with civilization. The charge that
the church bred disloyalty, that its theocratic penchant cut across the
nation's republican order, was genuinely threatening. But the fear
that Mormonism was corrupting the nation's homes overrode every
other terror. The actual magnitude of the peril was grossly and unfairly exaggerated.[153] But the impression took, and the crusade was
propelled by a righteous effrontery rooted in belief that Mormon
transgression spelled doom for Western man's quintessential achievement. When ladies of the Methodist Episcopal Women's Home Mission Society wished to show appreciation to Senator Edmunds for his
work against Mormon marriage, they sent his wife a silk bed quilt.
This, they said, was for the senator's efforts in behalf of a "better
civilization" in Utah.[154]

What Mormons, both those at the time and many writing on the subject today, have been unable fully to grasp was that concern lay less with the sexual derelictions of individuals than a sense that the *form* of the monogamous home was threatened. The purpose of anti-polygamy laws was to expunge the "semblance" of a competing, non-monogamic order of home life. This is why, in the face of Mormon consternation, convictions for plural marriage were allowed even when no sexual relations between spouses existed.[155] Replying to Mormon allegations of hypocrisy, that adulterers and prostitutes were allowed to vote under anti-polygamy laws while Mormons who married their companions were not, the Utah Commission restated Congress's purpose. They were attempting, said the commission, to meet what they saw as a conscious assault on "the most cherished institution of our civilization—the monogamic system." If plural marriage were tolerated, the commission explained, it could spread and weaken monogamy, which, they repeated, was the most important reason for "the advancement of civilization everywhere."[156]

The polemics mounted against Mormon plural marriage were so strident and, in many cases, distant from the views of our time that it is easy to dismiss them as hysterical or, in any case, unpersuasive. We must not forget, however, that nineteenth-century value constructions were as crucially felt as any of our own. In his summation in the Rudger Clawson case of 1884, Charles S. Varian referred to Mormonism as "teaching from its pulpits, speaking through its press, announcing through its oracles . . . that not only was it a right, but it was the duty of every man who could do so to enter into what was termed plural or celestial marriage."[157] And this, it was widely believed, directly threatened those structures that had won for Western civilization predominance abroad and civility at home. Polygamy, said Justice Stephen J. Field in 1889, confounded the "common sense" of his time.[158]

If Mormons were to successfully defend their marriage philosophy, they must do more than say they were under orders from heaven. They must speak to the "common sense" of their day. This required that they strike at the citadel of monogamy itself—a formidable task.

NOTES

1. Orson Pratt, "Celestial Marriage," *Seer* 1 (May 1853): 78. Richard Burton commented on the natural affinity in political philosophy of polygamous Mormons and the slave-holding South. *The City of the Saints and across the Rocky*

Mountains to California, ed. Fawn Brodie (1861; New York: Alfred A. Knopf, 1963), 277.

2. Brigham Young, quoted in Horace Greeley, *An Overland Journey, from New York to San Francisco in the Summer of 1859* (New York: Saxton & Barker, 1860), 211.

3. [Henry Charles Lea], *Bible View of Polygamy by Mizpah* (Philadelphia: n.p., n.d.), 1. Others who combined a defense of slavery with that of polygamy were Frederick A. Ross and John William Colenso, *Dr. Ross and Bishop Colenso; or, The Truth Restored in Regard to Polygamy and Slavery* . . . (Philadelphia: Henry B. Ashmead, 1857).

4. Mary Chesnut, quoted in *Mary Chesnut's Civil War,* ed. C. Vann Woodward (New Haven: Yale University Press, 1981), 308.

5. Charles Sumner's comments are in *Cong. Globe,* 33d Cong., 1st Sess., 268:1092–1114 (app. 1854). Smith's remarks to Stephens are in *Speeches of Gerrit Smith in Congress* (New York: Mason Brothers, 1856), 233.

6. For analysis of the sexual aspects of abolitionist thought in the antebellum period, see Ronald G. Walters, "The Erotic South: Civilization and Sexuality in American Abolitionism," *American Quarterly* 25 (May 1973): 177–201; and idem, *Primers for Prudery: Sexual Advice to Victorian America* (Englewood Cliffs, N.J.: Prentice-Hall, 1974), 98–109. Accounts of the Mormon question during these years, its connection with the slave controversy, and events leading to and during the "Utah War" are found in *CHC* 3:520–44, 4:181–451; Richard D. Poll, "The Mormon Question Enters National Politics, 1850–1856," *UHQ* 25 (Spring 1957): 117–31; Norman Furniss, *The Mormon Conflict, 1850–1859* (New Haven: Yale University Press, 1960); James B. Allen and Glen M. Leonard, *The Story of the Latter-day Saints* (Salt Lake City: Deseret Book, 1976), 258–63, 295–310; Davis Bitton, "Mormon Polygamy: A Review Article," *JMH* 4 (1977): 107–8; and David J. Whittaker, "Early Mormon Polygamy Defenses," *JMH* 11 (1984): 62–63. Mormon attitudes and circumstances during the Civil War are treated by E. B. Long, *The Saints and the Union: Utah Territory during the Civil War* (Urbana: University of Illinois Press, 1981). For Mormon thought and policy toward blacks, see Newell G. Bringhurst, *Saints, Slaves and Blacks: The Changing Place of Black People within Mormonism* (Westport, Conn.: Greenwood, 1981), 109–43.

7. Craig L. Foster, "Anti-Mormon Pamphleteering in Great Britain, 1837–1860" (M.A. thesis, BYU, 1989), 85, 102–11, 120–22, 133–52.

8. Encycl., *Arcanum Divinae Sapientiae,* sec. 13, 10 Feb. 1880. Regarding the extensive involvement of men of the cloth in defending slavery, see Larry E. Tise, *Proslavery: A History of the Defense of Slavery in America, 1701–1840* (Athens: University of Georgia Press, 1987), 371n.5.

9. John L. Thompson, *Mormonism—Increase of the Army. Speech of Hon. John Thompson of New York, Delivered in the House of Representatives, January 27, 1858* (Washington, D.C.: Buell & Blanchard, 1858), 5–6. The arguments of the Reverend Newman are found throughout *The Bible and Polygamy: Does the Bible Sanction Polygamy? A Discussion between Professor Orson Pratt . . . and Rev. Doctor*

J. P. Newman . . . (Salt Lake City: Deseret News, 1877). Even before Mormon polygamy became notorious, the practice was attacked in the United States as unscriptural by Sereno Edwards Dwight, *The Hebrew Wife; or, The Law of Marriage Examined in Relation to the Lawfulness of Polygamy and to the Extent of the Law of Incest* (New York: Leavitt & Lord, 1836). For a later example, see *Opinions Concerning the Bible Law of Marriage by One of the People* (Philadelphia: Claxton, Remson, & Haffelfinger, 1871). Criticisms of Mormon plurality as a system of organized lechery are instanced in Benjamin G. Ferris, *Utah and the Mormons* . . . (New York: Harper & Bros., 1854), 302–3, 306–7 passim; T. W. P. Taylder, *The Mormon's Own Book; or, Mormonism Tried by Its Own Standards* . . . (London: Partridge, 1857), 163–64 passim; A. E. D. DeRupert, *Californians and Mormons* (New York: John Wurtele Lovell, 1881), 161; Frederick Alphonso Noble, *The Mormon Iniquity* (Chicago: Jameson & Morse, 1884), 43 passim. An overview of these critiques is found in Charles A. Cannon, "The Awesome Power of Sex: The Polemical Campaign against Mormon Polygamy," *Pacific Historical Review* 43 (Feb. 1974): 61–82.

10. "The Governorship of Utah," *New York Times,* 30 March 1857; John Hyde, Jr., *Mormonism: Its Leaders and Designs* (New York: W. P. Fetridge, 1857), 74–75; Jules Remy and Julius Brenchley, *A Journey to Great Salt Lake City* . . . , 2 vols. (London: W. Jeffs, 1861), 2:150, 171; Newman, *The Bible and Polygamy,* 38; and George Whitfield Phillips, *The Mormon Menace* . . . (Worcester, Mass.: n.p., 1885), 7.

11. Regarding its non-democratic, enslaving effects, see the missives of Colonel Edward P. Conner, sent from Fort Douglas during the Civil War. U.S. War Department, *The War of the Rebellion: A Compilation of the Official Records of the Union and Confederate Armies,* 130 vols. (Washington, D.C.: G.P.O., 1880–1901), ser. 1, vol. 50, pt. 2:256, 318, 334, 370, 410, 492; and the remarks of Chief Justice Waite in *Reynolds v. U.S.,* 98 U.S. 145 (1879), at 166. For the threatening growth of Mormon population, see William Hepworth Dixon, *White Conquest,* 2 vols. (London: Chatto & Windus, 1876), 1:183; DeRupert, *Californians and Mormons,* 123; and Noble, *The Mormon Iniquity,* 9. Gerrit Smith said that "the Maker of the earth" had provided one home and one farm for each person, not two. *Speeches of Gerrit Smith,* 232.

12. "San Pete" to the editor, *Anti-Polygamy Standard* 1 (Oct. 1880): 45.

13. Daniel Wheelwright Gooch, *Polygamy in Utah: Speech of Hon. Daniel W. Gooch of Mass. Delivered in the House of Representatives, April 4, 1860* ([Washington, D.C., 1860]), 1–2. President James Buchanan concluded that Mormon polygamy was, in the words of one student, a "holy horror." Gwynn William Barrett, "John M. Bernhisel: Mormon Elder in Congress" (Ph.D. diss., BYU, 1968), 143–44.

14. This oft-quoted passage from a paper by Samuel A. Cartwright and Professor C. G. Forshey, based on the observations of Dr. Roberts Barthelow, received its most popular reading in a report of the proceedings of the New Orleans Academy of Science: "Hereditary Descent; or, Depravity of the Off-

spring of Polygamy among the Mormons," *DeBow's Review* 30 (1861): 203, 209–10. An examination of the report, as well as other nineteenth-century medical evaluations of the Mormons, is found in Lester E. Bush, Jr., "Mormon 'Physiology,' 1850–1875," *Bulletin of the History of Medicine* 56 (Summer 1982): 218–37. Other studies that devote some or all of their attention to the physiological critique made of Mormon polygamy are Cannon, "The Awesome Power of Sex," 61–82; Gary L. Bunker and Davis Bitton, "Polygamous Eyes: A Note on Mormon Physiognomy," *Dialogue* 12 (Fall 1979): 114–19; E. Victoria Grover-Swank, "Sex, Sickness and Statehood: The Influence of Victorian Medical Opinion on Self-Government in Utah" (M.A. thesis, BYU, 1980), 49–71; and Julie Dunfey, "'Living the Principle' of Plural Marriage: Mormon Women, Utopia, and Female Sexuality in the Nineteenth Century," *Feminist Studies* 10 (Fall 1984): 523–36.

15. DeRupert, *Californians and Mormons*, 161; and Samuel Bowles, *Across the Continent: A Summer's Journey to the Rocky Mountains, the Mormons, and the Pacific States, with Speaker Colfax* (New York: Hurd & Houghton, 1866), 124. Because of the practice, women were described as dull and idiotic in appearance. John G. Fackler Diary, 10 Aug. 1864, Missouri Historical Society, St. Louis, Mo. Also see Taylder, *The Mormon's Own Book*, xx passim; "The Woman's National Anti-Polygamy Society," *Anti-Polygamy Standard* 1 (Aug. 1880): 33; "Aggressive Mormonism," ibid. 2 (May 1881): 12; and the first annual message of President Chester A. Arthur, in *A Compilation of the Messages and Papers of the Presidents, 1789–1902*, comp. James D. Richardson, 20 vols. (New York: Bureau of National Literature, 1897–1921), 10:4644.

16. Peter Julius Christofferson, "Prison Life in the Detroit House of Correction," 1, typewritten manuscript, copy in possession of author.

17. "Persons and Things," *Chicago Evening Journal*, 9 Feb. 1880.

18. Utanus, "Squatter Sovereignty vs. the Constitution," *Kirk Anderson's Valley Tan*, 19 Nov. 1858. The same view was expressed in the anonymous tract *Opinions Concerning the Bible Law of Marriage*, 229.

19. Noble, *The Mormon Iniquity*, 3.

20. Phillips, *The Mormon Menace*, 2, 8, 10–11. One is reminded of Rebecca Latimer Felton's opinion, as paraphrased by Anne Firor Scott, that "the four years of bloody war was a fit penance for so many [sexual] sins." *The Southern Lady: From Pedestal to Politics, 1830–1930* (Chicago: University of Chicago Press, 1970), 53. I am indebted to Professor Klaus Hansen of Queen's University, Kingston, Ontario, Canada, for bringing this parallel to my attention.

21. "Separate Report of John A. McClernand," appended to "Annual Report of the Utah Commission" [1889], *Report of the Secretary of the Interior . . . ,* 5 vols. (Washington, D.C.: GPO, 1890), 3:207. Chief Justice Waite's remark is in *Reynolds vs. United States*, 98 U.S. 145 (1879), at 164.

22. Cannon, "The Awesome Power of Sex," 79.

23. Mrs. Benjamin G. Ferris, *Mormons at Home, with Some Incidents of Travel from Missouri to California, 1852–53, in a Series of Letters* (New York: Dix &

Edwards, 1856), 146–47, 200; Utanus, "Squatter Sovereignty vs. the Constitution," *Kirk Anderson's Valley Tan*, 19 Nov. 1858; Jennie Anderson Froiseth, *The Women of Mormonism; or, The Story of Polygamy as Told by the Victims Themselves* (Detroit, Mich.: C. G. G. Paine, 1882), 212 passim; William Hepworth Dixon, *Spiritual Wives* (London: Hurst & Blackett, 1868), 183–84; Christopher G. Tiedeman, *A Treatise on the Limitations of Police Power in the United States Considered from Both a Civil and Criminal Standpoint* (St. Louis: F. H. Thomas, 1886), 539; "Report of the Governor of Utah," *Report of the Secretary of the Interior . . .* , 5 vols. (Washington, D.C.: GPO, 1885), 2:1020. Also see Gary L. Bunker and Davis Bitton, *The Mormon Graphic Image, 1834–1914: Cartoons, Caricatures, and Illustrations* (Salt Lake City: University of Utah Press, 1983), 128.

24. See, e.g., the comments of Representative John Thompson in his *Mormonism—Increase of the Army*, 6; and especially the descriptions in "Celia Logan on Mormon Life—1" and "Celia Logan on Mormon Life—2," [New York] *Daily Graphic*, 28 and 29 Nov. 1873, respectively. Cf. the commentary in Richard I. Aaron, "Mormon Divorce and the Statute of 1852: Questions for Divorce in the 1980s," *Journal of Contemporary Law* 8 (1982): 23.

25. Edward Shorter, *The Making of the Modern Family* (New York: Basic Books, 1975), 227–54. Under the Victorians this led to a domestic architecture that made of the home a miniature church. Clifford Edward Clark, Jr., *The American Family Home, 1800–1960* (Chapel Hill: University of North Carolina Press, 1986), 25.

26. Lewis Henry Morgan, *Ancient Society; or, Researches in the Lines of Human Progress from Savagery through Barbarism to Civilization* (1877; New York: World Publishing, 1963), 58, 512. Also see John Haller, Jr., "Race and the Concept of Progress in Nineteenth-Century American Ethnology," *American Anthropologist* 73 (June 1971): 719.

27. Polygamy was linked with libertinage, license, and disease. See Michael Ryan, *The Philosophy of Marriage, in its Social, Moral, and Physical Relations . . .* (London: H. Bailliere, 1839), 125–26. This was Congressman John Thompson's meaning in 1858 when he represented Mormon polygamy as a threat to the American "hearthstone." *Mormonism—Increase of the Army*, 1, 5–6, 7–8. In his sentencing of Rudger Clawson in 1884, Judge Charles Zane emphasized that if monogamy failed the floodgates would be thrown open to confusion. See the discussion in Thomas G. Alexander, "Charles S. Zane . . . Apostle of the New Era," *UHQ* 34 (Fall 1966): 290–314. It was an enemy to American and European civilization. *Suppression of Polygamy in Utah*, House of Reps., 49th Cong., 1st sess., Report No. 2735 (1886): 3. As late as 1918 Arthur W. Calhoun referred to Mormonism as "a reversion" to "an earlier phase of racial experience." *A Social History of the American Family: From Colonial Times to the Present*, 3 vols. (Cleveland, Ohio: Arthur H. Clark, 1917–19), 2:155.

28. Ferris Jacobs, Jr., in *Cong. Rec.*, 47th Cong., 1st sess., 19 April 1882, 3057.

29. Samuel Cox, ibid., 47th Cong., 1st sess., 10 Jan. 1882, 338. Also see *Murphy v. Ramsey,* 114 U.S. 15 (1884), at 45.

30. Taylder, *The Mormons's Own Book,* 204. The magnitude of the danger was outlined by the Reverend Frederick Alphonso Noble: "Every tradition of our American life, every principle of our civil polity, every memory of what is sweetest and best in our homes, every aspiration for a worthy future for our nation is against this abomination." *The Mormon Iniquity,* 13.

31. The best-known exposition of this view is Barbara Welter, "The Cult of True Womanhood, 1820–1860," in *The American Family: A Social-Historical Perspective,* ed. Michael Gordon (New York: St. Martin's, 1973), 224–50. I am aware that qualifications and challenges to this description, as in so much of social history of the family, abound. See Nancy F. Cott, "Passionlessness: An Interpretation of Victorian Sexual Ideology, 1790–1850," in *A Heritage of Her Own: Toward a New Social History of American Women,* ed. Nancy F. Cott and Elizabeth H. Pleck (New York: Simon and Schuster, 1979), 162–82; Carl N. Degler, *At Odds: Women and the Family in America from the Revolution to the Present* (New York: Oxford University Press, 1980), 26–51; Estelle B. Freedman, "Sexuality in Nineteenth-Century America: Behavior, Ideology, and Politics," *Reviews in American History* 10 (Dec. 1982): 196–215; Karen Haltunen, *Confidence Men and Painted Women: A Study of Middle-Class Culture in America, 1830–1870* (New Haven: Yale University Press, 1982), 96; Peter Gay, *Education of the Senses,* Vol. 1: *The Bourgeois Experience: Victoria to Freud* (New York: Oxford University Press, 1984), 118–19, 124–27; all of Mabel Collins Donnelly, *The American Victorian Woman: The Myth and the Reality* (Westport, Conn.: Greenwood-Praeger, 1986); Nancy S. Landale and Avery M. Guest, "Ideology and Sexuality among Victorian Women," *Social Science History* 10 (Summer 1986): 147–70; and all of Karen Lystra, *Searching the Heart: Women, Men, and Romantic Love in Nineteenth-Century America* (New York: Oxford University Press, 1989).

32. Richardson, *Messages and Papers of the Presidents,* 10:4946–4947.

33. Hubert Howe Bancroft, *History of Utah* (San Francisco: History Co., 1889), 371–73.

34. Mark Wilcox Cannon, "The Mormon Issue in Congress, 1872–1882, Drawing on the Experience of Territorial Delegate George Q. Cannon" (Ph.D. diss., Harvard University, 1960), 127.

35. Paul Wilbur Tappan, "Mormon-Gentile Conflict: A Study of the Influence of Public Opinion on In-Group versus Out-Group Interaction with Special Reference to Polygamy" (Ph.D. diss., University of Wisconsin, 1939), 416–17.

36. Neal Lambert, "Saints, Sinners and Scribes: A Look at the Mormons in Fiction," *UHQ* 36 (Winter 1968): 63–76; Leonard J. Arrington and Jon Haupt, "Intolerable Zion: The Image of Mormonism in Nineteenth-Century American Literature," *Western Humanities Review* 22 (Summer 1969): 243–60; Richard H. Cracroft, "Distorting Polygamy for Fun and Profit: Artemus Ward

and Mark Twain among the Mormons," *BYU Studies* 14 (Winter 1974): 272–88; Douglas McKay, "The Puissant Procreator," *Sunstone* 7 (Nov.-Dec. 1982): 15–17.

37. James Washington Singleton, quoted from the *New York World*, in "The Prevailing Topic," *DN*, 20 Jan. 1882.

38. W. H. Babcock, "Our Monthly Gossip," *Lippincott's Monthly Magazine* 37 (June 1886): 664. Also see "Meddling with the Mormons," [New York] *Daily Graphic*, 9 Dec. 1873.

39. William Fraser Rae, *Westward by Rail: The New Route to the East* (New York: D. Appleton, 1871), 149; "Talmage on the Mormons," [New York] *Sun*, 27 Sept. 1880; and an editorial replying to the *Chicago Evening Journal*, in *Deseret News Weekly*, 4 Feb. 1880. The same Chicago paper urged that the United States take care of its Indian problem by colonizing tribes among the Mormons. "Persons and Things," *Chicago Evening Journal*, 4 Feb. 1880.

40. U.S., *Statutes at Large*, 12, ch. 126:501–2 (1862).

41. William Belmont Parker, *The Life and Public Services of Justin Smith Morrill* (Boston: Houghton Mifflin, 1924), 82–83, 87–89, 97–98.

42. President Chester A. Arthur said of the Morrill Act in 1881 that it had been "practically a dead letter." Richardson, *Compilation of the Messages and Papers of the Presidents*, 10:4644. Studies of problems associated with law enforcement in Utah at that time, including the Morrill Act, are extensive. See Edwin Brown Firmage and Richard Collin Mangrum, *Zion in the Courts: A Legal History of the Church of Jesus Christ of Latter-day Saints, 1830–1900* (Urbana: University of Illinois Press, 1988), 130–51; Leonard J. Arrington, "Crusade against Theocracy: The Reminiscences of Judge Jacob Smith Boreman of Utah, 1872–1877," *Huntington Library Quarterly* 24 (Nov. 1960): 1–45; idem, *Great Basin Kingdom* (Cambridge, Mass.: Harvard University Press, 1958), 356–57; Orma Linford, "The Mormons and the Law: The Polygamy Cases," *Utah Law Review* 9 (Winter 1964), pt. 1:316–17; Thomas G. Alexander, "Federal Authority versus Polygamic Theocracy," *Dialogue* 1 (Autumn 1966): 85–100; James B. Allen, "The Unusual Jurisdiction of County Probate Courts in the Territory of Utah," *UHQ* 36 (Spring 1968): 132–42; Gordon Morris Bakken, "Judicial Review in the Rocky Mountain Territorial Courts," *American Journal of Legal History* 15 (Jan. 1971): 57–59; Gustive O. Larson, *The "Americanization" of Utah for Statehood* (San Marino, Calif.: Huntington Library, 1971), 61–77; Elizabeth D. Gee, "Justice for All or for the 'Elect'? The Utah County Probate Court, 1855–72," *UHQ* 48 (Spring 1980): 129–47.

43. This was territorial Chief Justice James B. McKean. See Alexander, "Federal Authority versus Polygamic Theocracy," 89–90. Clear descriptions of the various proposed pieces of legislation, including the law named after Representative Luke Poland from Vermont, are available in Arrington, *Great Basin Kingdom*, 356–57; and Larson, *The "Americanization" of Utah*, 61–77. The Poland law can be read in U.S., *Statutes at Large*, 18, ch. 253 (1874).

44. "Old Laws Applied to New Conditions," *DN*, 13 Dec. 1880; "An Essen-

tial Difference," *DN*, 13 Oct. 1881; "We Do Not Believe in 'Polygamy,'" *DN*, 21 Dec. 1881; "Polygamy Is Not Bigamy," *DN*, 23 Jan. 1885; *JD* 24:45 (George Q. Cannon/1882); *JD* 26:94 (John Taylor/1882); *JD* 23:294–95 (Erastus Snow/1883); and "Are They in Earnest?" *SLT*, 18 Oct. 1884.

45. For a discussion of "cohabitation" as opposed to "bigamy," as finally developed by Congress, see Firmage and Mangrum, *Zion in the Courts*, 161, 167–75. Regarding the want of both records and law in connection with marriage in Utah Territory until 1888, see Carol Cornwall Madsen, "Beyond the Limits: Religion, Women and the Law in Territorial Utah" (Paper delivered before the Western Association of Women's Historians, Henry E. Huntington Library and Art Gallery, San Marino, Calif., 14 April 1984), 5.

46. *Reynolds vs. United States*, 98 U.S. 145 (1879). The best overview of circumstances surrounding the case, including the controversy over pre-trial agreements, is found in Bruce Arthur Van Orden, "George Reynolds: Secretary, Sacrificial Lamb, and Seventy" (Ph.D. diss, BYU, 1986), 53–93. Undiscussed by Van Orden is the account given by George Q. Cannon some eleven years after the case, in which he said his own marriages were first considered for the purpose of a test case, then those of Erastus Snow and Abraham M. Musser. For one reason or another, these were judged unsatisfactory and the younger, recently pluraled George Reynolds was selected with assurances from high officials that, if convicted, he would be pardoned. This was frustrated by one of the prosecuting attorneys, Robert N. Baskin. See "Remarks . . . ," *DN*, 11 Oct. 1890. Baskin's somewhat different account is in his *Reminiscences of Early Utah* ([Salt Lake City: Tribune-Reporter Printer], 1914), 61–72. Legal commentary on the case is voluminous. Some of the more important analyses, taking notice of the Mormon situation, are Linford, "The Mormons and the Law," pt. 1:331–41; C. Peter Magrath, "Chief Justice Waite and the 'Twin Relic': *Reynolds v. United States*," *Vanderbilt Law Review* 18 (1965): 507–43; Ray Jay Davis, "Plural Marriage and Religious Freedom: The Impact of *Reynolds v. U.S.*," *Arizona Law Review* 15 (1973): 287–306; Robert G. Dyer, "The Evolution of Social and Judicial Attitudes towards Polygamy," *Utah Bar Journal* 5 (Spring 1977): 35–45; Carol Weisbrod and Pamela Sheingorn, "*Reynolds v. United States:* Nineteenth-Century Forms of Marriage and the Status of Women," *Connecticut Law Review* 10 (Summer 1978): 828–57; Randall D. Guynn and Gene C. Schaerr, "The Mormon Polygamy Cases," *Sunstone* 11 (Sept. 1987): 8; James L. Clayton, "The Supreme Court, Polygamy, and the Enforcement of Morals in Nineteenth-Century America: An Analysis of *Reynolds v. United States*," *Dialogue* 12 (Winter 1979): 46–61; Mark S. Lee, "Legislating Morality: *Reynolds vs. United States*," *Sunstone* 10 (April 1985): 8–12; and Firmage and Mangrum, *Zion in the Courts*, 151–59.

47. *Clinton et al. v. Englebrecht*, 80 U.S. 434 (1871). Church leaders on several occasions said that they could not be shown to have broken the laws of the land: *JD* 6:19 (John Taylor/1857); *JD* 9:182 (Heber C. Kimball/1861); *JD* 9:331 (Brigham Young/1862); *JD* 20:3 (George Q. Cannon/1878).

48. Parley P. Pratt, *"Mormonism!" "Plurality of Wives!" An Especial Chapter, for the Edification of Certain Inquisitive News Editors, Etc.* (San Francisco, 1852), one-page flyer.

49. Wilford Woodruff, in *Wilford Woodruff's Journal*, ed. Scott G. Kenney, 9 vols. (Midvale, Utah: Signature Books, 1983–85), 6:518–19, 9 Jan. 1870.

50. Untitled editorial, *DN*, 2 April 1879; and "Shall Polygamy Be Put in Abeyance?" *DN*, 30 Aug. 1879.

51. See, for example, the account given of the pledge taken by Saints in St. George, in *Diary of Charles Lowell Walker*, ed. A. Karl Larson and Katharine Miles Larson, 2 vols. (Logan: Utah State University Press, 1980), 2:491–92, 27 March 1880. Also see the comments of Orson Pratt in *JD* 20:327 (1880).

52. [Dyer Daniel Lum], *Utah and Its People: Facts and Statistics Bearing on the "Mormon Problem"* . . . *by a Gentile* (New York: R. O. Ferrier, 1882), 41.

53. Miles's case was finally carried to the United States Supreme Court, where Caroline's testimony was ruled inadmissible. *Miles v. United States*, 103 U.S. 304 (1881). For an illustrated description of the Wells episode, see "The Great Mormon Demonstration," *Frank Leslie's Illustrated Newspaper*, Supplement, 31 May 1879. Also see the later account provided in *Inside of Mormonism: A Judicial Examination of the Endowment Oaths Administered in All the Mormon Temples* . . . (Salt Lake City: Utah Americans, 1903), 57–58; and Brigham H. Roberts's narrative in *CHC* 5:547–50. The sign painter's admission referred to in the text was that of Benjamin Franklin LeBaron, described in his "Autobiography," typewritten copy, 11, BYU Library. Whether the flag was purposely soiled in the parade was a question debated for decades. E.g., "Old Glory Was Trailed in Dust," *SLT*, 22 Oct. 1910.

54. *Defence of the Constitutional and Religious Rights of the People of Utah: Speeches of Senators Vest, Morgan, Call, Brown, Pendleton and Lamar.* ([Salt Lake City?]: n.p., 1882), 40.

55. The law is found in U.S., *Statutes at Large*, 22, ch. 47:30–32 (1882). Accounts of the legal and political circumstances surrounding passage of the Edmunds Act are available in Richard D. Poll, "The Political Reconstruction of Utah Territory, 1866–1890," *Pacific Historical Review* 27 (May 1958): 111–26; Linford, "The Mormons and the Law," pt. 1:317–18; Larson, *The "Americanization" of Utah*, 91–114; Edward Leo Lyman, *Political Deliverance: The Mormon Quest for Utah Statehood* (Urbana: University of Illinois Press, 1986), 19–40; Firmage and Mangrum, *Zion in the Courts*, 160–97.

56. Maurine Whipple's phrase was attributed to Apostle Erastus Snow in her novel, *The Giant Joshua* (1941; Salt Lake City: Western Epics, 1976), 446. For the question of the common law and its relevance for prosecuting polygamists in Utah Territory, see Michael W. Homer, "The Judiciary and the Common Law in Utah Territory, 1850–61," *Dialogue* 21 (Spring 1988): 97–108. A colorful account of the Young and Hawkins cases is provided in George Alfred Townsend, *The Mormon Trials at Salt Lake City* (New York: American News, 1871), 8–15. As George A. Smith pointed out in the year following these cases, the 1852 statute had never been intended for use

against polygamists, because those sitting in the territorial legislature that passed the act "were unanimously believers in, and four-fifths of them practical observers of, the law of celestial marriage." *The Rise, Progress and Travels of the Church* . . . , 2d rev. ed. (Salt Lake City: Deseret News, 1872), 69–70.

57. See the remarks of Senator Joseph Emerson Brown from Georgia, in *Defense of the Constitutional and Religious Rights,* 26–27; and those of Apostle Franklin D. Richards in *JD* 20:313, 23:113 (1880, 1883). More recently, see Poll, "The Political Reconstruction of Utah Territory," 114; Larson, *The "Americanization" of Utah,* 95; Magrath, "Chief Justice Waite," 517, 534; and Howard R. Lamar, "Statehood for Utah: A Different Path," *UHQ* 39 (Fall 1971): 312, 314. In considering the comparison with Reconstruction, one must keep in mind Thomas G. Alexander's point that a "pupilage" theory characterized nineteenth-century congressional dealings with all the western territories, Utah being no exception. See his *Clash of Interests: Interior Department and Mountain West, 1867–90* (Provo, Utah: BYU Press, 1977), 136, 173–74, 180–82.

58. The most thorough examination of the commission's work is that of Stewart Lofgren Grow, "A Study of the Utah Commission, 1882–96" (Ph.D. diss., University of Utah, 1954). Other helpful treatments are in Robert Joseph Dwyer, *The Gentile Comes to Utah: A Study in Religious and Social Conflict (1862–1890)* (Washington, D.C.: Catholic University Press, 1941), 215–30; Poll, "The Political Reconstruction of Utah Territory," 119–20; Larson, *The "Americanization" of Utah,* 98–103; Allen L. Shepherd, "Gentile in Zion: Algernon Sidney Paddock and the Utah Commission, 1882–1886," *Nebraska History* 57 (Fall 1976): 359–77; Alexander, *A Clash of Interests,* 133–35, 175. As examples of the storm raised by the Mormons over what they believed to be the moral hypocrisy of the oath, see "Gross Immorality at a Premium," *DN,* 11 April 1882; First Presidency, "An Address to the Members of the Church . . . ," 29 Aug. 1882, *Messages* 2:342–47; *JD* 24:107–8 (George Q. Cannon/1882); *JD* 23:268, 24:7 (John Taylor/1883, 1883); *JD* 25:111, 26:222–23 (Erastus Snow/1884,1885); "Discourse by President John Taylor," *DN,* 18 Oct. 1884; and "Discourse by Apostle Erastus Snow," *DN,* 13 June 1885.

59. *Murphy v. Ramsey,* 114 U.S. 15 (1885). On the numbers affected, see Larson, *The "Americanization" of Utah,* 98–103; and Firmage and Mangrum, *Zion in the Courts,* 231–33.

60. For accounts of the founding of the Anti-Polygamy Society, with names of officers and locations of chapters, see "The Ladies Anti-Polygamy Society of Utah," *Anti-Polygamy Standard* 1 (April 1880): 1; "Meeting of the Ladies Anti-Polygamy Society," ibid. 1 (May 1880): 9; "The Ladies Anti-Polygamy Society of Utah," ibid. 1 (July 1880): 25; "The Women's National Anti-Polygamy Society," ibid. 1 (Aug. 1880): 33; "Ladies Anti-Polygamy Movement," ibid. 1 (Sept. 1880): 43; "Work against Polygamy," ibid. 2 (July 1881): 30; "A Noble Society," *SLT,* 14 June 1880; "A Female Anti-'Mormon' Missionary," *DN,* 8 Nov. 1880; and Ernest Ingersoll, "Salt Lake City," *Harper's* 69 (Aug. 1884): 398–99. Sectarian opposition to polygamy inside Utah is

described in T. Edgar Lyon, "Religious Activities and Development in Utah, 1847–1910," *UHQ* 35 (Fall 1967): 298–99. For the genesis and history of the social purity movement, see David J. Pivar, *Purity Crusade: Sexual Morality and Social Control, 1868–1900* (Westport, Conn.: Greenwood, 1973). Kimball Young's comment is found in *Isn't One Wife Enough?* (New York: Henry Holt, 1954), 1. Proposals to amend the United States Constitution to prohibit polygamy date at least as early as the 1870s but acquired little momentum until the time of the Edmunds Act. See, e.g., *Cong. Rec.*, 47th Cong., 1st Sess., 1882, 13:293, 724; "Constitutional Amendment Craze," *DN*, 22 Nov. 1883.

61. For Joseph III's ordination at Amboy, Illinois, in 1860 as "Prophet, Seer, and Revelator" of the Reorganized Church and an account of his missionary and evidence-gathering visits to Utah, see Roger D. Launius, *Joseph Smith III: Pragmatic Prophet* (Urbana: University of Illinois Press, 1988), 115–19, 218–46; and Charles Millard Turner, "Joseph Smith III and the Mormons of Utah" (Ph.D. diss., Graduate Theological Union, Berkeley, Calif., 1985), 195, 291–300, 360–78, 388–90, 394–401. In a long letter to William Everest, Smith listed the reasons why he believed his father could not have been a polygamist. A major point, and one to which RLDS apologists would return for the better part of a century, was the seeming failure to find any children from such relationships, "not one!" Joseph Smith III to William Everest, 7 March 1889, P22, fd. 52, RLDS Library and Archives, Independence, Mo.

62. RLDS support for the crusade against polygamy is treated in Launius, *Joseph Smith III*, 247–72; and Turner, "Joseph Smith III and the Mormons of Utah," 333–39. Letters from RLDS missionaries in Australia, showing that the debate between the two factions extended abroad, are found in P24, fd. 28, RLDS Library and Archives. As an illustration of the coalescence of RLDS and national sentiment, see "A Boom against Utah Brighamy," *Chicago Evening Journal*, 16 Jan. 1880. Examples of attestations and affidavits gathered by the two churches to prove each other wrong are Joseph F. Smith, "Joseph the Seer's Plural Marriages," *DN*, 18 Oct. 1879; "Joseph Smith, Presidency and Plural Marriage," *DN*, 21 Aug. 1882; "Plural Wives in the Prophet's Day," *DN*, 3 July 1885; Joseph Smith III, *The Polygamic Revelation: Fraud! Fraud! Fraud!* . . . (Lamoni, Iowa: True Latter Day Saints' Herald Office, n.d.); idem, *Reply of Pres. Joseph Smith, to L. O. Littlefield in Refutation of the Doctrine of Plural Marriage* (Lamoni, Iowa: The Reorganized Church of Jesus Christ of Latter Day Saints, 1885); and, of course, the affirmations and denials adduced by both sides in the Temple Lot Case where, although Utah Mormons were not a formal party, they supported the Church of Christ and took an intense interest in the outcome: *Reorganized Church of Jesus Christ of Latter Day Saints, Complainant. vs. Church of Christ at Independence, Missouri; . . . Complainant's Abstract . . .* (Lamoni, Iowa: Herald Publishing House, 1893).

63. *Clawson v. United States*, 114 U.S. 477 (1885). Background on the Clawson prosecution can be read in "The Indictment for Polygamy," *DN*, 25 April 1884. Francis M. Lyman's statement was taken from his diary by Albert

Robison Lyman, "Francis Marion Lyman," typewritten manuscript, 24 Oct. 1941, p. 54, Church Archives.

64. On the number of polygamists sent to prison, see Larson, *The "Americanization" of Utah,* 104. And for sending Mormon pluralists to Michigan, see B. Carmon Hardy, "'The American Siberia': Mormon Prisoners in Detroit in the 1880s," *Michigan History* 50 (Sept. 1966): 197–210. Accounts of violence against Mormons are "The Dalton Murder," *Deseret News Weekly,* 29 Dec. 1886; "Persecution and Misrepresentation," *DN,* 18 July 1887; "Elders Wounded," *DN,* 14 Jan. 1888; *CHC* 6:89–102, 116–20; Fae Decker Dix, "Unwilling Martyr: The Death of Young Ed Dalton," *UHQ* 41 (Spring 1973): 162–77; and all of William Whitridge Hatch, *There Is No Law . . . : A History of Mormon Civil Relations in the Southern States, 1865–1905* (New York: Vantage, 1968).

65. "Polygamy in Utah," *DN,* 5 Oct. 1854; "'Mind Your Own Business,'" *Mormon* 1 (30 June 1855): n.p.; "The Chicago 'Times' at It Again," *DN,* 17 Aug. 1887. For an account of southern opposition to the Edmunds bill because of its approval of federal intervention in local affairs, see David Buice, "A Stench in the Nostrils of Honest Men: Southern Democrats and the Edmunds Act of 1882," *Dialogue* 21 (Fall 1988): 100–113.

66. Protest meetings by Mormon women, replete with speeches and petitions, were held on several occasions during the 1870s and 1880s. See Tullidge, *History of Salt Lake City,* 433–39; *CHC* 5:231–34, 6:115–16; William Mulder and A. Russell Mortensen, eds., *Among the Mormons: Historic Accounts by Contemporary Observers* (Lincoln: University of Nebraska Press, 1973), 404–8; Brigham H. Roberts, *The Life of John Taylor, Third President of the Church of Jesus Christ of Latter-day Saints* (Salt Lake City: George Q. Cannon & Sons, 1892), 356–57. For the other protests mentioned, see Larson and Larson *Diary of Charles Lowell Walker,* 2:653, 4 July 1885; Frederick Kessler Diary, 24 July 1886, University of Utah Library, Salt Lake City; Rose Berry West, "Pioneer Personal History," typescript, 4, UHi.

67. Wilford Woodruff, in *Wilford Woodruff's Journal,* ed. Kenney, 8:6–7, 19 Jan. 1881. This ceremony seems to have followed the prescription given Wilford Woodruff in a dream. See Fred C. Collier, comp., *Unpublished Revelations of the Prophets and Presidents of the Church of Jesus Christ of Latter-day Saints,* Vol. 1 (Salt Lake City: Collier's, 1981), pt. 79:124–25.

68. Editorial, *DN,* 23 April 1885; and "No Relinquishment," *DN,* 5 June 1885. Also see *JD* 25:191 (Brigham Young, Jr./1884); and "Effect of Persecution," *Contributor* 4 (Oct. 1882): 34.

69. The quote is from Senator John Tyler Morgan. *Cong. Rec.,* 49th Cong., 1st Sess., 1886, 17, pt. 1:511.

70. U.S., *Statutes at Large,* 24, ch. 397:635–41 (1887). The law was upheld in *Late Corporation of the Church of Jesus Christ of Latter-day Saints v. United States,* 136 U.S. 1 (1890).

71. Joy Lynn Wood Wetzel, "The Patriotic Priesthood: Mormonism and the Progressive Paradigm" (Ph.D. diss., University of Minnesota, 1977), 100;

Linford, "The Mormons and the Law," pt. 1:370. Also see Kenneth David Driggs, "The Mormon Church–State Confrontation in Nineteenth-Century America," *Journal of Church and State* 30 (Spring 1988): 273.

72. Austin E. Fife, "Folk Belief and Mormon Cultural Autonomy," *Journal of American Folklore* 61 (Jan.-March 1948): 29. It was Winslow R. Farr who was shipped in an organ crate. Mr. and Mrs. Joseph C. Clayson, "Winslow Farr, Jr.," in *Stalwarts South of the Border,* comp. Nelle Spilsbury Hatch and B. Carmon Hardy (Anaheim, Calif.: privately printed, 1985), 185–86. On the intrusive and sometimes humorous nature of the searches, see *Autobiography of Lorena Eugenia Washburn Larsen* (Provo, Utah: Published by Her Children and BYU Press, 1962), 65–66; "Ransacking the Temple," *DN,* 1 June 1887; "Cohabs vs. Deputies," in Larson, *The "Americanization" of Utah,* 115–38; and Juanita Brooks, "Cops and Co-Habs," *UHQ* 29 (Summer 1961): 294–96.

73. For a review of the inconveniences and occasional insults endured by the marshals, judges, and deputies, see Stephen Cresswell, "The U.S. Department of Justice in Utah Territory, 1870–1890," *UHQ* 53 (Summer 1985): 210–17.

74. Ruth Hawkins Dorset, "Hans Adolph Thompson," in Hatch and Hardy, *Stalwarts South of the Border,* 699–700. Also see Lula Mortensen, interviewed by Jessie L. Embry, 17 July 1976, p. 13, POHP.

75. "Report of the Governor of Utah," [1889] *Report of the Secretary of the Interior . . . ,* 5 vols. (Washington, D.C.: GPO, 1890), 3:499–500.

76. Mary Jane Mount Tanner, *A Fragment: The Autobiography of Mary Jane Mount Tanner,* ed. Margery W. Ward and George S. Tanner (Salt Lake City: Tanner Trust Fund and University of Utah Library, 1980), 186. In the words of a non-Mormon observer of the time, "The indignation which the Gentiles have displayed towards those who openly practiced Polygamy has tended more than anything else to confirm the Mormons in their notion as to the divinity of plural marriage." Rae, *Westward by Rail,* 175. This was a major theme of Paul Wilbur Tappan's study in the 1930s. See his "Mormon-Gentile Conflict." Linford suggested that the Edmunds and Edmunds-Tucker acts delayed the decline of polygamy among the Mormons. "The Polygamy Cases," pt. 2:589. Also see Burton, *The City of the Saints,* 478–79; and Dean L. May, "Mormons," in *Harvard Encyclopedia of American Ethnic Groups,* ed. Stephan Thernstrom (Cambridge, Mass.: Belknap Press, 1980), 729.

77. Helen Mar Whitney, *Why We Practice Plural Marriage . . .* (Salt Lake City: Juvenile Instructor's Office, 1884), 16.

78. Orson Pratt, in *Seer* 1 (May 1853): 75.

79. Comparisons with the ancient Jews and Christians, and interpretation of what was happening as threatening the Saints with bondage, or a condition as humiliating as that of the American Indians, was set forth repeatedly: Kenney, *Wilford Woodruff's Journals,* 7:51, 1 Jan. 1871; *JD* 22:178–79, 23:271–72, 26:42–43 (George Q. Cannon/1881, 1883, 1884); *JD* 26:159, 160 (George Reynolds/1885); Larson and Larson, *Diary of Charles Lowell Walker,* 2:555, 15

May 1881; Joseph F. Smith's comments in Andrew Jenson, "The Twelve Apostles," *Historical Record* 6 (May 1887): 195; Anna Eager Tenney to Ammon Tenney, 2 August 1885, Arizona Historical Society, Tucson; Henry Eyring, "Reminiscences," typescript, 63, 27 Jan. 1883, Church Archives; Gibson Condie, "Reminiscences and Diary," film, 3 March 1889, Church Archives.

80. *JD* 20:355 (John Taylor/1879). Also see *JD* 20:315 (Franklin D. Richards/1880). Woodruff's remark is in *Wilford Woodruff's Journal,* ed. Kenney, 7:123, 18 Feb. 1873.

81. Franklin D. Richards, quoted in *Salt Lake School of the Prophets Minute Book 1883,* ed. Merle Graffam (Palm Desert, Calif.: ULC Press, 1981), 18.

82. Numerous sermons were delivered in this vein. See, e.g., *JD* 20:296 (Charles W. Penrose/1880); *JD* 20:314–15 (Franklin D. Richards/1880); *JD* 20:374 (Erastus Snow/1880); *JD* 24:111 (Moses Thatcher/1883); *JD* 24:173 (Joseph F. Smith/1883); Larson and Larson, *Diary of Charles Lowell Walker,* 2:642, 25 Jan. 1885.

83. "Revelations Purportedly Given to John Taylor, 1882–1884," film, Church Archives; *Messages* 2:348–50, 354, 3:175–76; Collier, *Unpublished Revelations,* pts. 79–89:123–47.

84. "Celestial Marriage," 25 and 26 June 1882, in "Revelations Purportedly Given to John Taylor, 1882–1884;" Collier, *Unpublished Revelations,* pt. 80:129–32.

85. Collier, *Unpublished Revelations,* pt. 83:138, verse 4; "Revelation . . . ," 13 Oct. 1882, *Messages* 2:348–49.

86. See the copy of the revelation and accompanying note by Raymond Taylor in box 1, book 2, 548–49, John Taylor Papers, University of Utah Library; and statement by Raymond Taylor, indicating Joseph F. Smith, Jr., made a copy of the revelation on 3 Aug. 1909. Raymond Taylor to Dennis [Michael] Quinn, 14 May 1970, in John W. Taylor Correspondence, box 45, fd. 15, John Taylor Papers. A printed copy is available in Collier, *Unpublished Revelations,* pt. 86:145–46. In 1882, responding to the Edmunds Act, the First Presidency made it clear to church members that plural marriage was one of the requirements of Mormonism and that failure to comply with that obligation was likely to "incur the eternal displeasure of our Heavenly Father." "An Address to the Members of the Church . . . ," 29 Aug. 1882, *Messages* 2:343, 345.

87. *JD* 21:116 (John Taylor/1881).

88. "Funeral Services of Sister Elizabeth A. Whitney," *DN,* 17 Feb. 1882.

89. George Q. Cannon's statement is referred to in Larson and Larson, *Diary of Charles Lowell Walker,* 2:629, 26 April 1884. Also see Charles S. Smith Diary, typescript, 259, 26 April 1884, BYU Library. For other instances, see Heber C. Kimball's view that even two wives were not enough, as described in Stanley B. Kimball, *Heber C. Kimball: Mormon Patriarch and Pioneer* (Urbana: University of Illinois Press, 1981), 237; testimony of Daniel H. Wells in the *Reynolds* case before the territorial Third District Court, as described in Van Orden, "George Reynolds," 74; Kenney, *Wilford Woodruff's Journal,* 8:126–27,

14 Oct. 1882; ibid., 8:235, 9 March 1884; "Excerpts from the Journal of Douglas M. Todd, Sr.," typescript, 1, 27 Feb. 1887, Utah State University Library, Logan; John Morgan Diaries, 6 Oct. 1888, Church Archives; *JD* 20:99 (Orson Hyde/1880); *JD* 24:284–85 (Franklin D. Richards/1883); "Epistle of the First Presidency," 4 April 1885, *Messages* 3:10; George Q. Cannon, "Discourse," *DN*, 19 May 1883; the remarks of Francis M. Lyman in *Journal of Jesse Nathaniel Smith: The Life Story of a Mormon Pioneer, 1834–1906* (Salt Lake City: Jesse N. Smith Family Association, 1953), 287, 8 May 1884; Brigham H. Roberts, "Celestial Marriage and Acts of Congress," *Contributor* 6 (Nov. 1884-April 1885): 52, 107; and Annie Clark Tanner, *A Mormon Mother: An Autobiography*, rev. ed. (Salt Lake City: Tanner Trust Fund and University of Utah Library, 1973), 62.

90. Graffam, *Salt Lake School of the Prophets*, 37, 48, 57.

91. "A Brief Story of the Life of Joseph Eldridge Robinson," partly handwritten, partly typewritten manuscript, 11, Church Archives. The statement by Nels Anderson, repeated by Orma Linford, that Taylor advised the Saints not to fight "but to run," distorts Taylor's unyielding posture. Nels Anderson, *Desert Saints: The Mormon Frontier in Utah* (Chicago: University of Chicago Press, 1942), 318; Linford, "The Mormons and the Law," pt. 1:348. For more on these addresses and evidence of Taylor's firm stand, see Samuel W. Taylor, *The Kingdom or Nothing: The Life of John Taylor, Militant Mormon* (New York: Macmillan, 1976), 299, 334–35 passim.

92. Regarding economic adjustments, see Arrington, *Great Basin Kingdom*, 362–65. The church's legal strategy was discussed in Franklin S. Richards to presidents John Taylor and George Q. Cannon, 25 Sept. 1886, photocopy, Franklin S. Richards Correspondence, 1886–90, UHi. On public relations, see Lyman, *Political Deliverance*, 69–95.

93. See the comments of Franklin S. Richards to Carl A. Badger concerning Joseph F. Smith's remarks in Washington, D.C., in 1887, as reported in Carlos Ashby Badger Diaries, 21 Dec. 1904, Church Archives.

94. *Admission of Utah. Arguments in Favor of the Admission of Utah as a State* . . . (Washington, D.C.: GPO, 1888), 6–7; *Hearings before the Committee on Territories in Regard to the Admission of Utah as a State* (Washington, D.C.: GPO, 1889), 8. Also see the following: George Q. Cannon's interview with the Chicago *Times*, as reported in "Hon. George Q. Cannon Interviewed," *DN*, 17 Dec. 1881; "The Preaching and Practice of Polygamy," *DN*, 13 Dec. 1884; "Epistle of the First Presidency," 4 April 1885, *Messages* 3:11; Heber J. Grant in "Sunday Services," *DN*, 5 July 1887; "Polygamy Prohibited," *DN*, 5 July 1887; "More 'Chicago Times' Pettifogging," *DN*, 2 Aug. 1887; "What the 'Sun' Says," *DN*, 22 Aug. 1887; "The Church Suits," *DN*, 29 Feb. 1888; "The Jesperson [*sic*] Polygamy Case," *SLT*, 2 Oct. 1889; "A Strange Interview," ibid., 20 Oct. 1889; "Mormons Abandon Polygamy," *New York Herald*, 13 Oct. 1889.

95. Wilford Woodruff to Franklin S. Richards and Charles W. Penrose, 12 April 1888, Wilford Woodruff Letterbooks, Church Archives. Also see the

comment of Utah Commissioner Ambrose B. Carlton in his *Wonderlands of the Wild West, with Sketches of the Mormons* (n.p., 1891), 180.

96. John Taylor and George Q. Cannon to Charles W. Penrose and Franklin S. Richards, 19 Feb. 1887, Letterbooks, John Taylor Family Papers, Raymond Taylor typewritten transcription, University of Utah Library. The 1882 debate is referred to in Kenney, *Wilford Woodruff's Journal*, 8:92, 24 March 1882.

97. Thomas Cottam Romney, *The Mormon Colonies in Mexico* (Salt Lake City: Deseret Book, 1938), 49–59; B. Carmon Hardy, "The Mormon Colonies of Northern Mexico, 1885–1912" (Ph.D. diss., Wayne State University, 1963), 67–86; idem, "The Trek South: How the Mormons Went to Mexico," *Southwestern Historical Quarterly* 73 (July 1969): 1–5. For Canada, see Archie G. Wilcox, "Founding of the Mormon Community in Alberta" (M.A. thesis, University of Alberta, 1950); Lawrence B. Lee, "The Mormons Come to Canada, 1887–1902," *Pacific Northwest Quarterly* 59 (Jan. 1968): 11–22.

98. "The Polygamy Trial," and "Rudger Clawson's Trial," both in *DN,* 18 Oct. 1884. According to Samuel W. Taylor, a grandson of President John Taylor, the policy of dispersal was undertaken in 1882. See his *The Kingdom or Nothing,* 301–2, 305n; and the outline of events provided in the same author's *Rocky Mountain Empire: The Latter-day Saints Today* (New York: Macmillan, 1978), 20n.15.

99. See, e.g., Stanley B. Kimball, ed., *On the Potter's Wheel: The Diaries of Heber C. Kimball* (Salt Lake City: Signature Books in Association with Smith Research Associates, 1987), 87, 24 Sept. 1845; 94, 2 Feb. 1845; 140, 9 Nov. 1845; 143–44, 17 Nov. 1845; the instances and comments in Richard Edmond Bennett, "Mormons at the Missouri: A History of the Latter-day Saints at Winter Quarters and at Kanesville, 1846–52—A Study in American Overland Trail Migration," 2 vols. (Ph.D. diss., Wayne State University, 1984), 2:394–98; Kenney, *Wilford Woodruff's Journal*, 6:307–8, 26 Dec. 1866; 390, 24 Jan. 1868; *JD* 16:186 (Brigham Young/1873); *JD* 19:164 (Charles C. Rich/1878); *JD* 25:355–56 (John Taylor/1884). On the preference for performing sealings in temples or similar locations when convenient, see First Presidency, "To the Bishops and Members of the Church . . . ," 25 Oct. 1876, *Messages* 2:279. Brigham H. Roberts later said the sealing ceremony could be performed in two minutes or less. *Proceedings* 1:743.

100. James Burtrum Harvey, interviewed by Leonard R. Grover, 1 Dec. 1979, 1, POHP; and Lula Mortensen, "Reminiscences Spanning the Centuries," appendix to interview by Jessie L. Embry, 17 July 1976, p. 3, POHP. Also see Walter Clark, interviewed by Leonard R. Grover, 12 Oct. 1979, p. 3, POHP; Elna Hart Palmer, interviewed by Leonard R. Grover, 2 Feb. 1980, p. 17, POHP; Annie Clark Tanner, *A Mormon Mother,* 87, 120; and the account of the marriage of John H. Davies provided in Larson, *The "Americanization" of Utah,* 84–85. For summaries and accounts of the number convicted, see all of George A. Jenks, *Convictions for Polygamy in Utah and Idaho: Letter from the Acting Attorney-General, in Reply to the Resolution of the House in Relation to Convic-*

tions for Polygamy in Utah and Idaho, 50th Cong, 1st Sess., 13 Sept. 1888, House Exec. Doc. no. 447; and JoAnn W. Bair and Richard L. Jensen, "Prosecution of the Mormons in Arizona Territory in the 1880s," *Arizona and the West* 19 (Spring 1977): 25–46. An instance involving a plural marriage without sealing the couple for eternity is found in William L. Wyatt, interviewed by Jessie L. Embry, 19 June 1976, pp. 10–11, POHP.

101. This was art. 15, sec. 12 of the proposed constitution. For copies and discussion, see "Polygamy Prohibited," *DN,* 5 July 1887; "The Bigamy and Polygamy Provisions," *DN,* 6 July 1887; "The Constitution," *DN,* 8 July 1887. Also see Henry J. Wolfinger, "A Reexamination of the Woodruff Manifesto in the Light of Utah Constitutional History," *UHQ* 39 (Fall 1979): 341–42; all of Charles W. Watson, "John Willard Young and the 1887 Movement for Utah Statehood" (Ph.D. diss., BYU, 1984); and Lyman's chapter, "Another Attempt at Statehood: A Year of Preliminaries," in *Political Deliverance,* 41–68.

102. Franklin S. Richards to Joseph F. Smith, 28 June 1887, Richards Correspondence. Also see President John Taylor to William Packsman [Paxman], 4 Feb. 1887, First Presidency Letterbooks, Church Archives; Charles W. Penrose to President John Taylor, 16 Feb. 1887, John Taylor Papers, Raymond Taylor transcription.

103. "Report of the Utah Commission," *Report of the Secretary of the Interior . . . ,* 5 vols. (Washington, D.C.: GPO, 1887), 2:1333–1340, 1344–1345. Also see the comments of Robert Newton Baskin, *Reminiscences,* 187–92; and Larson, *The "Americanization" of Utah,* 222.

104. "An Act Regulating Marriage," *Compiled Laws of Utah* (1888), chap. 5, sec. 2584, sub-sections 2–3.

105. Larson and Larson, *Diary of Charles Lowell Walker,* 2:688, April 1888.

106. "Trying Times," *DN,* 14 Jan. 1888.

107. See, e.g., Charles W. Penrose, "Physical Regeneration," *Mill. Star* 29 (10 Aug. 1867): 497; "The Only Remedy," ibid. 29 (21 Sept. 1867): 593–94; Larson and Larson, *Diary of Charles Lowell Walker,* 1:433, 11 Nov. 1876; "Discourse by Prest. George Q. Cannon," *DN,* 25 June 1881; "We Do Not Believe in 'Polygamy,'" *DN,* 21 Dec. 1881; S. W. R., "Monogamy and Polygamy," *DN,* 24 Oct. 1885; *JD* 23:64 (John Taylor/1883).

108. Orson Spencer, *Letters Exhibiting the Most Prominent Doctrines of the Church of Jesus Christ of Latter-day Saints . . . ,* 3d ed. (Salt Lake City: Deseret News, 1889), 231–32.

109. Autobiography of William Adams, 1822–94, typewritten copy, p. 27, Henry E. Huntington Library.

110. "The Reynolds Test Polygamy Case—An Unconstitutional and Oppressive Decision," *Mill. Star* 41 (13 Jan. 1879): 24.

111. "An Address . . . ," 29 Aug. 1882, *Messages* 2:343.

112. "Celestial Marriage," 25 and 26 June 1882, in "Revelations Purportedly Given to John Taylor, 1882–1884," Church Archives; and Collier, *Unpublished Revelations,* pt. 80:130.

113. Graffam, *Salt Lake School of the Prophets,* 27. In 1879 Eliza R. Snow,

one of the Prophet Joseph Smith's polygamous widows, referred to the principle as "the revelation on celestial or plural marriage, and the eternity of the
marriage covenant." Affidavit, in Joseph F. Smith, "Joseph the Seer's Plural
Marriages," *DN*, 18 Oct. 1879. And Joseph F. Smith chided his anti-
polygamous cousin, Joseph Smith III (who eventually married, serially, three
women), that if he would accept the Mormon principle of eternal marriage he
could have all of them together in the hereafter. In his efforts at persuasion,
Joseph F. Smith used the phrase "celestial marriage, including a plurality of
wives." Joseph F. Smith to Joseph Smith III, 3 May 1889, P22, fd. 47, RLDS
Library and Archives.

114. Karl Skousen, interviewed by Leonard R. Grover, 31 Oct. 1979, p. 11,
POHP; Walter Clark, interviewed by Leonard R. Grover, 12 Oct. 1979, pp. 9–
10, POHP; Hortense Young Hammond, interviewed by Leonard R. Grover,
15 March 1980, p. 6, POHP.

115. *Admission of Utah. Arguments in Favor of the Admission of Utah as a State*,
14–18. Also see "Utah and Statehood," *DN*, 18 Feb. 1888; and the comments
of James E. Talmage, in "Dr. Jas. E. Talmage," *DN*, 23 Nov. 1889. The 1882
reference mentioned is found in "Anti-'Mormonism': A War upon Religion,"
DN, 29 July 1882.

116. Wolfinger, "Reexamination," 328–49; Lyman, *Political Deliverance*,
43–46, 60.

117. A forceful statement of this was provided by the Mormon press in
1882: "The 'social institution' [polygamy] which has been manufactured into
such a formidable bug-bear by persons interested in keeping Utah a vassal of
the Government, is not an institution of the Territory but of a church; it will
not be an institution of the state if Utah should be admitted. It is not in any
sense a feature of the political organization here and has nothing to do with it,
because those who are connected with the institution form and sustain their
domestic relations, not under any secular law or regulation, but solely and
entirely under Church ordinances, forms and rules, over which the Territory
or State has no jurisdiction whatever." "What We Contend For," *DN*, 14 July
1882. Also see "The 'Demand' upon the Mormon Church," *DN*, 19 July 1887.
Charles W. Penrose, in urging President Taylor's support for the proposed
1887 constitution with its anti-bigamy clause, argued for its acceptance as a
means of saving Mormon plural marriage almost entirely on this basis.
Charles W. Penrose to President John Taylor, 16 Feb. 1887, John Taylor
Papers, Raymond Taylor transcription. Franklin S. Richards, lobbying for the
church in Washington, D.C., was instructed by the leaders in Utah to preserve
the distinction between church and state in any promises he made concerning
Mormon conduct. Committee to Franklin S. Richards, 2 Feb. 1888, Richards
Correspondence. For more to this end, see Franklin S. Richards to presidents
Wilford Woodruff and George Q. Cannon, 28 Feb. 1888; and Franklin S.
Richards to Brother Mack [Joseph F. Smith], 1 May 1888, Richards Corre-
spondence. This distinction was also addressed by Brigham H. Roberts in
CHC 6:370.

118. John Henry Smith to Joseph F. Smith, 3 April 1888, John Henry Smith Letterbooks, George A. Smith Family Papers, University of Utah Library.

119. Lyman, *Political Deliverance*, 106.

120. "A Voice from Utah," *Woman's Journal* 19 (22 Sept. 1888): 302. Also see the remarks of Charles S. Varian in "United States vs. Rudger Clawson," *DN*, 20 Oct. 1884.

121. Brigham Young, quoted in *Proceedings* 1:15. There was also the report that in the 1860s Young said to William Henry Hooper, Utah's delegate to Congress: "Remember Brother Hooper, anything for Statehood, Promise anything for Statehood." "Success after Many Long Years," *Chicago Tribune*, 5 Jan. 1896. The argument that Brigham Young seriously contemplated the cessation of polygamy, as made by Max Anderson, fails to evaluate either Young's motives or the enormous importance attached to the tenet by Mormon leaders. J. Max Anderson, *The Polygamy Story: Fiction and Fact* (Salt Lake City: Publishers Press, 1979), 104. The more credible comment by Taylor concerning the First Presidency's historic commitment to the principle is found in John W. Taylor to Charles W. Penrose, 19 Feb. 1887, John Taylor Papers, Raymond Taylor transcription.

122. *D&C* 87 (1832) and 130:12–13 (1843). The study of Mormon millenarianism has only begun. See the opening chapter, "The Kingdom of God and the Millennial Tradition," in Klaus J. Hansen, *Quest for Empire: The Political Kingdom of God and the Council of Fifty in Mormon History* (East Lansing: Michigan State University Press, 1967), 3–23; Louis G. Reinwand, "An Interpretive Study of Mormon Millennialism during the Nineteenth Century with Emphasis on Millennial Developments in Utah" (M.A. thesis, BYU, 1971); Glen M. Leonard, "Early Saints and the Millennium," *Ensign* 9 (Aug. 1979): 42–47; Grant Underwood, "Seminal versus Sesquicentennial Saints: A Look at Mormon Millennialism," *Dialogue* 14 (Spring 1981): 32–44; idem, "Millenarianism and the Early Mormon Mind," *JMH* 9 (1982): 41–51; and Keith E. Norman, "How Long O Lord? The Delay of the Parousia in Mormonism," *Sunstone* 8 (Jan.–April 1983): 49–58.

123. Editorial, *Mill. Star* 26 (28 Oct. 1865): 681–83; "'Chain Gang of States,' Congress Inaugurating a Revolution—A War of Races in Prospect," ibid. 28 (21 April 1866): 246–48; *JD* 12:120, 242, 285 (Brigham Young/1867, 1868, 1868); "Wars and Rumors of Wars," *Mill. Star* 32 (16 Aug. 1870): 520–22; "War," ibid. 34 (10 Sept. 1877): 579–81; Kenney, *Wilford Woodruff's Journal*, 6:310–11, 1 Jan. 1867; Record of Andrew Jackson Allen, 21 Sept. 1873, UHi; George W. Laub Diary, 4 March 1877, Henry E. Huntington Library; John Druce to Brigham Young, 3 Feb. 1877, Brigham Young Incoming Correspondence, Church Archives; "Remarks by Prest. Geo. Q. Cannon," *DN*, 26 July 1884; "A Danger to the Nation," *DN*, 11 July 1890; "Joseph Smith a Prophet," *DN*, 30 Aug. 1890.

124. Luke William Gallup to Nancy Williams, 2 and 4 July 1862, Luke William Gallup, Reminiscence and Diary, Church Archives. Also see Cleland

and Brooks, *A Mormon Chronicle*, 1:255–56, 20 May 1860; and "Consequences of National Sin," *Mill. Star* 30 (15 Feb. 1868): 106.

125. Brigham Young to Daniel W. Jones, 22 Jan. 1876, in Daniel W. Jones, *Forty Years among the Indians: A True Yet Thrilling Narrative of the Author's Experiences among the Natives* (Salt Lake City: Juvenile Instructor Office, 1890), 261–62. Additionally, see James G. Bleak, "Annals of the Southern Utah Mission," typescript, book B, pt. 1:124, Washington County Library, St. George, Utah; Kenney, *Wilford Woodruff's Journal*, 7:94, 10 Nov. 1872, 7:261, 1 Jan. 1876; and Cleland and Brooks, *A Mormon Chronicle*, 2:235, 18 April 1873.

126. L. John Nuttall Diaries, 7 Jan. 1879.

127. On the 1882 law, see Kenney, *Wilford Woodruff's Journal*, 8:91, 14 March 1882, 351, 31 Dec. 1885, 378, 16 Feb. 1886; "They Refuse to See," *DN*, 6 June 1885; Larson and Larson, *Diary of Charles Lowell Walker*, 2:656–57, 7 Nov. 1885. And for that of 1887, Kenney, *Wilford Woodruff's Journal*, 8:420–21, 13 Jan. 1887, 9:94, 19 May 1890; and all of Robert Smith, *A Series of Lectures on the Signs of the Times . . . and the Last Judgment* (Payson, Utah: Juvenile Instructor Office, 1887). For Mormon disappointment in connection with millennialism at the time of the anti-polygamy crusade, see the comments of Keith E. Norman, "How Long O Lord?" 53.

128. *D&C* 130:15 (1843). See Scott H. Faulring, ed., *An American Prophet's Record: The Diaries and Journals of Joseph Smith* (Salt Lake City: Signature Books in Association with Smith Research Associates, 1987), 349. The weight of anticipation as the Saints looked toward 1890 is apparent from a statement by Wilford Woodruff at a church meeting in northern Arizona in 1879: "He did not Believe that any person who lived to see 1890 would be able to see any United States for He believed the Union would be broken by that time." Kenney, *Wilford Woodruff's Journal*, 7:537, 25 Dec. 1879. For more of the same, see "The Coming of the Messiah," *Mill. Star* 41 (7 April 1879): 716–19; "The Great Prophetic Pyramid: An Important Discovery by Prof. O. Pratt, Sen.," ibid. 41 (5 May 1879): 280–83; all of William Henry Harrison Sharp, *Prophetic History, and the Fulfillment of Prophecy from 600 Years B.C. to the Year of Our Lord A.D. 1891* (Salt Lake City: Deseret Home Co., 1883); and the comments of Brigham H. Roberts expressed at the October 1890 general conference of the church, as reported in "The Mormon Conference," *SLT*, 5 Oct. 1890. Caution and skepticism were also expressed, especially after the year passed. See, e.g., Larson and Larson, *Diary of Charles Lowell Walker*, 2:721–22, 3 Jan. 1891; and Marriner Wood Merrill Diaries, 8 March 1891, Church Archives. Seeming failure of the prediction notwithstanding, some believed Christ had already returned to earth but was working invisibly. Pacheco Ward Historical Record, book A1, 1892–93, 14 Feb. 1892, Church Archives.

129. "Anti-Polygamic Failures," *Mill. Star* 40 (1 April 1878): 197–98; "Further Reflections on Marriage," ibid. 40 (6 Oct. 1879): 630–31; "Shall Polygamy Be Put in Abeyance," *DN*, 30 Aug. 1879. This was a view in which the Mormons had several allies. See *Defence of the Constitutional and Religious*

Rights of the People of Utah: Speeches of Senators Vest, Morgan, Call, Brown, Pendleton and Lamar; and James Wells Stillman, *The Mormon Question: An Address by James W. Stillman, Delivered in Boston on Tuesday Evening, Feb. 12, 1884* (Boston: J. P. Mendum, 1884). Also see the studies by M. Paul Holsinger: "Senator George Graham Vest and the 'Menace' of Mormonism, 1882–1887," *Missouri Historical Review* 65 (Oct. 1970): 23–36; and idem, "Henry M. Teller and the Edmunds-Tucker Act," *Colorado Magazine* 48 (Spring 1971): 1–14.

130. *JD* 20:5–6, 23:104, 122–23 (George Q.Cannon/1878, 1881, 1881); George Q. Cannon, *The History of the Mormons: Their Persecutions and Travels . . .* (Salt Lake City: George Q. Cannon, 1891), 12–13. Also see Larson and Larson, *Diary of Charles Lowell Walker,* 2:522, 554, 21 Jan. and 13 May 1881; *JD.* 20:357, 22:229 (John Taylor/1880, 1881); *JD* 26:226 (Erastus Snow/1885); "Discourse by President John Taylor," *DN,* 14 Feb. 1885; "Discourse by Prest. George Q. Cannon," *DN,* 11 April 1885; "To the Presidents of Stakes and their Counselors . . . ," 26 May 1885, *Messages* 3:13–14.

131. Hansen, *Quest for Empire,* 179. While Hansen's entire work pursues this theme, it is especially developed in his chapter "The Kingdom of God vs. the Kingdoms of the World," ibid., 147–79. Gustive O. Larson subscribed to Hansen's thesis and built much of his *"Americanization" of Utah* around that view. Agreement was also expressed by Bruce L. Campbell and Eugene E. Campbell in their "Mormon Family," in *Ethnic Families in America: Patterns and Variations,* ed. Charles H. Mindel and Robert W. Habenstein (New York: Elsevier, 1976), 391. D. Michael Quinn's prosopographical study takes a similar approach but emphasizes that groups like the Council of Fifty and the School of the Prophets were appendages to the more controlling authority of the First Presidency and Quorum of Twelve Apostles. "The Mormon Hierarchy, 1832–1932: An American Elite" (Ph.D. diss., Yale University, 1976), 219–30. Firmage and Mangrum also emphasize political concerns as having greater priority with reformers than polygamy. See their *Zion in the Courts,* 159, 162–63. The political interpretation, as Hansen pointed out, is not entirely recent. See his *Quest for Empire,* 171n.61. In addition to sources identified there, it was the point of view of Paul Wilbur Tappan, a half-century ago, in his "Mormon-Gentile Conflict," 426. And Kimball Young said he had concluded that business and politics were more troublesome than polygamy as a source of Mormon-Gentile friction. "Polygamy in Utah: A Westerner's Reappraisal," *Westerners Brand Book* 11 (Jan. 1955): 81. After the publication of Lyman's *Political Deliverance,* with its emphasis on polygamy as the chief objection to statehood for Utah, the issue was raised by Vernon H. Jensen in "The Lyman Thesis," *Dialogue* 21 (Summer 1988): 9–11. Lyman replied in "Questioning the Jensen Thesis," ibid. 21 (Winter 1988): 9–10. The exchange closed with Jensen's "Reactions to Lyman's Reactions," ibid. 22 (Fall 1989): 5–6.

132. See, e.g., President Rutherford B. Hayes's "Fourth Annual Message," 6 Dec. 1880, in Richardson, *Messages and Papers of the Presidents,* 10:4558; "First Annual Message" of President Chester A. Arthur, 6 Dec. 1881, in ibid.,

10:4644–4645; "Political Aspects of Mormonism," *Harper's* 64 (Jan. 1882): 285–88; "Report of the Governor of Utah," *Report of the Secretary of the Interior . . .* , 5 vols. (Washington, D.C.: GPO, 1885), 2:1024; "Report of the Utah Commission," ibid., 2:885; "Report of the Governor of Utah" [1889], *Report of the Secretary of the Interior . . .* , 5 vols. (Washington, D.C.: GPO, 1890), 3:499.

133. Franklin S. Richards to presidents Wilford Woodruff and George Q. Cannon, 28 Feb. 1888, Richards Correspondence.

134. "Report of the Utah Commission" [1887], 2:1325.

135. "Fat Offices Wanted, Not Public Morality," *DN,* 14 March 1882; "The Real Object of Attack," *DN,* 12 April 1882; "The 'Press' and the Utah Revolutionists," *DN,* 12 Jan. 1883; "What the Spoilers Want," *DN,* 30 Nov. 1886; editorial, *DN,* 9 Aug. 1889; editorial, *DN,* 3 Oct. 1890; and John W. Young to "My Dear Sir," 29 July 1887, John W. Young Letterbooks, Church Archives. Examples of friendly non-Mormons who spoke in a similar vein are Bancroft, *History of Utah,* 361–67; all of Stillman, *The Mormon Question;* and the warning given Brigham Young by George Francis Train, "They cry Polygamy but mean plunder!" quoted in Davis Bitton, "George Francis Train and Brigham Young," *BYU Studies* 18 (Spring 1978): 415.

136. Thompson, *Mormonism—Increase of the Army,* 5.

137. John Taylor, *JD* 15:288–89 (1873).

138. Charles Smith Diary, Sept. 1866, BYU Library.

139. "Its Probable Effect," *DN,* 20 March 1882.

140. President John Taylor to William Packsman [Paxman], 4 Feb. 1887, First Presidency Letterbooks, Church Archives. Also see Kenney, *Wilford Woodruff's Journal,* 8:415, 31 Dec. 1886; and "Excerpts from a Journal or Sketch of the Life of Joel Hills Johnson (Brother to Benjamin F. Johnson)" (n.p., n.d.), 33, UHi.

141. Phil Robinson, *Sinners and Saints: A Tour across the States, and round Them; with Three Months among the Mormons* (Boston: Roberts Brothers, 1883), 97, 98. Sentiments of this kind were widespread and repeated. See, e.g., the following: *JD* 2:319, 9:331, 366, 12:285, 312 (Brigham Young/1855, 1862, 1862, 1868, 1868); *JD* 17:125, 24:103 (George Q. Cannon/1875, 1882); *JD* 23:209 (Moses Thatcher/1883); *JD* 26:344–45 (Franklin D. Richards/1885); "The Spirit of Persecution," *Mill. Star* 34 (13 Feb. 1872): 98–100; "Letter from Bishop Henry Lunt," ibid. 48 (11 Jan. 1886): 28; "Legislative Memorial to Congress," *DN,* 25 Feb. 1882; "The Convention," *DN,* 11 April 1882; "Discourse by Apostle Moses Thatcher," *DN,* 26 Aug. 1882; "The Dispatch Fiend at Work," *DN,* 22 Sept. 1890; "They Will Never Be Satisfied," *DN,* 4 Oct. 1890; "An Epistle of the First Presidency . . . ," March 1886, *Messages* 3:51–52; Larson and Larson, *Diary of Charles Lowell Walker,* 2:585, 10 Aug. 1882; Helen Mar Whitney, *Why We Practice Plural Marriage* . . . (Salt Lake City: Juvenile Instructor Office, 1884), 3–4; Benjamin Franklin Johnson, "Mormonism as an Issue," *Arizona Republican,* 25 June 1890. This view of the crusade yet lingers. See Duane E. Hiatt, "From Disdain to Distinction . . . ," *This People* 7 (Oct. 1986): 68.

142. The Henry J. Wolfinger essay is "An Irrepressible Conflict," *Dialogue* 6 (Autumn-Winter 1971): 124–31. Lyman makes the same point in his *Political Deliverance*, 180–81. For comparison of Utah political experience with that in other territories, see Kenneth N. Owens, "Pattern and Structure in Western Territorial Politics," in *The American Territorial System*, ed. John Porter Bloom (Athens: Ohio University Press, 1973), 161–79. On the economic dimensions of the matter, see Arrington's chapter "The Raid" in his *Great Basin Kingdom*, 351–79. Activities by Utah's non-Mormon clergymen are discussed in T. Edgar Lyon, "Religious Activities and Development in Utah, 1847–1910," *UHQ* 35 (Fall 1967): 292–306. And Governor Thomas's statement is found in "Report of the Governor of Utah" [1889], 3:494.

143. Carlton, *The Wonderlands of the Wild West*, 39. In the same work, Carlton said there was a coterie of gentile leaders in Utah who used polygamy as a mask for their own political goals. Ibid., 115–16, 119. Also see "Judge Carleton [*sic*] on the Mormon Question," *DN*, 30 Dec. 1889. In his own view, disloyalty to the United States was not a problem with the Saints, rather it was polygamy. And, he went on, if this were truly abandoned, "no just ground will remain for pursuing them with further hostile legislation." *Wonderlands of the Wild West*, 343. Also see the "Annual Report of the Utah Commission" [1889], *Report of the Secretary of the Interior . . . , 3:178–79.

144. Bunker and Bitton, *The Mormon Graphic Image*, 33–56. Other direct affirmations as to the primacy of polygamy as the source of contention are *JD* 6:22, 20:351–52 (John Taylor/1857, 1879); *JD* 9:263 (George A. Smith/1862); *JD* 17:339, 20:37 (George Q. Cannon/1875, 1878); Helen Mar Whitney, *Why We Practice Plural Marriage*, 51; James W. Barclay, "A New View of Mormonism," *Nineteenth Century* 15 (Jan. 1884): 177, 178.

145. "Meddling with the Mormons," [New York] *Daily Graphic*, 9 Dec. 1873.

146. James David Gillilan, *Thomas Corwin Iliff: Apostle of Home Missions in the Rocky Mountains* (New York: Methodist Book Concern, 1919); 81.

147. Quoted in Margery W. Ward, *A Life Divided: The Biography of Joseph Marion Tanner, 1859–1927* (Salt Lake City: Publishers Press, 1980), 23. Also see Autobiography of William Adams, 31; "More about Georgia Anti-Mormonism," *DN*, 21 Sept. 1881; and the comment of John Nicholson in his *Preceptor: Being a Simple System for Enabling Young Men to Acquire a Knowledge . . . of the Gospel . . . ,* 2d rev. ed. (Salt Lake City: Deseret News, 1883), 36.

148. Jabez Jenkins, *Jenkin's Vest-Pocket Lexicon . . .* (Philadelphia: Lippincott, 1862), 315.

149. "Dastardly Tale about Polygamy," *DN*, 31 Oct. 1905.

150. John Tyler Morgan, *Cong. Rec.*, 49th Cong., 1st sess., 1886, 17, pt. 1:511.

151. "The Citadel of Mormonism," *Chicago Evening Journal*, 6 Feb. 1880.

152. "Success after Many Long Years," *Chicago Tribune*, 5 Jan. 1896. Other examples of post-1890 comments, still associating Mormonism's unpopularity with plural marriage, are Emmeline B. Wells to Devereux Blake, 18 Sept.

1893, Lillie Devereux Blake Papers, Missouri Historical Society, St. Louis, Missouri; Florence A. Merriam, *My Summer in a Mormon Village* (Boston: Houghton Mifflin, 1894), 127; "The Mormon Question up to Date," *American Monthly Review of Reviews* 19 (Feb. 1899): 143; "Mormons" in the encyclopedic index to Richardson, *Messages and Papers of the Presidents,* 20:n.p.; *Proceedings* 2:715, 953; "Mormons of Mexico," *World's Work* 31 (March 1916): 484; William Earl LaRue, *The Foundations of Mormonism: A Study of the Fundamental Facts in the History and Doctrines of the Mormons from Original Sources* (New York: Fleming H. Revell, 1919), 234.

153. George A. Meears's comment is relevant here: "Every bit of sexual wrong is hinted at . . . and then embellished for the delectation of the rabid haters of anything Mormon." "A Gentile Exodus," *Tullidge's Quarterly Magazine* 3 (Oct. 1883): 186. Jan Shipps, in her study of the Mormon image, acknowledged that Mormon control in politics and commerce deeply offended many. But it was polygamy that rancored most. JoAnn Barnett Shipps, "From Satyr to Saint: American Attitudes toward the Mormons, 1860–1960" (Paper presented before the Organization of American Historians, Chicago, Ill., 1973), 15, 18, 22, 23 passim.

154. Untitled, *Frank Leslie's Illustrated Newspaper* 54 (29 April 1882): 155.

155. *Cannon v. United States,* 116 U.S. 72 (1886). For the same reason, if a man lived with only one of his wives, but remained married to others, they bearing his name, he could be convicted for unlawful cohabitation. *United States v. Clark,* 6 Utah 120; 21 Pac. 463 (1889).

156. "Report of the Utah Commission" [1885], *Report of the Secretary of the Interior,* 2:887–88.

157. Charles S. Varian, in "United States vs. Rudger Clawson," *DN,* 20 Oct. 1884.

158. *Davis v. Beason* 133 U.S. 333 (1889), at 342. Also see the remarks of Judge Charles S. Zane, made when sentencing Rudger Clawson, in "In the Pen," *SLT,* 4 Nov. 1884. In discussing this case, as throughout their book, Firmage and Mangrum display an impatience with the social arguments made against polygamy and, therewith, failure to fully grasp the nature of the threat plural marriage presented to the Victorian mind. *Zion in the Courts,* 234–35. Also see the dismissal of anti-polygamy sentiment as "amorphous" in Edwin B. Firmage, "The Judicial Campaign against Polygamy," 95, 98, 102–5.

3

Blessings of the Abrahamic Household

Not only did the church's attachment to the principle of plural marriage intensify as the nation's attacks upon it escalated but Mormon arguments for the social advantages of the practice acquired particular significance. While scriptural and revelatory authority were always of primary importance, naturalistic and theological considerations were conflated, so that for many Mormons nothing was more essential than their marriage system's supposed hygienic effects. Despite extensive study of Mormon polygamic commentary, this dimension of the subject has received little attention. An investigation into what one church leader described as perhaps the "strongest" argument in plurality's favor will illustrate not only the reflexive nature of their apologetics but the extraordinary role polygamy was expected to play in Mormonism's restoration movement.[1]

The Mormon question was part of a larger dialogue occurring in American society. Some said it illuminated the great problems of the age—the "conjugal relation" and social purity.[2] While recognizing the offensiveness that polygamy represented to many, we must, at the same time, not lose sight of the extent to which, and in what ways, agreement existed. The theme of majoritarian triumph and Mormon surrender can easily obscure zones of concurrence in which important assumptions were shared. The Saints spoke directly to questions absorbing many others at the time—sexuality, health, and home life. They fully subscribed to the paramount significance these things held for mankind. Drawing on the work of others, they recycled non-Mormon thought into their own armory, using it to defend the principle. This was but an extension of the Saints' ready appropriation of polygamous sanctions by earlier reformers and writers.[3]

Martin Madan's multi-volume, eighteenth-century defense of the practice was especially influential because it not only contained scriptural justifications but argued plurality to be a practical antidote for contemporary social ills. We know from David Whittaker's study that Madan was owned, read, and used by the Mormons.[4] Apostle John Henry Smith urged his monogamous cousin, Joseph Smith III, to read Madan's work, contending that "no mortal man can overturn the arguments of the author."[5] Another writer, David O. Allen, although personally opposed to plurality, favored the baptism of polygamous converts from India, so long as they were given no conspicuous roles in church services and did not marry plurally again. Mormons not only cited Allen's book as reinforcement but pointed to the intolerance of those denominations that disagreed with him, thereby consigning large portions of the human family to an existence outside the perimeter of Christian fellowship.[6] Other works, like Mercer Davies's study of concubinage and polygamy in the Old Testament, also found their way into Latter-day Saint discourse.[7]

The Mormons were never without allies of one stripe or another.[8] John J. Howard, for example, not only referred to the asymmetry of the sex ratio by the time men and women reached marriageable age but called on contemporary assumptions concerning women to justify plurality. Nature, he said, had made woman physically dependent on man. She was constituted as a "perpetual invalid" and was intellectually inferior as well. Her one gift was a keen moral sensibility. Clearly, woman's "sphere" was the kitchen, the parlor, and the nursery. Unable to compete with man outside the home, she must find ways to accommodate her proclivities inside one. Polygamy, said Howard, had worked for many ancient societies. Why should it not in the present? Urging that the Mormons be allowed to proceed, he said polygamy "cut the Gordion knot of the difficult woman-question," alone promising to solve the social problems of the day.[9] There were also private communications like that of Reuben Garten to President John Taylor. Garten, a sex theorist and lecturer, praised polygamy because it accommodated the comparatively greater sexual needs of men, resulted in improved physical health, and made for more vigorous children.[10]

Not all endorsed polygamy, but in their critiques of domestic malaise, they generated materials on which Mormons could draw in preparing arguments for their system. Henry C. Wright saw contemporary society as awash in self-pollution and careless sexual expenditure. The use of marriage for selfish gratification instead of reproduction was the institution's downfall. Stephen Pearl Andrews, on the other hand, argued for liberalizing the marital ethic as the only way to more adequately accommodate nature, thereby diminishing prostitution. Charles S. Woodruff believed that nearly all that was wrong in the world was due to contemporary marriage practice. Widespread want of amative harmony, he said, robbed mankind of enormous draughts of energy, causing disease and physical decline. Societies arose and fell according to sexual happiness. Marriage, he said, was the true "holy of holies." Men and women participated with God when they engaged in the procreative act. The human species was the literal, physical off-spring of God, and Jesus had been a perfect man because of the amative harmony of his parents. Like William Alcott, he argued that one must become a "second Adam," closely hearkening to the laws of sexual nature, if he wished to redeem his health and elevate his progeny.[11]

None probably influenced the Mormons more, however, than a Baptist minister writing under the pseudonym of E. N. Jencks. Troubled by the practice of Christian missionaries who required converts from polygamous societies to give up all wives save one, Jencks undertook an examination of the Bible and a survey of non-Western societies. Like others before him, he concluded that such a requirement had no basis in either scripture or nature.[12] Not only were there more women than men, he said, but plural marriage was far more ancient than monogamy and was practiced by the most enduring societies, especially in Asia.[13] Problems resulting from the large number of women who could never marry were compounded by the comparatively greater sexual needs of men. Repeatedly turning to this as the primary cause of prostitution, Jencks asked: "What can the poor monogamist do? The healthful currents of vigorous life impel him to amorous desire; and he cannot afford to shut down the gates . . . so the poor heart-broken and back-broken wife must submit to torture . . . [while] other men . . . steal away . . . wasting their health and strength upon vile prostitutes." He concluded that "an honest monogamy" was impossible.[14]

Affirming that marriage was the only proper and divinely approved condition under which sexual activity should occur, Jencks argued that polygamy alone assured sexual purity.[15] He blamed the Greeks and Romans for introducing Western man to monogamy. Corrupted by these societies, Christianity was further debilitated by its addition of ascetic celibacy. The result was physical inertia, prostitution, and social decline. Only through polygamy could the deleterious influence of male sexual repression be avoided, all women given honorable husbands, and the divine ukase commanding fecundity be fulfilled.[16] Although Jencks, in the first edition of his work, stated that he was unfamiliar with other supporters of the practice, it is clear from certain remarks that he was acquainted with the Mormons and their attempts to establish plural marriage.[17] In 1882 he published a stirring defence of them on grounds of religious liberty, pleading that the rights of the Saints in this regard were the rights of all.[18] While Mormon belief in the health benefits of polygamy preceded Jencks's publication, they subsequently made ample use of what he had to say.[19]

Fundamental to the Mormon argument, and identical to that of Jencks, was the assumption that men possessed greater sexual drive than women and that appropriation of this disparate condition was necessary if civilization were to survive. Whether or not it was due, as some have said, to a deep anxiety concerning female erotic capacity, Mormons, no less than non-Mormons, characterized women as both naturally and ideally without sexual desire.[20] In the words of the American physician Dr. George Napheys, it was an accepted truth that "only in very rare instances do women experience one tithe of the sexual feeling which is familiar to most men. Many of them," he said, "are entirely frigid, and not even in marriage do they ever perceive any real desire."[21] By contrast, as Margaret Fuller put it, man was assumed to be so sexually driven, so possessed by need, "that he must indulge his passions or die."[22]

Throughout the nineteenth century, there was no controversy between Mormon and non-Mormon on this point. Indeed, Latter-day Saints saw the difference of sexual need as an evidence for nature's approval of their system. In what was probably the earliest pamphlet defense of Mormon polygamy, it was said that "the marriage bed is shorter than that a man can stretch himself on it; and the covering is narrower than that he can wrap himself in it."[23] Belinda Marden Pratt said that men, unlike women, had no "draw back" on their sexual ardor. Nature had given them, she said, to move sexually "in a wider sphere."[24] A man's sexual powers, said another, were comparatively inexhaustible, whereas women lost even their fecundity at mid-life.[25] It came down to the fact, as another Mormon writer put it, that "the two sexes . . . are different in their tendencies; and . . . upon this very difference turns the whole question of the propriety of plural marriage. Women are endowed with monogamic tendencies and men with polygamic ones."[26]

This, however, was not argument enough. Critics of Mormon polygamy were quite willing to grant that it permitted greater accommodation of male sexual desire. But that was the problem. Monogamy was exalted precisely because it bridled men in this way, saving the community from sexual riot and conforming their energies to the building and refining vocations of genteel society. This was the basis of those correlations Peter T. Cominos found in the English Victorian mind between socioeconomic status and sexual behavior, or the idea of the gentleman—the "athlete of continence"—Charles E. Rosenberg saw emerging in the United States after 1830. Western civilization was the gift of "spermatic economy."[27] Abolitionist criticism of southern sexual degradation, as described by Ronald G. Walters, was now turned upon the Mormon. Both represented, by their want of restraint, a threat to orderly civilized life.[28]

Not only did Mormon polygamy portend destruction of Victorian marital safeguards, but, as we saw, it was believed to threaten society with actual physical deterioration. The common belief in a generative biology of fixed capacities held that an inverse relationship existed between spermatic depletion and man's health and energy. Those careless with such treasure suffered lassitude in both mind and body. And, it was believed, a measure of deprivation was passed to their descendants.[29] Thus, while "sapping" the people, polygamy was "dwarfing their physical proportions."[30] Hence the resemblance alleged between the Mormon polygamous product and sexual derelicts of other kinds and other races. All were guilty of a willful hemorrhaging of the precious seed. All could be expected to develop the same dreaded symptoms: sunken, lusterless eyes; a diminished physical frame; indolence; premature disease and death.

Again, the Saints had no quarrel with warnings concerning the dangers of spermatic waste. But here they took up the issue in a way that turned the argument to their favor. Sexual congress should occur only for the purpose of reproduction. That was clearly nature's intent with the act. But because of the want of parity in the sexual needs of men and women, monogamy, with its "unnatural matrimonial restraint," left men no alternative but to fruitlessly impose upon their wives or go outside the home, seducing the innocent and consorting with prostitutes.[31] In this way, sex was turned aside from its proper reproductive employment and life-giving fluids were prodigally lost. The result was a "great leakage of vital force, sapping the strength and vigor of the race."[32] As a Mormon apostle was reported to have told the French observer Jules Remy, monogamy forced upon men an alternative that was contrary to "the laws of nature, and to the great principle that nothing should be done in vain."[33]

Plural marriage permitted men to fulfill themselves sexually while creating new life. This comported with Mormonism's strict stand on sexual morality. "The necessity" that men pleaded in monogamous society, said George Q. Cannon, did not exist among the Latter-day Saints. "We close the door on one side," he declared, "and say that whoredoms, seductions and adulteries must not be committed among us . . . at the same time we open the door in the other direction and make plural marriage honorable."[34] The need for prostitution, as argued by some Victorians as a means for preserving homes from the disordering crises of male appetite, was seized on by Mormons as evidence that monogamy was manifestly an incorrect system of marriage.[35] It was monogamy's proscriptions that drove man to "desperation and all manner of iniquity."[36] In a formal epistle from the First Presidency in 1885, traditional marriage practice was attacked as having "dammed up" the natural channels God created for male sexual expression. The result was that women were degraded, prostitution encouraged, and disease abetted.[37] Mormonism's insistent linkage of sexuality to reproduction was an important part of their critique of monogamy, which, by its frustration of male need, was seen to foster social and physiological ruin.

From the 1850s until the end of the century, Mormon writers and speakers struck at what they considered their detractors' hypocrisy for criticizing Mormon marriage when, as the First Presidency affirmed in 1886, adultery and prostitution were the consequences of the monogamic arrangement.[38] George Q. Cannon told the story of a Mormon elder in Washington, D.C., who, when asked how many wives he had, replied, "I have such a plenty of my own that I have no occasion to trouble my neighbors." In Cannon's words, this was "a home shot." Not only did it speak to the advantage of polygamy in preserving public morality, but he and others were convinced that those who made the greatest stir concerning it were often those most tainted by sexual sin.[39] The faithful Latter-day Saint who married two or more wives, it was claimed, did more for humanity and redemption of the race than "ten thousand monogamists who write and preach about morality and virtue."[40]

It was commonly believed that during coition men transmitted to the embryo an impression of their thought and psychophysiological condition. Females, too, were capable of such imprinting, not only before birth but as long as lactation continued.[41] From the 1840s until the early twentieth century, Mormon authorities repeatedly warned against sexual relations when mothers were carrying and nursing children. Women free from the embraces of their husbands during pregnancy were known from science, it was said, to produce healthier and stronger offspring. In a letter to an unconverted friend, a Mormon mother reaffirmed the reproductive purpose of sexuality and emphasized the importance of female restraint during gestation because the developing embryo, near the mother's heart, "should be pure."[42] And polygamy, another Saint pointed out, "certainly favors this consummation more than monogamy."[43] As an unnamed Mormon correspondent told E. N. Jencks, if a man desired additional women, let him marry them. But, he said, let him then "observe the physiological laws, which even the brutes observe, and have no commerce during gestation. Then we shall have a race . . . not, as now, too frequently born with unbridled lusts engendered, while in a pre-natal state, by the excesses of their parents."[44]

This is not to say that breach of judgment did not occur in polygamous relations too. Indeed, there are grounds for believing that it occasioned troubled consciences in many instances. George Q. Cannon was probably referring to Mormons as well as outsiders in asserting that "many women are sent to the grave prematurely through the evils they have to endure from their husbands during pregnancy and lactation, and . . . their children often sustain irremediable injury."[45] And Heber C. Kimball, upbraiding the Saints for sexual misconduct, warned that many excited desire in their wives "at the most improper and unwise times."[46] Apostle Erastus Snow was reported to comment on "the folly of a man entailing disease and suffering on his posterity through not governing himself during the times when his wife was bearing children or nursing them."[47] But, the argument ran, the system of a plurality of wives acted to allay reasons for men being overcome from want of appropriate sexual outlet. As the Mormon press declared, for every "polygamous brute in Utah, a hundred monogamic brutes can be found in communities of equal number."[48]

These issues logically raise the question as to whether and to what degree Mormons granted erotic pleasure any role in marriage. This was an uneasy issue for many Americans throughout the nineteenth century. Anxiety was sharpened by the fact that at the very time methods of birth control were becoming better known and romance and affective relationships were acquiring added approval, medical advice manuals warned of the dangers sexual indulgence could bring.[49] Although contemporary Mormons yet display an unusually high birth rate, they are undoubtedly less anxious about such questions than their forebears of two or three generations past.[50] While the question is susceptible to argument, it seems there was something of a rigoristic shift away from the acceptance of sexual enjoyment in marriage that one encounters before the departure from Nauvoo. Oliver Cowdery once told his wife that not even maternal responsibilities should interfere with a married couple's personal relationship, for they were one flesh, as "bone and bone."[51] And Parley P. Pratt recalled that the Prophet Joseph Smith spoke to him approvingly of affection and intimacy in marriage.[52] After the move west, however, and as arguments for polygamy acquired greater importance, leaders granted a lesser role to pleasure in sexual activity. Reproduction was set forth consistently and emphatically as the near-exclusive function of sexual relations. Like other reformers of the age, their prescriptions reflected a predominantly conservative, reproductionist appropriation of conjugal response.[53]

Except for expressions of outrage over gentile hypocrisy, it is unlikely that any subject connected with sexuality occupied Mormon spokesmen more often than denials that gratification of the flesh had anything to do with plural marriage.[54] Beyond this, men were told not to "commit sin" with their spouses but to promote and multiply life. Heber C. Kimball pointed to husbands who continued to sleep with barren wives as adulterers, telling them that by so doing they were depleting their health.[55] Outside visitors commented on Mormon continence during pregnancy and lactation as part of their marital philosophy. Thus, said John Williams Gunnison, the time of weaning was an occasion of joy, like the celebration of a new marriage, when "patriarchal times" could return.[56] As James Dunn put it, in one of the few novels written in praise of the Mormon institution, "No marriage but what was founded in love—no love but for increase."[57]

Church authorities condemned monogamy in part because it held husbands and wives hostage to each other's attentions. Such affections were mutable and too easily transformed into lust. Spiritual duty, ecclesiastical authority, and regard for the general good alone deserved effusion. "Elders," said Brigham Young, "never love your wives one hair's breadth further than they adorn the Gospel, never love them so but that you can leave them at a moment's warning without shedding a tear. Should you love a child any more than this? No."[58] Wives, he said, should put aside all desire for the exclusive and romantic company of their husbands. Rather, they should simply "receive, conceive, bear, and bring forth in the name of Israel's God." They should not be concerned with whether they were loved "a particle" by their companions. That was not what the principle was about.[59] The explanation given by nineteenth-century practitioners (and fundamentalists defending the principle today), saying that one's love for multiple wives was no more difficult to understand than a parent's love for several children, if accepted as an honest statement of their feelings, illustrates the point. Sexual interest is, by definition and custom, ordinarily absent from parental love. If, in fact, men and women loved each other only in the same way they loved their children, a decline in erotic emphasis during the decades after 1852, when the principle was most actively preached and when such comparisons were adduced, is to be expected.

There is little surprise, then, that many observed a cool atmosphere in Mormon polygamous households.[60] In an article disparaging female reliance on marital affection, Emmeline B. Wells, sounding more the nun than the wife, said women of Utah should look for what their hearts craved in the hereafter.[61] Such attitudes echoed past the official cessation of polygamy into the twentieth century. Brigham H. Roberts, defending Mormon plural marriage in his *Comprehensive History of the Church,* praised it for delivering husbands and wives from that "uxorious sentimentality" that so often made monogamy half, if not entirely, "contemptible."[62] Given this, we can assume the faithful did what they could to confine their ardors to the divine injunction to reproduce.[63]

This does not mean that romantic love ceased to exist, for it did not. It would be an error to look upon the Mormons as either emotionally or sexually ascetic. They permitted more than many of their contemporaries. The case for a prudent sexuality had been carried to absurd extremes by theorists and physicians in both the United States and Europe.[64] With the Mormons, only wasted or vain emissions were to be avoided. Indeed, the persistence of romantic proclivities, combined with other monogamous assumptions, is credited with many of the difficulties encountered by polygamous spouses.[65] Nevertheless, while husbands were admonished to court their wives and sermons were given imploring tenderness between partners, it was not a topic of any popularity with the leaders.[66] Many must often have been unsure what they ought, or ought not, to feel.

If instructions were followed, however, reproductively purposed sexual activity was said to augment one's strength and alertness. As one Mormon pluralist wrote to a friend, "I wish you were a polyomist [*sic*] there is Something immensely [*sic*] Godlike in it   it increases the powers of the mind, [and] brings forth inbolden relief all the powers of the human Soul."[67] And there was the well-known statement by Heber C. Kimball that he could promise sixty-year-old men, if they would enter polygamy, that it would "renew" their age. For, he said, "I have noticed that a man who has but one wife, and is inclined to that doctrine, soon begins to wither and dry up, while a man who goes into

plurality looks fresh, young and sprightly."[68] Joseph E. Robinson recalled that President Lorenzo Snow told him that he had fathered a
child in his eighty-eighth year. Robinson said that when Snow told
him this, although past ninety, he was yet physically and mentally
vibrant.[69] And Snow himself told a Mormon gathering in 1899 that it
would not be long before the Saints would commonly live beyond the
age of one hundred.[70] Rather than fearing for their health, with a
modicum of restraint, Mormon patriarchs could green their old age
while, like Abraham, fathering nations of children.

In a sermon delivered in Springville, Utah, in 1857, Apostle Orson
Hyde graphically instructed his listeners in many of these principles.
Why was it, he asked, that men and women did not live as long as the
ancients? Apologizing that to give the answer he must speak plainly,
Hyde began by affirming that everything must be used as it was intended by nature. When a man confined sexual intercourse to no
more than what was required for conception, he said, his strength and
energy were not betrayed. This assured that his reserves were equal to
the challenge of disease, adding years to his life. One who indulged
himself beyond what was necessary for reproduction was sure to invite
physical prostration and weakness of mind. Parents and children alike
were enfeebled by such habits. This, said Hyde, accounted for the
birth of idiots and cripples. It explained what he saw in contemporary
society as a race of scrubby children. He said that those who were
drunkards, thieves, liars, and idlers were, as often as not, the issue of
parents who had given way to their passions. Moreover, he added,
sexual activity beyond conception was useless. It brought forth nothing. It was, he said, like sowing squash seeds on bare ground in the
autumn.[71] It is also significant that Hyde's remarks were addressed to
the practices of his Mormon audience. He called on them to repent of
their "secret sins," for they were a kind of murder. When men and
women were sexually prodigal, Hyde said, unborn spirits were disappointed and were forced to return to the Father, where they complained that they had been wronged and their mission frustrated.
Admitting that even in polygamy, especially in its early years, many
children died because of sexual excess, the apostle said that he himself
found it necessary to pray for assistance, that the entire matter constituted a difficult subject.[72]

Mormons expressed their views to more than assemblies of their
own people. James Bodell, a British soldier visiting Utah at the time of
the anti-polygamy crusade, was astonished to be lectured on his sins as
a monogamist. During a two-hour conversation with one of the Saints,
Bodell was told: "Do you know you Gentiles practice grievous sin in

what way you take unto yourself one wife? . . . All you Gentiles sow your seed on unfruitful places, having to do with a woman when she is bearing a child is against the laws of God." On the other hand, the elder said, Mormons suspended all sexual relations with a woman after she had conceived and further remained aloof for nine months after the child was born, permitting the mother to give her strength to the new infant. The Mormon elder told Bodell that he was sixty-three years old, had two wives, and was thinking of taking a third. Bodell said there was truth in the man's argument and that it about persuaded him to become a Mormon.[73]

Like others in both Europe and the United States, Latter-day Saints believed that members of the white race had dwindled from their former size.[74] One of the inaugural epiphanies of the Mormon church involved the appearance to Joseph Smith of an ancient American inhabitant, Moroni, who, as the young prophet later remembered, was larger than the ordinary man of Smith's generation.[75] Part of Mormonism's restorationist vision, even before the period of the church's settlement in the West, involved recovery of the longevity and physical powers of the ancients.[76] Luke William Gallup, not yet a polygamist but one who wrote valiantly in its behalf, cited non-Mormon authorities on European and American sexual behavior to persuade his unconverted father of the physical decline afflicting Western societies because of dissipation.[77] Another Mormon declared that the best of those who followed Sheridan in the Civil War could not have borne up a day under the heavy armor of their ancestors.[78] And Charles W. Penrose, an ardent expositor of the new faith, spoke of the "fact which must be patent to all, that the present generation of men are much more feeble, undersized and shorter lived than their ancestors of a few generations ago. . . . The great majority are small of stature, slight of limb, and look like boys turned old suddenly."[79] Many in the United States feared that, due to poor dietary habits, sexual dissipation, or failure to reproduce in sufficient numbers, their race was dying out.[80]

Advocates of Mormon polygamy played to the lamentations of those who, as David Pivar has shown, transformed antebellum abolitionism into crusades against sexual sin.[81] Because so many ills were viewed as arising from two-faced Victorian behavior, the times begged correction. Helen Mar Whitney, a Mormon polygamous wife for three decades, argued that historically polygamy had always neutralized moral evil and fostered sexual health.[82] The deleterious effects of the monogamous ethic were thought to be almost immediate. President

John Taylor once told a circle of faithful Mormons, for example, that prostitutes could be expected to die within five years and whoremongers and adulterers were stricken with diarrhea.[83] Health reform, sexual purity, and marriage relations remained popular issues with Americans well into the twentieth century.[84] Mormon sexual thought arose from this milieu and partook of these anxieties. Official church communications agreed with those predicting that the nation's "primitive Puritanic stock" was threatened with extinction. Plural marriage was the great need of the age, asserted one authority, because it promised to reverse the terrible downward physical course monogamous Christianity had taken.[85]

Church leaders made it clear that an effective program of reform involved such things as diet and personal cleanliness as well as polygamy. But modern man's fearful decline could be abated only when it was understood that the laws of health and the laws of God were the same and that nothing had been so corrupting as departure from the divine economy of the sexes provided for in plural marriage.[86] If their doctrines were adopted, Mormons were confident salubrious effects could be discerned in a single generation. As evidence, they cited the example of their own offspring. Their children, they held, were stronger, better looking, and more athletic. It was said that teachers from the East were astonished at how quickly Mormon children learned. And how could anyone question the transforming powers of polygamy, asked the *Deseret News*, "when we daily meet boys," the result of such unions, "weighing over 200 pounds and their parents perhaps not over 150."[87] Apostle Moses Thatcher appropriated Darwinian imagery in behalf of the tenet, declaring that upon natural, scientific grounds polygamy would be shown to be the better way. With their keener minds and stronger bodies, Mormon young people would eventually come to govern the rest of the world by "force of the 'survival of the fittest.'"[88] George A. Smith said he once spoke with an eastern professor who admitted that, if persistent with their health doctrines including polygamy, within about seventy years the Mormons would "produce a race of men who would be able to walk the rest of the human race under foot." And that, said Smith, was what they expected to do.[89]

As the non-Mormon writer Dyer Daniel Lum indicated, the Saints had turned the question around, stolen from their enemies the role of accuser, and placed monogamy on trial.[90] Using the same language as those critical of polygamy, Mormons characterized monogamous society as filled with languorous, vigorless, effeminate men. It mattered not that some labeled these claims "an insolent fallacy"; Mormons were certain they were true.[91] Mary Mount Tanner wrote to her non-Mormon aunt in 1880: "It is asserted by the world that the offspring of poligamy [sic] cannot be strong and vigorous both in mind and body. We have proved that they are . . . and Phisialogical [sic] reasons . . . bear out our theory . . . and facts demonstrate it."[92] Through polygamy, the Mormons believed they were nurturing "a more than Spartan race."[93] They were producing in the Great Basin a renewed society of "stalwart sons and fair and robust daughters." Because of their sexual practices, said one defender, Mormons in the Rocky Mountains would soon confront the rest of the world with a race of giants. A new and higher order of men had appeared. "The mountain boys of Utah, powerful and well developed," were "the first fruits of the Lord's great work of physical regeneration."[94]

Brigham Young, who once said he hoped to live to be 135 to 150 years of age, took pride that God had preserved him "in the vigor of youth" and that he was in his sixth decade yet "as active as a boy."[95] That such endowments were associated, in his mind, with his image as a sexual partner is clear from his remarks at the time the apostate Thomas Marsh was reaccepted into the church. Young chided Marsh on having once fretted about plural marriage. There was no need to worry, Young said, for Marsh was so feeble a man he probably could not have obtained a wife anyway. By contrast, although but a year and a half Marsh's junior, Young boasted that he could find more girls who would choose him for a husband than most younger men in the church.[96]

Mormon pluralists were undoubtedly flattered that not only did the predictions concerning polygamy's supposed vicious consequences fail to occur but, as time passed, increasing numbers of outsiders acknowledged their general good health and youthful appearance. Beyond the example of Brigham Young, or the spurious "Mormon Elders Damiana Wafers" huckstered by Gentiles to the gullible on the assumption that Mormon men possessed extraordinary sexual powers, more sober testimony existed that could be taken as confirming their hygienic success.[97] There was, for example, the remark of Lady Duffus Hardy that although she thought Mormon men coarse and sensual she also found them full of physical strength and good health. "One cannot imagine," she said, "a bad or ill-regulated liver among them."[98] The Britisher Phil Robinson was full of praise for the physical acquirements of polygamy's product. Not only did the daughters of Utah's "hardy sires" have figures that would make Parisians envious but, said Robinson, their young men promised what it was Plato had dreamed for in his guardians.[99] As late as 1902 a non-

Mormon visitor to Salt Lake City commented on the physical and mental achievements of the Saints under their system of plural marriage.[100]

Mormon commitment to polygamy became so embracing that, after the manner of Madan and Jencks, it was used to explain the success and failure of past societies. The Abrahamic prototype of a male-centered polygamous household was looked upon as heaven-ordained and as a model for individual and social health in every era of the world's history. The habits of Old Testament patriarchs were more than precedentally significant. Modern revelation, it was argued, opened their examples to a new and enlarged understanding of biosocial truths. Nowhere was this better explained than in an 1853 pamphlet by Orson Spencer.[101]

Central to the entire matter, said Spencer, was the story of Abraham. As a reward for his righteousness and in response to his childless condition, Abraham was given wives and concubines. This was done with the consent of Sarah, his first wife, who was then blessed with child herself. God was so pleased with Abraham that he made with him an everlasting covenant. The agreement was to be renewed by following generations and carried a promise of eternal family organization and eternal family increase. "And I will make my covenant between me and thee and will multiply thee exceedingly."[102] It was this that assured a more provident fulfillment of God's first and greatest commandment—to multiply and replenish the earth. To enter into such an arrangement, with permission from God or his prophets, was the Abrahamic law. To consent to one's husband taking additional wives, when done in righteousness, was the law of Sarah.[103]

Like the antebellum southerner in his scriptural defense of slaveholding, Mormons placed great store by the friendship between plural-wived Abraham and the Deity. As one who talked and dined with God, he had been instructed in heavenly ways. Thus, Spencer observed, "the family order which God established with Abraham and the patriarchs was the order observed among celestial beings, in the celestial world."[104] Mankind's chief exemplars had lived the principle, both patriarchally and polygamously. Christ, it was argued, had descended through polygamous forefathers and, according to some, engaged in plural marriage himself.[105] Critics who found the Latter-day Saint notion of a sentient man-become-god difficult, already embarrassed by the suggestion that He kept bed, were thunderstruck to be told it was with a plurality of companions.[106] But Mormons believed they had been shown the things of eternity. Institutions and society, they argued, could endure only to the degree they resembled or were built upon divine models.

It is important that emphasis be given to the equation made by Mormon writers between patriarchal home life and heavenly government. "The grand design of God in bringing the spirits of men and women to occupy bodies upon this earth," said Orson Spencer, "was to establish a system of perfect Patriarchal government, according to the pattern of the family of Heaven."[107] One writer referred to the 1852 announcement concerning polygamy as "the doctrine of Celestial Family Organization" now "made plain to the Saints."[108] By restoring the patriarchal polygamous home, the Saints opened to human view more than a superior arrangement between the sexes. They were laying a foundation for the polity of the gods.[109] It was, said Charles W. Penrose, "the dream of the Prophets, the prediction of the Seers, the theme of the inspired Bards. . . . A divine social system which will grow into a universal political system."[110]

An essential ingredient of the arrangement was the subordination of women to their husbands. In a series of articles appearing in the *Deseret News*, a visitor to Salt Lake City was led to ask if the "jars, jealousies and rivalries" so common in monogamous families did not reach unendurable proportions in polygamy. The visitor's Mormon host, appropriately named "Elder Freeman," replied that such a consequence was impossible because of the Saints' firm adherence to patriarchal rule. The absence of such a principle, said Freeman, accounted for not only anarchy in many domestic circles but, emanating upward, unsettled civil government as well. It was what Freeman called the "perilous and delightful service" of reordering family structure along patriarchal lines that constituted the Mormon mission.[111]

When asked why women should not have a right to additional spouses, as did their husbands, the answer was that women were not constituted by nature for such relationships. Not only were they more limited than males in their sexual desire and capacity for reproduction but multiple partners would, as in prostitution, lead to degeneracy and confusion of their natures. Luke William Gallup said, "I can think of only one way that it might be made to work both ways, & that is for the Almighty to send us all back to this earth again, after we leave it, and give us an exchange of sexual organization."[112] John T. Caine, Utah's territorial delegate, told Congress that polyandry was unacceptable to Mormons because of physical reasons preventing it.[113] Some argued that by enduring the trials of polygamy women could emancipate themselves from the curse of Eve, which Brigham Young once described as a strict subjection to their husbands. What this might connote for polygamy, if anything, was never said.[114]

Official Latter-day Saint attitudes toward women, especially when discussing male prerogative, could be sharply stated. Talk then taking place about women's rights, according to one Mormon authority, was so much "nonsense."[115] Heber C. Kimball had no regard for men who surrendered to what he called "pettycoat government."[116] Women were told they were not to take the lead from their husbands even in holding family prayer. Men permitting themselves to be dominated by their wives were "just a little better in appearance and in their habits than a little black boy. They live in filth and nastiness, they eat it and drink it and they are filthy all over."[117] And wives seeking fulfillment apart from the direction of their husbands were violating the pattern of divine domestic government. "Sisters," said Brigham Young, "do not ask whether you can make yourselves happy, but whether you can do your husband's will, if he is a good man."[118] Those "strong-minded" women and "weak-minded" men who went about passing resolutions on female equality were "ridiculous." And women who attacked the patriarchal order itself, condemning plural marriage, were without natural female inclinations, wanting faith and unworthy of the blessings of Sarah. Such had forgotten "the natural use of women, as revealed from heaven" and were hardened against divine order.[119]

It is difficult not to conclude that a major reason for the Mormon position regarding woman's subordinate role—and thus, in their eyes, the wisdom of God in ordaining the patriarchal order—was belief in an innate inferiority of the female sex. Explicit statements to this effect were made by church writers and speakers on numerous occasions. Charles W. Penrose echoed the sentiments of many in saying, "Much as it has been disputed by agitators for 'woman's rights,' man, as a sex, by reason of greater physical and mental strength, is placed by nature above woman in the scale of being."[120] More directly, Benjamin Franklin Johnson asked, "Where upon the 'pages of inspiration,' is there one evidence that woman was designed to fill a sphere equal with man?"[121] In the latter half of the nineteenth century Mormon churchmen were unhalting in urging strict adherence to patriarchal authority. Failure to uphold such a rule, it was said, was one of the reasons for spiritual apostasy and social decline in the past.[122] And throughout the entire period of the Mormon experiment, polygamous husbands seem to have displayed an especially passionate pride in the multiplication of sons.

Not only had the Israelites waxed and waned as they emulated or wandered from heaven's patriarchal, polygamous family standard but other non-Western societies had benefited from the natural advantages of this superior arrangement. Such nations were said to possess larger populations and to be less afflicted with prostitution and its attendant evils. As George Q. Cannon explained, "The history of the world goes to prove that the practice of this principle, even by nations ignorant of the Gospel, has resulted in greater good to them than the practice of monogamy or the one-wife system in the so-called Christian nations."[123] The assumption that European and American cultures were more advanced and more enduring was false. Older societies, yet adhering to the most ancient pattern, displayed greater vigor and better health. "Today," claimed the Mormon press, "the most stalwart and physically powerful men known are not found in Christian monogamous nations, but in polygamic Asia."[124]

Departure from the polygamous home after the time of Christ was especially fateful. Some said Jesus' crucifixion was due to unpopularity because of his supposed polygamous activities.[125] But Rome was made to bear more responsibility than all others for the loss of plural marriage. Brigham Young was scathing in his account of how the Romans came to endorse monogamy. No more than buccaneers, he said, they had been unable to steal enough women for all to have as many as they wanted, so they prohibited any from having more than one. This, he declared, commenced the undoing of plurality in the ancient world.[126]

The alliance between Christian religion and the Roman government, it was said, led to Catholicism's rejection of the principle. Some Mormons considered this to be an important element in the apostasy from divine truths that they believed had afflicted the early church.[127] Monogamy then brought with it the usual train of evils, including the decline of Rome, depopulation, prostitution, and disease. Appropriately enough, it was what George Q. Cannon called "the vigorous polygamic hordes of the north" that swept away the rotting carcass of the Roman imperial state.[128] With conversion of the barbarians to Christianity and its marriage practices, however, the declension continued. All Catholic Europe fell heir to the curse. By enforcing monogamy against both divine law and human nature, the Roman church fulfilled the Revelator's vision and became "the mother of harlots."[129]

Reestablishment of plural marriage as a perfect biological and social formula had to occur if the earth were to be cleansed and mankind prepared for the Second Coming of Christ.[130] Errors of the past, such as the tradition of monogamous marriage, were to be replaced by institutions of divine pattern. Those who accused the Saints of innovation were, said the Mormons, misconstruing their work. "We deny having a new marriage system," they argued. Rather, they were but "striving to restore the old," saying that it was first the church of Rome, then the Protestants, that had fallen away from the earlier and better plan.[131] Mormon superiority arose from conformity to the domestic manners of the ancient patriarchs, the friends of God.[132] Having reinstituted heaven's own domestic ways, the world had no alternative, as one Mormon put it, but to "take sides with the mother of harlots, and with her monogamy, and celibacy, and prostitution, or take sides with the Almighty, and with His holy law of polygamy, and sexual purity."[133]

At a century's removal it is difficult to appreciate the intensity of Mormonism's denigration of the monogamous ethic. A French writer, reviewing nineteenth-century church writings, caught the spirit of their attack: "Monogamy was unrelentingly condemned, and in the most insulting terms. Not only was it responsible for European decadence, but Mormon polygamists alone were to become the sons of God."[134] Only the noble and great of the earth, those able to escape the confining attitudes of traditional morality, could adequately appreciate the plural system. And few were more punishing, more disparaging than George A. Smith: "We have the best looking men and the handsomest women," he said, "for they are a poor, narrow-minded, pinch-backed race of men, who chain themselves down to the law of monogamy, and live all their days under the dominion of one wife."[135] The Mormon course was clear. "Contracted Romish principles of monogamy" must not "hinder the sons of progress in the great work of social reformation and regeneration."[136]

Mormon zeal for physically restoring the race took support from another Latter-day Saint belief—the contention that matter and spirit were intimately linked and that to care for one was to cultivate the other.[137] As one editorialist explained, Mormonism taught that man's ploughing was as holy as his preaching, and physical labor was true worship. "In whatever manner he advances the cause of humanity . . . he is advancing the cause of heaven."[138] The all-inclusive nature of nineteenth-century Mormonism bundled the things of this world and the next together, promising the faithful, by "the same felicitous means, a bushel of potatoes, an extra wife, and a promise of life everlasting."[139] Daniel H. Wells said it was a mistake to believe that glorification took place only after death. Exaltation, he said, begins in this world.[140] Brigham Young affirmed that, by adapting their habits to heaven's formula, men and women could "merge into immortality."[141] If the instructions given were faithfully observed, promised George Q. Cannon, "here in these valleys, we shall raise a race of men who will be the joy of the earth, whose complexions will be the complexions of angels."[142] Mormons looked to so reform enough of mankind that Christ could return, comfortably take up residence with them, and assume the reins of an already perfected society.[143]

Like Orson Hyde, who said that to talk of potatoes, hay, and wheat was to talk of things spiritual, so a story published in the *Deseret News* in 1853 argued the interchangeability of temporal and heavenly truths.[144] A boy was described as asking his father the meaning of the word *physiology*. The parent explained that it meant the study of man for the purpose of promoting health, longevity, and good memory. The youth then inquired why it was not given the attention in Mormon schools that it received elsewhere. The boy's father answered that, in fact, it was given a preeminent place among the Saints. Knowledge of the Gospel *was* knowledge of physiology. "I want you to understand," he declared, "that all transgression is directly in opposition to physiology." The father then illustrated his lesson with the story of a young man possessing a leaky "pipe of valuable wine." Because of the church's teachings, he said, a wise youth would know better than to "stop the gimlet holes and leave the bung out; but [instead] . . . would first stop the bung hole and at the earliest convenience plug up the lesser apertures."[145] By restoring the practice of a plurality of wives and urging that sex be used for procreative purposes, the Saints were placing a governor on what they believed was an uncontrolled, enfeebling spill. With such remedies, they were administering not only to the body but, *pari passu*, were engaged in a calisthenic of the spirit.

Latter-day Saint commitment to physically refining the body is exampled by the well-known early Mormon concern with diet.[146] It is further illustrated by teachings given in the Council of Health. This organization, commenced by the Mormon pioneers in early 1849, devoted itself to a variety of medical subjects. Among other things, members of the society were instructed in the health advantages of avoiding sexual intercourse during periods of pregnancy and nursing, of the dependence of longevity on proper sexual behavior, and on the best means for achieving "the most perfect development and the greatest amount of vital power in the shortest period."[147] Mormon views conceptually anticipated the late-nineteenth and early-twentieth-century eugenics movement. Building on the work of Francis Galton, men like Karl Pearson in England and Amzi Benedict Davenport in the United States pleaded for the ameliorative potentials of a socially conscious hereditarianism. While Mormons drew primarily on theories of acquired characteristics, they were, nevertheless, making the case for the use of sexual behavior to obtain an improved physical product.[148] Amasa M. Lyman, for example, commented: "Let us get the body improved first that the spirit may live and dwell in a perfect tabernacle. When this is done, we can go and cultivate the spirit as much as is needful."[149] Near the end of the century, when asked by a journalist what it was that Mormonism was seeking to accomplish, a church member replied: "To produce a perfect race of men, and to make each generation more nearly perfect than the last. The perfection that men can reach is of the physical sort: the morals God looks after. He puts good souls only in fit bodies."[150]

Adapting what they could from the Gentile, the Saints claimed to have commenced the millennial work of altering the world's order. With its bold promise to transfigure man's corrupted form and harmonize the genders, plural marriage acquired a central role in nineteenth-century Mormonism's restorationist intent. A writer for the *Philadelphia Press,* describing life among the Saints in the early 1870s, remarked that they spoke less regarding the spiritual origins of polygamy than they did about "its superiority as a social system." Another commented that, when discussing the subject, religion was brought in only at "the fag end of the argument."[151] What neither understood was that, so far as Mormonism was concerned, the two were identical. Life, here and hereafter, was an uninterrupted continuum. Theirs was the task of preparing the world for its eternal glory. "Our business," said Joseph F. Smith, "is to reclaim this earth. We have set out to regenerate the human family."[152]

At the time the movement against Mormon polygamy was acquiring greatest momentum, Eliza R. Snow, successively a plural wife to Joseph Smith and Brigham Young, declared that the principle was perhaps the most important thing preached by the restored church. It promised, she said, a "more perfect type of manhood mentally and physically" and offered to renew the longevity of Biblical patriarchs. Should the United States forbid its practice, she warned, the cost to humanity would be such that the American people must shoulder a heavier burden than any nation except the ancient Jews.[153] Mary Elizabeth Rollins Lightner, another of the Prophet Joseph Smith's wives, was urged in 1887 to write a biographical sketch memorializing her role as "among the first honored of God to help lay the foundation of this great work of regeneration."[154] And when testifying in the mid-1890s on the principle, Lucy W. Kimball, yet another of the first Prophet's plural wives, subsequently married to Heber C. Kimball, delivered herself of one of those confessions that, by its sudden, revealing nature, tells us more than was perhaps intended. Annoyed with the interrogator and chafing from her church's recent repudiation of the practice, she asserted: "There was not any love in the union between myself and Kimball, and it is my business entirely whether there was any courtship or not. It was the principle of plural marriage that we were trying to establish . . . and if we had established it, it would have been for the benefit of the whole human race, and the race will say so yet."[155]

However pronounced their differences over family structure, the Mormon considered civilization no less owing to correct sexual usage than did his Victorian monogamist foe. Both were convinced of the controlling significance sexual behavior had for individual and social health. Both were keenly attentive to theories of racial improvement. Spermatic government was as saving for one as the other. It was only that Mormons attributed to purely reproductive sex what others claimed for seminal reservation altogether. Whether to strengthen the home or amend the race, few in his day would have disagreed with George Q. Cannon in the comment that all must "begin in the marriage bed."[156]

Jan Shipps is undoubtedly correct that nineteenth-century Mormons believed themselves to be participating in a frame of sacred time and space.[157] But they also trafficked extensively in the thought of their day. Mormonism's theocratic cell had permeable walls. This meant, of course, that they were aware of criticisms made of their system and, as will later be suggested, were susceptible to such views. But in the toils of conflict, like the champions of slavery during the Civil War, they consecrated everything to a defense of the polygamous way.

As a part of this process, the Mormon principle of a plurality of wives acquired enormous importance. It was more than just another sectarian scriptural tenet. As the alleged order of heaven, it promised improved health, family peace, and social vigor. With such a device, God had introduced the Saints to the company of heavenly society. Writing to his reluctant cousin in the spring of 1889, Joseph F. Smith said that polygamous marriage was the "acme of Divine Purity," that, as one of the most sacred of all laws, it would continue forever.[158]

Victorian America, however, frowning at such claims, fiercely insisted monogamy alone promised men and women a better world.

NOTES

1. It was George Q. Cannon who said that such considerations were perhaps the most important. *JD* 13:206 (1869). David J. Whittaker, in his excellent overview of Mormon apologies for plural marriage, refers to the "social" arguments made in behalf of the practice. "Early Mormon Polygamy Defenses," *JMH* 11 (1984): 51–53, 55–56, 59; and idem, "The Bone in the Throat: Orson Pratt and the Public Announcement of Plural Marriage," *Western Historical Quarterly* 18 (July 1987): 303, 309–11. Also see Lester E. Bush, Jr., "The Mormon Tradition," in *Caring and Curing: Health and Medicine in the Western Religious Traditions,* ed. Ronald L. Numbers and Darrel W. Amundsen (New York: Macmillan, 1986), 406. The most recent book-length studies of Mormon polygamy are also brief in their mention of the matter: Lawrence Foster, *Religion and Sexuality: Three American Communal Experiments* (New York: Oxford University Press, 1981), 202–4; Richard S. Van Wagoner, *Mormon Polygamy: A History* (Salt Lake City: Signature Books, 1986), 90; and Jessie L. Embry, *Mormon Polygamous Families: Life in the Principle,* Vol. 1, Publications in Mormon Studies (Salt Lake City: University of Utah Press, 1987), 46–47.

2. James T. Cobb, "Mrs. Stearns and Mormonism," *Tullidge's Quarterly Magazine* 1 (April 1881): 523–24.

3. In addition to the discussion in chap. 1 of this volume, see Orson Pratt, "Christian Polygamy in the Sixteenth Century," *Seer* 1 (Dec. 1853): 177–83; "Luther on Polygamy," *DN,* 24 Nov. 1853; "Milton on Polygamy," *DN,* 10 Aug. 1854; "Luther on Polygamy (From Michelet's Life of Luther)," *Mill. Star* 15 (6 Aug. 1853): 526–27; "Milton on Polygamy," ibid. 16 (27 May 1854, 3 June 1854): 321–24, 342–45; Alexander Ott, "Polygamy among the Jews," ibid. 29 (20 July 1867): 451–52; H. Henriod, "Polygamy as Practiced by the Jews in Algeria, and Recognized by the French Government," ibid. 29 (3 Aug. 1867): 485–88; Veritas, "Plural Marriage," ibid. 36 (22 Sept. 1874): 593–97; "Notes Concerning Marriage," ibid. 36 (13 Oct. 1874): 644–47; "The 'Daily Mail' and Plural Marriage," ibid. 38 (14 Feb. 1876): 105; G. S., "John Milton on Plural Marriage," ibid. 38 (13 March 1876): 161–65; *JD* 11:127 (Brigham Young/1865). The Mormon appropriation of Milton has been explored in two articles by John S. Tanner: "Making a Mormon of Milton," *BYU Studies* 24 (Spring 1984): 191–206; and "Milton and the Early Mormon Defenses of Polygamy," *Milton Quarterly* 21 (May 1987): 41–46.

4. [Martin Madan], *Thelypthora; or, A Treatise on Female Ruin . . . ,* 3 vols. (London: J. Dodsley, 1780–81); and Whittaker, "Early Mormon Polygamy Defenses," 61n.57.

5. John Henry Smith to Joseph Smith III, 21 April 1886, RLDS Library and Archives.

6. David O. Allen, *India, Ancient and Modern, Geographical, Historical, Political, Social, and Religious; with a Particular Account of the State and Prospects of Christianity* (Boston: John P. Jewett, 1856), 459, 462, 464–65, 602–3, 604–9. For Mormon notice and discussion of Allen's work, see "Church of England (Episcopalians), Presbyterians, Baptists, and Congregationalists Turned Po-

lygamists," *Mormon* 2 (23 Feb. 1856): n.p.; "Free Love in the Church," ibid. 2 (23 Feb. 1856): n.p.; "A Protestant Minister's Arguments from the Bible in Favour of Polygamy," *Mill. Star* 18 (19 April 1856): 636–39; Parley P. Pratt, "Marriage and Morals in Utah," *Western Standard* 2 (10 May 1856): n.p.; George A. Smith, *The Rise, Progress and Travels of the Church of Jesus Christ of Latter-day Saints . . .* , 2d ed. rev. (Salt Lake City: Deseret News, 1872), 48–55.

7. Reverend Mercer Davies, *Hagar; or, Scripture Facts Concerning Marriage, esp. in Reference to Polygamy, Concubinage, Divorce, Marital Authority, etc.* (London: Wertheimer, Lea and Co., 1881). Mormon reference to the work is made in "'Concubinage' and the Church of England," *DN*, 11 Aug. 1882. Another non-Mormon defense of ancient plurality is the anonymously authored *Jezreel: The Problem of Judaism and Christianity Solved* (Ann Arbor, Mich.: Irvin Moore, n.d.). Mormon notice of the work occurs in "Polygamy," *DN*, 5 April 1884.

8. Because the Saints were keen on finding friends, it is relatively easy to trace their allies in Mormonism's public prints. E.g., "Mrs. [Jane] Swisshelm on Polygamy," *Mill. Star* 16 (1 April 1854): 206; "George Francis Train Defending Brigham Young and Mormonism on Scriptural and Moral Grounds," ibid. 31 (5 June 1869): 368–69; "Polygamy in England," ibid. 35 (7 Oct. 1873): 625–26; "The Men and Women of Utah," ibid. 25 (21 Oct. 1873): 657–58; "Concubinage and the Church of England," *DN*, 11 Aug. 1882; "Polygamy," *DN*, 5 April 1884. Also see "Life among the Mormons," [New York] *Sun*, 27 Feb. 1881; and W. H. Babcock, "Our Monthly Gossip," *Lippincott's Monthly Magazine* 37 (June 1886): 664. For the friendship and support of the eccentric George Francis Train, see Bitton Davis, "George Francis Train and Brigham Young," *BYU Studies* 18 (Spring 1978): 410–27; and for that of the socialist Dyer Daniel Lum, see John S. McCormick, "An Anarchist Defends the Mormons: The Case of Dyer D. Lum," *UHQ* 44 (Spring 1976): 156–69.

9. John J. Howard, *A Plea for Polygamy: Being an Attempt at a Solution of the Woman-Question* (Boston: printed by the author, 1875).

10. Reuben Garten to President John Taylor and twelve apostles, 15 March 1886, Taylor Family Papers, Letterbook, Raymond Taylor typewritten transcription, University of Utah Library, Salt Lake City.

11. Henry C. Wright, *Marriage and Parentage; or, The Reproductive Element in Man, as a Means to His Elevation and Happiness* (Boston: Bela Marsh, 1855); Stephen Pearl Andrews, ed., *Love, Marriage, and Divorce, and the Sovereignty of the Individual . . .* (New York: Stringer & Townsend, 1853); Charles S. Woodruff, *Legalized Prostitution; or, Marriage as It Is and Marriage as It Should Be, Philosophically Considered* (Boston: Bela Marsh, 1862), 17, 27, 30, 88, 92, 94–97, 102–3, 137, 146–47; and William A. Alcott, *The Physiology of Marriage* (Boston: Dinsmoor, 1866), 140.

12. E. N. Jencks [pseud.], *History and Philosophy of Marriage; or, Polygamy and Monogamy Compared by a Christian Philanthropist* (Boston: James Campbell, 1869), 16–22, 62–77. This work was republished in 1875 and again in 1885

by Joseph H. Parry in Salt Lake City, including extracts from Madan, Orson Pratt, Richard Burton, and Joseph Smith's 1843 revelation on polygamy. It was again published, under the same title, by Charles Carrington in Paris in 1898. Then, as a novelty item, it appeared as *A Plea for Polygamy* (New York: Panurge Press, 1929).

13. Jencks, *History and Philosophy of Marriage* (1869), 45–53, 60–62 passim.

14. Ibid., 169–71, 175.

15. Ibid., 44–50.

16. Ibid., 58–60, 78–143.

17. Ibid., 14, 61, 150.

18. E. N. Jencks [pseud.], *The Mormon Problem: A Letter to the Massachusetts Members of Congress on Plural Marriage, Its Morality and Lawfulness, by a Citizen of Massachusetts* (Boston: James Campbell, 1882).

19. For references to Jencks's book in Mormon writings, where the author is often referred to as James Campbell, see the series "A Christian Plea for Plurality of Wives," *Mill. Star* 31 (27 Oct. 1869): 699–701, 31 (10 Nov. 1869): 735–37, 32 (1 Feb. 1870): 65–66, 32 (8 Feb. 1870): 83–86. Also see "'Is Polygamy a Blessing?'" ibid. 32 (15 March 1870): 166–67; "The 'Daily Mail' and Plural Marriage," ibid. 38 (14 Feb. 1876): 105; "Presbyterians and Polygamy," *DN*, 18 Dec. 1879; and Scott G. Kenney, ed., *Wilford Woodruff's Journal*, 9 vols. (Midvale, Utah: Signature Books, 1983–85), 7:476, 29 March 1879. Helen Mar Whitney, after quoting extensively from Jencks's book, said that he expressed "a great deal of what we Latter-day Saints believe." *Plural Marriage as Taught by the Prophet Joseph: A Reply to Joseph Smith, Editor of the Lamoni (Iowa) "Herald"* (Salt Lake City: Juvenile Instructor, 1882), 53.

20. Peter Gay has suggested that the nineteenth-century characterization of female sexual disinterest may have been a reaction formation, rooted in fear of its opposite. *Education of the Senses*, Vol. 1, *The Bourgeois Experience: Victoria to Freud* (New York: Oxford University Press, 1984), 197. A different explanation is provided by Edmund Leites in his theory of a "hierarchy of gender." *The Puritan Conscience and Modern Sexuality* (New Haven: Yale University Press, 1986), 116–20, 148–49. Also see the near-classic study by Keith Thomas, "The Double Standard," *Journal of the History of Ideas* 20 (April 1959): 195–216; Louis J. Kern's *An Ordered Love: Sex Roles and Sexuality in Victorian Utopias—the Shakers, the Mormons, and the Oneida Community* (Chapel Hill: University of North Carolina Press, 1981), 34–49; John D'Emilio and Estelle B. Freedman, *Intimate Matters: A History of Sexuality in America* (New York: Harper & Row, 1988), 76–84; and the writings cited above in chap. 2, note 31.

21. George Napheys, *The Transmission of Life: Counsels on the Nature and Hygiene of the Masculine Function*, 6th ed. rev. (Philadelphia: J. G. Fergus, 1871), 173–74. Also see Anna Fergurson, *The Young Lady; or, Guide to Knowledge, Virtue, and Happiness* (Boston: G. W. Cottrell, 1848), 117; and, probably best known, the affirmations of the English physicians: T. L. Nichols, *Esoteric Anthropology (The Mysteries of Man): A Comprehensive and Confidential Treatise on the Structure, Functions, Passional Attractions, and Perversions . . . of Men and*

Women (London: Nichols, 1853), 97–98, 99, 102; and William Acton, *The Functions and Disorder of the Reproductive Organs in Childhood, Youth, Adult Age, and Advanced Life, Considered in Their Physiological, Social, and Moral Relations* (Philadelphia: Lindsay & Blackiston, 1865), 133.

22. Margaret Fuller, *Woman in the Nineteenth Century* (1855; New York: Norton, 1971), 150.

23. [Udney Hay Jacob], *An Extract, from a Manuscript Entitled "The Peace Maker," the Doctrines of the Millennium:* . . . (Nauvoo, Ill.: J. Smith, 1842), 37.

24. Belinda Marden Pratt, *Defense of Polygamy, by a Lady of Utah, in a Letter to Her Sister in New Hampshire* (Salt Lake City: n.p., [1854]), 6.

25. Abraham M. Musser, "Polygamy," *Mill. Star* 39 (11 June 1877): 390.

26. "Woman and Plural Marriage," *Utah Magazine* 2 (19 Dec. 1868): 150–51. The expression of this sentiment by a journal and its editor that took strong exception to the economic policies of Brigham Young illustrates the broad acceptance arguments of this kind enjoyed. Other statements indicating Mormon belief in the comparatively greater sexual drive of men are *JD* 2:83 (Orson Hyde/1854); *JD* 13:206 (George Q. Cannon/1869); the comments of Jules Remy in *A Journey to Great Salt Lake City . . . with a Sketch of the History, Religion, and Customs of the Mormons . . .* , 2 vols. (London: W. Jeffs, 1861), 2:103; and Joseph Birch, "Is Polygamy Unnatural?" *Mill. Star* 36 (20 Jan. 1874): 35.

27. The phrase was first used by G. J. Barker-Benfield in "The Spermatic Economy: A Nineteenth-Century View of Sexuality," in *The American Family in Social-Historical Perspective,* ed. Michael Gordon (New York: St. Martin's Press, 1973), 336–72. Also see idem, *The Horrors of the Half-Known Life: Male Attitudes toward Women and Sexuality in Nineteenth-Century America* (New York: Harper & Row, 1976), 175–88. Peter T. Cominos's study is "Late-Victorian Respectability and the Social System," *International Review of Social History* 8 (1963): pt. 1:18–48, pt. 2:216–50. That of Charles E. Rosenberg is "Sexuality, Class and Role in Nineteenth-Century America," *American Quarterly* 25 (May 1973): 131–53. Ellen K. Rothman discussed restraints expected of women in courtship, suggesting that they were not as "passionless" as supposed, in her "Sex and Self-Control: Middle-Class Courtship in America, 1770–1870," *Journal of Social History* 15 (Spring 1982): 409–25. Also see John S. Haller and Robin M. Haller, *The Physician and Sexuality in Victorian America* (New York: Norton, 1974), 191–234.

28. Ronald G. Walters, "The Erotic South: Civilization and Sexuality in American Abolitionism," *American Quarterly* 25 (May 1973): 177–201.

29. It is difficult to overstate the extraordinary importance attributed to semen by nineteenth-century writers, European and American alike. With regard to the dangers of spermatorrhoea and masturbation, the most influential early authority was the Swiss writer Samuel Auguste André David Tissot, whose Latin treatise, "Tentamen de morbis ex manustupratione," in his *Dissertatio de febribus biliosis* (Lausanne: n.p., 1758), was translated into English

under the title *Onanism: or, A Treatise upon the Disorders Produced by Masturbation, or, the Dangerous Effects of Secret and Excessive Venery, by M. Tissot.* (London: A. Hume, 1766). In the words of another frequently quoted European, "totus homo semen est." Alexander Mayer, *Des rapports conjugaux considérés sous le triple point de vue de la population, de la santé et de la morale publique* (Paris: J. B. Baillière, 1857), 367–68. Sylvester Graham referred to it as "the essential oil of animal liquors—the rectified spirit—the most subtile and spirituous part of the animal frame." *A Lecture to Young Men, on Chastity. Intended Also for the Serious Consideration of Parents and Guardians* (Boston: George W. Light, 1839), 51. The number of publications warning of the terrible effects sure to follow those who engaged in sexual profligacy was considerable. This was especially true of ultraists like Orson Squire Fowler, in his *Fowler on Matrimony . . .* (New York: O. S. and L. N. Fowler, 1842), 79–81; Russel Thacher Trall, *Home-Treatment for Sexual Abuses: A Practical Treatise* (New York: Fowler & Wells, 1853), 27–35; or Wesley Grindle, *New Medical Revelations, Being a Popular Work on the Reproductive System, Its Debility and Diseases* (Philadelphia: n.p., 1857), 43–73. But also see Alcott, *The Physiology of Marriage*, 26, 68–69; Nicholas Francis Cooke, *Satan in Society* (Cincinnati: C. F. Vent, 1876), 91–116, 173–75; and Joseph W. Howe, *Excessive Venery, Masturbation and Continence: The Etiology, Pathology, and Treatment of the Diseases Resulting from Venereal Excesses, Masturbation and Continence* (New York: E. B. Treat, 1887), 67–68, 72–73. Similar consequences were believed to occur with sexually careless women except that they were less visible, hiding "the ravages of their vice under 'general nervous excitement'" and "hysteria." Howe, *Excessive Venery*, 67. See Carol Smith-Rosenberg, "The Hysterical Woman: Sex Roles and Role Conflict in Nineteenth-Century America," *Social Research* 39 (Dec. 1972): 667–70; and Haller and Haller, *The Physician and Sexuality in Nineteenth-Century America*, 96–137.

30. *Cong. Globe*, 36th Cong., 1st sess., 1860, 1514; "Report of the Utah Commission," *Report of the Secretary of the Interior . . .* , 5 vols. (Washington, D.C.: GPO, 1887), 2:1351.

31. "Polygamy vs. Monogamy," *Mormon* 1 (8 Dec. 1853): n.p.

32. "'Mormonism' Not Sensual," *Mill. Star* 39 (3 Dec. 1877): 790.

33. Remy, *A Journey*, 2:109.

34. *JD* 24:144–45 (George Q. Cannon/1883). Also see Cannon's defense of plurality when he was territorial delegate to Congress, in *Cong. Rec.*, 47th Cong., 1st sess., 19 April 1882, 3068. This was Amasa M. Lyman's meaning, as well, in contending that polygamy permitted "a response to every requirement of nature, without stepping aside from the path of virtue and honor." *JD* 11:206 (1866). Benjamin Ferris said that a major argument he heard while in Utah, as justification for a plurality of wives, was that it reduced male sexual need to such a level that men had "no temptation to wander in forbidden paths." *Utah and the Mormons . . .* (New York: Harper & Brothers, 1854), 251.

35. The most frequently cited example of those saying that prostitution

was necessary for preserving public morals was Edward Hartpole Lecky, *History of European Morals from Augustus to Charlemagne*, 2 vols. (1869; New York: George Braziller, 1955), 2:283.

36. "Baptism and Plurality of Wives," *Mill. Star* 17 (30 Oct. 1855): 645.

37. "Epistle of the First Presidency," 4 April 1885, *Messages* 3:11. Also see earlier comments in "The New York *Sun* on the 'Mormons,'" *Mill. Star* 26 (4 Nov. 1865): 693–96.

38. "An Epistle of the First Presidency . . . ," March 1886, *Messages* 3:68. The charge of hypocrisy is emphatic and recurring in Mormon literature on polygamy. The following is but a sample: "Family Relations," *Mill. Star* 17 (17 Nov. 1855): 724–25; *JD* 5:89–90 (Heber C. Kimball/1857); *JD* 11:261 (Brigham Young/1866); *JD* 11:223, 342, 23:56–57 (John Taylor/1866, 1867, 1883); *JD* 24:58 (George Q. Cannon/1869); "Relics of Barbarism," *DN*, 23 Aug. 1879; "Deceivers and Being Deceived," *DN*, 28 Feb. 1881; "A Mormon Eater's Disgrace," *DN*, 25 Aug. 1881; "New England Bigamy and Utah Polygamy," *DN*, 22 June 1882; "Discourse of Apostle Erastus Snow," *DN*, 15 March 1884.

39. *JD* 14:58, 15:38–39 (George Q. Cannon/1869, 1880). Also see "The Great Sin of the Age," *DN*, 11 Aug. 1883; "Discourse by Apostle F. D. Richards," *DN*, 31 Oct. 1885; and the note penciled by Luke William Gallup on a clipping from the *Deseret News* for 3 Aug. 1870: "Congress had better look at home before they make war on us—the only difference between us and them, is that we practice the Lord's poligamy [*sic*] or Ancient Patriarchal Marriage while members of Congress & others of the same Stripe practice the Devil's Poligamy [*sic*]. Thats the exact difference between them and us." Luke William Gallup Collection, P26–28, fd. 1, RLDS Library & Archives.

40. Editorial, *DN*, 31 July 1867.

41. Lydia Maria Child, *The Mother's Book* (Boston: Carter, Hendee, & Babcock, 1831), 4; John B. Newman, *The Philosophy of Generation: Its Abuses, with their Causes, Prevention, and Cure* (New York: Fowler & Wells, 1853), 32–33, 36–38, 80; Nichols, *Esoteric Anthropology*, 88, 98, 280; and Napheys, *The Transmission*, 174. An extended discussion of this is found in Charles E. Rosenberg, "The Bitter Fruit: Heredity, Disease, and Social Thought in Nineteeth-Century America," in *Perspectives in American History*, ed. Donald Fleming and Bernard Bailyn (Cambridge, Mass.: Charles Warren Center for Studies in American History, 1974), 191–94.

42. Adelia B. Kimball to Dear Cousin Mary [Charlotte Bond], 21 March 1895, P22, fd. 11, RLDS Library and Archives.

43. Musser, "Polygamy," 390. Also see the following as illustrating the importance of avoiding sexual relations during pregnancy and lactation: Remy, *A Journey*, 2:101–2; Kenney, *Wilford Woodruff's Journal*, 3:242, 28 July 1847, 5:7–8, 11 Jan. 1857; "Principles of Physiology," *DN*, 1 Dec. 1853; Benjamin Franklin Johnson, *A Glance at Scripture and Reason, in Answer to an Attack through the Polynesian, upon the Saints for Polygamy* (San Francisco: Excelsior, 1854), 19; "Plurality of Wives—Physiologically and Socially," *Mill. Star*

28 (2 June 1866): 340; Robert Glass Cleland and Juanita Brooks, eds., *A Mormon Chronicle: The Diaries of John D. Lee, 1848–1876*, 2 vols. (San Marino, Calif.: Huntington Library, 1955), 2:115, 30 April 1869; Birch, "Is Polygamy Unnatural?" 50; Blanche Beechwood [Emmeline B. Wells], "A Mormon Woman's View of Marriage," *Woman's Exponent* 6 (1 Sept. 1877): 54; A. Karl Larson and Katherine Miles Larson, eds., *Diary of Charles Lowell Walker*, 2 vols. (Logan: Utah State University Press, 1980), 2:621, 3 Nov. 1883; W. R. Nelson, "Maternal Influence," *Woman's Exponent* 18 (15 July 1889): 29; and remarks by Apostle John W. Taylor, in Juarez Stake Historical Record, 1901–6, 12 March 1904, Church Archives.

44. Jencks, *The Mormon Problem,* 27. Also see "Plurality of Wives—Physiologically and Socially," 340; "Elder Joseph Birch Defends Polygamy," *Mill. Star* 25 (23 Dec. 1873): 804.

45. *JD* 13:207–8 (George Q. Cannon/1869); and Richard Ballantyne, *Dialogue between A. and B. on Polygamy* (Madras, India: Oriental Press, 1854), 5.

46. *JD* 4:278 (Heber C. Kimball/1857). This entire sermon bewailed sexual sin among the Saints.

47. Erastus Snow, as reported in *Diary of Charles Lowell Walker,* ed. Larson and Larson, 2:620, 3 Nov. 1883. The number of remarks in this vein is quite large. See, e.g., the conversation reported in Remy, *A Journey,* 2:101–2; Orson Pratt, "Celestial Marriage," *Seer* 1 (Oct. 1853): 155; *JD* 1:284 (Orson Pratt/1852); *JD* 2:21, 270, 8:61–62, 12:152 (Brigham Young/1854, 1855, 1860, 1867); *JD* 13:207 (George Q. Cannon/1869); *JD* 24:15 (Moses Thatcher/1883); Belinda Marden Pratt, *Defense of Polygamy,* 4; Birch, "Is Polygamy Unnatural?" 50; Nelson, "Maternal Influence," 29; and Moses Thatcher, as quoted in the Abraham Hoagland Cannon Diaries, 1 Oct. 1890, BYU Library.

There was a difficulty, however, and one clear to individuals like Apostle Erastus Snow. If a mother's thoughts and desires were transmitted to and implanted in the foetus, rather than allowing sexual need to grow, wouldn't it be best to indulge and so allay the effect on the unborn child? While Brigham Young told women that such desires were to be met with frequent prayer and strengthened resolve, Snow, on at least one occasion, condoned "the propriety of gratifying women during pregnancy where it was right and consistent that they might not entail on their offspring unholy desires and appetites." Larson and Larson, *Diary of Charles Lowell Walker,* 2:621, 3 Nov. 1883. The oft-cited statement by Brigham Young that, regarding intercourse during pregnancy, men may do "just as they please about that," must, in my view, be seen as an exception or lapse from the more frequently stated position set forth above. Cf. Klaus Hansen, "Mormon Sexuality and American Culture," *Dialogue* 10 (Autumn 1976): 51; and Lester E. Bush, Jr., "Birth Control among the Mormons: Introduction to an Insistent Question," ibid., 10 (Autumn 1976): 18–19.

48. "Relics of Barbarism," *DN,* 23 Aug. 1879. Also see Orson Pratt, "Celestial Marriage," *Seer* 1 (March 1853): 42; *JD* 11:271 (Brigham Young/1866).

49. This is a major theme pursued by Louis J. Kern in his *Ordered Love*, 9, 32–33 passim. Also see Gay, *Education of the Senses*, 48, 253, 310, 422.

50. See the graph displaying a heightened but curvilinear fertility for the Mormon-American, white birth rate in Bush, "Birth Control among the Mormons," 23; and the commentary in Bruce L. Campbell and Eugene E. Campbell, "The Mormon Family," in *Ethnic Families in America: Patterns and Variations,* ed. Charles H. Mindel and Robert W. Habenstein (New York: Elsevier, 1976), 394–96.

51. Oliver Cowdery to Elizabeth Cowdery, 4 May 1834, Oliver Cowdery Letterbook, Huntington Library, San Marino, Calif.

52. Parley Parker Pratt, *The Autobiography of Parley P. Pratt . . . Edited by His Son, Parley P. Pratt* (1874; Salt Lake City: Deseret Book, 1985), 259–60.

53. See the treatment given this as it related to social purity and feminist reformers in Hal D. Sears, "The Sex Radicals in High Victorian America," *Virginia Quarterly Review* 48 (Summer 1972): 379–81; and idem, *The Sex Radicals: Free Love in High Victorian America* (Lawrence: Regents Press of Kansas, 1977), 22–23. Late nineteenth-century efforts to scientifically justify nonreproductive sexual indulgence are discussed by Anita Clair Fellman and Michael Fellman, "The Rule of Moderation in Late Nineteenth-Century American Sexual Ideology," *Journal of Sex Research* 17 (Aug. 1981): 238–55.

54. As but a sample, see *JD* 2:76 (Orson Hyde/1854); *JD* 4:278, 11:210 (Heber C. Kimball/1857, 1866); *JD* 3:266, 8:118, 9:36 (Brigham Young/1856, 1860, 1861); *JD* 20:26 (Joseph F. Smith/1880); *JD* 22:97, 25:227 (Charles W. Penrose/1880, 1884); *JD* 23:228 (Erastus Snow/1883); "The Sin of Adultery," *Mill. Star* 30 (5 Dec. 1868): 776–79; "'Mormonism' Not Sensual," ibid., 39 (3 Dec. 1877): 789–90; Kenney, *Wilford Woodruff's Journal*, 5:563, 7 April 1861; Abraham H. Cannon Diaries, 8 Sept. 1890.

55. *JD* 4:278 (Heber C. Kimball/1857); also see Brigham Young, "A Few Words of Doctrine," 8 Oct. 1861, unpublished discourse, Church Archives.

56. Lieut. John Williams Gunnison, *The Mormons; or, Latter-day Saints, in the Valley of the Great Salt Lake . . .* (Philadelphia: J. P. Lippincott, 1856), 69. And see the comments of Richard F. Burton, *The City of the Saints and across the Rocky Mountains to California,* ed. Fawn Brodie (1861; New York: Alfred A. Knopf, 1963), 479. One is reminded here of Westermarck's observation that the first reason accounting for polygamy has always been that monogamy imposed periodic continence on men. Edward Westermarck, *The History of Human Marriage*, 3 vols; 5th ed. rev. (New York: Allerton, 1922), 3:64.

57. James Dunn, *Janet Dixon, the Plural Wife: A True Story of Mormon Polygamy* (Tooele, Utah: James Dunn, 1896), 57.

58. *JD* 3:360–61 (Brigham Young/1856). Also see "Men and Women," reprinted from the *Pall Mall Gazette*, in *Mill. Star* 35 (11 Feb. 1873): 83–85.

59. *JD* 9:37 (Brigham Young/1861). Also see *JD* 4:56, 6:276 (Brigham Young/1856, 1852); *JD* 22:126 (George Q. Cannon/1880); Kenney, *Wilford Woodruff Journals*, 3:104, 23 Dec. 1846.

60. Remy, *A Journey*, 2:91–92, 138–39, 141–42, 163. Numbers of others,

both at the time and since, made similar observations. See "Celia Logan on Mormon Life—1," [New York] *Daily Graphic*, 28 Nov. 1873; William Chandless, *A Visit to Salt Lake: Being a Journey across the Plains and a Residence in the Mormon Settlements at Utah* (London: Smith, Elder, 1857), 259; Burton, *City of the Saints*, 481; Phil Robinson, *Sinners and Saints: A Tour across the States, and Round Them; with Three Months among the Mormons* (Boston: Roberts Brothers, 1883), 96, 186; Walter M. Gallichan, *Women under Polygamy* (London: Holden & Hardingham, 1914), 304–5; Kimball Young, *Isn't One Wife Enough?* (New York: Henry Holt, 1954), 174; Dean L. May, "Mormons," in *Harvard Encyclopedia of American Ethnic Groups*, ed. Stephan Thernstrom (Cambridge, Mass.: Belknap Press, 1980), 729; Foster, *Religion and Sexuality*, 209–11; Stanley B. Kimball, *Heber C. Kimball: Mormon Patriarch and Pioneer* (Urbana: University of Illinois Press, 1981), 231; Julie Dunfey, "'Living the Principle' of Plural Marriage: Mormon Women, Utopia, and Female Sexuality in the Nineteenth Century," *Feminist Studies* 10 (Fall 1984): 532–33; and Joan Iverson, "Feminist Implications of Mormon Polygamy," ibid. 10 (Fall 1984): 515–16.

61. Blanche Beechwood [Emmeline B. Wells], "Why? Ah! Why?" *Woman's Exponent* 3 (1 Oct. 1874): 67. But, as Carol Cornwall Madsen shows, the authoress privately harbored quite different feelings. "A Mormon Woman in Victorian America" (Ph.D. thesis, University of Utah, 1985), 57–73, 166n.33. Also see Gilbert Clements, "The Relation of Parents and Children: Fragment of a Lecture on the Coming Forth of Elijah the Prophet," *Mill. Star* 15 (15 Oct. 1853): 673.

62. *CHC* 5:299. Ignoring such preachment, some have projected contemporary views back upon the nineteenth century, contending for a consistent Mormon approval of romantic love. See Leonard J. Arrington and Davis Bitton, *The Mormon Experience: A History of the Latter-day Saints* (New York: Alfred A. Knopf, 1979), 187.

63. Eugene E. Campbell and Bruce L. Campbell, "Divorce among Mormon Polygamists: Extent and Explanations," *UHQ* 46 (Winter 1978): 13, 15; and Kern, *An Ordered Love*, 144–45, 153–54, 179–84. Circumstances attending the campaign against polygamy, hardships on the frontier, and the complexities of dealing with multiple wives in the same household undoubtedly also burdened spontaneity in male-female relations. See the entire chapter "Plural Wives" by Stephanie Smith Goodson, in *Mormon Sisters: Women in Early Utah,* ed. Claudia L. Bushman (Cambridge, Mass.: Emmeline Press, 1976), 89–111. As late as 1935 one Mormon authority wrote: "If the light of truth could be turned upon the monogamist families of the world you would be surprised how few of them would find favor in the sight of God. And why would they not find favor? Because they are not the result of holy desires." LeGrand Richards to Mary S. Gilstrap, 22 Nov. 1935, P22, fd. 78, RLDS Library and Archives.

64. Sylvester Graham, for example, claiming "the most careful and thorough investigation," recommended that healthy, robust husbands never exceed twelve indulgences a year and indicated that a perfectly conditioned,

morally upright man could avoid any seminal emission throughout life. *A Lecture to Young Men*, 83–86, 188. Respectable gentlemen should be continent even in their dreams! Cominos, "Late Victorian Sexual Respectability," 32. In what is perhaps the best-known adage of this sort, a European writer was reported to have warned that, past age fifty, every time one spent "la liqueur séminale" it amounted to a shovel of graveyard dirt on the head. See the Abbé Maury as quoted in Mayer, *Des rapports*, 373.

65. The persistence of monogamous feelings was a primary thesis in the studies of James Edward Hulett, Jr. See his "Social Role and Personal Security in Mormon Polygamy," *American Journal of Sociology* 45 (Jan. 1940): 542–53; and "The Social Role of the Mormon Polygamous Male," *American Sociological Review* 8 (June 1943): 279–87. It was acknowledged by Kimball Young, *Isn't One Wife Enough?* 291–93; reaffirmed by Vicky Burgess Olson, "Family Structure and Dynamics in Early Utah Families, 1847–1885" (Ph.D. diss., Northwestern University, 1975), 61–62; and is to be inferred from the general agreement of polygamous and monogamous life-styles described by Embry throughout her *Mormon Polygamous Families*. The decline of affection between marriage partners was a traditional critique made of polygamous arrangements. See, e.g., William Paley, *The Principles of Moral and Political Philosophy*, 2 vols., 9th ed. rev. (London: R. Faulder, 1793), 1:320. It has also been remarked in connection with certain polygamous societies of Africa. Lila Abu-Lughod, "Bedouin Blues," *Natural History* 96 (July 1987): 28–29. It is not clear to what degree Mormons were influenced by the more direct, unceremonious ways of the American West. Diminished romance seems to have afflicted courtship and marriage among many non-Mormons on the nineteenth-century American frontier. John Mack Faragher, *Women and Men on the Overland Trail* (New Haven: Yale University Press, 1979), 146–48, 158, 180.

66. *JD* 19:339, 20:170 (John Taylor/1878, 1880); *JD* 24:226 (George Q. Cannon/1883); and Apostle George Teasdale, as quoted in Pacheco Ward Historical Record, 10 March 1895, Church Archives. For contentions that nineteenth-century Mormons held an essentially approbative view of sex, see Hansen, "Mormon Sexuality and American Culture," 45–56; E. Victoria Grover-Swank, "Sex, Sickness and Statehood: The Influence of Victorian Medical Opinion on Self-Government in Utah" (M.A. thesis, BYU, 1980), 113; and O. Kendall White, "Ideology of the Family in Nineteenth-Century Mormonism," *Sociological Spectrum* 6 (Autumn 1986): 296–302. Regarding equivocal feelings about sexuality in contemporary Mormon society, as an inheritance of its past, see Marybeth Raynes, "Mormon Marriages in an American Context," in *Sisters in Spirit: Mormon Women in Historical and Cultural Perspective*, ed. Maureen Ursenbach Beecher and Lavina Fielding Anderson (Urbana: University of Illinois Press, 1987), 238–42; and Romel W. Mackelprang, "Sexuality and the Mormon Family: Just Procreation or Pro-Fun Too?" (Paper presented before a Sunstone Symposium, Salt Lake City, Utah, 25 Aug. 1990).

67. Charles Smith to Henry Eyring, Feb. 1869, Charles Smith Diaries, copy, BYU Library.

68. *JD* 5:22 (Heber C. Kimball/1857). Additionally, see the comments of Stanley B. Kimball, *Heber C. Kimball: Mormon Patriarch and Pioneer* (Urbana: University of Illinois Press, 1981), 237–38.

69. "A Brief Story of the Life of Joseph Eldridge Robinson," partly handwritten, partly typewritten manuscript, 18, Church Archives.

70. Lorenzo Snow, quoted in Rudger Clawson Diaries, 8 July 1899, Rudger Clawson Collection, University of Utah Library.

71. Orson Hyde, quoted by Luke William Gallup, Reminiscence and Diary, May 1841-March 1891, entry for 11 Feb. 1857, film, Church Archives. Gallup usually copied or summarized the letters he wrote to his non-Mormon family in Connecticut. I am indebted to Professor Lowell "Ben" Bennion of Humboldt State University at Arcata, Calif., for bringing this collection to my attention.

72. Gallup, Reminiscence and Diary, 11 Feb. 1857. The idea that spirits were frustrated when coition did not lead to conception drew on more than the Mormon doctrine of pre-mortal existence. Writing in the same year as Hyde's sermon, Wesley Grindle, urging the dangers of spermatorrhoea, reminded readers of the cost when even the smallest seepage occurred. Every drop that escapes, he said, "is the habitation of living beings." *New Medical Revelations*, 45.

73. Keith Sinclair, ed., *A Soldier's View of Empire: The Reminiscences of James Bodell, 1831–92* (London: The Bodley Head, 1982), 194.

74. Concern with a presumed decline in man's vigor from want of proper health habits and ignorance of the laws governing reproduction was a common theme among antebellum ultraists. Lorenzo Niles Fowler, for example, believed that, before leaving the Garden of Eden, Adam and Eve had sexual relations and had enjoyed exquisite health and happiness. They stood at the head of the human family as a model from which mankind had strayed and toward which they must return. *Marriage: Its History and Ceremonies, with a Phrenological and Physiological Exposition of the Functions and Qualifications for Happy Marriages* (New York: Fowler & Wells, 1847), 10–11, 12. Such concerns continued and in some ways intensified in the years after mid-century. Writers such as the Frenchman Benedict Morel argued that man had steadily degenerated over the centuries. For some account of Morel and the large influence his degeneration thesis had on American reform hereditarianism, see Mark H. Haller, *Eugenics: Hereditarian Attitudes in American Thought* (New Brunswick, N.J.: Rutgers University Press, 1963), 14–17; and Charles Rosenberg's "The Bitter Fruit," 191–94. For an example of contemporary debate on the question, see "Have Americans Degenerated?" [New York] *Daily Graphic*, 21 Nov. 1873.

75. Oliver Cowdery, "Letter IV. to W. W. Phelps, Esq.," *Latter Day Saints' Messenger and Advocate* 1 (Feb. 1835): 79.

76. Andrew F. Ehat, "Joseph Smith's Introduction of Temple Ordinances

and the 1844 Mormon Succession Question" (M.A. thesis, BYU, 1981), 17–19; and Heber C. Kimball's statement in 1846 that he intended to live to be 150 years of age. Journal of Heber C. Kimball, 17 July 1846, Church Archives.

77. Luke William Gallup to his father, Dec. 1861, Luke William Gallup Reminiscence and Diary. Also see Gallup's summary of a recent letter to his family in the East, Dec. 1866, in his Reminiscence and Diary; and Luke William Gallup to Warren S. Wheeler, 16 Oct. 1871, Luke William Gallup Collection, P26–28, fd. 1, RLDS Library and Archives.

78. "Plurality of Wives—Physiologically and Socially," 340–43.

79. Charles W. Penrose, "Physical Regeneration," *Mill. Star* 29 (10 Aug. 1867): 497. Also see "A Chapter on Restitution," *DN*, 12 Jan. 1854.

80. Augustus K. Gardner, in the introduction to his 1870 book on sexual relations, said that he had written the work as a warning "that the American race is fast dying out, and that its place is being filled by emigrants." *Conjugal Sins against the Laws of Life and Health and Their Effects upon the Father, Mother and Child* (New York: J. S. Redfield, 1870), 8. Much the same was expressed by Orson S. Fowler in his *Sexual Science; Including Manhood, Womanhood, and their Mutual Interrelations;* . . . (Cincinnati: National, 1870), 274–75. Many agreed with Theodore Roosevelt that "old-stock Americans" and their Western European counterparts were confronted with decline and possible extinction if they did not win the "war of the cradle." See the chapter "Race Suicide" in Thomas G. Dyer, *Theodore Roosevelt and the Idea of Race* (Baton Rouge: Louisiana State University Press, 1980), 143–67.

81. David J. Pivar, *Purity Crusade: Sexual Morality and Social Control, 1868–1900* (Westport, Conn.: Greenwood Press, 1973).

82. Helen Mar Whitney, *Why We Practice Plural Marriage* . . . (Salt Lake City: Juvenile Instructor Office, 1884), 7.

83. Merle H. Graffam, ed., *Salt Lake School of the Prophets Minute Book 1883* (Palm Desert, Calif.: ULC Press, 1981), 54–55.

84. The Grahams, the Alcotts, the Kelloggs, and an army of others not only urged the importance of nutritive knowledge but argued as well that sexual relations must be better understood if the race were to be preserved. Sexuality, no less than digestion, was said to be subject to natural laws. The physiology of sex, in fact, had with most of these reformers a special priority. According to one writer, sexuality was "the master problem" confronting mankind. Orson Squire Fowler, *Sexual Science*, v. Although I have found James C. Whorton's book *Crusaders for Fitness: The History of American Health Reformers* (Princeton, N.J.: Princeton University Press, 1982) particularly helpful, the number of studies dealing with various aspects of the subject or with individual reformers—all tending to reveal the surprisingly large interest of Victorian society in bodily health and functions—is considerable. Among them are William Walker, "The Health Reform Movement in the United States, 1830–1870" (Ph.D. diss., Johns Hopkins University, 1955); John D. Davies, *Phrenology, Fad and Science: A Nineteenth-Century Crusade* (New Haven,

Conn.: Yale University Press, 1955); Numbers, *Prophetess of Health;* and Stephen Nissenbaum, *Sex, Diet, and Debility in Jacksonian America: Sylvester Graham and Health Reform* (Westport, Conn.: Greenwood Press, 1980). For explorations of the concern with birth control, see Carroll Smith-Rosenberg and Charles Rosenberg, "The Female Animal: Medical and Biological Views of Woman and Her Role in Nineteenth-Century America," *Journal of American History* 40 (Sept. 1973): 343–53; Daniel Scott Smith, "Family Limitation, Sexual Control, and Domestic Feminism in Victorian America," *Clio's Consciousness Raised: New Perspectives in the History of Women,* ed. Mary S. Hartman and Lois Banner (New York: Harper Torchbooks, 1974), 119–36; and Carl N. Degler, *At Odds: Women and the Family in America from the Revolution to the Present* (New York: Oxford University Press, 1980), 195–248. For a discussion of the relationship of the question to demographic and immigration patterns, see the chapter "Revolutions in Childbearing in Nineteenth-Century America" in Robert V. Wells, *Uncle Sam's Family Issues in and Perspectives on American Demographic History* (Albany: State University of New York Press, 1985), 28–56. Concerning eugenic interests of the time, see Richard Harrison Shyrock, *The Development of Modern Medicine: An Interpretation of the Social and Scientific Factors Involved* (Philadelphia: University of Pennsylvania Press, 1936), 297–98; Haller, *Eugenics;* Daniel J. Kevles, *In the Name of Eugenics: Genetics and the Uses of Human Heredity* (New York: Alfred A. Knopf, 1985).

85. "Epistle of the First Presidency," 4 April 1885, *Messages* 3:11; *JD* 11:200–208 (Amasa M. Lyman/1866); "Decimation of Americans," *Mill. Star* 35 (7 Jan. 1873): 11–12; and Luke William Gallup to his father and family, 8 July 1860, and Luke William Gallup to Aunt Nancy Williams, 2 and 4 July 1862, Luke William Gallup, Reminiscence and Diary. For a mirror image of these views, in a non-Mormon organ of the early twentieth century, see "American Destiny Menaced by Race Suicide," *Washington [D.C.] Times,* 11 Dec. 1904.

86. Paulos, "A Chapter on Restitution," *DN,* 12 Jan. 1854. Also see E. L. T. Harrison, "Tokens of Divinity in Mormonism," *Mill. Star* 23 (9 Feb. 1861): 83; *JD* 8:61, 63–64, 12:118–19 (Brigham Young/1860, 1867); *JD* 11:207 (Amasa M. Lyman/1866).

87. "Mormon Polygamy from a Philosophical Standpoint," *DN,* 15 Feb. 1881. Also see remarks by George Q. Cannon in JH, 20 March 1882.

88. "Discourse by Elder Moses Thatcher," *DN,* 26 May 1883. Also see the same author's *La poligamia mormona y la monogamia Cristiana comparadas . . . por el Elder Moisés Thatcher* (Mexico, D. F.: E. D. Orozco, 1881), 28, 33, 40; and *JD* 24:46, 58–59 (George Q. Cannon/1882, 1883). Some years later, the American Consul in Ciudad Juarez, Mexico, describing conversations with Mormon polygamists who had colonized in the area, was astonished at Mormon confidence in their eventual triumph throughout North America. This was to come about, they told him, because of the principle of "survival of the fittest." Charles W. Kindrick, "The Mormons in Mexico," *American Monthly Review of Reviews* 19 (June 1899): 705. Also see *JD* 14:43 (Brigham Young/1870); John

Druce to Brigham Young, 3 Feb. 1877, Incoming Correspondence, Brigham Young Papers, Church Archives; "Discourse by President Joseph F. Smith," *DN,* 24 Feb. 1883.

89. *JD* 12:144 (George A. Smith/1867).

90. [Dyer Daniel Lum], *Utah and Its People: Facts and Statistics Bearing on the "Mormon Problem" . . . by a Gentile* (New York: R. O. Ferrier, 1882), 41.

91. Ellen E. Dickinson, *New Light on Mormonism* (New York: Funk & Wagnalls, 1885), 148.

92. Tanner, *A Fragment,* 189. Attempts to restore strength through exercise would not do, the Mormons said, because it failed to reach the root of the problem: an absence of correct understanding concerning the reproductive function. Charles W. Penrose, "Polygamy and the Visit of the Sultan," *Mill. Star* 29 (3 Aug. 1867): 492–93; *JD* 1:348 (Jedediah Grant/1853); *JD* 12:144 (George A. Smith/1867).

93. From "The Women of the Everlasting Covenant," in Whitney, *Why We Practice Plural Marriage,* 68.

94. The statements made, in the order of their appearance, are found in Charles W. Penrose, "Physical Regeneration," 497–99; L[ouis] A[lphonse] Bertrand, *Mémoires d'un Mormon* (Paris: E. Jung-Treuttel, [1862]), 208; and Whitney, *Why We Practice Plural Marriage,* 54.

95. *JD* 5:210, 8:62 (Brigham Young/1857, 1860). Additionally, see Young's remarks at *JD* 12:119, 14:43 (1867, 1873); and Kenney, *Wilford Woodruff's Journal,* 6:250, 26 Sept. 1865.

96. *JD* 8:198 (Brigham Young/1860). Young did impress others with his youthful appearance. See Burton, *The City of the Saints,* 264; and *Wilford Woodruff's Journal,* 6:247, 17 Sept. 1865. For an account of the Thomas Marsh episode, see Richard Van Wagoner and Steven C. Walter, "The Return of Thomas B. Marsh," *Sunstone* 6 (July-Aug. 1981): 28–30. Statements of the sort made by Young, as quoted in the text, perhaps accounted for remarks like that attributed to some punster, that pretty girls in Utah almost always married Young. Frank L. Klement, "Mormons in the Trans-Mississippi West, 1837–1860," *Westerners Brand Book* 25 (Feb. 1969): 96. Ann Eliza Young, who left the Mormon leader and made a career lecturing about it, stated that Brigham Young's greatest weakness was the vanity he felt in connection with his attractiveness to women. *Wife No. 19; or, The Story of a Life in Bondage, Being a Complete Exposé of Mormonism . . .* (Hartford, Conn.: Dustin, Gilman, 1876), 375–76.

97. F. B. Crouch, *The Mormon Elders Damiana Wafers* (New York, n.d.). Also see the comments of Joseph L. Lyon and Steven Nelson, "Mormon Health," *Dialogue* 12 (Fall 1979): 85.

98. Lady Duffus Hardy, *Through Cities and Prairie Lands: Sketches of an American Tour* (New York: R. Worthington, 1881), 105–6, 115.

99. Phil Robinson, *Sinners and Saints: A Tour across the States, and Round them; with Three Months among the Mormons* (Boston: Roberts Brothers, 1883), 97, 103, 170, 232–33. Richard Burton, in addition to observing that Mormon

sexual behavior was enjoined more for hygienic than religious purposes, was reminded of "the splendid physical development of the Kaffir race in South Africa," which some had attributed "to a rule of continence like that of the Mormons, and to a lactation prolonged for two years." *City of the Saints,* 479.

100. James L. Hughes, "My Misconceptions Regarding the Mormons," *Canadian Magazine* 23 (1904): 9–16.

101. Orson Spencer, *Patriarchal Order; or, Plurality of Wives!* (Liverpool: S. W. Richards, 1853). David Whittaker provides a biographical sketch of Spencer, along with a summary of his defense of polygamy, in "Early Mormon Pamphleteering" (Ph.D. diss., BYU, 1982), 359–63.

102. Genesis 17:2.

103. Spencer, *Patriarchal Order,* 3–7 passim. The need to obey the law of Abraham was mentioned by Orson Pratt in the opening salvo of 1852. *JD* 1:59–63 (1852). Yet another Mormon, calling himself Living Stream, referred to the principle as the "Procreative Law." See "A Bird's-eye Glance; or, Preface to the Law of Progression or Procreation," *DN,* 25 Dec. 1852. Also see "Tabernacle . . . Sermon by Parley P. Pratt," *DN,* 19 Jan. 1854. And, of course, the importance of men following the example of Abraham and women becoming the "daughters of Sarah" was a major theme in Jacob's *"The Peace Maker,"* 11 passim; and *D&C* 132:32, 34, 65 (1843).

104. Spencer, *Patriarchal Order,* 1–2 passim. Also see *JD* 11:269, 271, 16:166 (Brigham Young/1866, 1873); *JD* 20:28 (Joseph F. Smith/1878).

105. Orson Pratt, "Celestial Marriage," *Seer* 1 (10 Oct. 1853): 159–60; Spencer, *Patriarchal Order,* 15; Johnson, *A Glance at Scripture and Reason,* 11–14; *JD* 1:345–46 (Jedediah Grant/1853); *JD* 2:82–83, 4:259–60 (Orson Hyde/1854, n.d.); and Gunnison's comment in *The Mormons,* 68. David Whittaker, in his dissertation, has conveniently organized Mormon arguments for Jesus' marriage, along with the sources where they appear. "Early Mormon Pamphleteering," 378–79n.62.

106. Taylder, *The Mormon's Own Book,* 179; and Chandless, *A Visit to Salt Lake,* 159.

107. Spencer, *Patriarchal Order,* 14.

108. "The New Year," *Mill. Star* 16 (7 Jan. 1854): 1.

109. Udney Hay Jacob's 1842 pamphlet title is relevant here: *An Extract from a Manuscript Entitled "The Peace Maker"; or, The Doctrines of the Millennium: Being a treatise on Religion and Jurisprudence or a New System of Religion and Politics.* For other statements indicating that family organization and priesthood authority constituted the government of heaven, see Spencer, *Patriarchal Order,* 1, 8; Orson Pratt, "Celestial Marriage," *Seer* 1 (June 1853): 91; Brigham Young, "Remarks," *DN,* 26 Oct. 1854; "The Priesthood," *Mill. Star* 18 (8 March 1856): 129–48; "True Policy or Legitimate Government," ibid., 22 (27 Oct. 1860): 673; *JD* 11:338, 13:208 (George Q. Cannon/1867, 1869); *JD* 12:153 (Brigham Young/1868); and the comments of Whittaker, "The Bone in the Throat," 299–301.

110. Charles W. Penrose, "Woman's Mission," *Mill. Star* 30 (1 Aug. 1868):

482; and idem, "Physical Regeneration," ibid. 29 (10 Aug. 1867): 497–98. Also see "Family Relations," ibid. 17 (17 Nov. 1855): 721; Spencer, *Patriarchal Order,* 8; *JD* 11:335–36 (George Q. Cannon/1867).

111. "Dialogue between Elder Freeman and a Visitor from Abroad," *DN,* 12 Jan. 1854.

112. Luke William Gallup to his father, 25 Dec. 1867. Also see his "Thoughts," Dec. 1866, both in Luke William Gallup, Reminiscence and Diary. Mormon comment on this question was extensive: *JD* 1:361 (Brigham Young/1852); *JD* 13:206 (George Q. Cannon/1869); *JD* 18:55–56 (Orson Pratt/1877); *JD* 19:270 (Erastus Snow/1878); "Discourse by Elder Naisbitt," *DN,* 28 March 1885; Orson Pratt, "Celestial Marriage," *Seer* 1 (Oct. 1853): 154; Belinda Marden Pratt, *Defense of Polygamy,* 5; Orson Pratt, in *The Bible and Polygamy: Does the Bible Sanction Polygamy? A Discussion between Professor Orson Pratt . . . and Rev. Doctor J. P. Newman . . .* (Salt Lake City: Deseret News, 1877), 32–33; "Polygamy and Polyandry," *Mill. Star* 37 (31 May 1875): 340–41; Musser, "Polygamy," 374–75. Mary Bennion Powell later recalled that her polygamous father, Heber Bennion, told her that Joseph Smith taught that if women were permitted to have a plurality of spouses all would die of syphilis. Mary Bennion Powell to Dr. George Stewart, 228-page transcript, composed between 26 Jan. and 25 Feb. 1952, 129, Huntington Library.

113. John T. Caine, quoted in *Hearings before the Committee on Territories in Regard to the Admission of Utah as a State* (Washington, D.C.: GPO, 1889), 70.

114. *JD* 4:57 (Brigham Young/1856). On this subject, see the essay of Jolene Edmunds Rockwood, "The Redemption of Eve," in Beecher and Anderson, *Sisters in Spirit,* 10–13; and Madsen, "A Mormon Woman in Victorian America," 177–83.

115. Penrose, "Woman's Mission," 481.

116. Stanley B. Kimball, *Heber C. Kimball,* 231, 236.

117. *JD* 4:50, 9:248–49, 11:271 (Brigham Young/1856, 1862, 1866); *JD* 4:83, 6:127 (Heber C. Kimball/1856, 1857); *JD* 4:128 (Jedediah M. Grant/1856).

118. *JD* 9:38 (Brigham Young/1861); and Heber C. Kimball, in *JD* 6:67 (1857).

119. Penrose, "Woman's Mission," 481; Spencer, *Patriarchal Order,* 12; *JD* 12:97–98, 312, 15:132–33, 17:159 (Brigham Young/1867, 1868, 1873, 1875); *JD* 13:189, 17:225 (Orson Pratt/1869, 1875); *Bible and Polygamy,* 77; Larson and Larson, *Diary of Charles Lowell Walker,* 1:254, 18 March 1866.

120. Charles W. Penrose, in "Family Government," *Mill. Star* 30 (16 May 1868): 307.

121. Johnson, *A Glance at Scripture and Reason,* 18. The number of instances displaying such attitudes is quite overwhelming. See, as only exemplary, Cleland and Brooks, *A Mormon Chronicle,* 1:10, 19 March 1848, 2:26, 12 Aug. 1866; Brigham Young, "A Few Words on Doctrine," 8 Oct. 1861, unpublished discourse, Church Archives; *JD* 5:17 (remark of Heber C. Kimball during sermon by Orson Hyde/1857); *JD* 3:52, 7:280, 9:308, 14:106 (Brig-

ham Young/1855, 1859, 1862, 1869); Juanita Brooks, *Not by Bread Alone: The Journal of Martha Spence Heywood, 1850–1856* (Salt Lake City: Utah State Historical Society, 1978), 122, 27 April 1856; S. George Ellsworth, *Dear Ellen: Two Mormon Women and Their Letters* (Salt Lake City: University of Utah Tanner Trust Fund, 1974), 38; Annie Clark Tanner, *A Mormon Mother: An Autobiography*, rev. ed. (Salt Lake City: University of Utah Tanner Trust Fund, 1973), 29, 62, 116–17, 169; "Excerpts from a Journal or Sketch of the Life of Joel Hills Johnson (Brother to Benjamin F. Johnson)," bound, printed copy, 33, 14 Feb. 1882, UHi; Larson and Larson, *Charles Walker Diary*, 2:619, 1 Nov. 1883; Burton, *City of the Saints*, 443; Chandless, *Visit to Salt Lake*, 191.

122. "When the servants of God in any age have consented to follow a woman for a leader, either in a public or a family capacity, they have sunk beneath the standard their organization has fitted them for; when a people of God submit to that, their priesthood is taken from them, and they become as any other people." *JD* 9:308 (Brigham Young/1862). For additional urging in behalf of patriarchal family government, see Spencer, *Patriarchal Order*, 13–14; Pratt, "Celestial Marriage," *Seer* 1 (Oct. 1853): 157; *JD* 1:68, 77, 4:55, 56, 6:45, 11:136, 14:106 (Brigham Young/1852, 1853, 1856, 1857, 1865, 1872); *JD* 4:81, 82, 10:104, 11:211, 12:190 (Heber C. Kimball/1856, 1862, 1866, 1868); *JD* 4:155 (Lorenzo Snow/1857); *JD* 16:247 (Joseph F. Smith/1873); *JD* 25:368–69 (George Q. Cannon/1884); "Discourse by Elder Henry W. Naisbitt," *DN*, 28 March 1885; "President Woodruff's Communication," *DN*, 20 Aug. 1887; Martha Spence Heywood's reference to her husband as "my Lord" in Brooks, *Not by Bread Alone*, 120, 13 April 1856; and the same usage by one of the wives of Heber C. Kimball as reported in Stanley B. Kimball, *Heber C. Kimball*, 239. The psychological basis for female subjection is a major theme of Louis Kern's study, *An Ordered Love*, 144–57.

Memories of polygamous home life, as told to oral historians and others, attest to the extent to which male authority (that of both fathers and sons) was often carried: Seth Budge, interviewed by Jessie L. Embry, 4 May 1976, p. 5, POHP; Celia R. Geertsen, interviewed by Jessie L. Embry, 5 May 1976, p. 13, POHP; Winnie Haynie Mortensen, interviewed by Leonard R. Grover, 26 Jan. 1980, p. 4, POHP; Lorin "Dutch" Leavitt, interviewed by Leonard R. Grover, 3 Jan. 1980, p. 15, POHP; Richard Ivins Bentley, interviewed by Leonard R. Grover, 5 Jan. 1980, p. 4, POHP; Elizabeth H. Packer, interviewed by Jessie L. Embry, 1 Sept. 1976, p. 4, POHP. Also see Michael E. Christensen, "Charles W. Nibley: A Case Study of Polygamy," *JMH* 7 (1980): 110; Juanita Brooks, "A Close-Up of Polygamy," *Harpers* 168 (Feb. 1934): 303; James Edward Hulett, Jr., "The Sociological and Social Psychological Aspects of the Mormon Polygamous Family" (Ph.D. diss., University of Wisconsin, 1939), 73–74, 83–84.

Responding to the heightened interest in women's history, numbers of scholars have found the status of women to have oscillated in the Mormon past. See, e.g., Maureen Ursenbach Beecher, "Women in Winter Quarters," *Sunstone* 8 (July-Aug. 1983): 11–19; Carol Cornwall Madsen, "Mormon

Women and the Temple: Toward a New Understanding," in *Sisters in Spirit,* ed. Beecher and Anderson, 80–110; and Nola W. Wallace, "The Contingency of Woman," *Sunstone* 13 (April 1989): 7–10. In pioneer Utah, despite Mormonism's patriarchal penchant, women seemed to play a greater role in many aspects of Mormon life than did their counterparts after the turn of the century. See the essays by Heather Symmes Cannon, "Practical Politicians," and Judith Rasmussen Dushku, "Feminists," both in *Mormon Sisters,* ed. Bushman, 157–75, 177–97; and that of Linda King Newell, "Gifts of the Spirit: Women's Share," in *Sisters in Spirit,* ed. Beecher and Anderson, 111–50. This agrees with Sandra L. Myres, who said that women in the west were generally more active in community affairs, more entrepreneurial and involved outside the home, than women in the east. See all of her *Westering Women and the Frontier Experience, 1800–1915* (Albuquerque: University of New Mexico Press, 1982). Some view contemporary Mormon attitudes toward women as still needing improvement. One woman writer said she yet feels "the church's devaluation of women and things female must result from the inherent lesser worth of femaleness compared with maleness." Alison Walker, "Theological Foundations of Patriarchy," *Dialogue* 23 (Fall 1990): 81.

123. *JD* 13:202–3 (George Q. Cannon/1869).

124. "Plurality of Wives—Physiologically and Socially," 342. Also see *JD* 13:202 (George Q. Cannon/1869); *Bible and Polygamy,* 100; Spencer, *Patriarchal Order,* 7; and Orson Pratt, "Celestial Marriage," *Seer* 1 (Aug. 1853): 124.

125. Parley P. Pratt, "Marriage and Morals in Utah," 356–57; *JD* 1:346 (Jedediah M. Grant/1853).

126. *JD* 9:322, 11:127–28, 12:262 (Brigham Young/1862, 1865, 1868). This view of history was shared by others, including Parley P. Pratt, "Marriage and Morals in Utah," 357, and George Q. Cannon, who enlarged the indictment to cover Greece, in *JD* 20:200–201 (1880). Also see "Monogamy, Polygamy, and Christianity," *DN,* 24 Nov. 1853; *JD* 23:298 (Erastus Snow/1883); the contentions of both George Q. Cannon and Orson Pratt, with the comments of the Reverend John P. Newman, in *Bible and Polygamy,* 63, 83, 98; Larson and Larson, *Diary of Charles Walker,* 2:581, 21 May 1882; "Elder Joseph Birch Defends Polygamy," 802; William Budge, *The Marriage Institution* (Liverpool: Latter-day Saints' Printing, Publishing, and Emigration Office, 1879), 14; and Franklin D. Richards and James A. Little, comps., *A Compendium of the Doctrines of the Gospel* (Salt Lake City: George Q. Cannon and Sons, 1898), 124.

127. Kenney, *Wilford Woodruff's Journal,* 4:152–53, 21 Nov. 1852; "A Reply to the 'Christian Herald' on the Plurality of Wives," *Zion's Watchman* 1 (4 March 1854): 79; "The Opinion of the Reformers on the Law of Marriage," ibid. 1 (15 Jan. 1855): 208–9; Robbins, "Baptism and Plurality of Wives," 644–45; Luke William Gallup to Melinda and family, 10 Nov. 1861, Luke William Gallup Reminiscence and Diary; Belinda Marden Pratt, *Defense of Polygamy,* 5; John Nicholson, *The Preceptor . . .* (Salt Lake City: Deseret News,

1883), 50; Benjamin Franklin Johnson, "Mormonism as an Issue," *Arizona Republican*, 25 June 1890; and *Ready References . . . for the Use of Missionaries and Scripture Students* (Salt Lake City: Deseret News, 1887), 136–37.

128. George Q. Cannon, in *Bible and Polygamy*, 99. Also see Jencks, *The History and Philosophy of Marriage*, 59–60, 241.

129. Rev. 17:1–2. See Spencer, *Patriarchal Order*, 7, 9 passim; Orson Pratt, "Celestial Marriage," *Seer* 1 (May 1853): 80; Belinda Marden Pratt, *Defense of Polygamy*, 5; "Chastity in Roman Catholic Countries," *DN*, 20 Feb. 1856; *JD* 13:194 (Orson Pratt/1869); *JD* 26:315 (Moses Thatcher/1885). But cf. Jacob, *"The Peace Maker,"* 17, 25–26.

130. Orson Pratt, "Christian Polygamy in the Sixteenth Century," *Seer* 1 (Dec. 1853): 182; *JD* 1:308 (Parley P. Pratt/1853); *JD* 1:231–32 (John Taylor/1853); *JD* 1:309 (Brigham Young/1853); *JD* 7:81, 220–21 (Orson Pratt/1859, 1875); *JD* 24:164–65 (Erastus Snow/1883); "Remarks by Elder Charles W. Penrose," *DN*, 20 Sept. 1879; L. John Nuttall Diary, typewritten copy, 13 Aug. 1881, BYU Library.

131. Alexander F. Macdonald, "A Marriage Law and Practice," *Mill. Star* 41 (28 April 1879): 258; Orson Pratt, "Celestial Marriage," *Seer* 1 (May 1853): 80; Musser, "Polygamy," 390; Whitney, *Why We Practice Plural Marriage*, 7–8.

132. "Plural Marriage, Treated Chiefly from an Historical Standpoint," reprinted from the *Utah Journal*, in *DN*, 19 May 1886.

133. "Monogamy, Polygamy, and Christianity," *Mill. Star* 15 (6 Aug. 1853): 515.

134. Alain Gillette, *Les Mormons: théocrates du désert* (Paris: Brouwer, 1985), 87.

135. *JD* 3:291 (George A. Smith/1856); and Charles Smith to Henry Eyring, Feb. 1869, Charles Smith Diaries, typewritten copy, BYU Library.

136. John Jaques, "A Mormonite's Plea for Polygamy," *Mill. Star* 16 (25 Nov. 1854): 747.

137. *D&C* 29:34–35 (1830), 131:7–8 (1843). For an exploration of Mormon metaphysics, especially in relation to the unity of spirit and matter, see Sterling M. McMurrin, *The Philosophical Foundations of Mormon Theology* (Salt Lake City: University of Utah Press, 1959), 17–20.

138. "Practical Nature of the Gospel Contrasted with That of Human Systems," *Mill. Star* 27 (20 May 1865): 316; *JD* 9:289 (Brigham Young/1867).

139. "The Mahomet of the West," *Overland Monthly* 7 (Sept. 1871): 237.

140. *JD* 9:362 (Daniel H. Wells/1862).

141. Young was not saying that death would disappear but that palpable degrees of perfection were possible before, as well as after, the grave. See his remarks in *JD* 10:30 (1862). Also see *JD* 4:53 (Charles C. Rich/1857); and Larson and Larson, *Diary of Charles Lowell Walker*, 1:168, 3 March 1861. More than forty years later, it was still being said that Mormonism would "evolve harmoniously into the Millennium." Nels L. Nelson, "Why This Magazine Is Needed," *Mormon Point of View* 1 (1 Jan. 1904): 12.

142. *JD* 12:224 (George Q. Cannon/1868). Also see "A Chapter on Restitution," *DN,* 12 Jan. 1854; and "Discourse by President George Q. Cannon," *DN,* 19 May 1883.

143. Although I am convinced the postmillennialist interpretation expressed here was dominant, especially in late nineteenth-century Mormon thought, it is necessary to acknowledge the presence in Mormon utterances of much that was clearly premillennial—particularly in the early years of the church's history. Like most religious traditions, Mormonism is rich with contradictory strains. For discussion of this issue, see Klaus J. Hansen, "The Kingdom of God and the Millennial Tradition," in his *Quest for Empire: The Political Kingdom of God and the Council of Fifty in Mormon History* (East Lansing: Michigan State University Press, 1967), 3–23; idem, *Mormonism and the American Experience* (Chicago: University of Chicago Press, 1981), 113–22; Louis G. Reinwand, "An Interpretive Study of Mormon Millennialism during the Nineteenth Century with Emphasis on Millennial Developments in Utah" (M.A. thesis, BYU, 1971); Ronald W. Walker, "Sheaves, Bucklers and the State: Mormon Leaders Respond to the Dilemmas of War," *Sunstone* 7 (July-Aug. 1982): 43–56; Thomas G. Alexander, "Between Revivalism and the Social Gospel: The Latter-day Saint Social Advisory Committee," *BYU Studies* 23 (Winter 1983): 20–23; and Grant Underwood's studies: "Millennarianism and the Early Mormon Mind," *JMH* 9 (1982): 41–51; "Early Mormon Millennarianism: Another Look," *Church History* 54 (June 1985): 215–29; "Early Mormon Perceptions of Contemporary America, 1830–1846," *BYU Studies* 26 (Summer 1986): 53–55.

144. "Discourse by Elder Orson Hyde," *DN,* 5 Oct. 1854.

145. "Dialogue between Father and Son, on Physiology," *DN,* 1 Dec. 1853.

146. *D&C* 89 (1833). Scholarly commentary on Mormon health practices is extensive and growing. For accounts dealing with the historical experience of the code, see Leonard J. Arrington, "An Economic Interpretation of the Word of Wisdom," *BYU Studies* 1 (Winter 1959): 37–49; Paul H. Peterson, "An Historical Analysis of the Word of Wisdom" (M.A. thesis, BYU, 1972); Robert T. Divett, "Medicine and the Mormons: A Historical Perspective," *Dialogue* 12 (Autumn 1979): 16–25; Thomas G. Alexander, "The Word of Wisdom: From Principle to Requirement," ibid. 14 (Autumn 1981): 78–88; and Lester E. Bush, Jr., "The Word of Wisdom in Early Nineteenth-Century Perspective," ibid. 14 (Autumn 1981): 46–65.

147. For a brief account of the origin of the council, which had been founded "by and with the advice of the authorities of the church," see untitled, *DN,* 15 June 1850. References to what was discussed are made in "Extracts from J. W. Cummings' Address before the 'Council of Health' and Their Friends, on Ensign Hill, June 16," *DN,* 10 July 1852; "Council of Health," ibid., 24 July 1852; "Council of Health," ibid., 4 Sept. 1852. It was the 24 July 1852 meeting involving an address by William W. Phelps that Benjamin Ferris criticized as devoted to enlightening "the mothers and daughters in Israel as to the proper time and manner in which the work of

generation should be carried on, with a minuteness of detail and vulgarity of language which could scarcely have been more broad had he denuded himself by way of illustration. . . . [Since that time] when any thing a little richer than common has been elicited, it is said to be almost equal to 'Phelps' sermon on the Mount.'" *Utah and the Mormons,* 303.

148. Kevles, *In the Name of Eugenics;* Haller, *Eugenics,* 14–16 passim.

149. *JD* 11:208 (Amasa M. Lyman/1866).

150. Julian Ralph, "A Week with the Mormons," *Harper's* 37 (8 April 1893): 330. Brigham H. Roberts, writing in the twentieth century of his Church's polygamous passage, argued that the practice was justified as preferable to monogamy only if it resulted in a superior physical product. *CHC* 5:297–99.

151. The *Philadelphia Press* article was reprinted as "The Men and Women of Utah," *Mill. Star* 35 (21 Oct. 1873): 657–58. The second quotation is from "Celia Logan on Mormon Life—1."

152. Joseph F. Smith, as quoted at a Church meeting in Woodruff, Ariz., in *Journal of Jesse Nathaniel Smith: The Life Story of a Mormon Pioneer, 1834–1906* (Salt Lake City: Jesse N. Smith Family Association, 1953), 295. The Saints thought of themselves as bold innovators, as pioneering scientists who found it necessary to fight prejudice in their efforts to bring truth to mankind. "The Only Remedy," *Mill. Star* 29 (21 Sept. 1867): 594; *JD* 15:206–7 (George Q. Cannon/1873); Whitney, *Why We Practice Polygamy,* 53. They were certain they had loosed the complicated knot of gender relations, family life, and racial decline. Polygamy was, affirmed Orson Hyde, an idea that could "revolutionize the whole world." "Lecture," *DN,* 19 Oct. 1854, reprinted as "The Marriage Relations," in *JD* 2:75–87 (1854). Also see Moses Thatcher, in *JD* 24:116 (1883); and Erastus Snow, in *JD* 23:232–33 (1883). The Mormons, said a daughter of Brigham Young, had worked hard at the problem of human sexuality. Plural marriage, she urged, would be "a grand factor" in bringing about a useful and happy millennium. Susa Young Gates, "Family Life among the Mormons," *North American Review* 150 (March 1890): 349. A brief discussion of plurality's role in Mormonism's restorationist agenda is found in David J. Whittaker, "Early Mormon Pamphleteering," 328–29.

153. Eliza R. Snow, as quoted by Joseph F. Smith, in "Joseph the Seer's Plural Marriages," *DN,* 18 Oct. 1879; and Spencer J. Palmer, "Eliza R. Snow's 'Sketch of My Life': Reminiscences of One of Joseph Smith's Plural Wives," *BYU Studies* 12 (Autumn 1971): 129–30.

154. Zina D. H. Young to Mary Elizabeth (Rollins) Lightner, 22 June 1887, copy included with Biographical Sketch of Mary Elizabeth (Rollins) Lightner, typewritten copy, Huntington Library.

155. Lucy W. Kimball, quoted in *Reorganized Church of Jesus Christ of Latter Day Saints, Complainant. vs. Church of Christ at Independence, Missouri; . . . Complainant's Abstract . . .* (Lamoni, Iowa: Herald Publishing House, 1893), 375.

156. George Q. Cannon, in "The Improvement of Our Species," *Western Standard* 2 (7 Aug. 1857): n.p.

157. "In and Out of Time," Jan [JoAnn Barnett] Shipps, *Mormonism: The Story of a New Religious Tradition* (Urbana: University of Illinois Press, 1985), 109–29. Also see O. Kendall White, Jr., "Ideology of the Family in Nineteenth-Century Mormonism," 290–92.

158. Joseph F. Smith to Joseph Smith III, 3 May 1889, P22, fd. 47, RLDS Library and Archives.

4

Tactical Retreat: The Manifesto of 1890

During the year and a half before President Woodruff's 1890 Manifesto, Mormons endured blow after blow from anti-polygamy forces. Attempts to thwart escheat of its properties failed and the church soon faced a near-empty treasury.[1] A changing Mormon/Gentile population ratio in Utah, reflected in victories by the non-Mormon Liberal party in local elections, was also threatening. Idaho's first state constitution, adopted in 1889, denied voting rights to immigrant Chinese and Mongolians, American Indians who had not "adopted the habits of civilization"—and Mormons.[2] When an older Idaho law designed to exclude the Saints from the polls was upheld by the United States Supreme Court, and a bill extending the same screen to Utah introduced in Congress, Mormon attitudes sobered even more. Emissaries and lobbyists working for the church brought a single response from the nation's capital: there would be no compromise. Mormon polygamy must end.[3] The Manifesto of 1890, successful as an answer to some of these events, presented other questions of its own.

Since the mid-1880s the church had responded to unfriendly developments by publicly presenting itself as increasingly obedient while privately refusing surrender.[4] Utah's territorial governor, Arthur L. Thomas, took particular offense at Mormon pretensions. He said that every evasion, while giving the impression that plural marriages were no longer performed, was employed to obscure their continuance. Referring to the necessity forced upon them by the Reorganized Church to prove plurality had existed in Illinois, Thomas said such admissions eroded Mormon claims that they had broken no laws and had been driven from their homes in the Midwest without excuse. "Mendacity and deceit," he concluded, were part of the Mormon tradition.[5] The Utah Commission in its report for 1889 observed that polygamy was yet taught and admonished, not by reference to sermons of earlier authorities alone but by those leading the church in the present day.[6]

Attempting to refute such reports, in mid-October 1889 President Woodruff made a statement to the press, insisting that since becoming church president he had neither approved new polygamous marriages nor permitted the principle to be taught. Woodruff stated that since passage of the Edmunds-Tucker Act Mormon authorities had instructed their followers that plural contractions were not to be performed. The church, he said, was determined to obey the law.[7] Late the next month John W. Young recommended that church leaders seriously proceed with such prohibitions. Instead, they deferred to a revelation of President Woodruff's, urging continued faithfulness to God's commandments.[8] This agreed with a private statement by Woodruff the year before indicating that divine revocation of polygamy would never occur.[9] Behind Mormon reluctance to abandon the principle lay an expectation that something dramatic and saving would happen. In 1888, for example, Woodruff said the practice would continue until Christ's return, an event many believed at their doors.[10]

The church was under siege not only for the practice of polygamy but also for allegations that oaths involving threats of death were taken in the temples and that secret promises to avenge the martyrdom of early Mormon leaders were made. On the strength of testimony concerning these allegations, Judge Thomas J. Anderson of the third judicial district of Utah ruled that Mormon aliens were not fit to enter the United States at full parity with other citizens. While some had urged for years that the government exclude Mormons from abroad, new support for the idea occurred in the late 1880s.[11] The First Presidency responded by assigning Charles W. Penrose to write a manifesto assuring non-Mormons that the Latter-day Saints were committed to a separation of church and state. This "official declaration" was issued to the public under the signatures of the First Presidency, members of the Quorum of Twelve Apostles, and others on 12 December 1889.[12] It is questionable whether the document succeeded in its intent, however, for immigration restrictions relating to the advocacy and practice of polygamy were enacted in 1891. And the lurid testimony given in Judge Anderson's court was cited for years as evidence of the Mormon threat.[13]

The policy of officially denying that polygamous contractions were approved while privately commending them inevitably caught some in the scissors of contradiction. Such was the fate of Hans Jespersen. A resident of Goshen, Utah, in April 1889 Jespersen took Alice Horton as a plural wife. When questioned, Mrs. Horton admitted she and Jespersen were married in the Endowment House in Salt Lake City by an individual purposely disguised so that they could only hear his voice. They considered themselves properly married, however, and Alice had become pregnant. Jespersen, too, claimed he could not identify the man who performed the ceremony. Church authorities, consistent with the language used in such instances, said that a recommend may have been given for going to the temple, but no one was authorized to marry a plural wife. President Woodruff expressed astonishment when told of the case. He then ordered demolition of the Endowment House as proof of his determination to bring such things to an end.[14]

Mormon commitment, however, was little changed. This was illustrated in an 1890 description of a Mormon Sunday school by G. Frederick Wright. He told how, as in most denominations, teachers quizzed their students on the work of great men in their church. "Where is such a one?" they were asked. "A missionary in California," came the reply. And so followed a recitation of the work of others, illustrating Mormon evangelism around the world. "And where is such a one?" referring to a gentleman from their community imprisoned for polygamy. "In the *pen*," was the quick, proud response. As Wright concluded, it would take drastic measures to uproot such early anchored regard for Mormonism's stalwarts.[15]

An editorial in the *Deseret News* in early February 1890 argued that those urging formal renunciation of plural marriage were asking too much. It stated that the church had already conformed itself to the laws outwardly. Polygamy remained a revelation, however, and nothing men might do could wipe it away. At the least, a Mormon's *conscience* should be his own. Similar statements followed in succeeding months.[16] In April President Woodruff and George Q. Cannon wrote to Apostle George Teasdale in England, saying that if Congress should pass the Cullom-Struble bill, disfranchising church members, it would not be an unmixed evil. It would, they said, have the effect of drawing a line between the Saints and the rest of the world, further moving things toward the long-awaited consummation.[17]

The hope felt among the leaders was poignantly illustrated in a comment by Apostle Brigham Young, Jr., in the spring of 1890. At a meeting of the apostles and First Presidency in which the subject was debated, it was decided that they could not ask church members to obey the law and repudiate their plural wives. Then, while yet in meeting, Apostle Young said he felt the spirit come over him. He was given to see, he said, that he and his brethren would outlast the anti-polygamy campaign and would soon be able to ride through the streets of Salt Lake City with their polygamous wives and children beside them.[18] And in early August President Woodruff was yet telling church members that persecution was a consequence of being among the chosen. He said that things in the earth were hastening to their end and God would cut short his work. The Saints need only persevere.[19] As late as mid-September 1890, a week before the Manifesto, Apostle John Henry Smith declared that "no principle or revelation that God ever gave to his people was to be laid on the shelf as a thing of the past."[20]

Then, on September 24, 1890, President Woodruff produced his famous Manifesto, advising church members to obey the laws of the land as they related to polygamy.[21] After all the debate, the Manifesto could not be described as unexpected. In many ways, it differed little from earlier statements made by the leaders. What precipitated the action seems to have been nothing more than realization that something of the sort was desperately needed. The document was issued one week before an important election in Idaho, where the Mormon question had been cause for bitter debate. With the Idaho test oath now approved by the United States Supreme Court, even non-polygamous Mormons could be excluded from the polls.[22] A recent amendment to Canadian law also criminalized Mormon plural marriage there.[23] And the annual report of the Utah Commission had been submitted to the Secretary of the Interior a month before. Although it had not been made public, rumors of its contents indicated the commission alleged polygamous marriages were being approved in Utah. The commissioners unanimously expressed regret that nothing of an "authoritative and explicit" nature had yet been said by the church concerning abandonment of the principle. The report strongly recommended legislation that would deny the right to vote to all members of the church.[24] Action by Congress had been delayed only because Mormon spokesmen assured national leaders they could depend on something being done to end the practice soon.[25]

Finally, President Woodruff was subject to intense solicitation from both Mormon and non-Mormon friends, apprising him that nothing less than formal cessation of polygamy would bring relief.[26] Joseph Henry Dean, visiting with members of the First Presidency on the day the Manifesto was written, described the frantic atmosphere. He said President Woodruff told him they felt like drowning men, clutching at every prospect for help.[27] If, as Frank Cannon claimed, President

Woodruff was as helpless "as a nun" in dealing with political matters, he was sufficiently astute to comprehend the serious nature of difficulties confronting him then.[28]

Dispute as to whether it was President Woodruff, a committee of individuals, or someone else who wrote the statement now seems settled as a result of the impressive study by D. Michael Quinn. He established that, even if amended by others, the document was overwhelmingly the composition of the president himself.[29] In one conspicuous matter of form, the Manifesto of 1890 was different from the official declaration on blood atonement and state-church relations issued by authorities the previous December. The earlier declaration was issued under the signatures of all members of the First Presidency, all twelve of the apostles, and John W. Young and Daniel H. Wells, "Counsellors." The official declaration on polygamy carried the name of President Woodruff alone.[30] It has been alleged that Woodruff's counselors, George Q. Cannon and Joseph F. Smith, did not sign the document because of strong reservations on the part of Smith. For Cannon alone to have signed, it is said, would have made President Smith's dissent too conspicuous, hence neither signed.[31] Although Joseph F. Smith was absent from the general conference at which the Manifesto was presented, this interpretation seems unlikely because of the independent testimonies of Franklin D. Richards and Marriner W. Merrill that both counselors were consulted and gave their assent to the document on the day it was prepared.[32]

Woodruff consulted with three apostles—Franklin D. Richards, Moses Thatcher, and Marriner W. Merrill—on September 24, the day before the Manifesto's publication. According to Merrill, all gave at least tentative approval to the statement.[33] The apostles met as a quorum on three occasions after its publication and prior to general conference: September 30, October 1, and October 2. While we do not have a complete record of what was said, it seems that the eight or nine members present on those occasions also expressed at least tentative concurrence with the document.[34] This is not to say that all felt unqualified allegiance to the declaration. We know that some were troubled by the move. But according to John Henry Smith, even those who had questions were, in these meetings, willing to give the statement their general endorsement.[35]

This notwithstanding, ill feeling erupted. There may have been something of this in Apostle Abraham H. Cannon's reference to the fault finding that came to his ears almost immediately after publication of the Manifesto.[36] Returning by train from church assignments south of Salt Lake City, Cannon, Francis M. Lyman, John Henry

Smith, and John W. Taylor, as well as Brigham H. Roberts, learned together of the Manifesto from a newspaper. Roberts, who said he read the headlines with astonishment, looked upon the document as "a kind of cowardly proceeding," and, he said, "the more I thought of it the less I liked it." While Lyman and Cannon were unruffled, Taylor and Smith seemed to share at least some of Roberts's discontent with President Woodruff's move.[37] John Mills Whitaker, who worked in the church historian's office where much of the business at that time was transacted, said that following the Manifesto's issuance considerable bitterness and mumbling occurred there, some saying they refused to accept it.[38]

To understand the apostles' responses it will be helpful to explore the views held by some concerning President Woodruff's leadership. In the cases of Brigham Young and John Taylor, succession of the senior apostle to the presidency of the church occurred only after delays of years. And during President Taylor's last sickness at least one of the apostles raised the question as to how binding the precedent was that would elevate Woodruff to the presidency of the church.[39] While all united in his appointment as church president on April 5, 1889, this was preceded by a delay of more than twenty months after the death of President Taylor and by considerable disagreement, including criticism of Woodruff himself. Animosities were so great that Woodruff compared the situation to the bitterness and divisions of the Kirtland period.[40]

Discontent with Woodruff seemed to arise first from what Apostle Erastus Snow referred to as his "toadyism." The comment was made as part of a larger attack on the influence and decisions of George Q. Cannon. There is no question but that Cannon was a leading figure in the church's hierarchy. More than one observer commented that after the death of Brigham Young no one exercised greater power in both civic and church affairs in Utah than Cannon.[41] Theodore Schroeder, a non-Mormon residing in Salt Lake City, later published a long article in the New York Times describing Cannon as not only the most powerful figure in the church but one of the most important in the American West.[42] Two weeks before the Manifesto was issued, Utah's governor, Arthur L. Thomas, said that while Woodruff was nominally Mormonism's president, Cannon was the church's actual leader.[43] His ascendancy became especially pronounced during the last stages of President Taylor's administration. It may have been because some felt Woodruff too amenable to Cannon's influence that they resisted organizing the First Presidency when he raised the question with them in the spring of 1888.[44] Ronald Walker has shown that a number of issues divided the leaders, including organizational friction between the First Presidency and the Quorum of Twelve Apostles, tensions due to differences of age, bitterness arising from suspicioned misappropriation of investments, as well as resentment of Cannon's authority.[45]

Some apparently entertained reservations about President Woodruff's intellectual capacity. Despite his prodigious diary keeping, his assistance with church historical materials, and his support for amateur science, he seems to have been particularly handicapped in formal literary exposition. If it was because he was overburdened with work that he almost immediately resigned his appointment to oversee publication of the *Deseret News* in 1872, there was also the remark made by George Reynolds that President Woodruff was an extraordinarily poor writer.[46] Whatever is to be made of this, it can hardly be considered a serious criticism of one who spent so much of his life pioneering and who, as already said, is remarkable for the quality of his journal record.

There remains, however, a sense that not all judged Woodruff to be intellectually equal to the task of running the church. Frank Cannon portrayed Woodruff as having not only an aged but a naive mind.[47] Apostle Moses Thatcher reportedly opposed Woodruff as president of the church because he lacked "smartness."[48] In late 1895, at a stake conference in Kaysville, Utah, Apostle John W. Taylor publicly stated that Woodruff's condition was such that "as well might a baby be placed at the head of the Church as Pres. Woodruff without the aid of Presidents Cannon and Smith."[49] It is possible to see how such reservations could have blended with those alleging an excessive vulnerability to the influence of George Q. Cannon. It is also possible to infer that some apostles, not having been consulted on so important a declaration as the 1890 Manifesto and already dubious of Woodruff's independent capacity, could feel only a qualified enthusiasm for the document.

Whatever the disposition of apostles in late September and early October 1890, the Manifesto already had been issued. Any response they might have had, except that of the three who were consulted on September 24, was after the fact. It seems clear that President Woodruff felt constrained to make the declaration public as quickly as possible. Evidence of haste arises from the expeditious manner in which the document was sent to the press and forwarded to government officials. On the day of its issuance in Salt Lake City, L. John Nuttall, who was then in the nation's capital, recorded that it was telegraphed to him and John T. Caine, territorial delegate. They immediately had it published in Washington newspapers and circulated to the President of the United States, cabinet members, congressmen, and others.[50]

The hasty, pre-conference issuance of the Manifesto suggests Woodruff did not initially plan to present it to the church at large for its approval.[51] The Official Declaration of 1889 had not been submitted to a body of the church for its acceptance. Something of the attitude of church leaders toward the Manifesto, and the question of its formal presentation, may be derived from remarks made at the conference itself. On Sunday morning, October 5, President Cannon, still speaking to the revolutionary effects of plural marriage, emphasized the importance of obtaining a testimony concerning it. While there was no explicit reference to polygamy, he was undoubtedly talking about this, for he referred to those things that "startle" the world and that were contrary to tradition. The Saints, he said, had introduced a "new condition of things" to oppose the tide of sexual sin, infanticide, and abortion. The nation, however, had interposed itself and frustrated the Mormon mission. While bowing to the law, the church would continue to protest against the evils of the day and do all they could to redeem the world from its misguided ways.[52]

In the afternoon session of the same day, President Woodruff, too, bemoaned the sexual error and wickedness of society. He told members that if they felt deprived of their privileges, they should know that God would hold responsible those who had brought about the "curtailment." As with Cannon's address, there was a tone of perseverance, if not defiance, in what was said. Congress had adjourned only days before without passing the Cullom-Struble bill. The Manifesto had accomplished one of its major purposes. Could it be that church leaders were leaving the document behind as part of another crisis met and passed? Remarks of the kind made by Cannon and Woodruff were little different from those made for years before the Manifesto was given to the press.[53]

It was a communication from John T. Caine in Washington, D.C., that persuaded authorities to take the Manifesto before a conference session itself. On October 5, the day of the comments reported above and one day before the conference's conclusion, Caine telegraphed that the Secretary of the Interior, on the advice of Governor Arthur L. Thomas, would not accept the Manifesto as binding unless it were presented to a conference of the church.[54] Failure to formalize the document in that way could give credibility to reports by the Utah Commission. Consequently, the Manifesto was made a matter of business the next morning, Monday, October 6, 1890. Bishop Orson F. Whitney first read the Articles of Faith, which included a declaration by church members that they believed in "obeying, honoring and sustaining the law." While the Articles had been a part of Mormon theological literature for half a century, it seemed a convenient time to sustain them as the official rule of conduct for the church. This was done on a motion by Apostle Franklin D. Richards. Bishop Whitney then took the stand again and read the Manifesto. Thereupon, Apostle Lorenzo Snow moved that President Woodruff's Official Declaration be approved and accepted "as authoritative and binding." The assembly was then asked to vote on the motion.[55]

At a century's distance it is difficult to ascertain precisely what the strength of the vote was. The official report in the *Deseret News,* and accounts given since in publications of the church, say that approval of the Manifesto was unanimous. Statements in other accounts, also friendly to the church, describe the vote as "near unanimous."[56] It was, of course, either unanimous or it was not. What seems to be involved is the manner in which one reports a response where some members voted neither for nor against. While we know of one confirmed contrary vote,[57] there is evidence that some refused to vote either way, including at least one of the general authorities. This was Brigham H. Roberts, who, reflecting on the propriety of presenting the Manifesto in conference at all, said: "During the Conference I saw that movements were on foot to have the whole people support it[,] a proceeding I viewed with alarm. When the crisis came I felt heartbroken but remained silent. It seemed to me to be the awfulest moment in my life, my arm was like lead when the motion was put; I could not vote for it, and did not."[58]

While Michael Quinn's judgment that only a minority present voted for the declaration seems extreme, it is clear that many did abstain.[59] Had a majority refrained, it is likely there would have been a large number of explicit reports to this effect in both journals and published commentaries. And the *Salt Lake Tribune* would never have overlooked so auspicious an opportunity to embarrass the leaders.[60] That numbers kept their hands in their laps, however, is certain from descriptions provided by Apostle Marriner W. Merrill and others.[61] An anonymous, undated, untitled typescript in the papers of Anthony W. Ivins provides what is probably the best description of what happened: "Both the members of the ch. & the genl. authorities *for the most part* voted for the manifesto with indiv. reservations" [emphasis added].[62]

A word about Mormon voting practice is appropriate here. It is less a "vote," in the sense the term is ordinarily employed, than a referendum on choices already made by those in authority. Whether, as one scholar described it, nineteenth-century Mormonism was an "authoritarian democracy," as opposed to twentieth-century Mormonism's "authoritarian oligarchy," the emphasis in both cases is on "authoritarian."[63] In almost all instances, there is an absence of general debate on what is proposed and a remarkable record of unanimous assents. Even though Joseph F. Smith once contended that Mormons were among the "freest and most independent" of Christian sects, it is also true, as another student of the church's decision-making process said, that very few in the organization have ever seen a dissenting vote cast on proposals submitted by the hierarchy.[64] Judge Orlando W. Powers indicated to the Smoot committee that while many Mormons privately told him of objections to their leaders' policies, when they were brought to vote upon such things, "not one of them seemed to dare to say that his soul was his own."[65]

There is, in the first place, a margin of disinterest that must ever accompany predetermined elections. For decades Mormons have made jocular comments regarding the absurdities possible during such votes because of the somnambulant effect they produce. The Reverend J. M. Buckley, generally favorable to the church during the Smoot hearings, remarked on the inevitability of unanimous votes among the Saints and how, when a mistake was made, the vote was the same before as it was after the mistake was corrected. It was, he said, "a great forest of hands raised with mechanical precision."[66]

At the presentation of the Manifesto in October 1890, however, there was no somnambulance on the part of those present. It was an issue of electric significance in the minds of everyone. Rather, it is another effect such procedures have that may give us insight into the vote that day. This is the coopting influence such methods cultivate. That which is unchallenged and exercised as habit rapidly becomes ritual. When this occurs, dissent becomes an object of surprise, if not resentment. There is an illustration of this in the journal of Charles Walker, who told of an instance in St. George where, after the names of church authorities were presented to a congregation for their approval, one person raised his hand in opposition. Walker remarked that this was something "very rare and caused many to stare in the direction of the contrary vote with wonder."[67] And Angus M. Cannon, a local Mormon authority, testified to the Smoot investigating committee in Washington, D.C., that he would not approve of any person expressing objection at the time of such decisions.[68]

There may well have been individuals who, although personally opposed, voted for the Manifesto or were brave enough not to vote at all, who yielded to the intimidation of custom and numbers. This, more than supernatural forces, may explain behavior like that of Samuel Bateman, who, his daughter recalled, went to conference deeply opposed to the Woodruff document. When it was presented for a vote, however, some "power" led him to raise his hand in support of the declaration. After so voting, he said, he felt peace and contentment.[69] The wish to avoid visible contrariety and, with it, a resignation to the ways of Providence are further illustrated by William Henry Gibbs, Sr. Gibbs said his feelings were so confused at the time of the vote that he could not easily express them. He at first was disposed against the measure, but after a moment's thought decided it was not his part to "steady the ark" and so voted with the rest of the congregation, leaving resolution of the matter to God.[70]

Not everyone felt the relief experienced by Bateman. Abbie Hyde Cowley said, after the vote was taken and the document sustained, "a gloom came over the people."[71] Gibson Condie said sadness and shaken faith ran through the congregation.[72] Joseph H. Dean spoke of the confusion felt by many before the vote was called for, wishing to dissent but fearing to oppose something already promulgated by their prophet. After noting that numbers refused to vote either way, he added: "A great many of the sisters weeped [*sic*] silently, and seemed to feel worse than the brethren."[73] John W. Whitaker, official recorder at the conference, said there was "great sadness and sorrow in the hearts of many," that some authorities themselves were opposed to the Manifesto, and that he heard some at the conference say they did not sustain the president in what he did and had strong reasons for saying so.[74] Distressed consciences continued to haunt some for years. Lucy W. Kimball, when asked in the Temple Lot case why her church had reneged on the practice if it was a divine principle, shot back: "Well, the church will see the day when it will apologize for that. Yes, sir, I did consent to the Manifesto with the rest of the church to President Woodruff, much to my regret, but I am not going to acknowledge it again; the time will surely come for that principle to rule."[75]

The argument, sometimes made by Mormon fundamentalists, that President Woodruff both expected and hoped that the conference audience would reject the Manifesto and thus provide an escape from pressures upon him is erroneous.[76] Such an explanation ignores the fact that the Manifesto was prepared, made public, and distributed to government officials days before the conference met; that it was presented in conference on the last day only because of urgings from government authorities; that special efforts, such as reading the Articles of Faith, were made before presentation of the writing to increase the likelihood of its approval; and, as we have seen, the vote on the document was reported in the most approbative language possible. So far as President Woodruff is concerned, a contrary vote, rather than helping, would have left him in very embarrassing circumstances.

Not only had everything possible been done to increase the likelihood for approval of the statement but, after the vote was taken, yet more was said to render what had been done acceptable. President Woodruff's first counselor, George Q. Cannon, recounted for nearly thirty minutes the experience of the Latter-day Saints in connection with the anti-polygamy crusade. Reversing what had been said before, he pointed to the 1841 revelation to Joseph Smith relieving the Saints from further trial when prevented by others from carrying out the commandments given them. Admitting that plural marriages had continued after the highest court in the land declared anti-polygamy statutes constitutional, he said this was because the principle was so important, "dearer . . . than life," and that they had believed they would be damned if they did not live it. Only in the Lord's good time was President Woodruff moved to dictate the Manifesto.[77]

Then the president himself spoke, indicating that what he had written was preceded by "a long season" of earnest prayer and that, given his nearness to the grave, people could be sure he had no reason to do anything for which he could not answer on the other side. He too referred to the revelation excepting the Saints from commandments frustrated by their enemies. It was the nation, with its unfriendly anti-polygamy laws, that must now answer to God. Ominous signs were to be seen in both heaven and earth. The Saints were on the edge of momentous developments. The Lord, he affirmed, would not allow him to lead the church astray. God would replace him before permitting such a thing to happen.[78]

Whatever the vote and the intentions of those who presented the Manifesto, the document deserves close examination. It consisted of five comparatively brief paragraphs. Of these, the first three, constituting nearly two-thirds of the declaration, addressed rumors relating to the about-to-be-released Utah Commission's annual report. In it, more than forty cases of polygamous marriage were cited by the commission's registration officers as having been discovered during the previous year. Notwithstanding some of these may have occurred years before, or outside Utah, notice of their detection acted to undermine church denials that such marriages were taking place.[79] The bulk of the 1890 Manifesto was an attempt, "in the most solemn manner," to contradict newspaper stories describing these findings and so disabuse Congress of impressions that new polygamous marriages were being performed or that the principle was yet being taught.

Not only does Michael Quinn's research in temple and Endowment House records reveal a dozen plural marriages in Utah during the period referred to by the Manifesto, ten of which were performed by Apostle Franklin D. Richards, but Apostle Marriner W. Merrill took a plural wife during this period, as did Matthias F. Cowley, who was called to be an apostle less than a decade later. The Manifesto's credibility is further eroded by the fact that both Richards and Merrill were among those consulted on the document before it was released to the press.[80] If it is said, in connection with teaching the doctrine, that Woodruff was denying only that *public* urging had occurred, the president's own words made no such qualification. He flatly said: "We are not teaching polygamy or plural marriage, nor permitting any person to enter its practice."[81] It is difficult to understand how, by denying that those marriages found by the Utah Commission "or any other number" had occurred, Woodruff could expect any comprehending observer to view his document as an honest description of fact.

The problem of reconciling the Manifesto's denials with known truth is heightened by another official statement issued slightly more than a year later. This was the petition for amnesty which, if prepared by the editors of the *Salt Lake Tribune,* was signed by the First Presidency and ten of the apostles in December 1891. In their preface the petitioners forthrightly stated that they had taught "polygamy, or celestial marriage" to be a commandment of God. They had not only taught this but, in the words of the petition, they also preached "that it was a necessity to man's highest exaltation in the life to come." The petition also said that polygamy, since its public announcement under Brigham Young, "was steadily taught and impressed upon the Latter Day Saints up to a short time before September, 1890." And, said the leaders, because Mormons were a sincere and devout people, they had dutifully embraced and practiced such teachings.[82]

In paragraph three of his statement Woodruff referred to a plural marriage alleged to have been performed in the Salt Lake City Endowment House in the spring of 1889. This was, unquestionably, the marriage of Hans Jespersen, referred to above. Journalistic attention to the case was extensive, and it would have been difficult to make denials as sweeping as those contained in the Manifesto without saying something about the incident. Woodruff's comment was that he had been unable to learn who performed the ceremony, that whatever happened was done without his knowledge, and that he had "in consequence of this alleged occurrence" ordered the Endowment House dismantled. Apostle Franklin D. Richards, who performed the ceremony, was one of those consulted by the president about the Manifesto before its release.[83] Destruction of the Endowment House did, in fact, take place. Anyone familiar with Mormon practice, however, must have recognized how meaningless such a gesture was. Not only were the St. George, Manti, and Logan temples all available for couples wishing to be married but, as already shown, monogamous and polygamous sealings alike could be performed anywhere. No special edifice was necessary.[84]

In the next to last paragraph Woodruff said that because laws prohibiting polygamy had been sustained by the Supreme Court, he intended to submit to such laws and would try to influence others to do the same. The Reynolds case of 1879 aside, prohibition of unlawful cohabitation, as defined in the Edmunds Act, had been sustained by the United States Supreme Court a half-decade previously.[85] Woodruff's resolution was years late. While other contests continued until 1890 and beyond, these involved questions such as enfranchisement, inheritance, and escheatment. After 1885 there was no justiciable basis for questioning the federal government's constitutional authority to criminalize polygamous marriages in territories of the United States.

In the final paragraph of the Manifesto, Woodruff denied a second time that he or his associates had taught the principle of polygamy during the previous year and said that anyone so doing had been reproved. Then followed, as the last sentence of the entire document, its most significant and oft-quoted part: "And I now publicly declare that my advise [sic] to the Latter-day Saints is to refrain from contracting any marriage forbidden by the law of the land."

Woodruff's characterization of his message as "advise" provoked derision. The Salt Lake Tribune commented that such language was unauthoritative, personal, and certainly not oracular. President Benjamin Harrison said Woodruff's choice of words undercut their persuasiveness.[86] When Governor Arthur L. Thomas was quoted as saying that the document had an evasive tone, Charles W. Penrose, editor of the Deseret News and one of those who assisted in preparation of the Manifesto, responded with a vicious attack. Thomas was described as a "light mental weight" and compared to an insect. "Nothing," Penrose said, "could be more direct and unambiguous than the language of President Woodruff, nor could anything be more authoritative."[87]

It was less what was said than what was not said, however, that first brought difficulty for the Manifesto. While it advised against new polygamous marriages where against the law, it said nothing about continued cohabitation with wives of older ones. This had been identified by both Congress and the courts as a punishable offense. It lay at the heart of what was considered wrong with the Mormon plural arrangement—its visible affront to the monogamous ethic. Inasmuch as the Manifesto said nothing about earlier polygamous unions, church members might logically have believed that, although forbidden by the law, such relationships were yet approved by the church. There was good reason for this assumption. During the crusade against polygamy, church authorities condemned men who left their plural families in order to comply with the law.[88] Not only had President Woodruff once said he would rather be shot or struck by lightning than to desert his polygamous wives but Apostle Abraham Cannon remarked directly on the subject's absence from the Manifesto. On the day after its publication, 26 September 1890, he observed that "there is no renunciation of principle nor abandonment of families recommended, as some fault-finders try to make it appear."[89]

This was reaffirmed in the meeting of the apostles held on 30 September 1890. Apostle Francis M. Lyman there declared: "I design [to continue] to live with and have children by my wives, using the wisdom God gives me to avoid being captured by the officers of the law." Others said much the same thing.[90] There was also a statement by President Woodruff, made at a meeting the day following conference, as reported by Apostle Marriner Wood Merrill, that brethren should not abandon their families but, if possible, be kinder to them than in the past. And Abraham Cannon recorded that at the same gathering President Woodruff emphatically stated: "This Manifesto only refers to future marriages, and does not affect past conditions. I did not, could not and would not promise that you would desert your wives and children. This you cannot do in honor."[91]

It is difficult to imagine Mormon leaders taking any other course. To have turned their backs on their wives, whatever the age or circumstances of the women, would have been more than dishonorable. It would have been cruel. For decades part of the Mormon apologia in behalf of polygamy had been that, unlike the rest of the world, Mormon elders did not abandon their companions once they had taken pleasure with them. Instead, they supported them as wives and raised up honorable families by them. To insist that, at the least, there would be no departure from this commitment is what one would expect from men of the kind we are dealing with here.

It seems to have been on these grounds and with these sentiments in mind that, in the week following the October 1890 conference, George Q. Cannon spoke with Charles S. Varian, United States Attorney in Salt Lake City. Cannon explained to Varian the reluctance Mormons felt about abandoning their families under the Manifesto. Varian is reported to have understood this and to have favored a suspension of the laws for a year or so for the purpose of seeing if Mormons would carry out the Manifesto in good faith. If this proved the case, he is supposed to have favored an arrangement that would allow Mormons to acknowledge and care for their plural wives so long as there was no "criminal intercourse" between them. While most leaders were unwilling to forego such relations, no such indication was given to Varian. Apostle Abraham Cannon, our source for the conversation between his father and Varian, also related comments by quorum members to the effect that brethren then promising to abstain from both new polygamous marriages and polygamous cohabitation were placing "too broad a construction" on the Manifesto.[92]

The result was misunderstanding. Varian, assuming that polygamists would provide only material support for their wives, pledged to do what he could to prevent the prosecution of such men. As a delegate to Utah's 1895 constitutional convention, in explaining the irrevocable clause in the new constitution prohibiting polygamy, he stated that cohabitation should be exempt from its application. Some church authorities took this to mean that gentile leaders were willing to permit Mormon polygamists to continue to live with their plural wives. This stretched Varian's intention too far and later led to charges of broken promises on both sides.[93]

In the spring of 1891 the situation was further complicated by Hans Jespersen, who had attracted so much public attention by his polygamous marriage in 1889. Now in prison, Jespersen became impatient and threatened to tell who it was that performed the ceremony unless church authorities did more to expedite his release. The leaders advised him to telegraph both the Attorney General in Washington, D.C., and United States Attorney Charles S. Varian, telling them that he would obey the law in the future. In other words, church authorities advised a course of action they had previously criticized. At the same time, public officials were reinforced in the impression that Mormons intended to discontinue criminal cohabitation altogether.[94]

After the Jespersen episode the Utah Commission issued its report for 1891. The commissioners said that while the Manifesto was a forward step in the struggle between civilization and "Oriental lust and barbarism," polygamous marriages were yet performed in Utah and unlawful cohabitation was especially prominent.[95] This raised doubt as to the sincerity of the church and impaired the case for statehood. The Latter-day Saint press issued more rebuttals, denying rumors that the Saints were emigrating to Mexico for the purpose of perpetuating polygamy there.[96] The leaders also used the autumn 1891 conference to refute the commissioners' charges. In a special set of committee resolutions submitted to and accepted by the conference, allegations that the church dominated Utah politics were emphatically denied. With regard to polygamy, however, they said only: "We do not believe there have been any polygamous marriages solemnized among Latter-day Saints during the period named by the Utah Commission."[97] Not only was this a feeble answer when compared to that bearing on church-state relations but it said nothing about polygamous cohabitation, which the commissioners pointed to as Utah's most common offense. By omitting reference to the matter, contrary to the advice given Hans Jespersen, the leaders inferred approval of those yet living with their plural wives. Where, many must have asked, did the church really stand?

Church leaders also decided to take advantage of the hearings before Master in Chancery Charles F. Loofbourow concerning the disposition of escheated church property. The hearings arose because of a court order directing that church properties taken under terms of the Edmunds-Tucker Act be appropriated for charitable use.[98] Although their appearance at the hearings was not required, the leaders decided that the Mormon image could be brightened if such a forum were properly used. Notwithstanding one apostle's fear that questions might be asked that would lead to difficulty, all went ahead with preparation and rehearsals for the event.[99]

At the proceedings Woodruff was maneuvered into saying that the prohibition on new plural marriages applied to Latter-day Saints "everywhere and in every nation and country." Those found in violation of this rule, he said, were liable to be severed from the church. He also said he believed the document was inspired by God. Presidents George Q. Cannon and Joseph F. Smith, as well as apostles Lorenzo Snow and Anthon H. Lund, were also examined. All concurred that they had no expectation of seeing new polygamous marriages restored, according to Apostle Snow at least, until Christ's Second Coming. Finally, following President Woodruff's lead, all agreed that the

Manifesto prohibited cohabitation with plural wives. In President Woodruff's words, the document interdicted "whatever there is in the law of the land with regard to it [i.e., polygamy]."[100] Witnesses for the church had not expected to be pressed so far. For his part, Woodruff later confessed to the Quorum of Twelve Apostles that "he was placed in such a position on the witness stand that he could not answer other than he did." Privately, however, he admonished them not to neglect their plural wives, only taking care not to be caught.[101]

Publicly, the leaders tried to remain consistent. This accounts for discourses such as that at a church conference in Logan, Utah, held a few days after the chancery proceedings. There, President Woodruff and his counselors repeated that not only new polygamous marriages but cohabitation with the wives of older ones must be halted.[102] It accounts for the lack of church opposition to a legislative enactment in 1892 that made polygamous cohabitation a crime under territorial law.[103] And it explains the willingness of the First Presidency and most of the twelve apostles in 1893 to accept special grants of presidential amnesty, promising thereby to obey the Edmunds Act, including provisions regarding unlawful cohabitation.[104]

Uneasiness due to this alternation of signals can be discerned in meetings by the apostles themselves. In early April 1892 Apostle Lorenzo Snow recalled to the quorum that when the Manifesto was first issued there was no idea that it would be interpreted to exclude them from the company of their plural wives. At the same meeting Apostle John W. Taylor remarked that, although he had voted to sustain President Woodruff in the issuance of the Manifesto, he was still not certain "that thing was right."[105] The sharpest comments came from Apostle Heber J. Grant. He had expressed himself privately to Abraham Cannon the previous autumn, following President Woodruff's testimony before the master in chancery, saying he feared the leaders must now give up their plural families or be looked upon as "a set of base deceivers."[106] At the spring meeting Grant reminded everyone that President Woodruff had said, early on, that the Manifesto should never be interpreted as applying to cohabitation with earlier wives and that "he would see them [gentile opponents] damned in hell before he would agree to cease living with his wives or advise any other person to do so." Yet, Grant went on, they had been led by degrees to that very circumstance.[107]

If statements by Mormon authorities were contradictory, their private life-styles were even more so. Some ceased living with their plural wives in strict accordance with public comments about the meaning of the Manifesto.[108] Most, however, did not. The only study made of continued cohabitation among general authorities of the church after 1890 found that "a substantial majority" continued the practice.[109] Given public utterances indicating that the Manifesto prohibited such relationships, their examples could only result in confusion, if not cynicism. After the chancery proceedings, Charles Walker in St. George and L. John Nuttall in Salt Lake City both spoke of discouragement and uncertainty brought by Woodruff's answers.[110] Similar responses followed the petition for and acceptance of amnesty.[111]

The persistence of polygamous cohabitation was the subject of debate in a meeting of Utah's first state legislature during the spring of 1896. A measure was proposed that would make polygamous offspring born since 1890 legitimate. Some opposed the bill on grounds that, by admitting the existence of and providing for such children, the sincerity of the Manifesto and the interpretations placed upon it were impeached. One Mormon legislator, favoring the proposed law, called for merciful behavior. Those who yet cohabited with their plural wives and parented children by them could hardly be blamed, he said, for acting on a half-century of religious teachings. Others carried the discussion back to a consideration of the Manifesto itself. William Gibson took the occasion to say he had voted against the Manifesto when it was presented in conference. He claimed to have vocally corrected George Q. Cannon's declaration that it carried unanimously with "all but one, right here." Gibson defended his opposition to the Manifesto and his support for the measure before the legislature by recalling traditional Mormon arguments in behalf of the principle. Sexual sin had existed since the beginning of time, he said, but the best antidote, polygamy, now had been abolished.[112]

The chief problem was a want of clear direction from church authorities. Some members took advantage of the situation to abandon women with whom they had become weary or who created excessive economic burdens. Others simply found public pressure too great to resist. Such cases, gratefully few, must be counted as the most tragic consequence of the Manifesto and the interpretations sometimes placed upon it.[113] There was trouble enough for those not shorn from their husbands or left to fend alone. Even a first wife could cry from fear of what the Manifesto held.[114] As one church member put it, they could not tell whether they were expected to leave their plural families or not. They could not, he said, get explanation from the leaders "for they would not commit themselves."[115] The First Presidency and apostles decided on one occasion in 1899 to advise brethren under indictment for continued cohabitation not to promise future obedience to the law. A little more than a month later, however, President Snow told the apostles that, out of respect for the law, all polygamous cohabitation in the church must come to an end. Apostle Reed Smoot admitted he was still confused on the question as late as 1905.[116]

In fairness, it should be said that the church asked no one to forsake or abandon his wives. Rather, they were told to continue to support them but not to live with them except in lands where it was permitted by the law. Joseph F. Smith suggested that pluralists move permanently with their families to Mexico.[117] Numbers of individuals did so. Most, however, including general authorities of the church, did not. Had Smith and others taken his own counsel, it would have saved both themselves and the church great embarrassment. As Judge William M. McCarty later commented, referring to Joseph F. Smith, the influence of his personal example on members was undoubtedly considerable.[118]

There was also a question as to whether the Manifesto was to be accepted as a revelation, an inspired guide, or something less. When the document first appeared in the *Deseret News* on 25 September 1890, there was nothing to suggest it was a formal communication from heaven. It closely resembled a statement issued by authorities less than eleven months previously dealing with questions of church and state and rumors concerning the temple ceremony.[119] Each involved the hand of Charles W. Penrose. Both carried the title "Official Declaration." And both were referred to as a "Manifesto." Both were addressed "To Whom It May Concern" and appeared in the editorial columns of the *Deseret News*. Both followed a similar line of argument, amounting to rebuttal of charges made in the non-Mormon press. In 1891 George Q. Cannon published a pamphlet history of the church containing both documents, setting them side by side, and referring to them as "the two Manifestoes." The reader was to infer that one was no more important than the other.[120] Certainly, the disputes and cavils that raged among authorities about the 1890 statement suggest nothing like the regard one would expect for the Word of God.

This was an important consideration, for the question of the Manifesto's species affected the force it would carry with members of the church. Between the time of its first printing and its presentation in conference, the question received considerable attention in the press. The *Salt Lake Tribune* said it was not only vague and insincere but nothing more than the personal advice of a visionary old man.[121] Added to this, how was one to judge the Manifesto as "advise" when weighed against the resolute admonitions of the First Presidency five years before? At that time the Saints were reminded that there was no salvation in the celestial kingdom except by obedience to the commandment concerning plural marriage and that damnation was the penalty of those who refused to obey it.[122] There was also the revelation President Woodruff received less than a year before the Manifesto—a communication whose style and format clearly suggested its putative heavenly origin. In that document the Saints were urged to remain faithful to the commandments they had received.[123] When the Manifesto is compared to such conveyances, incredulity on the part of critics, especially their hesitancy to view the document as more than exigent, is easy to understand.

The issue was later raised during the Smoot investigation. While questioning President Joseph F. Smith, Senator Joseph Weldon Bailey not only commented on the absence of anything in the Manifesto's language suggesting its divine origin but chided Smith by saying he thought a Christian would "go to the stake" before abandoning so vital a tenet of his creed. When Smith remonstrated that the Manifesto did not contradict a former revelation but only forbade the "practice" of polygamy, Bailey answered that such an interpretation was "a distinction without a difference." Bailey further told Smith he had little regard for revelations of convenience, that the circumstances surrounding issuance of the Manifesto made it difficult to believe anyone could be required to "accept it as a revelation."[124]

Comments by Mormons themselves are important in tracing perceptions of the document's provenance. Especially revealing was the editorial attached to the column in the *Deseret News* in which the Manifesto first appeared. After printing a copy of the statement and saying that it had been sent to the Associated Press for distribution, the editor of the *News* reported that it was the full document released by President Woodruff, albeit condensed from a longer draft. The editor also stated, with astonishing candor, that the piece only "poorly" conveyed "the sentiments of the writer."[125] One is left to conclude that, if the Manifesto was a revelation, editor Charles W. Penrose believed either God a poor stylist or Wilford Woodruff an inadequate stenographer. More likely, Penrose, who had assisted with writing the Manifesto, was apologizing for what he believed was something less than a finished literary product—a judgment too bold, surely, were the document considered a revelation at that time.

George Reynolds, who was involved with Charles W. Penrose and John R. Winder in editing President Woodruff's initial draft, was interrogated on the subject at the Smoot hearings a decade and a half later.[126] Reynolds explained that he believed that, although Woodruff was a poor writer, he had been inspired in his initial preparation of the manuscript. Senator Julius Caesar Burrows then asked Reynolds if he was not reluctant to alter something inspired from on high. Reynolds answered that "it had nothing to do with correcting what the Lord had said."[127] There were degrees of inspiration, he indicated, including one in which the vision is simply transcribed in one's own words. This, he believed, is what Woodruff did. Reynolds said he did not believe the writing to be a revelation in the sense that it began, "Thus saith the Lord." Therefore, he viewed it as neither contradicting the original 1843 revelation authorizing polygamy nor on a parity with other revelations in the *Doctrine and Covenants*.[128] Brigham H. Roberts granted even less. He described it to the senators as "an official act of the church . . . binding upon the members of the church." Somewhat equivocal, Roberts said he believed Woodruff was inspired to take a course of action. But he called the document itself an "administrative act."[129]

More relevant, perhaps, were articles in the *Deseret News* the week following appearance of the Manifesto. On 1 October an editorial addressed recent statements by a member of the Utah Commission who had said that, to solve the "Mormon problem," President Woodruff needed to have a revelation suspending polygamy. The *News* indicated that revelations were not such things as could be produced on demand. "When President Woodruff receives anything from a Divine source for the Church over which he presides," said the article, "he will be sure to deliver the message."[130] This, five days after publication of the Woodruff statement!

Nevertheless, appropriation of the Manifesto as a revelation began as early as the remarks by George Q. Cannon in the Tabernacle on 6 October 1890. President Woodruff had prepared the Manifesto, Cannon said, under the influence of the "Spirit." Secondly, he rhetorically affirmed, "when God speaks and when God makes known His mind and will, I hope that I and all Latter-day Saints will bow in submission to it." If this fell short of saying the Manifesto had been divinely dictated, it yet granted a special aura to the event. It is true that President Woodruff, in his own conference remarks, spoke only of the want of wisdom in further opposing United States anti-polygamy laws and said that the step had followed earnest prayer. Neither speaker anywhere used the word *revelation* in connection with the Manifesto, but a foundation was laid on which argument for this view could be built.[131]

It was Governor Arthur L. Thomas who, along with the *Salt Lake Tribune*, badgered the leaders into an unqualified, revelatory origin for the document. As the *Tribune* pointed out, if the statement were only President Woodruff's private counsel, it carried no weight against the 1843 revelation. A reading of *Tribune* articles makes it clear that they began referring to the Manifesto as a revelation before the *Deseret News* or any Mormon authority did so. They were even rebuked by the *Salt Lake Herald* for granting more to Woodruff's declaration than Woodruff himself. The *Tribune* responded that if it were not a revelation then the whole thing was a "swindle."[132] *Tribune* writers deserve as much credit as anyone for maneuvering the church into giving the Manifesto a fully divine attribution.

Within a year's time President Woodruff took the full step at proceedings before Master in Chancery Loofbourow in October 1891. On that occasion Woodruff said the Manifesto was issued by "inspiration." He was then led to say that, in his view, inspiration and revelation were the same thing.[133] Within days, Woodruff affirmed before a conference of Saints in Brigham City, Utah, that, while he had not used the words "thus saith the Lord," what he had done was, nevertheless, the will of God.[134] A week later Woodruff made a similar affirmation at a conference in Logan, Utah. Again, he said that the Lord had shown him "by vision and revelation" what would happen to the Latter-day Saints if they continued to resist the government over the question of polygamy. The issuing of the Manifesto, he said, was exactly what the Lord had wanted done, notwithstanding "some leading men" felt he had lost the spirit and was leading the church astray. All—the writing of the Manifesto, its approval by those counselors and apostles to whom it was shown, and the sustaining of the document at conference in October 1890—was done, he said, by "the Spirit of God and the revelations of Jesus Christ."[135]

While such language was intended to assuage doubt, it later made difficulty for Saints found to have entered polygamous marriages after the document was written. Some of those questioned at the time of the Smoot hearings were placed in the awkward circumstance of reconciling their behavior with a divine prohibition. When Senator Reed Smoot asked Apostle John Henry Smith "why in the world President Woodruff ever made that Logan speech in which he declared the manifesto to be a revelation," Smith replied that he "did not know!!!"[136] Both question and answer were disingenuous. Smoot and Smith certainly knew that Woodruff was pressed to do all he could to convince critics that he had been divinely led in turning the church down another road.

Efforts to give the Manifesto a supernatural attribution were continued in the amnesty petition of late 1891. There, the First Presidency and ten of the apostles said that it had come in answer to prayer and had suspended the 1843 commandment. This placed one nearly on a level with the other.[137] In the next few years President Woodruff repeated that the Manifesto was the result of visions of the spirit to him. Church speakers and writers have perpetuated his claim.[138] Probably as an attempt to contradict the arguments of Mormon fundamentalists, some of Woodruff's remarks have been added to the section containing the Manifesto in recent editions of the *Doctrine and Covenants*.[139]

It is clear that the Manifesto *evolved* to its present status as a revelation of God—a deference it did not originally claim. There is an entry in the diary of Apostle Marriner W. Merrill in 1891 indicating that a special meeting of the First Presidency and Quorum of Twelve Apostles had been called to determine if the Manifesto was to be understood as requiring a permanent abandonment by the church of plural marriage. Merrill answered that he could not "accede to or endorse Nor vote for [such an interpretation] as I do Not believe the Manifesto was a revelation from God but was formulated by Prest. Woodruff and endorsed by His Councilors and the Twelve Apostles for expediency to meet the present situation of affairs in the Nation or those against the Church."[140] Beyond this, three different individuals, on three different occasions, said that similar comments were made to them by Charles W. Penrose, in which he indicated that the Manifesto was not a divine production but something manufactured to outwit the church's enemies.[141] Attestations by Merrill and Penrose carry special weight because they were among the few consulted on the Manifesto before it was sent to the press.

The nature of the revelatory process in Mormonism has yet to be adequately studied.[142] It is complicated in the case of Woodruff because, to a degree greater than others, he often ran inspiration, revelation, and common experience together. The shift in Mormonism from a society rich with open, dramatic visions in its early years to one characterized by subdued personal experience in the late nineteenth century, as described by Thomas G. Alexander, is only partially helpful here.[143] While Alexander's study is insightful and provides assistance in understanding the late-nineteenth-century Mormon mind, this author does not see the changes he describes as so marked in Woodruff himself, the chief type or model he employs. Rather, Woodruff seems, early and late, to have been unusually susceptible to mystical transport. With him, there was always a subscription to belief that impressions of any kind on the part of Mormon holy men were possessed of more than earthly significance.

He was not peculiar in this tendency, to be sure. If it was difficult, as Orson Hyde once admitted, to distinguish between promptings of the spirit and one's own desires, this seems not to have inhibited leaders from affirming, again and again, that their views and pronouncements were messages from God.[144] Living in "the blaze of the Gospel day," as John Taylor once put it, Mormons were entitled to a constant flow of heavenly direction, making revelation as common, Brigham Young said, as "weeds in the garden."[145] If such a comparison lacked felicity and augured vulnerability to antinomian challenge, it allowed church leaders to move easily from one world to the other.

In his 1891 address in Logan, Utah, Woodruff provided an example of how everyday experience and the notion of inspiration were conflated. He told listeners that God had shown him that many Mormons were sorely tried because of the Manifesto.[146] Anyone reasonably attentive to affairs in Utah could have drawn the same conclusion based on nothing more than the gifts of literacy and hearing. On that and other occasions the president also described the subject of his inspiration as a vision of what would happen to the church if there were not a change in the course of events.[147] It matters not that loss of the temples and impairment of church functions—what it was that Woodruff said had been vouchsafed to him in vision—were also what friends and advisers had been telling him were likely to befall the Saints for some time. For Woodruff, these warnings were the premonstrations of heaven.

It seems most reasonable, and entirely consistent with what Woodruff believed, to say that all he intended was to "give counsel" to stop practicing polygamy. "As many words may not have been used, perhaps, in this matter as some might suppose should have been," but what he had told the church was "by inspiration, as I view it—by the mind and will of the Lord."[148] In other words, while his text might have been better written, thus admitting that part of the event to have been the performance of a man, what it was that Woodruff "intended" to do was to submit to guidance and inspiration from the Almighty. If the text of his declaration was flawed, or the ring of divine authority wanting, this did not compromise the inspiration of his *intent*.

One Mormon enthusiast said the Manifesto exceeded the abilities of European politicians and that Woodruff's acumen constituted the "ne plus ultra" of diplomatic skill.[149] Without subscribing to such hyperbole, we might consider the possibility that President Woodruff was more perceiving, cleverer than many then or since have believed. We must remember he was convinced the Second Coming of Christ was near at hand. Woodruff had been promised in his Patriarchal Blessing that he would "stand in the flesh & witness the winding up scene of this generation," that he would see the Saviour come in clouds of glory. With such anticipations, the Manifesto may have been all he sought—a device to secure time. If so, it succeeded. Woodruff's communication saved the temples and, for years beyond his own life, plural marriage too.[150]

Such questions aside, the larger gentile response to the Manifesto was increasingly favorable. Not the least of those converted was the territorial governor, Arthur L. Thomas, who had been viewed by Mormons as one of the foe. After initial hesitation Thomas, along with two Utah commissioners, judged the Manifesto to be the Mormon equivalent of a revelation and, with the confirming vote of conference members, fulfillment of what was asked of the Saints.[151] Judge Charles S. Zane, also considered an enemy, joined his support with that of the governor.[152] The sweep of acceptance soon led to other things. The United States Supreme Court in 1891 reversed a previous decision barring children born of polygamous unions from inheriting their father's estates.[153] This was followed the next year with passage of a territorial law, patterned after the Edmunds Act, criminalizing polygamy in language that anyone would find difficult to get around. With this, the remaining members of the Utah Commission were persuaded and statehood was virtually assured.[154] Luck seemed finally to be running for the Saints.

The second "relic of barbarism" subdued, the nation could in good conscience honor Utah's long-standing request for admission to the Union. With help from non-Mormon friends and recommendations from the Utah Commission, an enabling act was passed by Congress in the summer of 1894. It provided that Utah could be admitted with one proviso: "that polygamous or plural marriages are forever prohibited."[155] A constitutional convention met in Salt Lake City in the spring of 1895. A constitution was prepared and the famous "irrevocable" clause inserted, forever outlawing plural marriages in Utah.[156] As a gesture of good faith, church authorities agreed the next year to a suggestion by Charles W. Penrose that the 1890 Manifesto be published again.[157]

Much of the approbation derived from a sense that progress had simply had its way. When the Manifesto first appeared in the press, Senator George Frisbie Hoar described it as a victory over "sectionalism."[158] The dominant sentiment, summed up by Governor Thomas, was that the nation could congratulate itself on "the triumph of the

Christian home in Utah."[159] Some, however, planted pennants on ground not won. Local non-Mormon officials, persuaded that those yet living with plural wives were the last of their kind, seemed content to charitably look away and let the institution die. And the House Committee on Territories, recommending statehood, said Mormon leaders had promised not only to cease the practice of polygamy but to forever renounce it as "a doctrine of faith."[160]

It is difficult to see Mormon acquiescence to the terms imposed upon them as more than a genuflection. Of the seventy-seven church members sitting in the 1895 constitutional convention, thirty were polygamists. But even non-pluralists smarted because of the surrender. One delegate, Anthony W. Ivins, in a letter to his wife, said a great debt was due the Saints for all the broken hearts and broken families they had suffered. The laws enacted to coerce and punish them, he said, were a rebuke to the supposed civility and freedom of their age. If it were up to him, Ivins said, he would disregard the rest of the country and refuse to include the irrevocable clause in the state constitution. But, he concluded, it was the counsel of the leaders that such a step was necessary.[161] Ivins's comments are more telling considering the fact that he was a lifelong monogamist. On the other hand, as we will see, he was able to avenge the accommodation through a career that assisted in the perpetuation of polygamy to an extent greater than all but a few other Mormons of his time.

To most outside the church, however, Mormonism appeared honestly and forever to have put its greatest evil away. The Manifesto had succeeded in its intent and Utah had won its star in the flag. After decades of conflict, a calm settled over the valleys of the mountains and Gentile and Saint seemed finally to enter a peaceable kingdom together.

NOTES

1. *The Late Corporation of the Church of Jesus Christ of Latter-day Saints v. United States*, 136 U.S. 1 (1890). For commentary see Edwin Brown Firmage and Richard Collin Mangrum, *Zion in the Courts: A Legal History of the Church of Jesus Christ of Latter-day Saints, 1830–1900* (Urbana: University of Illinois Press, 1988), 251–60; Leonard J. Arrington, *Great Basin Kingdom: An Economic History of the Latter-day Saints, 1830–1900* (Cambridge, Mass.: Harvard University Press, 1958), 365–79; and Gustive O. Larson, *The "Americanization" of Utah for Statehood* (San Marino, Calif.: Huntington Library, 1971), 213–16, 254.

2. *Constitution of the State of Idaho* (1889), art. 6, sec. 3. Also see "Report of the Governor of Idaho," *Report of the Secretary of the Interior. . . . ,* 5 vols. (Wash-

ington, D.C.: GPO, 1890), 3:427; and the remarks of John D. Hicks, "The Constitutions of the Northwest States," *University Studies Published by the University of Nebraska* 23 (Jan.-April, 1923): 138–39.

3. The Idaho test oath act was upheld in *Davis v. Beason,* 133 U.S. 333 (1890). The best accounts of Mormon/non-Mormon conflict in Idaho are Merle W. Wells, *Anti-Mormonism in Idaho, 1872–92* (Provo, Utah: BYU Press, 1978), 133–54; and the same author's "Law in the Service of Politics: Anti-Mormonism in Idaho Territory," *Idaho Yesterdays* 25 (Spring 1981): 33–43. Regarding the declining ratio of Mormons to non-Mormons, see Richard D. Poll et al., *Utah's History* (Provo, Utah: BYU Press, 1978), 692, Table H; and Dean L. May, "A Demographic Portrait of the Mormons, 1830–1980," in *After 150 Years: The Latter-day Saints in Sesquicentennial Perspective,* ed. Thomas G. Alexander and Jessie L. Embry, Charles Redd Monographs in Western History, No. 13 (Provo, Utah: Charles Redd Center for Western Studies, 1983), 51. A general survey of the darkening picture, so far as the Mormons were concerned, including accounts of victories by non-Mormon forces at the polls, is to be found in Orson F. Whitney, *History of Utah,* 4 vols. (Salt Lake City: George Q. Cannon, 1892–1904), 3:687–743; *CHC* 5:203–9; 6:210–19; Larson, *The "Americanization" of Utah,* 246–59; and, most impressively, Edward Leo Lyman, *Political Deliverance: The Mormon Quest for Utah Statehood* (Urbana: University of Illinois Press, 1986), 111–20, 124–35.

4. There are not only those temple records of contractions in the United States, identified by D. Michael Quinn in his "LDS Church Authority and New Plural Marriages, 1890–1904" (*Dialogue* 18 [Spring 1985]: 46), but attestations of others, or their children, saying that between 1887 and 1890 permission was given to enter the principle in Mexico, some returning to Utah. As but a small sample, see Irvin R. Jackson, interviewed by Tillman S. Boxwell, 9 Oct. 1978, p. 14, POHP, [Joseph Jackson and Mary Ann Stowell/1887]; Orson F. Whitney, *Through Memory's Halls: The Life Story of Orson F. Whitney as Told by Himself* (Independence, Mo.: Zion's Printing and Publishing, 1930), 194–95 [Orson F. Whitney and Mary Wells/1888]; Rudger H. Daines, interviewed by Jessie L. Embry, 16 July 1976, p. 18, POHP, [William Moroni Daines and Chloe Viola Hatch/1889]; Benjamin Julius Johnson FGS [Benjamin Julius Johnson and Harriet Jane Hakes/1889]; James L. Wyatt, interviewed by Jessie L. Embry, 18 June 1976, pp. 2, 6, POHP [John Horsecroft Wyatt and Betsy Leavitt/1890]; Josiah Hickman, *Proceedings* 2:95–96 [Josiah Hickman and Martha A. Lawisch/1890].

5. "Report of the Governor of Utah" [1889], *Report of the Secretary of the Interior; . . . ,* 5 vols. (Washington, D.C.: GPO, 1890), 3:496–97.

6. "Annual Report of the Utah Commission" [1889], ibid., 3:495.

7. "Mormons Abandon Polygamy," *New York Herald,* 13 Oct. 1889.

8. For John W. Young's suggestion, see L. John Nuttall Diaries, typewritten copy, 23–24 Nov. 1889, BYU Library. President Woodruff's revelation may be read in *Unpublished Revelations of the Prophets and Presidents of the Church of Jesus Christ of Latter-day Saints,* comp. Fred C. Collier, Vol. 1 (Salt Lake City:

Collier's, 1981), pt. 89:146–47; and "Revelation to President Wilford Woodruff, Sunday, Nov. 24th, 1889," *Messages* 3:175–76.

9. As quoted from the journal of Heber J. Grant, in Lyman, *Political Deliverance,* 106.

10. President Wilford Woodruff's remark is taken from Jean Bickmore White, "The Making of the Convention President: The Political Education of John Henry Smith," *UHQ* 39 (Fall 1971): 359. For a discussion of millennial attitudes among the Saints at this time, see chap. 2 of this volume.

11. "The Avengers of Blood," *SLT,* 19 Nov. 1889. For accounts of attempts to restrict the flow of Mormons into the United States from abroad because of polygamy, see *CHC* 5:550–55; and William Mulder, "Immigration and the 'Mormon Question': An International Episode," *Western Political Quarterly* 9 (1956): 418–22ff. An excellent overview of the Mormon experience with immigration generally during these years is that of Richard L. Jensen, "Steaming Through: Arrangements for Mormon Emigration from Europe, 1869–1887," *JMH* 9 (1982): 3–23.

12. *Messages* 3:183–87.

13. U.S., *Statutes at Large,* 51st Cong., sess. 2, ch. 551, sec. 1 (1891). For examples of the sensationalist use to which descriptions of Mormon temple ceremonies were put, see Henry G. McMillan, ed., *The Inside of Mormonism: A Judicial Examination of the Endowment Oaths Administered in All the Mormon Temples.* . . . (Salt Lake City: Utah Americans, 1903); S. E. Wishard, "Facts Concerning Mormonism To Be Known," *Herald and Presbyter* 84 (28 May 1913): 6; "Mormons Taking Oaths of Endowment House," *Washington [D.C.] Times,* 14 Dec. 1904; *Proceedings* 2:75–82, 148–49, 175–79, 426.

14. The Jespersen case is reviewed, along with excerpts from local newspapers, in "Annual Report of the Utah Commission," *Report of the Secretary of the Interior* . . . , 5 vols. (Washington. D.C.: G.P.O., 1890), 3:417–18. Also see Woodruff's remarks in "Mormons Abandon Polygamy."

15. G. Frederick Wright, "The Mormon Muddle in Utah," *Nation* 51 (30 Oct. 1890): 338–39.

16. Editorial, *DN,* 10 Feb. 1890; "Sunday Services," *DN,* 14 July 1890; "Utah's Pioneer Day," *DN,* 25 July 1890; "Discourse . . . ," *DN,* 16 Aug. 1890; "The 'Mormon' Perplexity," *DN,* 23 Sept. 1890.

17. Wilford Woodruff and George Q. Cannon to George Teasdale, 12 April 1890, in *Messages* 3:189–91.

18. Brigham Young, [Jr.], Diaries, 24 April 1890, Church Archives.

19. "Discourse," *DN,* 16 Aug. 1890.

20. John Henry Smith, quoted in *Diary of Charles Lowell Walker,* ed. A. Karl Larson and Katherine Miles Larson, 2 vols. (Logan: Utah State University Press, 1980), 2:718, 16 Sept. 1890.

21. "Official Declaration," *DN,* 25 Sept. 1890; Scott G. Kenney, ed., *Wilford Woodruff's Journal, 1833–1898,* 9 vols. (Midvale, Utah: Signature Books, 1983–85), 9:112–16, 24–25 Sept. 1890; *Messages* 3:191–93.

22. Wells, *Anti-Mormonism in Idaho,* 155–77.

23. "The Canadian Colony," *DN,* 24 Sept. 1890. The Canadian law is found at 53 Victoria, ch. 37, sec. 11, subsections a-d (1890). This was subsequently incorporated into the *Revised Statutes of Canada,* pt. 5, sec. 278, 104–5 (1892).

24. "Annual Report of the Utah Commission" [1890], 414, 420–21. For evidence of Mormon distress concerning these reports, see "The 'Mormon' Perplexity," *DN,* 23 Sept. 1890; "The Latest 'Liberal' Trick Exposed," *DN,* 26 Sept. 1890; Robert Newton Baskin, *Reminiscences of Early Utah* ([Salt Lake City: Tribune-Reporter Printer], 1914), 184–85; Whitney, *History of Utah,* 3:743.

25. Frank J. Cannon and Harvey J. O'Higgins, *Under the Prophet in Utah: The National Menace of a Political Priestcraft* (Boston: C. M. Clark, 1911), 87–93 passim; Baskin, *Reminiscences,* 184; Larson, *The "Americanization" of Utah,* 255–64; Lyman, *Political Deliverance,* 131–33.

26. Whitney, *History of Utah,* 3:747; and Lyman, *Political Deliverance,* 130–35.

27. Joseph Henry Dean Diaries, 24 Sept. 1890, film, Church Archives.

28. Cannon and O'Higgins, *Under the Prophet in Utah,* 84.

29. Quinn, "New Plural Marriages," 44–46.

30. "Official Declaration," *DN,* 25 Sept. 1890.

31. [Gilbert Fulton and Rulon Allred], *The Most Holy Principle,* 4 vols. (Murray, Utah: Gems, 1970–75), 4:47.

32. Abraham Hoagland Cannon Diaries, 30 Sept. 1890, BYU Library; Melvin Clarence Merrill, ed., *Marriner Wood Merrill and His Family* (n.p., 1937), 127. Regarding Smith's absence at the conference ten days later, see the roll of those present in "General Conference," *DN,* 4 Oct. 1890. Brigham H. Roberts, initially quite unhappy with the Manifesto, noting that Woodruff alone signed the statement, said he "concluded that [President Woodruff decided] . . . to carry the responsibility alone, and I had begun to be reconciled to the Manifesto on that ground." As reported in Ronald W. Walker, "B. H. Roberts and the Woodruff Manifesto," *BYU Studies* 22 (Summer 1982): 365. Even the *Tribune* reported that Cannon, in his conference remarks after the vote on the declaration, stated that he and Counselor Joseph F. Smith had approved the document. "The Address Is Endorsed," *SLT,* 7 Oct. 1890.

33. Merrill, *Marriner Wood Merrill and His Family,* 127.

34. John Henry Smith Diaries, entries for 30 Sept. 1890, 1 Oct. 1890, and 2 Oct. 1890, George A. Smith Family Papers, University of Utah Library, Salt Lake City.

35. Ibid.

36. Abraham H. Cannon Diaries, 26 Sept. 1890.

37. This according to Brigham H. Roberts, as quoted in Walker, "B. H. Roberts and the Woodruff Manifesto," 363–66. Hugh B. Brown remembered, as a young man in Canada, that Apostle John W. Taylor, who often spent time there, looked upon the Manifesto as "rather a cowardly submission" on the part of Woodruff. Edwin B. Firmage, *The Memoirs of Hugh B. Brown* (Salt Lake City: Signature Books, 1988), 30.

38. John Mills Whitaker, *Efforts of the Church to Control Polygamy after the Manifesto* (Provo, Utah: BYU Press, n.d.), 2.

39. This was Heber J. Grant. Kenney, *Wilford Woodruff's Journal*, 7:431, 28 March 1887.

40. Ibid., 8:489–91, 20–26 March 1888.

41. "Annual Report of the Utah Commission" [1889], *Report of the Secretary of the Interior*, 3:180–81; Eugene Young, "Polygamy Is Reviving," *New York Herald*, 5 Feb. 1899; the account of Cannon's charisma in Gordon B. Hinckley, *James Henry Moyle: The Story of a Distinguished American and an Honored Churchman* (Salt Lake City: Deseret Book, 1951), 213; and Lyman's remarks in *Political Deliverance*, 17.

42. [Theodore Schroeder], "Sold to Republicans," *New-York Times*, 13 Feb. 1895.

43. "Report of the Governor of Utah," *Report of the Secretary of the Interior . . .* , 5 vols. (Washington, D.C.: G.P.O., 1890), 3:665.

44. Kenney, *Wilford Woodruff's Journal*, 8:489, 20 March 1888. As late as 1899, Apostle Heber J. Grant told fellow quorum members that he had overcome his hard feelings toward George Q. Cannon and could break bread with him. Rudger Clawson Diaries, 4 April 1899, Rudger Clawson Collection, University of Utah Library.

45. Ronald W. Walker, "The Presidential Succession of 1887" (Paper delivered before the Mormon History Association, Logan, Utah, 7 May 1988).

46. George Reynolds, in *Proceedings* 2:52.

47. "He was a gentle, earnest old man, patiently ingenuous and simpleminded, with a faith in the guidance of heaven that was only greater than my father's [George Q. Cannon] because it was unmixed with any earthly sagacity. He had the mind, and the appearance, of a country preacher, and even when he was 'on the underground' he used to do his daily 'stint' of farm labor, secretly, either at night or in the very early morning. He was a successful farmer (born in Connecticut), of a Yankee shrewdness and industry. He recognized that in order to get a crop of wheat, it was necessary to do something more than trust in the Lord. But in administering the affairs of the Church, he seemed to have no such sophistication.

"I can see him yet, at the meetings of the Presidency, opening his mild blue eyes in surprised horror at a report of some new danger threatening us. 'My conscience! My conscience!' he would cry. 'Is that so, brother!' When he was assured that it was so, he would say, resignedly: 'The Lord will look after us!' And then, after a silence, turning to his First Councillor, he would ask: 'What do you think we ought to do, Brother George Q.?'" Cannon and O'Higgins, *Under the Prophet in Utah*, 84–85. Also see the comments of Matthias F. Cowley in his *Wilford Woodruff, Fourth President of the Church of Jesus Christ of Latter-day Saints: History of His Life and Labors as Recorded in His Daily Journals . . .* (Salt Lake City: Deseret News, 1909), 594–95.

48. Lorenzo Snow to Messrs. Morris, Glauque, Barns, Badger, and Clawson, 30 Nov. 1896, as published in *Proceedings* 1:1023.

49. As reported in Abraham H. Cannon Diaries, 8 Dec. 1895.

50. L. John Nuttall Diaries, 25, 27, and 30 Sept. 1890.

51. Abraham H. Cannon Diaries, 2 Oct. 1890.

52. George Cannon, "General Conference," *DN*, 6 Oct. 1890.

53. Wilford Woodruff in ibid. Also see the editorial "'The Mormons Will Not Promise,'" *DN*, 29 Sept. 1890. Two days before conference, the *News* acknowledged the church's victory over those attempting to take away their voting rights by way of the Cullom-Struble bill, in "Not Yet," *DN*, 2 Oct. 1890. For questions at the time as to whether the Manifesto constituted a genuine departure from the past, see "Why the Devious Way?" *SLT*, 25 Sept. 1890; "That Manifesto," ibid., 27 Sept. 1890; "The Great Which Is It," ibid., 3 Oct. 1890.

54. Abraham H. Cannon Diaries, 5 Oct. 1890. The *Tribune* contended that it was John T. Caine who nudged President Woodruff to write the Manifesto in the first place. "A Frantic Mormon Lobby," *SLT*, 26 Sept. 1890.

55. Ibid., 6 Oct. 1890; "General Conference," *DN*, 6 Oct. 1890; *President Woodruff's MANIFESTO: Proceedings at the Semi-Annual General Conference of the Church of Jesus Christ of Latter-day Saints, Monday Forenoon, October 6, 1890* ([Salt Lake City, 1890]); Whitney, *History of Utah*, 3:745–46. For the original formulation of the Articles of Faith, see Joseph Smith's 1841 letter to John Wentworth, in "Church History," *Times and Seasons* 3 (1 March 1842): 709–10.

56. "General Conference," *DN*, 6 Oct. 1890; Whitney, *History of Utah*, 3:744; Brigham Young, [Jr.], "Shall the Mormon Question Be Revived," *Harper's* 43 (16 Dec. 1899): 3; "Official Statement from the First Presidency . . . ," 17 June 1933, *Messages* 5:324; Joseph Fielding Smith, *Essentials in Church History*, rev. ed. (Salt Lake City: Deseret Book, 1971), 495. "Near unanimous" claims are found in *CHC* 6:222; Hyrum M. Smith and Janne M. Sjodahl, eds., *The Doctrine and Covenants Containing Revelations Given to Joseph Smith, Jr., the Prophet, with an Introduction and Historical and Exegetical Notes*, rev. ed. (Salt Lake City: Deseret Book, 1957), 836.

57. See the statement of William Gibson that he voted against the Manifesto, in "Polygamous Issues," *DN*, 28 March 1896.

58. Brigham H. Roberts, as quoted from a diary entry by Roberts on 10 Feb. 1893, in Walker, "B. H. Roberts and the Woodruff Manifesto," 365.

59. Quinn, "New Plural Marriages," 48.

60. From the beginning of its reporting on the Manifesto, the *Tribune* was consistently sarcastic, never passing an opportunity to poke fun at or denigrate what Woodruff had done. In its account of the vote, it said only that the mood in the Tabernacle was one of "gloom," that someone in the gallery called for a second reading of the resolution to approve the document, and that after the vote George Q. Cannon said the resolution had "carried." See "The Address Is Endorsed," *SLT*, 7 Oct. 1890.

61. Marriner Wood Merrill Diaries, 6 Oct. 1890, Church Archives. Abra-

ham Cannon said only that "the vote was unanimous." Abraham H. Cannon Diaries, 6 Oct. 1890.

62. Anthony W. Ivins Collection, box 7, fd. 10, p. 9, UHi. Also see George Q. Cannon's comment a year later that, while he knew many had shed tears on the occasion, he was pleased with the "unanimity" displayed by the vote. "Remarks . . . ," *DN,* 14 Nov. 1891.

63. D. Michael Quinn, "From Sacred Grove to Sacral Power Structure," *Dialogue* 17 (Summer 1984): 16.

64. Joseph F. Smith's remark is found in *Proceedings* 1:97, 98. It was Gaylon Loray Caldwell, characterizing Mormonism as a "theo-democracy," who said that few members have witnessed a formal dissent in church gatherings. "Mormon Conceptions of Individual Rights and Political Obligation" (Ph.D. diss., Stanford University, 1952), 122, 123.

65. Orlando W. Powers, quoted in *Proceedings* 1:923.

66. J. M. Buckley, in ibid. 2:7.

67. Larson and Larson, *Diary of Charles Lowell Walker,* 2:544, 19 March 1881.

68. Angus M. Cannon, in *Proceedings* 1:778.

69. Juliaetta Bateman Jensen, *Little Gold Pieces: The Story of My Mormon Mother's Life* (Salt Lake City: Stanway, 1948), 129–30.

70. William Henry Gibbs, Sr., Diary, 6 Oct. 1890, Church Archives.

71. Abbie Hyde Cowley Diaries, 6 Oct. 1890, Church Archives.

72. Gibson Condie Diary, film, 108–9, Church Archives. Also see Horace Hall Cummings Autobiography, photoduplication of typewritten originals, fd. 2, Church Archives; Larson and Larson, *Diary of Charles Lowell Walker,* 2:720, 12 Oct. 1890; and the interview reported by Kimball Young, in his *Isn't One Wife Enough?* (New York: Henry Holt, 1954), 411.

73. Joseph Henry Dean Diaries, 6 Oct. 1890.

74. John Mills Whitaker Diaries, 6 Oct. 1890, typewritten transcription, John Mills Whitaker Papers, 1867–1963, University of Utah Library.

75. Lucy W. Kimball, quoted in *Reorganized Church of Jesus Christ of Latter Day Saints, Complainant. vs. Church of Christ . . . Complainant's Abstract . . .* (Lamoni, Iowa: Herald Publishing House, 1893), 375.

76. E.g., B. Harvey Allred, *A Leaf in Review of the Words and Acts of God and Man Relative to the Fullness of the Gospel,* 2d ed. rev. (Draper, Utah: Review & Preview, 1980), 196.

77. "Remarks by President George Q. Cannon and President Wilford Woodruff . . . ," *DN,* 11 Oct. 1890. The 1841 revelation referred to is *D&C* 124:49.

78. "Remarks by President George Q. Cannon and President Wilford Woodruff . . . ," *DN,* 11 Oct. 1890.

79. "Annual Report of the Utah Commission" [1890], 3:419.

80. Quinn, "New Plural Marriages," 46. Also see Endowment House Sealing Records, Special Collections, film #183402–25165, pt. 22, FHL.

81. Wilford Woodruff, in *D&C*, "Official Declaration—1" (1982 ed.). Both the commission and the governor accused Mormon leaders of continuing to urge the doctrine on their followers. "Annual Report of the Utah Commission" [1890], 3:414; "Report of the Governor of Utah" [1890], 3:661.

82. "Application for Amnesty," *DN*, 15 Feb. 1892; and "Amnesty Petition to the President [of the United States]," 19 Dec. 1891, *Messages* 3:230. For the *Tribune*'s version of the petition's history, see "True History of the Amnesty Proclamation," *SLT*, 6 Sept. 1899.

83. Endowment House Sealing Records, Special Collections film #183402–25165, pt. 22, FHL; and Quinn, who mistakenly and consistently identified Jespersen as "Jorgenson." "New Plural Marriages," 45, 46.

84. All of which was duly noted by *Tribune* writers. "The Manifesto," *SLT*, 2 Oct. 1890.

85. *Clawson v. United States*, 114 U.S. 477 (1885).

86. "That Manifesto," *SLT*, 26 Sept. 1890. For Harrison's comments, see James D. Richardson, comp., *A Compilation of the Messages and Papers of the Presidents*, 20 vols. (New York: Bureau of National Literature, 1897–1911), 11:118.

87. Charles W. Penrose, "Governor Thomas and the 'Declaration,'" *DN*, 30 Sept. 1890, and "Both Definite and Authoritative," *DN*, 3 Oct. 1890.

88. E.g., "What Shall the Mormon Church Do?" *DN*, 6 Sept. 1879; "The Only Consistent Course," *DN*, 23 April 1885; *JD* 26:225 (Erastus Snow/1885); Larson and Larson, *Diary of Charles Lowell Walker*, 2:646, 648, 7 and 21 May 1885.

89. Kenney, *Wilford Woodruff's Journal*, 8:337, 3 Oct. 1885; Abraham H. Cannon Journals, 26 Sept. 1890.

90. See Lyman's remarks and those of others, as recorded in Abraham H. Cannon Diaries, 30 Sept. and 1 Oct. 1890. Frank J. Cannon, a half-brother to Abraham H. Cannon, was deeply involved in Utah politics at the time of the Manifesto and in 1911 said he recalled meeting with President Woodruff just before the Manifesto was issued. He said the church president told him that it was intended to stop all polygamy, old as well as new. Cannon and O'Higgins, *Under the Prophet in Utah*, 100–102. Remarkable as Frank Cannon's memory was, he seems to have been in error here. At least one prominent Mormon historian accepted it as true, however. See Larson, *The "Americanization" of Utah*, 261–62, 265.

91. Merrill Diaries, 7 Oct. 1890; and Abraham H. Cannon Diaries, 7 Oct. 1890. Cf. the cleverly worded "The Mormons Will Not Promise," *DN*, 29 Sept. 1890.

92. Abraham H. Cannon Diaries, 14 Oct. 1890.

93. *Official Report of the Proceedings and Debates of the Convention Assembled at Salt Lake City on the Fourth Day of March, 1895, To Adopt a Constitution for the State of Utah*, 2 vols. (Salt Lake City: Star, 1898), 2:1738; *Proceedings* 1:153; 2:316–17, 679–80; Cannon and O'Higgins, *Under the Prophet in Utah*, 34;

Robert N. Baskin, *Reminiscences of Early Utah,* 245; Reed Smoot, "The Passing of Polygamy," *North American Review* 187 (Jan. 1908): 118–19. For allegations of Mormon misinterpretation of these agreements, see "True History of the Amnesty Proclamation," *SLT,* 6 Sept. 1899; and "The Case Is Made Up," ibid., 7 Sept. 1899.

94. The case is discussed in the Abraham H. Cannon Diaries, 9 April 1891.

95. "Annual Report of the Utah Commission" [1891], *Report of the Secretary of the Interior . . . ,* 5 vols. (Washington, D.C.: G.P.O., 1892), 3:426–28.

96. "Defending the 'Mormon,'" *Deseret Weekly,* 12 Sept. 1891; "A Sensible View," ibid., 26 Sept. 1891; "A Story-Telling Commissioner," ibid., 3 Oct. 1891; "On Utah," ibid., 10 Oct. 1891. For denials of Mormon removal to Mexico, see "'Mormon' Colonizers," ibid., 5 Sept. 1891; "'The Irrepressible Mormons,'" ibid., 19 Sept. 1891; "Mexico and the 'Mormons,'" ibid., 10 Oct. 1891.

97. "Committee Report," *Deseret Weekly,* 10 Oct. 1891.

98. *Late Corporation of the Church of Jesus Christ of Latter-day Saints v. United States,* 140 U.S. 665 (1890). Also see Firmage and Mangrum, *Zion in the Courts,* 257–59.

99. Abraham H. Cannon Diaries, 6, 20, and 22 Aug. 1891, respectively; Kenney, *Wilford Woodruff's Journal,* 9:165, 12 Oct. 1891.

100. The proceedings and testimony cited here are taken from "The Church Cases," *Deseret Weekly,* 24 Oct. 1891; and "The Escheated Property," *SLT,* 20 Oct. 1891.

101. Woodruff, quoted in the Abraham H. Cannon Diaries, 12 Nov. 1891.

102. "Remarks," *Deseret Weekly,* 14 Nov. 1891; and Merrill Diaries, 1 Nov. 1891.

103. "An Act to Punish Polygamy and Kindred Offenses," *Laws of the Territory of Utah* (1892), 30th sess., ch. 8, sec. 2:5–7.

104. The petition for amnesty submitted by church leaders in late 1891, significantly, did not explicitly pledge obedience to the unlawful cohabitation provisions of the law. "Amnesty Petition," 19 Dec. 1891, *Messages* 3:229–31. The grants of amnesty from presidents Benjamin F. Harrison and Grover Cleveland, however, did impose the requirement as a condition of forgiveness. See Proclamation no. 42, U.S., *Statutes at Large* 27:1058 (4 Jan. 1893), and Proclamation no. 14, U.S., *Statutes at Large* 28:1257 (25 Sept. 1894). For assistance given by prominent Gentiles in the preparation and presentation of the petition, see John Henry Smith Diaries, 22 Dec. 1891; "True History of the Amnesty Petition: An Open Letter from the *Tribune* to the Mormon People," *SLT,* 6 Sept. 1899; and Lyman, *Political Deliverance,* 189–90.

105. John W. Taylor, quoted in Abraham H. Cannon Diaries, 1 April 1892.

106. Heber J. Grant, in ibid., 11 and 12 Nov. 1891.

107. Heber J. Grant, in ibid., 1 April 1892.

108. See, e.g., Seymour B. Young, as affirmed by Hortense Young Ham-

mond, interviewed by Leonard R. Grover, 15 March 1980, POHP, 9–10; or George Q. Cannon, as reported by Clawson Y. Cannon, Sr., interviewed by Jerry D. Lee, 5, 7, 19, and 20 Feb. 1974, pp. 37–38, POHP.

109. Kenneth L. Cannon II, "Beyond the Manifesto: Polygamous Cohabitation among LDS General Authorities after 1890," *UHQ* 46 (Winter 1978): 24–36. See the parallel conclusion of Jessie L. Embry based on her survey of oral histories in "Families in Religion: Mormon Polygamy and Monogamy, Late Nineteenth and Early Twentieth Century" (Paper delivered before the Organization of American Historians, Reno, Nev., 26 March 1988). In the minds of some, failure to fully observe their plural covenants at this time was freighted with moral significance. Sarah Hendricks, whose father had two wives, recalled that "all the respectable men in the church that married for the principle kept their wives. It was those that were just in it for the lust that turned their wives away." Sarah Hendricks, interviewed by James Comish, 26 Jan. 1980, POHP, 9. Also see Orson R. Clark, interviewed by Leonard R. Grover, 20 Aug. 1980, p. 6, POHP. There is virtually no evidence to support the contention of one writer that most Mormon polygamists ceased living with their plural wives when the first Edmunds Act was passed in 1882. Paul E. Reimann, *Plural Marriage Limited* (Salt Lake City: Utah Printing, 1974), 130–32, 134–35.

110. Larson and Larson, *Diary of Charles Lowell Walker*, 2:728, 20 Oct. 1891; L. John Nuttall Diaries, 26 Oct. 1891; and "Fear Not for Zion," *Woman's Exponent* 20 (15 Nov. 1891): 76.

111. Matilda Ellen Pickton Teasdale to Elmina S. Taylor, 20 March 1893, Letters of Matilda Ellen Pickton Teasdale, 1892–93, Church Archives; Larson and Larson, *Diary of Charles Lowell Walker*, 2:755, 10 Jan. 1893; and Abraham H. Cannon Diaries, 27 Sept. 1894.

112. William Gibson, quoted in "Polygamous Issues," *DN*, 28 March 1896.

113. For examples, see *Autobiography of Lorena Eugenia Washburn Larsen* (Provo, Utah: Published by Her Children and BYU, 1962), 105–6, 110–11; the case of Amos Maycock and Mary Hurst in Sarah H. Jones, *The Life of Philip Hurst, 1836 to 1901, as He Lived It in England, Utah, and Mexico* (n.p., 1964), 7. This case was particularly sad because it was Mary's third marriage, each time as a plural wife. Her first husband died; the second divorced her; the third left her because of the Manifesto. Also see [William A. Moulton], "History of Mary J. Moulton," copy of typewritten manuscript, n.d., p. 19, Church Archives; Annie Clark Tanner, *A Mormon Mother: An Autobiography*, rev. ed. (Salt Lake City: Tanner Trust Fund and University of Utah Library, 1973), 236–37; the comments of Charles Walker in Larson and Larson, *Diary of Charles Lowell Walker*, 2:728, 20 Oct. 1891; Emma Burnham, as described by Guy C. Wilson, Jr., *Memories of a Venerable Father and Other Reminiscences* (Fullerton: California State University at Fullerton Oral History Program, 1988), 123–24; and the case of Joel Sixtus Eagar (Appendix II, #66) who, leaving his wife in 1893, made sure he took his recommend with him to ensure admittance to Mormon society elsewhere. Woodruff, Arizona R of M, 1891–96, FHL, 136.

114. See the recollection of Lorin "Dutch" Leavitt, interviewed by Leonard R. Grover, 3 Jan. 1980, p. 3, POHP.

115. *Autobiography of Andrew Janus Hansen, 1852–1932* (Provo, Utah: Andrew Janus Hansen Family Organization, 1969), 116–17.

116. For comment in the Mexican colonies, see Isaac Washington Pierce Diaries, 24 Dec. 1890, Church Archives. The 1899 discussions among apostles are noted in the Rudger Clawson Diaries, 23 Nov. and 30 Dec. 1899. Reed Smoot's remarks are in *Proceedings* 3:287, 294, 300. Also see the comments of George Reynolds, in ibid. 2:42, 51; those of Elias Smith, ibid. 2:840; and Richard W. Young, ibid. 2:968. Uncertainty about the Manifesto in regard to continued cohabitation is also remembered by the descendants of plural families. See, e.g., Pearl J. Augustus, interviewed by Jessie L. Embry, 1 June 1976, p. 7, POHP; and Albert L. Payne, interviewed by Jessie L. Embry, 8 June 1976, pp. 9–10, POHP. Years later, when the church achieved greater acceptance and had moved to a position of strong hostility toward plural marriage, the First Presidency admitted in an official statement that amnesty had been accepted "with the *definite* understanding that the *practice* of plural marriage was to be discontinued" (emphasis added). Moreover, the statement indicated, all members of the church were honor bound to be faithful to the agreement. "Official Statement," 17 June 1933, *Messages* 5:321, 330.

117. As reported in Abraham H. Cannon Diaries, 7 Oct. 1891.

118. William M. McCarty, in *Proceedings* 2:922.

119. "Official Declaration," *DN*, 14 Dec. 1889; *Messages* 3:183–87.

120. George Q. Cannon, *The History of the Mormons, Their Persecutions and Travels, by President George Q. Cannon. Also the Two Manifestoes of the Presidency of the Church of Jesus Christ of Latter-day Saints and Members of the Council of the Apostles.* (Salt Lake City: George Q. Cannon & Sons, 1891), 17–20.

121. "That Manifesto," *SLT*, 26 Sept. 1890; "That Manifesto," ibid., 27 Sept. 1890; "More Rubbish Concerning Polygamy," ibid., 1 Oct. 1890; "The Great Which Is It," ibid., 3 Oct. 1890. Also see comments by members of the Utah Commission in "Annual Report of the Utah Commission" [1891], 425–26.

122. "An Epistle from the First Presidency," 6 Oct. 1885, *Messages* 3:27, 32–33.

123. Collier, *Unpublished Revelations,* pt. 89:146–47; and "Revelation to President Wilford Woodruff, Sunday, Nov. 24th, 1889," *Messages* 3:175–76.

124. Joseph Weldon Bailey, quoted in *Proceedings* 1:554–57.

125. "Official Declaration," *DN*, 25 Sept. 1890.

126. For Reynolds's editorial role, see Quinn, "New Plural Marriages," 44–45.

127. George Reynolds, quoted in *Proceedings* 2:53.

128. Ibid. 2:53–54.

129. Brigham H. Roberts, quoted in ibid. 1:719, 721. Cf. Roberts in *CHC* 6:224–25.

130. "A Utah Commissioner's Perversions," *DN*, 1 Oct. 1890. There was

more in this tone during the next several days. Readers of the *News* were told that it was President Woodruff's manner to work by "persuasion, by counsel, by instruction." The declaration's language was the president's way of making his position known on a "timely" issue. "Both Definite and Authoritative," *DN*, 2 Oct. 1890; "They Will Never Be Satisfied," *DN*, 4 Oct. 1890; Charles Ellis, "Concerning Revelation," *DN*, 4 Oct. 1890. Also see "The 'Mormon' Perplexity," *Deseret News Weekly*, 4 Oct. 1890. Even after the conference, there was nothing said to give the impression that a divinely authorized alteration of affairs had occurred. See "The Recent Conference," *DN*, 8 Oct. 1890; and "Semi-Annual Conference," *Woman's Exponent* 19 (15 Oct. 1890): 68.

131. "Remarks . . . ," *Deseret Weekly*, 18 Oct. 1890.

132. "The Pronunciamento," *SLT*, 8 Oct. 1890; "The Results of the Action," ibid., 9 Oct. 1890; "Was It a Revelation?" ibid., 10 Oct. 1890. Also see Governor Arthur Thomas in "Local Government for the Territory of Utah," U.S. House, 52nd Cong., 1st sess., 1892, Report no. 943: 12.

133. "The Church Cases," *Deseret Weekly*, 24 Oct. 1891; "The Escheated Property," *SLT*, 20 Oct. 1891.

134. Kenney, *Wilford Woodruff's Journal*, 9:168–71, 25 Oct. 1891. Also see "Remarks . . . ," *DN*, 14 Nov. 1891.

135. Wilford Woodruff, quoted in "Remarks . . . ," *DN*, 14 Nov. 1891.

136. As reported by Senator Smoot's secretary, Carlos Ashby Badger Diaries, 19 Feb. 1905, Church Archives.

137. "Amnesty Petition," *Messages* 3:230.

138. For Woodruff's claims, see Abraham H. Cannon Diaries, 7 April 1892; Larson and Larson, *Diary of Charles Lowell Walker*, 2:743, 13 June 1892, 2:815, 13 April 1896. Perpetuation of this view is found in *Proceedings* 1:108 (Joseph F. Smith); ibid. 1:430 (Francis M. Lyman); ibid. 3:294–95 (Reed Smoot); John A. Widtsoe, "Was the 'Manifesto' Based on Revelation?" *Evidences and Reconciliations: Aids to Faith in a Modern Day* (Salt Lake City: Murray & Gee, 1943), 86, 89; Smith, *Essentials in Church History*, 494; Bruce R. McConkie, *Mormon Doctrine*, rev. ed. (Salt Lake City: Bookcraft, 1966), 578.

139. "Excerpts from Three Addresses by President Wilford Woodruff Regarding the Manifesto," *D&C* (1982), 292–93. Jan Shipps has concluded, "There is no question that, from a doctrinal standpoint, President Woodruff's Manifesto now has comparable status with the revelations in the Doctrine and Covenants." *Mormonism: The Story of a New Religious Tradition* (Urbana: University of Illinois Press, 1985), 114. As an illustration of fundamentalist views, see editorial, *Truth* 4 (Jan. 1939): 149.

140. Marriner Wood Merrill Diaries, 20 Aug. 1891. Also see Abraham H. Cannon Diaries, 20 Aug. 1891.

141. Thomas J. Rosser claimed that Penrose told a missionary conference in Bristol, England, in 1908 of his role in writing the Manifesto, saying that it was not a revelation but a contrivance to outsmart their enemies. Thomas J. Rosser to Robert C. Newson, 4 Aug. 1956, as printed in Robert C. Newson, *Is the Manifesto a Revelation?* (n.p., 1956), 6–8. Evidence for the Bristol con-

ference on the day Rosser said it was held, along with evidence that both Rosser and Penrose were present, is found in "Minutes of the Bristol Conference," *Mill. Star* 70 (28 May 1908): 348–50. Similar remarks were made by Penrose to Ada L. Shepherd. See Ada L. Shepherd statement, made before William J. Barrette, Notary Public, Salt Lake County, 7 Dec. 1912, printed in Oscar Franklyn Davis, *A World-Wide Survey of Present Day Mormonism as Made by a National Commission under the Direction of the National Reform Association and Presented to the Second World's Christian Citizenship Conference, Portland, Oregon, July 3d, 1913* (Pittsburgh, Pa.: National Reform Association, 1913), 13. And Apostle Matthias F. Cowley reported nearly the same remarks in 1911 when his polygamous activities were investigated by the Quorum of Apostles. *Trials.*

142. But see George Bartholomew Arbaugh, *Revelation in Mormonism: Its Character and Changing Forms* (Chicago: University of Chicago Press, 1932); William E. Berrett, *Teachings of the Doctrine and Covenants* (Salt Lake City: Deseret Book, 1956), 19–27; Donald Q. Cannon, Larry E. Dahl, and John W. Welch, "The Restoration of Major Doctrines through Joseph Smith: Godhead, Mankind, and the Creation," *Ensign* 19 (Jan. 1989): 27; Blake Ostler's "expansionist" theory, in his "Book of Mormon as a Modern Expansion of an Ancient Source," *Dialogue* 20 (Spring 1987): 66–123; and the developmental tracings in Thomas G. Alexander, "The Reconstruction of Mormon Doctrine: From Joseph Smith to Progressive Theology," *Sunstone* 5 (July-Aug. 1980): 24–33.

143. Thomas G. Alexander, "Wilford Woodruff and the Changing Nature of Mormon Religious Experience," *Church History* 45 (March 1976): 56–69. Also see Lorin K. Hansen, "Some Concepts of Divine Revelation," *Sunstone* 10 (May 1985): 51–57.

144. For the comment by Hyde and a similar observation by George Q. Cannon, see, respectively, Kenney, *Wilford Woodruff's Journal*, 5:255, 13 Dec. 1858; and *JD* 22:104 (1880). Brigham Young seems to have been close to the same thing when he said, "I don't profess to be such a Prophet as were Joseph Smith and Daniel; but I am a Yankee guesser." *JD* 5:77 (1857).

145. *JD* 18:142 (John Taylor/1877); and for Brigham Young's remark, see Kenney, *Wilford Woodruff's Journal*, 6:302, 4 Nov. 1866.

146. Wilford Woodruff, "Remarks," *Deseret Weekly*, 14 Nov. 1891.

147. Woodruff, in "Box Elder Stake Conference," ibid., 7 Nov. 1891, and "Remarks," ibid., 14 Nov. 1891.

148. Woodruff, in "The Church Cases," ibid., 24 Oct. 1891.

149. This by James Dunn, in his novel *Janet Dixon, The Plural Wife: A True Story of Mormon Polygamy* (Tooele, Utah: James Dunn, 1896), 50.

150. Kenney, *Wilford Woodruff's Journal*, 3:586, 20 Dec. 1850. The contextual importance of Woodruff's millennialism in connection with the Manifesto was emphasized in Alexander, "Wilford Woodruff," 64–66, 68–69, and referred to by James B. Allen and Glen M. Leonard, in *Story of the Latter-day Saints* (Salt Lake City: Deseret Book, 1976), 413.

151. Arthur L. Thomas, in "Report of the Governor of Utah" [1891],

Report of the Secretary of the Interior, 5 vols. (Washington, D.C.: GPO, 1892), 3:399–401; also see comments of the Secretary of the Interior, John W. Noble, in "Annual Report of the Secretary of the Interior," ibid. 1:cxiv.

152. "Judge Zane and the Manifesto," *DN,* 7 Oct. 1890; the statements in *Admission of Utah,* U.S., House, 53d Cong., 1st sess., 2 Nov. 1893, Report no. 162:4–5, 8; and Judge William M. McCarty, in *Proceedings* 2:918.

153. *Cope v. Cope,* 137 U.S. 682 (1890). See the commentary provided in Firmage and Mangrum, *Zion in the Courts,* 240–41.

154. "An Act to Punish Polygamy and Kindred Offenses," *Laws of the Territory of Utah (1892),* 30th sess., ch. 8, sec. 2, pp. 5–7.

155. See all of *Admission of Utah* and the enabling act, U.S., *Statutes at Large,* 27, ch. 138, sec. 19:112 (1894). For the work of non-Mormons in behalf of Utah statehood, see Edward Leo Lyman, "Isaac Trumbo and the Politics of Utah Statehood," *UHQ* 41 (Spring 1973): 128–49; and the same author's *Political Deliverance,* 185–254.

156. *Utah Constitution* (1895), Art. III, sec. 1; and *Official Report of the Proceedings and Debates of the Convention Assembled at Salt Lake City on the Fourth Day of March, 1895, to Adopt a Constitution for the State of Utah,* 2 vols. (Salt Lake City: Star, 1898), 2:1857, art. 3, sec. 1.

157. Charles William Penrose Diaries, 7 Jan. 1896, UHi.

158. Charles Frisbie Hoar, quoted in "The New Revelation," *SLT,* 9 Oct. 1890.

159. Arthur Thomas, "The Results of the Action," *SLT,* 20 Oct. 1890.

160. *Admission of Utah,* 20.

161. Anthony W. Ivins to Elizabeth Ashby Snow Ivins, 12 March 1895, Anthony W. Ivins Correspondence, box 2, fd. 12, Church Archives.

5

The Principle Continued Abroad and at Home

No better evidence for the power of Mormonism's commitment to plural marriage can be found than in authorizations given to continue it after 1890. While plural contractions were common in Mexico, they also occurred in Canada, albeit to a greatly reduced degree. Authorized ceremonies joining couples in polygamous relationships also took place in the United States. Despite the presumption of periodic slowing, as during the administration of Church President Lorenzo Snow (1898–1901), the approved performance of polygamous unions continued. The Manifesto of 1890, including President Woodruff's interpretation that it applied to Mormons throughout the world, did not mark a cessation anywhere of such unions performed by authorized representatives of the church.

Exploring expeditions into Mexico for the purpose of colonizing Great Basin Saints south of the United States border date from the mid-1870s. A mission under the direction of Apostle Moses Thatcher was established in Mexico City in 1879.[1] In the mid-1880s George Q. Cannon and President John Taylor hoped that removal of pluralists to Mexico would eliminate objections to statehood for Utah. Little urging was required. After convictions under the Edmunds Act commenced, there was a near stampede for the border. By 1890 three major communities, numbering hundreds of colonists, existed in Chihuahua. An additional six settlements appeared in the next two decades, including three in Sonora.[2]

Notwithstanding this was one of the largest colonization efforts undertaken by the church, Mormon spokesmen did what they could to diminish notice of the project. Every attempt was made to say as little as possible about it to outsiders. The church's official newspaper denied that anything like a large-scale movement to Mexico was happening. Mormon farmers were simply trying to improve their circumstances and were doing so only as individuals, it was said. All connection between the migration and polygamy was ignored or denied.[3]

Similar policies were followed by the colonists themselves. Apostle George Teasdale, who in 1889 succeeded Erastus Snow as the authority responsible for directing affairs in Mexico, appointed an official "entertainer of strangers" to monitor visitors. Colonists were instructed neither to associate nor to communicate with outsiders any more than necessary. Residents were asked to sign restrictive covenants agreeing not to sell property to non-Mormons. Plural wives were to identify themselves to strangers as single women, as sisters, or relatives visiting temporarily. W. Derby Johnson, Jr., bishop in Colonia Diaz, summarized in his diary the substance of talks to church members there: "Those who come to join us must have recommends. Parties in School House Mexicans must not be invited [n]or we go to their dances," and "Keep our mouths shut."[4]

Regardless of what was said to the press, everyone acquainted with the settlements knew plural marriage was the primary reason for the Mormon presence in northern Mexico. As the daughter of one colonist put it when asked why her father took a second wife south of the border: "because that's what they were down there for. That's what they told them. It was from the authorities. It was a commandment and they had been told to do that."[5] Those apostles chiefly involved were George Teasdale, Brigham Young, Jr., Matthias F. Cowley, and Abraham O. Woodruff. Others besides apostles possessed authority to perform such marriages, however. Alexander F. Macdonald, for example, acted in this role. Macdonald was an important Mormon official in Arizona before going to Mexico in 1885. From 1890 to 1895 he served as a counselor to George Teasdale, president of the Mexican Mission. Subsequently ordained a patriarch, Macdonald solemnized numbers of contractions for men and women wishing to enter polygamy.[6]

As news of these practices spread, Mormon leaders feared it might undermine credibility of the church in the United States. As early as April 1890 a directive was issued by the church president requiring any who went to Mexico for the purpose of entering polygamy to remain there—the new wife at the very least.[7] Even then, leaders sometimes displayed astonishing openness in the matter. The son of one Mormon polygamist recalled how Apostle Brigham Young, Jr., told bishops in Utah that if anyone in their wards wished to enter the principle they need only take a certain train to the Mexican-American border and "the brethren down there would marry them."[8]

In the months following presentation of the Manifesto in conference, several plural marriages authorized by the First Presidency were performed in Mexico. The polygamous contraction of Anson Bowen Call (Appendix II, #34) and his second wife, Harriet Cazier, in early December 1890 was one of them. A daughter by another wife, Mildred Call Hurst, said that her father told the story of this marriage many times. He had taken Harriet to the Logan Temple but was turned away because of the Manifesto. After a delay of some weeks, Call went to Salt Lake City for an interview with President Woodruff. He found the president at home, working in his front yard. Woodruff said he would approve the marriage but the couple must be willing to move to, and remain in, Mexico. Call was then given a letter authorizing the union. After arriving in Colonia Juarez, the couple went to the residence of Alexander F. Macdonald, where the ceremony was performed so peremptorily that Harriet had no opportunity even to change into the wedding dress she brought from Wyoming.[9]

Not every petitioner was successful, however, and in the first years after the Manifesto a pattern of uncertainty occurred. When Samuel F. Ball (Appendix II, #8), a Salt Lake City restauranteur, approached George Q. Cannon for permission to take a third wife in Mexico, Cannon refused the request. Ball was told that another church member, having received approval, returned from Mexico and allowed word of his marriage to circulate in Utah. Cannon decided, therefore, to temporarily withhold permission for such unions and so "make the brethren more appreciative of [their] . . . blessings."[10] Heber Bennion (Appendix II, #17), after returning from a mission for the church and becoming simultaneously engaged to two girls, was refused on the same grounds. Cannon told Bennion that church authorities were surprised by the number of intending couples "caught on the wing" by the Manifesto and regretted that, because of indiscretion, not all could be accommodated. Cannon told Bennion not to end his engagement to the women, however, as the "door might be opened again."[11] Later in the decade both Ball and Bennion took plural wives with the sanction of church officials.

Despite a broken pattern, plural unions continued to occur during the early 1890s. Most of them received official approval and were performed by men such as apostles George Teasdale and Brigham Young, Jr., as well as Macdonald. Most occurred in Mexico.[12] One of the contractions was discovered and became the subject of considerable attention at the time of the Smoot investigation a decade later.[13] This lay in the future, however. At the time, Saints south of the border were confident they were purposely set apart to keep the principle alive. Apostle Teasdale reassured them of his own unwavering allegiance, saying he believed the church was imperfect without plural marriage, and counseled Mormon men to ask the Lord for additional wives.[14]

The case of Joseph C. Bentley (Appendix II, #18) illustrates how such marriages came about. Sometime during 1891 Bentley, a resident of St. George, Utah, obtained his first wife's permission to take her cousin, Gladys Elizabeth Woodmansee, as a plural spouse. Bentley had business relations with Apostle Moses Thatcher and asked him to obtain permission for the marriage. Thatcher was unsuccessful, however, and Bentley was then referred by his former mission president, Samuel Roskelley, to Apostle Franklin D. Richards in Ogden, Utah. Richards treated Bentley with great kindness but, after repeated attempts, said he too was unable to obtain approval for the marriage. The only remaining possibility, Richards advised, was a personal meeting between Bentley and President Woodruff, which was arranged.[15] After learning Bentley's purpose, Woodruff turned him over to George Q. Cannon, who told young Bentley that he had been well acquainted with his father and that the only reason the elder Bentley had not been advanced in the church was because he had not taken additional wives. He also said that the First Presidency was pleased so many young men were yet interested in the principle. This notwithstanding, nothing could be done at the moment because of sensitivities associated with the statehood movement, and Bentley was asked to return in a week. This he did, but because of anxieties about discovery, Cannon postponed giving permission again.

In early 1892 Bentley settled his affairs in St. George and moved with his wife and three children to Colonia Juarez in Mexico. Gladys, the prospective second wife, was left behind. After arriving in Mexico, Bentley established himself in business and actively engaged in church affairs. After some time Gladys came to the colonies for a visit. Bentley then spoke to Alexander F. Macdonald, who said that, while he could not perform the marriage, Bentley might consider an alternative. We are uncertain what this involved, but Bentley said he preferred not to take Macdonald's advice. Gladys remained, however, and soon Apostle Teasdale informed the couple that he had received approval to perform the marriage. The ceremony took place in the autumn of 1894.[16] In 1901 Bentley was married to another plural wife, Mary Maud Taylor, by Apostle Matthias F. Cowley.[17]

In 1895 Apostle George Teasdale was replaced as the presiding authority in the Mexican colonies by Anthony W. Ivins. Although not a polygamist himself, Ivins was told he would be called on to perform such contractions for others. Like Teasdale and Macdonald, he was given authority to unite couples, both monogamously and polygamously, probably in the spring of 1896.[18] A form letter was agreed upon that, when presented to Ivins, would apprise him that the intending couple had obtained consent from an appropriate church official. Such letters were employed before the time of Ivins's administration in the colonies and were used much as a "recommend" is employed in the Mormon church today. Albeit, they were worded so that their real intent would have been unclear to a stranger.[19] A number of such letters have been found. Two of them, written by George Q. Cannon from Salt Lake City, are illustrative. Dated within about one month of each other, in late 1897 and early 1898, both are vague, requesting that Ivins give what aid he could to the bearer. These are certainly forms used and sent when Ivins was expected to seal a man and woman in a polygamous relationship.[20] Ivins's son, Heber Grant Ivins, said he believed his father always insisted on such authorizing letters and refused couples without them.[21]

An example of the procedure was provided in the testimony of Walter M. Wolfe at the time of the Smoot hearings. Wolfe told how one of his students at the Brigham Young Academy, Ovena Jorgensen, consented to become the plural wife of William C. Ockey (Appendix II, #146). Miss Jorgensen related how Ockey approached President Woodruff, who, as in the case of Joseph C. Bentley, refused to have anything to do with the marriage but referred them to George Q. Cannon. Cannon then gave the couple a letter addressed to Anthony W. Ivins, who, when contacted in Mexico, performed the marriage there in the late summer of 1898.[22] Similarly, Joseph H. Dean (Appendix II, #61), a former mission president in Samoa, asked Cannon for permission to marry Amanda Anderson as a plural wife in 1897. Cannon consented and told Dean that when he was ready to go to Mexico he would provide him with the required papers. The necessary letter was prepared, and in the spring of 1898 the two were married by Ivins in Colonia Juarez, Mexico.[23]

While there were exceptions when Ivins acted without authorization from the leaders in Salt Lake City, as a rule he was strict in requiring such approval. The inconvenience and delay that this involved for those living in Mexico is shown in the experience of Miles A. Romney (Appendix II, #162). In March of 1898 Romney wrote to Apostle John Henry Smith asking for his assistance in obtaining permission to take another wife. He enclosed his temple recommend in the letter. By mid-May, having received no reply, he wrote Smith again. Failing yet to receive word, he wrote a third time in July. In all three letters Romney referred to a previous conversation with Smith during one of the apostle's visits to Mexico. It is clear that Smith had, on that occasion, instructed Romney to write to him on the matter and to include his recommend with the letter. Romney also referred to the need for Smith to authorize Anthony W. Ivins to perform the ceremony, confirming again the pattern followed in such things. Romney's request was finally granted and on 23 October 1898, in Colonia Juarez with Ivins officiating, he was married to Lilly Burrell as his second wife.[24]

John T. Whetten (Appendix II, #205), a bishop in Colonia Garcia, required more than a year to obtain consent. Whetten, already a polygamist, acquired the reputation of taking care of the widows in his ward by marrying them. In July of 1900 he hand-penciled a note to Alexander F. Macdonald, who was leaving on a journey to Salt Lake City. In his note Whetten explained that he had been taking care of "the Foutz woman" and her five children for a year. Many in the community believed he had already married her. There was, in Whetten's words, a round of "general gossip" in the ward concerning the arrangement. Whetten asked Macdonald to lay his petition before the president of the church, Lorenzo Snow, with a view to obtaining consent to marry her. Because of President Snow's general disapproval of such marriages, permission was slow in coming. The request was eventually granted, however, probably by First Presidency member Joseph F. Smith. Bishop Whetten was married to Lorainia Nelson Foutz by Alexander F. Macdonald on 18 October 1901. On 6 March 1903 he married another widow, Ludie Ellis Hassell, as a fourth wife.[25]

Although Ivins reportedly destroyed papers associated with his responsibilities in connection with post-Manifesto marriages to keep them from the Smoot investigation, considerable evidence survives. This includes not only the form letters described above but an actual record containing over forty polygamous marriages performed by Ivins between 1897 and 1904. This latter document, perhaps, substantiates Ivins's comment, made years later when he was a member of the First Presidency, that he had sealed more men and women into polygamy after the Woodruff Manifesto than anyone else in the church.[26] These materials, together with private memoirs, genealogical data, oral interviews, and findings generated by investigations such as the Smoot case, provide a rich and persuasive record of officially sanctioned Mormon polygamy in the post-Manifesto years. The increase of such contractions after Ivins's appointment is undoubtedly related to events in Utah. An obvious congruence existed between the renewed pace of such marriages and Utah's graduation to statehood.

It is commonly believed that polygamy was legal in Mexico. In the words of a recent writer: "LDS Church President John Taylor advised many of the polygamous families to migrate to Mexico where President Porfirio Diaz assured the church there were no laws against polygamy."[27] The presumed absence of conflict with Mexican law permitted an illusion of consistency with the Woodruff Manifesto while preserving the principle. Not only were formal bigamous contractions forbidden in Mexico, however, but privately solemnized polygamous marriages, as performed by the Mormons, fell athwart Mexican legal *intent* as well. This is clear from a review of legislation on the subject.

Mexican statutes relating to marriage were largely based on Spanish codes. Although the sources of Spanish law were of a mixed and sometimes conflicting nature, the influences of Roman and canon law combined to produce a vigorous condemnation of polygamy. It was looked upon as a heinous crime, *sumamente perniciosa*. Condign punishment was authorized, including branding, loss of property, and forced service in galleys of the Spanish navy.[28] Hostility to polygamy was rooted in ancient Spanish concern for unsullied lines of patriarchal descent. Additionally, those commenting on Spanish law justified their aversion by saying that it was unfair to women, reducing them to slaves; that some men would have several wives while others would have none; and, most importantly, that it was contrary to the tradition of the Christian monogamous home.[29]

Mexican national law was slow to take form due to repeated paroxysms of political disturbance. But even with secularization of the marriage ceremony in the late 1850s, there was no departure from the traditional Spanish commitment to matrimony as an ideal, "uniting one sole man to one sole woman."[30] Spanish compilations, with their opposition to polygamous marriage, still served as the basis for legal procedure everywhere in the republic.[31] Mexican federal codes not only reiterated Spanish opposition to polygamy but affirmed their allegiance to monogamous marriage as an obligation of high, sacramental importance by forbidding divorce except under narrowly defined circumstances.[32] Divorce, like polygamy, was believed to corrupt the family and, therewith, society.[33]

Mexican federal codes frequently doubled as the basis for law in the states. Chihuahua, for example, adopted the federal criminal code as its own in 1883, two years before Mormons began arriving in large numbers. Sonora, where additional Mormon colonies came to be located, contrived a document more closely adapted to its particular needs in 1884. Both states developed new penal codes of their own in 1897 and 1909, respectively. And both included absolute prohibitions against *bigamia* or *matrimonio doble*—that is, against formally contracted plural marriages.[34]

As the products of private religious ceremonies, however, Mormon plural arrangements were not, strictly speaking, in violation of Mexican law. This, unquestionably, is why so many assumed they could practice polygamy in Mexico with a peaceful conscience. The problem is that this practice confounded the purpose for which the Mexican statutes were drawn. This is illustrated by what the laws did with adultery. Determined to preserve the traditional monogamous household against such things as polygamy, Spanish and Mexican legal authors made allowances for sexual irregularities. They recognized that men were likely sometimes to lapse in sexual fidelity to their wives. Consequently, if discreet, men were permitted to consort with mistresses without calling into question the structural durability of their monogamous unions. Adultery, in the case of men, did not categorically constitute grounds for dishonor or divorce.[35] And formal provision was made for heritable rights by children born as the result of such alliances.[36] For men, as one authority put it, the act of adultery was not the crime of adultery. This assured that the monogamous home would remain formally intact, whatever personal crises arose to unsettle it.[37]

One finds here a circumstance not unlike that in the United States at the time of the crusade against polygamy, where, as we saw, national laws passed against the practice were largely indifferent to private morality.[38] Rather, the object of such legislation was to secure the monogamous home as a social ideal. With the Mormons, however, polygamy was a conscious philosophy—one they believed preferable to monogamy. With their extensive and socially approved polygamous arrangements, the Saints were at cross purposes with both United States and Mexican socio-legal intent. What was counted as tolerable error, in Mexico at least, was cultivated in the Mormon colonies as the ideal. It was not a matter of Mormons taking advantage of Mexican moral laxity as permitted by exceptions in their laws. By ignoring the purpose behind those exceptions, Mormons were substituting the precise order of marriage Mexican legal allowances were designed to prevent.

Even before the colonies were established, Mexicans feared that if Mormon immigration to Mexico should occur it would threaten Mexico's commitment to monogamy as the only acceptable configuration of formal family life.[39] After the first colonists arrived, Mexican writers warned that, because of polygamy, members of the sect violated Mexican laws and insulted Mexican moral custom.[40] Such comments were made for years, characterizing the Saints as fanatical, anti-social, anti-family, and disobedient to the laws.[41] As the editor of a prominent Mexican journal expressed it in the late 1880s, if Mormons in Mexico practiced polygamy, they were both criminal and unchristian.[42] In a United States case in 1886 involving Apostle Lorenzo Snow, Mormons were reminded that polygamy had been against the law in Mexico ever since they first entered Mexican territory in the late 1840s. And the *Salt Lake Tribune* told readers the same thing.[43]

Comments by Mormons themselves suggest that at least some were aware of what the laws of Mexico required. In 1885 John W. Young apprised two Mormon apostles that he was told by a Mexican congressman that statutes forbidding polygamy existed in Mexico and the Mormons needed to take care.[44] In 1891 Apostle Brigham Young, Jr., admitted to reporters that polygamy was against the law in Mexico and that Mormons living there were abiding by those laws "in every particular."[45] W. Derby Johnson, Jr., a Mormon bishop in Colonia Diaz and the husband of three living wives, told a journalist from the United States that polygamy was not being practiced by the colonists because it was against Mexican law.[46] In yet another interview Bishop Johnson reassured Mexican reporters that "there is neither intention nor possibility of introducing the practice of polygamy in Mexico. That is as impossible under Mexican laws as under those of the United States."[47] And in 1906 a Mormon from Colonia Dublan, another of the colonies, denied to a Mexican newspaper that any of the colonists were living in polygamy because, as he expressed it, although Mormons believed plural marriage to be a divine institution, it was not practiced because it was against the laws of both Mexico and the United States.[48]

To understand why Mexican authorities tolerated Mormon polygamy, despite its unlawfulness, we must explore an episode that took place shortly after the first Mormon camps were established in the Casas Grandes Valley in the spring of 1885. At that time local Mexican officials issued an order expelling Mormon colonists from the country.[49] While there were several reasons for this, at least one is likely to have been hostility toward the polygamous habits of the settlers.[50] Hoping to have the order rescinded, Mormon apostles Erastus Snow and Moses Thatcher traveled to Mexico City for talks with national officials. Once there, and with the assistance of Mission President Helaman Pratt as interpreter, they gained an audience with cabinet-level officers and with the president of the Republic, Porfirio Diaz.

We have in Pratt's diary the most complete summary of what the Mormon leaders were told over the several days they were in the capital. In the first place, the secretary of public works, Carlos Pacheco, directed that the expulsion order be canceled. A major part of Diaz's plans for developing the nation's economy involved the establishment of foreign colonists on Mexican soil, especially on arid lands of the northern provinces. The Mormon reputation for being good farmers filled the prescription Mexican leaders built into laws governing colonization. The Saints were assured they could remain.[51]

According to Pratt, it was not until the third day, again in a meeting with Secretary Pacheco, that the subject of polygamy was discussed. The minister told the Mormon leaders that they could bring their plural wives and families to Mexico but they were to do it quietly. He indicated that he personally wished Mexico's laws could be changed. That not being possible, he made it clear that if attention were brought to the Saints' marriage practices, they would be vulnerable to legal action. He assured them, however, that monogamous Mormons need have no fear of persecution in Mexico. Pratt's final entry concerning this conversation was to paraphrase Secretary Pacheco as repeating that the Mormons and their plural families were welcome, they could come and colonize in peace, but they were to do it quietly.[52]

This interview is important for several reasons. In the first place, the meeting with Pacheco in which polygamy was discussed did not include President Diaz. It was more than a week after this occasion before the Mormons were introduced to the nation's president. And, when this occurred, Pratt's notes give no indication that anything at all was said about plural marriage.[53] This does not mean that the president would have opposed the Mormons on account of their polygamy. It is only that, contrary to later Mormon comments, there is no first-hand evidence that President Diaz personally gave them permission to ignore Mexican law. This is reinforced by remarks made to Anthony W. Ivins by George Q. Cannon when Ivins was instructed in the manner by which couples would be sent to him to be married in plural relationships. According to Ivins's son, Cannon said: "Now Brother Ivins, if you have occasion to meet Porfirio Diaz . . . we want you to tell him that we are NOT practicing polygamy in Mexico."[54]

Secondly, it is clear from Pacheco's advice that he knew Mormon family arrangements cut across Mexican legal intentions. This is why he repeatedly counseled them to be private and quiet about it. This is supported by a statement credited to Joseph F. Smith shortly after the Manifesto was drafted, in which he supposedly remarked: "There is a tacit understanding between the church and the Mexican government, that we may practice plural marriage but must outwardly appear to have but one wife."[55] We can also understand why officials of the Mexican government were among those to whom copies of the Manifesto were sent at the time of its issuance. Mormons needed to be seen as law-abiding in Mexico as well as the United States.[56]

It is also important to notice that Pratt's account of this conversation refers only to the safety colonists might feel in bringing already existing plural families to Mexico. Nothing of an equally explicit nature was said in connection with new plural marriages. The welcoming spirit of Mexican government officials may have led some to believe they had been given the right to marry new wives. But if this was the case, it was entirely inferential. Some years later Burton J. Hendrick, a non-Mormon journalist, claimed to have information that reinforces this view. Mexican officials, he said, gave the Mormon representatives to understand that they could bring already existing polygamous wives to Mexico but there were to be no new plural unions contracted on Mexican soil.[57]

The Pacheco interview and facts concerning Mexican law also help explain a question that has long troubled students of the Mormon experience with polygamy: why did Anthony W. Ivins never take additional wives of his own? Beyond performing the ceremony for others, including the plural marriage of his own daughter, Ivins was known to encourage some to enter the order.[58] Yet he stood apart, conspicuously so, from the practice in his own life. Not only did his son and daughter recall that family members were taunted by neighbor children, saying that their father's monogamy would keep them out of the celestial kingdom, but they remembered that apostles John W. Taylor and Matthias F. Cowley were especially insistent that Ivins embrace the principle.[59]

Many years later, when Heber J. Grant was president of the church, he was interviewed by Raymond Taylor for a biography of his father, the former apostle John W. Taylor. Grant disparaged the project, asking why anyone would want to write a history of one who stood against the church. As an instance, Grant said he remembered that apostles Taylor and Cowley "ganged-up" on Anthony W. Ivins in an effort to intimidate him to become a polygamist, telling him he could not advance in the hereafter unless he did. And, Grant commented to

Raymond Taylor, "you know that that is a lie!"[60] Grant seemed to have forgotten that he had earlier urged Ivins to do the same thing, telling him that unless he entered the principle the two were unlikely to associate in the celestial kingdom after death.[61]

Numbers of reasons have been given for Ivins's reluctance, including his mother's hostility toward the practice, pleadings by his wife, fear that if he became a pluralist he would have to remain indefinitely in Mexico, and personal indisposition.[62] While all of these may have been influences, it is equally probable that his role as official spokesman for the colonists would have been compromised had he been a polygamist. A reputation for respectful obedience to Mexican law was important for anyone dealing with the government as a formal representative of the colonies. This is supported by Melissa Wilson, a sister wife to Ivins's daughter. She claimed Ivins's wife, Elizabeth, told her that she and her husband were on the edge of entering polygamy before Ivins was called to preside over the Mexican settlements in 1895. But the First Presidency, Elizabeth said, wanted a monogamist as liaison in that position.[63]

What we know of negotiations between Mormon authorities and government leaders in Mexico, then, explains the subdued nature of Mormon statements concerning their settlements in Chihuahua and Sonora. Efforts to disguise the movement as inconsiderable and denials concerning the practice of polygamy not only comported with Mormon strategies of defense in the United States but also were in harmony with what they were advised to do by Mexican officials. We can also conclude that a good deal of myth developed suggesting that plural marriage in Mexico was legal. Rather, what the Mormons were doing was quite out of harmony with at least the purpose, if not the letter, of laws south of the border. And despite a long tradition asserting otherwise, both Mexican officials and Mormon leaders at the time knew it.

Latter-day Saint settlement in Alberta commenced in 1887, only two years after the Mormon entry into Mexico. In little more than a decade, seven Canadian settlements were founded, with others to follow in succeeding years. Most importantly, as with those who went to Mexico, the search for refuge from the crusade against polygamy in the United States constituted a major reason for the movement. As with the Mexican experience, leaders denied that Mormon interest in Canada had anything to do with plural marriage. Every effort was made to represent the migration north as inconsequential, as but the result of farmers looking about to improve their lot.[64] And as with the situation in Mexico, there has been misunderstanding about Canadian law. Some, for example, have said that prior to the Mormon entry anti-polygamy legislation did not exist in Canada.[65]

As with Mexico in its borrowings from Spain, Canada was strongly influenced by English legal practice and custom. Conformity to the British model was a conscious legislative policy in Canada. By the time of the Mormon arrival, not only had the British North American Act lodged the regulation of marriage throughout the Dominion with the central government but the Consolidation Act of 1869 reaffirmed English statutes prohibiting polygamy, precedents for which extended as far back as the seventeenth century.[66] Beyond this, in 1886, one year before Mormons began arriving in Alberta, the Parliament in Ottawa declared: "Every one who being married, marries any other person during the life of the former husband or wife, whether the second marriage takes place in Canada, or elsewhere, is guilty of felony, and liable to seven years' imprisonment."[67] In other words, the situation in Canada was the same as that in Mexico at the time of the Mormon arrival there in 1885 and in the United States prior to 1882. The question was whether unions arranged by the Mormons in their own private ceremonies would be any more acceptable than the officially performed polygamous marriages condemned by Canada's laws.

Canadian critics quickly focused on the issue.[68] Due to this and because of their experience in the United States, where, after 1882, laws were changed to comprehend private contractions, Mormon leaders took steps to obviate such a development in Canada. Reminiscent of their experience with the Mexican government, church authorities decided to approach Canadian officials directly and ask for permission to bring their plural families into the Dominion. Mormon leaders undoubtedly hoped they would be given the same kind of blind they had obtained in Mexico. Canada, like Mexico, was anxious to develop its vast lands in the central and western parts of the nation. Perhaps, as in Mexico, the prospect of establishing a hardy population of Mormon farmers in those regions would persuade government leaders to ignore the intent of anti-polygamy laws.

With these objects in mind, a special delegation including apostles Francis M. Lyman and John W. Taylor traveled to Ottawa in early November 1888 to obtain whatever concessions possible. Lyman and Taylor brought special credentials to the assignment because they had been closely advised on the meetings held by Snow, Thatcher, and Pratt with Secretary Pacheco in 1885. They had also spent time themselves in Mexico City discussing Mormon interests with cabinet-level ministers.[69] So far as their mission in Canada is concerned, we have a record of the experience in the diaries of Charles Ora Card, the presiding Mormon authority at Lee's Creek (later Cardston), who accompanied the two apostles to the Canadian capital.[70]

Upon arriving in Ottawa, the group obtained an appointment with Prime Minister Sir John Alexander Macdonald. After asking for the right to settle in Canada, Apostle Lyman made a special plea that Mormons be allowed to bring their plural families with them. Macdonald, keen to what it was the laws were drawn to do, asked if plural marriage as the Mormons practiced it was not the same as bigamy. That is, he was inquiring if multiple unions by the Latter-day Saints were not the kinds of households Canadian laws were intended to prevent. Lyman explained that there was a difference. Bigamy, as usually construed, involved deception of the women. With the Mormons, on the other hand, all gave their consent and there was no deceit. At this point, according to Card, the prime minister signaled a kind of understanding with his head and the conversation moved to other things. There is some evidence in Card's account that would suggest the Mormons interpreted this gesture as indicating approval for what they were asking.[71] It was, after all, the kind of thing— indirect consent, where nothing forthrightly illegal could later be alleged—that was looked for by the Mormons. It was very much the sort of approval that apostles Lyman and Taylor were told had been obtained from Mexican officials only three years before.

If, as hinted in his account, Card hoped Macdonald had semaphored approval on the question of plural marriage, he was incorrect. Reporting a year and a half later to Parliament on what was said in the interview, Macdonald claimed he was unequivocal in warning the delegation that, as Mormons, they were as welcome as Mohammedans. But in neither case would plural marriage be permitted. Whatever their religion, he said, "they must obey the laws of Canada." This was confirmed later by Apostle Lyman when he told fellow apostles that Macdonald had made it clear the Saints could look for protection under the law, so far as the law would permit, but that no settler would be allowed to live in Canada with more than one wife. Beyond this, in meetings with other government ministers, the Mormon delegation was again refused their request. Whatever a technical reading of the statutes might permit, the government was unwilling to temporize with the historical commitment to monogamy those laws were designed to protect.[72]

The privilege of engaging in plural marriage in Canada was not the only request made by the Mormons in Ottawa. They were also interested in such things as water rights, import duties, and postal service. But anxiety over the reception Canadians were likely to give plural marriage remained the major reason for their trip. Before leaving the capital, they prepared a written petition containing, once more, a prayer for immunity from prosecution and freedom to bring their plural families to Canada. Again, the request was denied.[73] Equally disappointing, newspapers soon got word of their discussions and began drumming on "Mormon importunity." That the new settlers would request special treatment in connection with the suspension of duties on farm machinery brought from south of the border was bad enough, but to ask for permission to practice polygamy was nothing less than "audacious." Badly as Canada needed settlers, the Mormons, it was stated, would be worse than no settlers at all.[74]

Not only did the Mormons fail with their petitions and suffer the attentions of a critical press but a later report by the Mounted Police indicated certain knowledge that polygamy was being practiced in Mormon villages. This led to demands that, in the words of the *Winnipeg Free Press,* "the law in this country is that a man shall have but one wife at a time, and that law must be made to apply to Mormons as well as the Gentiles."[75] The result, as in the United States, was that Canada's 1886 anti-bigamy statute was amended to criminalize such unions when contracted "in any . . . manner or form whatsoever, and whether in a manner recognized by law as a binding form of marriage or not." This amendment was more particular and careful in its language than the Edmunds law in the United States from which it was borrowed. But to make sure there was no confusion, the enactment specifically stated that it was "persons commonly called Mormons" and their practice of "spiritual or plural marriage" with which it was concerned.[76] Finally, illustrating Canadian congruence with views in Mexico and the United States that it was the *appearance* of plural family life that must be repressed, provision was made for convictions with or without evidence of sexual relations between spouses.[77]

Despite efforts to imitate and profit from their experience, the Saints in Canada failed to obtain the license granted them in Mexico. With the amendment of Canadian law in 1890, identifying the private ceremonies employed in Mormon polygamous ritual as prohibited, Canadian intent was made explicit. Unlike in Mexico, where legal intent existed but was never reified, the Canadians moved to meet Mormon plural marriage in the same way it had been done in the United States with the Edmunds Act of 1882 and its strictures against "unlawful cohabitation."

The result was that, although plural family life existed in Canada after 1890, the number of plural families were fewer and the incidence of plural contractions much less frequent than elsewhere. Nevertheless, a study based chiefly on the polygamy oral history project at Brigham Young University and relevant genealogical records makes it clear that not only were numbers of those who first went to Canada practicing polygamists (often taking only a single family with them, however) but a significant proportion of those in leadership positions through the 1890s and beyond were also pluralists. Only a few polygamous marriages were actually performed in Canada. But the importance of the principle was spoken on in church meetings.[78] And Mormon missionaries affirmed before Canadian audiences that plurality was yet a Latter-day Saint doctrine. Such public statements in Canada provoked another bitter exchange between the Reorganized and Utah branches of the church shortly after 1900.[79] For more than a half-century, Canada's criminal code preserved both the ban on private, polygamous marriage and the reference to Mormons as the group with which the law was particularly concerned.[80]

A surprising number of post-Manifesto plural marriages occurred in the United States (see table 1). Less than four years after his 1890 declaration, President Wilford Woodruff told a meeting of the First Presidency and Quorum of Twelve Apostles that the day would soon arrive when good men would again be able to marry plural wives.[81] Commitment to the principle was such, however, that many—church authorities and lay members alike—felt it was unnecessary to wait. Apostles John Henry Smith and John W. Taylor sealed several couples in polygamy during a trip through Arizona in the late 1890s.[82] Ellen Steffensen Cannon (Appendix II, #37) told how she and others were secretly sealed as plural wives to their husbands in a special room dedicated for that purpose in the Constitution Building in Salt Lake City.[83] And Arthur William Hart (Appendix II, #85) of Preston, Idaho, whose plural marriage to Evadyna Henderson in 1903 was performed by Matthias F. Cowley, said the apostle told him he was instructed to choose a "few select people" to carry on the work. This marriage was later declared acceptable by Church President Harold B. Lee.[84]

When such cases were brought to light, the church commonly denied that an approved ceremony had occurred, branding the relationships as adulterous, shifting responsibility to participants. This seems to be what happened with Loren Harmer (Appendix II, #84). The husband of two wives, at age forty-three Harmer took a third, Ellen Anderson, on 19 November 1897. In spite of Harmer's standing as a

Table 1
Post-Manifesto Polygamous Marriages
Period Covered from October 6, 1890 – December 31, 1910

	1890	1891	1892	1893	1894	1895	1896	1897	1898	1899	1900	1901	1902	1903	1904	1905	1906	1907	1908	1909	1910	unk*	TOTALS
Canada		1	1	1	1					2	6	1		4	2	2	1	4		4	2		11
United States	1	1	1	1	2		2	5	5	2	6	15	4	7	8	1	1	4		4	2		72
Mexico	5		3	2	6	3	2	10	13	5	9	14	19	27	6		2	2	3	5			127
Unknown			1	1	2	1		1	1	4	6	3	5	2	3	1	1	2	3			10	52
TOTALS	6	2	6	4	11	4	4	16	19	11	21	33	28	40	19	4	4	6	3	9	2	10	262

*Marriages for which a specific date and place are unknown but which occured during this time period
Information based on data provided in Appendix II

bishop and member of the Springville, Utah, City Council, complaints about the relationship led to his arrest in the autumn of 1899. While Harmer had previously referred to Ellen as his plural wife, when brought before the court he pleaded guilty to adultery and was sentenced to a year's imprisonment.[85] This notwithstanding, church authorities were loath to bring moral charges. Beyond that, others testified publicly that Harmer's was a polygamous marriage.[86] Secretary to the First Presidency of the Church, George F. Gibbs, later testified that not only did Harmer marry Ellen Anderson in Mexico but when Harmer was arrested for adultery, President Lorenzo Snow expressed admiration for the man's willingness to take "his medicine."[87]

Perhaps the most poignant instance of this kind was that of David Eccles (Appendix II, #67) and Margaret Cullen Geddes. Margaret was a Scottish convert to the church who emigrated to Utah in 1884. That same year, at the age of nineteen, she married William S. Geddes as a plural wife. They moved to North Powder, Oregon, where Geddes was employed as a bookkeeper by David Eccles. In 1891 Geddes died. Seven years after the death of her husband, Mrs. Geddes was joined to David Eccles as his plural wife and on 21 May 1899 gave birth to a son whom they named Albert.[88]

Because the boy was born nearly a decade after the death of her husband and because her marriage to Eccles was secret, Margaret was charged by local Mormon authorities in Plain City, Utah, where she resided, with adultery. During the hearing before the bishopric, Margaret steadfastly refused to give the name of the child's father, despite threats of excommunication.[89] At this point, David Eccles contacted George F. Gibbs, who, in addition to being a personal friend, was secretary to the First Presidency of the church. Eccles asked Gibbs to request that President Lorenzo Snow order Mormon leaders in Plain City to withdraw their charges.[90] President Snow sent a letter to the Plain City bishopric telling them to accept Margaret's statements as sufficient, forgiving her with no further requirement. President Snow also advised that Eccles and Margaret move to Mexico. Thereupon, local church authorities dropped the case.[91]

Margaret Geddes's ordeal had only begun, however. Rumors persisted and reached the ears of the anti-Mormon sleuth Charles Mostyn Owen, ever alert to such things. She was then summoned as a witness at the time of the Reed Smoot investigation. As described at the Eccles estate trial years later, before Margaret departed for the hearings, David Eccles and others asked her to sully her own reputation, to do everything possible to conceal the real father's name. After tearful pleas that she not be made "a bad woman" in the eyes of her children, she was finally brought to agree she would do what she could.[92] On 13 December 1904 Margaret arrived in Washington, D.C., by train, entirely alone. Unaided, she found her way to the capitol building where the Smoot hearings were held and, unmet and uncared for, waited her turn as a witness. While admitting she had given birth to a son some years after Geddes's death, she refused to give the father's name. When asked if his name was "Echols," she answered, "No sir."[93] Margaret's testimony was a confession of adultery with no suggestion that Eccles, the church, or anyone else was responsible. When David Eccles appeared before the same committee six weeks later, while admitting that William Geddes had been one of his employees and that he had contributed to Margaret's support, he flatly denied he had married her, or anyone else, since the Manifesto.[94]

Margaret's humiliations were not yet at an end. After spending an evening with her in 1912, David Eccles died. When his estate was to be settled, no provision was found for either Margaret or her son. Margaret was aware that, as a plural wife, she had no legal claim on Eccles's considerable fortune. She did, however, expect something for Albert. After years of silence, Margaret Geddes decided to bring suit for a just distribution of the estate. In the course of the trial, she spared no one. She told how most of her adult life had been spent as a polygamous wife, shifting from place to place under assumed names to protect her husbands, William Geddes and David Eccles. She revealed that it was Apostle Marriner W. Merrill who married her to Eccles in August of 1898. She described the ceremony as brief and one in which the word *union* instead of *marriage* was employed so that, if later questioned, all could deny that a "marriage" had been performed. She also said Eccles promised that both she and Albert would be handsomely cared for in the event of his death. In the end, after a hard-fought case, Albert was declared a legal heir to the estate.[95]

The Eccles-Geddes plural marriage occurred less than a month before the death of President Wilford Woodruff. Lorenzo Snow, who succeeded Woodruff, seemed determined to diminish, if not halt, new plural marriages in the church. Although it is difficult to establish all that lay behind Snow's policies, some of the reasons can be identified. The autumn of 1898, for example, witnessed the entry of Brigham H. Roberts (Appendix II, #159) into the race for congressional office. Because Roberts was a polygamist, his candidacy provoked widespread criticism.[96] In the spring of 1899 Eugene Young, a grandson of Brigham Young and a journalist, published a lengthy article in the *New York Herald,* including an interview with First Presidency counselor George Q. Cannon. Cannon virtually admitted the renewal of polygamy, saying that Mexico and Canada were places where such unions might occur. The article described several polygamous marriages in the 1890s, including that of Brigham H. Roberts.[97] A longer publication, by the same writer, followed in the *North American Review*. Attacking the church for its political domination as well as for recommencing the practice of polygamy, Young said that his investigation found twenty cases of new polygamous marriages and that these could be multiplied "many-fold."[98] Although Apostle Brigham Young, Jr., the reporter's uncle, prepared what was expected to be a rebuttal, it was an unconvincing effort, only repeating statements made by the church for years, nowhere addressing the evidence adduced in Eugene Young's account.[99] The Roberts and Eugene Young developments undoubtedly contributed to Snow's resolution to adhere more closely to what was promised at the time of the Manifesto.

After conference in the autumn of 1898, Anthony W. Ivins told the Juarez Stake High Council that President Snow wanted no more plural marriages performed anywhere, including in Mexico.[100] A press release published in the New York *World* in late December of the same year quoted Snow as emphatically denying that the church was teaching or encouraging polygamy. He insisted there had been no new plural contractions since the Woodruff Manifesto. The furor surrounding Congressman-elect Brigham H. Roberts, he said, had nothing to do with Mormonism's official policies. "There have been no polygamous marriages since 1890. There is no movement in the Church for the revival of such unions."[101] When told that there were many widows and unmarried young women in the church who needed husbands, Snow said that God would recompense them for their faithful waiting in the next life.[102] In early 1900 Snow denied again that plural marriages were occurring with his permission, declaring that no member or officer had authority to perform the ceremony or to so marry himself.[103] When similar instructions were given to the twelve apostles in one of their meetings, George Q. Cannon moved they be accepted as the mind and will of the Lord.[104]

While Snow must have known his statements denying the performance of new plural marriages since the Manifesto were untrue, he does seem to have determined that closer agreement between public profession and private fact should prevail.[105] There was also the message Snow sent to Alexander F. Macdonald in Mexico, directing that he discontinue performing such marriages there at the risk of losing his fellowship in the church.[106]

Nevertheless, at least four apostles, including Brigham Young, Jr., took new plural wives during Snow's term as church president. Most of these, as well as polygamous marriages by other men, were performed within the nation's boundaries.[107] And Alexander F. Macdonald solemnized at least ten plural marriages between 1898 and 1903, the year of his death. The possibility that Snow vacillated in his resolution might be suggested by the fact that Apostle Heber J. Grant, before his departure for a mission to Japan in 1901, felt that the president intimated to him that he could take an additional wife. Although Grant eventually decided Snow had withdrawn his permission, there was the later testimony of Apostle Cowley that President Snow told him he would not interfere with marriages already approved by Wilford Woodruff and George Q. Cannon.[108] To have countenanced even these, however, impeaches Snow's public assurances to the contrary.

Snow's statements notwithstanding, plural marriages continued to be performed and actually increased to an extent greater than during the later years of Wilford Woodruff's tenure as church president (see graph on p. 317). Michael Quinn's research shows that Snow's counselors, Joseph F. Smith and George Q. Cannon, worked around the president, giving authorizations apart from Snow's knowledge or consent.[109] Cannon, for example, repeatedly urged Guy C. Wilson (Appendix II, #210) to enter polygamy during the Snow years. Eventually, in the spring of 1902, after Snow's death, Wilson was married by Anthony W. Ivins to a former student, Melissa Stevens, as his second living wife. A year later Ivins performed the ceremony again, sealing his own daughter, Anna Lowrie Ivins, to Wilson as wife number three.[110] But even before Snow's passing, Cannon's determination to keep the principle alive overpowered whatever was placed in its way. Hugh J. Cannon (Appendix II, #38) is remembered by family members to have been told by his father, George Q. Cannon, to take a plural wife during Lorenzo Snow's presidency, despite the objections and grief of the younger Cannon's wife.[111] And notwithstanding explicit refusal from President Snow, Counselor Joseph F. Smith authorized Benjamin Cluff (Appendix II, #53) to proceed with a plural marriage to Florence Reynolds. The ceremony was performed in Colonia Diaz by Seymour B. Young in the summer of 1900.[112]

It was not that Lorenzo Snow lost attachment to the principle. He only believed that times required greater circumspection, if not temporary suspension of the practice. In one meeting Snow told apostles that the Manifesto was one of the greatest sacrifices God had imposed on the Saints, but not to worry. They would yet have posterity as numerous as the stars in heaven.[113] There is also a clear impression in

Snow's statements that, more indelibly than before, a line was drawn between the policies of the church and the activities of individuals. Referring to polygamous cohabitation, the president said in late 1899 that while the church was doing everything it could to submit to the law of the land, it was left to individuals to decide about associating with their polygamous families.[114] In another statement to the press, Snow said: "If, therefore, any member disobeys the law, either as to polygamy or unlawful cohabitation, he must bear his own burden; or . . . be answerable to the tribunals of the land for his own action pertaining thereto."[115] Apostle Matthias F. Cowley later said that he was instructed not to tell other apostles of the authority given him to perform plural marriages.[116] This suggests a compartmentalization, if not privatization, within the Quorum of Twelve Apostles itself.

Finally, millennial expectations were an important part of President Snow's thinking. We referred to this as a theme affecting Mormon attitudes during the crusade as well as one that entered President Woodruff's calculations in connection with the Manifesto.[117] The period of the 1890s and shortly after was intense in its preoccupation with the subject. Elders sent on missions were told to warn people that destruction and judgment were imminent.[118] Charles Walker, in St. George, Utah, filled his diary in these years with commentary on the apocalyptic implication of everything from cyclones to train wrecks.[119] Dedication of the Salt Lake Temple in 1893 was looked upon as evidence that the Second Coming was near: some believed the edifice especially constructed to receive Christ. Apostle Anthon H. Lund was sent to Palestine in 1897 to make preparations for the establishment of an "eastern" Zion there.[120] At a celebration of President Woodruff's ninetieth birthday in 1897, before the largest crowd to fill the Tabernacle to that time, he declared many then living would see the Savior return. Similar promises were made on other occasions, marking Coxey's Army, the Spanish American War, fires and floods all as intimations that time was short and fearful events at the door.[121] In a statement reminiscent of family linkages emphasized during the Nauvoo period of the church, and illustrative perhaps of the excited atmosphere, faithful members were told at a solemn assembly in 1899 that some were literal descendants of the ancient apostles and of Jesus himself, "for he had seed, and in time they shall be known."[122]

Planning was undertaken for the long-awaited Mormon return to Missouri. At more than one meeting President Snow said that numbers of Saints then living would participate in the trek and that it would occur sooner than most believed.[123] Assuring others they would soon be eating and drinking with Jesus, President Snow gave his attention to the payment of tithes, linking them with purchase of Missouri properties where the Center Stake of Zion was to be established. Talk of this was so common that one Saint sent a letter pledging $100 to the costs of redeeming lands and erecting a temple structure there. Another was reported to be holding $1,000 in reserve for the same reason.[124] Apostle John W. Taylor told members of the Forest Dale Ward that Isaiah's prophecy about seven women taking hold of one man was about to be fulfilled. And George Q. Cannon said at a meeting of the First Presidency and apostles that the Savior would soon make himself known to the leaders, providing them with personal direction.[125] Apprehensions so pointed allowed Snow to look on forfeitures brought by enforcement of the Manifesto as trials of short duration.

The president's cautions notwithstanding, other leaders sometimes spoke with surprising boldness. At a San Pete conference in September 1899, George Q. Cannon, employing the arguments of earlier years, told members that while the rest of the world may not believe in "breeding," the Mormons did, and because of it unbelievers would be displaced by the Saints.[126] At a stake conference in northern Utah in the summer of 1900, Apostle Matthias F. Cowley spoke on plural marriage and referred to the "evils of monogamy."[127] Heber J. Grant allegedly said in the office of the *Salt Lake Herald* that "I am a law breaker; so is Bishop Whitney; so is B. H. Roberts. My wives have brought me only daughters. I propose to marry until I get wives who will bring me sons."[128] A few years later, at a fund-raising function at the University of Utah, Grant told of giving $50 for himself and an additional $50 for each of his two wives, expressing regret that he did not have a greater number so that he could contribute more.[129]

The most defiant of such remarks, however, were those made to New York reporter Annie Laurie during an interview with Grant, Charles W. Penrose, and Joseph F. Smith in 1899. The interview was given for the purpose of discussing the challenge to Brigham H. Roberts's right to political office. After stating that no one had any business telling the people of Utah whom to elect, polygamist or not, Grant went on to declare that the state could enact a statute legalizing polygamy if it wished. If it did so, he added, neither the United States president, Congress, nor "all the committees of clergymen and women in America could do anything about it."[130] When in 1900 word reached the First Presidency that some members accused others of adultery for living with their plural spouses, George Q. Cannon not only said the accusers were wrong but affirmed that plurality was yet a doctrine of the church and that new plural unions were permissible in lands where it was not against the law.[131] It was said that only those who lived in plural marriage would become gods.[132] At a quarterly conference in Colonia Juarez, Apostle Abraham O. Woodruff prophesied that "no year will ever pass, whether it be in this country [Mexico], in India, or wherever, from now until the coming of the Saviour, when children will not be born in plural marriage. And I make this prophecy in the name of Jesus Christ."[133]

For many Mormons, as we saw in connection with polygamous cohabitation, there was confusion as to what was and was not permissible. Numbers believed church authorities when they said all polygamy had come to an end. At the same time, evidence that new plural marriages were approved, combined with strong statements from their leaders supporting the principle, created doubt. For the most part, rumors concerning new plural marriages were looked upon by church members as falsehood or evil gossip. Polygamous marriage was increasingly viewed as an embarrassment, something many preferred not to discuss. This fracture-line in the attitudes of lay members was one of the most significant features of Mormon life in the years surrounding the turn of the century.

Despite all uncertainty and contradiction, however, the principle survived. As Apostle Marriner W. Merrill said in 1900, plural marriage had "come to stay in some form or another."[134] That such marriages were not confined to a scattering of dissenters at odds with the leadership of the church is exampled by apostles and First Presidency members who themselves took post-Manifesto wives. We turn to their cases next.

NOTES

Portions of this chapter appeared in B. Carmon Hardy, "Mormon Polygamy in Mexico and Canada: A Legal and Historiographical Review," in *The Mormon Presence in Canada,* ed. Brigham Y. Card et al. (Edmonton: University of Alberta Press, 1990), 186–209. It is by kind permission of the University of Alberta that those portions are reprinted here.

1. Thomas Cottam Romney, *The Mormon Colonies in Mexico* (Salt Lake City: Deseret Book, 1938), 37–59; B. Carmon Hardy, "The Mormon Colonies of Northern Mexico: A History, 1885–1912" (Ph.D. diss., Wayne State University, 1963), 40–66; F. LaMond Tullis, "Early Mormon Exploration and Missionary Activities in Mexico," *BYU Studies* 22 (Summer 1982): 289–310.

2. This information is based on conversations between Cannon and Taylor, as related in Cannon's diaries, according to Mark Wilcox Cannon, "Mor-

mon Issue in Congress, 1872–1882: Drawing on the Territorial Delegate George Q. Cannon" (Ph.D. diss., Harvard University, 1960), 208.

3. "The Mormons Are Not Gone Yet," *DN,* 4 Feb. 1885; "Expressions from the People," *DN,* 8 April 1885; "Expressions from the People," *DN,* 14 April 1885; "Conflicting Reports," *DN,* 25 Aug. 1890; "Not an Exodus," *Deseret Weekly,* 22 June 1889; "Not Moving to Mexico," ibid., 10 Jan. 1891. Additionally, see Henry Lunt, as quoted by Warner P. Sutton, United States Consul-General at Matamoros, Mexico, in "Mormons," Consular Reports, no. 97, U.S. Cong., *House Miscellaneous Documents,* 50th Cong., 1st sess., 1887–88, 23:576; the comments of John W. Young, in [New York] *Evening Sun,* 10 Nov. 1888; "President Woodruff: His Views on the Present Situation," *Woman's Exponent* 18 (Feb. 1890): 141; and clippings in JH, 14 Sept. 1885 and 7 Oct. 1888.

4. W. Derby Johnson, Jr., Diaries, 25 Dec. 1887 and 15 July 1888, in possession of Mrs. Beth Simper, Holbrook, Ariz. Also see Nelle Spilsbury Hatch, "George Teasdale," in *Stalwarts South of the Border,* comp. Nelle Spilsbury Hatch and B. Carmon Hardy (Anaheim, Calif.: privately printed, 1985), 683; Joel H. Martineau, "The Mormon Colonies in Mexico, 1876–1929," typewritten manuscript, pt. 4:6, 8, 19–20, 35, Church Archives; "Mary Eliza Tracy Allred," typewritten dictation to Emily Black, Collection of Mormon Biographies, box 9, fd. 11, #5, 6–7, Church Archives; Juarez Stake High Council Minutes, 1895–1917, 29 Sept. 1900 and 25 May 1901, Church Archives. The theme of self-enclosure is further pursued in B. Carmon Hardy, "Cultural 'Encystment' as a Cause of the Mormon Exodus from Mexico in 1912," *Pacific Historical Review* 39 (Nov. 1965): 439–54.

5. Asenath Skousen Walser, interviewed by Jessie L. Embry, 26 May 1976, p. 22, POHP. Also see the comment of Anthony W. Ivins, in Juarez Stake High Council Minutes Historical Record, 1895–1903, 21 Feb. 1896, Church Archives.

6. Andrew Jenson, comp., *Latter-day Saint Biographical Encyclopedia: A Compilation of Biographical Sketches of Prominent Men and Women in the Church of Jesus Christ of Latter-day Saints,* 4 vols. (Salt Lake City: Andrew Jenson History Co. and Deseret News, 1901–36), 1:557–58.

7. Abraham Hoagland Cannon Diaries, 10 April 1890 and 2 Nov. 1890, BYU Library.

8. William L. Wyatt, interviewed by Jessie L. Embry, 19 June 1976, p. 10, POHP.

9. Mildred Call Hurst, interviewed by Jessie L. Embry, 12 July 1976, pp. 12–13, POHP. Also see Anson Bowen Call, "Life Story of Anson Bowen Call," typewritten manuscript, 2–3, Nelle Spilsbury Hatch Collection, BYU Library. For other marriages at this time, see D. Michael Quinn, "LDS Church Authority and New Plural Marriages, 1890–1904," *Dialogue* 18 (Spring 1985): 57, 59–61.

10. Abraham H. Cannon Diaries, 2 Nov. 1890. Denied in 1890, Samuel Ball was polygamously married to Margaret O. Brown by Anthony W. Ivins

on 16 Sept. 1897. Ivins R of M, box 16, fd. 7, Anthony Woodward Ivins Collection, UHi. The Ivins record of marriages was given to the LDS Church Historical Department by Anthony W. Ivins's son Antoine after his father's death. Before the book was relinquished, another son, Stanley, copied from it onto some five typewritten pages the data for more than fifty couples married by his father in Mexico between 1897 and 1904, many but not all of whom appear to have been polygamous. There is another copy of the list in "Polygamy B. F. Johnson Letter," Stanley Snow Ivins Collection, box 8, fd. 10, UHi.

11. Heber Bennion to Heber J. Grant, 9 July 1929, copy, Brigham H. Roberts Letterbox 7, folder titled "polygamy," Church Archives. Contrary to Cannon's encouragement, Bennion broke the engagements and the women married other men.

12. See the pattern and sources described by Quinn, "New Plural Marriages," 57, 62.

13. This was the case of James F. Johnson (Appendix II, #107) and Clara Mabel Kennedy. At the hearings Clara identified Apostle Brigham Young, Jr., as the authority who performed the ceremony. *Proceedings* 1:389–91, 395–400, 403–6, 420–21, 422, 424. Although the relevant portions of Young's diary are missing, other accounts confirm, at the least, that he and others mentioned by Clara were in Colonia Juarez at the time she was married. See Juarez Sabbath School Minute Book, 1893–95, 20 May 1894, Church Archives; the report submitted by the committee on land matters in Mexico that met at Alexander F. Macdonald's home two weeks after the marriage, in box 2, Brigham Young, Jr., Collection, Church Archives; Diaz Ward Historical Records, 1885–1912, March 1894, Church Archives; "Diary of Winslow Farr, 1856–1899," typewritten copy, 18 May 1894, BYU Library; John Henry Smith Diaries, 20–21 March 1894, George A. Smith Family Papers, University of Utah Library, Salt Lake City.

14. Pacheco Ward Historical Records, 1892–1912, 24 July 1892, 18 Feb. 1894, 5 Aug. 1894, Church Archives.

15. This description is based on the account and compilation by a son, Joseph T. Bentley, in his *Life and Letters of Joseph Charles Bentley* (n.p., [1977]), 77–85.

16. Ibid.; Harold W. Bentley, interviewed by Tillman S. Boxell, 15 Aug. and 9 Sept. 1978, p. 7, POHP.

17. Joseph Charles Bentley FGS; Joseph Taylor Bentley, interviewed by Gordon Irving, June-July, 1976, 1, James Moyle Oral History Program, Church Archives.

18. Quinn indicates that Ivins was not commissioned to perform polygamous marriages until the spring of 1897. "New Plural Marriages," 79. It seems more likely that this occurred a year earlier. A guarded entry in the "Journal History of the Church" indicates that Ivins was given authority to seal for time and eternity "in a single marriage, persons unable to go to the temple." JH, 7 April 1896. While it is true that Ivins seems not to have performed a plural marriage until mid-1897, members of the Ivins family

remembered permission to solemnize such unions was granted by George Q. Cannon, on the occasion referred to above, in 1896. Heber Grant Ivins, interviewed by Victor W. Jorgensen, 18 July 1972, 32, Oral History Collection, California State University, Fullerton; Florence Ivins Hyde, interviewed by Victor W. Jorgensen, 18–19 Aug. 1972, transcript in private possession. Also see Anthony W. Ivins Journal, 1:252, 7 April 1896, Anthony Woodward Ivins Collection, box 5, fd. 3, UHi.

For Teasdale's replacement by Ivins, see Andrew Jenson, comp., "Juarez Stake Manuscript History and Historical Reports, 1895–," non-paginated, Church Archives; and Anthony Woodward Ivins Journal, 1:223–27, 9 Oct. 1895.

19. See the discussion provided in Quinn, "New Plural Marriages," 75–80.

20. George Q. Cannon to Anthony W. Ivins, 27 Dec. 1897, on letterhead of the First Presidency of the Church of Jesus Christ of Latter-day Saints, Anthony Woodward Ivins Collection, box 5, fd. 10, UHi; and George Q. Cannon to Anthony W. Ivins, 1 Feb. 1898, on letterhead of the Pioneer Electric Power Company of Utah [of which Cannon was an officer], 1 Feb. 1898, box 107, fd. 13, George A. Smith Family Papers. Also see the footnote in box 10, fd. 1, item 10, Anthony Woodward Ivins Collection, UHi.

21. Heber Grant Ivins, "Polygamy in Mexico as Practiced by the Mormon Church, 1895–1905," unpublished typescript, 11, University of Utah Library; and Anthony W. Ivins to Heber Grant Ivins, 7 March 1911, bound original letters from Anthony W. Ivins to Heber Grant Ivins, 1910–14, UHi.

22. Walter M. Wolfe, in *Proceedings* 4:11. Wolfe, in his testimony, mistakenly indicated the date of the Ockey-Jorgensen marriage to have been in 1897. For the actual date, 14 Sept. 1898, see William C. Ockey FGS; and Ivins R of M.

23. Joseph Henry Dean Diaries, 25, 26, and 28 Oct., 3 Dec. 1897, 23 April, 3 May, 10 May, 17 June 1898, Church Archives.

24. Miles A. Romney to Apostle John Henry Smith, 16 March, 14 May, and 15 July 1898, John Henry Smith Letterbooks, George A. Smith Family Papers; Ivins R of M; Miles Archibald Romney FGS.

25. John T. Whetten note, 12 July 1900, Alexander Finlay Macdonald Correspondence, Church Archives; John Thomas Whetten FGS; Bertha W. Shupe, "John Thomas Whetten," in *Stalwarts South of the Border*, comp. Hatch and Hardy, 756. It was Quinn who established the likely role of Joseph F. Smith in granting permission for the 1901 Whetten marriage. "New Plural Marriages," 88. Quinn gives 1900, rather than 1901, as the date of the marriage.

26. Reference to the destruction of Ivins's records has been made by two of Ivins's children: Florence Ivins Hyde interview; and Heber Grant Ivins, "Polygamy in Mexico," 6. Ivins's statement that he had married more into the principle since 1890 than anyone else was made to Mary Minerva Clark, plural wife of Edwin Turpin Bennion (Appendix II, #16), and reported by her son, Theodore C. Bennion, interviewed by Jessie L. Embry, 9 June 1976,

p. 2, POHP. As hinted in the text, this is questionable. Both Apostle Matthias F. Cowley and Alexander F. Macdonald may have solemnized more plural unions than Ivins.

27. Annette Carroll, "Mormons in Mexico: Refuge, Revolution, and Rejection," *Blue Mountain Shadows* 1 (Fall 1987): 6. As only a sample of the many who have taken this view, see the inference of such belief in Romney, *The Mormon Colonies*, 51–52, 267; and Kimball Young, *Isn't One Wife Enough?* (New York: Henry Holt, 1954), 419. Direct affirmations of the legality of polygamy in Mexico are found in Jerold A. Hilton, "Polygamy in Utah and Surrounding Area since the Manifesto of 1890" (M.A. thesis, BYU, 1965), 6, 13, 18; James B. Allen and Richard O. Cowan, *Mormonism in the Twentieth Century*, rev. ed. (Provo, Utah: BYU Press, 1969), 19; Kenneth W. Godfrey, "The Coming of the Manifesto," *Dialogue* 5 (Autumn 1970): 15; Annie R. Johnson, *Heartbeats of Colonia Diaz* (Mesa, Ariz.: privately published, 1972), 14; Davis Bitton, "Mormon Polygamy: A Review Article," *JMH* 4 (1977): 111; and Elva R. Shumway, interviewed by Leonard R. Grover, 24 April 1980, p. 8, POHP.

28. Canons of the church directly influenced compilations of European and New World nations, turning monogamy into what one scholar called the "Grundsatz" of Western Christian society. Erich Vogel, "Das Ehehindernis des Ehebruchs: Eine rechtsvergleichende Arbeit" (Diss., University of Heidelberg, 1928), 92. Catholic emphasis on monogamy was especially great in Spain. Joaquin Francisco Pacheco, *El Código penal concordado y comentado*, rev. ed., 4 vols. (Madrid: Manuel Tello, 1870), 3:226; Rafael Altamira y Crevea, *Cuestiones de historia del derecho y de legislación comparada*, 4 vols. (Barcelona: Herederos de Juan Gile, 1913), 2:98–100, sec. 463; Luis Fernández Clérigo, *El Derecho de familia en la legislación comparada* (Mexico: Union tipografica editorial Hispano-Americana, 1947), 37. For statutory examples of repeated sanctions against polygamy in Spanish law, see "De los adúlteros, y bígamos," with references to earlier codes, in *Novisima recopilación de las leyes de España*. . . . (Madrid, 1805–7), lib. 12, tít. 28, leyes 6–9.

29. See the note attached to Carlos III's castigation of bigamy in 1770: *Nov. recop.*, lib. 12, tít. 28, ley 10. Also see the discussion in J. Francisco Pacheco's commentaries on the Spanish legal reform of 1870, in his *El Código*, 3:21; the same in Pedro Gomez de la Serna, *Elementos del derecho civil y penal de España* . . . , rev. ed. by Juan Manuel Montalban (Madrid: Sanchez, 1877), 3:348–49, 364; and Joaquin Escriche, *Diccionario razonado de legislación y jurisprudencia*, rev. ed. (Paris: Ch. Bouret, 1888), 378, 1356.

30. Jorge Vera Estañol, "Juridical Evolution," in *Mexico: Its Social Evolution* . . . , ed. Justo Sierra, trans. G. Sintiñón, 2 vols. in 3 (Mexico: J. Ballescá, 1900–1904), 2:742.

31. D. Manuel Mateos Alarcon, *La Evolución del derecho civil Mexicano desde la independencia hasta nuestros dias* (Mexico: F. Díaz de Leon, 1911), 5–7; Toribio Esquivel Obregón, *Influencia de España y los Estados Unidos sobre México* (Madrid: Calleja, 1918), 22; Miguel S. Macedo, *Apuntes para la historia del*

derecho penal Mexicano (Mexico: "Cultura," 1931), 199–210, 272; Jose M. Ots y Capdequi, *Historia del derecho Español en America y del derecho indiano* (Madrid: Aguila, 1969), 30–36, 43, 45–48.

32. *Redacción del código civil de México que se contiene en las leyes Españolas . . . por . . . Vicente González Castro,* Vol. 1 (Guadalajara: Mario Melendez y Muñoz, 1839); lib. 1, tít. 4, cap. 2, sec. 1, arts. 60, 63, 99, 102; *Código civil del imperio Mexicano* (Mexico: M. Villanueva, 1866), lib. 1, tít. 4, cap. 6, arts. 185, 191; *Código civil del Distrito Federal y Territorio de Baja California* (Mexico: José Batiza, 1870), lib. 1, tít. 5, cap. 1, arts. 159, 163, secs. 4–5, 9; *Código penal para el Distrito Federal y Territorio de Baja California sobre delitos del fuero común, y para toda la republica sobre delitos contra la federación* (Mexico: Imprenta del gobierno, 1871), lib. 3, tít. 6, cap. 7, arts. 831, 832, 838; *Código civil del Distrito Federal y Territorio de la Baja California reformado en virtud de la autorización concedida al ejecutivo por decreto de 14 de Diciembre de 1883* (Mexico: Francisco Diaz de Leon, 1884), lib. 1, tít. 1, cap. 1, arts. 155, 159, sec. 9; cap. 6, art. 268. As in Spain, divorce was not legally possible in Mexico until the twentieth century. *Código civil* (Mexico, 1884), lib. 1, tít. 5, cap. 5, art. 226.

33. Alberto Gaxiola G., "Notas sobre la evolución juridico-social de la familia en México" (thesis, U.A. de México, 1936), 28.

34. *Código penal para el Distrito Federal y territorio de la Baja California . . .* (Chihuahua: Donato Miramontes, 1883); *Código penal del estado de Sonora* (Hermosillo: Imprento del gobierno, 1884). The later codes, with their penalties for polygamy, were *Código penal del estado libre y soberano de Chihuahua,* primera ed. oficial (Chihuahua: Imprente del gobierno, 1897), lib. 3, tít. 6, cap. 7, arts. 781–88; *Código penal del estado de Sonora* (Hermosillo: Imprenta del gobierno, 1909), lib. 3, tít. 6, cap. 7, arts. 724–27.

35. Spain: *Nov. recop.,* lib. 12, tít. 26, art. 1; and the commentaries of Pacheco, *El Código,* 4:292–94; Gomez de la Serna, *Elementos,* 3:343–44; and Rafael Altamira y Crevea, *Historia de España y de la civilización Española,* rev. ed., 4 vols. (Barcelona: Herederos de Juan Giles, 1913), 1:462–63, sec. 307.

Mexico: *Código penal* (1871), lib. 3, tít. 6, cap. 6, art. 821; *Código civil* (1884), lib. 1, tít. 5, cap. 5, art. 228. Also see Manuel Andrade, *Código civil del Distrito Federal y territorios reformado . . .* (Mexico: Botas é hijo, 1925), 41; Gaxiola G., "Notas," 27; and Francisco Gonzalez de la Vega, *Derecho penal Mexicanos los delitos,* 3 vols. (Mexico: Porrua, 1944–45), 3:232–33.

36. As regards "las barraganas" and "los hijos naturales" in Spain, see Gomez de la Serna, *Elementos,* 1:95, 308n; 2:75–82. In Mexico, see *Código civil* (1884), lib. 4, tít. 1, art. 3236; ibid., lib. 4, tít. 4, cap. 3, art. 3592; and the discussion by Don Luis Mendez et al., in *Código civil del Distrito Federal anotado y concordado con . . . otras códigos Mexicanos y extranjeros . . .* (Mexico: Escalante, 1871), 31; Mateos Alarcon, *La Evolución,* 22–41.

37. D. Yndalecio Sanchez et al., *Código penal para el Distrito Federal y Territorio de la Baja California . . . anotado y concordado* (Mexico: Ignacio Escalante, 1872), 11. Also see Pacheco, *El Código,* 3:108–9; Gomez de la Serna, *Elementos,* 1:308n; Escriche, *Diccionario,* 98; "Adulterio," in Antonio de Jesús Lozano,

Diccionario razonado de legislación y jurisprudencia Mexicanas . . . (México: J. Ballescá, 1905), 95–96; and Gonzalez de la Vega, *Derecho*, 3:228.

38. See above in chap. 2.

39. "Mormones," *El Monitor Republicano*, 5 Feb. 1880.

40. "Teorías mormonicas," *La Patria: Diario de México*, 30 July 1886; "Mormonism in Mexico," *Mexican Financier*, 31 Jan. 1885; editorial, ibid., 2 May 1885; editorial, ibid., 14 March 1885; and the summary of attitudes provided in Warner P. Sutton, "Mormons," 576.

41. "Chihuahua antes y hoy," *El Correo de Chihuahua*, 27 Feb. 1905; "La Poligamia en México," ibid., 30 Jan. 1906; "Doce mil mormones para México," *El Tiempo Diario Católico*, 14 Sept. 1906; the letter from the Mexican minister of public works in William Alexander Linn, *The Story of the Mormons: From the Date of Their Origin to the Year 1901* (New York: Macmillan, 1902), 614–15; and the citations and comments of Moisés González Navarro, *La Vida social: Historia moderna de México. El Porfiriato*, ed. Cosio Villegas et al., 8 vols. (Mexico: Editorial Hermes, 1948–65), 4:179–80.

42. As reported in Sutton, "Mormons," 576.

43. See *U.S. v. Snow*, 9 Pac. 697 (1886), at 699; and "More Democratic Insults," *SLT*, 14 Nov. 1895.

44. John W. Young to apostles Brigham Young, Jr., and Moses Thatcher, 21 May 1885, John W. Young Collection, Church Archives.

45. Brigham Young, Jr., in "The Mormons in Mexico," *Deseret Weekly*, 17 Jan. 1891. Also see the interview of Luis Hüller in the Chicago *Tribune*, reported in "The Colonies and Railroads in Mexico," *DN*, 2 Feb. 1891; and that with John W. Young, in "Chihuahua, Sonora and Sinaloa," *Mexican Financier*, 7 March 1891.

46. W. Derby Johnson, Jr., in "Information about Mexico," *Deseret Weekly*, 24 Jan. 1891.

47. "The Mormon Colonies," *Mexican Financier*, 7 Feb. 1891.

48. "La Poligamia en México," *El Correo de Chihuahua*, 30 Jan. 1906. Also see the comments about Mormon problems with inheritance under Mexican law, as made by Anthony W. Ivins, in "Historical Record, Juarez Stake, 1901–1906," 23 Feb. 1901, Church Archives; and the remarks of John Henry Smith, in "Juarez Stake Historical Record, 1907–1932," 7 March 1908, Church Archives.

49. A translated copy of the expulsion order is found in Jenson, "Juarez Stake Manuscript History," 17 March 1885.

50. "Mormones," *La Época*, 5 May 1885; "The Mexican Plan for Settling the Mormon Question," *Mexican Financier*, 2 May 1885; and "Against the Mormons," *Salt Lake Herald*, 27 Sept. 1885.

51. Helaman Pratt Diaries, 12 and 13 May 1885, Helaman Pratt Collection, Church Archives. For the Mexican policy governing colonization on vacant lands, see "Ley sobre colonización y deslinde de terrenos baldíos," in *Legislación Mexicana; ó, colleción completa de las disposiciones legislativas expedidas desde la independencia de la república . . . 1867–1910*, ed. oficial . . . , Vols. 1–34

(1876–1904) by Manuel Dublán and José Maria Lozano, Vols. 31–42 edited as "Colleción Legislativa" by Agustín Verdugo, A. Dublan, and A. Esteva, 42 vols. in 50 (Mexico: Imp. Gob., 1876–1912), 16:663–67, no. 8887, 15 Dec. 1883.

52. Pratt Diaries, 14 May 1885.

53. Ibid., 22 May 1885.

54. Heber Grant Ivins, "Polygamy in Mexico," 22; and Heber Grant Ivins, Jorgensen interview, 11.

55. Joseph F. Smith, in Joseph Henry Dean Diaries, 24 Sept. 1890.

56. See untitled notice in *Diario oficial,* no. 102, 27 Oct. 1890.

57. Burton J. Hendrick, "The Mormon Revival of Polygamy," *McClure's* 36 (Jan. 1911): 459–60. There may have been concern by Mexican officials in 1901 that Mormons were not abiding by the requirement, as suggested in a report by John Henry Smith to the twelve apostles, as recorded in Rudger Clawson Diaries, 11 July 1901, Rudger Clawson Collection, University of Utah Library.

58. For the marriage of Anna Lowrie Ivins to Guy C. Wilson in 1903, as Wilson's third living wife, see Guy Carlton Wilson FGS. For an instance of Ivins encouraging another to enter plurality, as told by the plural wife herself, see Sarah Ann Spilsbury Skousen, "Daniel Skousen," (Appendix II, #170) in Hatch and Hardy, *Stalwarts South of the Border,* 612. Also see the case of Joseph Jackson (Appendix II, #101) and Maria Jones Ray, as told in Harriet Viola Jackson Stevens, "Joseph Jackson," ibid., 319.

59. Heber Grant Ivins, "Polygamy in Mexico," 11; Heber Grant Ivins, Jorgensen interview, 10, 25, 28; Heber Grant Ivins, interviewed by Justin Stewart, 27 June 1971, 5, box 1, fd. 5, Heber Grant Ivins Collection, UHi; Florence Ivins Hyde interview.

60. Raymond Taylor to Samuel Taylor, 28 Feb. 1938, included with Samuel Taylor, "Interviews with Nettie [Janet] M. Taylor," BYU Library.

61. Harold Bentley said he possessed a letter from Heber J. Grant to Anthony W. Ivins, telling him he would not reach the highest kingdom in the hereafter unless he took another wife. Harold W. Bentley, interviewed by Tillman S. Boxell, 15 Aug. and 9 Sept. 1978, p. 65, POHP. Ivins's daughter Florence remembered the same event. Florence Ivins Hyde interview.

62. Harold W. Bentley, interviewed by Tillman S. Boxell, 20, 63, 64, 66; Guy C. Wilson, Jr., *Memories of a Venerable Father and Other Reminiscences* (Fullerton: Oral History Program, California State University, 1988), 22; Heber Grant Ivins, Jorgensen interview, 25.

63. Melissa Wilson, "Looking Backward, 1962–1902," typewritten manuscript, unnumbered insertion after page 2, Church Archives.

64. Those accounts on which this section chiefly relies for Mormon colonization in Canada are "Brief Account of the Early History of the Canadian Mission, 1887–1895," Alberta Temple Historical Record, typewritten manuscript, Church Archives; Carl Addington Dawson, *Group Settlement: Ethnic Communities in Western Canada,* Vol. 7, *Canadian Frontiers of Settlement* (Toron-

to: Macmillan, 1936), 175–272; Archie G. Wilcox, "Founding of the Mormon Community in Alberta" (M.A. thesis, University of Alberta, 1950); Lowry Nelson, *The Mormon Village: A Pattern and Technique of Land Settlement* (Salt Lake City: University of Utah Press, 1952), 219–71; Melvin S. Tagg et al., *A History of the Mormon Church in Canada* (Lethbridge: Lethbridge Herald, 1968); Lawrence B. Lee, "The Mormons Come to Canada, 1887–1902," *Pacific Northwest Quarterly* 59 (Jan. 1968): 11–22; L. A. Rosenvall, "The Transfer of Mormon Culture to Alberta," *American Review of Canadian Studies* 12 (Summer 1982): 51–63; and Donald G. Godfrey, "'Canada's Brigham Young': Charles Ora Card, Southern Alberta Pioneer," ibid. 18 (Summer 1988): 223–38. For Mormon efforts to mask the connection between removal to Canada and the anti-polygamy crusade in the United States, see "Not an Exodus," *Deseret Weekly*, 22 June 1889; "The 'Mormons' in Canada," *DN*, 26 Aug. 1889; "Mormons in Canada," *Deseret Weekly*, 7 Sept. 1889; "Mormons in Canada," ibid., 14 Dec. 1889; "Mormons in Canada," *DN*, 25 Nov. 1889; "The 'Mormons' in Canada," *Deseret Weekly*, 20 Dec. 1890.

65. See the inference of such views in *CHC* 6:259, 276n.15. Firmer allegations are found in Austin and Alta Fife, *Saints of Sage and Saddle* (Bloomington: Indiana University Press, 1956), 171; Hilton, "Polygamy in Utah," 6, 13, 18; Lee, "The Mormons Come to Canada," 16; Godfrey, "The Coming of the Manifesto," 15; J. Max Anderson, *The Polygamy Story: Fiction and Fact* (Salt Lake City: Publisher's Press, 1979), 122; Brian Champion, "The Press, Parliament and Polygamy: The Mormons Come to Canada," *Thetian* (1981): 24; idem, "Mormon Polygamy Parliamentary Comments, 1889–90," *Alberta History* 35 (Spring 1987): 11.

66. "An Acte to restrayne all psons from Marriage until their former Wyves and former Husbands be deade," 1 Jac. 1, ch. 11 (1603–4); 26 Geo. 11, ch. 33 (1740), and 9 Geo. IV, ch. 31, sec. 1 (1833). The Consolidation Act, with its condemnation of bigamy, is at 32–33 Victoria, ch. 20, sec. 58. The slightly older English prohibition is 24–25 Victoria, ch. 100, sec. 57, Imp. And the British North American Act, as it relates to marriage, is read at 30 Victoria, ch. 3, sec. 91.

67. "An Act Respecting Offenses Relating to the Law of Marriage," 49 Victoria, ch. 161, sec. 4. Even before this, the lieutenant-governor of the Northwest Territories, of which Alberta was a part, issued a decree prohibiting bigamous contractions. "An Ordinance Respecting Marriages," no. 9, 1878, in David Laird [Lieutenant-Governor], *Ordinances of the Northwest Territories, Passed in the Years 1878 and 1879* (Regina: Nicholas Flood Dawn, 1884), 45.

68. Untitled, *Edmonton Bulletin*, 3 Sept. 1887; untitled, ibid., 31 March 1888; and the comments made in Parliament by M. P. Doyon, in Canada, House of Commons, 28 *Debates*: 980, 3 April 1889. Some Mormons were reported to have told all who inquired that they had "eschewed polygamy." "Lee's Creek Mormons," *Calgary Tribune*, 14 Nov. 1888.

69. Jenson, "Juarez Stake Manuscript History," 5 June, 3 and 15 July, 13

Aug. 1885; Albert R. Lyman, *Biography: Francis Marion Lyman, 1840–1916, Apostle, 1880–1916* (Delta, Utah: Melvin A. Lyman, 1958), 108.

70. Charles Ora Card was the leading Mormon pioneer to the Alberta settlements. An overview focusing on Card's background and motivations is provided in John C. Lehr, "Polygamy, Patrimony, and Prophecy: The Mormon Colonization of Cardston," *Dialogue* 21 (Winter 1988): 114–21.

71. Charles Ora Card Diaries, 10 and 16 Nov. 1888, film, Church Archives.

72. Macdonald's remarks are found in Canada, House of Commons, 31 *Debates*: 3180, 10 April 1890; and those of Lyman in *Trials*. As Donald G. Godfrey has shown, Card confirmed this understanding in later correspondence with government officials. "'Canada's Brigham Young,'" 232–33. For the unsuccessful conversations with other cabinet ministers, see the Card Diaries, 14 Nov. 1888.

73. Card Diaries, 16 Nov. 1888. A printed copy of the petition is contained in Dawson, *Group Settlement*, 203–4.

74. "Mormon Importunity," *Calgary Tribune*, 14 Nov. 1888; "The Mormon Question," and "Ottawa," both in ibid., 21 Nov. 1888; "The Mormon Demands," *Lethbridge News*, 12 Dec. 1888; letters and editorials in ibid., 12 and 26 Dec. 1888.

75. Editorial, *Winnipeg Free Press*, 18 Oct. 1889. Also see "That Mormon Visit," *Macleod Gazette*, 31 Oct. 1889; untitled, ibid., 6 Feb. 1890; "Mormons in Canada," *Edmonton Bulletin*, 21 Dec. 1889; editorial, *Regina Leader*, 17 Feb. 1890; editorial, *Saskatchewan Herald*, 19 March 1890. A brief account of the surveillance conducted by the Northwest Mounted Police and their continuing suspicions of the Mormons is found in R. C. Macleod, *The NWMP and Law Enforcement, 1873–1905* (Toronto: University of Toronto Press, 1976), 155–56.

76. 53 Victoria, ch. 37, sec. 11, subsections a–d. This enactment was incorporated into Canada's first criminal code (55–56 Victoria, ch. 29) in the *Revised Statutes of Canada*, pt. 5, sec. 278, 104–5 (1892). Despite the Canadian statute's greater particularity, there is no doubt that it was inspired by the purpose, if not the language, of the Edmunds Act in the United States. See the comments of Sir John Thompson, minister of justice and author of the law, in Canada, House of Commons, 31 *Debates*: 3173, 10 April 1890; and James Crankshaw, *The Criminal Code of Canada and the Canada Evidence Act . . .*, rev. ed. (Toronto: Carswell, 1910), 349. A recent study makes it clear that the Mormon-Canadian apologist Anthony Maitland Stenhouse influenced the lawmakers' language by the arguments he presented. See Robert J. McCue, "Anthony Maitland Stenhouse, Bachelor 'Polygamist,'" *Dialogue* 23 (Spring 1990): 120–22. To further ensure that plural marriages as performed by the Mormons could not legally occur, an 1892 law was added prohibiting the "solemnization" of any marriage except by those officers properly authorized by the state. 55–56 Victoria, ch. 29, sec. 279; *Revised Statutes of Canada*, pt. 22, sec. 279, p. 288 (1892). That this was aimed directly at polygamous Mormons

from Utah, see W. J. Tremeear, *The Criminal Code and the Law of Criminal Evidence in Canada* . . . (Toronto: Canada Law Book Co., 1908), 255. The United States Congress placed a similar provision in the Edmunds-Tucker Act: U.S., *Statutes at Large*, vol. 24, ch. 397, sec. 9 (1887).

77. 55–56 Victoria, ch. 29, sec. 279; *Revised Statutes of Canada*, pt. 6, sec. 311, p. 255 (1892).

78. Jessie L. Embry, "Exiles for the Principle: LDS Polygamy in Canada," *Dialogue* 18 (Fall 1985): 108–16. Also see idem, "Two Legal Wives: Mormon Polygamy in Canada, the United States, and Mexico" (Paper presented at the Conference on the Mormon Presence in Canada, 8 May 1987, University of Alberta, Edmonton, Canada).

79. See the compilation, with commentary, of exchanges first appearing in the Toronto *Daily Star*, in Joseph F. Smith, Jr., *Blood Atonement and the Origin of Plural Marriage: A Discussion* (Salt Lake City: Deseret, 1905). There was also a brief sensation when monogamous marriages performed by Mormon elders in Canada in 1924 were invalidated. JH, 18 June and 1 July, 1924.

80. *Revised Statutes of Canada*, pt. 6, ch. 146, sec. 310, pp. 253–54; in the 1927 general revision of the criminal code, it was preserved in "Offenses against Conjugal Rights," *Revised Statutes of Canada*, pt. 6, sec. 310, pp. 404–5. Explicit reference to the Mormons was finally deleted from the law. 2–3 Elizabeth II, ch. 51, sec. 243 (1953–54).

81. Abraham Hoagland Cannon Diaries, 5 April 1894, BYU Library. Also see the remarks of President Woodruff's counselor, George Q. Cannon, at the same gathering. Ibid.

82. Smith was given the sealing authority on an earlier occasion, in 1891. John Mills Whitaker Journals, 7 Nov. 1891, University of Utah Library. For its use, see John Henry Smith Diaries, 16 Feb. 1894 and 9 March 1898; and the comments of John W. Taylor in *Trials*.

83. Ellen Cannon to Katherine C. Thomas, 28 Dec. 1953, typewritten copy in possession of the author.

84. See the testimonies and information provided by Hart's children: Marcus Fielding Hart, interviewed by Jessie L. Embry, 31 May 1976, p. 16, POHP; Adelbert Mickey Hart, interviewed by Leonard R. Grover, 5 Jan. 1980, p. 5, POHP; Elna Hart Palmer, interviewed by Leonard R. Grover, 2 Feb. 1980, pp. 14–16, POHP; Rhea Hart Grandy, interviewed by Leonard R. Grover, 16 Feb. 1980, pp. 9–11, POHP. Also see Evadyna's FGS, which says the ceremony took place in Salt Lake City.

85. *State of Utah v. Loren H. Harmer*, complaint dated 1 Nov. 1899, signed by Sheriff George A. Storrs, fourth judicial district, Utah County, criminal division, case no. 132; *Minute Book*, fourth judicial district, Utah County, vol. 9, 1898–1903, entry for 4 Dec. 1899, pp. 163, 167, 172. Also see "Charged with Adultery," *SLT*, 31 Oct. 1899; "Bishop Harmer's Case," ibid., 1 Nov. 1899.

86. "Bishop Harmer Guilty," *SLT*, 10 Dec. 1899. But cf. Record of the

High Council, Utah Stake, book G, 1889–1910, 12 Jan. 1900, Church Archives. For testimony that Harmer's relationship was a plural marriage, see *Proceedings* 1:501–5; 2:1009–1010; and the typewritten statement provided by George Sutherland on 25 Feb. 1903, before sub-committee no. 1 of the Committee on the Judiciary, 2–3, George Sutherland Papers, box 8, Library of Congress; and U.S. Senate, *Cong. Rec.,* 59th Cong., 2d sess., 1907, 41:944. For a case similar to that of Loren Harmer, see that of Peter Droubay (Appendix II, #63), *Proceedings* 2:717.

87. See testimony in the David Eccles estate case, as reported in "Swears Eccles Acknowledged Geddes Child," *SLT,* 3 July 1915.

88. Cleo G. Geddes, "The Eccles Case" (Report no. 2 in partial fulfillment of requirements for the Master of Science degree in History, plan B, Utah State University, Logan, Utah, 1969), 3–6. This thirty-page paper is good for information on the inheritance suit of Albert Eccles, son of Margaret Geddes, versus the estate of David Eccles. Also see *Proceedings* 2:103–5.

89. See the accounts and testimony provided on the Eccles estate case in "Mrs. Geddes Tells of Moving to Salt Lake," *Ogden Standard,* 29 June 1915; "David Eccles Planned to Bring Libel Suit against *Tribune,*" ibid., 30 June 1915; "Dr. J. M. Tanner Testifies in Eccles Case for Mrs. Geddes," ibid., 5 July 1915; and "Non-Suit Motion Denied by Court," *DN,* 7 July 1915.

90. "Gibbs Testifies in Eccles Case," *DN,* 2 July 1915; "Authorship of President Snow's Declaration," ibid., 2 July 1915; "Gibbs Appears as Witness in Eccles Trial," *Ogden Standard,* 3 July 1915.

91. Presidents Lorenzo Snow and George Q. Cannon to Bishop George W. Bramwell, 17 May 1900, Lorenzo Snow Letterbooks, Church Archives. A verbatim copy of the letter can also be read in "Gibbs Appears as Witness in Eccles Trial," *Ogden Standard,* 3 July 1915. For Margaret's testimony that, after the letter from the First Presidency, Plain City churchmen dropped charges, see "Eccles' Provision for Woman and Son" and "Mrs. Geddes Is Still on Stand," both in *DN,* 1 July 1915.

92. "Mrs. Geddes Tells the Story of Her Life," *SLT,* 23 June 1915.

93. Margaret Cullen Geddes, in *Proceedings* 2:105. Also see testimony by George F. Gibbs that Mrs. Geddes lied before the Senate committee to shield David Eccles, in "Swears Eccles Acknowledged Geddes Child," *SLT,* 3 July 1915.

94. *Proceedings* 3:449–50.

95. *Albert Geddes Eccles vs. David Eccles estate,* Second Judicial District Court, Weber County, Ogden, Utah, probate division, case 2169; Cleo Geddes, "Eccles Case," 9; Reed Smoot Diaries, 23 June 1915, BYU Library; "Jury Chosen in Eccles Estate Contest," *SLT,* 22 June 1915; "Mrs. Geddes Tells the Story of Her Life," ibid., 23 June 1915; "Eccles' Provision for Woman and Son," and "Mrs. Geddes Is Still on Stand," both in *DN,* 1 July 1915; "Eccles Heirs Have Dark Hair and Eyes," *SLT,* 9 July 1915;

96. See below in chap. 7.

97. Eugene Young, "Polygamy Is Reviving," *New York Herald*, 5 Feb. 1899.

98. Eugene Young, "Revival of the Mormon Problem," *North American Review* 168 (April 1899): 476–89.

99. Brigham Young, [Jr.], "Shall the Mormon Question Be Revived?" *Harper's* 43 (16 Dec. 1899): 3–4.

100. Anthony W. Ivins, in Juarez Stake High Council Minutes, 1895–1917, 19 Oct. 1898, Church Archives.

101. Lorenzo Snow, in "Mormon Head to the World," [New York] *World*, 30 Dec. 1898.

102. Lorenzo Snow, in "Discourse . . . ," *DN*, 3 June 1899.

103. Lorenzo Snow, in "Polygamy and Unlawful Cohabitation," *DN*, 8 Jan. 1900; "Abandon Polygamy: President Snow to Mormons," *New York Evening Journal*, 9 Jan. 1900. For once, Mormon fundamentalist and Mormon church authority agree on something concerning post-Manifesto polygamy. Mark E. Peterson and Gilbert A. Fulton both said that President Snow's public statements imposed restrictions only in the United States. Mark E. Peterson, *The Way of the Master* (Salt Lake City: Bookcraft, 1974), 53; Gilbert A. Fulton, *That Manifesto* (Kearns, Utah: Deseret Publishing Co., 1974), 184–85. Both are wrong. After reflecting on the command given Joseph Smith, Jr., by the angel with a drawn sword, Snow said in late 1899: "I do not wish to convey that plural marriages are now being contracted *in any place in the world by the Church of Jesus Christ of Latter-day Saints, but to the contrary*. I do most solemnly testify that during my administration as President of the Church no such marriages have been contracted, neither to my knowledge have any such marriages been contracted since the Manifesto was issued by President Woodruff" [emphasis added]. "Reminiscences of the Prophet Joseph Smith," *DN*, 23 Dec. 1899. Also see Brigham Young [Jr.], "Shall the Mormon Question Be Revived," 3, 4.

104. George Q. Cannon, in JH, 11 Jan. 1900.

105. Brigham Young, Jr., Diary, 1900–1902, 13 March 1901, New York Public Library, film in Church Archives.

106. Snow to Macdonald, recorded in John Henry Smith Diaries, 27 May 1901; and *Proceedings* 2:295–96. This interdiction seemed still to be in force in 1903, when Apostle John W. Taylor told the Mexican colonists that no one but Anthony W. Ivins had authority to perform plural marriages there at that time. Historical Record, Juarez Stake, book E, 1901–6, 7 March 1903, Church Archives.

107. Quinn, "New Plural Marriages," 72–73, 88–90.

108. *Trials*; Quinn, "New Plural Marriages," 73. Snow told Grant at a meeting of the Quorum of Twelve Apostles and First Presidency not to worry about the fact that he had only daughters and was unable to acquire another wife to remedy the circumstance. The Lord, he said, would make him "rich in due time." As quoted in Rudger Clawson Diaries, 11 July 1901, Rudger Clawson Collection. Some years later the secretary to the First Presidency George F. Gibbs testified under oath that while Snow "rigidly" adhered to a policy of refusing permission for polygamous marriages in the United States,

he permitted it in Mexico, insisting only that the new plural wife remain south of the border. He also testified that one of President Snow's public statements declaring against further polygamous unions in the church was written by Judge George W. Bartch, a non-Mormon, but signed by President Snow. "Swears Eccles Acknowledged Geddes Child," *SLT*, 3 July 1915.

109. Quinn, "New Plural Marriages," 71–73, 86–91.

110. Guy Carlton Wilson FGS; and B. Carmon Hardy, "Guy Carlton Wilson," in *Stalwarts South of the Border,* comp. Hatch and Hardy, 781–88.

111. Information provided by Guy C. Wilson, Jr., whose first wife, Constance Quale Cannon, was a daughter of Hugh J. and May Wilcken Cannon, 13 April 1984, Pasadena, Calif.

112. The best reconstruction of the Cluff affair is that of Quinn, "New Plural Marriages," 69–70, 86–87.

113. Lorenzo Snow, in Clawson Diaries, 8 July 1899.

114. "A Chat with President Snow," *DN*, 30 Dec. 1899.

115. Lorenzo Snow, in "Polygamy and Unlawful Cohabitation," *DN*, 8 Jan. 1900. This was reinforced by an editorial in the same issue. There it was stated that while there may be "derelictions" by "erring individuals," "the church teaches obedience to secular law. It does not advise nor encourage any species of lawlessness." "Prest. Snow's Declaration," *DN*, 8 Jan. 1900.

116. Matthias F. Cowley, in *Trials.*

117. See above in chap. 2 and in chap. 4. This author disagrees with Louis Reinwand's contention that Mormon thinking about the millennium became progressively diffuse in the decades between the end of the Civil War and the turn of the century. Louis G. Reinwand, "An Interpretive Study of Mormon Millennialism during the Nineteenth Century with Emphasis on Millennial Developments in Utah" (M.A. thesis, BYU, 1971), 138.

118. "Fulfillment of Prophecy," *DN*, 6 Aug. 1892.

119. As only a sampling, see A. Karl Larson and Katherine Miles Larson, eds., *Diary of Charles Lowell Walker,* 2 vols. (Logan: Utah State University Press, 1980), 2:742, 13 June 1892, 2:801, 27 Sept. 1895, 2:821, 13 July 1896, 2:831, 30 Dec. 1896, 2:835, 26 Feb. 1897, 2:842, 30 April 1897, 2:868, 9 April 1898.

120. Ibid., 2:860, 13 Dec. 1897; W. Derby Johnson, Jr., Diaries, 13 April 1893. The large significance that dedication of the Salt Lake Temple had in Mormon thinking at the time was explored by Brian H. Stuy in "The Salt Lake Temple Dedication of 1893," Sunstone Symposium, Pasadena, Calif., 3 March 1990. For reference to Lund's mission to Palestine, see JH, 29 Dec. 1897.

121. "Ninety Years of Age," *Deseret News Semi-Weekly,* 2 March 1897; Scott G. Kenney, ed., *Wilford Woodruff's Journal, 1833–98,* 9 vols. (Midvale, Utah: Signature Books, 1983–85), 9:300, 1 May 1894, 9:307, 24 June 1894, 9:404, 28 May 1896; "Discourse," *DN*, 7 May 1898. Also see Woodruff's remarks as reported in Larson and Larson, *Diary of Charles Lowell Walker,* 2:742, 13 June 1892, 2:868, 9 April 1898; and the sermons reported in Joseph W. Musser Diaries, 19 Sept. 1901, Church Archives; David Fisk Stout Diaries, 9 Feb. 1902, film, Church Archives; and Ivins Diaries, 9 March 1902. In a long epic

poem published in 1904, Orson F. Whitney indicated the time was near when slaves would yet rise and Indians vex the Gentiles, events men then living would see. Orson Ferguson Whitney, *Elias, An Epic of the Ages* (New York: Knickerbocker Press, 1904), 141, 143–44.

122. Ivins Diaries, 2 July 1899; Clawson Diaries, 2 July 1899. Also see Steven Faux, "Genetic Self Interest & Mormon Polygamy," *Sunstone* 8 (July-Aug. 1983): 39.

123. Lorenzo Snow, in "Discourse . . . ," *DN,* 3 June 1899; Clawson Diaries, 2 July 1899; Whitaker Journals, 7 Nov. 1900. At a conference in Mexico in 1899 Apostle Brigham Young, Jr., told bishops and others to prepare themselves for returning to Jackson County, Missouri. "Winslow Farr Diary, 1856–1899," 242–43, July 1899, typewritten copy, BYU Library.

124. Ivins Diaries, 2 July 1899 and 13 July 1901. For private pledges and sequestering of monies for the trek to Missouri, see George C. Naegle pledge letter, 1 Sept. 1903, Anthony Woodward Ivins Collection, box 10, fd. 5, UHi; and the remarks of Rudger Clawson reported in Musser Diaries, 18 May 1901. The relationship of President Snow's emphasis on the tithing principle and its revenues to "redeeming" the Missouri lands has been insufficiently appreciated. All was a part of intense millennialist expectations, especially among the hierarchy, at the time. See the sermons and remarks reported in Ivins Diaries, 22 July 1899, 6 April and 9 April 1900, 8 April 1901, and 7 April 1902; Clawson Diaries, 12 June 1899; Musser Diaries, 16 June and 13 July 1901, 7 April 1902; and Rudger Clawson, "Memoirs of the Life of Rudger Clawson Written by Himself," 387–92, typescript, 1926, UHi.

125. Musser Diaries, 15 Sept. 1901; and Clawson Diaries, 11 Jan. 1900, respectively.

126. This and similar comments by other authorities are reported in *Proceedings* 1:9. Also see Brigham H. Roberts, "Comment on Dr. Reiner's Letter," *Improvement Era* 1 (May 1898): 472, 475, 478, 482; remarks quoted from the wife of Apostle John Henry Smith in "A Chat with President Snow," *DN,* 30 Dec. 1899; and "What Luther Did Say," *DN,* 30 Jan. 1900.

127. Matthias F. Cowley, in Clawson Diaries, 25 Aug. 1900.

128. "That Awful Mouth Again," *SLT,* 8 Sept. 1899; and "The Grant Declaration," ibid., 9 Sept. 1899. Grant, who acquired something of a reputation for indiscretion, while presiding over the Mormon mission in Japan in 1901 also said that honorable men should be permitted to marry multiple wives. Ronald W. Walker, "Strangers in a Strange Land: Heber J. Grant and the Opening of the Japanese Mission" (Paper presented before the Pacific Coast Branch of the American Historical Association, 17 Aug. 1986, Honolulu, Hawaii).

129. "Heber J. Grant's Gift," *SLT,* 5 Nov. 1903. "Apostle Grant Gives Up $1,150," *DN,* 5 Nov. 1903. Grant's speech was the subject of commentary at the time of the Smoot investigation. *Proceedings* 1:932, 935, 2:401–2.

130. Heber J. Grant, quoted in "Church Officials Talk," *SLT,* 9 Jan. 1899.

131. George Q. Cannon, in JH, 16 Aug. 1900.

132. Musser Diaries, 8 July 1901; and the comments of bishopric member Newell K. Young, in Pacheco Ward History, Record E, 26 June 1904, Church Archives.

133. Abraham O. Woodruff, as quoted by the clerk of the conference, Joseph Charles Bentley, "Journal and Notes," 61, 18–19 Nov. 1900, Church Archives. Woodruff's prophecy found a precedent in, and may have been a repetition of, nearly identical remarks the previous year by Apostle Marriner W. Merrill. Clawson Diaries, 11 July 1899.

134. Marriner W. Merrill, as quoted in Clawson Diaries, 9 Jan. 1900.

6

Church Leaders and Post-Manifesto Polygamy

Apostle John W. Taylor (Appendix II, #191) was the first of the Quorum of Twelve Apostles to marry polygamously after the Manifesto. Ordained an apostle in 1884 and known for his candor, Taylor was also one of the quorum's most devoted advocates of the principle. On 10 October 1890—only four days after the Manifesto was presented to the church in conference—he espoused Janet Maria Woolley as his third wife. As Janet later recalled, her marriage to Taylor was solemnized by Apostle Francis M. Lyman as they drove around in a carriage in Salt Lake City's Liberty Park at night.[1]

This was one of several marriages performed either by or with the consent of general authorities in the months immediately following President Wilford Woodruff's famous declaration. It is likely that most of these, including Taylor's, were in the planning stages before the document was published. As already indicated, President George Q. Cannon told Heber Bennion that the authorities were surprised by the number of couples "caught on the wing" by the Woodruff statement.[2] Taylor was undoubtedly such an instance and one they believed should be allowed to proceed. In later genealogical records the family intentionally predated the marriage to 10 October 1889—a year before the Manifesto. Others would employ the same stratagem. Taylor's bride remembered the ruse, however, and discussed it with her son many years later, justifying the action by stating that "John said that marriage was consummated on engagement and not on ceremony; and at any rate this marriage date . . . came in blanket amnesty later."[3]

Taylor further increased the number of his wives to five when, on 29 August 1901, he married two half-sisters, Rhoda and Roxie Welling, both on the same day. Apostle Matthias F. Cowley performed the weddings at the Taylor home in Farmington, Utah. According to Janet, Taylor was given permission to marry the Welling girls by Joseph F. Smith, a counselor in the First Presidency. Smith conveyed approval, Janet said, by speaking in parables. There was no doubt of his intent, however. Concluding the discussion, she said, Smith patted Taylor on the back and said, "Be careful, John."[4] As an active defender of the doctrine, Taylor was reluctant to accept policies of retrenchment, including the 1890 Manifesto. He not only urged individuals in Canada and elsewhere to enter the principle after 1890 but also performed the ceremony for others.[5]

The role of fellow apostle Francis M. Lyman in contracting Taylor's marriage in the park requires comment. He was, perhaps, a logical choice for the task because he had joined Taylor to his second wife, Nellie Eva Todd, aboard the ship *Premier* on Puget Sound, 25 September 1888.[6] Yet Lyman later became one of the most outspoken of the apostles in opposing new polygamy. This attitude, however, developed gradually. Not only was he willing to perform Taylor's plural marriage within a week of the Manifesto's approval in conference but, at St. George in 1894, he upbraided elders there for allowing so many "golden opportunities" to have passed before the Manifesto was issued.[7] Finally, years later, when Lyman and others were attempting to bring such contractions under control, the *Salt Lake Tribune* recorded an encounter between the apostle and a stake president, Reuben Miller, who had entered such a marriage. While he was chastising Miller, the man's wife interrupted Lyman: "Don't you say a word! Don't you say a word! . . . You know very well that you proposed to me to become your plural wife since the manifesto, and I refused you! Don't you say a word against us! You proposed to me, and I have the black and white to show for it! You keep quiet!"[8] Without independent proof for such an episode, one cannot be certain that it happened as reported by the *Tribune*. As will later be shown, however, Lyman was not the only authority to display a selective memory when it came to post-Manifesto ardors.

Apostle Brigham Young, Jr., (Appendix II, #219) presents us with another example of post-Manifesto polygamous marriage by a high authority in the church. Young, who was ordained an apostle by his father in 1868, served as president of the Quorum of Twelve Apostles from 1901 until his death in 1903. Despite President Woodruff's insistence in the Manifesto that no such marriages had occurred, Young was one of several church members who took plural wives in the year before the Woodruff document was published.[9] He was married again in August of 1901 by Matthias F. Cowley.[10] Beyond this, Young performed a post-Manifesto plural contraction for at least one other couple and encouraged allegiance to the principle in his sermons.[11]

The case of Apostle Young is interesting because, at the time of the controversy surrounding the seating of Brigham H. Roberts in Congress, he publicly reaffirmed President Snow's denials regarding polygamy in the church. In his article in *Harper's* in late 1899, Young stated that the Woodruff Manifesto was binding on members of the church everywhere in the world, that the promises associated with it had been "scrupulously kept," and that an "estoppel" had been placed on all plural marriages since 1890.[12] Given the fact that he had performed at least one polygamous ceremony for others during that time period and may have been contemplating another plural marriage of his own, such affirmations strain credulity. They are more difficult to understand because of the reputation Young enjoyed as one who had "naught but contempt for all forms of hypocrisy or deceit," as one who, in the words of his half-sister, "would not gain the whole world were it to be secured through policy or subterfuge. He can keep still but must not deceive."[13]

Marriner W. Merrill (Appendix II, #132), who was ordained to the apostleship in 1889, also took a plural wife well after the Manifesto. The woman involved was Hilda Maria Erickson, a Swedish immigrant who was joined to Merrill by fellow apostle Matthias F. Cowley in the Logan Temple in 1901. Although Merrill denied to the Smoot investigating committee that he had married Hilda after 1890, evidence to the contrary is overwhelming.[14] He also performed the ceremony for his daughter, Hattie L. Merrill, who became the plural wife of John W. Barnett in 1894 and, as Quinn has put it, for "several [other] unambiguously polygamous" couples, after the Manifesto, in the Logan Temple.[15]

Abraham Owen Woodruff (Appendix II, #213), son of President Wilford Woodruff, also took a plural wife in those late years. Born on 23 November 1872 and ordained an apostle on 7 October 1897, Woodruff, at age twenty-four, was the youngest quorum member at the time. He married Helen May Winters as his first bride the same year he became an apostle. Then, in 1901, probably in January, he took eighteen-year-old Eliza Avery Clark as a plural wife. It has been said that Avery, living with her family in Wyoming, was already engaged to a young man when approached by Woodruff. He and Matthias F. Cowley spoke to her of the blessings she would receive by marrying the apostle. Avery was persuaded. She broke her engagement and married Woodruff, the ceremony being performed by Cowley in Preston, Idaho. Avery then moved to a Mormon community in Mexico, where her relationship with Woodruff was less likely to be discovered.[16] Hugh B. Brown remembered Woodruff, together with Apostle Hyrum M. Smith, a son of Joseph F. Smith, urging continued plural marriage among the Saints in Canada.[17] The strong comments Woodruff made in behalf of post-Manifesto polygamy, as well as his own polygamous marriage, must have been at least indirectly representative of the sentiments of his late father, President Wilford Woodruff.[18] In his biographical account of the apostle, Nephi L. Morris spoke of the extraordinary closeness that existed between the two. "They were," he said, "most confidential one toward the other."[19]

Matthias F. Cowley (Appendix II, #56) was perhaps the most frequently employed of the church's high leaders in performing polygamous marriages for his brethren. He was elevated to the apostleship in 1897, at the same conference as Abraham O. Woodruff. Cowley, whose maternal grandmother was a sister to Wilford Woodruff's first wife, was close to the Woodruff family and a biographer of the church president.[20] His first post-Manifesto plural wife was Harriet Bennion of Salt Lake City, a widow whom he married in 1899. When quorum members later asked who performed the ceremony, Cowley replied: "Brother [Marriner W.] Merrill put me under a solemn covenant binding me not to tell; I was married in the Logan Temple, so leave you to guess the rest."[21] Since Merrill was temple president at the time, the inference is clear that it was he who solemnized the marriage. Cowley's second post-Manifesto marriage was to Lenora Mary Taylor, whom he married in 1905 as his fourth and last wife. In this case the wedding occurred in Canada, the ceremony being performed by a local Mormon patriarch.[22]

Like others of his brethren, Cowley felt a strong loyalty to the tenet. In a talk given in Logan, Utah, in early 1901, he said none of the revelations given to the prophets were to be set aside. Every bearer of the priesthood was obliged to acquaint himself with such principles and teach them both by "example and precept." If there were some among them who taught disregard for any doctrine, "plural marriage and all," the apostle said they should "turn them out."[23] Cowley seems to have been instructed by George Q. Cannon of the church's First Presidency in most of the cases in which he officiated. As we will see, the exercise of this authority contributed to later conflicts between Cowley and other apostles.

Rudger Clawson (Appendix II, #51) is also likely to have married a plural wife after the Manifesto, in the late spring or summer of 1904. Born in 1857, he became one of Mormonism's best-known person-

alities because of an encounter with a Georgia mob that shot his missionary companion to death in 1879. Clawson survived Georgia, but
after an 1884 conviction for polygamous marriage, he served more
than three years in prison in Utah. Distinguished for valor in behalf of
the principle, Clawson was ordained an apostle on 10 October 1898 at
forty-one years of age.[24] His first and legal spouse, Florence Ann
Dinwoodey, had divorced him during his prison term. Lydia Spencer,
whom he married as a plural companion in 1883, remained for nineteen years his only wife. Then, in 1904, with Lydia's consent, he added
Pearl Udall to his family.[25]

Evidence for Clawson's marriage to Miss Udall arises first from a
guarded entry in his diaries that points to important conversations
with Pearl's father, David K. Udall (Appendix II, #201) of St. Johns,
Arizona, who married a plural wife himself in 1903. After returning
from an assignment in Arizona, Clawson told his apostolic colleagues
of expressions of interest by an unnamed young woman in the area
who, still committed to the principle, stated that she and others
"would much prefer to take a married man in the church who had
proved his faithfulness and integrity than to marry a single young
man who was untried."[26] In the same meeting at which Clawson reported these sentiments, after "freely" partaking of sacramental bread
and wine, Apostle Marriner W. Merrill testified to the divinity of the
principle. Speaking directly to younger members of the quorum
whom he identified by name—apostles Hyrum M. Smith, Abraham
O. Woodruff, and Clawson himself—Merrill advised them not to neglect opportunities to build up their kingdoms. If they wished exaltation and glory, they should lay the foundations "and not wait until old
age comes on."[27] There is no question Merrill was urging his junior
associates to think seriously about taking additional wives. And
Clawson was never indifferent to advice from ecclesiastical leaders.
Nephi Anderson once quoted him as saying that whatever success he
enjoyed in life was due to "a fixed and unyielding determination . . .
to seek and abide by counsel."[28]

Nine days after the comments by Apostle Merrill, Clawson spoke to
his wife on the subject and she gave consent for him to marry again.
In the following weeks correspondence and gifts passed between the
apostle and his intended, although in his diary accounts she is nowhere identified by name.[29] In May of 1904 Miss Udall traveled to
Salt Lake City, where she likely visited with Clawson and obtained her
temple endowments.[30] Following this ceremony, a ritual usually undertaken by young Mormon women shortly before marriage, the se-
quence of events becomes obscure. After conferring with Apostle

Merrill in Smithfield, Utah, in mid-May and obtaining his counsel and blessings in the matter, Clawson made a flying trip to Grand Junction, Colorado, in early August, returning the same day. It seems most likely that while in Grand Junction, Rudger and Pearl met with Apostle Matthias F. Cowley, who performed the sealing ceremony for them. At this time, Pearl was twenty-three years of age. Clawson was forty-seven.[31]

Because Cowley is known to have assisted other apostles in this way, and because of his presence in Grand Junction at the time, it is reasonable to assume that it was he who solemnized the marriage. It is also possible, however, that Clawson falsified his diary entries to mask the event. It may have been that Apostle Merrill, whom Clawson visited in mid-May, advised his junior colleague to eliminate all mention of Pearl in his diary and to construe his entries to mislead investigators. Not only were the Smoot hearings underway, with witnesses and documents regularly subpoenaed, but Merrill is likely to have falsified his own diary in connection with the plural marriage he performed in 1898 for David Eccles and Margaret Geddes.[32] Omissions, deletions, and distortions, as we will subsequently see, occurred in the records of other authorities as they related to post-Manifesto polygamous activities.

Difficulties with Clawson's record arise from the fact that, according to what seems to have been a retrospective entry, he spent most of 1 and 2 August 1904 at home with an ailing wife and baby. On the evening of 2 August he claimed to have taken his wife out riding. Then, on 3 August, his diary says: "I went to Grand Junction to meet Brother Cowley, and returned in the evening."[33] Presumably, it was while in Grand Junction that Apostle Clawson was sealed to Pearl Udall, returning, according to his journal, to Salt Lake City the same evening. His entry for the next day, Thursday, 4 August 1904, indicates he attended a 10:00 A.M. meeting of the apostles in the temple, with his diary describing the opening prayer, reading of minutes, and other activities at the meeting's start.[34] The problem is that, had Clawson taken the earliest train from Salt Lake City on 3 August 1904 (the fastest method of travel at the time), without delay or other complication, he could not have arrived in Grand Junction before 6:35 P.M. And the next returning train did not leave until after midnight, arriving in Salt Lake City at 10:40 A.M. the next morning.[35] Clearly, Clawson could not, as his diary describes, have returned to Salt Lake City the same evening as his departure for Grand Junction. Neither could he have been present in time for the beginning of the gathering of apostles the next morning. If we surmise that the day or two pre-

vious to his journey was actually spent in Grand Junction (or elsewhere) and that his account of the activities of his quorum in their 4
August meeting were borrowed and filled in after the fact, we are yet
left, at the least, with a diary account that is improbable.

Another, if less likely, possibility involves a marriage between
Clawson and Udall on water off the California coast. According to
Clawson's biographers, a tradition in the Udall family held that
Rudger and Pearl were married on shipboard, between Los Angeles
and Catalina Island, in the spring of 1904 by the California Mission
president, Joseph Robinson. Clawson's diary makes no allowance for
such an occasion, but Pearl did go to Los Angeles soon after receiving
her endowments in May.[36] Not only had Joseph Robinson (Appendix
II, #160) married two plural wives himself since the Manifesto but
after his Arizona visit in the early autumn of 1903, Clawson spent time
with Robinson in California, visiting Mormon congregations there.[37]
Later, after journeying to England, where Clawson was British Mission president, Pearl decided to withdraw from the relationship with
him and wrote to her parents, referring to counsel and encouragement in the matter from a "Bro. R." in Los Angeles.[38] This, reinforced
by family tradition, suggests that, while it is more likely Apostle
Cowley united the two in Colorado—whatever the actual calendar of
events—it is also possible that the marriage may have occurred, with
the assistance of Joseph Robinson, off the coast of California, a location where other polygamous marriages took place as well.

The case of Abraham Hoagland Cannon (Appendix II, #36) presents us with not only another instance of post-Manifesto plural marriage among the apostles but one of such interest and instruction that
it requires considerable attention. A son of George Q. Cannon, Abraham had been in charge of the *Juvenile Instructor* and other church
publications since 1882. Later, with his brother John Q. Cannon, he
assumed responsibility for publication of the *Deseret News*. On 17 October 1878 he married Sarah Ann Jenkins. Almost exactly a year later,
he took his cousin, Wilhelmina, a daughter of Angus M. Cannon, as a
plural spouse. In 1887 he married yet another wife, Mary E. Croxall,
in Mexico. At the October conference in 1889, during his thirty-first
year, Abraham was called to be an apostle.[39]

At the time of the Manifesto, then, Cannon had three living wives
and had served time in the penitentiary because of it.[40] On more than
one occasion during the 1890s, he considered marrying yet again. An
early instance involving *disinclination* to proceed with such a union
occurred in September 1891. Twenty-two-year-old Mary Davis, a resi-

dent in Salt Lake City's Nineteenth Ward, developed an affection for Cannon and was determined to marry him and no one else. When told of the young woman's feelings, Cannon went to the Davis home to speak with her. He visited with Mary and told her it was useless to think of him, inasmuch as he was already married. Besides, he reminded her, under existing rules in the church, polygamous marriages were no longer permitted.[41]

Somewhat more than a year later, Abraham's brother David died suddenly while serving in the Swiss-German Mission. The boy's father, George Q. Cannon, was especially grieved because his son was left without posterity. Aware of Mary Davis's interest in Abraham, the elder Cannon decided that Abraham should consider marrying her to raise a family in his brother David's behalf. He told Abraham to think about the proposal, inasmuch as President Woodruff said such a marriage could be performed in Mexico.[42] Abraham was amenable to the suggestion, except that Mary Davis was not the one he wanted. Less than a week later Abraham went to President Woodruff's office to discuss the matter further with his father and others. The name of Annie Cannon, a daughter of his uncle and father-in-law, Angus M. Cannon, was brought into the conversation. Annie's father was present at the time and said he had no objections so long as his daughter were willing. Presidents Wilford Woodruff and Joseph F. Smith both gave their consent, President Woodruff promising the Lord's blessings in the undertaking.[43]

This meeting took place on a Wednesday. The following Saturday Abraham went to the home of his Uncle Angus to discuss the proposed marriage with Annie. Abraham reported in his diary that his uncle gave his consent, saying that he was free to ask Annie if she would like "to become the wife of David."[44] When discussing the matter with the First Presidency, Abraham used the phrase "taking a wife for David." Who, we might ask, was it that the proposed marriage contemplated as Annie's actual husband—Abraham or David? And if David, how was Annie to espouse a dead man?

What was involved resembles the ancient Jewish practice of a levirate marriage—a custom, common among not only the early Jews but other societies, by which a brother or close relative to a deceased man was expected to marry his widow. This assured posterity for, or perpetuation of, the name of the decedent. President Cannon's anxiety lest his dead son be left without "seed," combined with Mormonism's penchant for the restoration of early Judeo-Christian forms, suggests it was the levirate that was contemplated.[45] Mormon apologists had argued for years that, like polygamy, the practice of raising a family by

proxy for another continued after the time of Moses and was not
repudiated by Jesus.[46] A Mormon editorial once said that asking the
Latter-day Saints to give up polygamy was like asking a faithful Jew in
antiquity not to marry the childless widow of his deceased brother.[47]
We also know that Mormons sometimes entered into this arrangement to ensure the survival of a man's name and to provide him with a
surrogate family.[48] In his 1899 interview with Eugene Young, George
Q. Cannon stated that this "old Hebraic principle" was a tenet of the
Mormon Church.[49] Inasmuch as Cannon is known to have unsuccessfully approached an older son first, before turning to Abraham
for the purpose of raising up posterity for David, we are further
reminded of the Jewish practice where such seniority was followed.[50]

It is also possible, however, that instead of the levirate, the contemplated relationship between Abraham and his cousin Annie was
an instance of concubinage. In the first place, in its strictest but not
invariable sense, the levirate involved marriage to a deceased brother's
wife. And Annie was not David's widow. Secondly, neither President
Cannon, Abraham, nor Annie, so far as we know, used the term
"levirate marriage." The more informal tradition of concubinage may
have been considered the better solution. Rather than a "wife" in the
way that polygamous and levirate spouses were usually looked upon,
Annie could be taken under conditions of greater privacy and secrecy
as Abraham's concubine. In ancient societies concubines were often
used to secure posterity when a man was unable to have children by
his barren wife. Although this was not the circumstance of David
Cannon, the device could be discreetly used to vicariously raise a
family to his name.[51]

Mormon authorities had periodically examined the propriety of
concubinage from at least the time of Joseph Smith's 1843 revelation
on plural marriage. That communication opened by saying that it was
in answer to inquiries by Joseph regarding the "many wives and concubines" of early patriarchs. And in a later passage the use of concubinage by those worthies was explicitly approved.[52] Later, because
the word was used pejoratively by critics of the church, Mormons
sometimes denied they had anything to do with concubines. All, they
insisted, were honorable "wives."[53] At the same time, there are numbers of statements suggesting that church leaders looked upon polygamy as comprehending more than a single order of spousal relationships. Quite apart from those who alleged Joseph Smith had sought to
organize female companions into different classes, the question of
concubinage was raised on several occasions after the Saints removed
to the Great Basin.[54] It was pointed out that concubinage was a cus-

tom practiced by ancient holy men. The burden of Mormon comments was uniformly to describe concubines as more than mistresses, taken only for promiscuous pleasure. If not the same as wives, they were nevertheless respectable companions, fully approved by God.[55]

Some months before the October 1894 discussion with Abraham, during a meeting with the Quorum of Twelve Apostles and First Presidency, George Q. Cannon said he felt something needed to be done to remedy circumstances created by the Manifesto: "My son David died without seed," he said, "and his brothers cannot do a work for him in rearing children to bear his name because of the Manifesto. I believe in concubinage, or some plan whereby men and women can live together under sacred ordinances and vows until they can be married." He went on to say that such relationships would have to be kept secret until the government changed its laws to permit formal polygamous marriages to be performed. If approved, he said, concubinage would open the way to take care of "our surplus girls" and fulfill the commandment to multiply and replenish the earth.[56] President Wilford Woodruff gave his blessing, saying it was an acceptable resort until men were again able to openly embrace plural marriage.[57] On yet another occasion, Cannon was reported to have told a church member who had only daughters, whose name was likely to die with him, that he must privately make a covenant with some woman and in that way have male offspring.[58] There is also the possibility that Cannon himself, in the year before his death, entered into a concubinage-like relationship with another woman. Albeit in this case the person involved, Amelia Madsen, seems to have been chosen for reasons apart from her capacity to rear children inasmuch as she was past child-bearing age.[59]

Regarding Abraham and Annie, it is unfortunate that we have no known record of her response to Abraham's proposal. There may have been something more said about this in a missing portion of Abraham's diary. Fifteen lines were cut from his entry for 30 October 1894. This was three days after his visit with Annie in his Uncle Angus's home. It is conceivable, but speculative only, that the deleted portion related to Annie's answer. There were many such excisions in his record—whether made by Abraham or someone else is uncertain—and we can only guess at their contents. His diary does indicate that during the next several months Annie was often included in excursions and activities in the company of Abraham's family. In these entries no distinction is made between Annie and Abraham's wives.[60] It is also significant that, although Annie lived to be seventy-nine years of age, there is no formal record of her ever having married. She must have been reasonably intelligent and attractive or the handsome and much-sought-after Abraham Cannon likely would have shown little interest in her—as with Mary Davis. Indeed, some time after these events, she refused a proposal for marriage from another prominent Latter-day Saint, Heber Bennion.[61] President Cannon, we must recall, had said that those who took concubines must do so in secrecy and through private agreement with one another. This may explain a great deal.

At the same time, this could appear as morally questionable and excessively off-hand to some. One might ask if this was the arrangement suggested to Joseph C. Bentley (Appendix II, #18) at the time he wished to marry Gladys Woodmansee as a plural wife. It will be recalled that, because of the church's sense of vulnerability during the early 1890s, his petition to marry Gladys was at first refused. After Bentley moved to Mexico and was still unable to enter polygamy, Alexander F. Macdonald suggested a solution to the problem, in response to which Bentley said only, "I felt I could not follow [it]." As it turned out, Bentley was finally given permission to marry Gladys in the autumn of 1894.[62] Given the fact that concubinage was being discussed by church authorities at this time, could that have been what Macdonald suggested to Bentley?

There is less mystery in connection with Abraham Cannon's next connubial venture. This was the marriage to Lilian Hamlin as his fourth known wife. Indeed, far from the secret contraction intended, this relationship became the object of national attention. Abraham first referred to Lilian in his diary at the time of his brother David's funeral, on 13 November 1892. Lilian had been David's fiancée. After the funeral ceremonies Lilian and others went to Abraham's home, where they spent the afternoon and evening.[63] She is next mentioned in Abraham's journal three years later. On this occasion he was in Provo for the purpose of receiving a Patriarchal Blessing from Patriarch Charles D. Evans. Coincidentally, Lilian and a friend, Leah Dunford, were also there to receive their blessings. Abraham and the two young women returned to Salt Lake City on the train together.[64]

Our ability to follow events after this is more difficult because Abraham's extant journals end with the year 1895. He had been a faithful diarist for many years and it is likely that he continued to be so into 1896. But the location of his records for that year are unknown. We do know that in the spring of 1896 he was courting Lilian and, on several occasions, took her for buggy rides in Salt Lake City.[65] We also know, based on testimony given before the United States Senate eight years later, that on or about 9 June 1896, he began talking to his wife

Wilhelmina concerning his wish to marry Lilian. Interestingly, Abraham told Wilhelmina that because of Lilian's earlier engagement to David, he intended to marry her in David's stead. "He told me he was going to marry her for time," said Wilhelmina, "and that she would be David's wife for eternity."[66]

At this point one must ask if this was not the purpose of Abraham's interest in Annie Cannon. There are at least three possibilities that would account for what seemed to be happening. In the first place, Abraham may well have vicariously taken both Annie and Lilian as wives for his brother David. There was nothing in Mormon theology that would preclude Abraham from marrying both women for time, while designating them as David's spouses in the hereafter. Secondly, it is possible that, if Abraham took Annie as a wife or concubine, she had not been able to conceive. There is no record of her having children. He may have wished to marry Lilian, again in David's stead, for the purpose of raising up a posterity for him. A third possibility is that no marriage whatever took place between Annie and Abraham. If this were so, then Lilian was the only one intended to fulfill that role.[67]

Whatever motives were involved, Wilhelmina strenuously objected. She reminded Abraham that the Manifesto had made further polygamous marriages impossible.[68] This was probably an argument of desperation, however, for she had long been unhappy in Abraham Cannon's polygamous household. Six years earlier, in 1890, she had considered divorce. Abraham once recorded that Wilhelmina told him that she felt herself in disgrace because she was a polygamous wife and that she would as soon be a prostitute. On another occasion he told how she threatened to leave him because, in her words, she "could no longer endure the marriage system in which we are living."[69] If these rumbles reveal instability in the households of the faithful, they also attest to the continuing strength of the principle in the face of domestic opposition.

On 12 June 1896 Abraham was at Wilhelmina's home, celebrating the birthday of a daughter. When previously discussing his intentions with regard to Lilian, he had said such a marriage could be performed outside the United States. He now told Wilhelmina that he and Lilian were going to California, presumably to be married, that President Joseph F. Smith would accompany them, and he needed assistance in packing his bags.[70] According to the *Deseret News*, Cannon departed by rail on 18 June with business associates for the purpose of filing articles of incorporation for a railway venture in Carson City, Nevada. Later, after his return, the *News* reported that only some of the party went to Carson City. Cannon, it said, branched off on the way and journeyed to Los Angeles.[71] When testifying before the Smoot investigating committee some years later, Joseph F. Smith said he met with Abraham Cannon in Los Angeles for the purpose of signing important mining papers. Yet, in none of the contemporary accounts was anything said about mining. Rather, newspapers indicated the trip was taken in connection with the projected Utah and California and Nevada Southern Railroad lines.[72] It is clear that much, if not all, of the newspaper story was manufactured as a cover for Abraham's marriage to and honeymoon with Lilian.

The night before their departure, 17 June 1896, Lilian Hamlin received her endowments in the Salt Lake Temple.[73] Then, as now, this ordinance commonly preceded marriages between Mormon couples if one or both had not already been endowed. The rituals of marriage and sealing, as indicated earlier, could be performed anywhere.[74] How Lilian traveled to Los Angeles is uncertain, although it is likely she was on the same train with Abraham. President Joseph F. Smith and one of his wives left Salt Lake City a day later, on 19 June.[75] While in Los Angeles the two couples decided to visit Catalina Island. All four made the trip by excursion vessel across the channel.[76]

Sometime during their stay in California, perhaps while at Catalina harbor, Abraham got water in his ear while relaxing on the beach. This aggravated an earlier condition, causing him great distress, and soon led to serious complications. After returning to Salt Lake City, he suffered from intense head and ear pain that grew progressively worse. His condition deteriorated rapidly, despite repeated administrations and blessings from fellow apostle Brigham Young, Jr. On 19 July 1896, with family members and President Joseph F. Smith at his side, Abraham died.[77] During the illness, Abraham stayed at the home of his plural wife Wilhelmina. Sometime before he died, asking Wilhelmina's forgiveness, he confirmed to her that he had indeed married Lilian. He further said that he had not had a healthy day since the marriage took place.[78]

Wilhelmina stated that she was not told who it was that performed the ceremony or where it had taken place. She nevertheless inferred that it was Joseph F. Smith who united the couple. Although she felt constrained to believe President Smith's testimony before the Smoot investigating committee, in which he denied having anything to do with the marriage, there were good grounds for Wilhelmina's assumptions. To begin with, when she objected to Abraham's intended marriage because of the Manifesto, Abraham had replied that it could be done outside the United States. When the trip was taken to the coast, where the couple, with President Smith and his wife, could easily escape the nation's land boundaries, Wilhelmina's inference that Smith was involved was a conclusion reasonably drawn. So far as the time and location of the marriage are concerned, we should remember that after his return, Abraham told Wilhelmina that he had not been well *since* he married Lilian.[79] Inasmuch as his last illness was precipitated by sea bathing, one could fairly conclude that all three events—sea bathing, the ear infection, and Abraham's marriage—occurred at or very near the same time.

John Henry Hamlin, Lilian's brother, held the same views as Wilhelmina—that it was Joseph F. Smith who married his sister to Abraham Cannon and that it took place "on the Pacific Coast" or, as he put it another time, "on the high seas." John said this was told to him by his wife, who was a close friend of Lilian, and that it was generally accepted as fact by the family.[80] Before the stir caused by the Smoot hearings, many in the community considered it common knowledge that Abraham had gone to southern California to take a plural wife. Utah Congressman George Sutherland, a non-Mormon, testified in 1903 that, after Abraham Cannon's death, word of the case came to his ears and that it was said to be a post-Manifesto contraction performed on the "high seas."[81]

The widespread nature of rumor concerning the Cannon-Hamlin marriage made it necessary for President Smith to answer questions about it in his testimony during the Smoot hearings. This is also why, after his appearance in Washington, he sent Senator Smoot additional material on the case, hoping to buttress both his and the senator's testimonies. Smith's original statements to the committee amounted to an unconvincing series of denials either as to his knowledge of the marriage in California or his complicity in it.[82] Smith's claim that there was never an opportunity during the time both couples were on the boat when he could have performed the ceremony is particularly implausible. The ritual for sealing couples in polygamy was very brief. Brigham H. Roberts once said it took about two minutes.[83] There would have been little problem with such a performance, *sotto voce,* either while standing or strolling about on board the vessel.

In a document sent to Smoot, Smith stated that he had received information from a mutual friend who reported that Lilian positively denied "that Steamboat story." She had further declared, Smith said, that he (Smith) was not present when "she was sealed to A. H. Cannon," that he had "no part in it."[84] This was a curious and hardly convincing submission. One can only ask why Smith would send something that, in Smoot's hands, amounted to no more than third-hand hearsay? And why was Smith unable to get the testimony he reported from Lilian herself? Having a contact that knew of her whereabouts should have permitted him to quote Lilian directly, or even obtain from her an affidavit. One also suspects Smith's use of language in quoting Lilian. If Abraham took Lilian in David Cannon's stead, then she was probably "sealed" to David, not to Abraham. Eugene Young, in his 1899 article on Mormon polygamy, said this was the understanding in the Cannon family, that by employing one of Mormonism's "quibbles," Lilian was not sealed to Abraham but, through him, to his dead brother David.[85]

As another alternative the author was told by a senior member in the Church Historical Department that he had seen a document indicating that it was George Q. Cannon who married his son Abraham to Lilian. In 1911 the apostles directed that a special folder be prepared on the Cannon-Hamlin marriage. This was not to be made public but was for the apostles' use and reference. This may have been the source identifying George Q. Cannon as the authority performing the ceremony.[86] Apostle Francis M. Lyman told Joseph W. Musser in 1914 that President Cannon was responsible for the marriage. Whether this meant that he formally united the couple or simply gave his approval is not clear from Musser's report.[87] For his part Cannon publicly denied any knowledge of the case, saying he had never been consulted in the matter.[88] If the senior Cannon did unite his son and Lilian, the marriage must have occurred before the party's departure for California.

Yet another possibility is that President Smith stood proxy for Abraham, with Abraham performing the ceremony. No one at the Smoot hearings seems to have thought to ask Joseph F. Smith if it were he that had married Lilian![89] It could also be that someone quite unknown conducted the ritual. Again, at the time of the Smoot investigation President Smith hinted this may have occurred, and Carl A. Badger, Smoot's secretary, referred to this possibility as well. Badger was told that Orson Smith, president of Cache Stake, may have married Abraham and Lilian.[90] This could have occurred in a private ceremony somewhere on the evening of 17 June 1896, after Lilian received her endowments. Michael Quinn believes that Orson Smith was but code for Joseph F. Smith and that the latter indeed performed the marriage, but in Salt Lake City.[91] There was also speculation that James H. Anderson, a friend and companion to the deceased David Cannon, performed the marriage as early as 1893.[92] This latter hypothesis has little to support it. The initial discussions between Abraham, his father, and his uncle, as we saw, did not take place until 1894.

While it seems most likely that the marriage was performed off the California coastline, that resort raises a puzzling issue. Such an undertaking invites the supposition that it provided a shelter from the nation's laws prohibiting such unions. But this was not so. It is true that at that time the federal government had largely relinquished police power functions in territorial waters to littoral states. And California, at the time, had no statute criminalizing polygamous cohabitation. But this gained couples nothing after their return to Utah, where both polygamous marriages and polygamous cohabitation were forbidden.[93] And, while in coastal jurisdictions like California, they were vulnerable to that state's criminal code on adultery.[94] Even if the vessel were of foreign registry and the ceremony performed in international waters, polygamous marriage by individuals intending to return to United States residences constituted one of the few exceptions to the rule of *lex loci contractus:* the principle of comity whereby a state recognizes marriages and divorces approved elsewhere when such performances cannot be undertaken at home. As one distinguished nineteenth-century jurist put it, polygamous and incestuous relations were exceptions to that rule "because they are condemned by the common voice of civilized nations, which establishes a common law forbidding them."[95] The polygamous marriage of Abraham Cannon and Lilian Hamlin—even if solemnized by a magistrate of the state, which it was not—was no more valid upon their return than if it had been performed in Salt Lake City.

Inasmuch as polygamous ceremonies at sea brought no legal advantage to participants, one can only conclude that their single purpose was an attempt at consistency with the Woodruff Manifesto. That document had advised the Saints to "refrain from contracting any marriage forbidden by the law of the land." It mattered not, in other words, that from a legal standpoint maritime resorts offered Utah residents no more than what was available in their home state. They could in any case say they had been literally obedient to the Manifesto in its concern with laws of the *land*.

This does not, however, fully explain why some Mormons went to the trouble of having plural marriages solemnized outside the nation's land boundaries. As we saw, at least one such union—that of John W. Taylor on Puget Sound—occurred in 1888.[96] The date of this marriage precludes an interest in the Manifesto's language. There was also the polygamous contraction of Benjamin Julius Johnson with Harriet Jane Hakes in 1889. That ceremony was performed by Alexander F. Macdonald in what Johnson later told Kimball Young was "no man's land" between Mexico and the United States.[97] Such a zone was, of course, non-existent and even more fictive a sanctuary than coastal seas for illegal activity. These cases may only illustrate a Mormon illusion that sites located at the nation's edge enjoyed some degree of immunity from its laws. In any case, and despite rumor among certain church members that Mormon authorities approved plural marriages if solemnized at sea, polygamous contractions on the water constituted only a fraction of such unions after 1890.[98] Few though they were, because off-land locations were employed for the performance of other plural unions near the same time, this constitutes additional support for believing the Cannon-Hamlin marriage took place there as well.

After Abraham's death Lilian attended a teacher-training institute in the East. She then returned to teach at the Brigham Young Academy in Provo, Utah. In 1902 she married another member of the Cannon family, Lewis Mousley Cannon, once again as a plural wife.[99] So far as David's posterity is concerned, Lilian gave birth to her first child on 22 March 1897.[100] This date fell almost exactly nine months from the time of her honeymoon with Abraham in California the previous year. Lilian named the little girl Marba—Abram spelled backwards. If all that happened was for the purpose of raising up a posterity to the name of David Cannon—what it was that set the entire train of events in motion—Lilian seemed determined to leave some hint as to who it was that did the work.

The marriages of Apostle George Teasdale (Appendix II, #192) are as complicated and fraught with question as those of Abraham Cannon. Most members of the church today know little of the man. He was born in London, England, on 8 December 1831 and was baptized a member of the church in 1852. He emigrated in 1861 and crossed the plains in a company led by Sixtus E. Johnson. In October of 1882 he was called to the apostleship, serving much of his time assisting with the colonies in Mexico.[101]

Apostle Teasdale was remembered as genial and kindly, giving considerable time to the instruction of children, emphasizing the importance of the Word of Wisdom, and cultivating an appreciation for music. He was also remembered as timid—so frightened by thunder that during electric storms he would tent himself inside a house with blankets. He took great care with his appearance, dying his hair and always wearing a duster out of doors to preserve the cleanliness of his clothing.[102] The chief ecclesiastical authority in Mexico during the early years of the church's colonization efforts there, Teasdale was, in many ways, too delicate for such a calling. He was, nevertheless, fiercely devoted to the principle. During his years in Mexico, on more than one occasion and well after the Manifesto, he testified to the divinity of plural marriage, declaring that the church was imperfect without it. He urged the brethren there to ask the Lord to give them additional wives.[103] In 1902 he told a meeting of patriarchs in Salt Lake City that they were expected to believe in the tenet, that Jesus Christ had been a polygamist, and that only wicked people opposed the practice.[104]

Teasdale's first wife was Emma Emily Brown, whom he married in England in 1853. She bore seven children before dying, at the age of forty-two, in 1874. A year and a half later, on 14 October 1875, Teasdale married Lillias Hook in Salt Lake City. Lillias thus became George's legal wife. As we will see, this marriage became the source of controversy and some mystery. The apostle later married Mary Lauretta Picton and her sister Matilda Ellen Picton. Both went with Teasdale to Mexico when he relocated there in the mid-1880s. Tragically, both died in Mexico, leaving the apostle to care for five small children.[105]

George Teasdale's next wife was Marion Eliza Scoles. Thirty-four years his junior, she, like George, was born in London, England. On 12 September 1891 Marion and her mother sailed from England on the *S.S. Wyoming* with their stated destination as Logan, Utah.[106] This departure date is important because it later became an issue of some significance during the Smoot hearings. Indeed, it was Reed Smoot who put the two women on the boat in England in 1891, making him a witness that she could not have married Teasdale before the Manifesto of 1890. Before commencement of the inquiry, Smoot nervously reminded President Joseph F. Smith of this fact, hoping to patch together a convincing argument that he was innocent of knowledge that Teasdale, his fellow apostle, had engaged in post-Manifesto polygamous activity.[107]

Arriving in Logan, Marion taught school for a period of four years then moved with her mother to Nephi, Utah. There she was employed by Teasdale, caring for his motherless children. After a year of this, she agreed to become the apostle's wife. Inasmuch as Lillias Hook was yet living and legally married to Teasdale, Marion's status was that of a plural spouse. According to temple records the marriage occurred on 25 October 1897, somewhere "on the Pacific Ocean."[108] Not only does this resemble the case of Apostle Abraham Cannon and Lilian Hamlin of only slightly more than a year before, but an additional similarity exists. The Journal History in the church's archives describes Teasdale and fellow apostle Anthon H. Lund as absent, "filling an appointment in the North," at the time of Teasdale's marriage. When Joseph F. Smith and Abraham Cannon made their journey to Los Angeles, the Journal History stated that Smith was gone on a journey "through the North."[109] In both cases the location and purposes of the parties were concealed by an identical ubiquity.

While we do not have as much detail concerning the Teasdale marriage as we do with Abraham Cannon's, it seems certain that Teasdale was attempting to circumvent the Manifesto in the same way as Cannon—by having the illicit marriage performed outside the nation's land boundaries. Whether it was done, as with Abraham and Lilian, in the channel between Los Angeles and Catalina Island or somewhere else cannot be determined. Teasdale's journal is unavailable to researchers, and Lund, who presumably performed the marriage and whose diaries are otherwise remarkably complete, deletes entries for the period of 23 October through October 28, 1897—the precise days he and Teasdale were absent together and during which Teasdale was married to Marion Scoles.[110]

The employment of marine locations to get around the Manifesto, and Apostle Lund's use of such a method in the Teasdale marriage, finds another parallel a few months later in the case of Ferdinand Friis Hintze (Appendix II, #95). Hintze had served as president of the Turkish Mission some years before and was returning to the Middle East as Lund's assistant to determine the feasibility of colonizing Armenian Saints in the Holy Land. The idea was eventually rejected, but on their way east Lund married Hintze to a plural wife, probably on waters separating the United States and Canada near Detroit, Michigan.[111] Lund was thus accessory to at least two post-Manifesto marriages, both of which he performed on the water. We have no record indicating he entered such contractions himself. It was rumored that he never took a plural spouse because his first wife would not permit it.[112] Clearly, however, this did not deter him from providing help to his friends—including fellow apostle George Teasdale.

Teasdale and Marion Scoles were quite aware that their marriage ceremony, even if performed on the Pacific Ocean, was illicit. Marion, for example, continued to use her maiden name both in the community in which she lived in Utah as well as in the Mormon colonies in Mexico.[113] There was even an attempt to obscure her relationship to Teasdale at the time of her death in mid-December 1898. Marion died giving birth to her first child. Local doctors, friendly to Teasdale and his secret, certified that she died of heart failure. Having lost four of his five wives in death, Teasdale was especially grieved. Indifferent to consequences, he erected a fine tombstone over her grave, inscribing on the monument: "In Memory of Marion E. Scoles Teasdale, Beloved Wife of Apostle Geo. Teasdale."[114]

Neither matrimonial adventure nor the trial and difficulty associated with it were at an end for the apostle, however. On 17 May 1900, at sixty-eight years of age, Teasdale married again. On this occasion it was to twenty-three-year-old Letitia Dolly Thomas. The ceremony was performed in the temple in Logan, Utah.[115] Ever alert to the opportunity for trumpeting new plural marriages, the *Salt Lake Tribune* began reminding readers that the inveterate Teasdale still had what they believed was a living wife—Lillias Hook—in Salt Lake City and that the union with young Letitia was thus polygamous. In this case, however, they were wrong. Teasdale's marriage to Letitia Thomas as his sixth wife was not polygamous. Before taking the new bride, he formally divorced Lillias to preclude the very sort of scandal savored by *Tribune* writers.[116]

The relationship with Lillias Hook is not so easily set aside, however. When asked about the matter, President Joseph F. Smith told the Smoot investigating committee that Lillias had never been a real wife to Teasdale. Rather, he said, she had been only an elderly, deformed housekeeper, working in the apostle's home for years. Teasdale, Smith claimed, had her "sealed to him for eternity" only, both understanding that it was for the hereafter and that there was to be no sexual relationship between them in the present life. Teasdale's association with her, Smith said, was as "chaste as if she were his sister or a stranger to him." Therefore, Smith insisted, Teasdale had been at liberty to marry again.[117]

Smith's explanation poses a number of problems. To begin with, Teasdale's alliances with each of his other wives, except Letitia Thomas, were polygamous and thus illegal, whatever his personal relationship to Lillias Hook. Beyond this, at the time of her marriage Lillias can hardly be described as an "elderly" lady. Born on 19 March 1840, she was thirty-five years of age, more than eight years younger than Teasdale himself. Regarding the allegation that she was deformed, we find in Teasdale's 1899 divorce complaint that this involved her inability to have sexual intercourse, an impediment he discovered "immediately after said marriage took place."[118] Rather than the charitable arrangement described by President Smith before a United States Senate committee in 1904, this suggests Teasdale entered the relationship fully expecting Lillias to be his legal wife in every sense. The divorce complaint makes it clear that if Lillias's incapacity really existed, Teasdale was unaware of it until after the marriage ceremony was performed. Not only must one ask why he delayed so long to terminate the relationship (almost a quarter century) but why, if he had not considered it a bona fide marriage, had he gone to such lengths to obscure subsequent unions?

There is a further complication. Lillias and George had something of a family. Records of the Twentieth Ward in Salt Lake City, where Lillias lived, list one George Vivian Teasdale as born on 11 June 1896 and identify George and Lillias Teasdale as the parents.[119] The boy died of marasmus when only four months old but was buried under the name of George Vivian Allen.[120] While the death certificate listed George and Alice H. Allen as the parents, there is nothing in the city's register of births concerning either a Teasdale or Allen child at or near the time of the infant's birth. Eugene Young remarked that one of the things making detection of polygamous marriages difficult during those years was that records of births in Salt Lake City were so poorly kept.[121] The place of death on the death certificate, however, was given as 579 South Temple, Salt Lake City—the residence of George and Lillias Teasdale.[122] Twentieth Ward records also indicate that George and Lillias were the "adopted parents" of a girl, Sarah Ann Teasdale, born 31 July 1870.[123] But there is nothing in the record to indicate an adoption was involved with young George Vivian.[124] Unless Lillias was something of a modern Sarah, however, it is highly unlikely that she gave birth to the infant. She was fifty-six years of age at the time.

If Apostle Teasdale buried a child that was his own under an assumed name, the undertaker, Joseph E. Taylor, was a logical choice for the task. Taylor had been similarly employed in 1891 by Abraham Cannon and one of his plural wives. Cannon arranged with Taylor to bury his son, Gene Croxall Cannon, as "Gene Crawford from Farmer's Ward."[125] But with Lillias as a legal wife, why should Teasdale have needed an alias for the youngster at all? Whether young George Vivian was an adopted child, the natural offspring of George and Lillias, or the product of an alliance between Apostle Teasdale and an as yet unidentified plural spouse, it seems to have been their clear intention to raise the boy, like the earlier adopted daughter, Sarah Ann, as a part of their family.

It is also possible that the divorce between George and Lillias was agreed to by both partners only as an expedient permitting the apostle to marry Letitia Thomas with a minimum of disadvantage to Lillias. Bogus divorce was not unknown in Mormon polygamous families and seems likely here for two reasons.[126] To begin with, Lillias did not contest the divorce. Secondly, at least in later years, she continued to be acknowledged as George's wife. After Teasdale's death in 1907 the

Salt Lake City Directory listed both Lillias and Letitia as his widows.[127] The church census of 1914 identified Lillias as Teasdale's widow.[128] And when she died in 1921, her obituary read: "Mrs. Lillias Hook Teasdale, widow of the late Apostle George Teasdale, died Friday evening, Feb. 11, 1921."[129] Given the priority attached to plural marriage, both Lillias and George may have agreed on the divorce as a maneuver permitting the apostle to marry again and so augment both their spiritual estates. Besides, according to Mormon theology, earthly divorces have no binding authority in heaven anyway.

The case of Apostle George Teasdale closes on a note as curious as any in the complicated story of his several marriages. When he died in 1907, Letitia was forty-five years his junior. Although the two had had no children, during their residence in Nephi, Utah, Letitia cared for five of George's youngsters by wives who had passed away. When the family relocated in Salt Lake City, three of the children continued to live at home. One of them, George Washington Teasdale, eventually married his father's widow. The marriage probably occurred about 1915, when Letitia was thirty-eight and George W. twenty-seven. The two parented at least three children of their own.[130]

It is likely that President Wilford Woodruff (Appendix II, #214) also took a new plural companion in 1897, one year before his death. The woman involved was Lydia Mamreoff von Finkelstein Mountford. Born in Jerusalem in 1848, Madame Mountford was baptized in the Anglican church as a child and from her youth on dreamed of evangelizing in behalf of Christ.[131] Her oldest brother emigrated to the United States after the American Civil War and became a private secretary to William Henry Seward. The rest of the family, except for the father, who had died, soon followed. Madame Mountford began writing for various American periodicals and lecturing on scriptural interpretation, employing illustrated scenes and references to life in Palestine, both ancient and modern. In addition to meeting important persons such as Frances Willard, Elizabeth Cady Stanton, and Susan B. Anthony, she impressed Henry Ward Beecher with her eloquence, which led to an invitation to lecture on the Chautauqua circuit. This was followed by a journey to England, where she gave hundreds of illustrated lectures and was awarded a gold Maltese Cross for her service. She then toured Australia, Ceylon, and India, returning to the United States at the time of the Columbian World's Fair. After another visit to England, she recommenced lecturing in the United States, meeting with responsive audiences everywhere she went.[132]

Madame Mountford first visited Salt Lake City in the winter of 1897. Dr. James E. Talmage, who had previously heard her in New York City, organized a series of lectures for her in the Tabernacle. Audiences filled that vast structure nearly every night for three weeks to hear Madame Mountford speak. She also made an appearance at the Brigham Young Academy in Provo, Utah, after which President Benjamin Cluff made arrangements for her to tour the entire state. Her dramatic and vocal powers seemed to profoundly affect everyone who heard her. The Mormon population found her especially winning because she told how, in the early 1840s, her father had entertained and befriended Apostle Orson Hyde in Jerusalem when he was sent there to dedicate Palestine for the return of the Jews. She remembered her father's interest in the young man and had long wished to visit the Saints herself. She also had chosen to be rebaptized by immersion when eighteen years of age. And she claimed to be descended through her father from Ephraim and on her mother's side from Melchizedek.[133]

President Wilford Woodruff attended her lectures and was impressed with her magnetic personality. The two were introduced, and she seems to have found an interest in him. After their first visit in early February 1897, the number of such meetings multiplied, becoming increasingly private.[134] On the occasion of Woodruff's birthday in March, Mountford was one of the speakers at what was described as the largest assembly ever to meet in the Tabernacle. She said President Woodruff was her president and that she was honored to be in the Zion of the Western Hemisphere.[135] She was soon baptized into the church, and by July Woodruff recorded that she called at his home "and gave me a sample of her massage treatment."[136] The two corresponded frequently when she was away from Salt Lake City in connection with her lectures. At this time the blonde, blue-eyed Mountford was forty-nine years of age. Woodruff was ninety.[137]

Woodruff suffered from a number of maladies, most painfully from prostatic hypertrophy. During the late spring of 1897 his doctors advised him that he needed a vacation from his work and that relaxation at sea level would be helpful. Woodruff began contemplating a visit to the Pacific coast at that time.[138] He not only corresponded about the trip with Madame Mountford (who spent part of the spring and summer on the coast herself) but arranged with L. John Nuttall to accompany him "on the quiet and [to] avoid newspaper men and interviews."[139] When Woodruff told his wife Emma and daughter Alice of his plans, both asked to go with him and were annoyed that he refused them.[140]

Departing by train on September 9, Woodruff spoke with Nuttall the next day "confidentially in regard to some of . . . [his] personal affairs."[141] Nuttall's own extensive diaries are, unfortunately, non-existent for the period between 1894 and 1899. Woodruff's journal entries provide almost everything we know of this episode. When the two arrived in Portland, Oregon, Woodruff said they registered at a hotel under assumed names. On 16 September they took rail passage south to San Francisco, where they arrived on Saturday, 18 September 1897.[142] The following Monday, 20 September, after only two days in San Francisco, Woodruff's record says they started back to Portland but, on this leg, by water. It seems most likely that while on the steamer, between 20 and 22 September, Nuttall joined President Woodruff and Madame Mountford in marriage or a marriage-like relationship.[143]

Woodruff left Portland on 23 September, arriving in Salt Lake City two days later. While two weeks were consumed by the trip, so much time was spent moving about that it could not have provided the convalescence for which the journey was ostensibly undertaken. Madame Mountford remained on the coast, lecturing in California's bay area during October and journeying to Los Angeles in November.[144] In the year that followed, more than fifty letters passed between them. Woodruff invariably referred to her in his diary as "M"; no other subject, with the exception of his health, received such consistent attention.[145] In late December Madame Mountford returned to Salt Lake City, where she paid several visits to Woodruff and delivered an address in the Tabernacle that included a discussion of Jesus' parable of the talents—a biblical allegory often used by Mormons in defense of polygamy. She then told the Tabernacle audience she would soon leave for a visit to her home in Palestine, thanked them for their kindness, stated that she knew President Woodruff was a man of God, and urged the people to pay him homage.[146] Before leaving the city for Jerusalem in mid-January, she made suggestions in regard to the mission to Palestine involving Apostle Anthon H. Lund and Elder Ferdinand Hintze.[147] After this, apart from their continued correspondence, Woodruff and Mountford never saw each other again.

If Mountford married Woodruff as a plural wife, it was undertaken while her first husband was yet alive. She espoused Charles Edwin Mountford, an English civil servant, in Delhi, India, on 3 February 1890. The appellation "Madame" carried no special connotation in England and was probably used only to impress American audiences. Their only child, a boy, died when very young after the couple had come to America at the time of the Columbian Exposition. Her husband lost his health near this same date and returned to England.[148] But Charles Edwin Mountford did not die until 21 May 1916. There is no English record of divorce between the two, and despite their years apart Madame Mountford erected a headstone on his grave that read: "My Dear Husband Charles Edwin Mountford."[149] Although plural marriage to women undivorced from earlier husbands was not unknown in Mormonism, this constitutes the latest such instance known to the author.[150]

While she lived for nearly two decades after the assumed relationship with Woodruff, one cannot easily follow Madame Mountford's life in detail. After returning from Palestine and assisting Apostle Lund and Ferdinand Hintze there, she resumed lecturing, especially in the Midwest and East. She made appearances in England again and gave a return lecture in Salt Lake City in 1912.[151] Notwithstanding she was baptized into the church, it is difficult to know what importance she attached to this. One of the themes in her lectures was ecumenical tolerance and recognition of the different meanings Jesus' life held for different people. She believed Christ united in himself all grades and species of religious philosophy.[152] What this meant for her own life values cannot be determined. Except for the help given Apostle Lund in connection with the mission to Palestine, nothing would indicate that she used her evangelical tours to advance Mormonism. And in a 1911 publication of her lectures, she went to some length to contradict the notion that Jesus was married—a seeming reversal of views inferred in her Tabernacle address of 1898.[153] She died in Lakeland, Florida, where she kept a summer home, in 1917.

On 13 August 1898, a half-year after Mountford's departure from Salt Lake City, President Woodruff left for another visit to San Francisco, this time taking his wife Emma. Rather than improving, the prostate problem only became worse, the president sometimes suffering acutely. There was none of the excitement of the excursion a year before. He spoke in public on two occasions and visited with friends. But Woodruff's strength was rapidly draining away. Painful but unsuccessful attempts were made by a physician to obtain relief from his affliction. On 2 September 1898 church authorities in Salt Lake City were sent a telegram from California announcing that the church president was dead.[154]

Although much concerning the Woodruff-Mountford relationship is unclear, the evidence suggests a union of some kind between the two at a time when such marriages were occurring and in a location chosen by others for similar purposes—on water outside the nation's land boundaries. Apostle Matthias F. Cowley said in 1911 that he was

Table 2

Post-Manifesto Plural Marriages of Apostles and First Presidency Members
Period Covered from October 6, 1890 – December 31, 1909

	1890	1891	1892	1893	1894	1895	1896	1897	1898	1899	1900	1901	1902	1903	1904	1905	1906	1907	1908	1909	TOTALS
Abraham H. Cannon							1														1
Rudger Clawson															1						1
Matthias F. Cowley										1						1					2
Marriner W. Merrill												1									1
John W. Taylor	1											2								1	4
George Teasdale								1													1
Abraham O. Woodruff												1									1
Wilford Woodruff								1													1
Brigham Young, Jr.												1									1
TOTALS	1						1	2		1		5			1	1				1	13

Table 3

Post-Manifesto Plural Marriages Performed By Apostles
Period Covered from October 6, 1890 – December 31, 1909

	1890	1891	1892	1893	1894	1895	1896	1897	1898	1899	1900	1901	1902	1903	1904	1905	1906	1907	1908	1909	TOTALS
Matthias F. Cowley								1	3	1	6	15	7	6	3		1			1	43
Anthon H. Lund								1	1												2
Francis M. Lyman	1																				1
Marriner W. Merrill					1				1	1											3
John W. Taylor									5			1		1							7
George Teasdale			1	1			1														4
Abraham O. Woodruff										1				3							4
Brigham Young, Jr.					2	1															3
TOTALS	1		1	1	4	1	1	1	10	3	6	16	7	10	3		1			1	67

persuaded President Woodruff had married another wife the year before he died.[155] Apostle Anthon H. Lund, during his preparation to lead the mission to Palestine, told how, in early December 1897, President Woodruff took him aside and spoke to him about Madame Mountford. Lund's comment was: "I was rather astonished."[156] It could well be that Lund's surprise at hearing of President Woodruff's relationship with Madame Mountford, if indeed that is what he was told, was only part of the conversation. For sometime before he left for the Middle East, as already shown, he was given authority to perform the plural contraction for his companion, Ferdinand Hintze, on waters separating Canada and the United States. Mormon fundamentalists also have long contended that Woodruff married again after the Manifesto, identifying Madame Mountford by name.[157] And finally, it has been reported that there is evidence the marriage was solemnized, by proxy, in the Salt Lake Temple in 1920.[158]

The significance of a plural marriage, or plural-like union, at this time by the president of the church, by the author of the Manifesto, is obvious. It was more than once remarked by outsiders that whatever the circumstances with others, it was certain President Woodruff had always been faithful to his 1890 declaration.[159] As one of more than a dozen polygamous or polygamous-like relationships undertaken by apostles and members of the First Presidency after 1890, it raises serious question about the church's claims to have done away with the practice. When we add to these cases those individuals who, if innocent of taking new wives, spoke in behalf of the principle or were instrumental in joining others in such unions, we have powerful testimony to the continued practice of the doctrine (see tables 2 and 3).

Events of the late 1890s and first years of the new century, however, were soon to overtake the church. Many of their secrets were found out and "new polygamy" became the basis for another crusade against Mormonism.

NOTES

1. John Whitaker Taylor's first wife was May Leona Rich, whom he married 19 Oct. 1882. John Whitaker Taylor FGS; Samuel W. Taylor, "Interviews with Nettie [Janet] M. Taylor," July 1947, 8–9, BYU Library; and "John Whitaker Taylor," in *Latter-Day Saint Biographical Encyclopedia: A Compilation of Biographical Sketches of Prominent Men and Women in the Church of Jesus Christ of Latter-day Saints,* ed. Andrew Jenson, 4 vols. (Salt Lake City: Andrew Jenson History Co. and Deseret News, 1901–36), 1:151–56.

2. Heber Bennion to Heber J. Grant, 9 July 1929, copy, Brigham H. Roberts Letterbox 7, folder titled "polygamy," Church Archives.

3. Samuel W. Taylor, "Interviews with Nettie [Janet] M. Taylor," 8–9.

4. Ibid., 18–21; John Whitaker Taylor FGS; *Trials; Proceedings,* 1:1051–1058.

5. John Henry Smith Diaries, 16 Feb. 1894 and 9 March 1898, George A. Smith Family Papers, University of Utah Library, Salt Lake City; *Trials;* Edwin B. Firmage, *The Memoirs of Hugh B. Brown* (Salt Lake City: Signature Books, 1988), 30.

6. John Whitaker Taylor FGS; Samuel W. Taylor, "Interviews with Nettie [Janet] M. Taylor," 8–9.

7. Francis M. Lyman, in *Diary of Charles Lowell Walker,* ed. A. Karl Larson and Katherine Miles Larson, 2 vols. (Logan: Utah State University Press, 1980), 2:781, 8 Sept. 1894.

8. "One on Lyman," *SLT,* 9 Dec. 1910; and "Points on Sporadicism," ibid., 28 Oct. 1910.

9. Young's plural wife was Helen Armstrong, whom he married in Colonia Juarez, Mexico, on 7 June 1890. Ephraim North Ward, Sanpete Stake R of M, book C, Early to 1923, FHL; Brigham Young, [Jr.], Diaries, 7 June 1890, Church Archives. This marriage occurred in the company of several others who journeyed to Mexico under Young's leadership for the same reason. See James L. Wyatt, interviewed by Jessie L. Embry, 18 June 1976, p. 6, POHP; and William L. Wyatt, interviewed by Jessie L. Embry, 19 June 1976, p. 21, POHP.

10. Cowley's testimony that he performed this marriage is in *Trials.* Also see D. Michael Quinn, "LDS Church Authority and New Plural Marriages, 1890–1904," *Dialogue* 18 (Spring 1985): 72–73.

11. Young's performance of a plural union for James F. Johnson (Appendix II, #107) and Clara Mabel Kennedy was described above, chap. 5. For an instance of Young's continued urging of the doctrine, see Joseph W. Musser Diaries, 11 Nov. 1901, Church Archives.

12. Brigham Young, [Jr.], "Shall the Mormon Question Be Revived?" *Harper's* 43 (16 Dec. 1899): 3–4.

13. Susa Young Gates, "Apostle Brigham Young," in *Lives of Our Leaders: Character Sketches of Living Presidents and Apostles of the Church of Jesus Christ of Latter-day Saints* (Salt Lake City: Deseret News, 1901), 102.

14. Melvin C. Merrill, *Utah Pioneer: Apostle Marriner Wood Merrill and His Family* (n.p., 1937), 501; and Charles Mostyn Owen to Dr. William Paden, 11 Oct. 1904, Letterbook, Charles Mostyn Owen Collection, Church Archives. When Cowley later recalled the marriage before the Quorum of Twelve Apostles, he thought he remembered performing the ceremony sometime in 1903. *Trials.* It is more likely to have occurred in mid-1901, inasmuch as Hilda's first and only child was born 17 April 1902. Logan 7th Ward R of M, 1910, FHL. This same record indicates the child was confirmed on 14 June 1910 and identifies the child's father (then deceased) as Marriner W. Merrill and the

mother as Hilda M. Erickson. Merrill recorded that on 2 July 1901 he took Hilda Erickson to district court in Logan to file her naturalization papers. *Marriner Wood Merrill Diaries*, 2 July 1901, Church Archives. Nearly three years elapsed before she was mentioned again in Merrill's diary, and then not as Hilda Erickson, as in 1901 and before, but as Hilda M. Merrill. *Merrill Diaries*, 15 June 1904. Merrill's denials are in *Proceedings* 3:439–43.

15. *Proceedings* 1:408–18; Quinn, "New Plural Marriages," 77n.273. At the Smoot committee hearings, Charles Merrill (Appendix II, #131), a son of Apostle Merrill, testified that he married his first wife in 1887 then took Anna Stoddard as a plural wife in 1888. Because the first wife died in 1889, he married Chloe Hendricks as his legal wife in 1891. Charles said the marriage to Anna was secret, that she lived with her parents and he with his mother. He said that Anna probably did not enter the Merrill home more than once a year, even though she lived only a mile and a half away. This explanation seems unlikely inasmuch as no reason for secrecy existed after the death of his first wife. As his only wife after 1889, why had Anna any reason for remaining with her parents? It is more likely, all other dates remaining the same, that he married Anna on 22 March 1893, as stated on her FGS. Anna's first child, born in 1896, seems more likely to have followed an 1893 marriage than one in 1888, especially in a Mormon community. Hence, the probability is that, when Charles married in 1891, it was not a plural marriage, as was the marriage to Anna in 1893.

16. That Avery took her temple endowments on 1 Nov. 1900 suggests her marriage followed soon after. See Abraham Owen Woodruff FGS and Logan Temple Records, B/25/881, FHL. Cowley later said he married the two sometime in 1903. *Trials*. That year seems too late, the more likely date being sometime in 1901. See Quinn, "New Plural Marriages," 72n.254. For Avery's recollections, see the Eliza Avery Clark Woodruff Papers, 1900–1952, 32, 33, 42, 43, Church Archives. Comment on Woodruff's courtship with Avery was made by Mary Bennion Muhs, interviewed by Victor W. Jorgensen, 22 Jan. 1972, 31–33, Oral History Collection, California State University, Fullerton. Mrs. Muhs was a niece of Apostle Woodruff, her mother being sister to his first wife. Avery's child, a girl, was born 11 April 1904 in Colonia Juarez. See Abraham Owen Woodruff FGS, FHL; and Florence Ivins Hyde, interviewed by Victor W. Jorgensen, 19 Aug. 1972, transcription in private possession.

17. Firmage, *Memoirs of Hugh B. Brown*, 30.

18. Regarding Woodruff's remarks to a church audience in Mexico, see above in chap. 5. Also see Wayne Earl Carroll, interviewed by Marsha Martin, 1983, p. 26, POHP; and the discussion in Quinn, "New Plural Marriages," 89n.317.

19. Nephi L. Morris, "Abraham Owen Woodruff," *Lives of Our Leaders*, 238.

20. Matthias F. Cowley, *Wilford Woodruff, Fourth President of the Church of Jesus Christ of Latter-day Saints: History of His Life and Labors as Recorded in His Daily Journals* . . . (Salt Lake City: Deseret News, 1909).

21. Matthias F. Cowley, in *Trials*.

22. Ibid.; and Anthony W. Ivins Diaries, 25 Jan. 1911, Anthony Woodward Ivins Collection, UHi. The patriarch who married Cowley in 1905 was John Anthony Woolf, a former bishop and member of the stake presidency in Cardston, Alberta. Woolf was ordained a patriarch by Apostle John W. Taylor in 1899. "John Anthony Woolf," in *Latter-Day Saint Biographical Encyclopedia*, ed. Jenson, 2:17.

23. Matthias F. Cowley, as reported in *Proceedings* 1:8.

24. Information on Rudger Clawson is based chiefly on Roy Hoopes, "My Grandfather, the Mormon Apostle," *American Heritage* 41 (Feb. 1990): 82–92; and David Hoopes and Roy Hoopes, *The Making of a Mormon Apostle: The Story of Rudger Clawson* (Lanham: Madison Books, 1990). Stan Larson, Religion Archives specialist at the University of Utah Library, must also be acknowledged for having first alerted me to the likelihood of Clawson's post-Manifesto plural marriage.

25. Hoopes and Hoopes, *The Making of a Mormon Apostle*, 215–27.

26. Rudger Clawson Diaries, 23 Aug. and 1 Oct. 1903, Rudger Clawson Collection, University of Utah Library.

27. Ibid., 1 Oct. 1903.

28. Nephi Anderson, "Rudger Clawson," *Lives of Our Leaders*, 252.

29. Clawson Diaries, 11 Oct. (referring to events of the previous day), 6 Nov. and 19 Dec. 1903.

30. David King Udall FGS; Clawson Diaries, 10 May 1904.

31. Clawson Diaries, 16 May 1904 and events described in Hoopes and Hoopes, *The Making of a Mormon Apostle*, 225, 227.

32. See the discrepancy between Merrill's diary entries, produced in court, and the testimony provided by Margaret Geddes, as described in "Eccles Heirs Have Dark Hair and Eyes," *SLT*, 9 July 1915. For an account of the Eccles-Geddes episode, see above, chap. 5.

33. Clawson Diaries, 1–3 Aug. 1904.

34. Ibid., 4 Aug. 1904.

35. Denver and Rio Grande timetable, summer 1904, Denver–Rio Grande Collection, box 72, Colorado Historical Society, Denver, Colo.

36. Hoopes and Hoopes, *The Making of a Mormon Apostle*, 225, 227–28.

37. Clawson Diaries, 1 Oct. 1903.

38. Pearl Udall to her parents, 19 Oct. 1912, as referred to in Hoopes and Hoopes, *The Making of a Mormon Apostle*, 279–80, 314.

39. "Abraham Hoagland Cannon," in Jenson, *Latter-Day Saint Biographical Encyclopedia*, 1:167–68.

40. William C. Seifrit, "The Prison Experience of Abraham H. Cannon," *UHQ* 53 (Summer 1985): 223–36.

41. Abraham Hoagland Cannon Diaries, 8 and 11 Sept. 1891, BYU Library.

42. Ibid., 19 Oct. 1894.

43. Ibid., 24 Oct. 1894.

44. Ibid., 27 Oct. 1894.

45. Deuteronomy 25:5–10; "Levirate Marriage," *Interpreter's Dictionary of the Bible,* 4 vols. (New York: Abingdon Press, 1962), 3:282–83; Louis Isaac Rabinowitz, "Levirate Marriage and Halizah," in *Encyclopaedia Judaica,* ed. Cecil Roth et al., 16 vols. (Jerusalem: Keter, 1971), 11: cols. 122–31; Theodore H. Gaster, *Myth, Legend, and Custom in the Old Testament: A Comparative Study with Chapters from Sir James G. Frazer's "Folklore in the Old Testament,"* 2 vols. (New York: Harper Torchbooks, 1975), 2:447.

46. John Jaques, "Polygamy: Is It Consistent with the Bible, the Book of Mormon, and the Doctrine and Covenants of the Church of Jesus Christ of Latter-day Saints?" *Mill. Star* 15 (12 Feb. 1853): 99, 147; and idem, "Polygamy," ibid. 15 (5 March 1853): 147–48. Also see the comments of Leonard Arrington in his account of Brigham Young's marriage to the widows of Joseph Smith. *Brigham Young: American Moses* (New York: Alfred A. Knopf, 1985), 121.

47. Editorial, *DN,* 24 July 1867.

48. See, e.g., the case of brothers John and Elias Morris, John marrying Elias's widow for the express purpose of raising a family for the latter after his death. Katherine Cannon Thomas, interviewed by Leonard Grover, 25 March 1980, p. 2, POHP. Although not an example of the levirate, barren Mormon wives sometimes urged their husbands to marry plurally as a way of assuring perpetuation of their name. See the case of John Fielding Burton (Appendix II, #33).

49. Eugene Young, "Polygamy Is Reviving," *New York Herald,* 5 Feb. 1899.

50. For the choice of an older son as George Q. Cannon's initial preference, see George F. Gibbs affidavit, sworn before Arthur Winter, public notary, 10 Jan. 1912, George F. Gibbs Correspondence, Church Archives. Also see Rabinowitz, "Levirate Marriage," col. 123.

51. Anson Rainey, "Concubine," in *Encyclopaedia Judaica,* ed. Roth et al., 5:862–63; "Concubine," *Interpreter's Dictionary of the Bible,* 1:666. The practice was followed for centuries in medieval Christian Europe. See Christopher N. L. Brooke, "Marriage and Society in the Central Middle Ages," in *Marriage and Society: Studies in the Social History of Marriage,* ed. R. B. Outhwaite (New York: St. Martin's, 1981): 23–24; Michael Siegfried, "Research Note: The Skewed Sex Ratio in a Medieval Population: A Reinterpretation," *Social Science History* 10 (Summer 1986): 198–200; James A. Brundage, "Concubinage and Marriage in Medieval Canon Law," *Journal of Medieval History* 1 (1975): 1–17; and idem, *Law, Sex, and Christian Society in Medieval Europe* (Chicago: University of Chicago Press, 1987), 245, 297, 341–43.

52. *D&C* 132:1, 37–39 (1843).

53. See, e.g., the comments made in "'Concubinage' and the Church of England," *DN,* 11 Aug. 1882; Hubert Howe Bancroft, *History of Utah* (San Francisco: History Co., 1889), 370; and Orson F. Whitney, *Through Memory's Halls: The Life Story of Orson F. Whitney as Told by Himself* (Independence, Miss.: Zion's Printing and Publishing, 1930), 190–91. This view has been perpetu-

ated by Bruce R. McConkie, a late Mormon authority who asserted that "there were no concubines connected with the practice of plural marriage in this dispensation, because the caste system which caused some wives to be so designated did not exist." *Mormon Doctrine*, rev. ed. (Salt Lake City: Bookcraft, 1966), 154–55.

54. "The Mormon Seraglio," in John C. Bennett, *The History of the Saints; or, An Exposé of Joe Smith and Mormonism* (Boston: Leland & Whiting, 1842), 217–25; and Pomeroy Tucker, *Origin, Rise, and Progress of Mormonism: Biography of Its Founders and History of Its Church, Personal Remembrances and Historical Collections Hitherto Unwritten.* (New York: D. Appleton, 1867), 272–74. The best treatment of this matter remains that of Lawrence Foster, *Religion and Sexuality: Three American Communal Experiments of the Nineteenth Century* (New York: Oxford University Press, 1981), 163–66. Also see the comments of Samuel and Raymond Taylor in *The John Taylor Papers: Records of the Last Utah Pioneer*, 2 vols. (Redwood City, Calif.: Taylor Trust, 1984–85), 1:58–59, 86n.3; and the remark of Apostle Franklin D. Richards that there was more yet to be revealed concerning male-female relations than was contained in Joseph's 1843 revelation. "Discourse by Apostle F. D. Richards," *DN*, 18 April 1885.

55. Jaques, "Polygamy: Is It Consistent?" 99; Orson Pratt, "Celestial Marriage," *Seer* 1 (April 1853): 61–64; "Wives and Concubines," *DN*, 6 Nov. 1879; "Discourse by Apostle Erastus Snow," *DN*, 9 Sept. 1882; *JD* 26:330–31 (Moses Thatcher/1885).

56. George Q. Cannon, as reported in the Abraham H. Cannon Diaries, 5 April 1894.

57. Wilford Woodruff, in ibid., 5 April 1894.

58. Carlos Ashby Badger Diaries, 18 Sept. 1905, Church Archives.

59. Quinn, "New Plural Marriages," 81–82.

60. Abraham H. Cannon Diaries, 21 Nov., 11 Dec. 1894, 23–24 July 1895, 17 Dec. 1895.

61. Mary Bennion Powell to George R. Stewart, 228-page transcript composed between 26 Jan. and 25 Feb. 1952, Henry E. Huntington Library, San Marino, Calif., 198.

62. See above in chap. 5.

63. Abraham H. Cannon Diaries, 13 Nov. 1892.

64. Ibid., 28 Dec. 1895.

65. *Proceedings* 1:1060–1061, 1079; 2:142.

66. Ibid., 2:142–43.

67. Some years later, another of the sons of George Q. Cannon, Frank Cannon, accused President Joseph F. Smith of reinstituting the practice of polygamy within the church and, specifically, to have commenced the renewal with the marriage of his brother Abraham to Lilian Hamlin. In response to Frank Cannon's allegations, Lilian was found and persuaded to make a statement to the press. In it she said nothing as to where the ceremony was performed. But, she declared, "Joseph F. Smith did not perform the marriage

ceremony between Abram H. Cannon and myself." She went on to further offer to exonerate anyone who in the future might be falsely charged with "performing the ceremony which united Abram H. Cannon and myself in plural marriage." "Lilian Hamlin Says Jos. F. Smith Did Not Perform the Ceremony," *DN,* 2 March 1911.

Both Frank Cannon's article, published in *Everybody's* magazine and later included in his and Harvey J. O'Higgins's book, and Lilian's response are interesting. Not only did Lilian's denial employ phrases the church had long since become expert in using to obscure the truth but Frank Cannon engaged in some humorous prevarication of his own. In his account he quoted himself, upon hearing of the marriage between Abraham and Lilian, as saying to his father, George Q. Cannon: "'Father!' I cried. 'Has this thing [polygamy] come back again!'" President Cannon, who had actually instigated the entire affair, was then represented to say: "I know—its awful. I would have prevented it if I could." Frank J. Cannon and Harvey J. O'Higgins, *Under the Prophet in Utah: The National Menace of a Political Priestcraft* (Boston: C. M. Clark, 1911), 177. More ironic, we learn from an affidavit drawn in 1912 that Frank, on hearing about his father's idea of raising up "seed" for his deceased brother David, actually volunteered *himself* as a candidate and offered to marry Lilian in polygamy. Although Hugh J. Cannon, an older son, was considered as the first prospect, family opposition developed and Abraham was the one finally authorized. Frank, the affidavit reveals, was turned down by his father as morally unworthy. George F. Gibbs affidavit, sworn before Arthur Winter, public notary, Salt Lake City, Utah, 10 Jan. 1912, George F. Gibbs Correspondence, Church Archives.

68. *Proceedings* 2:142–43.

69. Abraham H. Cannon Diaries, 8 July 1890, 14–15 Sept. 1891, 30 May 1892, 18 Oct. 1890.

70. *Proceedings* 2:142–43.

71. "Off for Reno, Nevada," *DN,* 18 June 1896; "From Los Angeles," *DN,* 2 July 1896.

72. *Proceedings* 1:110–11; "Off for Reno, Nevada"; and "From Los Angeles."

73. "Living Endowments, Salt Lake Temple," book A, p. 131, no. 4710, film, FHL.

74. See above in chap. 2.

75. JH, 1 July 1896.

76. *Proceedings* 1:128, 177; Joseph F. Smith to Reed Smoot, 9 April 1904, p. 10, Reed Smoot Correspondence, 1903–19, film, Church Archives.

77. "Abraham Hoagland Cannon," *DN,* 20 July 1896; "Abraham Cannon Dead," *SLT,* 20 July 1896; Brigham Young, [Jr.], Diaries, 10–16 July 1896, Church Archives.

78. This information was provided by Wilhelmina at the Smoot hearings. *Proceedings* 1:1067, 2:143, 146.

79. Ibid. 2:142–44, 147.

80. Ibid. 2:68–72.

81. As reported in a six-page, typewritten deposition entitled "*Polygamy, Statement of Representative George Sutherland of Utah.* At hearing on Wednesday, February 25, 1903, before Sub-Committee No. 1 of the Committee on Judiciary, House of Representatives." George Sutherland Papers, box 8, Library of Congress. Also see *Proceedings* 2:694.

82. *Proceedings* 1:110–12, 127.

83. See Roberts's testimony in *Proceedings* 1:743. Lenora Taylor, when sealed to Apostle Matthias F. Cowley in 1905, also was surprised by the peremptory nature of the ceremony. Ivins Diaries, 25 June 1911.

84. Joseph F. Smith to Reed Smoot, 24 April 1904, Joseph F. Smith Letterbook, Church Archives.

85. Eugene Young, "Polygamy Is Reviving," *New York Herald,* 5 Feb. 1899.

86. Charles William Penrose Diaries, 19 July 1911, UHi.

87. Joseph W. Musser Diaries, 16 Feb. 1914, Church Archives.

88. See Cannon's statements in Young, "Polygamy Is Reviving."

89. For reference to this as a Mormon stratagem in other cases, see the comments of Edward B. Critchlow at the time of the Smoot hearings as contained in Badger Diaries, 18 April 1904.

90. Badger Diaries, 9 Dec. 1905; *Proceedings* 1:110–11.

91. Quinn, "New Plural Marriages," 83–84.

92. Carl A. Badger to Rose Badger, 29 Dec. 1904, in Carlos Ashby Badger Letterbook, Church Archives; and Badger Diaries, 22 Dec. 1904.

93. The Utah law was "An Act to Punish Polygamy and Kindred Offenses," *Laws of the Territory of Utah* (1892), 30th sess., 8, sec. 2:5–7. For commentary on its continuance after statehood, see Orma Linford, "The Mormons and the Law: The Polygamy Cases—Part II," *Utah Law Review* 9 (Summer 1965): 585n.172. With regard to the applicability of common-law restrictions on plural marriage in Utah and elsewhere prior to 1898, see all of G. W. Bartholomew, "Recognition of Polygamous Marriages in America," *International and Comparative Law Quarterly* 13 (July 1964): 1022–1075; and Michael W. Homer, "The Judiciary and the Common Law in Utah Territory, 1850–61," *Dialogue* 21 (Spring 1988): 97–108.

94. "An Act to Punish Adultery," *Statutes of California,* ch. 271, pp. 380–81 (1871–72). A review of the question of state-federal jurisdiction in territorial possessions, including territorial waters, was provided by the United States Supreme Court in *Utah Power & Light Co. v. U.S.,* 243 U.S. 389, 404–5 (1916); and *U.S. v. California,* 332 U.S. 19 (1947).

95. *Hutchins v. Kimmell,* 31 Mich. 126 (1875). For cases more nearly parallel to the situation of the Mormons, see *Holmes v. Holmes et al.,* 1 Sawy. 99, 1 Abb. (U.S.) 525. Circuit Court, D. Oregon (1870); and *Norman v. Norman,* 121 Cal. 620 (1898). Joel Prentiss Bishop, a leading commentator of the time, was explicit in excepting polygamy from the common-law rule that would recog-

nize marriage and divorce arrangements undertaken outside an individual's state. *New Commentaries on Marriage, Divorce, and Separation as to the Law . . . ,* 2 vols. (Chicago: T. H. Flood, 1891), 1:128–29, 311n.1, 368, 370, 729.

96. See above in chap. 2.

97. "Johnson, Benjamin Julius," Kimball Young Collection, box 2, fd. 33, p. 1, Garrett Evangelical Theological Library, Evanston, Ill. Also see Isabella Johnson Sevey, "Benjamin Julius Johnson," in *Stalwarts South of the Border,* comp. Nelle Spilsbury Hatch and B. Carmon Hardy (Anaheim, Calif.: privately printed, 1985), 341.

98. Herbert L. James to John M. Cannon, 15 Dec. 1901, and 10 Jan. 1902, copies of John M. Cannon legal correspondence in private possession. Also see Young, "Polygamy Is Reviving."

99. See Appendix II, #40; Young, "Polygamy Is Reviving"; *Proceedings* 2:97–98.

100. Abraham Hoagland Cannon FGS.

101. "The Late Elder George Teasdale," *Juvenile Instructor* 142 (1 July 1907): 400–401.

102. Hugh J. Cannon, "Apostle George Teasdale," *Lives of Our Leaders,* 148–49; Nelle Spilsbury Hatch, "George Teasdale," in *Stalwarts South of the Border,* comp. Hatch and Hardy, 682–84; Heber Grant Ivins, interviewed by Victor W. Jorgensen, 18 July 1972, p. 12, Oral History Collection, California State University, Fullerton.

103. Pacheco Ward Historical Records, 24 July 1892, Feb. 1894, 5 Aug. 1894, Church Archives.

104. George Teasdale, quoted in Musser Diaries, 8 Feb. 1902.

105. Information provided in divorce complaint, *George Teasdale, Plaintiff, vs. Lillias H. Teasdale, Defendant,* District Court of the Fifth Judicial District, State of Utah, County of Juab, complaint dated 9 Dec. 1899 (hereafter cited as Teasdale's Divorce Complaint); *Orders and Decrees in Probate,* Fifth District Court, Juab County, book 1, 1896–1901, pp. 8, 9, 44, 189, 227, Nephi, Utah; index cards to temple records for Mary Lauretta Picton and Matilda Ellen Picton, FHL; George Teasdale FGS; Hatch, "George Teasdale," 684.

106. See information provided under "Scoles, Hannah," in "Emigrations from Europe," film 298437, FHL.

107. Reed Smoot to Joseph F. Smith, 19 Jan. 1904, Reed Smoot Correspondence, Church Archives. Also see Smith's responses on the Teasdale-Scoles marriage in *Proceedings* 1:144.

108. "Living Sealings, Book C, Salt Lake Temple, Sealings Performed Elsewhere, 5 Feb. 1900 to 11 Sept. 1904," p. 33, no. 594, FHL. For information on Marion Scoles's early years in Logan and Nephi, see "Into the Great Beyond: Marion E. Scoles, Wife of Apostle George Teasdale, Passes Away at Nephi," *DN,* 19 Dec. 1898; "Obituary," *DN,* 24 Dec. 1898; "One of the Cases," *SLT,* 19 April 1899.

109. JH, 1 July 1896 and 28 Oct. 1897.

110. Anthon Hendrik Lund Diaries, 6 Sept. 1897 to 23 March 1898, Church Archives.

111. For references to the Lund-Hintze mission, see JH, 29 Dec. 1897; Lund Diaries, 29 Dec. 1897; and "Higher Spiritual Thoughts: A Treatise in Advanced Theology," undated, unpublished manuscript, quoted and edited by Henry S. Florence, Jr., "A Hintze Compilation, Begun August 27, 1983 at the Annual Family Reunion," p. 2, copy in possession of Victor W. Jorgensen, Logan, Utah. Evidence of Hintze's plural marriage and Apostle Lund's involvement with it arises from inferences in extant portions of the Ferdinand Friis Hintze Diaries, 1 and 2 Jan. 1898, Church Archives. That unavailable passages in Hintze's diary describe the marriage is known from the candor of remarks by family members on Hintze's FGS. There it states: "F. F. HINTZE's Journal records that they [Hintze and Nora Mikkelsen] were married 'on a ferry boat between U.S. and Canada by Anthon H. Lund.' Nora told her children they were sworn to secrecy." Ferdinand Friis Hintze FGS, as included in "A Hintze Compilation." Further corroborating evidence is provided by Mary Bennion Muhs, interviewed by Victor W. Jorgensen, 22 Jan. 1972, pp. 16, 20, Oral History Collection, California State University, Fullerton; and Eulale J. Hintze to Victor W. Jorgensen, 23 Feb. 1984, letter in possession of Victor W. Jorgensen.

112. *Proceedings* 1:611.

113. See, for example, the bid, in her own name, to obtain property owned by the three children of Mary Picton Teasdale. *Orders and Decrees in Probate,* Fifth District Court, Juab County, book 1, 1896–1901, p. 227. Also see "One of the Cases," *SLT,* 19 April 1899.

114. This headstone, yet standing, is to be seen in the Vine Bluff Cemetery in Nephi, Utah. Regarding Marion's death, see "Obituary," *DN,* 24 Dec. 1898; and "One of the Cases," *SLT,* 19 April 1899. That both Marion and her infant died in childbirth is confirmed in Nephi, 2d Ward, Historical Record, book 1877–1901, p. 300, FHL.

115. Marriage License Record, Cache County, book 4, 1895–1901, FHL.

116. Teasdale Divorce Complaint. The *Tribune* articles were "Apostle Teasdale Weds," *SLT,* 19 May 1900; and "Looks Like Polygamy," ibid., 20 May 1900.

117. Joseph F. Smith, in *Proceedings* 1:487, 491.

118. Teasdale Divorce Complaint. There is a summary of the divorce proceedings, as agreed upon by the attorneys, in the Smoot hearings. *Proceedings* 3:457.

119. "A Record of Births, Blessings, Baptisms, Confirmations, Re-Baptisms, Re-Confirmations, Ordinations, Received, Removed, Died, and Cut off," Twentieth Ward, ROM Early to 1912, p. 56, no. 1338, FHL.

120. Death Certificate D7499, Salt Lake City, Utah Death Records (1895–1908), p. 39, no. 1467, FHL.

121. Eugene Young, "Polygamy Is Reviving."

122. Death Certificate D7499.

123. Twentieth Ward ROM Early to 1912, no. 2623, FHL.

124. Neither is there record of an adoption for George Vivian Teasdale in 1896 in "Probate Record A, Adoption of Children, Salt Lake County, 1884–1902," FHL.

125. Abraham H. Cannon Diaries, 14 and 21 Sept. 1891, respectively.

126. See, for example, the "sham" divorce granted David Cazier and his wife Eliza Ann Naylor in 1892, albeit Eliza was a plural wife and the divorcement a church action only. David Cazier Autobiography, 21 Jan. 1913, BYU Library.

127. *R. L. Polks Salt Lake City Directory* (1908), 1069.

128. "1914 Census of the LDS Church," film 24282, FHL.

129. "Handcart Pioneer Answers Death Call," *DN*, 12 Feb. 1921.

130. "Letitia Thomas Teasdale," in Jenson, *Latter-Day Saint Biographical Encyclopedia*, 4:268; Sugar House Ward ROM, 1901–17, FHL; LDS Church Census, 1920, FHL.

131. [Lydia Maria Olive Mamreoff von Finkelstein], *The Life Sketch of Lydia Mamreoff von Finkelstein (Madame Mountford) with Original Photographic Views Taken by the Author in the Holy Land, "The Glory of All Lands" Ezekiel: 20:6* (Washington, D.C.: published by the author, 1911), 7–24.

132. Ibid., 25–33.

133. "Oriental Scenes," *Deseret News, Semi-Weekly*, 16 Feb. 1897; "Madame Lydia von F. Mountford," *Relief Society Magazine* 8 (Feb. 1921): 71–73; Finkelstein, *The Life*, 7–12, 25. On Hyde's mission to Palestine, see *CHC* 2:44–45.

134. See the several references in Scott G. Kenney, ed., *Wilford Woodruff's Journal, 1833–1898*, 9 vols. (Midvale, Utah: Signature Books, 1983–85), 9:446, 450, 454, 455, 456, 472, 473, 493, 494, 495, 496, 497.

135. Lydia Mountford, quoted in "Ninety Years of Age," *Deseret News, Semi-Weekly*, 2 March 1897; Cowley, *Wilford Woodruff*, 604–5.

136. Kenney, *Wilford Woodruff's Journal*, 9:493, 21 July 1897; "Madame Lydia von F. Mountford," 76.

137. Kenney, *Wilford Woodruff's Journal*, 9:487, 15 June 1897, 9:490, 5 July 1897, 9:491, 13 July 1897, 9:498, 12 Aug. 1897; Finkelstein, *The Life*, 18.

138. Kenney, *Wilford Woodruff's Journal*, 9:486–87, 14 June 1897.

139. Ibid., 9:488, 489, 23 and 25 June 1897, 9:506, 5 Sept. 1897.

140. Ibid., 9:507, 8 Sept. 1897.

141. Ibid., 9:507, 10 Sept. 1897.

142. Ibid., 9:509, 18 Sept. 1897.

143. The entries in Woodruff's diary indicate little except that, during his nights on the boat, he slept well. Kenney, *Wilford Woodruff's Journal*, 9:510–11, 20–22 Sept. 1897.

144. Kenney, *Wilford Woodruff's Journal*, 9:511, 25 Sept. 1897, 9:520, 17 Nov. 1897; "Veale Shot Himself," *Los Angeles Daily Times*, 9 Nov. 1897.

145. Kenney, *Wilford Woodruff's Journal*, 9:515ff.

146. Ibid., 9:527–28, 9 Jan. 1898. Apostle Erastus Snow said Joseph Smith taught that Jesus' parable of the talents referred to a man who had but one wife and would not take another. Ibid., 8:126–27, 14 Oct. 1882. Mountford's Tabernacle address was reported in "Services at the Tabernacle," *DN*, 10 Jan. 1898.

147. Kenney, *Wilford Woodruff's Journal*, 9:528, 11 Jan. 1898.

148. "Madame Lydia von F. Mountford," 76–77; Finkelstein, *The Life*, 32–33. Notice of the marriage is found in India Office Records, N/1/211/193, India Office Library, London, England.

149. Certificate of death for Charles Edwin Mountford, 21 May 1916, Thanet, County of Kent, General Register Office, London, England. The grave is located in St. Peters Churchyard, Broadstairs and St. Peters, row 17, no. 44.

150. See, e.g., Richard Van Wagoner, "Mormon Polyandry in Nauvoo," *Dialogue* 18 (Fall 1985): 67–83.

151. See the letters to associates, handbills, and newspaper notices for the years 1905–10, in fds. 1–5, Lydia Mary Olive von Finkelstein Mountford Collection, Church Archives; and "Madame Lydia von F. Mountford," 71, 76–77.

152. Finkelstein, *The Life*, 37–38; editorial, [Calif.] *Santa Cruz Surf*, 20 Oct. 1897.

153. Mme. Lydia M. von Finkelstein Mountford, *Jesus Christ in His Homeland* (Cincinnati: Jennings & Graham, 1911), 114–18.

154. Kenney, *Wilford Woodruff's Journal*, 9:558–63, 13 Aug. 1898–2 Sept. 1898.

155. Matthias F. Cowley, in *Trials*.

156. Lund Diaries, 1 Dec. 1897.

157. Charles F. Zitting, *A Discussion between President Anthony W. Ivins and Charles F. Zitting* (n.p., n.d.), 4.

158. See statements attributed to D. Michael Quinn, made before the B. H. Roberts Society in May 1990, as reported in "'Living the Principle': Then and Now," *Sunstone* 14 (Aug. 1990): 62.

159. Untitled statement, Charles Mostyn Owen Collection, Church Archives; *Proceedings* 2:702, 736. Also see Apostle Brigham Young, Jr.'s comment in his "Shall the Mormon Question Be Revived," *Harper's* 43 (16 Dec. 1899): 3. In the autumn of 1889, to illustrate his obedience to the laws, Woodruff told a reporter that he had been strict in staying away from the homes of his plural wives for five years. "Mormons Abandon Polygamy," *New York Herald*, 13 Oct. 1889.

7

The Leaders Divide:
Roberts and Smoot, Taylor and Cowley

When President Wilford Woodruff died on September 2, 1898, criticism of the church was rapidly reviving. Mormons were accused of defaulting on their promises concerning polygamy. These allegations, as already suggested, contributed to the conservative policies of Woodruff's successor, Lorenzo Snow, even though during his brief administration several new plural marriages were performed (see graph, 317). After Joseph F. Smith succeeded to the presidency of the church on 17 October 1901, they occurred in yet greater numbers. Concurrently, in response to growing rumor, attacks on the church mounted. This led to the ordeals of the Brigham H. Roberts and Reed Smoot hearings in Congress. These, in turn, precipitated a painful division among church leaders themselves.

Most of the initial criticism arose in connection with continued cohabitation by Mormon men with their plural wives. Charles Mostyn Owen said in 1899 that he could not find a half-dozen cases where polygamists in Utah had lived up to the cohabitation restrictions imposed by amnesty.[1] Church members, on the other hand, argued that an "understanding" had been struck with gentile leaders permitting cohabitation so long as new polygamous marriages were brought to an end.[2] Mormon assumptions were reinforced by a spirit of general toleration. When Charles L. Walker was convicted for unlawful cohabitation in 1892, for example, he was fined six pennies for his crime.[3] There was also what appeared to be an intentional failure by Utah's first state legislature to implement a territorial law of 1892 prohibiting polygamy and unlawful cohabitation.[4] This was read as a signal to men living with older polygamous wives that they would be left alone so long as new ones were not added to their families.

Lulled by such tolerance and insufficiently sensitive to differences of interpretation concerning the "understanding," the church failed to prevent reenactment in 1898 of the 1892 territorial statute into the new state's criminal code. Inasmuch as the commission overseeing the codification included devoted Mormons, and considering the influence the church enjoyed in state government, to have allowed repassage of the 1892 law was a blunder.[5] An instrument now existed permitting anyone to bring information for the purpose of prosecuting men cohabiting with women other than their legal wives. Hoping to undo the effects of the measure, Mormons took steps to amend it. A committee of church leaders worked with state legislators to fashion a provision prohibiting prosecution for adultery and unlawful cohabitation unless such action were brought on complaint by an immediate relative, such as an offended wife. Inasmuch as polygamous marriages were presumed to consist of voluntary participants on all sides, the likelihood that any would commence legal action against husbands was greatly diminished.[6]

In a discussion of some sharpness among First Presidency members and apostles, George Q. Cannon opposed the move as likely to result in hostility toward the church.[7] Nevertheless, it was decided that if the legislature could be brought to amend the code, it would spare those living with and caring for polygamous companions from being taken to court on information provided by apostates and paid "spotters." As Joseph F. Smith, a supporter of the plan, explained later, it was designed to save Utah from a return to the troubles of the 1880s. Moreover, by confining those able to bring charges for adultery to offended family members, Utah was aligning itself with the practices of other states.[8]

While state legislator Abel John Evans was the official sponsor of the proposal, it is clear from the diaries of Apostle John Henry Smith that the writing of the amendment, as well as maneuvering for its passage, was largely overseen by church authorities.[9] These efforts were frustrated, however, by Governor Heber M. Wells, who, like George Q. Cannon, foresaw an angry reaction if the measure passed. He referred to the possibility for a revival of the movement for incorporating an anti-polygamy amendment into the United States Constitution. Hence, Wells vetoed the law. Even then, criticisms were heard condemning the attempt as evidence of political intrusion by Mormon leaders in behalf of polygamy.[10] The church, of course, said talk of plurality was only an excuse, as it had always been. The real object of critics, they said, was destruction of Mormonism itself.[11]

One of the more strident of the church's new opponents was Theodore Schroeder. He began as a gentile lawyer in Salt Lake City in the late 1880s and early 1890s, when the controversy surrounding Mormon polygamy was at its height. An initial sympathy for the church declined as he became persuaded Mormons were engaged in an elaborate system of deceit. Although he later moved to New York City, where he actively advocated First Amendment liberties and helped found the Free Speech League, a forerunner of the American Civil Liberties Union, he is best remembered in Mormon annals for his literary fusillades against the Saints.[12]

Beginning in late 1897 and continuing through the next year, Schroeder filled the columns of his publication, *The Kinsman,* with essays devoted to the subject of continued Mormon polygamy. Tracing its history from the Kirtland and Nauvoo periods to the time of the Manifesto, he sought to show how the church had always dissimulated in its responses to public inquiry concerning the practice. He said that, despite statements to the contrary, polygamy was preached and practiced in the church yet. Mormons, he said, not only had transformed the "understanding" into a contract but, under the guise of caring for their families, were continuing to produce children by plural spouses just as they had before the Manifesto and the promises made in connection with it. If the agreement had not been understood by the Saints to exclude continued cohabitation, he asked, why had they permitted the enactment of those portions of the 1898 code criminalizing such activity?[13]

There was also Charles Mostyn Owen. For more than a decade he traveled throughout Utah, southern Idaho, and western Wyoming as an engineer. During that time he interviewed numerous individuals, Mormon and non-Mormon, concerning the marital status of residents in the areas he visited. Owen kept extensive records and asked for written affidavits whenever possible. He seems to have had a mischievous personality, delighting in any discomfort he could create for those implicated in polygamy. By late 1899 he said he was ready to organize the names of guilty polygamists into groups of five, releasing evidence about them to civil authorities throughout the state. This, he expected, would keep recently married polygamists in a state of anxiety. Already, he said, the Mormon community was nervous as to whose marriages were likely to be found out and made public.[14]

Owen described his method for obtaining evidence as involving information furnished by either apostates or church members who disapproved of those yet engaging in polygamy. After learning of such activities from a witness, he said he "checked and checked and checked" to be sure that what he had been told was correct. Thereupon, he approached the county attorney with the evidence gathered. If the legal officer hesitated to prosecute, Owen provided newspapers such as the *Salt Lake Tribune* with his findings. This usually pressured such officers to take action. In this way, a number of prominent individuals were criminally indicted. These included Apostle Heber J. Grant; Angus M. Cannon, president of the Salt Lake Stake; and church president Joseph F. Smith.[15] Owen's activities as a professional snoop won him little love from the Saints.

The Brigham H. Roberts case not only brought the work of men like Schroeder and Owen into play but was a harbinger of the Smoot investigation.[16] A member of the First Council of Seventy and a polygamist, Roberts entered the electoral race for Congress in the autumn of 1898. George Q. Cannon had objected on grounds that a "whip" would be made of Roberts's domestic affairs to the injury of the church.[17] Utah's first state governor, Heber M. Wells, himself a Mormon and the son of a polygamist, opposed Roberts's nomination for the same reason. In the end, with a majority of high churchmen behind him, Roberts ran and won the election handily.

Roberts (Appendix II, #159) not only cohabited with his wives, Louisa Smith and Celia Dibble, fathering children by them after 1890, but he probably took a third wife during those years as well. The woman concerned was Dr. Margaret Curtis Shipp, a former polygamous wife of Dr. Milford Shipp. At the time of the Smoot hearings, Roberts said he married Shipp in April 1890, thus contradicting President Wilford Woodruff's statement that no such marriages had occurred in the year preceding the Manifesto.[18] Roberts testified that Daniel H. Wells performed the ceremony solemnizing his marriage in a private home in Salt Lake City and that there were no witnesses. Roberts also stated that neither of his first two wives learned of the marriage until two or three years after the event and that Wells himself had died the year following the marriage.[19] The 1890 date seems doubtful because of indications Dr. Shipp was yet living with her first husband until at least 1892. Not only is this inferred by the Salt Lake City Directory for those years, but Senator Smoot told Carl A. Badger he was reliably informed this was true. On the basis of the chronology of Mrs. Shipp's residences and the beginning dates for her use of the name Mrs. Roberts, Charles Mostyn Owen concluded the marriage occurred in the spring of 1894.[20]

Some of Roberts's friends defended the relationship with Shipp as only platonic, resulting from Roberts's need for greater intellectual companionship than was available in his other marriages.[21] Shipp, however, was more candid. In a lecture given to young women shortly

before Roberts's nomination for Congress, she reportedly told them
to look for "affinity" with a man, even if he already had other wives.
The excitement from the touch of his hand, she said, would tell each
that she had met her true love. The law could not prevent her from
having the man of her choice, she declared, and they should feel
equally free.[22] Years later, when Roberts married Shipp legally in
Illinois, it disturbed some in Utah who believed the two were indis-
crete and should have formalized their union inconspicuously at
home.[23]

Despite his domestic circumstances, Roberts was active in church
and civic affairs throughout the 1890s. The comparative freedom he
enjoyed in Utah's public life seemed to support Mormon interpretation of the "understanding." He also argued that other polygamists
had been appointed to federal positions such as postmasters and sur-
veyors. This demonstrated, he said, that the arrangement Mormons
worked out with the local gentile population was respected, justifying
his own candidacy for public office.[24] Opposition of large proportions, however, developed soon after his election.

The Methodist leader Thomas Corwin Iliff and Dr. William M.
Paden, a Utah Presbyterian, lectured from Maine to California to
arouse opposition to Roberts.[25] Both sectarian and non-religious societies responded to the call. These included the Protestant Ministerial
Alliance of Utah, the Women's Board of Home Missions of the Presbyterian Church, the National Congress of Mothers, the National
Council for Women, the American Female Guardian Society, the
League for Social Service, the National Anti-Polygamy League, and
numerous individual crusaders such as Theodore Schroeder. Newspapers and magazines blazoned arguments against seating the polygamous congressman to their readers across the country.[26] "It was
perfectly understood," said an 1899 writer, "that the one condition of
Utah's admission to the Union was the complete abandonment in all
good faith of the institution and practice of polygamy." This notwithstanding, said another, "church leaders scarcely waited for Statehood
to be perfected before they began pressing forward the old polygamy
doctrine."[27]

As before the Manifesto, the cry was that the American home was
in jeopardy. Some said the presence of Roberts in Congress constituted the most serious attack on the sacredness of marriage in a
generation. In the words of Theodore Schroeder, the Mormons had
"buncoed" the nation. They had only pretended to give up polygamy
to obtain statehood and were now sending a near "erotomaniac" to the
nation's capital.[28] Tolerance for cohabitation, it was said, would only

smooth "the way for the announcement that new polygamous marriages are being made, and that the doctrine is being taught within the church with its old vigor"—a development some said had already commenced.[29] The question provoked a new round of calls for a constitutional amendment that would forever exorcise the "disease" of polygamy from the American commonwealth. Congressmen urging passage of the measure reminded the public that if Utah were allowed to revive polygamy and send pluralists to Congress, it would introduce into their midst a home system that would doom society as they knew it. "Such a union between the Asiatic type and European-American type of civilized life would be incompatible and fatal to our peace and progress."[30] Anti-Roberts broadsides recapitulated all that was laid against Mormon polygamy for two generations. By threatening the purity of womanhood and of the home, all that was most precious to Americans was in danger. Most fearfully, to allow Roberts into Congress augured the "enthronement and deification of human passion."[31]

The *New York Evening Journal,* a Hearst publication, took the lead as coordinator of a new crusade. As one of the largest circulating dailies in the United States, its influence was considerable. It began the campaign in early 1899 with a serial adaptation of Arthur Conan Doyle's "A Study in Scarlet," publishing it under the title "Mormons; or, The Curse of Utah."[32] The paper employed Charles Mostyn Owen to provide it with information; articles critical of Roberts and the Saints began appearing regularly in October. Roberts credited the *Journal* and the research of Owen with much of the success that the attack against him carried.[33]

A petition demanding Roberts be denied his seat in the national legislature produced 7,000,000 signatures. It was sent to Congress on twenty-eight rolls, each two feet in diameter and encased in an American flag. When the scrolls were placed before the speaker's desk in the House of Representatives, the *Journal* described as "thrilling" the scene presented by women jostling in the galleries to gaze at the offering.[34] It mattered not that many of the signatures were those of children or that some signed more than once; the petition had the hoped-for effect.[35]

Acting on the recommendation of a committee chaired by Representative Robert Walker Tayler from Ohio, the House overwhelmingly voted to exclude Roberts from their chamber. In its investigation the committee confirmed that Roberts was engaged in polygamous cohabitation and indicated that one of the three women involved had likely become his wife since the Manifesto. This, they said, constituted a "notorious and defiant violation of the law of the land." Roberts, the report said, had flouted not only society's legal codes but his church's promises as well. His election as Utah's representative was "an explicit and offensive violation of the understanding by which Utah was admitted as a state."[36] The *Journal's* account described Roberts's exclusion as the greatest victory so far achieved by twentieth-century journalism in defense of womanhood and social purity in the home.[37] The *New York Times* said it better: "the vast mob" of women who "bawled for the shutting out of Roberts" had their way.[38]

It was a costly miscalculation for the Mormon leaders to have allowed Roberts to run for office. They had inadequately assayed the residue of national sentiment against plural marriage. As one female activist expressed it, polygamy was "utterly and unspeakably opposed to the American idea of the home, which with us is a sacred word."[39] The fears of George Q. Cannon and Governor Wells had proved correct. Theodore Schroeder and Charles Mostyn Owen, whose murmuring had been confined largely to local audiences, now were given a national platform by their work in the Roberts hearings. Their efforts, combined with the jeremiads of religious and women's organizations, cranked the rhetoric of the 1880s into circulation again.

In the midst of this, the controversy between Utah Mormonism and the Reorganized Church of Jesus Christ of Latter Day Saints flared once more. Events like the Roberts case and debate surrounding the Evans law incited the bickering. There was a humorous, but confusing, character to the contest because at the time both churches had leaders named Joseph Smith, both of whom were related and claimed descent either from Joseph Smith the prophet or from his brother Hyrum, and both of whom wrote aggressively in their respective church's behalf. The spectacle acquired few friends for either party. John T. Bridwell, a Progressive journalist, spoke for most non-Mormons when he said the altercation between the cousins was not only noisy but disgusting. It reminded one, he said, of the youngster employed by an amusement concern to keep an eye on the freaks. The boy soon came running to the proprietor, shouting: "Mister! Mister! The two-headed monster is a-fightin' with herself, and a-pullin' out all her hair!" "Long," said Bridwell, "may she fight!"[40]

These episodes crested in the investigation made of Senator Reed Smoot. While the vast majority of Americans, including Mormons, have no memory of the affair, it was an event of high drama at the time. It began when Apostle Reed Smoot, again with the approval of church leaders, was elected to the United States Senate by the Utah legislature in 1903. Smoot and President Joseph F. Smith both believed that God had specially chosen the senator for his role and that he could perform valuable services for the church in that capacity.[41] After his election, protests were drawn up almost immediately, as in the recent case of Brigham H. Roberts, to prevent Smoot from taking his seat. What was called a "tidal wave" of letters was sent to Congress asking that the Utah senator be barred from their councils.[42] Protestant church groups and women's organizations such as the Women's Christian Temperance Union and National Congress of Mothers were especially aroused. They were not alone. Ray Stannard Baker, admiring the Saints in other regards, said Mormon polygamy was so common that leaders in Salt Lake City could take a street car in any direction and arrive home.[43]

The primary objection against Smoot was that, as an apostle, he was a member of Mormonism's highest governing body, and under its leadership polygamy and unlawful cohabitation were yet approved and practiced.[44] Complaints of this nature were sent to Washington, D.C., in such volume that it was estimated it would take a half-dozen men to carry the documents to the senate chamber where the Committee on Privileges and Elections opened its inquiry into Smoot's qualifications on 16 January 1904.[45] Although a majority on the committee were, like Smoot, Republican, the flood of letters ran so overwhelmingly against him that party allegiance offered little solace. The committee's chairman, Julius Caesar Burrows of Michigan, had squinted at Mormon practices since the Edmunds law of 1882 and was expected to exploit the sensational nature of Smoot's problem for his own political advantage.[46]

Former Ohio Congressman Robert Walker Tayler was retained by the protestants as counsel. Tayler was an able prosecutor and chaired the committee that had successfully excluded Brigham H. Roberts from the House of Representatives. His files proved invaluable, for, as he later said, nearly everything adduced against Smoot had been raised in connection with Roberts four years earlier.[47] Remembering the services rendered by Charles Mostyn Owen in the Roberts case, the anti-Smoot petitioners retained him as well. He proved so crucial that Senator George Sutherland referred to him as the "master of ceremonies" over the entire affair.[48] Before Smoot's ordeal passed, the investigation lasted more than three years, consumed in excess of 3,000 pages of printed testimony, and ranged far beyond the immediate question of Smoot, broadening its inquiry to include the history, theology, and culture of Mormonism itself. More than one student has suggested that the episode constituted the most searching, and perhaps bigoted, congressional investigation of any religious body in American history.[49]

Recognizing the implications involved, Mormon leaders assigned the church's legal counsel, Franklin S. Richards, to assist Smoot with his defense. A non-Mormon, the Washington, D.C., attorney A. S. Worthington, was retained as Smoot's counsel before the committee. He was assisted by Salt Lake City attorney Waldemar Van Cott. These men attempted to narrow the inquiry to whether Smoot was individually guilty so far as the practice of polygamy was concerned. This was expected to be an easy task. Not only did Smoot solemnly deny under oath that he either was or ever had been a polygamist but no one, during the entire three-year proceeding, appeared with evidence or testimony to refute the claim.[50] While it is quite likely that Smoot was indeed a monogamist, we know from the records of fellow apostle Rudger Clawson that the senator had at least some susceptibility to polygamous sentiments. At a gathering of the First Presidency and the Quorum of Twelve Apostles in 1902, Smoot praised the plural family life of his father and said that, if universally observed, polygamy would save mankind much pain and difficulty. Beyond this, he said he looked forward to the time when practice of the principle could be resumed.[51]

If nothing was introduced to incriminate Senator Smoot at the hearings, there was yet the problem of plural marriages and continued polygamous cohabitation by his associates. If found privy to such things, he could be charged as *particeps criminis*—that is, constructively involved in unlawful activity and subject to disqualification from public office. As a rule, most who testified in behalf of Smoot, especially high church officials, took the same tack, denying any knowledge of each other's domestic arrangements.[52] While this resulted in astonishing claims, such as statements that the apostles never discussed polygamous cohabitation when they met, Smoot, at least, was finally brought to admit he knew that members of the apostolate and First Presidency had continued to live with their plural wives despite promises they would not.[53]

President of the Church Joseph F. Smith said he welcomed the inquiry. Indicating that Mormons had been trying to tell the world about themselves for more than a half-century, he said he had no fear of standing before Congress and discussing his faith. So robust a response prompted Smoot's secretary, Carl A. Badger, to proudly say his church president had answered like a warrior.[54] Smith, who was the first witness called in the hearings, fell short of what Badger and others looked for, however. His testimony was one of the most damaging of the entire investigation. It must have been difficult for Senator Smoot, who with his wife sat at the same table with Smith, to hear his leader plead, on the one hand, an incredible ignorance concerning the polygamous activities of Smoot's fellow apostles while, on the other, admitting to having cohabited with and fathered children with all five of his own wives since 1890.[55] After saying the Manifesto was divinely received and that it comprehended continued cohabitation with po- lygamous wives, Smith had to admit he was living in defiance of not only secular law but the revelations of Deity.[56] Statements like these led one reporter to say that "every one of [Smith's] . . . damaging and candid admissions" was "a nail in the coffin of his candidate."[57]

The church president repeatedly and categorically denied that he or either of his predecessors, Wilford Woodruff and Lorenzo Snow, had authorized new polygamous marriages since the Manifesto. Nei- ther had any such contractions taken place with the "consent or knowledge or approval of the church." He was emphatic in denying that secret marriages had occurred anywhere in the world with official Mormon sanction. Smith went so far as to say he had not heard any- one "advocate, encourage or recommend" plural marriage since the Manifesto.[58] If some were shocked by Smith's admissions concerning cohabitation with his wives, others were dumbfounded that he would deny what many knew to be true so far as the polygamous marriages of others was concerned. This led one witness to say that Smith must be employing his words differently from the way most men ordinarily use them.[59]

There is almost no basis for saying that President Smith's "quiet calm," as one historian put it, made a positive impression on observers at the hearings.[60] Rather, his responses increased hostility toward himself, Smoot, and Mormonism. The Women's Christian Tem- perance Union described his admissions as a "brazen stand," justifying a continuation of the "anti-Polygamy Crusade."[61] Nels Lars Nelson, in Provo, Utah, admitted that Smith's testimony left "the whole country agog with astonishment and curiosity."[62] After the appearances of Smith and Apostle Francis M. Lyman before the committee, Smoot wrote home in despair, saying congressmen were directly accusing Smith of insincerity. Smoot told his leader: "I must admit that it is the hardest thing that I have had to meet in my life."[63] Another faithful young Mormon, George Q. Morris, said Smith's presentation left Mormonism never so much disliked in its history.[64]

Unlikely affirmations and inconsistencies were not the lot of Presi- dent Smith alone. George Reynolds, appellant in the famous United States Supreme Court case, did not know when his own daughter became the polygamous wife of Benjamin Cluff (Appendix II, #53), president of Brigham Young Academy. He further stated that, in the more than thirteen years since the Manifesto of 1890, he had spoken to no one either for or against the practice of polygamy—indeed, that he had never preached for or against it in his life. Smoot reported that Reynolds originally intended to testify that he had no knowledge that his daughter was married and had shown indifference as to who had fathered her child. He was persuaded to back away from such statements, however, because it was feared that such an account would have been too "shocking . . . to the public conscience."[65] Apostle Hyrum M. Smith, a son of President Joseph F. Smith, affirmed, like his father, that he had no memory of the subjects of new polygamy and polygamous cohabitation being discussed at meetings of the apostles. Then, contradicting himself, he assured the committee that, when the subject did arise, apostles were urged to do all they could to stamp it out.[66]

The most pointed instance of this kind occurred when Apostle Francis M. Lyman, seeking to protect Smoot, said that while his (Lyman's) continued cohabitation with plural wives was common knowledge in Utah, he did not think Smoot himself was aware of the fact. Senator George Frisbie Hoar then asked if Lyman was saying that Senator Smoot was less informed than Utah society generally. Lyman said no, confessing that Smoot probably knew of his domestic arrangements as well as any. Admitting he had contradicted himself, he compounded the dilemma under further interrogation by saying he was guided in his answers by the spirit of the Lord. When Hoar asked if the Lord was also responsible for the contradiction, Lyman had no reply.[67] But, he said, polygamy was one of the mysteries of the kingdom. And like President Smith he admitted that by continuing to cohabit with plural wives he was violating the law, not only of man but of God. When asked if as a transgressor he had repented, Lyman could only say, "not yet." The apostle's clumsiness provoked laughter from the committee and a lecture from Senator Hoar on the need to take greater care with his answers.[68]

Apostle John Henry Smith probably outdid everyone with his amnesia for names and events, saying at one point he had trouble remembering his own birth date.[69] Apostle Marriner W. Merrill, who took a plural wife in 1901, risked charges of perjury by submitting an affidavit in which he swore that he had taken no additional wives since the Manifesto.[70] Mormon witnesses commonly answered so quietly that Senator Burrows, at one point, said there must be something in the air in Utah that affected the voice.[71] Reed Smoot, the principal of the investigation, declared he had no knowledge that "any apostle or any member of the Presidency" had taken a plural wife since 1890, except as it had been revealed in the course of the hearings. It was his belief, for example, that Abraham Cannon and Lillian Hamlin were married sometime before 1890! In other instances, however, Smoot was brought to admit personal knowledge of continued cohabitation by church officers, acknowledging their violation of the terms of amnesty to which they had subscribed.[72]

In their defense, Smoot's counsel called respectable gentile citizens from both Utah and Idaho to testify that polygamy was "as dead as slavery." The question of continued cohabitation was eloquently addressed, demonstrating that, if only from concern for the women and children, the policy of a blind eye was humanely motivated. So far as new polygamous marriages were concerned, they were described as sporadic, with the number of extant plural households small and declining. When asked what was meant by "sporadic," the answer was twenty or thirty cases in the entire church, and those mostly outside Utah. It was repeatedly stated that the younger generation of Mormons was overwhelmingly opposed to polygamy. And, numbers affirmed, Senator Smoot had a reputation for being firmly against the practice.[73]

The long-nagging question of Mormon loyalty to the nation and church involvement in commercial and political affairs was also raised. Some testified that these were greater obstacles to Americanization in Utah, and free government in neighboring states such as Idaho, than polygamy.[74] To refute these charges, friendly non-Mormons were summoned to say there was no evidence the church was dictating political preferences to its members—that, in fact, in proportion to their numbers, more Gentiles than Mormons held public office in Utah. There was, they remarked, a genuinely fervent strain of patriotism in Mormon thought and behavior.[75] For his part, ignoring instructions given at the time of his apostolic ordination, in which he was told that loyalty to his quorum must supersede all other allegiances, Smoot declared absolutely against personal susceptibility to church influence in his work as a senator.[76]

Throughout the hearings, Reorganized Church leaders followed developments closely. Joseph Smith III made a fifth visit to Utah in 1905, speaking on the case of Senator Smoot. Reorganite authorities periodically attempted to bring their views to the attention of the investigating committee, and RLDS apostle Francis M. Sheehy sat through most of its sessions. Both he and President Joseph Smith III spoke with the committee chairman, Senator Julius C. Burrows, and at one point consideration was given to inviting the RLDS president to testify.[77] When rumor of this reached Utah leaders, they took alarm. Smoot's secretary, Carl A. Badger, said they were more sensitive to RLDS claims that Joseph Smith, Mormonism's founder, had nothing to do with plurality than they were to charges that polygamy was yet practiced in Utah.[78] As it turned out, no "Josephites" were summoned and Senator Smoot's lawyers were spared the labor of disproving that polygamy was an invention of "Brighamites" in the West.

An especially portentous issue arising from the hearings involved summoning those authorities suspected of entering post-Manifesto polygamous marriages or of performing them for others. President Smith was diffident toward their cases, saying church inquiries into such things should commence at the local, rather than all-church, level. He did, however, promise to do what he could to have them appear and speak for themselves in Washington, D.C.[79] After his return to Salt Lake City, Smith wrote to Senator Burrows, committee chairman, saying he was unable to obtain the attendance of George Teasdale, John Henry Smith, and Marriner W. Merrill, on account of illness.[80] John Henry Smith later traveled to the nation's capital, where, as we indicated, he gave a remarkable display of failed memory. His appearance occurred over the objections of Senator Smoot, however, who preferred that he not appear at all. The decision that he testify is evidence of the orchestrating role played by leaders in Salt Lake City.[81] Marriner W. Merrill (Appendix II, #132), as we saw, pleaded illness and submitted an affidavit denying any complicity in new plural marriages.[82] Apostle George Teasdale (Appendix II, #192) also sent a letter, alleging incapacity for travel to the East. Apostles John W. Taylor (Appendix II, #191) and Matthias F. Cowley (Appendix II, #56), according to President Smith, were simply unwilling to testify. He expressed "sincere regret" to Burrows for his inability to persuade the two men to appear before the committee.[83]

President Smith's "sincere regret" is questionable, and his efforts to have Teasdale, Cowley, and Taylor testify were quite pretended. Teasdale, who celebrated his seventy-third birthday in 1904, may have been in declining health. He seems always to have been fragile. Yet, in the spring of 1904, at the time President Smith told the committee Teasdale was too frail to make the trip to Washington, the apostle was directed to hasten south into Mexico—an ordeal involving at least as much, and probably more, physical strain than a rail journey east. In the late summer Teasdale was healthy enough to travel north and attend three stake conferences in Arizona. In the letter containing these assignments, the apostle was instructed to see that no reports of his presence in Arizona were released to newspapers. Neither was he to let it be known what his intended course of travels was. Secretary to the First Presidency George F. Gibbs, who had a penchant for injecting his own style into official communications, wrote Teasdale that the First Presidency wished him to return to Mexico "without unnecessarily offending the righteous sensibilities of the righteous people of this the greatest nation on the top of the earth."[84]

In a subsequent letter Teasdale, who was still in Mexico, was advised that his so-called medical advisers in Salt Lake City felt the weather yet inappropriate for his return to Utah. These same advisers had determined that if he desired a change of scenery, he could travel to Canada for a few months. Why Canada, as far from Utah as Mexico, was acceptable was undoubtedly clear to Teasdale. The communication closed by reminding the apostle that he had previously indicated that he wished to be only where the Lord wanted him to be. And that, he was being told, was to stay out of the way.[85] Teasdale was an apostle known to have married plurally since the Manifesto, and the fact that in his testimony in Washington, D.C., President Smith had provided a dubious scenario concerning Teasdale's domestic affairs, more than anything associated with his health, accounted for the time the apostle spent south of the border.[86]

Regarding apostles Taylor and Cowley, it is true both men asked to be excused from attending the hearings. Cowley, for example, wrote Smith that he wished to avoid the humiliation of exposing his family affairs to the nation's eyes. Moreover, he said that whatever he could add to the record would but confirm what President Smith had already said in his testimony. At the same time, Cowley's letter stated that, while he would not volunteer, he would go to Washington if subpoenaed.[87] This was clearly a less defiant posture than that represented by President Smith to Senator Burrows.

Taylor, in his reply to the president, was more pointed, saying he felt "positive disinclinations" about going. Because of his residence in Canada at the time, he undoubtedly felt greater safety from the committee's summons.[88] After receiving the letters of both men from President Smith, Smoot cut out "the whitened sepulchers" from Taylor's letter and read them to members of the committee. The senators agreed, after hearing them, that Taylor and Cowley were both beyond President Smith's control and that he could not force them to testify in Washington.[89]

From the beginning there was an unmistakable note of equivocation in President Smith's attitude about the prudence of having Taylor and Cowley testify. In the presence of Senator Smoot and his secretary, Carl A. Badger, he remarked that he felt he could persuade them to appear in Washington, provided they were not guilty of involvement in post-Manifesto marriages.[90] That Smith, in making such a comment, was hedging against the discovery of what he knew to be fact was not lost on Senator Smoot. Badger recorded in his journal that Smoot volunteered, if President Smith thought best, to resign his senatorial office rather than bring sorrow on the church. Anthon H. Lund, President Smith's counselor, said less than a month later that the First Presidency took concern when it was rumored that someone was likely to be subpoenaed who could testify to the certainty of Taylor's post-Manifesto marriages.[91] It was also said that Taylor even agreed to testify in Washington but stated that he would not compromise the truth in what he said. Supposedly, he was actually departing for Washington, D.C., when recalled by Apostle Francis M. Lyman, who, on the authority of a warning dream, told him to stay in Canada.[92] As much as two years later, Smoot wrote President Smith that it yet seemed best for Taylor and Cowley to remain out of reach of Congress until the investigating committee finished its work and the opportunity for successfully serving them with subpoenas had passed.[93]

Efforts to sequester knowledge of Mormon polygamous activities naturally involved those living in Mexico. During the Smoot investigation pluralists relocated south of the United States border in such numbers that it was noticed by the Mexican press.[94] Mormon residents remembered the new refugees for decades, referring to them as the "exiles." Some who spent time there, apart from George Teasdale, were Apostle John W. Taylor and three of his wives; Apostle Matthias F. Cowley and one of his wives; two of the wives of California Mission president Joseph E. Robinson (Appendix II, #160); a plural wife of George M. Cannon (Appendix II, #37); and one of the spouses of John M. Cannon (Appendix II, #39).[95]

It was inevitable that in their search the Smoot committee would run across these and other cases from the colonies. Mrs. Clara Mabel Barber Kennedy (Appendix II, #107), for example, told the senators that she was joined to her first husband in a plural marriage by Apostle Brigham Young, Jr., in Mexico after the Manifesto.[96] Professor Walter M. Wolfe told of the plural marriage in Mexico between Benjamin Cluff (Appendix II, #53), president of Brigham Young Academy, and an academy student, Florence Reynolds. He also reported the post-Manifesto marriage there of William C. Ockey (Appendix II, #146) and Ovena Jorgensen. And he stated that he had seen numbers of young, recently married, plural wives in the colonies, some telling him that if they could not have married a polygamist they would not have married at all.[97]

In an effort to controvert such findings, church leaders prepared an affidavit and sent it to Anthony W. Ivins, asking that he sign, notarize, and forward the statement to Senator Smoot.[98] Ivins responded that he could not do as requested. In the first place, he said facts in the affidavit were untrue. Secondly, it was his judgment that such a document, were he to sign it, would result in greater, rather than less, inquiry into affairs in the colonies by both Mexican and American governments. And this, he said, could have serious consequences.[99] Ivins was not only concerned with legal sensitivities relating to polygamy under Mexican law, a circumstance we have explored before, but he was a man of firm conscience and resisted engaging in anything dishonest. He did urge circumspection on the colonists regarding their plural relationships, but when asked to appear as a witness in behalf of Smoot, knowing what was expected, he declined, telling his family that he refused to perjure himself. His son later remarked that this was probably the only time Ivins ever dissented from the wishes of his ecclesiastical superiors.[100] Painful to historians now, however, he did destroy papers relating to activities in Mexico.[101]

Church authorities were keenly aware of the reproachful attitudes emerging from the hearings. As early as March 1904, after Smith and Lyman appeared, Senator Smoot urged that something be said at the forthcoming April conference to redress the Mormon reputation. Franklin S. Richards, who worked closely with Smoot in his defense, also favored the idea.[102] The result was a statement prepared by President Smith denying charges of new plural marriages in the church. The document was read before the apostles and First Council of Seventy, both groups giving their approval. In the course of their discussions, however, questions were raised. Apostles Abraham Owen Woodruff and Rudger Clawson, for example, expressed reservation about the step, Woodruff fearing it would tend to obliterate the principle.[103] In response to this and other remarks, President Smith assured his colleagues that the statement constituted nothing more or less than a confirmation of the Woodruff Manifesto in 1890. He repeated, however, that any who performed plural marriages since that time had done so without his knowledge or consent, and such individuals must answer to both the law of the land and the rule of the church.[104]

On the last day of the conference, in words similar to those President Woodruff used when presenting his document, Smith told the Saints they were living in "peculiar times" and that their circumstances required the employment of "peculiar wisdom and understanding."[105] After disposing of other business and listening to a hymn by the Tabernacle Choir, the president read his "Official Statement." Repeating charges that plural marriages were yet occurring, he declared "no such marriages have been solemnized with the sanction, consent or knowledge of the Church." He also repeated that any member who entered or performed such contractions was liable to be excommunicated. Referring to allegations during his appearance before the Smoot committee, he concluded: "They charge us with being dishonest and untrue to our word. They charge the church with having violated a 'compact' and all this sort of nonsense. I want to see today whether the Latter-day Saints representing the church in this solemn assembly will not seal these charges as false by their voice."[106]

A "Resolution of Endorsement" and seconding speeches were then presented. As one of those seconding the motion, Brigham H. Roberts commented on that part of Smith's statement referring to charges that the church had broken its compact with the nation. Roberts repeated the point that no compact was or could have been made between the church and the government. The only agreement possible was one between the government of Utah and the government of the United States. A vote was then taken and, according to the conference report, unanimously carried.[107]

Yet bearing scars from the hearings less than a month before, and with rumors at his back, President Smith seemed to have chiefly wanted reinforcement by church members for his testimony before Congress. Some have contended that the Smith statement sought to extend the 1890 Manifesto to Mormons outside the United States, to all the world.[108] The problem is that, on several occasions, including Smith's own testimony before the Smoot committee, the Woodruff Manifesto was said already to apply to Saints everywhere.[109] If it is said that the 1904 message was intended to formalize such an interpolation, we are yet left with the difficulty that there is no more in Smith's actual wording concerning a universal application of the policy than in the Manifesto of 1890. As Woodruff had done, Smith simply denied continued Mormon plural marriages and stated that members of the church were enjoined from entering or performing them. And, as in the Woodruff document, there was no reference to continued cohabitation.[110] Counselor Anthon H. Lund confirmed this in remarks made following the conference's vote. It was not, he said, "a new Manifesto." It simply refuted rumors and ratified Smith's testimony in Washington.[111]

Having been so emphatic with denials in the nation's capital, now reinforced by the formalizing gesture of a conference vote, President Smith would, at the least, need to follow a more cautious path. Evidence that this occurred is found in written instructions to apostles telling them to desist from either entering or contracting new plural unions. President of the Quorum of Twelve Apostles Francis M. Lyman was asked to oversee the notification of quorum members. The message he sent Apostle Teasdale was especially revealing. He said continued plural marriages after the Manifesto had shaken the confidence of many Latter-day Saints in their leaders. Lyman admitted to Teasdale that church leaders were looked upon as dishonest and untrustworthy. If credibility were to be restored, they must swing around and support the testimony given by President Smith before Congress. It was necessary, he said, to uphold the president and so redeem the reputation of the church.[112]

Anthony W. Ivins was told to carry word of the policy to Mexico.[113] Rumor of the impending announcement circulated well before conference time, however. There were at least two cases in Mexico in which couples intending plural unions were told to hurry with their plans before the retreat was implemented.[114] When one church member appeared in the colonies in June of 1904 with a woman to whom he wished to be polygamously joined, Ivins adamantly refused.[115] All this indicates that, whatever else might be said, the 1904 declaration constituted a genuine dividing line, resulting in a definite reduction, if not cessation, of approved polygamous marriages within the church.

The statement did little, however, to turn the current of anti-Mormonism undammed by the Smoot hearings. The old proposal that an amendment prohibiting polygamy be added to the United States Constitution was formally endorsed by the Democrats in their 1904 national party platform.[116] Throughout 1905 and 1906 public hostility reached such a level that talk was heard of disfranchising all Mormons, polygamous or not. Both Smoot and Franklin S. Richards said they could not remember a time when "the feeling was so strong and so universally opposed to the church as at the present." Smoot also said that whenever he was spoken to on the matter, apostles Taylor and Cowley were always pointed to as examples of Mormon duplicity.[117]

President Smith's 1904 "Official Statement" was not enough. Something more needed to be done. By this time at least a third of the Quorum of Twelve Apostles were new, younger men who, like Smoot, had only one wife and were anxious to acquit the hectored reputation of the church. Presumably mirroring Senator Smoot's views, Carl A. Badger told a friend that it was wrong that the entire church should submit to insult and suffering only to protect the reputation of a few.[118] Without their appearance in Washington, or other evidence to contradict allegations made concerning them, Senator Smoot told the committee in early 1905 that he had urged the apostles to undertake an investigation to determine if Taylor and Cowley had violated the Woodruff Manifesto. If they were found to be guilty, Smoot assured the senators, he would no longer sustain them as members of his quorum. Having so committed himself, and inasmuch as he and other Mormons had been accused of routinely raising their hands in support of whomever and whatever their leaders presented to them, the senator publicly withheld his vote from sustaining the quorum, as constituted, at the autumn conference of the church in 1905.[119]

Within days of the conference the apostles began holding meetings to discuss the division within their quorum. Brigham H. Roberts, who had been appointed to assist Smoot with his case, urged that some step be taken to separate any involved in late plural marriages from the structure of church authority. That was the only way Mormon supporters, both in and outside the church, could justify themselves. Although not present at the first meeting to discuss their cases, Taylor and Cowley attended subsequent gatherings which were held in the temple. At these meetings Roberts and others appealed to them to offer themselves, as a way out of the present difficulty, by taking responsibility for their acts without implicating the church. When inquiries were made as to the actual extent of their involvement in plural marriages, both were reticent, suggesting that it was best for everyone if they did not divulge all they knew. Both men insisted, however, that the 1904 "Official Statement" encompassed no more, geographically or otherwise, than the Woodruff Manifesto of 1890. After some disagreement and anger, especially on the part of Taylor, the two apostles agreed to resign from the quorum. Both men were asked to say nothing about the matter until the leaders decided it should be made public. Significantly, and illustrative of the concern with appearances that lay behind the action, both men were reassured it was only a separation from their quorum that was involved. Neither was stripped of his apostleship. This occurred on 28 October 1905.[120]

For more than a month, until mid-December 1905, the leaders were uncertain how to proceed. For his part, Smoot wanted to move quickly and, in his own mind, believed that a majority of his brethren agreed with him. The day following the meeting in which the resignations were tendered, Smoot told a stake conference audience that they should not be surprised if something unusual happened in the church.[121] President Smith and others, however, seem not to have been so certain. It was surely clear that Taylor and Cowley were not alone in the practice of post-Manifesto polygamous marriage. There also may have been concern that the appearance of division, however advantageous in an immediate sense, could widen into paralyzing conflict.[122]

The hesitation involved can be read in messages between Smoot and his associates at a time when continuation of the senate investigation was being debated. On 8 December the senator wired to say that a "nasty bitter feeling against the church" had become almost universal and that the hearings were likely to recommence. This was in response to a telegram the day before from Salt Lake City indicating that, if the inquiry reopened, he was not to use the resignations or mention them to anyone. Smoot responded by saying that the time when public notice of the resignations could have helped had passed. In an exchange with Apostle Francis M. Lyman, Smoot reiterated his feeling that the resignations should have been used immediately after they were written: "I hear [from other congressmen] nothing but T[aylor] and C[owley], T[aylor] and C[owley] and why are they not handled, and if the President of the Church won't stop polygamy we will." The senator went on to say publication of the resignations might secure the favor of President Theodore Roosevelt and that the brethren must remember that, in the event the government should mount another crusade against them, this time "we have not the full sympathy of our own people behind us."[123]

On the same day the telegram to Lyman was sent, George F. Gibbs, the secretary to the First Presidency, wired Smoot in code as follows: "Brethren beginning [to] feel [that] J. W. Taylor and Cowley should not be sacrificed unless required by C[ommittee] of P[rivileges] & E[lections to] save you."[124] Piqued by their equivocation, Smoot replied that he thought the quorum had agreed, early on, to proceed with an announcement. But now, he gathered, they felt the resignations should not be used at all unless it was necessary to save his seat in the senate. He did not, he said, want the two apostles to be sacrificed for his interests alone. Then followed this statement: "If Taylor and Cowley have done no wrong and their acts meet the approval of the Brethren for heavens sake don't handle them but let us take the consequences; but I cannot yet bring myself to believe that President Snow would time and again deceive the Quorum or that President Smith is an untruthful man. I would about as soon lose my life as become convinced of it. I want no sacrifice on the part of anyone."[125]

We read here what it is that will invite comment later—the inference of special knowledge, of secrets among the leaders themselves. So far as Smoot was concerned, he was told a week later in a telegram from Apostle Francis M. Lyman that he was finally at liberty to use the resignations when he felt best. The brethren in Salt Lake City had met the day before and decided to formally accept them, expelling Taylor and Cowley from their quorum. Then, to relieve Smoot's conscience, Lyman told him that the resignations were not to be looked upon as for his benefit alone but for "the relief of the Church."[126] Even then Smoot waited for those in Salt Lake City to make the first move. Formal announcement was made on the last day of the spring conference of the church, 8 April 1906. Presenting the names of the authorities to be sustained by the membership, Francis M. Lyman told the assembly that Taylor and Cowley had resigned from the quorum the previous October. They had done this, he said, because they were "out of harmony" with both the First Presidency and other apostles. In Lyman's words, their resignations had caused church leaders "the deepest sorrow."[127]

On the day of the announcement the *Salt Lake Herald* predicted Apostle Teasdale would be deposed as well because he, with Taylor and Cowley, had defied President Smith's requests to testify before Congress. All three, said the article, were outlaws to the church.[128] Considering the notoriety of Teasdale's domestic circumstances, his immunity infers that motives other than belief in their guilt actuated the leaders in their policy toward Taylor and Cowley. At the same time, however, Joseph Marion Tanner (Appendix II, #186), the superintendent of church schools and a well-known polygamist who had taken plural wives since the Manifesto, was not presented for a sustaining vote at the conference along with the two apostles. As with Taylor and Cowley, Tanner suffered no loss of priesthood authority and remained in demand as a church speaker for years.[129]

While rumors that certain leaders might be dropped had circulated for some time, the impact on church members at conference was dramatic. According to one of those in attendance, announcement that the two apostles had been excluded from their quorum evoked a wave of emotion. Crying and sadness swept through the congregation. One said she looked for a way to get out of the building so as to more freely express her feelings.[130] More than a half-century later a former bishop in one of the Mormon colonies in Mexico, and an acquaintance of Taylor and Cowley, remembered in what special affection they were held, saying their rejection fell like a heavy blow to the Saints.[131]

Smoot's counsel in Washington was notified on 11 April 1906 that the resignations had been received and accepted the previous autumn.[132] Another month passed, however, before Smoot was permitted to show copies of them to members of Congress.[133] Slow and halting in its execution, the "sacrifice," made public in both Salt Lake City and Washington, D.C., was at last complete. As it happened, the effect of the episode on the investigating committee was, if anything, reactionary. In the words of the majority report: "The dropping of Taylor and Cowley from the quorum of the twelve apostles was so evidently done for popular effect that the act merits no consideration whatever, except as an admission by the First Presidency and twelve apostles that Apostles Taylor and Cowley have each taken one or more plural wives since the manifesto."[134]

Many within the church viewed matters in much the same way as the committee. Eastern States Mission president John G. McQuarrie wrote to Apostle George Albert Smith that the action must have been a trial and that it was sad to see men fall because of their mistakes, "or to know that they are making a sacrifice for our good."[135] A resident of the Mormon colonies in Mexico described Taylor and Cowley as among the most faithful and respected of the leaders and said they were expelled to satisfy Mormonism's persecutors and so bring peace to the church.[136] In 1909 Apostle Orson F. Whitney was reported to have contradicted the statement that Taylor and Cowley were dropped because they were out of harmony with their quorum. Rather, he said, many believed their sacrifice necessary for the good of the church.[137] And Anthony W. Ivins later said it was commonly believed in Mexico that the two men were asked to resign "for political reasons only."[138]

Some church members felt the authorities went too far. A friend of Janet Taylor, one of John W. Taylor's plural wives, told her in 1911 that it was bad enough to be harassed from outside. But when church leaders began persecuting each other, it was much more painful to bear.[139] The official position taken by church authorities, however, was that the two apostles were mavericks, misguided in their interpretations, making the action against them necessary. In 1909 a letter from the First Presidency, intending to improve the Mormon image abroad, affirmed that since 1890 the church had not in any way sanctioned new plural marriages and that the two men were dropped from the quorum for violating that rule and for refusing to testify in Washington. There has been no official departure from that view since.[140]

So far as Taylor and Cowley were concerned, differences between themselves and the quorum grew as time passed. It was alleged that some apostles refused to socialize with them. It was also claimed that false rumors were circulated about them and that confidences were breached. Taylor became so enraged that he threatened to impose physical punishment on Apostle George Albert Smith if, in Taylor's words, "he did not stop talking against me." He accused Anthony W. Ivins of currying favor to secure his own appointment as an apostle in 1907. And there was rumor that Taylor took financial advantage of church members.[141] All this resulted in the two apostles being called again, in 1911, before the quorum to answer charges. In the course of the hearings a great deal of information was divulged, some of which has been used in this study to illuminate matters relating to Mormon polygamy in the post-Manifesto years. It did little to assist Taylor and Cowley, however. Taylor was excommunicated. Cowley, because of a penitent spirit, would have been forgiven altogether except for two apostles who demanded some mark of punishment. He was therefore deprived of the right to exercise priesthood authority.[142]

In the years that followed, both men felt they were unfairly used. Janet Taylor, John W.'s third wife, told her inquiring son that at the time of their resignations in 1905 Joseph F. Smith said to John W. of him and Cowley: "You brethren are called upon to make this sacrifice, but you will lose nothing from it. When things quiet down you will be reinstated."[143] Cowley expressed a similar view to Raymond Taylor, another of John W.'s sons, in 1937. As Taylor remembered it, Cowley said: "When we were in council relative to our trouble brother [Charles W.] Penrose remarked, 'These brethren (Cowley and Father) are not on trail [sic] nor have they committed any ofense [sic], but if they are willing to offer the sacrifice and stand the embarrassment, we will admit them back after the situation clears,' or words to that effect."[144] A daughter of Matthias F. Cowley remembered it in much the same way. She paraphrased one authority of the time to say: "When this trouble blows over, you'll be reinstated." Another, she added, said, "Amen to that."[145]

Confidence that these were more than expressions of self-justification arises from statements by Senator Smoot in 1906. When Apostle Heber J. Grant wrote the senator from England to say he had not been told the reasons for the resignations, Smoot remarked that a policy of reticence was purposeful because they expected some day to reinstate the men in the quorum. And less than a year later Carl A. Badger wrote of the senator's consternation that such a restoration might actually occur.[146] As time passed and the reinstatements did not happen, resentment deepened. "They held us up," Cowley told Raymond Taylor, "in the eyes of the lay members of the church, and the nation as the 'ring leaders' when in fact we were no more guilty than those who supposedly took action against us."[147]

Whatever was said about them, Taylor and Cowley continued to be held in high regard in Mormon society. Both remained popular as speakers at church gatherings. And despite the interdiction imposed upon him by his quorum, Cowley continued to perform priesthood functions. In 1936 he was readmitted as a fully functional member of the church.[148] Although no formal reconciliation with the quorum occurred during his lifetime, a story told in the Taylor family holds that before John W. died in 1916, in a ceremony on the shore of Lake Utah, Cowley rebaptized him into the church. Cowley had also performed the ceremony for yet another plural marriage by Taylor in 1909. This marriage and Taylor's unwillingness to discontinue relations with his later plural wives compounded differences between himself and some of the apostles.[149] This notwithstanding, it was said that President Joseph F. Smith, regretting all that had happened, called privately at the Nellie Taylor home in Salt Lake City on the evening of Taylor's death, giving Nellie a small parcel containing temple robes in which to bury the former apostle. Taylor's priesthood and blessings were posthumously restored in 1965.[150]

During the first two years of the Smoot hearings, regard for Senator Smoot and Mormonism steadily declined. It was publicly stated that a good Mormon simply could not be a good American.[151] Then, in early 1906, public sentiment began swinging in Smoot's favor. No less an adversary than Theodore Schroeder took the senator's part, arguing that he was innocent of personal wrongdoing and should not be judged by the misbehavior of others.[152] Testimony generally seemed less damaging. Perhaps, as Smoot's secretary suggested, this was because the inquiry did not probe deeply enough into the situation in Mexico.[153] In an article published in the *Deseret News* in mid-1906, the church came close to admitting that new polygamous marriages had occurred, especially outside the country. But these had nowhere been proved, they said, and even if true were not in violation of United States laws. Moreover, no connection had been made between such performances and Reed Smoot.[154] The investigating committee, however, remained convinced that the Mormon hierarchy permitted and encouraged polygamy and that Smoot must bear some responsibility for this. Consequently, they voted seven to five against accepting the Mormon apostle into Congress.[155]

When the committee's report was debated before the full Senate, in the midst of speeches for and against, an event happened that must have pinioned the attention of everyone present, Smoot more than others. Senator James H. Berry from Arkansas arose and provided a gripping account of the Mountain Meadows Massacre of 1857, in which a wagon train was attacked and nearly all its members slaughtered by a combined party of Mormons and Indians. Berry was from the county where the emigrant train originated and, as a teenager, had known some of the victims. Although the event occurred a half century earlier and more than four years before Reed Smoot was born, it was recalled as an accusing specter to show the nature of the organization of which Smoot was a presiding authority.[156] Nothing so illustrates the boundless extent the inquisition had acquired. Nothing better shows that it was less Reed Smoot than Mormonism that was on trial.

When the full Senate voted, aided by support from President Theodore Roosevelt, the two-thirds majority required to expel the senator failed.[157] Smoot was welcomed into full fellowship in the Congress, returned again and again by the Utah electorate for thirty years. But the episode brought Mormons before the public again, resurrecting what Senator Shelby M. Cullom called the Mormon sins of "polygamy and hierarchy."[158]

Perhaps no one saw the meaning of the Smoot proceedings so clearly as a professor of political science from the University of Illinois, James Wilford Garner. Writing in the *North American Review* a month before the vote was taken, Garner argued that the senator was individually innocent and ought to be granted his seat. At the same time, Garner pointed out, the hearings demonstrated that a majority of Mormonism's First Presidency and apostles were yet living with plural wives and that numbers of the women concerned had been married since 1890. Neither the Manifesto, terms of the grants of amnesty, nor other assurances given by the church were being observed. The leaders, he said, by example if not by precept, were assuring perpetuation of the practice.[159] To most Americans Mormonism and polygamy were yet synonymous.

NOTES

Portions of this chapter appeared in Victor W. Jorgensen and B. Carmon Hardy, "The Taylor-Cowley Affair and the Watershed of Mormon History,"

UHQ 48 (Winter 1980): 4–36. It is with the kind permission of the Utah State Historical Society that those portions are reprinted here.

1. Charles Mostyn Owen to J. W. Howe, 3 Oct. 1899, Charles Mostyn Owen Letterbook, Charles Mostyn Owen Collection, Church Archives. Also see comments made in *Cannon v. U.S.* 116 U.S. 72 (1885).

2. See the discussion above in chap. 4, and the comments by Apostle John Henry Smith, in *Proceedings* 2:316–17.

3. A. Karl Larson and Katherine Miles Larson, eds., *Diary of Charles Lowell Walker,* 2 vols. (Logan: Utah State University Press, 1980), 2:749–50, 13–14 Sept. 1892. Additionally, see the comments of judges and others in *Proceedings* 2:840, 910, 915.

4. Utah's 1892 law was "An Act to Punish Polygamy and Kindred Offenses," *Laws of the Territory of Utah* (1892), 30th sess., ch. 8, sec. 2:5–7. Congress's enabling act for Utah is found in U.S., *Statutes at Large,* 27, ch. 138, sec. 19:112 (1894).

5. The commission, which began its work after the achievement of statehood in 1896, consisted of Richard W. Young, Grant H. Smith, and William A. Lee. They described their activities in *Revised Statutes of the State of Utah* (1898), iii-vi. The statute concerned is found in ibid., tit. 75, ch. 24, sec. 4209:900.

6. Accounts are available in James B. Allen and Glen M. Leonard, *The Story of the Latter-day Saints* (Salt Lake City: Deseret Book, 1976), 439–40; Samuel W. Taylor, *Rocky Mountain Empire: The Latter-day Saints Today* (New York: Macmillan, 1978), 8–10; William Alexander Linn, *The Story of the Mormons from the Date of Their Origin to the Year 1901* (New York: Macmillan, 1902), 605.

7. Rudger Clawson Diaries, 26 and 28 Feb. 1901, Rudger Clawson Collection, University of Utah Library, Salt Lake City; John Henry Smith Diaries, 26 Feb. 1901, George A. Smith Family Papers, University of Utah Library.

8. First Presidency to Reed Smoot, 20 Jan. 1904, Correspondence between Senator Reed Smoot and the First Presidency and other General Authorities of the Church of Jesus Christ of Latter-day Saints, 1903–41, Private Papers of the Reed Smoot Collection, BYU Library (hereafter Reed Smoot–First Presidency Correspondence); and *Proceedings* 1:311, 678.

9. John Henry Smith Diaries, 4 Feb., 7 Feb., 23 Feb., 26 Feb. 1901. Also see "Law to Permit Polygamy: Bill Will Pass Utah Legislature Making Prosecution Impossible," *New York Times,* 9 March 1901. For Mormon political influence in the Utah judiciary, see L. John Nuttall Diaries, 4 March 1903, BYU Library.

10. "Utah Polygamy Law Vetoed," *New York Times,* 15 March 1901; Linn, *The Story of the Mormons,* 605; and the summary provided by Edward B. Critchlow at the time of the Smoot investigation, in *Proceedings* 1:580–84.

11. "Polygamy Is Only an Excuse," *DN,* 6 Feb. 1900.

12. David Brudnoy, "A Decade in Zion: Theodore Schroeder's Initial Assault on the Mormons," *Historian* 37 (Feb. 1975): 241–56; idem, "Of Sinners and Saints: Theodore Schroeder, Brigham Roberts, and Reed Smoot," *Journal of Church and State* 14 (Spring 1972): 261–62. Sidney Ditzion's remarks con-

cerning Schroeder are among the few in his account of the Mormons that are accurate. *Marriage, Morals, and Sex in America: A History of Ideas* (New York: Bookman, 1953), 215–20. The only book-length biography is that of Ralph Edward McCoy, *Theodore Schroeder: A Cold Enthusiast* (Carbondale: Southern Illinois University Press, 1973).

13. Theodor Schroeder, editorial, *The Kinsman* 1 (1 Oct. 1897): 2–3; the series entitled "Polygamy and Inspired Lies," ibid. 1 (29 Jan. 1898): 2; ibid. 1 (5 Feb. 1898): 2; ibid. 1 (12 Feb. 1898): 2; ibid. 1 (19 Feb. 1898): 2; ibid. 1 (26 Feb. 1898): 2; Marcus F. Jones, "The Present Situation in Utah as the Result of Statehood," ibid. 1 (5 Feb. 1898): 3; "What Is Polygamy?" ibid. 1 (16 April 1898): 1; N. E. Clemenson, "The Supremacy of Mormonism," ibid. 1 (14 May 1898): 2–3; "No Polygamy in Utah and Yet . . . !" ibid. 2 (3 July 1898): 3; "Polygamy and Cohabitation," ibid. 2 (17 Sept. 1898): 4–5; "The Present Status of Polygamy," ibid. 2 (1 Oct. 1898): 1–2; "Death to Polygamy," ibid. 2 (22 Oct. 1898): 4. For local ministerial criticism, see T. Edgar Lyon, "Religious Activities and Development in Utah, 1847–1910," *UHQ* 35 (Fall 1967): 302–4.

14. Charles M. Owen to J. W. Howe, 3 Oct. 1899, Charles Mostyn Owen Letterbook.

15. *Proceedings* 2:397, 402–5; the review of Owen's testimony provided in "Smoot Protestants Conclude Their Case," *New York Times,* 21 Dec. 1904; the account of Owen's affidavit concerning Angus and Martha Hughes Cannon, in "Baby Causes a Suit for Polygamy against Chief Mormon," *New York Evening Journal,* 8 July 1899; and the case of Joseph F. Smith treated in Thomas G. Alexander, *Mormonism in Transition: A History of the Latter-day Saints, 1890–1930* (Urbana: University of Illinois Press, 1986), 66.

16. The number of studies dealing with Roberts and his expulsion from Congress is considerable. His own account of the matter is in *CHC* 6:363–74. Also see R. Davis Bitton, "The B. H. Roberts Case of 1898–1900," *UHQ* 25 (Winter 1957): 27–46; Robert H. Mahan, *B. H. Roberts: A Biography* (Salt Lake City: Deseret Book, 1966): 62–77; W. Craig Mikhelsen, "The Politics of B. H. Roberts," *Dialogue* 9 (Summer 1974): 35; William Griffin White, Jr., "The Feminist Campaign for the Exclusion of Brigham Henry Roberts from the Fifty-Sixth Congress," *Journal of the West* 17 (Jan. 1978): 44–52; and Truman G. Madsen, *Defender of the Faith: The B. H. Roberts Story* (Salt Lake City: Bookcraft, 1980), 241–72.

17. This was stated by Joseph F. Smith in an interview, "Church Officials Talk," *SLT,* 9 Jan. 1899. Also see Frank J. Cannon and Harvey J. O'Higgins, *Under the Prophet in Utah: The National Menace of a Political Priestcraft* (Boston: C. M. Clark, 1911), 222–23.

In contrast to the concern expressed by George Q. Cannon, some authorities displayed an extraordinary insensitivity to the connection between Mormon marriage habits and national policies toward Utah. In the same interview cited above, Charles W. Penrose remarked, "What in the world has polygamy to do with politics?" "Church Officials Talk," *SLT,* 9 Jan. 1899.

18. See above in chap. 4.

19. *Proceedings* 1:710–13. Truman G. Madsen accepts without question Roberts's 1890 date for his marriage to Shipp in *Defender of the Faith*, 199–200. And Richard O. Cowan says Roberts married all three of his wives "before 1890." Richard O. Cowan, *The Church in the Twentieth Century* (Salt Lake City: Bookcraft, 1985), 28.

20. See *R. L. Polk & Co's Salt Lake City Directory* (1890), 554; and ibid. (1891–92), 633. Also see Carlos Ashby Badger Diaries, 3 March 1906, Church Archives; Charles M. Owen to J. W. Howe, 3 Oct. 1899, Charles Mostyn Owen Letterbook; and notations in fd. 12, Charles Mostyn Owen Collection. Also see the information provided by Elizabeth Felt, in box 4, fd. 21, Kimball Young Collection, Garrett Evangelical Theological Library, Evanston, Ill.; "Men from Utah Face Roberts," *New York Evening Journal*, 13 Dec. 1899; "Roberts Dodges; Miss Gould Acts," ibid., 19 Dec. 1899; and "Roberts Has Three Wives, Twelve Children," ibid., 20 Dec. 1899.

21. "Polygamist Is Worried," [New York] *World*, 29 Dec. 1898; "Roberts Defends His Polygamy," ibid., 30 Dec. 1898.

22. Margaret Curtis Shipp, reported in Eugene Young, "Polygamy Is Reviving," *New York Herald*, 5 Feb. 1899.

23. Susa Young Dunford to Leah E. Widtsoe, 24 Nov. 1923, copy in possession of Victor W. Jorgensen, Logan, Utah. The marriage between Roberts "of New York" and "Margaret Curtis of Chicago" was performed on 9 Nov. 1923 by a Cook County superior court judge. *Certificate of Marriage*, No. 1008494, 9 Nov. 1923, Cook County Bureau of Vital Statistics, Chicago, Ill.

24. Brigham H. Roberts, in "Did Not 'Peach' on Utah Polygamists," *DN*, 5 Feb. 1900; "On Polygamous Postmasters," *DN*, 9 Feb. 1900; "Postmasters in Idaho Living in Polygamy," U.S. Senate, 58th Cong., 3d sess. (4 Jan. 1905), doc. no. 62. Also see Isaac Russell, "Mr. Roosevelt to the Mormons: A Letter with an Explanatory Note," *Colliers* (15 April 1911): 28; Ruth and Reginald Kauffman, *The Latter-day Saints: A Study of the Mormons in the Light of Economic Conditions* (London: Williams & Norgate, 1912), 239; and Torrey L. Austin, interviewed by Jessie L. Embry, 18 June 1976, p. 5, POHP.

25. James David Gillilan, *Thomas Corwin Illif: Apostle of Home Missions in the Rocky Mountains* (New York: Methodist Book Concern, 1919), 87–90.

26. "Mormon Roberts Is Not a Citizen," [New York] *World*, 1 Jan. 1899; "Shall a Polygamist Sit in Congress?" *New Church Review* 6 (April 1899): 279; "Plan Now to Expel Roberts," *New York Times*, 4 April 1899; "Miss Gould Protests against Seating of Congressman Roberts, The Guardian Society Acts," ibid., 7 Oct. 1899; "Reply to Roberts Plea," ibid., 9 Dec. 1899; "The Utah Congressman-Elect," *American Monthly Review of Reviews* 20 (Dec. 1899): 654; "The Roberts Case," *Outlook* 64 (Jan. 1900): 201–2; "The Roberts Case," ibid. 64 (Feb. 1900): 235; A. Theodore Schroeder, "Polygamy in Congress," *Arena* 23 (Feb. 1900): 115–18. Roberts took a severe pillorying in the national press in the form of cartoons. See Gary L. Bunker and Davis Bitton, *The Mormon Graphic Image, 1834–1914: Cartoons, Caricatures, and Illustrations* (Salt

Lake City: University of Utah Press, 1983), 60–64. The best overview of women's organizations arrayed against Roberts is provided in White, "The Feminist Campaign for the Exclusion of Brigham Henry Roberts," 44–52. Roberts spoke for himself in "The Roberts Case in Congress," *New York Times,* 19 Nov. 1899; and "Congressman Roberts' Defense," *DN,* 30 Dec. 1899. The church not only published in behalf of Roberts but pleaded their own faithfulness to the law in "The Church and the Law," *DN,* 6 Jan. 1900; "Utah's Compact with the Nation," *DN,* 6 Jan. 1900; "Returning to Old Ways," *DN,* 29 Jan. 1900; and "Come to the Point," *DN,* 16 Feb. 1900. Non-Mormon support for Roberts came from Theodore W. Curtis, "Roberts: The Dreyfus of America," *Arena* 23 (Feb. 1900): 120–31; and A. L. Mearkle, "The Passing of the Mormon," ibid. 23 (April 1900): 378–89.

27. These statements, respectively, occur in "The Case of Roberts," *American Monthly Review of Reviews* 19 (Feb. 1899): 145; and Eugene Young, "Polygamy Is Reviving," *New York Herald,* 5 Feb. 1899.

28. A. Theodore Schroeder, "Polygamy in Congress," 115.

29. "Roberts Defends His Polygamy," 3; Eugene Young, "Revival of the Mormon Problem," *North American Review* 168 (April 1899): 484; Schroeder, "Polygamy in Congress," 118–20.

30. U.S. House of Representatives, 55th Cong., 3d sess., Committee on Election of President, Vice President, & Representatives in Congress, *Amendments to the Constitution Prohibiting Polygamy, Etc.,* Report no. 2307 (Washington, D.C.: GPO, 1899): 11 passim.

31. Representative Charles B. Landis, Indiana, as quoted in "The Journal's Poll of the House Shows that Roberts Is Doomed by an Overwhelming Vote," *New York Evening Journal,* 25 Jan. 1900.

32. "Mormons; or, The Curse of Utah," *New York Evening Journal,* 23–28 Jan. 1899; "No Polygamists in Congress," ibid., 24 Jan. 1899.

33. "All Due to Journal Crusade, Says Roberts," ibid., 7 Jan. 1900.

34. "Crowds View Anti-Roberts Petitions," ibid., 4 Dec. 1899.

35. White, "The Feminist Campaign for the Exclusion of Brigham Henry Roberts," 49.

36. "Case of Brigham H. Roberts of Utah," U.S., House of Representatives, 56th Cong., 1st sess., Rep't. 85, (20 Jan. 1900) pt. 1:2–3, 11–12, 40–45; *CHC* 6:367.

37. "No Seat in Congress for Roberts," *New York Evening Journal,* 26 Jan. 1900. Also see "'Roberts No Citizen,' Is Carlisle's Opinion," ibid., 6 Jan. 1900; "The Journal's Fight for the Purity of the Home and the Honor of American Womanhood is Won . . . ," ibid., 18 Jan. 1900; "Bar Roberts Is the Verdict," ibid., 18 Jan. 1900.

38. "The Greatest Question," *New York Times,* 27 Jan. 1900.

39. "Blow at Womanhood of America Averted," *New York Evening Journal,* 28 Jan. 1900.

40. John T. Bridwell, "Origin of American Polygamy," *Arena* 29 (May

1903): 472. This was the same muckraking journal in which the two denominations were most visible to the American public. See, e.g., Joseph Smith [Reorganite], "Origin of American Polygamy," *Arena* 28 (Aug. 1902): 160–67; Joseph F. Smith [Utah Mormon], "Real Origin of American Polygamy: A Reply," ibid. 28 (Nov. 1902): 490–98; Joseph F. Smith [Utah Mormon], "Mormonism and Polygamy," ibid. 29 (May 1903): 449–56; Joseph Smith [Reorganite], "Plural Marriage in America," ibid. 29 (May 1903): 456–65. In addition to remarks in chap. 2 above, see Alma R. Blair, "RLDS Views of Polygamy: Some Historiographical Notes," *John Whitmer Historical Association Journal* 5 (1985): 16–28; and Linda King Newell, "Cousins in Conflict: Joseph Smith III and Joseph F. Smith," ibid. 9 (1989): 3–16.

41. Milton R. Merrill, "Reed Smoot, Apostle-Senator," *UHQ* 28 (Oct. 1960): 345; idem, *Reed Smoot: Apostle in Politics* (Logan: Utah State University and Department of Political Science, 1990), 16–40; Thomas G. Alexander, "Reed Smoot, the LDS Church and Progressive Legislation, 1903–1933," *Dialogue* 7 (Spring 1972): 54.

42. "Smoot Protest National," *New York Times,* 17 Nov. 1903.

43. Ray Stannard Baker, "The Vitality of Mormonism," *Century* 68 (June 1904): 117. Also see "Mormonism," *Outlook* 70 (5 April 1902): 799–800; "The Opposition to a Mormon Senator," ibid. 72 (6 Dec. 1902): 760–61; "W.C.T.U. Denounces Smoot," *New York Times,* 18 Nov. 1903; and "Fight against Mormon Missionaries," ibid., 17 Jan. 1904. For general accounts and names of other protesting groups, see Merrill, *Reed Smoot,* 26–40; M. Paul Holsinger, "J. C. Burrows and the Fight against Mormonism, 1903–1907," *Michigan History* 52 (Fall 1968): 181–95; idem, "Philander C. Knox and the Crusade against Mormonism, 1904–1907," *Western Pennsylvania Historical Magazine* 52 (Jan. 1969): 47–55; idem, "For God and the American Home: The Attempt to Unseat Senator Reed Smoot, 1903–1907," *Pacific Northwest Quarterly* 60 (July 1969): 154–60; Gary J. Bergera, "Secretary to the Senator: Carl A. Badger and the Smoot Hearings," *Sunstone* 8 (Jan.-April 1983): 36–41; Alexander, *Mormonism in Transition,* 17–27, 241.

44. See the summary provided in Carl A. Badger to R. S. Collett, 21 March 1904 [unsent], Carlos Ashby Badger Letterbooks, Carlos Ashby Badger Collection, Church Archives. Formal charges by the protestants, with supporting documents, are in *Proceedings* 1:1–30. Smoot's formal denials follow in ibid. 1:31–40.

45. "Petitions against Smoot," *New York Times,* 11 Nov. 1903; *Proceedings* 1:40.

46. Holsinger, "J. C. Burrows and the Fight against Mormonism," 181–95.

47. Robert Walker Tayler, in *Proceedings* 3:371.

48. *Speech of Hon. George Sutherland, of Utah, in the Senate of the United States, Tuesday, January 22, 1907* (Washington, D.C.: GPO, 1907), 41. Also see *Proceedings* 2:395–97.

49. James Wilford Garner, "The Case of Senator Smoot and the Mormon Church," *North American Review* 184 (4 Jan. 1907): 46–47; Holsinger, "For God and the American Home," 154; Alexander, *Mormonism in Transition*, 19.

50. *Proceedings* 1:31, 49–50, 122, 3:183; Merrill, *Reed Smoot*, 35–40.

51. Reed Smoot, quoted in Clawson Diaries, 7 Jan. 1902.

52. As examples, see *Proceedings* 1:476, 479 (Joseph F. Smith), 1:438, 450–56 (Francis M. Lyman), 1:722 (Brigham H. Roberts), 1:785 (Angus Cannon), 2:50, 56, 58 (George Reynolds), 2:290–302 (John Henry Smith), 3:96 (James E. Talmage).

53. Ibid. 1:360, 510–11, 3:219–21.

54. Joseph F. Smith and Carl A. Badger, in Badger Diaries, 2 Feb. 1904.

55. Joseph F. Smith, in *Proceedings* 1:129–30; "Mormon Church Head Believes in Polygamy," *New York Times*, 3 March 1904.

56. Joseph F. Smith, in *Proceedings* 1:336–37.

57. "Smith vs. Smoot," *New York Times*, 6 March 1904.

58. Joseph F. Smith, in *Proceedings* 1:102, 143, 177, 178, 184, 211, 317–18, 485. Also see John Henry Smith, in ibid. 2:302–3.

59. Edward B. Critchlow, in ibid. 1:612–13.

60. Holsinger, "For God and the American Home," 60. Merrill was closer to the fact in describing Smith's testimony as "sensational." Merrill, *Reed Smoot*, 47, 50–51.

61. "Mormons at W.C.T.U. Session," *New York Times*, 15 March 1904. Also see "White Ribbons Score Mormons," *SLT*, 1 Nov. 1905; and Bunker and Bitton, *The Mormon Graphic Image*, 65–71.

62. Nels Lars Nelson, "The Mormon Family," *Mormon Point of View*, 1 (1 Oct. 1904): 335. Also see Reed Smoot to Joseph F. Smith, 23 March 1904, Reed Smoot–First Presidency Correspondence; Waldemar Van Cott to Karl [*sic*] A. Badger, 28 March 1904, Reed Smoot Incoming Correspondence, Church Archives; Carl A. Badger to R. S. Collett, 21 March 1904 [unsent], Carlos Ashby Badger Letterbooks. As the hearings dragged into a second year, Richard W. Young, a stake president, said he believed the body of the church, like himself, was "profoundly surprised" by the Smoot committee's findings. *Proceedings* 2:975.

63. Smoot to Smith, 23 March 1904, Reed Smoot–First Presidency Correspondence.

64. George Q. Morris to Karl [*sic*] A. Badger, 17 March 1904, Reed Smoot Incoming Correspondence. As yet another Mormon put it, remembering his impressions of President Smith's encounter with the committee, "They had him on the ropes there." Walter Ernest Young, interviewed by Victor W. Jorgensen, 14 Aug. 1972, p. 21, Church Archives.

65. Reed Smoot, in Badger Diaries, 11 Dec. 1904; *Proceedings* 2:37–39, 44–45.

66. Hyrum M. Smith, in *Proceedings* 1:510–11. Also see Smoot's comments, ibid. 3:191.

67. Francis M. Lyman and George Frisbie Hoar, in ibid. 1:451–52, 456–57.

68. Lyman and Hoar, in ibid. 1:451, 455–57.

69. John Henry Smith, in ibid. 2:284–85ff.

70. Marriner W. Merrill, in ibid. 3:442–43.

71. "Protestants Are Ready to Rest in Smoot Case," *Washington [D.C.] Times,* 20 Dec. 1904.

72. Reed Smoot, in *Proceedings* 3:192, 205–7, 210–27.

73. The volume of testimony supporting these claims was quite overwhelming: *Proceedings* 1:882 (Orlando W. Powers), 2:495, 508 (William J. McConnell), 2:550, 559 (Burton Lee French), 2:581 (F. H. Holzheimer), 2:607, 622 (Frank Martin), 2:647–55 (James H. Brady), 2:679, 705 (J. W. N. Whitecotton), 2:714–18 (Hiram E. Booth), 2:744 (Arthur Pratt), 2:754 (James E. Lynch), 2:757, 760–62 (Hugh M. Dougal), 2:785 (William Hatfield), 2:798–99 (John P. Meakin), 2:825–26 (W. D. Candland), 2:817, 831–32, 835 (James A. Miner), 2:822, 857–58 (William P. O'Meara), 2:888–90 (William M. McCarty), 2:936–44 (Amasa S. Condon), 2:1003 (Charles de Moisy). Specifically regarding the "understanding" and policies toward continued cohabitation, see the following: ibid. 2:558–62 (Burton Lee French), 2:587 (F. H. Holzheimer), 2:672–73, 679 (J. W. N. Whitecotton), 2:715–16, 729 (Hiram Booth), 2:883–86 (William J. McCarty).

74. See the official protest submitted by those opposing Smoot in *Proceedings* 1:1–6; the testimonies at ibid. 1:550–687 (Edward B. Critchlow), 1:691–97 (Ogden Hiles), 1:797–921 (Orlando Powers), and "Mormon Oaths Are Revealed," *Washington [D.C.] Times,* 13 Dec. 1904.

75. *Proceedings* 2:505, 510–13, 515 (William J. McConnell), 2:674 (J. W. N. Whitecotton), 2:708–9 (Hiram E. Booth), 2:770–71 (Alonzo A. Noon), 2:785 (William Hatfield), 2:800 (John P. Meakin), 2:843 (Elias A. Smith), 2:888–932 (William M. McMarty), 2:992–94 (E. D. R. Thompson), 2:1002–1010 (Charles De Moisy), 3:168–74 (Mary G. Coulter), 3:337 (J. U. Eldredge, Jr.), 3:358, 377 (Frank B. Stephens), 4:374 (William K. Henry).

76. Reed Smoot, in ibid. 3:187–89. Admonitions concerning the requirement for primary faithfulness to the leaders, in the cases of both Rudger Clawson and Reed Smoot, are described in Clawson Diaries, 10 Oct. 1898 and 8 April 1900 respectively.

77. Charles Millard Turner, "Joseph Smith III and the Mormons of Utah" (Ph.D. diss., Graduate Theological Union, Berkeley, Calif., 1985), 438–45, 447–61. Also see "Calls Brigham Young Names," *New York Times,* 14 March 1904.

78. Carl A. Badger to Rose Badger, 6 Feb. 1906, Badger Letterbooks.

79. Joseph F. Smith, *Proceedings* 1:476–78, 1057. Also see "Mormon Witnesses Failed to Appear," *New York Times,* 10 March 1904; "Smoot Protestants Conclude Their Case," ibid., 21 Dec. 1904; "Smoot Denies Church Controls His Politics," ibid., 21 Jan. 1905. In fairness to Smith, Professor Thomas G.

Alexander points out that, even before the Smoot investigation, the church president favored resolution of problems at the lowest possible level of ecclesiastical jurisdiction. *Mormonism in Transition,* 97.

80. Joseph F. Smith to Julius C. Burrows, 15 April 1904, copy in *Proceedings* 1:1057–1058; also see *Messages* 4:85–86.

81. Carl A. Badger to Rose Badger, 30 Jan. 1906, Badger Letterbooks.

82. Marriner W. Merrill, in *Proceedings* 3:442–43.

83. Smith to Burrows, ibid. 1:1057–1058.

84. George F. Gibbs to George Teasdale, 20 Aug. 1904, Joseph F. Smith Letterbooks, Church Archives. Theodore Schroeder once described Gibbs as a man "of [the] most ordinary parts, mentally as well as physically." "Sold to Republicans," *New York Times,* 13 Feb. 1895.

85. George F. Gibbs to George Teasdale, 16 Jan. 1905; First Presidency [Joseph F. Smith, John R. Winder, and Anthon H. Lund] to George Teasdale, 8 Feb. 1905; [George F. Gibbs] to George Teasdale, 17 May 1905, all in Joseph F. Smith Letterbooks; Reed Smoot to George Teasdale, 17 May 1905, Reed Smoot Letterbook, BYU Library.

86. Smith's explanations of Teasdale's marriages, given to the Smoot investigating committee, are to be read in *Proceedings* 1:143–44, 477, 486–88, 491.

87. Matthias F. Cowley to Joseph F. Smith, 28 March 1904, Reed Smoot–First Presidency Correspondence; Badger Diaries, 14 April 1904.

88. John W. Taylor to Joseph F. Smith, 16 March 1904, Reed Smoot Correspondence, Church Archives.

89. Badger Diaries, 14 and 18 April 1904.

90. Joseph F. Smith, in ibid., 22 March 1904.

91. Smith to Smoot, 9 April 1904, Reed Smoot–First Presidency Correspondence; Anthon Hendrik Lund Diaries, 15 April 1904, Church Archives.

92. Badger Diaries, 18 Sept. 1905; Lund Diaries, 8 Sept. 1905. Samuel W. Taylor claimed to hear the same story about Francis M. Lyman from his mother, Apostle Taylor's wife Janet, in 1947. Samuel W. Taylor, "Interviews with Nettie [Janet] M. Taylor," July 1947, p. 20, BYU Library. In an interview eleven years previously, however, Samuel Taylor said his mother knew nothing of the episode until he, Samuel, related it to her. "Interview with Nettie [Janet] M. Taylor," 14–15 Jan. 1936, p. 3, BYU Library. This is an example of evidence created by the interviewer/historian who, encountering his own creation some years later, then grants it an independent validity. Also see Taylor, *Rocky Mountain Empire,* 94n.24; and "Why Taylor Didn't Go," *SLT,* 16 Oct. 1910.

93. Smoot to Smith, 10 May 1906, Reed Smoot Correspondence, Church Archives; and Matthias F. Cowley to Jesse N. Smith, 22 April 1906, in *Journal of Jesse Nathaniel Smith: The Life Story of a Mormon Pioneer, 1834–1906* (Salt Lake City: Jesse N. Smith Family Association, 1953), 462. Senator Smoot also suggested in 1905 that Avery Woodruff, the post-Manifesto plural wife and widow of Apostle Abraham Owen Woodruff, be removed "to a safe place" so

as to be out of reach of the investigating committee. Smoot to Smith, 8 Dec. 1905, Reed Smoot–First Presidency Correspondence.

94. "Nuevas colonias mormonas," *Correo de Chihuahua*, 10 Sept. 1904.

95. Nancy Abigail Clement Williams, "Reminiscences and Diary," p. 88, autumn 1905, Church Archives; Ellen Cannon to Katherine C. Thomas, 28 Dec. 1953, copy in possession of author; Asenath Skousen Walser, interviewed by Jessie L. Embry, 26 May 1976, p. 7, POHP; Catherine S. Brown, interviewed by Jessie L. Embry, 3 May 1976, p. 16, POHP; Effie Redd Jameson, interviewed by Gary Shumway, 18 Aug. 1977, p. 34, POHP; Richard Ivins Bentley, interviewed by Leonard R. Grover, 5 Jan. 1980, p. 10, POHP; and Heber Grant Ivins, "Polygamy in Mexico as Practiced by the Mormon Church, 1895–1905," typewritten manuscript, pp. 14–17, University of Utah Library.

96. Clara Mabel Barber Kennedy, in *Proceedings* 1:388–408.

97. Walter M. Wolfe, in ibid. 4:4–6, 8–12, 15, 17–24; and comments by Wolfe quoted in "'Manifesto Only Trick to Beat Devil at Own Game,'" *SLT*, 16 Jan. 1906.

98. George F. Gibbs to Anthony W. Ivins, 22 Feb. 1906, Joseph F. Smith Letterbooks.

99. Anthony W. Ivins to George F. Gibbs, 6 March 1906, George F. Gibbs Letterbox, Church Archives.

100. Ivins's son, Heber Grant Ivins, told the story of his father refusing the request of his superiors on at least three separate occasions: Heber Grant Ivins, "Polygamy in Mexico," 5, 18, 20; Heber Grant Ivins, interviewed by Justin Stewart, 27 June 1971, p. 8, box 1, fd. 5, Heber Grant Ivins Collection, UHi; Heber Grant Ivins, interviewed by Victor W. Jorgensen, 18 July 1972, pp. 9, 36, Oral History Collection, California State University, Fullerton. Regarding Ivins's counsel to the Mexican colonists, see Juarez Stake Historical Record, 1901–6, 7 March 1903, Church Archives; and Juarez Stake High Council Minutes and Historical Record, 1895–1917, 25 Feb. 1905, Church Archives.

101. Two of Ivins's children separately attested to the destruction of records by their father at the time of the Smoot hearings. Heber Grant Ivins, "Polygamy in Mexico," 6; and Florence Ivins Hyde, interviewed by Victor W. Jorgensen, 18–19 Aug. 1972, transcript in private possession.

102. Smoot to Smith, 23 March 1904, Reed Smoot–First Presidency Correspondence; Clawson Diaries, 5 April 1904; Lund Diaries, 7 April 1904.

103. Abraham Owen Woodruff, in Lund Diaries, 6 April 1904.

104. Joseph F. Smith, in JH, 6 April 1904.

105. Joseph F. Smith, in *Seventy-fourth Annual Conference of the Church of Jesus Christ of Latter-day Saints Held in the Tabernacle, Salt Lake City, April 3rd, 4th and 6th, 1904, with a Full Report of the Discourses* (Salt Lake City: Deseret News, 1904), 74.

106. Ibid., 75–76.

107. Ibid., 76. The position taken by Roberts was consistent with that of

church spokesmen from before the time of the Manifesto. See above in chap. 2. Later, in a 1933 statement by the First Presidency, the leaders reversed themselves. President Heber J. Grant and his counselors argued that the Mormon people had indeed "sacredly covenanted with the Government of the United States that they would obey the civil law." "Official Statement," 17 June 1933, *Messages* 5:322.

108. E.g., Mark E. Peterson, *The Way of the Master* (Salt Lake City: Bookcraft, 1974), 54, 62; Eugene E. Campbell and Richard D. Poll, *Hugh B. Brown: His Life and Thought* (Salt Lake City: Bookcraft, 1975), 28.

109. *Proceedings* 1:177–78. Also see the testimonies of Andrew Jenson and George Reynolds in ibid. 1:540–41 and 2:47, respectively. President Woodruff himself said in 1891 that the Manifesto was binding on church members throughout the world. "The Church Cases," *Deseret Weekly*, 24 Oct. 1891. Snow reinforced this position during his administration. "Reminiscences of the Prophet Joseph Smith," *DN*, 23 Dec. 1899; and "Polygamy and Unlawful Cohabitation," *DN*, 8 Jan. 1900. In 1911 President Joseph F. Smith and his counselors reminded church members that Snow had extended the prohibition to all the world. They also said at that time that President Smith's 1904 declaration "reiterated" the restriction. "To the Officers and Members of the Church . . . ," 9 April 1911, *Messages* 4:226.

110. Angus Cannon later told the Smoot committee that he was among those who seconded the 1904 document when it was presented in conference and that he would not have done so if such relationships had been condemned. *Proceedings* 1:789.

111. *Seventy-fourth Annual Conference,* 76. On the day his declaration was presented, Smith assured conference visitors that it was only a reaffirmation of the Woodruff doctrine. JH, 6 April 1904.

112. Francis M. Lyman to George Teasdale, 8 July 1904, copy in Francis M. Lyman Letterbox, Church Archives. For other letters to the apostles, enjoining the same policy, see Francis M. Lyman to John W. Taylor, 3 May 1904, Joseph F. Smith Letterbooks; Francis M. Lyman to John Henry Smith, 5 May 1905, John Henry Smith Collection; and the comments of George H. Brimhall and Josiah Hickman regarding Lyman's letter to Reed Smoot, in *Proceedings* 2:89–90, and 100–101, respectively.

113. Anthony W. Ivins Diaries, 17 Dec. 1904, Anthony Woodward Ivins Collection, UHi; Juarez Stake High Council Minutes and Historical Record, 1895–1917, 26 Jan. 1907, Church Archives.

114. These were the marriages of Charles Edmund Richardson to Daisie Stout and Heber Farr to Hilda Bluth. See Annie Richardson Johnson and Elva Richardson Shumway, *Charles Edmund Richardson: Man of Destiny* (Tempe, Ariz.: Annie R. Johnson Irrevocable Present Interest Trust, 1982), 941–42; Elva R. Shumway, interviewed by Leonard R. Grover, 24 April 1980, p. 8, POHP; Hilda B. Farr, interviewed by Victor W. Jorgensen, 16 Jan. 1972, p. 3, Oral History Collection, California State University, Fullerton. Also see the case of Martha Cragun Cox, who had prior knowledge of the 1904 Manifesto,

as mentioned in Jan [JoAnn Barnett] Shipps, "The Principle Revoked: A Closer Look at the Demise of Plural Marriage," *JMH* 11 (1984): 71; and Carl A. Badger to E. E. Jenkins, 31 March 1904, Badger Letterbooks.

115. Lund Diaries, 18 June 1904.

116. Donald Bruce Johnson and Kirk H. Porter, comps., *National Party Platforms, 1840–1972*, rev. ed. (Urbana: University of Illinois Press, [1973]), 133.

117. Smoot to Smith, 7 Feb. 1905, Reed Smoot–First Presidency Correspondence; and the comments of Senator Fred Dubois, in *Cong. Rec.*, 59th Cong., 1st sess., 1906, 40, pt. 9:8401.

118. Carl A. Badger to E. E. Jenkins, 31 March 1904, Badger Letterbooks.

119. References to alleged polygamous activities by Taylor and Cowley, before the Smoot committee, are found in *Proceedings* 1:1051–1052, 2:386–91, 397, 427, 730–31, 3:192. Senator Smoot's account of the quorum's proposed self-examination is in ibid. 3:194–95, 235–39, 293. For Smoot's refusal to sustain the apostolate when presented to the church in the autumn of 1905, see Smoot to Badger, 11 Oct. 1905, Carlos Ashby Badger Collection; and Merrill, *Reed Smoot*, 57.

120. George Franklin Richards, "Record of Matters of Special Importance," as reproduced in Dale C. Mouritsen, "A Symbol of New Directions: George Franklin Richards and the Mormon Church, 1861–1950" (Ph.D. diss., BYU, 1982), Appendix D, 274–76. I have also used the recollection of Apostle Charles W. Penrose, as given in *Trials*. What appear to be handwritten reproductions of the resignations, on First Presidency stationery, both dated 28 October 1905, are found in Reed Smoot Correspondence, fd. 1, Church Archives. Although Taylor's is the longer of the two statements, both follow the same format and appear to be the work of a single mind. Also see "Are They Not Still Apostles?" *SLT*, 1 Jan. 1910; and Cannon and O'Higgins, *Under the Prophet*, 286–87.

121. Reed Smoot, in Joseph W. Musser Diaries, 29 Oct. 1905, Church Archives.

122. The period during which Taylor and Cowley were dropped was one of stress within the Quorum of Twelve Apostles generally. See Thomas G. Alexander, "'To Maintain Harmony': Adjusting to External and Internal Stress, 1890–1930," *Dialogue* 15 (Winter 1982): 51.

123. Smoot to George F. Gibbs, 6 Dec. 1905; Gibbs to Smoot, 7 Dec. 1905; Smoot to Joseph F. Smith, 8 Dec. 1905; Francis M. Lyman to Smoot, 8 Dec. 1905; Smoot to Lyman, 8 Dec. 1905, Reed Smoot–First Presidency Correspondence.

124. Gibbs to Smoot, 8 Dec. 1905, Reed Smoot–First Presidency Correspondence. Formulation of the code used by Smoot for communicating with church authorities is provided in Joseph Heinerman, "Reed Smoot's 'Secret Code,'" *UHQ* 52 (Summer 1989): 261–62.

125. Smoot to Joseph F. Smith, 8 Dec. 1905, Reed Smoot–First Presidency Correspondence.

126. Francis M. Lyman to Reed Smoot, 15 Dec. 1905, Reed Smoot–First Presidency Correspondence. Also see Lund Diaries, 14 Dec. 1905.

127. Francis M. Lyman, in *Seventy-Sixth Annual Conference of the Church of Jesus Christ of Latter-day Saints Convened in the Tabernacle, Salt Lake City* . . . (Salt Lake City: Deseret News, 1906), 93–94.

128. "Apostles Are in Open Rebellion," *Salt Lake Herald,* 8 April 1906. Due to the death of Apostle Marriner W. Merrill the previous February, three new appointments were made: George F. Richards, Orson F. Whitney, and David O. McKay.

129. Margery W. Ward, *A Life Divided: The Biography of Joseph Marion Tanner, 1859–1927* (Salt Lake City: Publishers Press, 1980), 46–49.

130. Mary Lois Walker Morris Diaries, 7 April 1906, Church Archives.

131. Walter Ernest Young, interviewed by Victor W. Jorgensen, 14 Aug. 1972, pp. 15–16, Church Archives.

132. George F. Gibbs to A. S. Worthington, 11 April 1906, Joseph F. Smith Letterbooks.

133. *Proceedings* 4:441. The leaders seem to have hoped that the dropping of Taylor and Cowley could be done with very little notice. They were undoubtedly looking ahead to readmission of the apostles and wanted the path as free as possible. Smoot, for example, was not permitted to show copies of the resignations to members of Congress for more than a month after Taylor and Cowley were formally excluded at the April 1906 conference. Smoot to Joseph F. Smith, 1 May 1906; First Presidency to Smoot, 9 May 1906; Smoot to Joseph F. Smith, 10 May 1906; and First Presidency to Smoot, 18 May 1906, all in Reed Smoot Correspondence, Church Archives. Before permission was given, an editorial in the *Deseret News* gave the impression that no charges had been filed against Taylor and Cowley and that, except for disagreement with other members of the quorum, they really had done nothing wrong. "Wrong and Irrational," *DN,* 1 May 1906. This added to the impression that removal of the two men was an empty ceremony. The *Deseret News* article resulted in something of a furor in Washington, D.C. George Sutherland, non-Mormon senator from Utah and a supporter of Smoot, told the latter that he thought it the most "unfortunate thing" to have happened since the hearings began. Another senator was quoted as saying: "The church is either honest in this matter [the dropping of Taylor and Cowley] or dishonest, and, damn them, I have about come to the conclusion that they are dishonest." Smoot to Joseph F. Smith, 10 May 1906, Reed Smoot Correspondence.

134. *Proceedings* 4:477.

135. John G. McQuarrie to George Albert Smith, 23 April 1905, George A. Smith Family Papers, University of Utah Library. Also see Carl A. Badger to Rose Badger, 13 April 1906, Carlos Ashby Badger Letterbooks.

136. Nancy Abigail Clement Williams, "Reminiscences and Diary," 114–15.

137. Orson F. Whitney, in Musser Diaries, 22 July 1909.

138. Anthony W. Ivins, in *Trials.*

139. Maggie Palmer to Janet Taylor, 18 May 1911, box 17, fd. 9, John W. Taylor Papers, University of Utah Library.

140. Joseph F. Smith, John R. Winder, and Anthon H. Lund to Henry H. Rolapp, 10 April 1909, Joseph F. Smith Letterbooks, Church Archives. Both official and unofficial statements have perpetuated the impression that cases discovered by the Smoot committee occurred in spite of warnings and efforts by the church to end polygamy. The committee's findings, explained almost as a surprise, are thus seen as what made the 1904 Manifesto and the move against zealots like Taylor and Cowley necessary. *CHC* 6:399–402; "An Address . . . ," May 1907, *Messages* 4:151–52; "To the Officers and Members of the Church . . . ," 9 April 1911, ibid. 4:226–27; "Official Statement from the First Presidency . . . ," 17 June 1933, ibid. 5:324; Joseph Fielding Smith, *Essentials in Church History . . .* , 22d ed. rev. (Salt Lake City: Deseret Book, 1971), 512–13; Ray Jay Davis, "Polygamous Prelude," *American Journal of Legal History* 6 (Jan. 1962): 24; Orma Linford, "The Mormons and the Law: The Polygamy Cases," *Utah Law Review* 9 (Summer 1965), pt. 2:583n.163; and Paul E. Reimann, *Plural Marriage Limited* (Salt Lake City: Utah Printing, 1974), 177–78.

141. For Taylor's remarks to George Albert Smith, see *Trials;* and John Henry Smith Diaries, 18 Feb. 1911. The other allegations are read in Ivins Diaries, 2 Sept. 1907; Carl A. Badger to Rose Badger, 19 April 1906, Badger Letterbooks; and George Franklin Richards Diaries, 28 March 1911, Church Archives. Cf. Samuel W. Taylor, "The Ultimate Disgrace," *Dialogue* 6 (Spring 1971): 114–16.

142. *Trials;* John Henry Smith Diaries, 28 March 1911; Richards Diaries, 28 March 1911; Charles William Penrose Diaries, 28 March and 11 May 1911, UHi; and the comments of Apostle Francis M. Lyman, recorded in Salt Lake High Council Minutes, 11 Feb. 1914, Church Archives.

143. Joseph F. Smith, quoted in Samuel W. Taylor, "Interviews with Nettie [Janet] M. Taylor," 14–15 Jan. 1936, p. 4. In the same interview Nettie Taylor said President Joseph F. Smith told John W. that restoration to the quorum would require that he give up seeing his last two wives. Taylor refused.

144. Charles W. Penrose, quoted in Raymond W. Taylor to Samuel W. Taylor, 3 May 1937, Raymond W. Taylor Collection, BYU Library.

145. Elna Cowley Austin, interviewed by Leonard R. Grover, 26 Jan. 1980, p. 12, POHP.

146. Badger Diaries, 24 May 1906; and Carl A. Badger to unnamed person, 21 Feb. 1907, Badger Collection.

147. Matthias F. Cowley, quoted in Raymond W. Taylor to Samuel W. Taylor, 3 May 1937, Raymond W. Taylor Collection. After a meeting with the apostles in 1909, Joseph W. Musser said that Apostle John Henry Smith admitted plural marriages were performed after the Manifesto but that Taylor and Cowley had gone wrong by performing them in the United States. Musser Diaries, 22 July 1909.

148. "Reconciliation, Letters Passing between the First Presidency and Elder Matthias F. Cowley," *DN*, 3 April 1936. For instances of both men exercising priesthood authority after their exclusion from the quorum and, in Cowley's case, after the 1911 interdiction, see Abbie Hyde Cowley Diaries, 1 Jan. 1913, 2 Aug. 1915, 22 April 1917, Church Archives; Sarah Elizabeth Johnson, Sr., "Reminiscences," n.p., Church Archives; *Excerpts from the Journal of Douglas M. Todd, Sr.* (Salt Lake City: n.p., 1972), 9, 23 Feb. 1908.

149. Samuel W. Taylor, "Interview with Nettie [Janet] M. Taylor," p. 5, 14–15 Jan. 1936; John W. Taylor FGS.

150. Samuel W. Taylor, "Interviews with Nettie [Janet] M. Taylor," 14–15 Jan. 1936, pp. 4, 7, 26–27. For Cowley's care and attentions to Taylor during the latter's final illness, see Abbie Hyde Cowley Diaries, 10 Oct. 1916. Taylor's reinstatement is documented in "Record of the Reinstatement of the Late Apostle John Whittaker Taylor, 1858–1916" (n.p., 1965), copy with other relevant documents contained in box 22, fds. 1–3, John W. Taylor Collection.

151. W. M. Raine and A. W. Dunn, "Mormon or Patriot," *Leslie's Monthly Magazine* 59 (March 1905): 536–47; Bruce Kinney, "The Present Situation among the Mormons," *Missionary Review of the World* 19 (August 1906): 616.

152. Brudnoy, "Of Sinners and Saints," 276–77. Also see the survey of periodical literature as it reflected the public's attitude toward Smoot, both at the time of the committee investigation and throughout the balance of his career, in Jan [JoAnn Barnett] Shipps, "The Public Image of Senator Reed Smoot, 1902–32," *UHQ* 45 (Fall 1977): 388–400.

153. Carl A. Badger to Rose Badger, 10 Feb. 1906, Badger Letterbooks. Evidence of Mormon fear that more marriages would be discovered is illustrated in a letter from Smoot to the church president warning him that opponents might hire detectives to unearth additional cases and that Smith should warn all concerned to be on their guard. Smoot to Smith, 7 Feb. 1905, Reed Smoot–First Presidency Correspondence.

154. "The Committee's Reports," *DN*, 6 June 1906.

155. The committee's majority and minority reports are bound in *Proceedings* 4:467–542.

156. *Speech of Hon. James H. Berry, of Arkansas, in the Senate of the United States, on the Question of Excluding Hon. Reed Smoot, of Utah, from the United States Senate, Monday, February 11, 1907* (Washington, D.C.: GPO, 1907), 12–23. The best study of this tragedy remains that of Juanita Brooks, *The Mountain Meadows Massacre* (1950; Norman: University of Oklahoma Press, 1962).

157. *Cong. Rec.*, Senate, 59th Cong., 2d sess., 20 Feb. 1907, 41:3429. For Roosevelt's impression of Smoot and his belief that the Mormon apostle deserved a place in the Senate, see Isaac Russell, "Mr. Roosevelt to the Mormons," 28, 36. Brigham H. Roberts said Roosevelt's partiality was evinced in early 1905 when he appointed Robert W. Tayler, chief counsel for the complainants against Smoot, to a federal judgeship, thus removing him from the hearings. *CHC* 6:396–97. Also see "Some Changes in the Smoot Case," *DN*, 2 Jan. 1905; and "Made History in State of Utah," *SLT*, 27 Nov. 1910. For

references to Smoot's gratitude for Roosevelt's help, see Heinerman, "Reed Smoot's 'Secret Code,'" 263. Milton R. Merrill, in his biography, said that without the aid of President Roosevelt and the Republican party, Smoot would have lost. *Reed Smoot,* 81–96. Perhaps the most popular explanation for the support given Smoot when the vote came is a remark attributed to Pennsylvania Senator Boies Penrose: "I don't see why we can't get along just as well with a polygamist who doesn't polyg as we do with a lot of monogamists who don't monog." From a reminiscence of Frances T. Plimpton at Amherst College, reported in *Readers' Digest* 72 (1 June 1958): 142.

158. Shelby Moore Cullom, "The Reed Smoot Decision," *North American Review* 184 (15 March 1907): 573.

159. Garner, "The Case of Senator Smoot and the Mormon Church," 46–58.

8

The Mormon-Progressive Encounter: A New Crusade

Increasingly congruent since at least the time of the 1890 Manifesto, Mormon and American value systems drew especially close between 1900 and 1920. Assimilation, of course, had been the goal of Gentiles all along. One observer optimistically noted that, after the death of Brigham Young, Mormons increasingly shopped in the same markets as non-Mormons, cultivated modern manners, and read the same newspapers.[1] And the Utah Commission in its report for 1890 forecast the captivating effect of the nation's monogamous example when combined with Mormonism's own "ambitious desire for social and political standing."[2] Progressive thought furthered the rapprochement, having, at once, an intimidating and seductive effect on Mormon society.

Reinterpretations of the Progressive Era have drawn our attention to the movement's diversity and splintered motivations. With political and economic reform, Progressivism was also, for many, an exercise in preservation and control.[3] Equally important was the role played by a newly emergent middle class—men keen on economy, technical expertise, and efficient organization.[4] Especially relevant for our inquiry was the era's preoccupation with moral concerns, particularly as they related to family life. Growing urban industrialism provoked reformers of many persuasions to attack almost anything believed to threaten the traditional domestic order, albeit, as John D. Buenker has shown, there was division here as well, some seeking change through coercive legislation, others pleading policies of greater pluralism.[5] For those of prescriptive inclination, the bottle and the bordello were only the most prominent of many evils to be met. Immigration with its supposed threat to the nation's race and institutions, white slavery, divorce, and birth control all received attention. Reformers often lacked precise definitions of their goals and many disagreed with one another. Moral issues partook of an astonishingly diffuse character. But alarm was reinforced by the fact that traditional values were, indeed, being questioned. Greater openness about sex and sex-related issues was especially unsettling.

Generally, however, the period's preservationist tendencies joined with its confidence in modernist, scientific solutions to focus on the family as the institution most essential for understanding human problems and needs. In 1901 Samuel W. Dike referred to the centrality of home life. It would, he said, soon occupy the same place in the social sciences as that of the cell in biology.[6] As Martha Elizabeth May has shown, the ideal of the American home—with the husband as provider, the wife as nurturer, a clean parlor, and an efficient budgetary regimen—lay behind most of the period's intrusive campaigns. Social order and monogamous, middle-class marriage were nearly synonymous for most Progressives.[7] These commitments led to attacks on Victorian acceptance of the double standard and the "conspiracy of silence." The Social Purity Alliance of the late nineteenth century was succeeded by groups like the League for the Protection of the Family, the National Vigilance Society, and the American Social Hygiene Association. These crusaders, in David Pivar's words, were possessed of a theocratic temper, folding programs and morality together into a kind of civil religion.[8]

It was quite to be expected, then, that Mormonism's best-known feature would yet attract the nation's attention. Despite efforts to obscure polygamy, the church was unable to stanch public curiosity about it. In 1901 John Fiske lumped Mormons together with buffaloes and red Indians as those American spectacles best known to travelers from abroad.[9] From the beginning of the decade through final disposition of the Smoot case in 1907, a steady flow of articles in journals and newspapers said that polygamy was yet encouraged, that homes in Utah were nothing more than harems, and that foreign female converts were regularly brought to the country as victims for Mormon lechery.[10] The Smoot hearings were but a three-year-long chronicle of what many considered the immoralities of the Mormon church. As late as 1910 the *Chicago Tribune* included Mormonism in a list of the world's "freak religions."[11] With a popular press at the height of its effectiveness, Progressive concerns with survival of the traditional family were bound to find in rumor of continued plural marriage an evil to be crushed.

Part of what made the Mormon-Progressive encounter so meaningful was the number of issues on which the church not only concurred but had preached for decades: frank acknowledgment of Victorian hypocrisy and the importance of social purity; condemnation of birth control; patriarchal family structure; women committed to childbearing; familial self-reliance and solvency.[12] To a rising generation of Mormons, already monogamous and "modern" in their pretensions, it stung to have their loyalty to these ideals questioned, to be associated with a marriage system considered immoral and un-American. The seepage of gentile views into Mormon social consciousness had an incalculable effect. Again and again during the Smoot proceedings, witnesses testified that Mormon youth were overwhelmingly opposed to a revival of polygamy.[13] John W. Judd, who was given a judicial appointment in Utah by President Grover Cleveland, described attitudes of Mormon young people in the 1890s to be forming as distinctly against plural marriage, in contrast to those of the older generation, as a "marked line . . . between the banks of the Mississippi River."[14] Claiming to have quit the practice, many Mormons craved full partnership with other Americans in support of their nation's highest values. The years after the turn of the century were additionally formative because the Mormon hierarchy, as Allen and Leonard have pointed out, was so broadly affected by the passing of older leaders.[15]

Andrew J. Hansen represented what was happening when, after moving from Utah to Idaho at the height of the Smoot investigation, he found his plural families snubbed by Mormons and non-Mormons alike. Wishing to mix with his neighbors, he said, "We courted their good will and pleasure, as well as their approbation." He and other Mormons wanted, he recalled, to take President Grover Cleveland's advice when he said, "I wish you people out there would be like us."[16] Juliaetta Bateman Jensen, whose older brother took a plural wife after 1904, told of the difficulty she had in understanding her brother's motivations. "Our ways of thinking," she said, "were separated by a generation of rapidly changing ideas."[17] And Carl A. Badger, himself born of a polygamous union and of a father who married plurally after 1890 (Appendix II, #6), reflected the transformation with his comment that he could no longer believe polygamy the best marriage arrangement. One man and one woman, both honorable and devoted to each other, he said, constituted the ideal marriage.[18]

Then, in 1909, the journalistic storm became more thundering on what Brigham H. Roberts called "that same old question of polygamy and polygamous living," riveting the nation's attention on what was represented as a vigorous renewal of the Mormon evil.[19] The *Salt Lake Tribune*, a caustic opponent of Mormonism for decades, led the way. Reflecting not only religious differences but political divisions arising from a resurrection of the old gentile Liberal party, now called the American party, hard-fisted articles ran across the *Tribune*'s pages in a flood.[20] Thomas Kearns, former United States senator from Utah and owner of the *Tribune,* believed church influence was used to deny him reelection, and in 1905 he spoke critically of Mormonism in an address before the United States Senate at the height of the Smoot controversy. After leaving public office, he used the *Tribune* to support the American party and to attack both polygamy and church influence in politics.

Municipal victories by the new party, beginning in 1905 and continuing through 1910, cheered the *Tribune* in its policies. With their initial triumph in Salt Lake City, Kearns's paper jubilantly ran headlines that, in Brigham H. Roberts's words, "must have exhausted the type font of its organ." It led with the huzzah "SALT LAKE IS AN AMERICAN CITY."[21] The next day the *Tribune* printed as its banner the full telegram from the National Congress of Mothers and National League of Woman's Organizations which concluded: "On behalf of womanhood and childhood, for love of home and freedom and our country, we rejoice in your victory."[22]

Kearns, whose literary capacity was severely limited, employed Frank J. Cannon as chief editorial writer for the paper. Cannon had served as one of Utah's first United States senators and, when sober, was widely regarded as a writer and speaker of extraordinary ability. Although a son of the late church leader George Q. Cannon, Frank became disenchanted with Mormonism and was especially embittered toward President Joseph F. Smith. A mercurial figure, he seemed able to attack or defend a cause, equally effective in either instance. It was said that his brother, Hugh, while editing the church's European publication, the *Millennial Star,* called on Frank for assistance in preparing a series of articles on Mormon theology. Frank complied. Impressed with their persuasiveness, Hugh asked his brother how it was that, without belief of his own, Frank could so powerfully defend the faith? Frank is supposed to have replied: "I wrote them for you, not me."[23]

Encouraged by a sense that the temporal power of Mormon leadership was in retreat, anti-Mormon forces held a large celebration in Salt Lake City in 1908 to honor former United States senator from Idaho Fred T. Dubois, a fierce critic of Mormonism. It was a grand affair with many dignitaries present, including Frank Cannon and Charles S. Varian. Numerous speeches were given, all of them echoing volleys

by the *Tribune* attacking the church on the familiar grounds of hierarchical control and plural marriage. Concluding the long evening,
Edward B. Critchlow, a prominent Salt Lake City attorney and civic
officer, presented a resolution calling for an amendment to the
United States Constitution that would everywhere prohibit both unlawful cohabitation and new plural marriages performed "by authority of the alleged revelation and with the formulas of the Mormon
Church."[24]

Beginning on 13 November 1909 and continuing into mid-January
1911, the *Tribune* published no less than 119 articles describing new
polygamous marriages since 1890. Maintaining a running tally of
offenders, the accounts eventually provided over 230 names. Because
of duplications and other errors, the *Tribune* lists are not wholly accurate. They are, however, a valuable source for reconstructing the
church's post-Manifesto polygamous experience. Referring to claims
made by friendly witnesses in the Smoot hearings that only a few
"sporadic" plural marriages had taken place, and using Apostle Francis M. Lyman's appellation of "skulldugger" for those who made such
contractions, the *Tribune* delighted in unveiling all the "sporadic
skullduggers" it could find.[25] Society was demoralized by the practice,
it was said, and cohabitation and new plural unions were denigrated as
the work of a "polygamous cult."[26]

Following the *Tribune*'s lead, various national journals took up the
cry. Frank J. Cannon teamed with Harvey J. O'Higgins, a former
protégé of Lincoln Steffens, to prepare a ten-part exposé for *Everybody's*, entitled "Under the Prophet in Utah: The National Menace of a
Political Priestcraft."[27] Drawing on his experience in politics and his
family's prominence in church circles, Cannon spun out a tale of
conspiracy, despotism, and betrayal. President Joseph F. Smith, he
said, reneged on the efforts of Wilford Woodruff and his father,
George Q. Cannon, to bring polygamy to an end. Smith, Cannon
asserted, was the one chiefly responsible for clandestine renewal of
the practice. Under Smith's leadership, the articles charged, Mormonism was not only administered for the material benefit of a few, but
new polygamy had revived to such a degree that more were living in
the arrangement than before the Manifesto. Contending that the *Tribune* lists constituted less than 10 percent of the total number of
offenders, Cannon said there were likely more than two thousand
who had entered plural marriage since 1890.[28] Cannon not only engaged in exaggeration but, hypocritically ignoring the important role
his father had played before dying in 1901, sought to lay the burden of

guilt for approving new polygamous unions overwhelmingly at the feet of Joseph F. Smith.

"New polygamy" became almost a shibboleth for writers hungry for scandal. In addition to the Cannon and O'Higgins series in *Everybody's,* the church was attacked as threatening the American home in *Pearson's, McClure's,* and *Cosmopolitan.* Writing for *Pearson's,* Richard Barry said that, except for polygamy, Mormonism had much about it that was praiseworthy. But because of its home practices, it had always been "an Ishmael church," shunned and driven for its immoralities. The years between the Manifesto and the granting of statehood had been an "opossum period" during which it only pretended to abandon the practice. Like the church's critics a half-century earlier, Barry played on racial and sexual anxieties of the day, saying that continued Mormon polygamy was "an issue ready-made" for Americans troubled by the outcome of the Jeffries-Johnson prize fight.[29] Alfred Henry Lewis exploited the concern with immigration and white slavery to warn, in *Cosmopolitan,* that by bringing female converts from overseas, Mormonism threatened "the whiteness of American womanhood."[30] Sarah Comstock, in *Collier's,* said polygamy was so common in southern Utah that Mormons there received mail addressed, "Brother L— and Wives."[31] Mormon plurality made appearances in the nation's fledgling film industry.[32] And alarm spread to Europe, where the Saints were sometimes jailed and forbidden to preach. In England Mormons were stoned, tarred, and feathered.[33]

The strident nature of journalistic statements aside, a credible basis existed for charges that church leaders continued to authorize men in the activity of plural marriage. Some who published in national periodicals were surprisingly accurate. Burton Hendrick, for example, in an article for *McClure's* described in detail how Mexico and Canada were used as part of the machinery by which men obtained additional wives. He told where many of them located after their return to Utah. He commented on Mormon belief in polygamous deities as necessarily sanctioning the practice among men. And he described how, so far as new polygamy was concerned, the church was often unable to control its own members.[34]

Neither could the Reorganized Church remain clear of the matter. It was bad enough that a persuasive refutation of RLDS claims was published in 1910, establishing the responsibility of Joseph Smith the prophet for "that polygamic system which has been one of the foulest blots upon our national escutcheon."[35] But Joseph Smith III, who as RLDS president denounced the practice to his deathbed, was outraged when *Everybody's* mistakenly used a photograph of *him* as a cover illustration for one of its 1911 issues on continued polygamy in Utah.[36]

Predictably, Mormon leaders took steps to answer allegations made against them. A notarized statement was prepared claiming that some of those named by the *Tribune* were falsely accused. If certain names were in error, it was pointed out, the entire assault lacked credibility.[37] Repeating assurances given by the First Presidency in a 1907 address, it was stated that polygamy was dying out. Charges that crime and immorality existed in Latter-day Saint society because of polygamy were denied. The Saints, they protested, were less afflicted with family problems than the rest of American society. Meetings sermonizing on purity were noted, the sanctity of marriage was preached, and loyalty to home and nation extolled. Critics of the church, they said, should first pluck the beams from their own eyes. No opportunity was lost to declare Mormonism's intense loyalty to the government and its belief that the United States Constitution was inspired by God. Consideration was given to using the new movie industry as a way to improve Mormonism's image. And, as part of the exercise, the Tabernacle Choir was sent on tour as a goodwill gesture.[38]

More importantly, when articles in the *Tribune* began appearing in 1909, a committee consisting of apostles Francis M. Lyman, John Henry Smith, and Heber J. Grant was organized to investigate the charges and consider what to do.[39] The work of the committee eventually came to involve the entire quorum. Attacks by journalists were so biting that every leader had an interest in the matter.[40] It was a complex undertaking, however, because some quorum members had direct knowledge of authorized polygamy well after the Manifesto. And due to Apostle Smoot's role as a senator, political considerations were not irrelevant.

Probably because of pressures from Reed Smoot and Apostle Francis M. Lyman, a consensus emerged that things were moving too slowly and greater efforts should be made to discipline offenders. Smoot insisted that all who took plural wives after 1890 be removed from positions of authority in the church. And he "strongly demand[ed]" that those married polygamously since 1904 be excommunicated. Most in the quorum, he felt, agreed with him but feared making "a wholesale slaughter." They felt it best simply to drop such men from leadership roles as fast as circumstances permitted "without making a great stir about it."[41] Complete harmony was yet wanting, however, some believing that the entire problem could have been avoided if the leaders had given their support to Thomas Kearns, owner of the *Tribune,* allowing him to keep his seat in the United States Senate.[42]

During the autumn and early winter of 1910 and 1911, individuals thought guilty of post-Manifesto polygamous contractions were brought before the apostles and questioned. Some were cooperative. Most were not. In the instance of Henry S. Tanner (Appendix II, #185), the quorum, reflecting perhaps their unwillingness to yield to the alarmed urgings of Smoot, refused to be bullied by "the Tribune clamor" and resolved to consider his case carefully.[43] After more than six months and repeated discussions, Tanner was disfellowshipped.[44] Bishop Daniel Muir (Appendix II, #139), who married polygamously in 1906, told the apostles he believed that neither the Woodruff Manifesto of 1890 nor the Smith statement of 1904 were sincerely intended to bring plural marriages to an end. Too many instances existed, he argued, in which late marriages were approved. Those who took the step knew they were at risk, he said, and if found out were prepared for excommunication from the church.[45]

Patriarch Judson Tolman (Appendix II, #198) acknowledged that he had solemnized fifteen such marriages but refused to give the names of those involved. Admitting he had taken a post-Manifesto plural wife of his own, he said he could not tell who performed the ceremony because the party concerned wore a mask.[46] When Joseph W. Summerhays (Appendix II, #184) identified President Joseph F. Smith as the one who gave him permission to engage in the activity, the quorum was stunned. Smoot and Lyman wanted Summerhays excommunicated. Despite President Smith's contradiction of Summerhays's testimony, however, the apostles decided only to drop him from all church positions.[47] Inquiries into the behavior of apostles John W. Taylor and Matthias F. Cowley also occurred at this time. Any explanation of their cases must take into consideration that they were part of the leaders' responses to a journalistic crusade. For Taylor and Cowley, the subjects of a similar interrogation conducted for similar reasons a half-dozen years previously, it must have seemed a cruel encore.

Through all this, Reed Smoot was most conspicuous. He was probably the best example of the church's new leadership—monogamous and untouched by officially authorized post-Manifesto polygamy. Journalistic interest in Mormon polygamy had led to renewed criticism of the senator.[48] Again and again, Smoot raised the question of "new polygamy" with his quorum, insisting that action be taken to suppress it. He also repeatedly met with the First Presidency to urge his views. Smoot recommended that a special circular be sent through-out the church calling for action against known offenders and that President Smith speak out more forcefully on the matter.

After the quorum decided in January 1911 that, short of compell-ing reasons, anyone married in polygamy before 1904 would not be molested by the church, Smoot returned from Washington, D.C., and reopened the question. At the least, he argued, all post-1890 pluralists should be dropped from church positions. This was the only way, he said, that their critics could be convinced the church was serious about stopping the practice.[49] And it was Smoot, more than anyone else, who insisted that those discovered to have taken plural wives since 1904 be cut off altogether. The impression created by the senator—as instigator of these measures and as one who often went beyond what others felt appropriate—led to a rumor that he was out of harmony with the rest of his quorum.[50]

If Smoot's motions crowded what some believed prudent, he per-suaded his colleagues more often than not. The recommended circu-lar, for example, was sent to all stake presidents and their counselors, directing them to try offenders for their membership in the church.[51] At a special priesthood meeting at the autumn general conference in 1910, at Smoot's urging, President Smith sharply rebuked those at-tempting to perpetuate new plural marriages.[52] Smoot also obtained agreement on the proposal to quietly remove men who had married after 1890 from positions of visibility in church organizations.[53] With few exceptions the quorum began excommunicating those involved in post-1904 plural marriages more vigorously than at any time pre-viously. And notices of the excommunications were printed in the *Deseret News*. As Smoot put it, "The crowd that have been marrying and getting others to marry plural wives are beginning to think the church is in earnest."[54]

There was, nevertheless, a sense on the part of the senator that he was forward of most other leaders on these issues and that President Smith especially needed prodding. The First Presidency was not alone in their inertia. Other authorities, including various bishoprics and presidencies of stakes, were loath to act.[55] It was determined in the spring of 1911 that, if a housecleaning were undertaken, some four-teen or fifteen men serving in stake presidencies throughout the church would need to step down. In two instances, those of Davis and Granite stakes, the entire stake presidencies would be affected.[56]

The senator's concerns, especially in connection with President Smith, are illustrated by a development in the spring of 1911. In mid-November 1910 Smoot told the First Presidency that in the event

President William Howard Taft or members of the Senate should ask, Smoot wanted to be positive in saying that all known cases of post-Manifesto polygamy had been acted upon, with those that occurred after 1904 resulting in excommunication. In mid-March 1911, as the result of magazine articles, especially those in *Everybody's* by Frank Cannon and Harvey J. O'Higgins, Smoot had a long meeting with the First Presidency on the same subject. Again he insisted that the only way for the church to clear itself was by summary action against all who were guilty. President Smith and his counselors seemed reluctant, however, taking the view that if the church had not approved the marriages, it could not be held responsible for them. They also expressed fear of responses by church members if "wholesale action" were taken.[57]

Two days later, on 16 March 1911, Smoot continued his entreaties at a meeting of the Quorum of Apostles in the temple. Once more he warned of potential injury to the church if those involved in late plural marriages were allowed to continue to occupy conspicuous church roles. He also said former president Theodore Roosevelt was preparing a letter or essay to answer charges that he had made improper political agreements at the time of the Smoot investigation. The piece was to be sent to the Mormon journalist Isaac Russell and to be published in *Collier's,* and the senator indicated he was uneasy about the venture. It could lead to questions about post-Manifesto polygamy, and as Smoot remarked, "we know there have been new cases." Later the same day, in a meeting with the First Presidency, he told of the Roosevelt essay, again urging that the church clear its reputation by taking action against all who had married plurally since 1890.[58]

After returning to Washington, D.C., at the end of the month, Smoot sent a long telegram to President Smith dilating on the same theme—the anti-Mormon magazine crusade and the need for action. Smoot then asked Smith what he should tell former president Roosevelt in the event he were to ask about post-Manifesto plural marriages. Because of Roosevelt's soon-expected publication on the Mormons, it was reasonable to believe he might consult Smoot about it. Given his sense that the church was moving tardily, anxious about both his and the church's reputations, Smoot was nervous as to what he would say.[59]

Smith's response by telegram disappointed the senator. It underlined differences between the two men in their perceptions of the problem. President Smith advised that if Roosevelt should ask the senator about charges of "new polygamy," Smoot should tell the truth. He should say that George Q. Cannon was the first to suggest that the practice could be kept alive by performing plural ceremonies in Mexico and Canada, where, according to Smith, it was legal to do so. Cannon had, Smith said, authorized such contractions and that was why men in the church had entered the principle since the Manifesto.[60] Nothing in the president's telegram indicated new efforts were being undertaken by the church to deal with polygamous offenders. Nothing was said about the measures Senator Smoot had proposed. There was nothing that could be taken even as assurance that new plural marriages were finally at an end. Senator Smoot recorded in his diary that Smith simply did not understand how strongly Americans felt about polygamy. He concluded: "It is evident no action against the persons taking polygamist wives before 1904 will be taken. If there is another investigation I do not know how [our] present position will be justified. . . . We are in a bad position for an examination or investigation."[61]

As it turned out, Roosevelt seems not to have consulted Smoot about new polygamy. His essay was written and sent in mid-February, well before the discussions between Smoot and his colleagues in Salt Lake City. When published, the essay was quite approbative. Roosevelt first absolved himself of any special favors to or arrangements with the Mormon leadership. He also reaffirmed his support for federal control of marriage practices including, if necessary, a constitutional amendment prohibiting polygamy. He emphatically warned that the Saints must not attempt a renewal of the practice. Roosevelt then stated that, from all he had observed, Mormon monogamous families adhered to a standard of morality higher than most. He found among them less prostitution, less sexual degradation, and less evidence of birth control than among their neighbors. It was a glowing vindication.[62]

Beyond this, Smith delivered another special address on the subject at the April 1911 conference of the church in Salt Lake City. Using arguments and phrases employed before, the president reminded everyone that the charge that Mormons had broken their compact with the federal government was false. The church had made no compact, nor could it. So far as new polygamous marriages were concerned, the church had forbidden them to be performed in the Manifesto of 1890. Because some had interpreted this to apply only to the United States, he asserted that the restriction was made applicable to Mormons everywhere. All found in violation of these rules were disciplined and, in some instances, excommunicated. Smith promised that these policies would be continued.[63] If the message was not all that Smoot wished, at least the president affirmed the church was holding course.

As frustrated as Smoot sometimes felt, the impact of his views was significant. When Benjamin E. Rich (Appendix II, #155), who had married polygamously since 1890, was nominated to replace a vacancy in the First Council of Seventy, Smoot urged that he be passed over for having taken a post-Manifesto wife. The result was that Levi Edgar Young was selected instead.[64] The lives of men at lesser levels were also altered. Arthur William Hart (Appendix II, #85), who married his two wives in 1900 and 1903 and was serving as a high councilman in the Oneida Stake in Idaho, was told by apostles to step down and confine his church work to a life of Christian integrity.[65] Hart's son, Mark, is reported to have twice refused a judgeship in the fifth judicial district of Idaho because of the family's involvement in post-1890 polygamous marriages.[66]

In 1912 an unexpected development thrust Mormon polygamy into the news again. The Mexican Revolution forced hundreds of Mormon families north into the United States.[67] The Mexican colonies constituted the richest preserve of Mormon polygamy, both old and new, in all the church. Not only did the event arouse interest at a time shortly following the rash of magazine criticism, but it left the displaced colonists in confusing circumstances. They were accustomed to view themselves as a special elite. In their minds, they had lived a higher principle and had sacrificed dearly to keep it alive. But now they found it necessary to sit quietly while bishops and stake authorities in the United States, faithful to instructions, sermonized on the error of those who failed to observe the Manifesto. Unaware of the special permission given, local leaders sometimes brought action against former colonists living in their wards. Refugees were routinely passed over for ecclesiastical advancement. Because the new policy was designed to veil the very specimen they represented, polygamous men and women found themselves drifting toward obscurity among their own people. Some encountered hostility from relatives who now considered plural marriage adulterous. One pluralist, after taking his wives into New Mexico from Texas, was accused of white slavery.[68]

Most trying was the sense of abandonment by the leaders. As a younger colonist recalled, whereas in Mexico the authorities had praised them, saying that a higher reward awaited them for living as they did, after the exodus to the United States this no longer was true.[69] Even those who later returned to Mexico found attitudes in the reestablished Mormon communities changed. One member who married polygamously long after the 1904 announcement was humiliated when, at a church meeting where the sexes were seated on opposite sides of the room, he was made to sit with the women.[70] The practice of turning away from those formerly looked upon as stalwarts continued as long as most of them lived. The son of one prominent polygamist from the colonies told how, as late as the 1960s, a general authority of the church refused to acknowledge his plural mother and her family at the funeral of another of his father's wives. Responding to the affront, he said: "I am persuaded that this was an attitude, if not directed by, at least symptomatic of, . . . the hierarchies. I resented it then and I still resent it."[71]

Mormon polygamous families returning from Mexico, along with other Americans forced to leave because of the revolution, precipitated a congressional inquiry. Junius Romney, the presiding ecclesiastical officer in Mexico at the time the Mormons left, assured senators that no plural marriages were being solemnized south of the border. The Mormons were there, he said, because of cheap land and a warm climate.[72] Many remained unconvinced, however, and problems arose with the United States Immigration and Naturalization Service. Mormon converts from abroad were sometimes accused of being either polygamous or, if women, destined for polygamous homes in Utah. White slaves were commonly thought to be of foreign origin. Given the near hysteria of some Progressives on the issue, it is not surprising that Mormon female immigrants invited question.[73]

Criticisms arose in other quarters as well. The decades-old call for a constitutional amendment that would prohibit plural marriage was also revived, especially by religious and womens' organizations. By 1913 petitions from state legislatures urging passage of the amendment were arriving in the nation's capital from both sides of the continent. At year's end all but five of the necessary number of states had ratified a proposal forbidding plural households in any state or territory subject to United States' jurisdiction.[74] In the same year a special commission on Mormonism established by the National Reform Association made its report. The commission referred to answers by Mormon witnesses before the Smoot investigating committee as evidence of Mormon defiance and remarked on the contrast of such behavior with the "suppliant" manner of church leaders before the granting of statehood. With other indictments the report noted that Mormonism simply was not "disposed to leave the Christian home alone." In addition to making a "wreck" of marriages by proselytizing and converting one or another of the partners, the report said Mormon teachings had such currency that citizens were asking "whether the unit of . . . society . . . in America is to be the harem or the home." Doing all they could to cultivate offense, the commissioners declared: "If Lincoln were still living he doubtless would say: 'The national house divided against itself will not endure. No nation can endure very long with its homes part polygamous and part monogamous, with its marriage system partly Moslem and partly Christian.'"[75]

In 1916 an international publication returned to the subject of Mormon settlements in northern Mexico, referring to them as "shrines established for the uninterrupted practice of polygamy."[76] The Methodist minister Thomas Iliff continued to lecture throughout the United States, warning that Mormonism was "the same old serpent," that polygamy was yet taught and practiced with church approval, and that Mormon leaders still craved temporal control.[77] And when Mormon representatives were invited to speak before the World's Christian Citizenship Conference at Pittsburgh in 1919, they were hooted down by an audience certain of Mormon sexual sin.[78]

Latter-day Saint efforts to appease did not commence with these events. They began, as already shown, years before. Comment on plural marriage, except to condemn its continuance, had long since largely disappeared from official Mormon sermons and writings. Reference to surviving plural households was also avoided. After the turn of the century, Mormonism's public flight from the practice escalated. Beyond the 1904 conference statement warning members to desist from plural marriage, at least eight other addresses of similar language were issued by the First Presidency in the next ten years.[79] And Mormons guilty of taking new plural wives, if found out, were formally and publicly disciplined. During the Smoot hearings Mormon witnesses were repeatedly reminded that, while the revelation approving polygamy (section 132) remained in the *Doctrine and Covenants*, the Manifesto by President Woodruff had not yet been included in the same organ.[80] This point was made by writers discussing polygamy in magazine articles. Richard Barry, for example, claimed that the 1906 printing of the work was purposely left undated to give the impression that no new edition had been issued requiring inclusion of Woodruff's statement.[81] Finally, and symbolic of Mormon-American détente, the 1890 document was put at the back of the volume in 1908.[82]

There was also a return to the question of what was meant by the term "celestial marriage." Attention was earlier given to alteration of the phrase, as part of the church's defensive tactics in the 1880s, to mean only a marriage that survived death.[83] It may have been sometime during the 1890s that wording in the superscript to section 132 of the *Doctrine and Covenants* was rewritten to more closely reflect this change.[84] Then, during the Smoot hearings, authorities declared again that "celestial marriage" was not used in Mormon parlance to connote polygamy. Unless directly enjoined from heaven as in the individual case of Joseph Smith, plurality was said not to have been a general command to the Saints. This was reiterated in subsequent conferences of the church.[85] The new meaning proved politically helpful in Idaho, where a constitutional prohibition existed disfranchising anyone practicing or teaching "celestial marriage."[86] Occasionally, however, slips occurred. In 1910 Apostle Francis M. Lyman told an out-of-state journalist that President Woodruff's Manifesto stated that Mormons "need not go into celestial marriage any longer" and that President Smith's 1904 official declaration had made that "the law of the church."[87]

Generally, however, the new emphasis held. In a 1905 work previewed and endorsed by church authorities including President Joseph F. Smith, John Henry Evans argued that eternity of the marriage covenant, not polygamy, was the chief theme of Joseph Smith's 1843 revelation. Plural marriage, he said, was not "obligatory upon the members of the Church generally."[88] Other Mormon writers, especially James E. Talmage, denied that polygamy had ever been a vital tenet of the church and repeated that it was not to be equated with eternal marriage.[89] It seems likely that this view was sincerely accepted by increasing numbers of the leaders. In early 1908 a committee consisting of Anthon H. Lund, Orson F. Whitney, Brigham H. Roberts, and James E. Talmage, after researching the question, recommended to the First Presidency that "celestial marriage" not be equated exclusively with "plural" or "patriarchal" marriage. The crucial, saving principle, said the report, was simply the eternal nature of the marriage covenant.[90] Word that an attempt was underway to have the 1843 revelation eliminated from the Mormon book of commandments altogether seems to have been a false rumor.[91] There was, however, discussion by the apostles of proposals that references to plural marriage in other Mormon publications be removed.[92]

These shifts, steering the church into closer alignment with common American belief about the family, were accompanied by reformulations unrelated to polygamy.[93] Thomas G. Alexander is certainly correct in suggesting that consequences of the 1890 Manifesto comprehended social mood, a greater susceptibility to American pluralism, and acceptance of the traditional disjunction of temporal and spiritual spheres.[94] But nothing repostured the church so dramatically as official changes associated with its views of marriage. Ironically, some of what the church set aside now was taken up by others. The eugenics movement of the late nineteenth century acquired its greatest support just as the church turned away from polygamy and the physiological arguments presented in its favor.[95] While many in the Eugenics Education Society and allied concerns found such views extreme, one is struck with how closely the comments of some eugenicists compared with apologies earlier adduced in behalf of Mormon polygamy—that racial improvement, to succeed, must acquire the power of a religious tenet; that monogamous marriage should be reexamined and alternative arrangements considered as more beneficial to society; and that not only were "foresight and self-control . . . of the essence of civilization" but procreation constituted the "supreme impulse" of man and should be regarded as "a sacred function, to be exercised in the light of scientific knowledge."[96] One of the evidences of Mormonism's capture by mainstream sentiments was its refusal, like Americans at large, to link arms with those advocating racial improvement through selective reproduction.

Latter-day Saint concerns with their public image brought the desired result. Notwithstanding many of those fleeing north at the time of the Mexican Revolution were polygamous, Congress appropriated $100,000 to assist in their relief.[97] The publication two years later of Walter M. Gallichan's survey of polygamy in different societies illustrates how non-Mormon attitudes were changing toward the Saints. Not only did the work employ an anthropological tone, anticipating the diffidence of society in coming years, but the chapter on Mormons, except in its view of the treatment of women, was quite approving.[98] Ruth Reed, writing on American marriage in the 1920s, praised Mormonism for its courage in experimenting with an institution needing reform.[99]

Encouraged by the church's denunciations of new plural marriages and by the deaths in 1918 of both Thomas Kearns and Joseph F. Smith, the *Salt Lake Tribune* embarked on a policy of respectful coexistence with Mormonism that has continued to the present day.[100] In 1919, responding to criticisms of the Saints by the World's Christian Citizenship Conference referred to above, speeches were made on the floor of the United States Senate defending the church. Non-Mormon senators praised Latter-day Saint morality, industry, and patriotism. One church authority said this was "doubtless the first unsolicited defense of the Latter-day Saints ever uttered in the Senate of the United States."[101]

The campaign for amending the constitution to prohibit polygamy continued, but with declining support. After cresting in 1913, at the time of the magazine crusade, enthusiasm for the idea faltered. Private organizations and church congregations still wrote their congressmen on the subject. Petitions describing the evils of Mormon polygamy, urging the need for a constitutional amendment, yet circulated at Chautauqua meetings. But after gilding the speeches of representatives and senators for a half-century, the movement to constitutionally enshrine judgment against the practice sputtered out in the 1920s.[102] In her study of the transformation of the Mormon image, Jan Shipps found that, although journalistic currents did not begin running strongly for the Mormons until the 1930s, by the end of World War I antagonism toward the Saints took a discernible plunge.[103]

Mormonism's image brightened by the year. Books by Mormon and non-Mormon minimized polygamy in the church's history, emphasizing instead the Saints' record as pioneers and agriculturalists. In his beautiful volume *Utah, the Land of Blossoming Valleys,* published in 1922, George Wharton James admitted that it was sometimes alleged that polygamous marriages were yet performed by the church, but there was not, he stated, "the slightest scintilla of evidence" for such a thing.[104] James worked with church leaders in the preparation of his manuscript, as did James H. McClintock in the writing of his *Mormon Settlement in Arizona.*[105] McClintock's account barely mentioned plural marriage. It was the Mormon's role as irrigator, road builder, and citizen that deserved historians' attention.

Levi Edgar Young, a church authority and faculty member at the University of Utah, wrote a popular history that, while claiming one of its primary objects to be the social experience of Utah, gave no mention whatever to plural family life among the Saints.[106] And in the mid-1930s Preston Nibley, in his biography of Brigham Young, accomplished what Thomas G. Alexander described as "the astounding feat of eulogizing the much-married prophet without mentioning polygamy in more than 500 pages."[107] Heber J. Grant, who succeeded Joseph F. Smith as the church's president in 1918, is supposed to have remarked at a church meeting in the late 1920s that harmony with outsiders had progressed to the point where the press could be depended on to publish whatever the church wanted.[108] This was an exaggeration, undoubtedly, but it illustrates the confidence Mormon leaders had acquired and the extent to which Mormon and non-Mormon could now agree.

Whatever the course by which Mormons arrived, there was a more personal consequence than restatement of policy, than a rewriting of the church's past, or the taking of cultural vows. For there were men and women yet living in polygamous families. And it was they who were the living cost of the bargain. The "hardest times," said one student after interviewing a plural family from that period, came during those years. "Until then," he said, those living the principle "had the consolation that they were doing right and living their religion. The persecution did not matter. But when the church renounced polygamy all the heroism was gone. The whole thing seemed to be in vain. Family life after that was a sort of extended underground. The attitude of [Mormons themselves] . . . changed and in a way there was a stigma attached to polygamist families."[109]

Loyal before the change, however, most who were polygamous remained devoted to the church after it. What if those once considered best were called to play a humbler role? God would know his own. It was the rapidly enlarging number of monogamists that could best serve Mormonism now. By postponing the taking of plural wives to another world, a snug agreement was struck in this one. The church purchased a season of peace unknown from its beginning. And in the meantime, few surpassed the Saints in implementing Progressivism's model family—monogamous, thrifty, patriarchal, and fecund.

NOTES

1. "Salt Lake City," *Harper's* 69 (Aug. 1884): 403.

2. "Annual Report of the Utah Commission," *Report of the Secretary of the Interior . . .* , 5 vols. (Washington, D.C.: GPO, 1890), 3:421.

3. On Progressive era historiography and suggestions for reinterpretation, see all of John D. Buenker, John C. Burnham, and Robert M. Crunden, *Progressivism* (Cambridge, Mass.: Schenkman, 1977).

4. David M. Kennedy, ed., *Progressivism: The Central Issues* (Boston: Little-Brown, 1971), xi; all of Samuel P. Hays, *The Response to Industrialism, 1885–1914* (Chicago: University of Chicago Press, 1957); idem, *Conservatism and the Gospel of Efficiency* (Cambridge, Mass.: Harvard University Press, 1959); and Robert H. Wiebe, *The Search for Order, 1877–1920* (New York: Hill & Wang, 1967).

5. See especially the chapter "An American Kulturkampf," in John D. Buenker, *Urban Liberalism and Progressive Reform* (New York: Charles Scribner's, 1973), 163–97. Also see John C. Burnham, "The Progressive Era: Revolution in American Attitudes toward Sex," *Journal of American History* 59 (March 1973): 887; and Paul Boyer, *Urban Masses and Moral Order in America, 1820–1920* (Cambridge, Mass.: Harvard University Press, 1978), 189–292.

6. Samuel W. Dike, "The Proposed Canons on Divorce," *Outlook* 69 (28 Sept. 1901): 232.

7. Martha Elizabeth May, "Home Life: Progressive Social Reformers' Pre-

scriptions for Social Stability, 1890–1920" (Ph.D. diss., State University of New York at Binghamton, 1984).

8. David Pivar, "Cleansing the Nation: The War on Prostitution, 1917–21," *Prologue* 1 (Spring 1980): 40. I have also found helpful the studies of John Higham, *Strangers in the Land: Patterns of American Nativism, 1860–1925* (New Brunswick, N.J.: Rutgers University Press, 1955), 158–93; Mark Thomas Connelly, *The Response to Prostitution in the Progressive Era* (Chapel Hill: University of North Carolina Press, 1980); Ruth Rosen, *The Lost Sisterhood: Prostitution in America, 1900–1918* (Baltimore: Johns Hopkins University Press, 1982); James C. Whorton, *Crusaders for Fitness: The History of American Health Reformers* (Princeton, N.J.: Princeton University Press, 1982), 140–41, 164–67; William O'Neill, *Divorce in the Progressive Era* (New Haven: Yale University Press, 1967); David Noble, *The Progressive Mind, 1890–1917* (Chicago: Rand McNally, 1971); and Robert M. Crunden, *Ministers of Reform: The Progressives' Achievement in American Civilization, 1889–1920* (New York: Basic Books, 1982).

9. John Fiske, *American Political Ideas* (New York: Harper & Brothers, 1901), 17. As Peter N. Carroll and David W. Noble suggested, Mormon polygamy was one of a panoply of threats that critics from the 1880s on associated with growing urban industrialism. See their *The Free and the Unfree: A New History of the United States* (London: Penguin, 1977), 240.

10. The following are but a sample: William R. Campbell, "Mormonism and Purity," *Missionary Review of the World* 15 (Feb. 1902): 133–37; "What Is Mormonism?" ibid. 18 (Nov. 1905): 853; Bruce Kinney, "The Present Situation among the Mormons," ibid. 19 (August 1906): 616–19; John T. Bridwell, "Origin of American Polygamy," *Arena* 29 (May 1903): 472; "Here to Study Mormonism," *New York Times,* 20 August 1906; Marie O. Corbin, "A Gentile Child among the Mormons," *Outlook* 84 (6 Oct. 1906): 324.

11. "Freak Religions from All over the World," *Chicago Tribune,* 6 Feb. 1910.

12. Much that occurred during the administration of Joseph F. Smith, 1901–18, coincided not only with Progressivism's dates but partook of Progressive values. There was greater attention to things like public health and welfare. The church also closed step with American society by moving toward greater centralization, increased bureaucratic control, and more efficient methods of accounting. See the studies of Thomas G. Alexander: "Reed Smoot, the L.D.S. Church and Progressive Legislation, 1903–1933," *Dialogue* 7 (Spring 1972): 47–55; and *Mormonism in Transition: A History of the Latter-day Saints, 1890–1930* (Urbana: University of Illinois Press, 1986), 126–56.

13. *Proceedings* 2:100, 508, 553, 559, 607, 635, 672, 679 passim.

14. John W. Judd, in ibid. 1:68.

15. James B. Allen and Glen M. Leonard, *The Story of the Latter-day Saints* (Salt Lake City: Deseret Book, 1976), 436.

16. Grover Cleveland, quoted in *Autobiography of Andrew Janus Hansen, 1852–1932* (Provo, Utah: A. J. Hansen Family Organization, 1969), 165.

17. Juliaetta Bateman Jensen, *Little Gold Pieces: The Story of My Mormon Mother's Life* (Salt Lake City: Stanway, 1948), 135.

18. Carl Badger to unidentified recipient, 22 June 1906, Carlos Ashby Badger Letterbooks, Church Archives.

19. *CHC* 6:413.

20. Thomas G. Alexander, "Political Patterns of Early Statehood, 1896–1919," in *Utah's History*, ed. Richard D. Poll et al. (Provo, Utah: BYU Press, 1978), 415–17.

21. *SLT*, 8 Nov. 1905. The election results were counted as a victory over both polygamy and church political control. See "Says 'It Is the Will of the Lord,'" ibid., 7 Nov. 1905; and "Individual Freedom," ibid., 8 Nov. 1905.

22. *SLT*, 9 Nov. 1905.

23. Frank J. Cannon, as quoted by O. N. Malmquist, *The First 100 Years: A History of the "Salt Lake Tribune," 1871-1971* (Salt Lake City: Utah State Historical Society, 1971), 243.

24. Edward B. Critchlow, quoted in "Great Banquet at Cullen [Hotel] in Honor of Senator Dubois," *SLT,* 22 Feb. 1908.

25. See, e.g., "Two More Transgressors," *SLT,* 29 Dec. 1910.

26. As examples, see "The Real Allegiance," *SLT,* 9 May 1910; "A Possible Evasion," ibid., 12 May 1910; "The Cloak for Immorality," ibid., 14 May 1910; "Carnality Leads to Incest," ibid., 29 Aug. 1910; "Polygamist v. Polygamy," ibid., 5 Oct. 1910; "Contempt for Women," ibid., 21 Sept. 1910.

27. Frank J. Cannon and Harvey J. O'Higgins, "Under the Prophet in Utah: The National Menace of a Political Priestcraft," *Everybody's* 23 (Dec. 1910): 723–37, 99–104 (advertising section); 24 (Jan. 1911): 29–45; 24 (Feb. 1911): 189–205; 24 (March 1911): 383–99; 24 (April 1911): 513–28; 24 (May 1911): 652–64; 24 (June 1911): 825–35; 25 (July 1911): 94–107; 25 (Aug. 1911): 209–22. The articles were gathered in book form under the same title (Boston, Mass.: C. M. Clark, 1911). Subsequent citations are from this latter publication.

28. Cannon and O'Higgins, *Under the Prophet,* 351–52. Another critic writing at the same time who employed the same large estimate for the number of new plural marriages since 1890 was William Edward Biederwolf, *Mormonism under the Searchlight* (Chicago: Glad Tidings, [1910]), 66.

29. Richard Barry, "The Mormon Evasion of Anti-Polygamy Laws," *Pearson's* 24 (Oct. 1910): 443–51.

30. Alfred Henry Lewis, "The Viper's Trail of Gold," *Cosmopolitan* 90 (May 1911): 833.

31. Sarah Comstock, "The Mormon Woman: Polygamy as It Works Out in the Daily Routine of the Family," *Collier's* 44 (6 Nov. 1909): 16.

32. Richard Alan Nelson, "From Antagonism to Acceptance: Mormons and the Silver Screen," *Dialogue* 10 (Spring 1977): 59–69. Also see the chapter "Uneasy Accommodation, 1890-1914" in Gary L. Bunker and Davis Bitton, *The Mormon Graphic Image, 1834–1914: Cartoons, Caricatures, and Illustrations* (Salt Lake City: University of Utah Press, 1983), 60–72.

33. JH, 21 July 1910; "'Mormonism Unmasked' in the Netherlands," *DN*, 29 Jan. 1910; "Mormon Missionaries Expelled from Prussia," *DN*, 22 July 1910; "Birmingham Anti-Mormon League" materials in box 8, fd. 5, Rudger Clawson Collection, University of Utah Library, Salt Lake City; Malcolm R. Thorp, "The British Government and the Mormon Question, 1910–1922," *Journal of Church and State* 21 (Spring 1979): 305–23; and Richard O. Cowan, *The Church in the Twentieth Century* (Salt Lake City: Bookcraft, 1985), 36–37.

34. Burton J. Hendrick, "The Mormon Revival of Polygamy," *McClure's* 36 (Jan. 1911), 245–61.

35. Charles Augustus Shook, *The True Origin of Mormon Polygamy, by Charles A. Shook* (Mendota, Ill.: W[estern] A[dvent] C[hristian] P[ublication] Ass'n., [1910]), iv.

36. See the account in Charles Millard Turner, "Joseph Smith III and the Mormons of Utah" (Ph.D. diss., Graduate Theological Union, Berkeley, Calif., 1985), 480, 488, 503.

37. Notarized statement by W. Derby Johnson, Jr., El Paso, Texas, 16 May 1910, W. Derby Johnson, Jr., Papers, Church Archives.

38. See, e.g., the long speech by Charles W. Penrose given in Atlanta, Ga., and reprinted in "Loyalty of the Mormons," *DN*, 16 Feb. 1908. All of which amounted to little more, as another organ pointed out, than belief that "the Lord is for that nation which is for the Lord." "Politics in the Pulpit," *Inter-Mountain Republican*, 17 Feb. 1908. The 1907 statement by the First Presidency is "An Address . . . ," 26 March 1907, *Messages* 4:143–55. Also see William Albert Morton, *Salt Lake City through a Camera, and What the Mormons Believe, by Charles W. Penrose.* (Liverpool: Millennial Star Office, [1909]), 31–32; John Phillips Meakin, *Leaves of Truth: Utah and the Mormons* (Salt Lake City, 1909), 27; "Not on the Move," *DN*, 10 Oct. 1910; "The Purity Meeting," *DN*, 17 Oct. 1911. Their attendance at Purity meetings had been pointed to at the time of the Smoot hearings as evidence of Mormon morality. *Proceedings* 3:347. For Mormon interest in the public relations potential of moving pictures, see JH, 30 June 1910. Regarding the Tabernacle Choir, see Allen and Leonard, *The Story of the Latter-day Saints*, 474–75.

39. George Franklin Richards Diaries, 14 July 1909 and 8 Feb. 1910, Church Archives; and the comments of Apostle Joseph F. Smith, Jr., as reported in Salt Lake Stake Historical Record, 1910–12, p. 91, Church Archives.

40. See, for example, references to various magazine articles in the Charles William Penrose Diaries, entries for 9 Aug. 1910, 20 Feb. 1911, and 28 July 1911, Charles William Penrose Collection, UHi; and Anthony W. Ivins Diaries, 10 April 1910, Anthony Woodward Ivins Collection, UHi.

41. Reed Smoot Diaries, 27 Sept. 1910, BYU Library; Ivins Diaries, 7 Jan. 1910.

42. Joseph W. Musser Diaries, 22 July 1909, Church Archives; and Smoot Diaries, 29 Sept. 1910.

43. John Henry Smith Diaries, 8 Nov. 1910 and 5 Jan. 1911, George A.

Smith Family Papers, University of Utah Library; Richards Diaries, 3 and 8 Oct. 1910; 1, 9, and 16 Nov. 1910; 7 Jan. 1911; Ivins Diaries, 7 Jan. 1911.

44. Penrose Diaries, 29 Oct. and 8 Nov. 1910, 6 June 1911.

45. Daniel Muir, in Smoot Diaries, 1 Oct. 1910.

46. Judson Tolman, in ibid., 1 Oct. 1910; Richards Diaries, 3 Oct. 1910.

47. Smoot Diaries, 12 Oct. 1910; Richards Diaries, 12 and 13 Oct. 1910; Penrose Diaries, 12 and 13 Oct. 1910.

48. Jan [JoAnn Barnett] Shipps, "The Public Image of Senator Reed Smoot, 1902–32," *UHQ* 45 (Fall 1979): 397; Cowan, *The Church in the Twentieth Century*, 291.

49. Ivins Diaries, 7 Jan. 1911; Anthon Hendrik Lund Diaries, 16 March 1911, Church Archives.

50. Smoot Diaries, 8 Oct. 1910. For other instances illustrating the urgings of Senator Smoot as described in the text, see Smoot Diaries, 27 and 28 Sept., 1 and 5 Oct., 15 Nov. 1910, 16 March 1911.

51. JH, 5 Oct. 1910; and "Letter," 5 Oct. 1910, *Messages* 4:216–18.

52. Smoot Diaries, 8 Oct. 1910; Richards Diaries, 8 Oct. 1910; Ivins Diaries, 9 Oct. 1910.

53. Smoot Diaries, 13 Oct. 1910.

54. Ibid. As examples of published excommunications, see those for Israel Barlow and Judson Tolman, respectively, in "Excommunication," *DN*, 28 Sept. 1910; and "Excommunication," *DN*, 3 Oct. 1910.

55. See the comments of Alexander, *Mormonism in Transition*, 68.

56. Smoot Diaries, 16 March 1911.

57. Ibid., 15 Nov. 1910, 14 March 1911; Penrose Diaries, 16 Nov. 1910.

58. Smoot Diaries, 16 March 1911; Lund Diaries, 16 March 1911.

59. Smoot Diaries, 31 March 1911.

60. Smith to Smoot, 1 April 1911, Reed Smoot Correspondence, BYU Library.

61. Smoot Diaries, 2 April 1911.

62. Isaac Russell, "Mr. Roosevelt to the Mormons: A Letter with an Explanatory Note," *Collier's* 47 (15 April 1911): 28, 36.

63. Joseph F. Smith, "To the Officers and Members of the Church . . . ," 9 April 1911, *Messages* 4:224–29.

64. George Franklin Richards, "Record of Matters of Special Importance," pp. 31–32, as reproduced in Dale C. Mouritsen, "A Symbol of New Directions: George Franklin Richards and the Mormon Church, 1861–1950" (Ph.D. diss., BYU, 1982), 97; JH, 23 Jan. 1910.

65. Adelbert Mickey Hart, interviewed by Leonard R. Grover, 5 Jan. 1980, p. 5, POHP; Elna Hart Palmer, interviewed by Leonard R. Grover, 2 Feb. 1980, p. 21, POHP.

66. Marcus Hart, interviewed by Jessie L. Embry, 1976, p. 7, POHP.

67. For general accounts of the "Exodus," see Thomas Cottam Romney, *The Mormon Colonies in Mexico* (Salt Lake City: Deseret Book, 1938), 149–200; B. Carmon Hardy, "The Mormon Colonies of Northern Mexico, 1885–1912"

(Ph.D. diss., Wayne State University, 1963), 164–72; F. LaMond Tullis, *Mormons in Mexico* (Logan: Utah State University Press, 1987), 87–108.

68. Halvan H. Farr, interviewed by Jessie L. Embry, 1 July 1976, pp. 23, 31, POHP; Abraham L. Stout, interviewed by Tillman S. Boxell, 5 Sept. 1978, p. 17, POHP; Karl Skousen, interviewed by Leonard R. Grover, 31 Oct. 1979, p. 4, POHP; Elva R. Shumway, interviewed by Leonard R. Grover, 24 April 1980, p. 20, POHP; the comments of Jessie L. Embry in her "'Isn't One Wife Enough': Life in an LDS Polygamous Family" (Paper presented at the Oral History Association Colloquium, Tamarron, Colo., 3 Oct. 1980, pp. 6–12); and idem, "Two Legal Wives: Mormon Polygamy in Canada, the United States, and Mexico" (Paper presented at a conference on the Mormon Presence in Canada, University of Alberta, 8 May 1987), p. 8. For earlier instances where men yet living with their plural wives, though married before the Manifesto, were looked upon as adulterous by church members, see JH, 16 Aug. 1900; and the cases cited by Kimball Young, in *Isn't One Wife Enough?* (New York: Henry Holt, 1954), 412–14.

69. Joseph C. Eyring, interviewed by Jessie L. Embry, 10 May 1976, p. 11, POHP. Also see H. H. Farr, interviewed by Jessie L. Embry, 1 July 1976, p. 23, POHP; Esther Jarvis Young, interviewed by Jessie L. Embry, 15 June 1976, p. 9, POHP; Erma Romney Haymore Greetham, interviewed by Jessie L. Embry, 7 June 1976, p. 13, POHP; Pearl J. Augustus, interviewed by Jessie L. Embry, 1 June 1976, p. 7, POHP; Elva R. Shumway, interviewed by Leonard R. Grover, 24 April 1980, pp. 14, 25, POHP; Bearl Fenn Gashler, "Life Story of Samuel Walter Jarvis," (1974), copy of typewritten manuscript in the author's possession, p. 17.

70. Merriner L. Jones, interviewed by Jessie L. Embry, 11 Jan. 1981, p. 12, POHP. The incident involved Merriner's father, Thomas Henry Jones, who married Leah Wall as a plural wife in Utah in 1926. Also see the comments of Heber Grant Ivins, interviewed by Justin Stewart, 27 June 1971, p. 14, Heber Grant Ivins Collection, box 1, fd. 5, UHi.

71. Guy C. Wilson, Jr., *Memories of a Venerable Father and Other Reminiscences* (Fullerton: California State University Oral History Program, 1988), 106–8, 111–12, 129–30.

72. Subcommittee of the Senate Committee on Foreign Relations, *Revolutions in Mexico,* Hearing Pursuant to S. Res. 335, 62nd Cong., 2nd sess., 1913, pp. 59–60.

73. Egal Feldman, "Prostitution, the Alien Woman, and the Progressive Imagination, 1910–1915," *American Quarterly* 19 (Summer 1967): 192–206; and Daniel J. Leab, "Women and the Mann Act," *Amerikastudien* 21 (Spring 1976): 55–65. For Mormon difficulties with the INS, see Alexander, *Mormonism in Transition,* 71, 198–99.

74. *Cong. Rec.,* Senate, 62nd Cong., 3rd sess., 1913, 49:1433, 2400. After the Brigham H. Roberts case in Congress, the subject of amending the United States Constitution to prohibit polygamy received sustained attention through the balance of the Progressive period. See, e.g., "Ministers Urge the Amend-

ment," *DN*, 13 Feb. 1900; "WCTU Denounces Smoot," *New York Times*, 18 Nov. 1903; Bruce Kinney, "The Present Situation among the Mormons," *Missionary Review of the World* 19 (Aug. 1906): 618–19; Mrs. John Paddock and Miss Elizabeth Vermilye, "Facts on Mormonism," ibid. 26 (Nov. 1913): 855; William Edward Biederwolf, *Mormonism under the Searchlight*, 69. For Mormon concern with growing interest in the amendment, see JH, 20 Jan., 2 Feb., 20 April 1912, 19 Jan. 1913; Smoot Diaries, 10 Dec. 1913.

75. Oscar Franklyn Davis, *A World-Wide Survey of Present-Day Mormonism as Made by a National Commission under the Direction of the National Reform Association and Presented to the Second World's Christian Citizenship Conference, Portland, Oregon, July 3d, 1913* (Pittsburgh, Pa.: National Reform Association, 1913), 8–9 passim.

76. "The Mormons of Mexico," *The World's Work* 31 (March 1916): 484.

77. Iliff's standard speech containing these views was reprinted in James David Gillilan, *Thomas Corwin Iliff: Apostle of Home Missions in the Rocky Mountains* (New York: Methodist Book Concern, 1919), 73–96.

78. An account of the experience was subsequently prepared by the church in *The Pittsburgh Conference on "Mormonism," by Dr. James E. Talmage, and Report of Proceedings in the United States Senate in Defense of the Latter-day Saints* (Salt Lake City: Bureau of Information, [1919]).

79. See the list compiled by James R. Clark in his *Messages* 4:194.

80. *Proceedings* 1:107–8, 336, 3:114, 126.

81. Barry, "The Mormon Evasion of Anti-Polygamy Laws," 444; Garner, "The Case of Senator Smoot," 48.

82. "Official Declaration," *D&C* (1908), 543–44. As Arbaugh pointed out long ago, while the old section enjoining monogamy was dropped from the *Doctrine and Covenants* in 1876 at the time section 132 was included, the revelation approving polygamy was neither eliminated nor altered when the Manifesto was added. George Bartholomew Arbaugh, *Revelation in Mormonism: Its Character and Changing Forms* (Chicago: University of Chicago Press, 1932), 182.

83. See above in chap. 2.

84. LaMar Petersen, *Problems in Mormon Text* (Salt Lake City: privately printed, 1957), 18. Cf. Dennis R. Short, *Questions on Plural Marriage* (Salt Lake City: published by the author, 1975), 35.

85. *Proceedings* 1:199–200, 210, 333, 3:45; "Powers of Mormon Head," *New York Times*, 19 Jan. 1905; *Speech of Hon. Reed Smoot, of Utah, in the Senate of the United States, Tuesday, February 19, 1907* (Washington, D.C.: GPO, 1907), 2. For reiteration of the interpretation, see Martha S. Bradley, "Changed Faces: The Official LDS Position on Polygamy, 1890–1990," *Sunstone* 14 (Feb. 1990): 28.

86. See the case of Alfred Budge described in Alexander, *Mormonism in Transition*, 35.

87. Francis M. Lyman, as reprinted in *Restoration News: Views and History of the Latter Day Saint Movement* 1 (Jan. 1982): 15. George Q. Cannon, in late

1891, described the Manifesto as relieving the Saints of the obligations of "celestial marriage." "Remarks Made by President George Q. Cannon," *DN*, 14 Nov. 1891. And Brigham H. Roberts made a similar equation of the phrases in his reference to "plurality of wives" as "more properly celestial marriage." See his "Comment on Dr. Reiner's Letter," *Improvement Era* 1 (May 1898): 478.

88. John Henry Evans, *One Hundred Years of Mormonism: A History of the Church of Jesus Christ of Latter-day Saints from 1805 to 1905* (Salt Lake City: Deseret Sunday School Union, 1905), 476–77.

89. James E. Talmage, *Story of "Mormonism"* (Liverpool: Mill. Star Office, 1907), 86; and Apostle Charles W. Penrose, in Morton, *Salt Lake City through a Camera, and What the Mormons Believe*, 16.

90. Copy of typewritten extract from a meeting of the twelve apostles, 17 Feb. 1908, box 11, fd. 10, Stanley Snow Ivins Collection, UHi.

91. Remarks made at Juarez Stake Conference, 17 June 1906, in Ivins Diaries, 17 June 1906.

92. John Henry Smith Diaries, 24 May 1911. An example of references to polygamy and discussions of its importance being deleted from one well-known Mormon work is Parley Parker Pratt's *Key to the Science of Theology* . . . (Liverpool: F. D. Richards, 1855). Compare it to all recent church-authorized editions of the book. The exact locations of the changes and deletions are described by Jerald and Sandra Tanner, *Changes in the Key to Theology* (Salt Lake City: Modern Microfilm, n.d.), 2–3 passim. Equally illustrative is the absence of any reference to plural marriage in a recent compilation of sermons and writings by one of Mormonism's foremost advocates of the principle, George Q. Cannon. Jerreld L. Newquist, comp., *Gospel Truth: Two Volumes in One: Discourses and Writings of George Q. Cannon* . . . , Classics in Mormon Literature Series (Salt Lake City: Deseret Book, 1974).

93. David John Buerger, "The Adam-God Doctrine," *Dialogue* 15 (Spring 1982): 14–58; Boyd Kirkland, "Jehovah as the Father: The Development of the Mormon Jehovah Doctrine," *Sunstone* 9 (Autumn 1984): 36–44; Thomas G. Alexander, "The Reconstruction of Mormon Doctrine: From Joseph Smith to Progressive Theology," *Sunstone* 5 (July-Aug. 1980): 28–29; and idem, *Mormonism in Transition*, 279–81.

94. Thomas G. Alexander, "The Manifesto: Mormondom's Watershed," *This People* 11 (Fall 1990): 21, 23–27; idem, "How the Manifesto Changed the Church" (Paper presented before a Sunstone Symposium, Salt Lake City, Utah, 24 Aug. 1990).

95. The two best treatments of the eugenics movement, focusing especially on the early twentieth century, are Mark H. Haller, *Eugenics: Hereditarian Attitudes in American Thought* (New Brunswick, N.J.: Rutgers University Press, 1963); and Daniel J. Kevles, *In the Name of Eugenics: Genetics and the Uses of Human Heredity* (New York: Alfred A. Knopf, 1985).

96. Haller, *Eugenics*, 16–20; Havelock Ellis, *The Task of Social Hygiene* (Boston: Houghton Mifflin, 1912), 16–18, 28. However, the church con-

tinued to agree generally with the ideal of racial improvement. See "Science of Eugenics," *DN*, 26 March 1910; and "Polygamy Is Again Upheld," *SLT*, 17 April 1910.

97. Senate Joint Resolution 129, 62d Cong., 2d sess. (1912). Senator Smoot was the primary instigator of this appropriation, but wishing not to be associated with polygamy in any way, he asked his colleague, Senator Joseph Weldon Bailey, to author the bill. Smoot Diaries, 2 Aug. 1912.

98. Walter M. Gallichan, *Women under Polygamy* (London: Holden & Hardingham, 1914), 299–312.

99. Ruth Reed, *The Modern Family* (New York: Alfred A. Knopf, 1929), 166–68.

100. Malmquist, *The First Hundred Years*, 298–301.

101. Reprinted in *The Pittsburgh Conference on "Mormonism,"* 16–25.

102. *Cong. Rec.*, 63rd Cong., 2nd sess., 1914, 51:1285, 1560, 2284, 8204; ibid., 64th Cong., 1st sess., 1915–16, 53:31, 491, 2442; ibid., 65th Cong., 2d sess., 1917–18, 56:103, 4627; ibid., 66th Cong., 1st sess., 1919, 58:381; ibid., 67th Cong., 1st sess., 1921, 61:1718, 1811–12; ibid., 68th Cong., 1st sess., 1923–24, 65:570.

103. JoAnn Barnett Shipps, "From Satyr to Saint: American Attitudes toward the Mormons, 1860–1960" (Paper presented before the Organization of American Historians, Chicago, Ill., 1973), 2n.1, 19–21.

104. George Wharton James, *Utah, the Land of Blossoming Valleys* (Boston: Page Co., 1922), 134.

105. James H. McClintock, *Mormon Settlement in Arizona: A Record of Peaceful Conquest of the Desert* (Phoenix, Ariz.: Manufacturing Stationers, 1921).

106. Levi Edgar Young, *The Founding of Utah* (New York: Charles Scribner's, 1923). For a later example arguing that polygamy had been given too much attention, overshadowing things like the great colonizing achievements of Brigham Young, see Theron Luke, "Utah's Forty Years of Historical Amnesia," *Westerner's Brand Book* 16 (April 1959): 9–11, 16.

107. Thomas G. Alexander, "Toward the New Mormon History: An Examination of the Literature on the Latter-day Saints in the Far West," in *Historians and the American West,* ed. Michael P. Malone (Lincoln: University of Nebraska Press, 1983), 346. Preston Nibley's work was *Brigham Young: The Man and His Work* (Salt Lake City: Deseret News, 1936).

108. Heber J. Grant, as reported in Alexander, *Mormonism in Transition*, 251.

109. This was Kimball Young, paraphrasing the sentiments of some of his interviewees. "B. F. Larsen interview," 9 April 1935, box 2, fd. 41, p. 2, Kimball Young Collection, Garrett Evangelical Theological Seminary, Evanston, Illinois.

9

Late Efforts
and Polygamy's Decline

By duress and winning solicitation, American society drew official Mormonism into further agreement on the constitution of the ideal family. The process, underway for some time, was hastened by a rising generation of younger Mormons, anxious for approval from their fellow citizens, and by the political interests of men like Senator Reed Smoot. But such changes are seldom the consequence of a single epochal transformation. More often, they are qualified and cumulative. This was the case with Mormon plural marriage. Surrender met with resistance at various levels. Not only was there never a formal repudiation of the doctrine but, during the early years of the new century, it displayed surprising resilience. Because of the surreptitious nature of what was said and done, however, our vision is interrupted. Among church authorities themselves, confidences were layered and dissimulation indulged.

After Joseph F. Smith became president in 1901, at both local and all-church levels voices were heard recalling the Saints to an acceptance of "all the principles of the Gospel." A member of the bishopric in one of the Mormon colonies in Mexico told a congregation there that only those who entered plural marriage would become gods.[1] Apostle George Teasdale said to a meeting of patriarchs in 1902 that they were unworthy of their office if they did not reverence belief in the principle. On another occasion he said the colonists in Mexico had been especially blessed because of their loyalty to it. In the same year Apostle Rudger Clawson urged that only women who believed in polygamy be appointed to church positions. And newly called members of certain stake presidencies were asked to declare their willingness to put the doctrine into practice.[2]

Church groups were instructed to pray for polygamy's revival, to prepare themselves for it, and told that Christ could not return until it was being "lived up to."[3] Apostle John Henry Smith, in a meeting of the First Presidency and apostles, said that it was in practicing polygamy that men learned "the true order of government." He pointed out that all who were then apostles had fathers who were successful pluralists. More than that, a majority of the quorum were the sons of plural wives. He said that it had been predicted that the offspring of the wicked would wither and die, whereas the children of polygamy would flourish. He saw in those constituting the quorum a fulfillment of that prediction.[4] Given the strength of these sentiments, it is hardly surprising that the number of new plural marriages leaped in the years between the start of Smith's presidency in 1901 and the Smoot investigation in 1904 (see graph, 317).

There was also a sense on the part of many that when Smith's 1904 declaration came, as with the Woodruff Manifesto, it was because of political pressures and that when those conditions changed freedom to engage in plural marriage would again be possible. At a conference in Mexico in March 1904, Apostle George Teasdale, anticipating the "Official Statement," told his audience that polygamy may be taken from them for a time but that it would be restored.[5] After the 1904 conference Anthony W. Ivins reported that President Smith told him the new policy resulted from the difficult situation associated with the Smoot hearings and that there were to be no more plural marriages anywhere in the church "for the time being."[6] In a talk to church members in Burlington, Wyoming, less than six months after the "Official Statement," President Smith spoke approvingly of the principle, saying that men could not enter the City of God except by gates named after the polygamic sons of Jacob.[7] And in the autumn of 1905, during a visit to the Mexican colonies, addressing the question again, Smith told his listeners: ". . . but men cannot marry plural wives at present with my consent or the consent of the church. The church is upon trial before the government of the United States, and we must be very careful."[8]

Such comments had an undeniably qualified ring. This may be why Apostle John W. Taylor, present in the colonies when Anthony W. Ivins returned from conference with the 1904 statement, gave his assent and urged support for President Smith's position.[9] Ivins's language, in representing the president, suggested that the cessation of new plural marriages, associated as it was with political events, was only "for the time being." It is also significant, as Mormon fundamentalists have pointed out, that the language used in these statements invariably linked abatement of polygamy with the institution of the church. It did not bind individual priesthood holders who had received authority in connection with polygamy from acting privately.[10]

At the same time, and apart from letters by Francis M. Lyman urging compliance with Smith's 1904 statement, new apostolic appointees were mostly monogamous and, as shown, generally committed to a cessation of the practice. While Reed Smoot is the best-known example of this, others stood beside him in their opposition to polygamy. George F. Richards, after his ordination to the apostolate in 1906, worked hard to bring stake presidents into line with the 1904 "Official Statement."[11] The strenuous and continued nature of such efforts, combined with official public pronouncements, is what leads some to affirm that approval for such marriages ceased in 1904.[12]

This notwithstanding, word continued to circulate that President Smith's statements were for appearance only. This invited a countercurrent of denials. In priesthood meetings held at both the spring and autumn general conferences in 1906, President Smith and other authorities denounced the whispering then taking place that individuals could yet marry polygamously. Such rumors, it was said, were "sapping the faith" of younger members. There was no "dealing in the dark," they declared, and both the Quorum of Twelve Apostles and the First Presidency were united in attempts to bring new polygamy to an end.[13] This was echoed by Anthony W. Ivins when he told the Mexican colonists in 1906 that he regretted there had been a misinterpretation of Smith's remarks. There was, said Ivins, to be no expectation of the renewal of plural marriage. Those who succeeded in having such unions performed did so with neither his nor President Smith's permission.[14] Apostle Francis M. Lyman made similar remarks later the same year. No one, asserted Lyman, had authority to perform polygamous marriages and anyone doing so was, by orders of President Smith, to be disfellowshipped.[15]

Still, rumors persisted that an inner circle existed in which the true policy of the church was better understood. Joseph W. Musser (Appendix II, #140), when interviewed by the apostles in 1909, said that church members by the hundreds believed plural contractions could be performed and that if one had the right connections it was yet possible to "get in."[16] The same year Musser made his remarks, certain bishops were found telling ward members that plural marriages were indeed being performed and that if they spoke to the right individuals they could undertake a plural union. As one bishop put it, Mormon fundamentals had not changed, only their "development."[17] Much of the problem arose from a sense that the church's policy was undefined, that leaders and members alike were divided. In her memory of those years, Annie Clark Tanner (Appendix II, #186) described the confusion of men like her husband who saw Mormonism shaken when polygamy, "the capstone" of the Gospel, was taken away. The faithful, she said, "were going, for a time, in both directions."[18] Some new plural unions seemed acceptable to the leaders. John Reese Evans (Appendix II, #71), who married Catherine Durfee as a plural wife in 1907, for example, was left uncensured.[19] On the other hand, Juliaetta Bateman Jensen, who as a girl witnessed the excommunication of an older brother for polygamy, spoke of her distress because others, equally guilty, were left alone.[20]

As another Mormon later described it, the Manifesto and excommunications notwithstanding, "there was a great many People that did not understand that there would be no more Poligemus [*sic*] Marriages but [believed] it could be done Sectrly [*sic*]."[21] The impression was shared by women as well as men. Florence Ivins, oldest daughter of Anthony W. Ivins, told how her aunt, a plural wife of Moses Thatcher, responded when Florence expressed doubt concerning new plural marriages after 1904: "Oh, but Libbie," said the aunt, "you're not on the inside. You don't know the facts of the thing—you're not on the inside."[22]

Rumor concerning an inner circle was not untrue. It arose from instances in which high church leaders approved and/or participated in perpetuating the practice. Such cases often involved permission from President Smith, albeit indirectly given. Individuals entering such relationships did so with an understanding of the risks involved. Knowledge of these activities had to be kept secret; in fact, oaths were sometimes administered binding the new married couple to silence. Language used in the ceremonies was often purposely chosen to make deception easier. All who entered such marriages understood that if discovery occurred the authorities would deny any part in the affair. Beyond this, it would be necessary, for the reputation and protection of the church, sometimes to disfellowship or excommunicate those who were found out. To complicate matters further, reminiscent of charges given the Relief Society in 1842, some leaders were expressly directed to ferret out new pluralists and implement action against them.

Despite these obstacles, numbers of Latter-day Saints were successful with their petitions. The case of William Gailey Sears (Appendix II, #165) is an example. Sears married his first wife in 1897, served as a mission president in the South Pacific and was, shortly after the turn of the century, employed by the church-owned sugar company. Because Sears's wife, Agnes McMurrin Sears, was unable to conceive, both partners considered polygamy an acceptable way to bring children into the family. President Joseph F. Smith, hearing of their situation, was reported to be sorrowed by the couple's childless condition and authorized Joseph W. Summerhays to join Sears to a plural wife. Exactly when and under what conditions this permission was given is unclear, but Sears left his position with the sugar company and moved with his first wife to Mexico. It was rumored that he made the trip to visit Thomas Hilton, who had also been a mission president in the South Pacific. After acting for a time as Salt Lake City chief of police and marrying a sister of Mrs. Sears as a plural wife in 1902, Hilton was living in the colonies. On 21 February 1906 Summerhays married eighteen-year-old Athelia Viola Call to Sears as his second living wife.[23]

Summerhays (Appendix II, #184) was a respected member of the Latter-day Saint community. Emigrating from England in the 1860s, he had crossed the plains as a young man, held numerous church and civic offices, and had, by the time of the 1890 Manifesto, married four wives of his own.[24] At a hearing before the Quorum of Twelve Apostles, as indicated in the previous chapter, Summerhays insisted Joseph F. Smith not only gave him authority to act in the Sears case but approved his own plural contraction in 1898. Smith denied this, flatly telling Apostle Reed Smoot that Summerhays's statements were false.[25] The apostles, unsettled by the contradictions, finally concluded only to release Summerhays from all church positions. It is reasonable to assume that if a majority believed Summerhays was lying, falsely accusing the church's president, he would have been excommunicated. He was not.[26]

Like William Gailey Sears's wife Agnes, Warren Longurst's first wife, Myra Irene Allred, was unable to have children. Longhurst (Appendix II, #119) and his wife also served a mission in the Samoan Islands. And, like the Searses, upon returning from the South Pacific shortly after the turn of the century, the Longhursts moved to Mexico, where they lived with Myra's family. There, in July of 1903, he was joined to a plural wife, Nellie Clark, by Anthony W. Ivins. This marriage, however, was also childless. Six years later, on 17 November 1909 Longhurst married his first wife's sister, Eva Allred, in Salt Lake City. This relationship resulted in five children, the oldest daughter being named after Longhurst's barren first wife, Myra.[27] The author cannot establish that President Smith was consulted in this instance or who it was that performed the ceremony, although fundamentalists claim it to have been John W. Woolley of Centerville, Utah.[28] The resemblance of what is known to circumstances in the Sears case, however, is striking.

Samuel J. Robinson (Appendix II, #161) also said he received approval from President Smith in 1907 to marry an additional wife. Robinson was born and raised in Payson, Utah. He married Minnie Amelia Stark as his first wife in the Logan Temple in 1886. After accepting a mission call to England but before departing in 1891, he visited the colonies in Mexico, where he was married to a second wife, Annie Elizabeth Walser, by Apostle George Teasdale. After returning from England, he moved both families to Mexico and was later chosen bishop of Colonia Dublan. In 1903, while giving birth to twins, Annie Elizabeth died.[29] Subsequently, Robinson claimed to visit with President Smith, who told him to search for a way and if someone were found to perform the ceremony, he could marry again—the president saying, "God bless you." Robinson took Maud Heder as a plural companion in 1907.[30]

When knowledge of the last Robinson marriage came to light, he was summoned before the Juarez Stake High Council, asked to resign his bishopric, and disfellowshipped. Anthony W. Ivins and others on the high council were annoyed with Robinson. It was later charged that peculation was involved and this weighed against him at the time of his hearing. While unaware of these circumstances, certain that he had received approval for his marriage, Apostle John W. Taylor declared the "disfellowshipping of Brother Robinson to be one of the greatest outrages perpetrated upon the Church."[31] Quorum members felt that Taylor unfairly implicated President Smith, obscuring his own responsibility with inferences of secrecy and oaths.[32] In the 1911 meeting in which the Robinson case and others were discussed, after referring to a private conversation with President Smith, Taylor told the apostles, "If I should turn my tongue loose, there would be the damndest time in this state you have ever had." Apostle Hyrum M. Smith, a son of the president, replied, "I think you are creating the damndest time by keeping still."[33]

As the graph charting post-Manifesto marriages suggests, there was a dramatic increase in permission given to engage in the practice during the early years of President Smith's administration (see 317). In accounting for the persistence of plural marriages after the 1904 "Official Statement" of President Smith, it is likely that, despite their diminished frequency, such contractions were inspired by the same reasons that had actuated them before, including a determination on the part of at least some authorities to keep the principle alive. Carl A.

Badger indicated, for example, that a friend of his, Alonzo Blair Irvine, said Apostle Abraham O. Woodruff told him that certain worthy individuals were being chosen to continue the principle.[34] This is close to the language one encounters in other cases both before and after the 1904 declaration. The children of Arthur William Hart (Appendix II, #85), who took a second wife in 1903, remembered that their father was told by Apostle Matthias F. Cowley that "select" individuals were being chosen to perpetuate the practice and that such unions could be performed outside the temples.[35] Heber Bennion (Appendix II, #17), bishop of Taylorsville Ward and the husband of two plural wives married in 1900 and 1902, told his daughter Mary that when he was ordained a seventy he was asked to take an oath that he would do what he could to continue the practice. He told her that one of the apostles personally spoke to him in behalf of the church president. He was informed that President Smith was determined to keep polygamy indefinitely alive. Bennion was told that word of this was being sent to "the most trusted young men in the church" and that they were expected to enter the principle. This was to be done secretly, however, and only those necessary for performing the ceremonies were to be present. Of greatest importance, he was told, President Smith was to have no direct knowledge of the marriages.[36]

A similar episode occurred in the life of John B. Cannon, a son of George Mousley Cannon (Appendix II, #37), in or near the year 1908. John recalled that his father took him aside in the library of their home and told him that polygamous living was a requirement if one wished to enter the highest level of the celestial kingdom. Unaware at that time that his father already had married two plural wives after the Manifesto, John later became convinced that, as a friend and business associate of President Smith, his father was counseled to enter the principle and had been instructed by Smith in the same sentiments expressed to him on the occasion of that visit in the library.[37]

It cannot be proved that President Smith gave permission for such ceremonies. Confidence that approval was granted in many, if not all, cases, however, arises from several indicators. Apart from those who named Smith as having given them consent, there was the determination he had shown after the Manifesto, during the administrations of presidents Woodruff and Snow, to perpetuate the principle in spite of denials by these men that such things were occurring.[38] There are also examples from the early years of his own tenure as church president when, contrary to his statements, permission for plural marriages was given. Anson Bowen Call (Appendix II, #34), who took a polygamous wife in 1903, was reassured by Anthony W. Ivins that approval for the

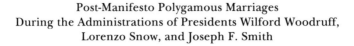

Post-Manifesto Polygamous Marriages
During the Administrations of Presidents Wilford Woodruff,
Lorenzo Snow, and Joseph F. Smith

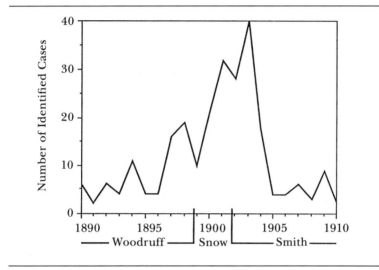

Information based on data provided in Appendix II

marriage originated with President Joseph F. Smith.[39] And there was the episode related by Orson P. Brown (Appendix II, #29). Some years after Brown married the daughter of Alexander F. Macdonald as a polygamous wife in 1901, he attempted to deliver to President Smith the record of marriages his father-in-law had performed in Mexico. Macdonald, it will be remembered, had solemnized plural unions before his death in 1903. According to Brown, Smith scanned the list and said: "Brother Brown, all of this work that Brother Macdonald performed was duly authorized by me." He then told Brown to keep the record himself in Mexico because of fear it would be requisitioned by enemies of the church investigating its practices. At the time of the Mormon exodus from Mexico in 1912, Brown gave the records to Anthony W. Ivins, who took them to Salt Lake City.[40]

On the other hand, in 1902 Smith told a senior apostle, Brigham Young, Jr., that all plural marriages had ceased. Similar statements were made before the quorum of apostles and other members of the First Presidency.[41] He also announced to a meeting of the apostles in 1903 that he had not given approval for anyone to enter plural relationships and that he had no knowledge of such marriages taking place.[42] The most likely explanation for such inconsistencies is that

Joseph F. Smith was simply traduced by events. To maintain his allegiance to the principle he was led into policies of constricted confidences and, perforce, prevarication. Such resorts did not begin with his tenure as church president. Some of what strengthens the conviction that they were engaged in during that time is the fact of their employment in connection with polygamy so many times before. As we have seen, wariness among themselves and the use of circuitous channels were commonplace during the administrations of presidents Taylor, Woodruff, and Snow. Matthias F. Cowley told Jesse N. Smith that part of the problem was that some did not understand all that was involved and that President Smith, "awfully tried," should not be held responsible for the difficulties "forced upon us."[43]

Formal gatherings of the leaders were increasingly looked upon as off limits for authorizations or approving discussions relating to the subject. Even private conversations were guarded. Apostle Reed Smoot was undoubtedly insulated on many occasions because of his role as a United States senator and sensitivities resulting from the prolonged investigation made by Senate members into his case. We get some hint as to the presence of such walls when, during the administration of President Snow, Apostle Marriner W. Merrill predicted to fellow apostles that the time would never come when children of polygamous parents would cease to be born in the church. The next day, again while meeting in the temple, Francis M. Lyman said he believed the Manifesto was inspired and deserved to be treated as a revelation.[44] Juxtapositions like this give credibility to the account by Byron Harvey Allred, Jr., (Appendix II, #3) as to how he was authorized to marry a plural wife in 1903. When Louis A. Kelsch (Appendix II, #113) of the First Council of Seventy was sent by President Joseph F. Smith to give permission for the marriage, according to Allred, Kelsch told him that Apostle Francis M. Lyman, traveling with Kelsch on church business was, by Smith's direction, to be kept ignorant in the matter.[45]

At the time of his and John W. Taylor's 1911 hearing, Matthias F. Cowley said he was once censured by a member of the First Presidency, George Q. Cannon, for telling other apostles of his activities. He was instructed to keep his own counsel in such matters. Furthermore, he was asked to take an oath of secrecy when another quorum member united him with a post-Manifesto spouse of his own.[46] So far as permission to perform such marriages was concerned, Cowley said it was given to him by his "file leaders," that the official statements of 1890 and 1904 were "bluffs," and that neither declaration took away authority already conferred.[47] Similar views were held by other apostles, even after Taylor and Cowley resigned from the quorum in 1905. In 1907 Senator Smoot was so angered to learn that such marriages were yet occurring in the United States that he told Carl A. Badger, his secretary, he was going to inform his fellow apostles that, if they were going to persist with polygamous activities, they must do it outside the country. Badger asked if Smoot was referring only to continued living with plural wives taken in previous years. The senator replied that he was not. Badger described himself as astonished that such things were happening.[48]

The history of officially sanctioned Mormon polygamy after the onset of the crusade in the early 1880s is one of increasing enclosure. Each successive crisis led to greater secrecy. Covert behavior following the Manifesto of 1890 reached its most obscure phase after 1904. Albeit a surprising number obtained permission after that date to commence or continue the practice. As the Quorum of Twelve Apostles grew to include a greater proportion of monogamists, unacquainted with concealments of the past, partitions among the leaders became even more necessary. Referring to the confusion besetting many in this period, H. Grant Ivins said of his father, Anthony W. Ivins, who became an apostle in 1907, "Even father wasn't convinced they meant what they said." Because he had been party to devices for continuing polygamy after 1890, Ivins was hardly to be blamed for wondering whether things were different from what they had been before.[49]

More than abstract doctrinal commitment accounted for continued polygamy in these late years. If wives were infertile or beyond childbearing age, the wish to enlarge one's eternal estate through additional progeny, especially sons, could be insistent. There was the influence provided by awareness that prominent men in the church yet lived in plural households. Nor can we discount the weight of habit arising from family precedent and example. These ingredients blended, quite naturally, with the inherent momentum acquired by decades of polygamous preachment. When sermons were heard, like that of Joseph E. Robinson in 1908, yet arguing for the scientific advantages of the principle, it would be unrealistic to expect pluralist psychology suddenly to cease.[50]

An example is Ernest Leander Taylor (Appendix II, #189). Post-Manifesto plural marriage pervaded his family. Maud, Taylor's oldest daughter by his third wife, was married to Joseph C. Bentley (Appendix II, #18) in 1901 as Bentley's third wife.[51] His daughter Lenora, the fifth child by his second wife, married Apostle Matthias F. Cowley

(Appendix II, #56) on 16 September 1905 in Canada as Cowley's fourth wife.[52] Ernest Guy Taylor (Appendix II, #188), a son by Ernest L.'s first wife, married a plural wife on 16 September 1905 in Cardston, Canada, perhaps in a double-ring ceremony with his half-sister Lenorah.[53] Finally, Alonzo Leander Taylor (Appendix II, #187), the oldest son of Ernest L.'s second wife, also married polygamously in 1906.[54] Ernest Leander, then, had considerable precedent for marrying Rozilla Roxanna Alexander Scott in the Logan Temple on 13 April 1910 as his own fourth wife.[55] After some dissent the stake high council excommunicated Taylor, reaccepting him into the church in 1916.[56]

Another reason for plurality's survival was, undoubtedly, sexual interest. While it is a difficult issue, it is reasonable to assume that sexual desire was no less a part of the lives of men and women then than now. Joseph Bates Noble, for example, who joined the church in 1832 and was a close associate of the Prophet Joseph Smith, could declare in 1893, in his eighty-third year, "I commenced hunting a wife in 1838, and don't know as I have quit yet."[57] President Joseph F. Smith alluded to this when asked by the Smoot investigating committee why he continued to cohabit with plural wives after the Manifesto. Smith replied, "That is just exactly the kernel in the nut."[58] Joyce Richardson Heder, the daughter of a polygamous marriage consummated in 1904, summarized her father's motivations by commenting that "polygamy was just part of his philosophy. When that is part of your philosophy and there are so many attractive young girls around, it isn't too hard to follow."[59] And Mary Bennion Powell, whose 228-page letter to Dr. George Stewart in the early 1950s was a therapeutic exercise undertaken to relieve pain associated with things she had witnessed as a girl in her father's post-Manifesto polygamous household, said she was told more than once that a reason justifying the system was that men, by nature, were "more passionate" than women. One should not immediately assume, however, that this was why her father, a bishop, once jokingly stated he had proposed to "every old maid" in town.[60]

In a 1902 article criticizing the church, William R. Campbell pointed to the dilemma created by Mormon apologetics. How, he asked, could the Saints be expected to discontinue plural unions when for so long they were told that man was stamped in his nature with polygamous needs and that it was a practice shared by the gods? How could they suddenly convert to a form of marriage they had been told was responsible for the "social evil" outside Mormon communities? Campbell's essay exaggerated immorality among the Saints but perceptively identified the inherent stubbornness of a marriage philosophy defended on the bases of biological and moral necessity.[61] Discussing new plural unions after the Manifesto, an anonymous typescript in the papers of Anthony W. Ivins referred to the conflict of motives actuating those who thought they were living a higher law and those who were only "marriage musts."[62] There was likely something of both in most entering such relationships—whether before or after the Manifesto.

The undefined nature of polygamous courtship joined with sexual desire to make matters more enigmatic yet. This is seen in the freedom of polygamous wives at Mormon entertainments. Outsiders had long noticed that traditional forms were modified, permitting men to dance with multiple female partners at the same time. We know that polygamous wives sometimes attended such occasions unescorted and were allowed to remain at the affairs after their husbands went home.[63] Sometimes a younger wife was taken to the event by the older son of an earlier marriage or by a gentleman unrelated to the family. At least some of these customs persisted into the post-Manifesto period. The child of one pluralist recalled that, because her father always went to bed early, when church dances were held his two wives would leave the man at home and "get over there and dance with all the young fellows just like the [other] young girls."[64] Because of secrecy surrounding such unions, suitors were confused as to who was and who was not available for serious courtship.[65] Some aspiring Jacobs, of course, claimed dreams and visions directed them in such difficulties.[66] But thought and psychology associated with the principle were not easily shut off. One young woman told how, as late as the 1920s, she was repeatedly approached at church dances by married men who wanted her to be their plural wife.[67]

Peremptory behavior took license from the want of guidelines. The 1909 elopement with a young lady by the member of a Salt Lake City bishopric, for example, suggests more of passion than religious deliberation.[68] And Heber Grant Ivins recalled an instance when, for want of an authorizing letter, his father refused to marry in polygamy a Utah couple who had traveled to Mexico for that purpose. When he offered them separate rooms for the night, Ivins was told it was unnecessary because, expecting soon to be married, they had slept together on the trip down. As the younger Ivins pointed out, the protocols of traditional courtship and marriage were blurred in the Mormon polygamous milieu.[69]

Mixed with these elements was the ubiquitous nature of authority to approve and perform plural contractions. Permission for solemnizing such marriages had been purposely dispersed since at least the early 1880s when President John Taylor and George Q. Cannon had pointed out that the sealing authority was the same whether joining one or several women to a man.[70] Delegation of such authority had been made not only to apostles but to men outside the quorum. We have seen how Anthony W. Ivins, Alexander F. Macdonald, and Joseph W. Summerhays were authorized in one or more cases to perform the ritual. Resting their authority on an 1841 revelation to Joseph Smith and taking encouragement from some of the leaders, men holding the office of patriarch also sometimes performed post-Manifesto plural marriages.[71] In the case of Patriarch John Anthony Woolf, who in 1905 performed marriages in Canada for Matthias F. Cowley and Ernest Guy Taylor, Apostle John W. Taylor admitted giving him authority to do so, saying, however, that he was acting as liaison for someone else.[72]

John Jacob Walser, a member of the Juarez Stake High Council, expressed distress at having to excommunicate men brought before the council for having gone around certain Mormon leaders in acquiring new plural wives. Because of statements once made to him by former church president John Taylor, Walser said he could not in good conscience automatically cut such individuals off from the church.[73] John Mills Whitaker told of discovering a post-1904 polygamous union in which the groom performed his own plural marriage in the temple.[74] Remembering that presidents Woodruff and Smith had asked to be left uninformed when new polygamous unions occurred, it is easy to see how the marriage machinery could get away from those setting it in motion.

An example involving indistinct authority, sexual interest, and religious devotion is Miles A. Romney (Appendix II, #162). Reference has already been made to the ways by which Romney obtained permission to marry Lilly Burrell as a polygamous spouse in 1898. He also married Elizabeth Burrell, Lilly's sister, in 1902.[75] Then, in 1909 he was sealed to the third sister, Emily Burrell, in the Manti Temple in Utah. According to information Romney provided the Juarez Stake High Council in early 1910, he commenced courting Emily several years previously, intending to have Apostle Abraham O. Woodruff marry them. Woodruff died unexpectedly in 1904, however, and Romney began looking for someone else to perform the ceremony. Describing to the high council the way he succeeded in having the marriage solemnized, he reminded them that some of the authorities said it could be done while others said it could not. He simply found one who would help him. This occurred, according to information gleaned from his trial, about 1906.[76]

There was considerable discussion about warm behavior on the part of Miles toward Emily before the marriage was formalized. By his own account, so much gossip arose concerning them that the authority who performed their marriage advised them not to live together until rumor died down. Some of those at the hearing testified that Romney's affectionate displays provoked special inquiries by the local bishopric. When invited to speak for himself, Romney said he was so deeply attached to the principle that he would die for it. At the same time, he conceded that his actions were sometimes imprudent. Although previously sealed by one he believed to have authority, he told of his decision to take Emily to a temple in Utah where she could obtain her endowments, and in case there was question about the person who first sealed them, the marriage could be properly solemnized in the temple.[77] The high council unanimously decided Miles should be disfellowshipped. Romney, a member of the council, voted with his brethren to sustain the judgment against him. He was readmitted to full fellowship less than a decade later.[78]

Devices used to camouflage polygamous marriages in earlier years were yet employed in this later period. The most visible of these was for a pluralist to legally remarry after the death of a first wife. George W. Willis (Appendix II, #208) provides a well-documented example of this stratagem. Brought before the Salt Lake Stake High Council on 17 August 1910, Willis explained that he was the husband of two wives until his first and legal wife died four years previously. The second wife, his plural, wished to live away from him so as to care for her mother. He then arranged to marry a recent English convert to the church, Louisa M. Patterson, as a new legal wife. As Willis explained, it was his understanding that the church had not really repudiated plural marriage but was only acting for the sake of appearances. If anyone could find a way to enter the principle secretly, he believed, it would be permitted.[79]

Insisting that he was acting in harmony with the commandments of God, Willis petitioned President Smith for permission to marry Louisa as his legal wife. President Smith replied, through an emissary, that he could not condone the step. Nevertheless, Willis obtained a marriage license and took Louisa Patterson to the Manti Temple. Upon describing his circumstances to temple president Lewis Anderson, he was told the sealing could not be performed unless he (Anderson) could obtain the consent of President Joseph F. Smith. Anderson contacted President Smith, who again sent word that Willis's marriage was not to occur in the Manti Temple. Anderson then advised the couple to go to a justice of the peace who could perform a civil ceremony. This they did, but wishing to be sealed before consummating their marriage, the two decided not to live with each other until approval was given by the church.

Willis then approached the leaders directly, contacting Apostle Francis M. Lyman. Lyman felt that even the civil marriage had been improper and initiated steps to discipline the couple. When the hearing occurred, a letter from temple president Lewis Anderson was read telling of Miss Patterson's insistent comments to him at the time of their meeting in Manti. According to Anderson, Patterson said that she knew such marriages were performed and could not see why she should be denied. Willis testified that Anderson told him that if they were first married by a civil authority, the church, having no responsibility for the contraction, could privately perform a sealing somewhere outside the temple. When asked why he ignored President Smith's denial of his petition, Willis answered that he believed President Smith had no choice in the matter for policy was to give the appearance that plural marriages were not approved even though many, Willis said, were being performed. Since his first wife had died, from a purely legal point of view Willis and Miss Patterson were within the law. It was only the church, recognizing the plural wife where the law did not, that shied from a new contraction. Willis was disfellowshipped.[80]

If George Willis and Louisa Patterson made a mistake, it was not in their assumption that such marriages as theirs were occurring and that President Smith privately wished to see the principle continued. It lay in assuming that all in the hierarchy were party to such intentions. On both occasions when the First Presidency was approached in his case, it was through an intermediary. When Willis himself contacted a high authority, after his civil marriage to Patterson, it was Francis M. Lyman with whom he spoke—a church leader who was strongly committed to enforcement of the 1904 "Official Statement." The case of one in Willis's circumstances was discussed during the congressional investigation of Senator Smoot and pronounced non-bigamous. Comments by witnesses in the hearings, as well as others, make it clear George Willis was not alone in attempting a plural marriage in this way. President Nephi L. Morris of the Salt Lake Stake said the Willis case was only one of many.[81]

Condemnation for adultery was also employed to distance the

church from the practice. We saw how this was used in the pre-1904 period in the cases of David Eccles (Appendix II, #67) and Loren Harmer (Appendix II, #84).[82] David Felt (Appendix II, #76), a resident of Salt Lake City, was discovered after marrying a plural wife and excommunicated for adultery with notice of the action published in the *Deseret News* in 1909. When the case came to light, Felt's bishop, George R. Jones, who likely assisted Felt in taking the new wife, immediately resigned his bishopric. Felt's son Vernon took offense from the public description of his father's excommunication, however, and lashed out at the church for what it had done. He called the account in the *Deseret News* "a garbled, dirty, damaging report," insisting that his father's actions were proper and in harmony with his religion. Church leaders were still privately conferring with Felt about his case two years later.[83]

Some collapsed the confusion into vigilance, hewing to the letter of the church's public statements. John Mills Whitaker, bishop of Sugar House Ward, made almost a career of hunting for post-1904 pluralists. In 1905 Whitaker was told by a member of his congregation, Nichol Hood, that Nichol's brother, John, claimed to have received permission from President Smith to take an additional wife. Whitaker marched with Hood directly to the president's office to confirm the story. They found Smith in a meeting with his counselors and ten of the apostles. Whitaker spoke directly to the church president: "President Smith, this is Nichol Hood, the man who has made the charge against you that you gave your consent for his brother, John Hood, to take a plural wife." According to Whitaker, Smith flatly but calmly denied Hood's story, saying he had given authority to no one since 1890 to enter polygamy.[84]

Over the years Bishop Whitaker told of finding fifteen different cases of men and women entering new plural relationships. In his words, "President [Heber J. Grant] was greatly wrought up over the many cases of polygamy I have taken to him . . . and thought it very remarkable to get first hand information, when in nearly all cases they deny with such vehemence [that] it is hard to obtain the facts."[85] Whitaker displayed such energy in their discovery that he came into conflict with his own stake presidency. It was probably due to his anti-polygamous activity that he was relieved as bishop and ordained a patriarch in 1914. This failed to deter him, however. Claiming special discernment, he continued to expose those involved in late plural unions. Encountering instance after instance, he was led to declare in 1917, "There must be something wrong somewhere."[86] Except that he reported these cases to his Mormon leaders, considering himself a dutiful servant, Whitaker reminds one of Charles Mostyn Owen, who, if possessing different ends, was a tireless laborer in the same field.[87]

The story of John Mills Whitaker has an interesting sequel, however—one that reveals the persistence of a psychology of polygamous expectation. Whitaker developed an attachment to another woman. But, according to his journal, he refused to disregard what he understood to be the policy of his church. He, his wife, and the lady concerned agreed they would be only good friends this side of the veil, postponing to the next life the joys of a married threesome. This, at least, is what we are led to assume. Whitaker closed his account of this relationship by saying that his "understanding" with the woman concerned was "*too sacred for the public to know*" (emphasis in original).[88]

Inconsistencies in the church's responses to new polygamy made for irritation on the part of those attempting to stamp it out. One can read the frustration of Francis M. Lyman when in 1914 he again questioned Joseph W. Musser concerning new cases of plural marriage. Musser remembered that Lyman came down hard, saying anyone who had taken an additional wife since 1890 had sinned. He charged that those apostles and leaders, including George Q. Cannon, who had authorized the activity brought embarrassment and reproach upon the church. Lyman told Musser that, in their efforts to identify those involved, President Smith resisted going back before the time his presidency began. And, Lyman added, Smith had about all he could take care of with cases arising during his own administration.[89] As one student commenting on the apostolate during these years described it, try as they might, the problem of new polygamy simply "would not go away."[90]

The decade and a half after 1904, even with the authorized plural unions that occurred, was a time of shifting currents, an interval anticipating the reverse rush following President Smith's death. Cases involving church authorities themselves were not handled consistently. Although Rudger Clawson, as we saw, married a plural wife after Joseph F. Smith's 1904 "Official Statement," he was never censured for the step and became president of the Quorum of Twelve Apostles in 1921.[91] Matthias F. Cowley's 1905 plural marriage to Lenora Taylor, on the other hand, undoubtedly contributed to differences between himself and other quorum members. And Apostle John W. Taylor's 1909 plural marriage to Ellen Sandberg compounded the case for his excommunication in 1911.[92] While there may have been a rationale governing such cases, to observing members of the church they partook of a blinkered pattern.

It is impossible after the turn of the century always to distinguish between those individuals properly authorized to enter polygamy and those who were not. The allegiance felt to oaths of silence imposed at that time was illustrated when Louetta Brown Tanner was interviewed at a Salt Lake City nursing home in 1973. She had been married as a plural wife to Henry S. Tanner (Appendix II, #185), a prominent Mormon attorney, in 1904. Admitting that the marriage took place in Salt Lake City, but outside the temple, and that it had been performed by one having authority, she still refused at that late date to identify who the individual was. "That," she said, "was one thing never spoke[n] of to anyone."[93]

Beyond oaths of secrecy, words and phrases were purposely equivocal. Messages intending approval acquired a semiotics of their own. Apostle John W. Taylor was given consent for one of his post-Manifesto marriages by President Smith in the form of a parable.[94] Heber Bennion, describing the permission he received, said that President Smith "let me know as well as I wanted to know, that he approved."[95] Melissa S. Wilson, who became a plural wife to Guy C. Wilson (Appendix II, #210) in 1902, recalled that "to be tapped on the shoulder" was a phrase used to indicate one was surreptitiously advised to enter the principle.[96] However confident such individuals may have been that they had deciphered the signal, communications of this nature were inevitably vulnerable to misunderstanding and exploitation.

The question of who besides President Smith was involved in condoning and performing such unions is equally difficult. Apart from individuals like John W. Taylor and Matthias F. Cowley, whose views, it has been suggested, were not out of harmony with Joseph F. Smith's, there must have been others. Men like Francis M. Lyman, Reed Smoot, and George F. Richards, who were especially active in bringing members into line with the church's putative stand on the issue, undoubtedly came to know more than they wished. Something of this was hinted in comments already cited from Smoot and Lyman.[97] Apostle Richards made perhaps the most intriguing remark when, in 1912, the quorum was engaged with its investigations into how so many members had entered plural marriage in recent years. Richards stated that they uncovered things of so startling a nature that he dared not record them in his diary.[98]

Neither can this investigator say when the practice ended. We might surmise that, with Smith's death in 1918, the last chapter in the story of approved polygamy came to a close. Some, however, allege that church officials were performing plural marriages and encouraging the practice in the 1920s.[99] There was also rumor that the excommunication of Apostle Richard R. Lyman in 1943 simply made use of the diverting charge of "unchastity" for what was actually polygamy, or a polygamous-like relationship. One commentator speculated that Lyman was influenced by Matthias F. Cowley and that this led to the complications in Lyman's affairs. Given the substance of Lyman's confession, now known from the diaries of Apostle George F. Richards, this seems unlikely.[100] On the other hand, remembering the lengths to which church officials had gone to obscure polygamous arrangements in the past, one cannot be certain. As Fawn Brodie put it at the time, she wondered if the unchastity with which Lyman was accused was of the form commonly assumed.[101] At the least, as Thomas G. Alexander has shown, there was a kind of half-way covenant by which authorities had dead women sealed to themselves as plural wives until at least 1925.[102]

So far as *approved* performances of new plural marriages are concerned, there is no doubt that numbers took place during the first decade of Joseph F. Smith's administration. They may have continued until Smith's death in 1918—and beyond. Reluctance to identify and tally such unions after 1910 arises from more than want of access to relevant archival materials, albeit this constitutes a large obstruction to understanding what occurred. One also hesitates to count polygamous marriages after that date because, even with available attestations, the print of authority for their performance becomes so diffuse. Increasingly, instances appearing to involve official permission are streaked by the nascent claims of Mormon fundamentalism. This does not mean such marriages were unapproved by church leaders. But it adds the complication of ulterior interest, of special claims upon the evidence, which, when combined with the qualified and faded nature of information attending many of them, leaves one understandably hesitant. Peter K. Lemmon, for example, doubted the efficacy of his own marriage to a plural wife in 1914 because of uncertainties associated with its performance by John W. Woolley, a patriarch tracing his authority to verbal encouragement from Matthias F. Cowley.[103] As suggested, it is not unreasonable to infer that the powerful impetus of polygamy was bled into some yet surviving subterranean channel. Certainly, the practice had persevered under difficult, near-invisible conditions before. So far as this study is concerned, however, the stream's current so dwindled that, after 1910, it sinks from *clear* view altogether.

However great the determination of plural aspirants, other, more powerful forces were at work. The church's long-standing public contention that it had undertaken a full compliance with the monogamous tradition was reshaping Mormonism itself. The country's best-known native religion was rapidly becoming a fully American church.

NOTES

1. Pacheco Ward Historical Record E, 26 June 1904, Church Archives.

2. For the Teasdale and Clawson comments, see respectively Joseph W. Musser Diaries, 11 and 17 Nov. 1901, 8 Feb. and 1 March 1902, Church Archives; and Rudger Clawson Diaries, 16 Jan. 1902 and 8 July 1903, Rudger Clawson Collection, University of Utah Library, Salt Lake City. Regarding the allegiance asked of stake authorities, see Theodore C. Bennion, interviewed by Jessie L. Embry, 9 June 1976, p. 2, POHP; and Mary Bennion Powell to George R. Stewart, 228-page transcript composed between 26 Jan. and 25 Feb. 1952, p. 24, Henry E. Huntington Library, San Marino, Calif. Also see the fascinating struggle such efforts at renewal precipitated with more modernist stake leaders, in Jessie L. Embry, "'All Things unto Me Are Spiritual': Contrasting Religious and Temporal Leadership Styles in Heber City, Utah" (Paper presented in the Charles Redd Center for Western Studies Lecture Series, 21 Jan. 1981, BYU).

3. Musser Diaries, 26 May 1902.

4. John Henry Smith, in Clawson Diaries, 7 Jan. 1902.

5. George Teasdale, in Juarez Stake Historical Record, 1901–6, 13 March 1904, Church Archives.

6. Juarez Stake High Council Minutes, 1895–1917, 30 April, 1904, Church Archives.

7. Anthony W. Ivins, quoted in Anthon Hendrick Lund Diaries, 14 Sept. 1904, Church Archives.

8. Joseph F. Smith, quoted in Juarez Stake Historical Record, 1901–6, 16 Sept. 1905.

9. Juarez Stake High Council Minutes, 1895–1906, 30 April 1904.

10. While the distinction between church and priesthood is referred to in most Mormon fundamentalist writings, perhaps the two most extensive and carefully developed expositions of the argument are found in Lynn L. Bishop and Steven L. Bishop, *The Keys of the Priesthood, Illustrated* (Draper, Utah: Review and Preview Publishers, 1971), 3–75, 201–3 passim; and all of Gilbert A. Fulton, *That Manifesto* (Kearns, Utah: Deseret Publishing, 1974).

11. George Franklin Richards Diaries, 10 April 1906, Church Archives. Also see the discussion in Dale C. Mouritsen, "A Symbol of New Directions:

George Franklin Richards and the Mormon Church, 1861–1950" (Ph.D. diss., BYU, 1982), 96.

12. J. Max Anderson, *The Polygamy Story: Fiction and Fact* (Salt Lake City: Publishers Press, 1979), 129.

13. Anthony Woodward Ivins Diaries, 9 April and 8 Oct. 1906, Anthony Woodward Ivins Collection, UHi.

14. Anthony W. Ivins, in Juarez Stake Historical Record, 1901–6, 16 June 1906, Church Archives.

15. Francis M. Lyman, in ibid., 9 Dec. 1906.

16. Musser Diaries, 22 July 1909.

17. Ivins Diaries, 19 Sept. 1909; and George F. Gibbs [secretary to the First Presidency] to Bishop Lorin Merrill, 8 Dec. 1909, Joseph F. Smith Letterbooks, Church Archives.

18. Annie Clark Tanner, *A Mormon Mother: An Autobiography,* rev. ed. (Salt Lake City: Tanner Trust Fund and University of Utah Library, 1973), 223, 225–26.

19. Walter Ernest Young, interviewed by Victor W. Jorgensen, 14 Aug. 1972, p. 14, Church Archives.

20. Juliaetta Bateman Jensen, *Little Gold Pieces: The Story of My Mormon Mother's Life* (Salt Lake City: Stanway, 1948), 134–35. Bishop Joseph C. Bentley was reported to be relieved that events surrounding the exodus of Mormon colonists from Mexico saved him the unpleasantness of proceeding against two men accused of post-1904 plural unions there. Melissa Wilson, "Looking Backward from 1962 to 1902," typewritten manuscript, p. 76, Church Archives. Also see H. Grant Ivins, interviewed by Victor W. Jorgensen, 18 July 1972, p. 40, Oral History Collection, California State University, Fullerton.

21. Retrospective comment in John Alfred Spendlove Journal, p. 49, copy, Church Archives.

22. Florence Ivins Hyde, interviewed by Victor W. Jorgensen, 18 August 1972, transcript in private possession.

23. Details concerning the Sears case were obtained from William Gailey Sears FGS; *Trials;* "Adding to the Roll," *SLT,* 25 April 1910; and information provided by Agnes E. Sears Jacobs, oldest child of William Gailey Sears and Athelia Viola Call, in Ronald Bateman and Raymond Dewey, interviewed by Victor W. Jorgensen, 14 Sept. and 25 Dec. 1974, record of interview in possession of Victor W. Jorgensen, Logan, Utah.

24. Andrew Jenson, *Latter-day Saint Biographical Encyclopedia . . . ,* 4 vols. (Salt Lake City: Andrew Jenson History Co., 1901–36), 4:64–65.

25. Reed Smoot Diaries, 27 Sept., 12 Oct., and 15 Nov. 1910, BYU Library; Ivins Diaries, 7 Jan. 1911.

26. Smoot Diaries, 12 Oct. 1910.

27. Warren Longhurst FGS; Ivins R of M; and Nelle Spilsbury Hatch, "Warren Longhurst," in *Stalwarts South of the Border,* comp. Nelle Spilsbury

Hatch and B. Carmon Hardy (Anaheim, Calif.: privately published, 1985), 409–12.

28. It has been said that Longhurst approached Anthony W. Ivins, who would not perform the ceremony but sent the couple to John W. Woolley of Centerville, Utah, and he solemnized the union. "A Biographical Sketch of the Life of Mary Evelyn Clark Allred," *Star of Truth* 2 (Nov. 1954): 301–2. Also see Bishop and Bishop, *The Keys of the Priesthood,* 180–81.

29. Lucille R. Taylor, "Samuel John Robinson," in *Stalwarts South of the Border,* comp. Hatch and Hardy, 575–77.

30. Testimony of John W. Taylor, in *Trials.* Robinson told much the same story when interviewed by Kimball Young, 28 Feb. 1939, box 11, fd. 13, Kimball Young Collection, Garrett Evangelical Theological Library, Evanston, Ill.

31. *Trials.* Also see Ivins Diaries, 30 Nov. 1907; and Juarez Stake High Council Minutes, 1895–1917, 26 Oct. 1907, Church Archives.

32. *Trials.*

33. John W. Taylor and Hyrum M. Smith, in ibid.

34. Carlos Ashby Badger Diaries, 8 Oct. 1904, Church Archives.

35. Elna Hart Palmer, interviewed by Leonard R. Grover, 2 Feb. 1980, p. 14, POHP; Rhea Hart Grandy, interviewed by Leonard R. Grover, 16 Feb. 1980, pp. 9, 11, POHP.

36. Heber Bennion, in Powell to Stewart, 26 Jan. 1952, pp. 24–25.

37. John Bennion Cannon, interviewed by Leonard R. Grover, 19 Jan. 1980, pp. 7–8, 14, POHP.

38. See above, in chaps. 5 and 7.

39. Anson Bowen Call, "Life Story of Anson Bowen Call," pp. 6–7, original in possession of Arnold Call, Colonia Dublan, copy in possession of author. Also see Lorna Call Alder, interviewed by Jessie L. Embry, 28 June 1976, p. 28, POHP.

40. Orson P. Brown Journal, typewritten copy, pp. 67–68, UHi. Also see the anecdote involving First Presidency member John R. Winder in Frank J. Cannon and Harvey J. O'Higgins, *Under the Prophet in Utah: The National Menace of a Political Priestcraft* (Boston: C. M. Clark, 1911), 350.

41. Brigham Young, Jr., Diary, 5 June 1902, film, Church Archives; Clawson Diaries, 17 April and 5 June 1902.

42. Joseph F. Smith, in JH, 19 Nov. 1903.

43. Matthias F. Cowley to Jesse N. Smith, 22 April 1906, in *Journal of Jesse Nathaniel Smith: The Life Story of a Mormon Pioneer, 1834–1906* (Salt Lake City: Jesse N. Smith Family Association, 1953), 462. Illustrating how knowledge of these things was kept even from family members of the leaders is an anecdote told by William Walser concerning a visit to the Mexican colonies by President Smith after his 1904 "Official Statement." Walser recalled that President Smith came to the colonies for the purpose of reinforcing and clarifying his policy and had brought his son, the future president of the church, Joseph Fielding

Smith, Jr., with him. Asked to speak but unaware of the special arrangement existing between Ivins and his father, Joseph Fielding attacked Ivins from the stand for his part in solemnizing plural marriages since the Manifesto, so many of which had embarrassed the church. Ivins defended himself by saying that not only had he been commissioned to perform such ceremonies but that none were undertaken without the approval of "that man that sits right there"—President Smith himself. William Walser, interviewed by Jessie L. Embry, 11 June 1976, p. 18, POHP.

44. Marriner W. Merrill and Francis M. Lyman, in Clawson Diaries, 11 and 12 July 1899.

45. Byron Harvey Allred, Jr., in "Biographical Sketch of the Life of Mary Evelyn Clark Allred," 298.

46. *Trials.*

47. Matthias F. Cowley, in Charles William Penrose Diaries, 10 May 1911, UHi.

48. Carlos Badger to Rose Badger, 21 Feb. 1907, Carlos Ashby Badger Letterbooks, Church Archives.

49. H. Grant Ivins, Jorgensen interview, p. 41.

50. Juarez Stake Historical Record, 1907–32, 8 March 1908, Church Archives.

51. Joseph Charles Bentley FGS.

52. *Trials;* Ivins Diaries, 25 Jan. 1911. Also see Appendix II, #56.

53. Earnest Guy Taylor FGS; and Appendix II, #188.

54. Alonzo Leander Taylor FGS; and Appendix II, #187.

55. Ernest Leander Taylor FGS; Penrose Diaries, 31 Oct. 1910.

56. Juarez Stake High Council Minutes and Historical Record, 1895–1917, 19 Nov. 1910; Hatch and Hardy, *Stalwarts South of the Border,* 680–81.

57. Joseph Bates Noble, quoted in *The Reorganized Church of Jesus Christ of Latter Day Saints, Complainant vs. The Church of Christ at Independence, Missouri; . . . Complainant's Abstract . . .* (Lamoni, Iowa: Herald Publishing House, 1893), 367.

58. Joseph F. Smith, in *Proceedings* 1:312, 334.

59. Joyce Richardson Heder, interviewed by Leonard R. Grover, 27 Aug. 1980, p. 9, POHP. Also see the comment of Bernal A. Harvey, interviewed by Jessie L. Embry, 27 July 1976, p. 6, POHP. Embry's conclusion in her own study that, without religious motivation, Mormon pluralists "would not have even considered the possibility" of such arrangements seems overstated to this author. Jessie L. Embry, *Mormon Polygamous Families: Life in the Principle,* Publications in Mormon Studies, Vol. 1 (Salt Lake City: University of Utah Press, 1987), 50.

60. Powell to Stewart, 29 Jan. 1952, pp. 56–57, 198.

61. William R. Campbell, "Mormonism and Purity," *Missionary Review of the World* 15 (Feb. 1902): 136.

62. Unsigned, untitled, undated typescript, Anthony Woodward Ivins Collection, box 7, fd. 10, p. 11, UHi.

63. Mrs. Benjamin G. Ferris, *Mormons at Home, with Some Incidents of Travel from Missouri to California, 1852–53, in a Series of Letters* (New York: Dix & Edwards; London: Sampson, Low, & Son, 1856), 159; William Chandless, *A Visit to Salt Lake: Being a Journey across the Plains and a Residence in the Mormon Settlements at Utah* (London: Smith, Elder, 1857), 258; Jules Remy, *A Journey to Great-Salt-Lake City . . .* , 2 vols. (London: W. Jeffs, 1861), 1:214, 2:180–81; George Alfred Townsend, *The Mormon Trial at Salt Lake City* (New York: American News, 1871), 43; Mrs. Thomas B. H. Stenhouse, *Exposé of Polygamy in Utah: A Lady's Life among the Mormons . . .* , (New York: American News, 1872), 91. These were undoubtedly among the reasons why Apostle Moses Thatcher declared that "nowhere in the world are women freer than in Utah." *JD* 26 (1885): 314.

64. Sarah Hendricks, interviewed by James Comish, 26 Jan. 1980, p. 11, POHP. For examples of wives escorted to and from home by men other than their husbands and attending dances without their husbands, see Juanita Brooks, ed., *Not by Bread Alone: The Journal of Martha Spence Heywood, 1850–56* (Salt Lake City: Utah State Historical Society, 1978), 49n.; Morris Hodges, interviewed by Jessie L. Embry, 17 July 1976, p. 9, POHP; Mary Pratt Parrish, "Helaman Pratt," in *Stalwarts South of the Border*, comp. Hatch and Hardy, 551.

65. See, e.g., the experience of one of the wives of Joseph Marion Tanner, described in Badger Diaries, 4 June 1906; and that related in Powell to Stewart, 10 Feb. 1952, p. 200.

66. Jensen, *Little Gold Pieces*, 135–39; Pearl J. Augustus, interviewed by Jessie L. Embry, 1 June 1976, p. 16, POHP; and Florence Ivins Hyde interview.

67. Pearl J. Augustus interview, p. 16.

68. "High Churchman Enters Polygamy," *SLT*, 27 July 1909; "But One of Many Cases," ibid., 28 July 1909; "Action Taken in Alpha J. Higgs Case," *DN*, 9 April 1910; "The Bluff as to Higgs," ibid., 12 April 1910; and "Mrs. Higgs Sues for Divorce," *SLT*, 7 Sept. 1910.

69. Heber Grant Ivins, Jorgensen interview, pp. 32–33.

70. See above, in chap. 2.

71. *D&C*, 124:124 (1841). For references to patriarchs involved in post-Manifesto polygamous marriages, see Ivins Diaries, 25 Jan. 1911; and President Heber J. Grant's 1921 comments, in "Concerning Marriage and Inspiration," *Messages* 5:196.

72. John W. Taylor, in Penrose Diaries, 22 Feb. 1911; *Trials*.

73. See Walser's comments in connection with the cases of Miles A. Romney and Ernest Leander Taylor, in Juarez Stake High Council Minutes, book D, 1908–11, 29 Jan. and 19 Nov. 1910, respectively.

74. John Mills Whitaker Journals, 6 March 1921, typewritten transcript, University of Utah Library. Many of Whitaker's entries are retrospective, though the marriage referenced seems to have occurred in 1921.

75. See above in chap. 5; and Appendix II, #162.

76. Juarez Stake Historical Record—High Council Minutes, Book D, 1908–11, 29 Jan. 1910, Church Archives.

77. Ibid.

78. Ibid. Also see Miles Archibald Romney FGS; Walter Ernest Young interview, pp. 17–18, Church Archives; Celia R. Geertsen, interviewed by Jessie L. Embry, 5 May 1976, p. 1, POHP.

79. George H. Willis, in Salt Lake Stake Historical Record, 1910–12, 17 Aug. 1910, Church Archives.

80. Ibid.

81. Nephi L. Morris, in Salt Lake Stake Historical Record, 17 Aug. 1910. For discussions of this approach and indications of its legality, see *Proceedings* 2:41, 693–94, 953–54; Charles Mostyn Owen to J. W. Howe, 3 Oct. 1899, Charles Mostyn Owen Letterbook, Charles Mostyn Owen Collection, Church Archives; Eugene Young, "Polygamy Is Reviving," *New York Herald*, 5 Feb. 1899. But cf. Judge William M. McCarty's opinion in *Proceedings* 2:919.

82. See above in chap. 5.

83. For continued discussions with Felt, see Penrose Diaries, 28 March 1911. Additional information, including comments by Vernon Felt, are found in Twenty-Third Ward Minutes, Salt Lake Stake Historical Record Book, 1906–9, 8 and 9 Aug. 1909; "Cut Off the Church," *DN*, 10 Aug. 1909; "David P. Felt Has Lived His Religion," *SLT*, 11 Aug. 1909; "The Sneaking Lawlessness," ibid., 22 Aug. 1909.

84. Whitaker Journals, entry for 8 Oct. 1906.

85. Ibid., 6 March 1921.

86. Ibid., 1 Nov. 1917.

87. Ibid., 13 Aug. 1909, 24 Sept. 1912, 22 Feb. 1914, 13 Sept. 1915, 6 March 1921. For an account of Charles Mostyn Owen, see above in chap. 7.

88. Whitaker Journals, 17 April 1915.

89. Francis M. Lyman, in Musser Diaries, 16 Feb. 1914.

90. Mouritsen, "A Symbol of New Directions," 104.

91. See the account of Clawson's marriage to Pearl Udall in chap. 6.

92. Regarding Taylor and Cowley's problems with other apostles, see chap. 7. For the issue of Taylor's 1909 plural marriage, see Samuel W. Taylor, "Interviews with Nettie [Janet] M. Taylor," 14–15 Jan. 1936, pp. 1, 5; and idem, "Interviews with Nettie [Janet] M. Taylor," July 1947, p. 25, BYU Library.

93. Louetta Brown Tanner, interviewed by Victor W. Jorgensen, 5 Feb. 1973, transcript in possession of Victor W. Jorgensen, Logan, Utah. A brief biographical sketch of Henry S. Tanner is contained in George S. Tanner, *John Tanner and His Family* (Salt Lake City: John Tanner Family Association, 1974), 328.

94. Samuel W. Taylor, "Interviews with Nettie [Janet] M. Taylor," July 1947, p. 20.

95. Heber Bennion to Heber J. Grant, 9 July 1929, Brigham H. Roberts Letterbox, folder labeled "Polygamy," Church Archives.

96. Wilson, "Looking Backward from 1962 to 1902," handwritten insert following p. 10.

97. See above, pp. 326, 327.

98. Richards Diaries, 16 Jan. 1912.

99. See the cases of Thomas Henry Jones and Frank Jones, described by Merriner L. Jones, interviewed by Jessie L. Embry, 11 Jan. 1981, pp. 1–3, 5, 11, 17 passim, POHP; and Elma Jane Anderson, interviewed by Rochelle Fairbourn, 20 Nov. 1981, pp. 1–2 passim, POHP. Also see Verlan M. LeBaron, *The LeBaron Story* (Lubbock, Texas: Keels, 1981), 42–43.

100. Mouritsen treats this issue in *A Symbol of New Directions*, 161–63. Also see Jerold A. Hilton, "Polygamy in Utah and Surrounding Area since the Manifesto of 1890" (M.A. thesis, BYU, 1965), 19; Edward L. Kimball and Andrew E. Kimball, Jr., *Spencer W. Kimball: Twelfth President of the Church of Jesus Christ of Latter-day Saints* (Salt Lake City, Utah: Bookcraft, 1977), 208–10; and the comments in Edwin B. Firmage, *The Memoirs of Hugh B. Brown* (Salt Lake City: Signature Books, 1988), 125. For the suggestion of Cowley's influence on Lyman, see Raymond Taylor to Dennis [Michael] Quinn, 14 May 1970, box 45, fd. 15, John W. Taylor Family Papers, University of Utah Library.

101. Fawn Brodie to Dale Morgan, 19 Nov. 1943, Fawn Brodie Papers, University of Utah Library. I am indebted to Professor Newell Bringhurst of the College of the Sequoias for bringing this letter to my attention.

102. Thomas G. Alexander, *A History of the Latter-day Saints, 1890–1930* (Urbana: University of Illinois Press, 1986), 300.

103. Copy of John W. Woolley affidavit, 16 Jan. 1914, box 11, fd. 21, Anthony Woodward Ivins Collection; same in box 11, fd. 9, Stanley Snow Ivins Collection, both in UHi; and Ivins Diaries, 1 March 1914.

10

Monogamous Triumph

In his diary Wilford Woodruff told of a time deposit made in the cornerstone of the yet uncompleted Salt Lake Temple in 1857. This was removed in 1862. At least one other gathering of books and photographs was placed beneath a copper plate, marking the near completion of the edifice in 1892. In both instances treatises were included that argued for and praised plural marriage, most notably Orson Spencer's famous tract, *Patriarchal Order; or, Plurality of Wives!*[1] A former Baptist minister, Spencer became one of the church's best-known missionaries, serving both in the United States and Europe. He was made chancellor of the University of Deseret in 1850 and was a member of Utah's territorial legislature. His *Letters* were long considered one of the greater of Mormonism's proselyting tools, especially his defense of polygamy.[2]

"The grand design of God," said Spencer, in bringing men and women to this earth was to teach and organize them "according to the pattern of the family of heaven." The nature of this arrangement was revealed to mankind in the patriarchal, polygamous household of Abraham, the friend of God. Every departure from this construction, including "monogamy, or the one-wife system," was a corruption, sure to lead to "debauchery and whoredoms." Those, he said, who hate the family order of Abraham hate God. Nothing in the Bible so provoked the Devil to opposition as plural marriage. If his voice were a trumpet, Spencer said, he would declare to all governments and authority on earth that to survive and prosper they must build on the divine foundations revealed in the polygamous habits of Abraham and the yielding example of his wife Sarah.[3]

These declarations in the hallowed mortar of the temple walls whisper very quietly anymore. They impose little restraint on the momentum with which the church continues to move away from the principle. With some Mormons the subject evokes embarrassment. Others, born to plural unions solemnized after 1890, have suffered ridicule from members of the church.[4] Among scholars there is widespread understanding that investigation into the matter is disapproved by Latter-day Saint authorities and those who are stewards of the church's archives and records. A former chairman of the History Department at Brigham Young University told a professional gathering in the early 1980s that he was instructed not to encourage studies of either polygamy or blacks and the priesthood.[5] This, combined with the near-complete absence of reference to plurality in official discourse at Mormon conferences, might persuade one that Orson Spencer belonged not only to a different time but to a different church.

We must, nevertheless, acknowledge how remarkably persevering the principle has been. If one dates its origins from the 1830s and includes contemporary Mormon fundamentalists in the time line, its practice has survived for more than a century and a half. Apart from fundamentalist adherents, there are individuals whose plural marriages were approved by church authorities and who were accepted as orthodox members in good standing, yet attending Mormon church services well into the second half of the twentieth century. We can revise the summary of Stanley Ivins. After saying that "only a few" privately solemnized plural marriages occurred between 1890 and 1904, he concluded, "The experiment was ten years in embryo, enjoyed a vigorous life of forty years, and took fifteen years to die."[6] Not only must we recede to a time before the 1890 Manifesto to mark the commencement of a strategy involving submersed perpetuation of the practice but, as shown, there are strong grounds for extending its duration beyond 1904, the date traditionally given for its arrest. And there were certainly more than "only a few" who took new plural wives after 1890. The entire story of plurality's later years must be reevaluated. Jan Shipps's statement that recent scholarship has profoundly altered our understanding of the system's beginning while leaving its closing chapter "virtually unchanged" then also needs amendment.[7]

To fully understand the transformation, we must recognize the cumulative consequences of the church's resort to pretense as a means for preserving plural marriage when it was under attack. John A. McClernand presciently saw, as he told President Grover Cleveland, that "the more often the Mormons commit themselves, whether regularly or irregularly, against polygamy, the more they will have increased the obstacles to a retreat from the path of reform."[8] Mormon leaders such as John W. Taylor and Abraham O. Woodruff, who feared the church's policies as irretrievable concessions, were correct. Although the principle was surreptitiously kept alive by hundreds of stalwarts, thousands more believed the public statements of their leaders. This, combined with the lure and pressure of the larger society's monogamous ethic, as well as sincere efforts at reformation by a growing number of Mormon authorities, led the church to a condition of estrangement from their polygamous past, to the near contradictory circumstance described by Fawn Brodie as one in which "polygamy shocks the Mormons."[9]

While there is growing scholarly interest in Mormon polygamy, and several important studies on the subject have appeared in recent years, official church publications have carefully stepped around it for decades.[10] This proclivity first arose, as we saw, in connection with church attempts during the anti-polygamy crusade to obscure the dimensions of its commitment to plural marriage. These efforts continued after the Manifesto and were especially pronounced at the times of the Roberts and Smoot cases.[11] By 1919 church doctrinal expositions had closed gait with contemporary domestic ideals to such an extent that Apostle James Talmage could not only condemn the double standard and sexual impurity without linking them to monogamy but affirm the propriety of each man having only one wife, the rightfulness of secular control of the marriage institution, and the equation of "celestial marriage" with a monogamous union for eternity.[12]

Since at least the 1930s Sunday-School manuals and other official Latter-day Saint writings uniformly display the kinds of guidelines for successful family life one would encounter in most traditional Christian denominations. References to polygamy are conspicuous by their absence. Discussion of the principle—except to say God directed a small number of church members to enter it in the past, a commandment since suspended—is carefully avoided. Brief narratives sometimes refer to plurality but almost always for the purpose of declaring its minuscule extent or instancing persecution. Nowhere does one read accounts of its superiority to monogamy or the advantages—spiritual, social, or physiological—that Mormon leaders once claimed for the practice. Illustrations and art work for these publications, indeed twentieth-century Mormon iconographies generally, project the ideal family as that of a single married couple with their children.[13] Even writings focusing on the restoration of the "fullness" of the

Gospel, the meaning of Old Testament teachings, or the significance of Old Testament prophets are shorn of reference to plural marriage.[14] And, of course, there is an almost unbroken silence regarding approved perpetuation of the practice after the Manifesto.

A doctrinal treatise by one apostle, while indicating that plurality will recommence with the Second Coming of Christ, reaffirms that the union of one man with one woman is now "the Lord's law of marriage" and any who engage in polygamy are guilty of "gross wickedness."[15] The traditional family is praised, sometimes referred to as "ideal," and Bible scriptures are summoned in support of it. Character sketches intended as models for both young men and young women never include polygamy as one of their components.[16] A study made in the mid-1950s described the Mormon family, while slightly more conservative, as quite similar in its practices and values to American families at large.[17] Another survey taken in the 1960s found that not only do contemporary church members overwhelmingly disapprove of polygamy but only two in five said they would enter the principle if commanded by the prophets. Nearly half said they would not practice it under any circumstances.[18] A more recent essay describes Mormon family problems, including increased divorce, as close to demographic and socio-psychological patterns in American society generally.[19]

Oral interviews with the children of officially approved plural unions also illustrate Mormon reluctance. While some believe polygamy will exist in the next life and say they think it a true principle, numbers voice strong reservation about having to revive it in the present. During one interview an elderly gentleman whose parents had been happy in plurality reflected that, because of their example, he could probably live comfortably in such an arrangement too. The man's wife, however, listening to the interview, broke in to say: "You could live it, but I couldn't!"[20] Plural marriage is "an awful thing to have to do," said a male polygamous child. And a sister of the same respondent said she believed that monogamy offered the greater possibility for happiness.[21] Hortense Young Hammond told of learning years after the church's putative abandonment of the practice that her own father had entered the principle. She did not believe in the system and was shocked at the discovery. "I had read about it [polygamy], of course . . . , but I never dreamed that Papa had another wife. It broke my heart. . . . I'll never forget it."[22]

The degree to which Latter-day Saint thinking has absorbed and come to reflect traditional attitudes toward the family is astonishing. In his 1930 *Comprehensive History of the Church*, Brigham H. Roberts said plurality must prove itself superior to monogamy on eugenic grounds or forfeit the contest altogether. Less than a decade later, Dr. Franklin L. West, church commissioner of education and assistant superintendent of the Latter-day Saint Young Men's Mutual Improvement Association, seemed to answer Roberts by declaring that Christian monogamy had proved itself "best in the experience of the race." Reversing arguments used by the nineteenth-century Saints, West said the one-wife system was rooted in "man's inherent nature," the needs of society, and religious sanction.[23]

In a recent essay Eugene England, a professor at Brigham Young University, questioned the preferred status of polygamy, either here or hereafter. England argued that there was nothing necessarily eternal about the principle, that it was required of the Saints for a time only as a "test," and that it was permanently rescinded in 1890. It is not, he said, a "celestial" order of family life. While England's article involves extensive historical distortion, it is an excellent illustration of the stage to which Mormon attitudes have arrived. Using criticisms of plurality remarkably similar to those made by nineteenth-century Gentiles, England argued that the scriptures reinforce monogamy more than polygamy. Exclusive, romantic love, he said, offers greater joy for married partners, whereas polygamous relationships incline to superficial emotional ties. Plural expectations lead to infidelity. And the polygamous configuration is inherently degrading to women.[24]

Unquestionably, pressures to establish full equality between women and men are having an effect on Mormonism only slightly less pronounced than on the rest of American society.[25] Assumptions undergirding the patriarchal, polygamous home grow increasingly faint. In 1899 a gentile reporter, Frank G. Carpenter, told of an interview with the first wife of Apostle John Henry Smith in which she spoke for the advantages of polygamy. She recalled traditional defenses, saying it assured greater sexual purity in marriage and made it possible for every woman to have a husband and a family. She then followed with the comment that if her husband did not come home at night, unlike many gentile wives she at least knew what they did not.[26] Quite apart from the acceptability of those differences of need between the genders that, in the Mormon mind, made polygamy a safeguard of sexual purity, the claim that she was advantaged through knowledge of her husband's other relationships would purchase little peace for most wives today. Indeed, the uncertainty deprecated as the lot of wives in monogamy is sure to pass as preferable to the knowledge she prized as plurality's gift. With her response the apostle's good wife illustrates the dramatic changes that have occurred between the end of the last century and the end of this one.

The first three presidents of the Mormon church. *Clockwise from left:* Joseph Smith, Jr., 1805–44; Brigham Young, 1801–77; John Taylor, 1808–87. Under their leadership polygamous marriage was inaugurated, justifications for the principle developed, and its practice vigorously defended. *Courtesy of the Utah State Historical Society.*

Frank Leslie's Illustrated Newspaper, 8 May 1886, 184.

"Life among the Mormons—The New Wife." During the anti-polygamy crusade, opponents portrayed the Saints as sensationally as their imaginations—and public taste—would permit.

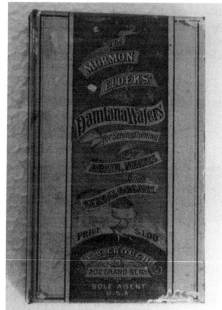

Photos by Goetz Photography, Cairo, New York

Mormon Elders' Damiana Wafers, a hucstering attempt, illustrates efforts to commercially exploit images associated with presumed Mormon sexual powers. The tin, which measures 3 x 1 3/4 x 1/2 inches, probably dates from the 1880s and is owned by Robert Uzzilia of Cairo, New York.

The Mormon church First Presidency at the time the Manifesto was issued in 1890. *Left to right:* George Q. Cannon, Wilford Woodruff, and Joseph F. Smith.

President Wilford Woodruff, 1807-98, and his third wife, Emma Smith, 1831-1912.

Mormon apostles and First Presidency, September 1898. *Back row, left to right:* Anthon H. Lund, John W. Taylor, John Henry Smith, Heber J. Grant, Francis M. Lyman, George Teasdale, and Marriner W. Merrill. *Middle row:* Brigham Young, Jr., George Q. Cannon, President Lorenzo Snow, Joseph F. Smith, and Franklin D. Richards. *Front row:* Matthias F. Cowley and Abraham Owen Woodruff.

The Mormon church First Presidency of Lorenzo Snow, 1898–1901. *Clockwise from left:* Lorenzo Snow, First Counselor George Q. Cannon, Second Counselor Joseph F. Smith. Despite Snow's efforts to halt new plural marriages, his counselors worked around him, approving such unions in greater numbers than at any time since the Manifesto. *Courtesy of the Utah State Historical Society*

Joseph F. Smith, 1838–1918, and the counselors of his later years. *Clockwise from left:* Joseph F. Smith, Anton H. Lund, Charles W. Penrose. In the early years of Smith's administration new plural marriages were performed in considerable numbers. These activities declined precipitously as a result of the Smoot investigation. *Courtesy of the Utah State Historical Society*

Courtesy of Victor W. Jorgensen

"The Exiles." These and other polygamous wives with their small children went to Mexico shortly after the turn of the century, especially during the Smoot investigation, to avoid discovery. Florence Ivins Hyde, a daughter of Anthony W. Ivins, gave copies of the picture to Victor W. Jorgensen and the LDS Church Archives. Florence said the picture was taken on the lawn of the Ivins home in Colonia Juarez, Mexico.

Alexander Finlay Macdonald, 1825-1903. As a patriarch in the Mormon colonies in Mexico, Macdonald performed numerous polygamous marriages between the time of the Manifesto in 1890 and his death in 1903.

Anthony Woodward Ivins, 1852-1934, leading authority in the Mormon colonies in Mexico, 1895-1907. By permission of the First Presidency in Salt Lake City, Ivins performed more than forty polygamous marriages during the years from 1897 to 1904. Ivins was made an apostle upon the death of George Teasdale and later became a member of the First Presidency itself.

George Q. Cannon, 1827-1901, with some of his sons. *Seated, left to right:* Lewis T., John Q., Angus J., George Q., Read T., Abraham H., and Mark (adopted). *Standing:* Brigham T., Hugh J., Frank J., Willard T., William T., Joseph J., Sylvester Q., and David H. Picture taken about 1892. George Q., a member of the First Presidency, authorized numerous polygamous marriages after the Manifesto. Abraham and Hugh both took plural wives after 1890.

Apostle Rudger Clawson, 1857-1943.

Pearl Udall Nelson, 1880-1950. It is likely that Pearl was joined to Apostle Rudger Clawson as a plural wife in 1904. She and the apostle later ended their relationship and Pearl married Joseph Nelson in 1919. She was a licensed osteopath and provided distinguished service throughout her life, not only in her profession, but in a variety of offices in her church.

Brigham H. Roberts, 1857-1933, a member of the First Council of Seventy, was denied his seat in Congress after being elected in 1898. He is likely to have married a polygamous wife after the Manifesto.

Apostle and United States senator Reed Smoot, 1862-1941. Smoot's responsibilities as a political officer undoubtedly stiffened his opposition to post-Manifesto polygamy, sometimes creating tension between himself and other high leaders of the church.

Leslie's Monthly Magazine, March 1905, 543

Robert W. Tayler, 1852-1910, chairman of the House committee dealing with the seating of Brigham H. Roberts and later chief counsel for the complainants in the Smoot hearings. Witty, relentless, possessed of a keen intellect and a comprehensive knowledge of Mormonism, Tayler provided invaluable service to those opposing the admission of Roberts and Smoot to Congress.

Perhaps the only known photograph of the anti-Mormon sleuth Charles Mostyn Owen, shown here disguised with beard and wig. This is a partial reproduction of one of three pictures appearing on the front page of the *Washington Times*, 14 December 1904. The other two, in which Owen was shown modeling Mormon temple costume, were considered inappropriate for use here. When the photographs were published, with accompanying excerpts from the Mormon temple endowment ceremony, both prosecuting and defending attorneys in the Smoot hearings were dismayed by the shenanigan. See *Proceedings* 2:426.

Courtesy of Southern Illinois University at Carbondale

Theodore Schroeder, 1864-1953. Schroeder's published criticism of continued Mormon polygamy contributed to the renewal of hostility toward the Saints during the late 1890s and early twentieth century. This photograph was probably taken between 1900 and 1909.

Heber J. Grant, 1856-1945, and his first wife, Lucy Stringham, 1858-1893. Despite Grant's earlier belief in and practice of the doctrine of plurality of wives, after succeeding Joseph F. Smith in 1918 as the church's president, he moved harshly against those seeking to continue the principle.

Most dramatically, the church's record of severity toward Mormon fundamentalism tells its reformation. While fundamentalist organizations became most visible in the 1930s, they had arisen from the environment of indistinct authority and inconsistent response surrounding Mormon plurality in the years following the Manifesto. It was during those years that some stalwarts began attaching large importance to a divine communication to former president John Taylor, in which he was told that plural marriage was an "everlasting covenant" and that its requirements could never be revoked.[27] Fundamentalists additionally said that Taylor charged certain individuals with perpetuating the practice until the millennium. Linked with this was a prediction that the church would fall into apostasy, captive to the appetites of modern secular society. Fundamentalists often portrayed the Manifesto of 1890 as a surrender and President Heber J. Grant as the leader most responsible for consummating the church's alliance with the world—a world on the edge of collapse, in good part, because of sexual sin.

Joseph W. Musser, one of those active in the fundamentalist movement, began editing the periodical *Truth* in 1935. Its opening issue, echoing church authorities of the previous century, said modern Christendom was in ruin because of the "monogamic order of marriage." *Truth* was dedicated to championing plurality as a great and redeeming "social law."[28] During the two decades of the magazine's publication, its pages were filled with accounts of approved post-Manifesto plural marriages, support for fundamentalist authority to perpetuate polygamy, and instances demonstrating the alleged betrayal by the modern church of the principles of early Mormonism. Yet affirming the socio-biological advantages of the principle, fundamentalists admonished men not to waste their "substance" through sexual association with older women or those unable to conceive. Prostitution, venereal disease, and general social chaos, they said, were the results of monogamy.[29]

After succeeding Joseph F. Smith as president of the church in 1918, Grant turned harshly against those contending for perpetuation of the principle. Although he had been a pluralist himself, Grant moved against those found to be contracting such unions with greater sharpness than any of his predecessors. Even those whose marriages were undeniably approved noticed the difference. Hilda Farr, who became the second living wife of Heber Farr in Mexico in 1904, commented on the greater severity displayed by President Grant in comparison to the ways of President Smith. Guy C. Wilson, it was rumored, was asked to disperse his plural families to different communities so as to reduce their visibility.[30] Grant seemed to blot from his memory the earlier, solemn commitment Mormonism had displayed toward plurality. With considerable success he cultivated an image he knew would please American audiences. In a 1925 speech before the Kansas City Chamber of Commerce, for example, he appropriated polygamy humorously by playing on prejudices that had contributed to its defeat. "They say that the stock runs out intellectually, physically and morally in plural marriage," he said, "and of course I have to acknowledge it, because I am the last son of the last wife (laughter)."[31]

There was little humor, however, in Grant's attitude toward fundamentalist attempts to renew the practice. This was illustrated by a document prepared by his counselor, J. Reuben Clark, and issued by the First Presidency in 1933. The message erroneously claimed it was not until 1874 that the federal government attempted to suppress the practice of polygamy. It also asserted that the church had, after all, made a compact with the United States government promising to cease plural marriage. It affirmed that the Manifesto of 1890 was unanimously sustained in the conference to which it was presented. It repeated that President Smith's 1904 "Official Statement" was precipitated by the misbehavior of "a few misguided members." The document held that President John Taylor's alleged 1886 revelation and authority for secret perpetuation of the practice were without historical or archival basis. And it reasserted that celestial marriage was not the same as plural marriage.[32] There is no doubt that the purpose of the address was to denounce groups in the church seeking to perpetuate polygamy and that it was part of a larger campaign, especially by President Grant and J. Reuben Clark, to quash such activities. Clark had long been offended by those violating the Manifesto and, for years after becoming an active member of the First Presidency in early 1933, worked closely with law enforcement agencies to quarantine the movement.[33]

So far as President Grant was concerned, the 1933 statement explicitly stipulated he had never authorized anyone to solemnize a plural marriage nor was he himself joining couples in such unions. This seems plausible enough. The message insisted, however, that Grant, neither presently nor in the past, had ever broken his pledge taken at the time of the Manifesto "to the church, to the world, and to our government." If Grant had forgotten his misgivings at the time the Manifesto was issued and his obstreperous statements made in support of his plural life-style at the turn of the century, had he also forgotten his impudent remarks before a local judicial officer that he had no intention of honoring the law or keeping the promises agreed to by his signature to the petition for amnesty? And if not this, had he lost all recollection that he pleaded guilty in court to unlawful polygamous cohabitation in 1899?[34] Perhaps, as Grant once admitted, he knew "little or nothing of History."[35]

During the 1930s and 1940s church leaders gave active support to civil authorities seeking to apprehend and prosecute polygamous fundamentalists. A loyalty oath was prescribed for a time and, according to one investigator, resulted in the excommunication of scores of Latter-day Saints who refused to sign it.[36] The Utah legislature, moving opposite from the earlier proposed, but failed, Evans bill, made unlawful cohabitation a felony and compelled all but the accused to testify.[37] Mormon officials authorized surveillance of suspected pluralists, urged their prosecution, denied church welfare assistance to their families, and advised that their children not be baptized until old enough to repudiate "the principle that gave them birth."[38] As Martha Bradley has shown, even private discussion of plural marriage became grounds for suspicion.[39]

Church leaders both assisted with and publicly applauded a mass arrest in 1944 designed to jail Utah polygamists and choke off the printing of *Truth* magazine. The publication was described as "obscene, lewd, lascivious, indecent, and immoral" because it advocated plural marriage.[40] Apostle Mark E. Peterson prepared a special statement admitting the church was giving assistance to the state in its prosecution of the accused polygamists. Peterson insisted that neither the fundamentalists nor their practices should be thought of as "fundamental" to the Mormon Church.[41] The *Deseret News* commenced a policy of consistently referring to polygamist adherents as "cultists," a tag reminiscent of the label used to denigrate Mormons themselves near the beginning of the century.[42]

Because national laws aimed at polygamy were applicable only to territories, it was necessary to show the accused individuals had transported their plural wives across state lines for "immoral" purposes, convicting them under the federal government's Mann Act. When the conviction was upheld on appeal to the United States Supreme Court, Justice William O. Douglas justified application of the federal law and its concern with commercialized sex to contemporary Mormon fundamentalists by citing those cases in which the church had been a losing party in the nineteenth century. Plural households, he repeated, were a threat to the community, to Christianity, and to civilization. The state had an interest, he declared, in protecting itself from regressions to "barbarism." His single concession to the convicted men was to say at the outset of his opinion that Mormon fundamentalists were those who practiced what other Latter-day Saints only believed.[43] Sent to jail, the convicted pluralists proved to be model prisoners and were given early parole on promise they would not resume their polygamous ways. Most promised. After the example of earlier Mormons, however, they quickly relapsed to regard for a higher law.[44]

The most celebrated episode of this kind occurred when the Arizona National Guard was used against fundamentalists in the rural settlement of Short Creek (since renamed Colorado City), just south of the Utah-Arizona border. The church had been involved in excommunications and other harassments of families there since the mid-1930s. With Mormon approval and support, along with detective work underwritten by a secret appropriation by the Arizona state legislature, Governor Howard J. Pyle planned a surprise assault on the town, which he said was a nest of white slavers. Word of the attack leaked out, however, and when the armed column of national guardsmen, law enforcement personnel, judges, doctors, nurses, and journalists arrived at 4:00 A.M. on 26 July 1953, the community's inhabitants were already assembled, peacefully raising the flag and singing "America." Despite their docility, residents were arrested, the town placed under marital law, and road blocks, field kitchens, and medical facilities erected. Men were jailed while women and children, under direction of the state's welfare agency, were relocated with foster families, many in orthodox Mormon homes.[45] Although some Arizona officials condemned the raid as farcical, the church's official publication, the *Deseret News,* approved the action as necessary for eradicating a "smudge" on the reputations of Utah and Arizona. The polygamists, it said, were a "cancer" on society.[46]

Subsequently, a plural wife from Short Creek residing in Utah was forcefully separated from her children by court order. The action was taken on grounds that the youngsters were being raised in an immoral environment and that their parents' polygamy was contributing to the delinquency of minors. Again, the *Deseret News* editorialized in support of the decree.[47] The church's stance soon began to try the respect of members themselves, however. The best-known example was the Utah historian Juanita Brooks. She condemned the taking of children from parents as inherently wicked, reminiscent of the treatment of slave families in the early republic, and the more shocking in this case because of church endorsement.[48] The only unfamiliar element in all this was the confederacy of official Mormonism with those attacking the principle. The most that can be said is that, since the 1960s, there has been a clear and seemingly purposeful decline in the number of prosecutions brought against polygamous fundamentalists living in Arizona and Utah.[49]

This is not to say feelings and arguments of earlier years were nowhere to be found among orthodox, twentieth-century church members themselves. The son of a Mormon pluralist recalled how shortly after World War I an older brother and sister of his, both tall and muscular, witnessed an outsider lecturing a crowd in Salt Lake City on the weakening effects of polygamy. The children of such unions, said the speaker, degenerated into little African-like people. Outraged, the brother and sister stepped to the front of the crowd, identified themselves as "polygamists," and asked the speaker to judge if they looked like "pygmies."[50] Brigham H. Roberts, for whom plural marriage was an old and favored cause, in his 1930 history of the church could yet say that the primary consideration in the Mormon polygamic system had been "race culture"; that the revelation commanding the practice was accepted as a "divinely ordered species of eugenics"; and that it was implemented as a means for revealing man's potential, "that the day of the super-man might come."[51] Annie Clark Tanner, after a life of disappointment as a polygamist wife, commented in 1941 that she yet heard it said that "all the headaches and heartaches caused by polygamy" were, to some degree, "compensated by the fine eugenic results."[52]

At a more private level one could encounter the old arguments in rather high places. The president of the Quorum of Twelve Apostles, Rudger Clawson, at a birthday party in the late 1920s, stated that he still believed plural marriage to be a true principle. The only reason it was "obnoxious" to the rest of the world, he said, was because they had been taught only in the tradition of monogamy.[53] And in a letter remarkable for its candor, Leah Eudora Dunford Widtsoe, wife of Apostle John A. Widtsoe, described to a Mormon convert some of plurality's advantages. If parenthood was accepted as life's primary goal, one could not ignore implications arising from the fact that men retain their reproductive abilities much longer than women. Nature, she said, therefore clearly endorsed the plural system. Then, referring to her own circumstances, Mrs. Widtsoe said that she and her husband had raised only daughters to adulthood. There were no sons to perpetuate her husband's name. His only brother had also died, leaving only daughters. Mrs. Widtsoe said she would have to overcome "selfishness" but would gladly try if her husband should take another wife to remedy the situation. It was more difficult, she said, "to know that his name, which he has done so much to honor, and his seed, must die out from the records of our Church forever." Of course, she added, the Manifesto had removed polygamy as a requirement in their time.[54]

But these are frail reminders. The status of the 1890 Manifesto as a divinely revealed, binding directive seems more secure than ever. Not only does it remain in force, interdicting polygamous marriage, but because of its presence in the *Doctrine and Covenants,* it shadows the 1843 revelation authorizing the principle. And that communication, section 132 of the canon, is now read by Mormons to connote, quite exclusively, that a monogamous union, sealed in the temple, constitutes celestial marriage. A private compilation of Mormonism's holy sayings also includes the 1904 "Official Statement" by President Joseph F. Smith, arranging it into verses, granting it the appearance of scripture.[55] The church's historical experience with plural marriage is almost always explained simply as the result of divine command. And by divine command it was suspended. Except for an occasional reference suggesting that it helped care for a presumed excess in the number of women in the church, its redeeming social and biological purposes receive no mention.

At the same time, and with some irony, the Saints' growing attachment to monogamy finds itself challenged by increasing numbers of non-Mormon voices favoring experiment with polygamy. Medical and psychological considerations are now given as reasons recommending plurality to elderly citizens. Not only is it said that polygamy would provide companionship for the large number of older females but it is suggested that it would contribute to improved health for both older men and women, bring a higher standard of living to their lives, diminish psychiatric problems, and lower insurance costs. Mormon fundamentalists, of course, have been quick to seize upon such claims, citing them as evidence that arguments made by Latter-day Saint defenders in the nineteenth century were correct—however forgotten and ignored by orthodox, monogamous members today.[56]

These views are complemented by a growing sense that the *Reynolds* decision must be qualified, if not overturned. Extension of the First Amendment's "free exercise" clause to an increasing number of activities, breaching the old division between belief and action, forecasts eventual decriminalization of the practice. Justice Douglas himself, spokesman for the court in the 1946 case upholding the conviction of polygamous fundamentalists, in a later dispute delphically proclaimed: "*Reynolds* will be overruled."[57] The freedom to marry is acquiring growing support as a constitutional right. G. Keith Nedrow is especially persuasive in contending that this must allow men and women who wish to do so to legally enter plural relationships. He and others further make the point that there is no evidence either that children are disadvantaged in such households or that pluralists make bad citizens. When combined with a frank recognition that nature does not necessarily prescribe monogamy, that indeed large segments of the world's population have and do yet practice polygamy, the nation's democratic social philosophy demands legal tolerance for this alternative life-style.[58]

Not only do such views resemble those adduced by the Saints a century ago but the change is given greater profile by contemporary Mormons who say *Reynolds* is best left in place as a guarantor for what is perceived as the cement of civilization—the traditional family![59] In a way, Mormonism finds itself again breasting the dominant cultural tide. Paul L. Murphy defined the nation's attitude in the nineteenth century as one in which rebellious behavior was permitted so long as there was orthodoxy of belief. And, conversely, differences of belief were permitted so long as personal behavior was orthodox.[60] Because they erred on both counts, citing conscience and God for their aberrant deeds, Mormons offended. Having conformed, the Saints must now contend with a larger society that has moved again. Modern reformers find more that is friendly in the old church, with its strong pleas for private liberty, than with those guardians of the monogamous order who preside in the new.

Mormon insularity is made more awkward by changes undertaken by the Reorganized Church of Jesus Christ of Latter Day Saints—a traditional enemy of the plural arrangement. Although the Reorganized Church looked upon the Manifesto as a triumph, and the issue of succession tended to replace polygamy as the major difference between the denominations, both churches continued to tilt at one another over the question of whether Joseph the prophet had or had not taken plural wives.[61] Reorganite insistence that no children could be found as evidence of the prophet's alleged alliances elicited, with few exceptions, rather weak responses from Utah. Some Mormon authorities, for example, suggested that because the times were so agitated, the women Joseph Smith visited were too nervous to conceive. Mormon president George Albert Smith reasoned that the prophet himself, "harassed and hounded," was unable to make connections with his plurals at the right times of month.[62]

The evidence for personal involvement by Smith and others in the principle was, nevertheless, overwhelming. Consequently, RLDS apologists cast as widely as possible for support. Considerable time was unsuccessfully devoted to an attempt to prove that Brigham

Young invented the entire system after reading the *Thelypthora* in a Manchester, England, library. Handwriting in the library copy turned out not to be that of Young, however, and the prospect for driving what was called, in a later context, "another nail in the Brighamite casket" was lost.[63] Disagreements continued until mid-century, with the RLDS president, Israel A. Smith, referring to arguments for the church founder's polygamy as the work of "twisting Utah historians."[64] The Utah Mormon Preston Nibley insouciantly told Smith: "This polygamy business seems to worry you people a great deal. Why don't you accept the facts as we do and stop worrying about it?" Smith responded: "'This polygamy business' ought to worry every Mormon dug out of its pit."[65]

It was less remarks like those of Nibley than evangelizing efforts in third-world nations that led to altered policies. As the result of both revelation and conference approval, but only after considerable debate, the Reorganized Church decided in the early 1970s to accept the baptism of polygamist converts from eastern India. Monogamy was yet the rule of the church, and further polygamous marriages after baptism would result in expulsion. But like other Christian denominations, where similar recommendations were being made, it was decided to receive plural families of non-Western cultures into their communion, while teaching monogamy in kindness and love.[66] This not only reversed the historical positions of these two churches but left Utah Mormons, in their own missionary efforts, occupying the almost identical ground and endorsing the almost identical policies of those they so harshly criticized for intolerance during the anti-polygamy crusade.[67]

The refitting of Mormonism's image recalls observations by Mark Leone and R. Laurence Moore. The church's assimilation into twentieth-century society, they suggest, required a forfeiture of memory. They believe the Saints never to have been far from the nation's own middle-class values. Most of what separated them were apologetics cultivated by the church to confirm its identity. Once this "rhetoric of deviance" was set aside, Mormonism's native resemblance to the larger society was apparent.[68] Related to this, conscious or unconscious, residual or imported, was the presence of Mormonism's own equivocation between monogamous and polygamous sentiment. However insistently they may have defended plurality and however persuasive the rationale used to justify it, Mormon men and women contended with emotions that were probably little different than if they had been Presbyterians. Such uncertainty made the movement away from polygamy both quicker and easier.

As Kenneth M. Stampp has argued regarding the South, indetermination and self-doubt so laced southern personal feelings about slavery that it maimed the Confederate will, contributing to both the outcome of the Civil War and the adjustments made in southern attitudes after it was over.[69] Mormonism, like the South, emerged from its struggle displaying more pronounced similarities than differences with the values of its former enemy. Just as the old apologies for slavery, both scriptural and scientific, were quickly set aside, so Mormonism has turned its memory away from the arsenal of proofs it assembled to support patriarchal marriage.[70] A selective aphasia, arising from social and psychological forces, has undoubtedly made it easier for many Saints to bridge the two centuries of their church's existence.

In like manner, so has sublimation. Attempting to salve believers concerning the Manifesto, George Q. Cannon once told them that limitations brought by the document would not interfere with their exaltation, for God judged men by the intentions of their hearts.[71] If this contradicted what had been said before and threatened church members with the treacheries of a morality conflicted by opposing religious ideals, it also made it easier to graduate polygamy's practice to another life. As with communitarian economics, which, although doctrinally respected, slumbers in incubation, plural marriage is coated with the chrysalis of a spiritual ideal and laid away for rebirth in a world beyond time. The modern Latter-day Saint, relieved of responsibility for living it, need only believe in his heart that he will be equal to the task when, once again, God requires it of the faithful.

But even heaven is not immune from changes on earth. The close, reflexive relationship existing between this life and the hereafter has been observed since at least the time of the ancient Greeks. To the present day, one of Mormonism's best-known features is its isomorphic appropriations of matter and spirit, heaven and earth. As a Latter-day Saint writer recently asserted, life in this world is a facsimile of what one can expect in the next. Heaven "will be a *counterpart* of all the most desirable activities and things mankind enjoyed while on earth." And the chiefmost of these in Mormon thought is the family. "The family here is *in similitude* of the family there."[72] In the first discussion undertaken by Mormon missionaries with prospective converts, there is a focus on the eternal nature of the family unit. Church-produced films, television, and radio programs grant a dominant role to family subjects. Unlike Joseph Smith, who often delayed giving the blessings of the sealing ordinance to husbands and wives, young couples are now urged to commence marriage by cementing their union forever with such rituals. As another Mormon writer explained, "The highest immortality is a family affair."[73] So much attention is given to family life as central to man's purpose in the world, along with its role as a vehicle for transporting him to the next, that at least one Latter-day Saint fears it is overburdened with expectation, that Mormonism has fallen victim to "familyolatry."[74]

This emphasis on the transcendent nature of domestic relationships seems to emerge from what McDannell and Lang found to be a commanding theme in the idea of heaven since the Renaissance—humanization of the next world. While some find this an encroachment of the profane, it can also be interpreted in the opposite way, as a suffusion of the divine, a sacralizing of the secular. Mormonism is only the foremost expression of a Western drift toward apotheosization of the family as the central feature of existence both before and after death.[75] We observed early in this study that Mormon projection of domestic relationships and affections into heaven mirrored contemporary sentiments in Romantic thought. Appropriating those expectations in their own way, the Saints answered the social perplexities of their era and the challenges of immense continental space with the potency of patriarchal dominion and plural marriage. Secured against time through ritualized sealings and energized by the alleged tonics of the plural arrangement, Mormon teachings offered health now and a promise to fill the universe with life and order hereafter. As Thomas F. O'Dea explained, plural marriage made reproductive sexuality the key to progress through eternity.[76]

Given Mormonism's return from a polygamous to a monogamic ethic, we might reasonably look for an installation of these new manners into the domestic circles of the gods. Reference has already been made to the essay by Eugene England directly challenging the ideal of patriarchal polygamy, favoring an exclusive, romantic monogamy.[77] Beyond this, the women's movement has led to greater emphasis on and attention to female stature in the Mormon parental dyad. There is increasing reference to "Mother in Heaven" and, reciprocally, to the nurturing role of fathers. The sealing ritual in Mormon temples has been changed to relieve brides from taking an oath of obedience to their husbands. Sex between married partners is approved as a non-reproductive resort for comfort and affection. Sexual desire in women is not only acknowledged but said sometimes to be greater than that in men.[78] Those formidable masculine powers called forth by Mormonism's nineteenth-century environment have yielded to twentieth-century urban society's craving for the reinforcements of sexual love and intimacy. If the replicative process between terrestrial and celestial spheres holds, even heaven may not long remain a preserve for the polygamous, Abrahamic household.

These developments infer changes of an even more profound nature. The transformation of romantic love and domestic enclosure into a kind of religion, one that Karen Lystra suggests aspired to a parity with love for God, was part of the late Victorian world view—a view intensely partial to the private, emotionally self-absorbed family.[79] As a consequence, Mormonism's embrace of monogamous values may have imported tendencies for which it did not bargain. As Lawrence Birken contends, the industrialized West has moved inexorably toward a value system of consumerism, or desire. Inherent in the ideology of nuclear, monogamic relationships of the late nineteenth and early twentieth centuries was an accreditation of pleasure, elevating the importance of affective reward. Validated by the hallowed regard for democracy and a shift from productionist/reproductionist to consumerist/pleasure-affirming goals, Western society is well advanced in its erosion of most traditional hierarchies. Paternalism generally, including the long-accepted subordination of children, is rapidly moderating. Personal reward is exalted in everything from the economy to religion. The hierarchical family is yielding to a pleasure-affirming, voluntaristic association of friends.[80] While this is a process yet fully to unfold, Diane Johnson's comment is appropriate: "Mormons can see in what the rest of American society is becoming what may await them too."[81]

The reconstruction of Mormonism's domestic ideal, nevertheless, remains a remarkable passage. Little more than a hundred years ago, the Saints were certain that plural marriage was both a revelation and a social necessity. It acted as a nexus for Latter-day Saint belief concerning Deity, priesthood, and the family. Along with Mormonism's theocratic tendencies, it was a major source for conflict between Gentile and Saint, posing as a decades-long obstacle to statehood for Utah. It was considered part of Mormonism's restorationist commitment, essential to the church's vision of its role as renovator of the earth. It revealed what was believed to be the patriarchal pattern of heavenly social organization. By the third and fourth decades of the twentieth century, however, official Mormon views were close to those of their erstwhile adversaries. Confronted by an obstreperous remnant determined to keep the principle alive, the church's leaders displayed even greater energy defending the monogamous way. Time's sprocket moved the contenders round until, in many ways, they seem to have exchanged fields.

All history is a palimpsest. The number of tracings is so great that none can ever be sure they have turned the last overlay or found the marking that reveals the tablet whole. The scholar's ever-refocusing glass assures revisions and rebuttals to eternity. If this study has given polygamy's track a brighter dye, it is a partial reading only, for the Mormon record, like that of all peoples, is susceptible to a multitude of renderings. However unlikely in any lasting sense, the author hopes to have imparted a heightened visibility to Mormon plurality and illuminated the trying passage of its decline. For, beyond the conceptual significance plural marriage enjoyed in the Saints' restorationist scheme, and the ordeal of halting subordination to which it was finally brought, we must remember there were thousands of devoted men, women, and children whose lives were given to its trial. The magnitude of that extraordinary aspiration, in emotional as much as other terms, justifies its claim to a place in the history of Western man.

By bending to a closer examination of the story's etching, we more fully recall its memory to a generation inclined to forget and a church that asked those once its heroes to stand down. Those pioneers, certain God was partner to their solemn covenant, praised by their leaders as heaven's own models, believed they had commenced the metamorphosis of mankind.

NOTES

1. Originally published in 1853, this letter to the Reverend William Crowel was included in later editions of Spencer's *Letters Exhibiting the Most Prominent Doctrines of the Church of Jesus Christ of Latter-day Saints . . .* , republished several times, in both Liverpool and Salt Lake City between 1866 and 1891. The 1889 printing, published by the Deseret News in Salt Lake City, is the edition cited here. Wilford Woodruff's accounts of time deposits made in the Salt Lake Temple are found in Scott G. Kenney, ed., *Wilford Woodruff's Journal, 1833–1898,* 9 vols. (Midvale, Utah: Signature Books, 1983–85), 5:75–76, 13 Aug. 1857, 6:53, 10 June 1862, and 9:194, 6 April 1892.

2. For a summary of Spencer's life, which ended in 1855, see David J. Whittaker, "Early Mormon Pamphleteering" (Ph.D. diss., BYU, 1982), 359–63. Brigham H. Roberts called Spencer's *Letters* a "New Dispensation Classic." *CHC* 4:118n.20.

3. Spencer, *Letters,* 248–49, 265, 267–68, 272 passim.

4. H. Grant Ivins gave this as one of the reasons he prepared his unpublished paper, "Polygamy in Mexico as Practiced by the Mormon Church,

1895–1905," typescript, p. 2, University of Utah Library, Salt Lake City. Also see the comments of Arthur B. Simmons, interviewed by Faye Ollerton, 14 Nov. 1935, Kimball Young Collection, box 3, fd. 46, Garrett Evangelical Theological Library, Evanston, Ill.; Anthony I. Bentley, interviewed by Jessie L. Embry, 27 April 1976, p. 8, POHP; Katherine Cannon Thomas, interviewed by Leonard R. Grover, 25 March 1980, pp. 7–9, POHP; Leroy Eyring, interviewed by Leonard R. Grover, 24 April 1980, pp. 9–10, POHP; Jessie L. Embry, "Interviewing Children of Polygamous Families: Does Oral History Only Produce Success Stories?" (Paper delivered before the Women's Oral History Conference, Denver, Colo., Nov. 1981), 4–5; and cases cited above, in chap. 8.

5. Eugene Campbell before a session of the American Historical Association, Los Angeles, Calif., 29 Dec. 1981.

6. Stanley Snow Ivins, "Notes on Mormon Polygamy," *Western Humanities Review* 10 (Summer 1956): 229.

7. Jan [JoAnn Barnett] Shipps, "The Principle Revoked: A Closer Look at the Demise of Plural Marriage," *JMH* 11 (1984): 65.

8. McClernand to Cleveland, 30 June 1887, as quoted in Edward Leo Lyman, *Political Deliverance: The Mormon Quest for Utah Statehood* (Urbana: University of Illinois Press, 1986), 66n.31.

9. Fawn M. Brodie, "Polygamy Shocks the Mormons," *American Mercury* 62 (April 1946): 399–404.

10. Perhaps the best-known recent scholarly treatments are the appropriate sections of Lawrence Foster, *Religion and Sexuality: Three American Communal Experiments of the Nineteenth Century* (New York: Oxford University Press, 1981); Louis J. Kern, *An Ordered Love: Sex Roles and Sexuality in Victorian Utopias—the Shakers, the Mormons, and the Oneida Community* (Chapel Hill: University of North Carolina Press, 1981); all of Richard S. Van Wagoner, *Mormon Polygamy: A History* (Salt Lake City: Signature Books, 1986); and Jessie L. Embry, *Mormon Polygamous Families: Life in the Principle* (Salt Lake City: University of Utah Press, 1987).

11. See, e.g., all of Brigham Young, [Jr.], "Shall the Mormon Question Be Revived?" *Harper's* 43 (16 Dec. 1899): 3–4; and Reed Smoot, "The Passing of Polygamy," *North American Review* 187 (Jan. 1908): 117–23.

12. James E. Talmage, *The Vitality of Mormonism: Brief Essays on Distinctive Doctrines of the Church of Jesus Christ of Latter-day Saints* (Boston: Richard G. Badger and Gorham Press, 1919), 220–33. Also see the parallel development of approval extended to Latter-day Saints in Jan [JoAnn Barnett] Shipps, "From Satyr to Saint: American Attitudes toward the Mormons, 1860–1960" (Paper given at the annual meeting of the Organization of American Historians, Chicago, Ill., 1973).

13. As examples, see the following: Franklin S. Harris, *Attitudes of the Latter-day Saints toward Home and Family; . . .* (Salt Lake City: Church of Jesus Christ of Latter-day Saints, [1932]); *Gospel Doctrine Sunday School Lessons . . .* (Salt Lake City: Deseret Sunday School Union Board, 1943), 74–84; Joseph

Fielding Smith, *The Restoration of All Things* . . . (Salt Lake City: Deseret News, [1945]); J. Reuben Clark, "The Perfect Earth Home," *DN,* 11 Feb. 1945; Charles A. Callis, *Fundamentals of Religion* (Independence, Mo.: Zion's Printing and Publishing, 1945); Thomas C. Romney, *The Gospel in Action* (Salt Lake City: Deseret Sunday School Union Board, 1949); Ariel S. Ballif, "The L.D.S. Family Organization," *The Latter-day Saint Family in Modern Society* . . . ([Salt Lake City]: Association of the Church of Jesus Christ of Latter-day Saints, 1951), 19 passim; William E. Berrett, *Teachings of the Doctrine and Covenants* (Salt Lake City: Deseret Sunday School General Board, 1954), 93–98; Gerrit DeJong, Jr., *Living the Gospel* (Salt Lake City: Deseret News, 1956), 185–200; William E. Berrett, *The Restored Church* (Salt Lake City: Deseret Book, 1965), 183; "An Era of Persecution," *My Kingdom Shall Roll Forth: Readings in Church History* (Salt Lake City: Church of Jesus Christ of Latter-day Saints, 1979), 53–60; "Home: A School for Eternity," and "Eternal Marriage—More Than Endless," *Preparing for Exaltation* . . . (Salt Lake City: Church of Jesus Christ of Latter-day Saints, 1984), 158–64; "The Eternal Family through Christ," *Ensign* 18 (Dec. 1988): 24–25; Gordon B. Hinckley, "The Order and Will of God," ibid. 19 (Jan. 1989): 2–5.

14. E.g., David J. Whittaker, "A Covenant People: Old Testament Light on Modern Covenants," *Ensign* 10 (Aug. 1980): 36–40; Dean L. Larsen, "Marriage and the Patriarchal Order," ibid., 12 (Sept. 1982): 6–13; Ronald K. Esplin, "'God Will Protect Me until My Work Is Done,'" ibid. 19 (Aug. 1989): 16–21; Robert J. Matthews, "The Fullness of Times," ibid. 19 (Dec. 1989): 46–51; Donald Q. Cannon, Larry E. Dahl, and John W. Welch, "The Restoration of Major Doctrines through Joseph Smith: Godhead, Mankind, and the Creation," ibid. 19 (Jan. 1989): 27–33; idem, "The Restoration of Major Doctrines through Joseph Smith: Priesthood, the Word of God, and the Temple," ibid. 19 (Feb. 1989): 7–13; and Kent P. Jackson, "The Abrahamic Covenant: A Blessing for All People," ibid. 20 (Feb. 1990): 50–53. The aversion displayed itself as complete silence on polygamous belief in an article comparing Moslems with Mormons. Mitch Davis, "Mormons and Moslems: Bridging the Gap," *BYU Today* 35 (Dec. 1981): 3–6. And in an account of nineteenth-century Mormon journeys to the St. George Temple from northern Arizona, despite the frequency with which polygamists were present in such pilgrimages, their identity as such was completely ignored. H. Dean Garrett, "The Honeymoon Trail," *Ensign* 19 (July 1989): 23–27.

15. Bruce R. McConkie, *Mormon Doctrine,* rev. ed. (Salt Lake City: Bookcraft, 1966), 577–79.

16. Guy C. Wilson, *Religion: A Way of Life,* Adult Department Guide and Manual 1933–34 (Salt Lake City: General Boards of the Mutual Improvement Associations, 1933), 54–57. Wilson, himself a pluralist, quoting from Mormon and non-Mormon sources, nowhere alludes to plurality as a desirable feature in his description of "the perfect man." For more recent examples, including use of scriptures, see Thomas S. Monson, "Heavenly Homes—Forever Families," *Ensign* 16 (June 1986): 3–6; Bruce C. Hafen, "The Family

and the Law," *BYU Today* 40 (Aug. 1986): 38; Gordon B. Hinckley, "Reverence and Morality," *Ensign* 17 (May 1987): 47; James M. Harper, " 'A Man . . . Shall Cleave unto His Wife': Marriage and Family Advice from the Old Testament," ibid. 20 (Jan. 1990): 28–31.

17. Ray Russell Canning, "Changing Patterns and Problems of Family Life in Provo, Utah, 1905 to 1955" (Ph.D. diss., University of Utah, 1956), 91–93.

18. John R. Christiansen, "Contemporary Mormons' Attitudes toward Polygynous Practices," *Journal of Marriage and the Family* 25 (May 1963): 167–70.

19. Carri P. Jenkins, "The Changing Family," *BYU Today* 44 (March 1990): 26–31, 42–43.

20. William K. Harvey, interviewed by Leonard R. Grover, 1 Dec. 1979, p. 13, POHP.

21. Leroy Eyring, interviewed by Leonard R. Grover, 24 April 1980, pp. 10–11, POHP; and Rose Eyring Calder, interviewed by Leonard Grover, 12 July 1980, p. 13, POHP, respectively. Also see similar comments by Zina Roskelley Bell, interviewed by Jessie L. Embry, 8 June 1976, p. 18, POHP; Abraham L. Stout, interviewed by Tillman S. Boxell, 5 Sept. 1978, p. 16, POHP; Rhea Hart Grandy, interviewed by Leonard R. Grover, 16 Feb. 1980, p. 17, POHP; Sarah Hendricks, interviewed by James Comish, 26 Jan. 1980, p. 14, POHP; and Winnie Haynie Mortensen, interviewed by Leonard R. Grover, 26 Jan. 1980, p. 21, POHP.

22. Hortense Young Hammond, interviewed by Leonard R. Grover, 15 March 1980, p. 6, POHP.

23. "Utah Liquor Chief Urges Effective Prohibition, at B.Y. Leadership Institute," *DN,* 27 Jan. 1937. Roberts's statement is found in *CHC* 5:298.

24. Eugene England, "On Fidelity, Polygamy, and Celestial Marriage," *Dialogue* 20 (Winter 1987): 138–54. Cf. comments by Joseph Michaels, "In Defense of Polygamy," *Sunstone* 14 (Oct. 1990): 6–7.

25. There is a vigorous and vocal minority contending for greater equality for the female sex in Mormon theology, church organization, and society. This is undoubtedly a harbinger of difficulties for the hierarchy in times to come. See the following as examples: Paul James Toscano, "The Call of Mormon Feminism" (Paper presented before the Mormon Women's Forum, Salt Lake City, Utah, 30 Nov. 1988); Lavina Fielding Anderson, "The Grammar of Inequity" (Paper presented before the Mormon Women's Forum, Salt Lake City, Utah, 30 Nov. 1988); Edwin B. Firmage, "Reconciliation," Monsignor McDougall Lecture, Cathedral of the Madeleine, Salt Lake City, Utah, 7 March 1989; Martha Pierce, "Reflections on God the Mother" (Paper presented before the Mormon Women's Forum, Salt Lake City, Utah, 7 Feb. 1989); Margaret Merrill Toscano, "Should Women Be Ordained?" (Paper presented before the Mormon Women's Forum, Salt Lake City, Utah, 8 June 1989); and the moving account of Amy L. Bentley, "Comforting the Motherless Children: The Alice Louise Reynolds Women's Forum," *Dialogue* 23 (Fall 1990): 39–61.

26. The interview referred to is contained in "A Chat with President Snow," *DN,* 30 Dec. 1899.

27. This was the revelation of 1886. See chap. 2 above. Also see the account in D. Michael Quinn, "LDS Church Authority and New Plural Marriages, 1890–1904," *Dialogue* 18 (Spring 1985): 28–29; and Richard S. Van Wagoner, *Mormon Polygamy: A History* (Salt Lake City: Signature Books, 1986), 190–91. No better introduction to the skirmishing between fundamentalist and orthodox Mormon over the issue of continued polygamy can be found than the exchanges between Joseph W. Musser and Apostle Joseph Fielding Smith in the late 1920s, reprinted in "Virile Correspondence," *Truth* 11 (Aug. 1945): 57–80. For more accessible reviews, see J. Max Anderson, *The Polygamy Story: Fiction and Fact* (Salt Lake City: Publishers Press, 1979), 128–47; Martha S. Bradley, "Changed Faces: The Official LDS Position on Polygamy, 1890–1990," *Sunstone* 14 (Feb. 1990): 26–33; and Ken[neth David] Driggs, "After the Manifesto: Modern Polygamy and Fundamentalist Mormons," *Journal of Church and State* 32 (Spring 1990): 367–89.

28. "Announcement," *Truth* 1 (June 1935): 1.

29. Examples of fundamentalist advertence to polygamy's eugenic advantages may be read in "Our Position," *Truth* 10 (March 1945): 268; "'I, Too, Am a Man,'" ibid. 10 (March 1945): 276; unpaginated foreword to Joseph W. Musser, comp., *Celestial or Plural Marriage* (Salt Lake City: privately printed, 1944); Lyn L. Bishop and Steven L. Bishop, *Keys of the Priesthood Illustrated* (Draper, Utah: Review and Preview Publishers, 1971), 321–24; Harold W. Blackmore, *All about Polygamy: Why and How to Live It!* (Hurricane, Utah: Patriarchal Society, 1978), 47–52; and Dorothy Solomon, "A Very Different Kind of Family," *Good Housekeeping,* April 1979, 246. For allegations concerning the Manifesto and President Heber J. Grant's supposed apostasy from traditional Mormon belief, see "Heber J. Grant Given Cause to Rejoice," *Truth* 1 (Jan. 1936): 101–2; "President Heber J. Grant and Polygamy," ibid. 3 (Sept. 1937): 49–56; all of Robert Newson, *Is the Manifesto a Revelation?* . . . (n.p., [1956?]); and Ogden Kraut, *Compromise and Concession* (n.p.: Kraut's Pioneer Press, 1977), 140–59. The most extensive effort to discountenance fundamentalist historical claims is Anderson, *The Polygamy Story.*

30. The relocation of Guy C. Wilson and one of his plural families to Provo, Utah, is told in A. C. Lambert, "Heber J. Grant Would Have Totally Ruined the Mormon Church," handwritten recollections of a conversation with Heber Grant Ivins, A. C. Lambert Collection, University of Utah Library. But cf. Guy C. Wilson, Jr., *Memories of a Venerable Father and Other Reminiscences* (Fullerton: Oral History Program, California State University, 1988), 105–6. For Grant's attitudes toward pre-1904 pluralists, see Hilda B. Farr, interviewed by Victor W. Jorgensen, 16 Jan. 1972, p. 7, Oral History Collection, California State University, Fullerton. Examples of President Grant's censure of those advocating and entering plural marriages are Heber J. Grant, "Concerning Marriage and Inspiration," April 1921, *Messages* 5:195–98; his comments at the April 1931 general conference of the church, re-

published under "President Grant," ibid. 5:292–300; and the reprint of these
and other remarks about polygamy in his very popular *Gospel Standards* . . .
(Salt Lake City: Improvement Era, 1941), 159.

31. Heber J. Grant, "Glimpses of 'Mormon' Life and Ideals," *Lloyd's of
America* 2 (May 1925): 23. Regarding the growing approval of Mormonism by
American audiences in these years, see Shipps, "From Satyr to Saint, 23–25.

32. "Official Statement," 17 June 1933, *Messages* 5:315–30.

33. D. Michael Quinn, *J. Reuben Clark: The Church Years* (Provo, Utah:
BYU Press, 1983), 179–86.

34. "Confession by Grant," *SLT,* 9 Sept. 1899. Charles Mostyn Owen, on
whose information Grant was indicted, described the matter in *Proceedings*
2:402–3. Also see Alexander, *Mormonism in Transition,* 66. For Grant's reservations at the time of the Woodruff Manifesto, his own post-Manifesto polygamous interests and defiant comments around the turn of the century, see
above, pp. 189, 342–43; and below at p. 375. The exchange with Judge John
W. Judd is recorded in Carlos Ashby Badger Diaries, 16 Jan. 1904, Church
Archives. Fundamentalist claims that in 1941 Grant sent a letter authorizing a
stake president to give permission to a certain church member to enter the
principle seems highly doubtful. [Gilbert Fulton and Rulon Allred], *The Most
Holy Principle,* 4 vols. (Murray, Utah: Gems, 1970–75), 4:88.

35. Heber J. Grant, as quoted by Ronald W. Walker in "Young Heber J.
Grant and His Call to the Apostleship," *BYU Studies* 18 (Fall 1977): 125.

36. See what appears to be a copy of the loyalty oath in box 12, fd. 13,
Stanley Snow Ivins Collection, UHi. Also see "Mass Excommunications,"
Truth 1 (March 1936): 114–21; "State Rests Case in Polygamy Trial," *SLT,* 11
Dec. 1935; and "Excommunications," *DN,* 29 March 1939. For commentary
on this as well as other church policies toward the fundamentalists, see Martha
Sontag Bradley, "Changed Faces: The Official LDS Position on Polygamy,
1890–1990," *Sunstone* 14 (Feb. 1990): 26–33.

37. "Unlawful Cohabitation," *Laws of the State of Utah* (1935), ch. 112, sec.
103–51–2.

38. See "An Official Letter," *Truth* 5 (Nov. 1939): 141–42; and Van Wagoner, *Mormon Polygamy,* 195–96.

39. Bradley, "Changed Faces," 31.

40. "Forty-Six Seized in Three-State Polygamy Drive," *SLT,* 8 March 1944.

41. The letter was reprinted in "The Mark E. Peterson Letter," *Truth* 10
(Jan. 1945): 207–8. Also see Van Wagoner, *Mormon Polygamy,* 197–98.

42. Examples of the church's employment of the term as a pejorative in
the columns of its official organ, the *Deseret News,* are both unvarying and
numerous. Following are a few instances only, selected from a single year:
"Cultists Lose in High Court," 6 Feb. 1945; "Cultists' Appeal Suffers Setback,"
6 March 1945; "Cultists Deny Trial Proved Any Polygamy," 1 May 1945;
"Cultist Case in Supreme Court," 25 May 1945. "15 Cult Members Begin
Terms in State Prison," 16 May 1945; "Cultists Deny Trial Proved Any Polygamy," 25 May 1945; "Cultists Case in Supreme Court," 9 Oct. 1945; "Freedom

Asked by Ten Cultists," 19 Oct. 1945; "Cultists Meet Pardon Board," 30 Oct. 1945.

43. William O. Douglas, in *Cleveland vs. U.S.*, 329 U.S. 14 (1946), at 16.

44. "Eleven Polygamists Win Paroles from Prison," and "Ten Cultists Sign Promise to Drop Polygamy Teaching," *SLT*, 27 and 30 Nov. 1945, respectively.

45. Accounts of the episode are provided in *Juvenile Delinquency (Plural Marriages) Hearings before the Subcommittee to Investigate Juvenile Delinquency of the Committee on the Judiciary, U.S. Senate, 84th Cong., 1st sess., Pursuant to S. Res. 62, Investigation of Juvenile Delinquency in the United States* (Washington, D.C.: GPO, 1955), 1–22; "Arizona: The Great Love-Nest Raid," *Time* 62 (3 Aug. 1953): 16; and Martha Sontag Bradley, "Women and the Raids: Short Creek, Arizona, 1953" (Paper presented before the Organization of American Historians, 26 March 1988, Reno, Nev.).

46. "Police Action at Short Creek," *DN*, 27 July 1953; "Arizona Solon Asks Short Creek Raid Probe," *SLT*, 14 Oct. 1953.

47. "Stamp Out Polygamy," *DN*, 28 Jan. 1956; "Children Suffer Most in Area's Polygamy Cults," *DN*, 19 Oct. 1956. The case is *In re Black*, 3 Utah 2d 315 P2d 887, cert. denied, 350 U.S. 923 (1955).

48. Levi S. Peterson, *Juanita Brooks: Mormon Woman Historian* (Salt Lake City: University of Utah and Tanner Trust Fund, University of Utah Library, 1988), 246–48. Also see "Too Many Wives?" *Newsweek* 46 (21 Nov. 1955): 98–99; and Van Wagoner, *Mormon Polygamy*, 205–7.

49. Regarding the decline in prosecution of polygamists, see the statement that, in both Utah and Arizona, fundamentalist polygamy has become a "dormant" issue, in "Town on Utah-Arizona Line Coy on Polygamy," *Los Angeles Times*, 24 Aug. 1969. Also see "State to Ease Campaign on Utah's Polygamists," *SLT*, 11 March 1962; "Polygamy, So What?" ibid., 19 June 1986; and Patrick Christian, "Feelings Run Deep in Utah Polygamist Custody Case," [Provo, Utah] *Daily Herald*, 9 Oct. 1988.

50. Lorin "Dutch" Leavitt, interviewed by Leonard R. Grover, 3 Jan. 1980, p. 6, POHP. See the similar experience described by Juanita Brooks in "A Close-Up of Polygamy," *Harpers* 168 (Feb. 1934): 299.

51. *CHC* 5:297–300. For examples of unofficial, and largely unconvincing, twentieth-century claims for the superiority of Mormonism's polygamous product, see Josiah E. Hickman, "The Offspring of the Mormon People," *Journal of Heredity* 15 (Feb. 1924): 55–68; Louis O. Turley, "The Affects [*sic*] of Plural Marriage upon the Present Membership of the Church" (M.A. thesis, BYU, 1950); and "The Fruit of Polygamy," in Mark Cannon, "The Mormon Issue in Congress, 1872–1882, Drawing on the Experience of Territorial Delegate George Q. Cannon" (Ph.D. diss., Harvard University, 1960), 135–38. A Mormon fundamentalist compilation of findings seeming to suggest that polygamous offspring are both socially and physiologically advantaged over monogamous ones is Knut J. Knuteson, "Science and Plural Marriage:

An In-Depth Study into the Scientific and Genetic Aspects of Plural Marriage," *Doctrines of the Priesthood* 6 (Jan. 1991): 1–43.

52. Annie Clark Tanner, *A Mormon Mother: An Autobiography by Annie Clark Tanner,* rev. ed. (Salt Lake City: Tanner Trust Fund and University of Utah Library, 1973), 23.

53. "President Rudger Clawson's Seventieth Celebration Held at His Home, Sunday, March 13, 1927," box 1, fd. 15, Rudger Clawson Collection, University of Utah Library.

54. Leah Eudora Dunford Widtsoe to Mrs. Picha, n.d., box 8, fd. 14, Widtsoe Family Collection, UHi. Mrs. Widtsoe's husband, Apostle John A. Widtsoe, wrote that not only had studies shown polygamous offspring to be above average physically and mentally but plural households were generally happier than monogamous ones. *Evidences and Reconciliations Aids to Faith in a Modern Day* (Salt Lake City: Murray & Gee, 1943), 310.

55. David M. Reay and Londa Lee Skousen Reay, comps., *Selected Manifestations: Being an Unofficial Collection of Temple Dedicatory Prayers, Revelations, Visions, Dreams, Doctrinal Expositions, and Other Inspired Declarations Not Presently Included in the Official Canon of Scriptures Known as the Four Standard Works of the Church of Jesus Christ of Latter-day Saints* (Oakland, Calif.: published by the authors, 1985), 163–64.

56. Victor Kassel, "Polygyny after Sixty," *Geriatrics* 21 (April 1966): 214–18; "Sociologist Sees Future Rebirth of Polygamy," *SLT,* 6 Nov. 1986.

57. William O. Douglas, in *Wisconsin v. Yoder et al.,* 406 U.S. 205 (1971), at 247.

58. G. Keith Nedrow, "Polygamy and the Right to Marry: New Life for an Old Lifestyle," *Memphis State University Law Review* 11 (Spring 1981): 303–49. Also see Harrop A. Freeman, "A Remonstrance for Conscience," *University of Pennsylvania Law Review* 106 (1957–58): 806–30; Henry Mark Holzer, "The True *Reynolds v. United States,*" *Harvard Journal of Law and Public Policy* 10 (1987): 43–46; Ralph Slovenko, "The De Facto Decriminalization of Bigamy," *Journal of Family Law* 17 (1978–79): 297–308; "Legalize Polygamy" *SLT,* 19 Feb. 1979; "ACLU Seeks Overturning of Polygamy Laws," *Sunstone* 14 (Oct. 1990): 63.

59. Mark S. Lee, "Legislating Morality: *Reynolds vs. United States,*" *Sunstone* 10 (April 1985): 8–12. Also see the contention that *Reynolds* is unlikely to be overturned, in Randall D. Guynn and Gene C. Schaerr, "The Mormon Polygamy Cases," *Sunstone* 11 (Sept. 1987): 8–17.

60. Paul L. Murphy, *The Meaning of Freedom of Speech: First Amendment Freedoms from Wilson to FDR* (Westport, Conn.: Greenwood Press, 1972), 16.

61. Charles Millard Turner, "Joseph Smith III and the Mormons of Utah" (Ph.D. diss., Graduate Theological Union, Berkeley, Calif., 1985), 405–28.

62. Harold H. Jenson to C. J. Hunt, 20 April 1946, copy, P22, fd. 41, RLDS Library and Archives, Independence, Mo.; G. T. Harrison to First Presidency of the Reorganized Church of Jesus Christ of Latter Day Saints, 16

May 1949, copy, P22, fd. 41, RLDS Library and Archives; [President] George Albert Smith to Glen Cargyle, 4 Oct. 1949, P22, fd. 41, RLDS Library and Archives; and the comments of Angus Cannon, cited in Turner, "Joseph Smith III," 454. These same explanations were discussed in the late nineteenth century. Thomas B. H. Stenhouse, *The Rocky Mountain Saints . . .* (New York: D. Appleton, 1873), 186. For the identification of polygamous children that Joseph the prophet may possibly have fathered, see Fawn M. Brodie, *No Man Knows My History: The Life of Joseph Smith, the Mormon Prophet,* rev. ed. (New York: Alfred A. Knopf, 1971), 344–47.

63. The phrase is that of Mark H. Siegfried, used in connection with the discovery of some inaccuracy in Utah writings about polygamy. Siegfried to President Israel A. Smith, 30 April 1949, P22, fd. 1, RLDS Library and Archives. Documentation for the *Thelypthora* project is found in P22, fd. 109, RLDS Library and Archives. A copy of the work, now in the Church Archives, seems first to have been given to Young by Samuel Whitney Richards in 1859.

64. [President] Israel A. Smith to Albert Embleton, 12 Feb. 1943, copy, P22, fd. 64, RLDS Library and Archives. For other examples of the continuing controversy, see J. F. Curtis, *The Polygamy Question Examined and Refuted* (Spokane, Wash.: privately printed, 1955); and the several pamphlets and inclusions in P57, fd. 4, RLDS Library and Archives.

65. Nibley to Smith, 21 June 1949, P22, fd. 1; and Smith to Nibley, 5 July 1949, P22, fd. 1, RLDS Library and Archives.

66. "Marriage in Relationship to World Mission," *Saint's Herald* 118 (Jan. 1971): 6, 61–62; "Special Report of the Council of Twelve," *World Conference Bulletin* (11 April 1972): 221–28; "Inspired Document," ibid. (15 April 1972): 264; "Official Minutes of Business Session," ibid. (14 April 1972): 265–68. Also see "RLDS Change Their Tune," *Sunstone Review* 3 (Nov.-Dec. 1983): 10; and "RLDS First Presidency Clarifies Polygamy Issue," ibid. 4 (Jan. 1984): 5. I am indebted to Mr. Donald Shaffer for assistance with this development in the Reorganized Church. For evidence of debate and recommendations of a similar nature in other denominations, see Eugene Hillman, *Polygamy Reconsidered: African Plural Marriage and the Christian Churches* (Maryknoll, N.Y.: Orbis Books, 1975).

67. For a statement by Jerry Cahill, director of public relations, that the church refused to baptize polygamous families in Africa, see Lin Ostler Strack, "Plight of the Polygamist," *Sunstone Review* 3 (June 1983): 9.

68. Mark P. Leone, *Roots of Modern Mormonism* (Cambridge: Harvard University Press, 1979), 194–226; R. Laurence Moore, *Religious Outsiders and the Making of Americans* (New York: Oxford University Press, 1986), 29–46. This same question was imaginatively addressed by Klaus J. Hansen in his "Epilogue: Mormonism and the Shifting Sands of Culture," *Mormonism and the American Experience* (Chicago: University of Chicago Press, 1981), 205–17.

69. Kenneth M. Stampp, "The Southern Road to Appomattox," in *Imperiled Union: Essays on the Background of the Civil War* (New York: Oxford University Press, 1980), 246–69. Also helpful in considering this parallel are the

observations made on Stampp's thesis by Peter Loewenberg, "Psychoanalytic Models of History: Freud and After," 39–41 (Paper presented to the Conference on History and Psychology: Recent Studies in the Family, Biography, and Theory, Stanford University, 7–9 May 1982).

70. It is important, in citing Stampp's thesis concerning the South and suggesting its applicability to Mormonism, that one distinguish, as did he, between slavery and racism. Slavery, as Stampp shows, was quickly set aside in theory as well as practice. Racism, of course, continued in all sections of the country. Stampp, *The Imperiled Union,* 263, 268–69.

71. "Remarks Made by President George Q. Cannon, . . ." *DN,* 14 Nov. 1891.

72. The quotations are from Allen H. Barber, *Celestial Symbols: Symbolism in Doctrine, Religious Traditions, and Temple Architecture* (Bountiful, Utah: Horizon, 1989), 51, 100. Also see Joseph Fielding Smith, *The Restoration of All Things,* 247; J. Reuben Clark, Jr., "Earth Home," *DN,* 11 Feb. 1945; and Boyd K. Packer, "A Tribute to Women," *Ensign* 19 (July 1989): 73. The Mormons are not peculiar in their projection of earthly family life into the hereafter. The World-Wide Church of God also says domestic relationships, including sexuality, will continue after death. "Sex the Big Risk?" *Plain Truth: A Magazine of Understanding* (April 1989): 3–6. For a provocative essay on implications of the Mormon closure of the traditional separation of matter and spirit, see Max Nolan, "Materialism and the Mormon Faith," *Dialogue* 22 (Winter 1989): 62–75.

73. Truman Madsen, "Distinctions in the Mormon Approach to Death and Dying," in *Deity and Death,* ed. Spencer J. Palmer (Provo, Utah: BYU Press, 1978), 69. On the gradual nature by which Joseph Smith inducted his followers into the sealing ritual, see Andrew F. Ehat, "Joseph Smith's Introduction of Temple Ordinances and the 1844 Mormon Succession Question" (M.A. thesis, BYU, 1981), 46–47.

74. Christian Ryder, "Familyolatry," *Sunstone* 10 (March 1985): 24–27; and Maurine Jensen Proctor, "Communicating the Church," *This People* 10 (Spring 1989): 23. But cf. "Mormonism Spotlighted," *Sunstone Review* 2 (Jan.-Feb. 1982): 9–10.

75. Colleen McDannell and Bernhard Lang, *Heaven: A History* (New Haven: Yale University Press, 1988), 313–22. Also see the work of Stephen A. McKnight, who has described the tradition of Western man as that of a spiritually aggrandizing terrestrial god. *Sacralizing the Secular: The Renaissance Origins of Modernity* (Baton Rouge: Louisiana State University Press, 1989).

76. Thomas F. O'Dea, *The Mormons* (Chicago: University of Chicago Press, 1957), 60.

77. England, "On Fidelity, Polygamy, and Celestial Marriage," discussed above, p. 340.

78. President Spencer W. Kimball, "The Lord's Plan for Men and Women," *Ensign* 5 (Oct. 1975): 4; Boyd K. Packer, *Eternal Love* (Salt Lake City: Deseret Book, 1973), 4, 6; idem, "Tribute to Women," *Ensign* 19 (July 1989):

72–75; Linda Wilcox, "The Mormon Concept of a Mother in Heaven," *Sunstone* 5 (Sept.-Oct. 1980): 14; Grethe B. Peterson, "The Mormon Concept of a Mother in Heaven: A Personal Response," ibid. 5 (Sept.-Oct. 1980): 16–17; the review of Sonia Johnson's *From Housewife to Heretic* in "Warrior in a Time of Women Warriors," *Sunstone Review* 1 (Dec. 1981): 25–26; "Is God Married?" ibid. 10 (Jan. 1985): 47; "Women's Rites: The Mormons Modernize a Supersecret Ceremony," *Time* 135 (14 May 1990): 67; Bruce C. Hafen, "The Gospel and Romantic Love," *Ensign* 12 (Oct. 1982): 64–69; idem, "The Family and the Law," *BYU Today* 40 (Aug. 1986): 36; and Brent A. Barlow, "They Twain Shall Be One: Thoughts on Intimacy in Marriage," ibid. 16 (Sept. 1986): 49–53. Also see the comments of Bruce L. Campbell and Eugene E. Campbell, "The Mormon Family," in *Ethnic Families in America: Patterns and Variations,* ed. Charles H. Mindel and Robert W. Habenstein (New York: Elsevier, 1976), 392–93. But cf. Romel W. Mackelprang, "Sexuality and the Mormon Family: Just Procreation or Pro-fun Too?" (Paper presented before the Sunstone Symposium, Salt Lake City, Utah, 25 Aug. 1990).

79. Karen Lystra, *Searching the Heart: Women, Men, and Romantic Love in Nineteenth-Century America* (New York: Oxford University Press, 1989), 227–58.

80. Lawrence Birken, *Consuming Desire: Sexual Science and the Emergence of a Culture of Abundance, 1871–1914* (Ithaca: Cornell University Press, 1988). Similar observations are made in Rowland Berthoff, *An Unsettled People: Social Order and Disorder in American History* (New York: Harper & Row, 1971), 396–410, 467, 477; Stephanie Coontz, *The Social Origins of Private Life: A History of American Families, 1600–1900* (London: Verso, 1988), 348–54; Steven Mintz and Susan Kellogg, *Domestic Revolutions: A Social History of American Family Life* (New York and London: Free Press, 1988), xv, 186–90; and the section entitled, "The Privatization of American Faith," in Robert Wuthnow, *The Struggle for America's Soul: Evangelicals, Liberals, and Secularism* (Grand Rapids, Mich.: William B. Eerdmans, 1989), 116–25.

81. Diane Johnson, "The Lost World of the Mormons," *New York Review of Books* 37 (15 March 1990): 31. In a recent article Armand L. Mauss suggested that Mormonism, increasingly wary of its assimilationist course, has taken steps to reaffirm a unique religious image. The return to polygamy, however, seems not to be on anyone's agenda. "Assimilation and Ambivalence: The Mormon Reaction to Americanization," *Dialogue* 22 (Spring 1989): 30–67.

Appendix I

Lying for the Lord: An Essay

Modern Mormonism's reputation for sobriety and honesty is prover-
bial. Latter-day Saint sermons are freighted with admonitions concerning the importance of upright, open dealing with one's neighbors. Like John Milton, Heber C. Kimball said that truth summoned
special powers of its own. There was, he said, no need for "any lies
being told, or of any misrepresentations being made."[1] The church,
like its Deity, said another leader, should use straight language. God's
words were "yea and amen, plain, pointed, definite, no two meanings
about them."[2] Those trafficking in deceit, warned George Q. Cannon,
lost the spirit of God as well as the trust of men.[3] "I do not care how
wise the man is, how long the prayer he may make, or how reverend
[*sic*] he may look," said John Morgan, "if he tells a lie, it is a lie, and
you cannot change or alter it."[4]

In early 1907 the First Presidency issued a major address in which
they specifically denied the use of duplicity in any of their dealings.
"Enlightened investigation," they said, had always been the goal of the
church. Again, in 1910, when the magazine crusade against new polygamy was reviving, an editorial in the *Deseret News* said that not only
had Latter-day Saints always been truthful but that they, of all people,
were most obliged to be so. They "cannot say one thing and do another."[5] Those adhering to the gospel must operate "in full light," said
Apostle John A. Widtsoe. "There is no secrecy about [Mormonism's]
. . . doctrine, aim, or work." The church, he said, had always fought
darkness, and, in its pursuit of knowledge, should let chips from "the
axe of truth" fall where they may.[6] A contemporary apostle repeated
these injunctions, declaring that there simply is "no justification for
lying."[7] And a member of the First Presidency, enlarging on the same
theme, warned that when one resorts to falsehood and deception,

even in behalf of a worthy cause, there is danger such practice will spread to other employments "like a disease that is endemic."[8]

Professions of this sort call into question the behavior we have seen attending Mormonism's contest with the world over polygamy. It is as if the church read from differing scripts. Depending on circumstances, Mormon authorities seemed to shift between registers of opposing values. So dramatic an inconsistency cannot fail to provoke inquiry. It fairly begs the scholar's attention.

Despite its declarations, Mormonism has always sequestered, in one way or another, a surprisingly large amount of its ritual and doings. The degree to which its revealments were connected with the occult in early America has been recently noticed.[9] Ceremonies associated with the endowment in Mormon temples have long been hidden and oath-protected. Council of Fifty gatherings were conducted in strict privacy.[10] In the nineteenth century men were chastised for publicly discussing what occurred in priesthood meetings and, early on, were told there were things best kept even from their wives.[11] Much of the discussion associated with reestablishment of the School of the Prophets in the early 1880s related to graded instruction for candidates at different levels of worthiness. Secret ceremonies were involved and initiates were told not to reveal what was said.[12] Deliberations and accounts by the church's highest leaders remain unavailable to the public to the present day.

These and other concealments suggest not only an equation between the secret and the sacred but an essentially defensive psychological posture. While this undoubtedly acted, as David Brion Davis pointed out, to confirm the worst suspicions of their enemies, it also strengthened the Mormon sense of community.[13] Church members' secrets set them apart from the world, sealed them up to one another through things arcane, and fortified them in their confidence that they were the special friends of God.[14]

We saw how church leaders at the time of Joseph Smith withheld knowledge concerning polygamy not only from the general public but from many of their own followers. There seems always to have been a special sensitivity about the subject—perhaps because rumor concerning sexual misconduct nagged the church with such stubbornness from its beginning. A month before he was killed, the Prophet Joseph Smith admitted that it seemed he had been married little more than five minutes to his wife Emma before it was charged that he had plural wives. Talk of spiritual wifery and adultery so plagued the church, he said, that "a man dares not speak or wink, for fear of being accused" of such things.[15] At the same time, the fact of plurality on the part of Joseph and his associates and the coloring of truth in connection with it has been reported by almost every student of the period.[16]

Outright denial was but one of several strategies employed. Declarations of fidelity to law, disapproval of those who married too quickly after the death of a first wife, and expressions of outrage when accused of departures from traditional morality were also used to obstruct an open view of what was happening.[17] Statements denying plurality were phrased either to permit more than one interpretation, or to avoid directly disallowing the possibility of such marriages if correctly authorized.[18] Words like *priesthood, sealing, giving counsel,* or urging attention to the parable of the talents carried special meanings for the initiated.[19]

Some have explained that the Saints properly condemned "spiritual wifery" or John C. Bennett's "secret Wife system." These were not the same, it is argued, as "plural marriage" or "celestial marriage"—what Mormon leaders actually preached. It has also been said that, in those instances in which Joseph and others denied that "the church" was teaching plural marriage, they were correct. Most of the general membership were unaware of what was happening, it had not been made an official doctrine, and those practicing it were doing so by private permission only.[20]

Not only do such defenses ignore repeated denials that they were engaging in the practice under any name but there are grounds for believing that the term *spiritual wife* was, in fact, employed by Mormons both before and after their exodus to the Great Basin.[21] Beyond this, later in the century, as part of the skirmishing between Utah and RLDS Mormons, the contradictions were acknowledged and described as "very wisely drawn," as one of the evidences that plurality was indeed in vogue among those close to the prophet.[22] There is testimony that instruction was expressly given on how to conceal it.[23] And one must confront pretzled language like that of the prophet when, though husband to scores of women, he exclaimed, "What a thing it is for a man to be accused of committing adultery, and having seven wives, when I can only find one."[24]

Given the mobbings, dispossessions, and murders that were so often the lot of the Saints, there is good reason for tendencies toward enclosure. We earlier remarked on the sense of insecurity and the formative significance of such things in early Mormonism generally.[25] This undoubtedly explains why the prophet laid such store by loyalty and friendship. Joseph's instruction to the Quorum of Twelve Apostles in 1839, born of cruel experience, was, above all else, "do not betray your *Friend.*"[26] A connection between secrecy and friendship was made in 1841 when he said that the reason more "secrets of the Lord" were not revealed was because so few could keep them. This was followed, once more, by emphasis on the need to observe and honor friendship even to death.[27] Justus Morse told how, as a Danite in Missouri in 1838, he and others were directed to assist each other when in difficulty by lying, "and to do it with such positiveness and assurance that no one would question our testimony."[28] The greatest of evils, Joseph said in his 1839 address to the apostles, were "sinning against the Holy Ghost and proving a traitor to the brethren."[29] Mosiah Hancock remembered that the prophet spoke on the subject in Nauvoo, lamenting that he had been betrayed by some who were closest to him.[30] Given the perils and social complexities involved, it is easy to understand why dissimulation was used in protecting the church's polygamous affairs.[31]

Neither Mormon nor Gentile, it was sometimes said, was able to absorb a full disclosure of the truth. Not only had Saint Paul indicated that new converts must be fed a modified doctrinal diet, but Joseph Smith, in an early revelation, referred to his followers as "little children," unable to "bear all things now."[32] On other occasions he spoke of the inexpedience of telling all, of the non-written nature of some of his revelations, and the great difficulty he had in teaching things contrary to tradition.[33] Brigham Young remembered that, as early as in Kirtland, the prophet told him that if he was open about what he had received from heaven, "not a man or woman would stay with me." And Levi Hancock recalled that Joseph once remarked to him that if he were to reveal all God had shown him, his own followers would seek his life.[34] The sense of peril, if all were made public, extended to a concern for the entire Mormon community. "What would it have done for us," asked Orson Hyde later, "if they had known that many of us had more than one wife when we lived in Illinois? They would have broken us up, doubtless, worse than they did!"[35]

Mormon leaders undoubtedly found the deceit involved an onerous condition. This may be why the prophet counseled the Female Relief Society not to be overzealous in their search for wrongdoing and to be charitable toward the accused. He was especially aggravated by stories about adultery and the taking of spiritual wives.[36] Discomfort with holding a curtain to the eyes of Mormons themselves prompted Joseph to attempt, on more than one occasion, a cautious unveiling of the practice. This was certainly the intention, for example, with issuance in 1842 of the Udney Hay Jacob pamphlet.[37] It also explains the prophet's reminder to his followers that part of his mission involved a breaking down of superstition and a reformation of what was considered sinful.[38]

Polygamous activities by the leaders, and the deceit considered necessary to shelter them, contributed directly to the assassinations of Joseph and Hyrum Smith.[39] During the city council debate over allegations in the *Expositor* concerning his doctrines and behavior toward women, Joseph found it necessary to double back upon himself, declaring he had not kept the doctrine secret but had taught it openly.[40] It was nearer the truth a few months later when, raging against the proposal that it was yet necessary to hide things about the church, the prophet's widow told William Clayton that "it was secret things which had cost Joseph and Hyrum their lives."[41]

Dissimulation did not cease when the Saints moved west. Although greater freedom existed as early as their stay in Iowa, there was still reticence about their marriage philosophy, and secrecy was enjoined on participants.[42] In a well-known 1850 debate with Protestant ministers in France, Apostle John Taylor, although the husband of ten wives, denied that polygamy was practiced in the church, saying that it was a thing "too outrageous to admit of belief."[43] Orson Pratt, on call to publicly champion the practice, bent facts about it.[44] And many years later Charles W. Penrose admitted that, after the prophet's death, some things about him were deleted from church publications "for prudential reasons."[45]

So far as the practice of plural marriage in the Great Basin is concerned, Brigham Young once said that, while some told the outside world it did not exist, he refused to blanket the facts. "I never deny it," he said. "I am perfectly willing that . . . [non-members] should know that I have more than one wife and they are pure before the Lord and are approved in his sight."[46] At the same time, in connection with his theories of the godhead, Young said he withheld much of what he knew. And George A. Smith revived the theme of a filtered exposure for those young in knowledge of the Gospel. The majority of things sacred and binding on the Saints, said another, properly remained unwritten.[47] Emphasis on the importance of protecting friends also continued. In 1859, probably as part of an effort to obscure church connection with the Mountain Meadows massacre, apostles Amasa Lyman and George A. Smith fulminated against doubting members who "sought to betray and expose their brethren into the hands of their enemies."[48]

Referring to the charge that Latter-day Saints in Utah resorted to falsehood when asked about their marriage patterns, Richard Burton repeated their answer, saying they wished only to deny imputation of any similarity between the Mormon practice of "true patriarchal marriage" and the "spiritual wifedom," "free loveism," and "Fanny Wrightism" familiar to outsiders.[49] Claims that the generality of people were unprepared to accept all truths received by God's oracles continued to be made to justify Mormon reservation. And the turning of words or attribution of qualified meanings to certain passages of language was defended as communicating truth in a way that "those who had the spirit of truth could understand."[50]

When the national campaign against Mormon polygamy became intense, the use of non-truths spread rapidly to the larger body of the church. In his account of the legislative and constitutional extremes to which Idaho legislators felt they must go, John D. Hicks described those Mormon tactics that provoked the response. It was alleged, he said, that "when polygamists were prohibited from voting, the Mormons promptly swore that they were not polygamists; when those who taught polygamy were discriminated against, everybody immediately became silent on the subject; and when members of organizations which advocated polygamy were denied the ballot, they withdrew . . . from the Mormon Church."[51] Children were instructed to deny knowledge of family relationships, of their parents' whereabouts, and even of their own last names.[52] One church authority was so concerned about the pervasiveness of intentional falsehood that he feared for its effect on the moral fiber of Mormon society. In a letter to President John Taylor in 1887, Charles W. Penrose expressed concern that "the endless subterfuges and prevarications which our present condition impose . . . threaten to make our rising generation a race of deceivers."[53]

A revealing instance arising from such policies occurred when committee hearings were conducted on Utah's proposed 1887 constitution and accompanying petition for statehood. Franklin S. Richards, a Mormon attorney who counseled the church in legal matters and a son of Apostle Franklin D. Richards, worked with the territorial delegate John T. Caine to present Utah's case. In a series of letters from the nation's capital to the First Presidency, Richards explained that he felt great anxiety about the assignment because certain questions, if not answered carefully, could prejudice congressmen against them and there was already suspicion that Mormons were not to be trusted. He was particularly worried about queries as to whether plural marriage was a commandment binding on the Saints. There was also concern as to whether a compact could be struck between the church and the government—that is, to what extent could official Mormonism be made responsible for the polygamous behavior of private citizens in Utah.[54]

By careful design Richards and Caine were able to work their way around these issues. This involved taking an aggressive, rather than defensive, stance at the hearings, allowing them to head off difficult questions. Caine also read the 1843 revelation to the congressmen in such a way and crafted his answers to their inquiries so as to give a modified impression of the truth. He stated that plurality was not a commandment to the Saints and that "celestial" and "plural" marriage were not the same thing; and he treated the idea of a "compact" between the church and the government so that leaders could later deny they were bound by it. Beyond this, Caine denied there was any mistruth in Mormon statements, calling such charges "the merest balderdash." He also said polygamy was "a dead issue" in Utah and that it would not be revived.[55] Richards, at least, believed his answers to have been guided by inspiration and thanked the First Presidency for approving his conduct.[56]

Not all were happy with this approach. Speaking at a church meeting in Nephi, Utah, Apostle John W. Taylor branded Caine's statement on the death of polygamy a "d----d lie." If plural marriage were dead, he declared, "the whole religion was dead." More importantly, Taylor devoted most of his reported remarks to the error of employing mistruth as a defense. In the first place, he said, it was impossible to deceive the nation in such things. The Saints were sure to be found out. More importantly, honesty was also a part of the Gospel. Instead of prevarication, Taylor said, Mormon spokesmen should tell the truth and take the consequences. Rather than bending and deceiving, they should declare firmly for polygamy as a Mormon essential, leaving members to conduct themselves according to their own consciences.[57] Deception as a part of Mormon strategy was an issue of growing difference between Apostle Taylor and other church leaders. Referring to the time of the Smoot investigation, his wife Janet said: "John was considered a little out of harmony because he didn't like this way of doing. He was a frank man and didn't like to say one thing aloud and another in a whisper."[58]

Taylor's dissent is significant, not only as an echo of anxieties already expressed by Charles W. Penrose but because of its agreement with one of the major themes of this book: the consequence of pragmatic resort to distortion, the opposition of public statement to private fact, and the growing acceptance by church members themselves of claims that polygamy was entirely a thing of the past—a belief suc-

cored by conviction that their leaders would not lie. Taylor's objection
to the Caine statement made little difference, however. A month and a
half after his comment in Nephi, President George Q. Cannon was
asked at a special church meeting which of the two was correct, John
T. Caine or Apostle Taylor. Cannon answered that both were right. In
a legal sense, polygamy was dead. Ecclesiastically, however, the principle remained alive. Another authority illustrated the church's approach by saying that he no longer gave recommends for marrying
plural wives but gave them for obtaining whatever blessings the Lord
might bestow.[59]

It was hardly unexpected, then, that the Woodruff Manifesto was
probably drawn, and certainly interpreted, with ulterior purposes in
view. Mormonism's continued support for polygamy after 1890, and
the use of devices to obscure it, was but a perpetuation of styles long
practiced. There was a difference, however, in that after 1890 leaders
found it necessary to exclude not only Gentiles but many church
members from a knowledge of newly authorized plural contractions.
This returned the church to circumstances analogous to those under
the Prophet Joseph Smith in Nauvoo. Whereas all Mormons, polygamous and non-polygamous, might take umbrage from attacks on the
church's tenets during the crusade, after 1890 they were divided into
two classes of their own: those who believed the leaders' pretensions
about the abandonment of polygamy and those who looked upon
such statements as a hedge against discovery of the truth. As in the
Nauvoo period, those aware of these things had to reconcile them as
best they could. Franklin S. Richards once told Carl A. Badger how he
appropriated purposeful inconsistencies by his leaders. He put such
problems aside, he said, by considering the good and the noble men
and women in the church, as opposed to what he would forfeit by
rejecting them for their faults.[60]

However large their church's treasury of merit, some Mormons still
balked at the practice of deceit. In a 1903 letter from Wiley Nebeker
of Afton, Wyoming, to Apostle John Henry Smith, Nebeker said he
was troubled by the fact that, although the church made official statements that plural marriages were no longer condoned, he frequently
heard of men and women, some from his own area, entering the
principle. Rumors to this effect were so common that both members
and non-members in Wyoming talked about it. It was even said, he
told Smith, that some were specially called by apostles to continue the
practice. Nebeker went on to say that, while he accepted the divine
origin of plural marriage and believed it to be as true as baptism and
repentance, he could not condone a duplicitous policy that said one

thing while doing another. "To be plain," Nebeker wrote, "while I am fully converted to the belief that this is a true principle, I am not converted to the idea that the Lord justifies deceit and falsehood." Surely, he declared, if God wanted the practice carried on, it would be better to openly admit as much, "even if it brings persecution upon us, because then there can be no reproach—we will not be under the necessity of apologizing to our own consciences."[61]

Because rumors of the kind referred to by Nebeker were so wide-spread, he suggested that Apostle Smith use his [Nebeker's] letter as the basis for a public statement on the subject, possibly in the columns of the *Deseret News*. At the least, he asked for private explanation in the matter. Smith replied within the week. Unless there was a verbal exchange or other yet undiscovered communication between the two, the apostle's response illustrates the wall of disinformation leaders constructed around the practice of post-Manifesto plural marriage. Smith told Nebeker that not only was permission presently unavailable for anyone in the church to enter the principle but since the Manifesto no one had been authorized to undertake a polygamous marriage. There may be a few who were plurally married before the Manifesto who could yet be found living together, Smith said, but that was the size of it. The doctrine was true but the practice was forbidden out of regard for laws of the land.[62] Whatever Wiley Nebeker thought of this answer, it is clear Smith felt it best not even to address the central issue raised—dishonesty. Instead, by providing no more than an unqualified repetition of church denials, the apostle perpetuated it.

The pressure on those undertaking plural marriages in the post-Manifesto years was extraordinarily intense. Katherine C. Thomas, whose father, George Mousley Cannon, had married her mother as a polygamous wife in 1901, said she and her siblings were told not to ask their parents about their plural relationship. As a child she was instructed to conceal from others the identity of her father, and as a first grader in Salt Lake City she was required to attend school using a false name.[63] Anthony W. Ivins's son, Heber Grant Ivins, told of his dismay as a youngster when a church officer visiting with one of his plural families in the Ivins home lectured one of his children on the need to give a false name when asked by others who she was. Later, after he became an apostle and moved to Salt Lake City, another of Ivins's children, Florence, described how, following a meeting with fellow apostles and the First Presidency, her father seemed upset. When Florence asked her mother what the matter was, Mrs. Ivins confided to her that during the meeting President Smith had said he "would lie any day to save [his] . . . brother." Ivins—who, as we saw at the time of the Smoot investigation, had always opposed deceit—was shaken. Florence said that she believed her father troubled over President Smith's statement for the rest of his life.[64]

With the world divided into those for and those against, suspicions sometimes partook of an intramural character, infecting relationships between quorum members themselves. At the time of the Smoot investigation, when great care was taken to coordinate answers and cloak Senator Smoot with the appearance of ignorance regarding the polygamous activities of his colleagues, for reasons yet unclear one of the plural wives of President Joseph F. Smith referred to Apostle Charles W. Penrose as "a Judas."[65] Uneasiness also led some leaders to caution their colleagues not to write everything that was said and done in their diaries. Referring specifically to the journals of George Q. Cannon and Abraham H. Cannon, Joseph F. Smith feared their enemies might gain access to and use such materials against them. For this reason some urged that no private record of what transpired in their meetings be kept by individual apostles at all.[66]

Men engaged in what they believe are great causes naturally order the data of their perceptions to vouchsafe their dearest goals. This is not always a conscious process. As Wingfield-Stratford said in his discussion of John Richard Green, a well-known English historian captive to the whig-liberal myth, he was an entirely honorable gentleman "who would have rather died than lied deliberately." Yet his biases were so deeply felt that, although contradictory, what he found and what he read were made to fit neatly into the frame of an already accepted historical scheme.[67] In the early 1890s, when Mormon leaders were attempting to organize church members along traditional party lines, they once instructed their followers that political commitment was less important than the appearance of division itself. When asked if such an approach were not insincere, George Q. Cannon said sincerity was irrelevant in the present case. Without such division, he said, more unfriendly legislation was likely. And security against this, he urged, was of greater priority.[68] However disingenuous they may have appeared to an outsider, it is unlikely Mormon leaders sensed anything but righteous consistency in their defensive adaptations for so high a cause as plural marriage.

Matthias F. Cowley provides another illustration of how malleable, in threatened circumstances, traditional values can be. At the time of his hearing before the Quorum of Twelve Apostles in 1911, describing how he had performed post-Manifesto plural marriages when authorized by George Q. Cannon and others, he related the chastisement he once received for consulting too broadly in certain cases. He also spoke of the practice of pre-dating post-1890 plural marriages so as to make them appear to have occurred before the Manifesto. "I mention these things," he said, "only to show the training I have had from those over me." He might have added that they were but drawing on the teachings of others before them.[69] Yet Cowley did not view himself as a dishonest man. In what would otherwise seem a non sequitur, he told the quorum: "I am not dishonest and not a liar and have always been true to the work and to the brethren. . . . We have always been taught that when the brethren were in a tight place that it would not be amiss to lie to help them out." Then, in words remarkably close to those that troubled Anthony W. Ivins (and those remembered from an earlier occasion by Justus Morse), Cowley said he had heard a member of the First Presidency say that "he would lie like hell to help the brethren."[70]

In addition to a commitment to friendship, and the capacity religious intensity has for blurring moral boundaries, Cowley's statements draw our attention to another feature of the Mormon belief system. Church authorities from the time of the prophet Joseph Smith onward placed great stress on the need for "following the brethren." Because men and women were thought not able always to see as far and as clearly as their leaders, church members were told that, when confronted with doubt or difference, they should subordinate their judgment to that of priesthood superiors. As Brooks Adams explained when discussing early New England, the power of the ministry lay in parishioners' belief that religious authorities possessed vision unavailable to the common run of men. When this belief combined with suspicion that disagreement with the ministers' views had a better than average chance of being the work of the Devil, ecclesiastical authorities found enormous forces in their hands.[71]

These assumptions made it possible for Mormon leaders to claim that the Lord's servants ought properly to "dictate" not only "in the greatest and what might be deemed the most trifling matters" but to impose judgment as well. Men refusing calls to go on church missions, for instance, were once told they should expect to forfeit their wives for insubordination.[72] Utah's territorial governor, Arthur L. Thomas, spoke to this very condition. He said it had nothing to do with the Saints' ethical character; but because of Mormon belief in the inspiration of their leaders, if they should "be told to sign a declaration [that] they were Mohammedans and that the priesthood understood the matter and it was for the advancement of the cause and the glory of God, they would probably do it."[73]

Latter-day Saint precept, with its rich and contradictory texture, occasionally urged men and women to dissent from church leadership if they believed it morally wrong.[74] More often they were told not to criticize their leaders, not to openly dispute their judgment, and, as Brigham Young once put it, to remember that "sheep must follow the Shepherd, not the shepherd follow the sheep."[75] The Prophet Joseph Smith provided an example when, after being refused, he attempted to persuade Nancy Rigdon to become his plural wife: "That which is wrong under one circumstance, may be, and often is, right under another. . . . Whatever God requires is right, no matter what it is, although we may not see the reason thereof till long after the events transpire. . . . But in obedience there is joy and peace unspotted."[76] This feature of Mormon society was, and continues to be, often discussed and criticized.[77] At the same time, it has been an important reason for Latter-day Saint communal success. It lent its weight to the survival of polygamy when the principle was under siege. As one Mormon explained in accounting for his polygamous father's forthright practice of the doctrine: "You don't question things. If the church says it, you don't say yes or no, you go along."[78] Adherence that is willingly blind necessarily relegates truth to a lesser order of priority.

To these explanations must be added another. In the minds of some, their circumstance was entirely involuntary. The Saints had been brought to a condition in which they must be true either to their religion, with its requirements, or to their country, with, in their view, its unrighteous laws. This unwanted dilemma is what gave them cloven speech and manners. Anxious justification was clearly what prompted President John Taylor to declare in 1880: "Have we done anything covertly? Not until we were forced to."[79] Richard W. Young, a prominent Salt Lake City attorney and stake president, struggled with the same issue before the Smoot investigating committee in accounting for false denials in the early church. Although uncomfortable with such things, Young explained them as the result of "exigency" and "circumstances."[80]

Men yet living with plural wives, contrary to the law and after the Manifesto was interpreted as prohibiting it, were, said another churchman, like one having to pull his ox from the mire on the sabbath.[81] Henry S. Tanner explained it best. The promises made by the Mormons to the government, he said, were extracted by force. It was like a man seized by a powerful foe and compelled to say things ordinarily repugnant as the only way to obtain his freedom. Under such circumstances, Tanner stated, the words had no binding power. Consequently, the Mormons were as free as if they had made no promises at all.[82] By interpreting anti-Mormon laws as Satanic artifice in which the Saints had become involuntarily ensnared, those who continued to marry and live polygamously were forced to prevaricate as the only way of escape.

The Book of Mormon prophet, Nephi, once was instructed to take the life of another that God's purposes might be fulfilled.[83] With His help the Saints could outwit the enemy again. Verbal contortions might be inspired. Church leaders sincerely believed that God sometimes led them by a different way when important things were at stake. When Heber J. Grant astonished Judge John W. Judd by telling him that he did not intend to observe the laws prohibiting polygamous cohabitation, Judd asked about Grant's signed promise that, if given amnesty, he would keep such laws. The apostle was reported to answer "that that made no difference, [because] every man who signed had to make his election of the force of his signature."[84] This was close to the thrust of Apostle John Henry Smith's alleged remark that the Woodruff Manifesto was but "a trick to beat the devil at his own game."[85] Like the Shia of Islam, Mormons believed that dissimulation for the cause really was not wrong. Because they were compelled, by lying with mental reservation the faithful were yet in the service of the Lord.[86]

History is generous with examples of individuals responding in similar ways when caught in circumstances like those confronting the Saints. Not only were there instances in scripture, like Abraham, who had such resorts forced upon them, but in every war there have been cases when to lie was construed as an act of patriotism.[87] And what is to be said of the deceit surrounding circumvention of things like British taxes in the colonial period or the fugitive slave laws? Heber Bennion, recalling President Heber J. Grant to memory of the Mormon practice of false denial in the past, reminded him that, depending on the circumstance, it could be quite acceptable. If such behavior were to be categorically condemned, what of the countless fibs told to children in the interest of benign myth? What was to be done with Jacob lying to obtain Esau's blessing? And, he asked, what of President Joseph F. Smith's purposeful misstatements before the Smoot investigating committee?[88] These same considerations led Anthony W. Ivins's son Grant to plead extenuation in the church's behalf.[89] Given the high priority attached to the practice of polygamy, one can understand the lengths to which Mormon determination was carried in preserving it.

These arguments have been addressed before, however. In the nineteenth century Thomas B. H. Stenhouse noted that not only must the Mormons bear greater responsibility for their dilemmas than they were inclined to do but, said Stenhouse, "if once admitted to be justifiable, how frequently and to what other ends may [such resorts] . . . not be used?"[90] This was a cogent reminder and one often remarked before. It was the essence of Montaigne's warning that purposeful misrepresentation usually leads to corruption in other things.[91] And Thomas Hutchinson, on the eve of the American Revolution, cautioned that lying could be excused in behalf of immorality as easily as principle. In any case, he said, it was "a scurvy trick at best."[92]

It was confusing enough to some young Mormons that the worthiest in their communities would surreptitiously engage in polygamy, knowing it was against the law.[93] But to subscribe to a policy of overt deceit by arguing for its service to a higher end compounded the evil. It was this to which Carl A. Badger referred when, smarting with embarrassment over statements by his leaders during the Smoot investigation, he lamented that, if only the church had been faithful to the promises they had made and to the Manifesto, all the world would have admired their integrity. As Badger described it, however, church leaders had decided there were some things more important than honesty. The result, he said, was moral confusion.[94] One wonders if the same thing was in the mind of George D. Kirby in 1910 when, writing in the *Improvement Era* of allegations that Mormons were deceitful, asked if, after all, there might be "truth in the charges."[95] This again reminds one of the fears expressed by Charles W. Penrose and John W. Taylor.

Most fundamentally, what brought these trials upon the church was the decision to project only the *appearance* of compromise. As Senator Joseph Bailey said when interrogating Joseph F. Smith in 1904, given the alleged gravity of their attachment to the doctrine, he would have thought that, as Christians, Mormons would have gone "to the stake" before temporizing with plurality.[96] A policy of pretense once taken, however, casuistry, secrecy, and moral contradiction necessarily followed. And this, just as certainly, invited charges of hypocritical behavior. After the turn of the century, outsiders more than once observed that Mormon leaders consistently stood for honest policies—so long as their own affairs were not involved. As one gentile resident was reported to express it, "When any of us sin . . . we sin for our own sakes." But when a Saint crossed the line, it was done "for Christ's sake."[97]

In 1897 someone pretending to be a church member, calling himself "Juab, a High Private in Israel," wrote a sardonic response to remarks about continued polygamy and Mormon deception that were made at a meeting of Methodist ministers. "Juab" faulted the pastors for their want of heavenly guidance. Otherwise, he said, they could easily interpret the Manifesto and other cases of Mormon "inspired phraseology." Everything the Mormons said and promised about polygamy had been prayerfully and thoughtfully written. If they found such documents confusing or contradictory, the ministers simply lacked a discerning spirit.[98] It was the Saints, of course, that "Juab" mocked. In 1898 Theodore Schroeder published a blistering series of articles entitled "Polygamy and Inspired Lies." In these installments he cited instance after instance, from the time of Joseph Smith the Prophet to Schroeder's own day, illustrating the church's use of mistruth as a way to hide polygamy. In the end he asked the question historically posed by others: "How can we ever know that the reasons which prompted falsehoods once, may not be inducing falsehoods to be told again?"[99]

Much of the *Salt Lake Tribune's* ferocity in these years was fueled by disgust that Mormon leaders would, while claiming their church to be the Lord's special vessel of truth, so frequently corrupt it. In 1899 the *Tribune* sarcastically reported comments by a local bishop to the effect that it may be necessary to distort facts to get Brigham H. Roberts elected to Congress. This was justified not only because the full truth could be told later but because the hand of the Lord was "in it all."[100] While the paper's allegations were sometimes extreme, it is difficult to refute their insistence that it was nearly "impossible for a Mormon Elder to be a new polygamist without at the same time being a liar."[101] Sensitive to such statements, the leaders responded with denial, affirming their honesty again and again.[102]

The inventive capacity of Mormons intent on entering polygamy by some means that would preserve a measure of ethical redemption is impressive. In addition to semantic usages such as *union* and *sealing,* thus permitting denials of plural *marriage,* reference has also been made to instances involving the marrying of two wives on the same day; reliance on the fact that women were always sealed to men, allowing their husbands to deny that *they* had married polygamously; use of proxies; marrying a new wife legally, after the death of a prior legal spouse, while maintaining relationships with earlier plurals; the performance of ceremonies at sea or in foreign countries; and resort to concubinage.[103] The variety of ruses employed will never fully be numbered. Guy C. Wilson, Jr., remembered the case of a Mormon couple intending a polygamous marriage; when asked by the magistrate if either had been married before, the groom answered "yes." "But," he added, "she's in the cemetery." His first wife was indeed in the local cemetery, standing up very much alive.[104]

Last of all, the use of mistruth as a device for assisting the survival of plurality provided a nursery for those who continue in polygamy today. Mormon fundamentalism is at least partially a consequence of such tactics. Contemporary polygamists place great reliance on President John Taylor's 1886 revelation, given when he was in hiding from United States marshals. In the revelation those wishing to receive the highest glory in the hereafter were admonished to continue to live the principle in spite of pressures brought upon them to bring it to an end.[105] Subsequently, certain individuals were said to have been specially commissioned to keep plural marriage alive until the millennium.[106] Many of those who practice plural marriage today trace their authority to this alleged commission. Inasmuch as President Taylor was living "on the underground" at the time these events are supposed to have occurred, and because the supposed commission was given from expectation that opposition would continue, the movement took a resistance to disclosure from its infancy.

Citing Mormon history as precedent, fundamentalists defend the propriety of reticence and false denial when dealing with the things of God, especially plural marriage. The use of codes and ciphers when threatened by hostile laws is approved. The priority of covenants and friendships is affirmed. And when placed in difficult circumstances, they have broken pledges to civil authorities to secure freedom for themselves and their families.[107] Dorothy Allred Solomon, recalling her upbringing in a prominent fundamentalist home, summarized the atmosphere by saying, "Although we were reared to treasure truth and 'cling to the light,' our way of life was filled with secrets." The resort to distortion, what was referred to as "Mormon logic," rested uncomfortably on every aspect of their existence. She remembered that this was justified by her father, a fundamentalist leader, with the aphorism "We must sometimes disobey a lesser law to keep a higher one."[108]

An important aspect of fundamentalist apologetics is the contention that plural marriage was never condemned by the Mormon *priesthood*. A careful reading of denials and statements suspending the practice, it is said, reveals that they were done only in the name of the *church*. The difference between priesthood and church allowed men, they say, to truthfully claim the church, as an organization, had discontinued plural marriage and would excommunicate any found disobedient to its rules. Individual priesthood holders, on the other hand, might yet take new wives acting on their own responsibility.[109] In other words, the church may have abandoned polygamy, issued the

Manifesto, and placed violators in danger of losing their membership, but the priesthood held firm with the principle.

As earlier suggested, during the late nineteenth and early twentieth centuries some Mormons thought that the church could find in its status as an entirely private organization fence enough to shelter the practice.[110] Because it acted as the official voice of Mormonism, however, the church was too easily caught on the cusp of formal, juxtaposing roles. A preferred solution was found in separating the church, *qua* church, from individual priesthood holders, thereby double casting those who led and spoke for the organization. Such a construction met the need nicely, allowing church leaders to act at chosen times as corporate spokesmen and at others as individual priesthood bearers, alternating personas as circumstance required.

Precedent for such a division could be found at least as far back as President John Taylor.[111] Near the turn of the century, rumor circulated among some stake presidents that plural marriages were still possible if they were performed "by the priesthood" outside the country.[112] At the time of the Smoot hearings, Carl A. Badger recorded that he heard the church was not involved with polygamy. President Smith, however, as a priesthood authority accountable to God, could perform plural ceremonies.[113] And Apostle John Taylor in 1911 affirmed that, as he saw it, since the time of his father's 1886 revelation and certainly since the Manifesto and the 1890s, the Lord had "put everybody upon his own responsibility" and had taken "the responsibility from the Church."[114] It was this that led a son of Apostle Taylor, Samuel W. Taylor, to describe the contrivance as a conspiracy, a "big secret."[115] Until the time of President Heber J. Grant, the argument goes, such a distinction provided a workable cover. With the succession of Grant to the church presidency, fundamentalists contend, this exchange of dress ceased and official Mormonism, impatient with the exercise, became an entirely monogamous society.[116]

Fundamentalism, as a phenomenon, is far from peculiar to Mormonism. It commonly occurs when institutions move away from earlier belief patterns. Scholars who study the subject suggest that, more than an attempt to restore, fundamentalism always has dynamic dependencies on the present and that its complexity is such that boundaries and models used for explaining it are necessarily heuristic.[117] Mormon fundamentalism—sharing with similar movements elsewhere an anxiety about things such as the purity and binding power of inherited text, fearfully scouting the meanings of cultural accommodation, and hungry for more authentic, spiritual experience within traditional walls—displays as its most visible feature a remarkable pre-occupation with polygamy. As with the nineteenth-century church, it is the most conspicuous tenet of a majority of non-conforming Mormon groups.

To the extent that they are genuinely artifactual, these dissenters provide confirmation for one of the book's central themes—the prized regard developed by the old church for marriage in polygamy. And this high priority, when threatened by an unfriendly environment, explains the resort to shielding apparel, coded communications, secrecy, and misleading denial. Because of the church's sometime approval of these flections, alternating voices and faces in purposeful illusion, they assured today's following of fundamentalist actors who believe the play neither is nor should be at an end.

NOTES

1. *JD* 8:241 (Heber C. Kimball/1860).

2. *JD* 23:163 (Orson Pratt/1883).

3. *JD* 24:225 (George Q. Cannon/1880).

4. *JD* 20:286 (John Morgan/1880).

5. For the 1907 "Address," dated 26 March 1907, and its denials of Mormon deceit, see *Messages* 4:145–46. The *Deseret News* editorial is found in *DN*, 19 March 1910.

6. John A. Widtsoe, *Evidences and Reconciliations: Aids to Faith in a Modern Day* (1943; Salt Lake City: Bookcraft, n.d.), 62, 208, 213 passim.

7. Dallin H. Oaks, "Criticism," *Ensign* 17 (Feb. 1987): 69.

8. Gordon B. Hinckley, "We Believe in Being Honest," *Ensign* 20 (Oct. 1990): 5.

9. D. Michael Quinn, *Early Mormonism and the Magic World View* (Salt Lake City: Signature Books, 1987).

10. Klaus J. Hansen, *Quest for Empire: The Political Kingdom of God and the Council of Fifty in Mormon History* (East Lansing: Michigan State University Press, 1967), 56–65 passim.

11. JH, 7 April 1897; Brigham Young and Willard Richards to Reuben Hedlock, 3 May 1844, *HC* 6:352–53; and Helen Mar Kimball's comments in Orson F. Whitney, *The Mormon Prophet's Tragedy* (Salt Lake City: Deseret News, 1905), 37.

12. Merle H. Graffam, ed., *Salt Lake School of the Prophets Minute Book, 1883* (Palm Desert, Calif.: ULC Press, 1981), 6, 8, 9, 13, 15, 16, 17, 52, 55, 57–60, 66.

13. David Brion Davis, "Some Themes of Counter-Subversion: An Analysis of Anti-Masonic, Anti-Catholic, and Anti-Mormon Literature," *Mississippi Valley Historical Review* 47 (Sept. 1960): 211–14.

14. See the commentary in this regard by R. Laurence Moore, *Religious Outsiders and the Making of Americans* (New York: Oxford University Press, 1986), 37–38.

15. Joseph Smith, in *HC* 6:410–11; and John Jaques, "Polygamy . . . ," *Mill. Star* 15 (12 March 1853): 164.

16. See the citations for these many denials gathered by David J. Whittaker, "Early Mormon Pamphleteering" (Ph.D. diss., BYU, 1982), 368–69n.3. Also see *HC* 5:286; Robert Bruce Flanders, *Nauvoo: Kingdom on the Mississippi* (Urbana: University of Illinois Press, 1965), 268–77; Bachman, "A Study," 189–96; Samuel W. Taylor, *The Kingdom or Nothing: The Life of John Taylor, Militant Mormon* (New York: Macmillan, 1976), 85; Linda King Newell and Valeen Tippets Avery, *Mormon Enigma: Emma Hale Smith, Prophet's Wife, "Elect Lady," Polygamy's Foe, 1804–1879* (Garden City, N.Y.: Doubleday, 1984), 128–29; and Richard S. Van Wagoner, *Mormon Polygamy: A History* (Salt Lake City: Signature Books, 1986), 27–35 passim.

17. *Elder's Journal* 1 (8 May 1838): 43; *HC* 2:214, 4:585–86; "From the Boston (Mass.) *Bee*," *Times and Seasons*, 4 (15 March 1843): 143.

18. *HC* 4:582–83, 6:46.

19. William Clayton's Nauvoo Journal, 7 March, 27 April, 26 May, 16 Aug. 1843, typewritten copy in private possession; testimony of Jason Briggs, given in the Temple Lot case and reprinted in Joseph F. Smith, Jr., *Blood Atonement and the Origin of Plural Marriage: A Discussion* (Salt Lake City: Deseret News, 1905), 54; Benjamin Franklin Johnson, *My Life's Review* (Independence, Mo.: Zion's Printing and Publishing, 1947), 95–96.

20. James B. Allen and Glen M. Leonard, *The Story of the Latter-day Saints* (Salt Lake City: Deseret Book, 1976), 171.

21. For examples of those contending that the leaders' denials were in order when semantically understood, see "Be Not Led Astray by Deceivers," *DN*, 13 Dec. 1879; Joseph F. Smith, "Joseph Smith and Celestial Marriage," *DN*, 20 May 1886; Wilford Woodruff's testimony in *The Reorganized Church of Jesus Christ of Latter Day Saints, Complainant vs. The Church of Christ at Independence, Missouri . . . Complainant's Abstract . . .* (Lamoni, Iowa: Herald Publishing House and Bindery, 1893), 303; and Paul E. Reimann, *Plural Marriage Limited* (Salt Lake City: Utah Printing, 1974), 93 passim.

The employment of double entendre in connection with the practice of polygamy in the early church has long been noticed: Thomas B. H. Stenhouse, *The Rocky Mountain Saints . . .* (New York: D. Appleton, 1873), 194; JoAnn Barnett Shipps, "The Mormons in Politics: The First Hundred Years," (Ph.D. diss., University of Colorado, 1965), 99; Samuel W. and Raymond W. Taylor, eds., *The John Taylor Papers: Records of the Last Utah Pioneer*, Vol. 1 (Redwood City, Calif: Taylor Trust Publisher, 1984): 58–59.

For use of the term "spiritual wife" in Nauvoo and later, see the quotation from Ebenezer Robinson in Lawrence Foster, *Religion and Sexuality: Three American Communal Experiments of the Nineteenth Century* (New York: Oxford University Press, 1981), 177; Helen Mar Whitney, *Plural Marriage as Taught by the Prophet Joseph* . . . (Salt Lake City: Juvenile Instructor Office, 1882), 15; and Mrs. Benjamin G. Ferris, *Mormons at Home* . . . (New York: Dix & Edwards; London: Sampson, Low & Son, 1856), 114.

22. John Henry Smith to Joseph Smith III, 21 April 1886, P22, fd. 331; and Joseph F. Smith to Joseph Smith III, 3 May 1889, P22, fd. 47, both in RLDS Library and Archives.

23. Ebenezer and Angeline E. Robinson affidavit, 29 Dec. 1873, copy, P31, fd. 7, RLDS Library and Archives.

24. Joseph Smith, in *HC* 6:411.

25. See above in chap. 1, 4.

26. Joseph Smith, in *Wilford Woodruff's Journal 1833–1898*, ed. Scott Kenney, 9 vols. (Midvale, Utah: Signature Books, 1983–85), 1:344, 2 July 1839.

27. Joseph Smith, in *HC* 4:478–79.

28. Justus Morse affidavit, 23 March 1887, contained and discussed in John E. Thompson, "The Justus Morse Affidavit: An Examination of Its Historicity and Significance," and Michael S. Riggs, "'Because of My Oath as a Danite': A Biographical and Sociological Sketch of Justus Morse" (Papers presented before the Mormon History Association, 1 June 1991, Claremont, Calif.). A copy of Morse's affidavit was also printed in Charles A. Shook, *The True Origin of Mormon Polygamy* (Cincinnati: Standard Publishing, 1914), 167–71.

29. Joseph Smith, in *HC* 3:385; Autobiography of Mosiah Lyman Hancock, typewritten copy, p. 18, BYU Library.

30. Mosiah Hancock, "The Prophet Joseph—Some of His Sayings," *DN*, 21 Feb. 1884.

31. For examples of dissimulation to protect the Prophet Joseph Smith in his polygamous relationships, see Bachman, "A Study," 194; and Richard S. Van Wagoner, "Sarah M. Pratt: The Shaping of an Apostate," *Dialogue* 19 (Summer 1986): 82, 97.

32. Saint Paul, in I Corinthians 3:2; Joseph Smith, in *D&C* 50:40 (1831).

33. Joseph Smith, in *HC* 1:220n, 2:477; Kenney, *Wilford Woodruff's Journal*, 2:342–43, 21 Jan. 1844; the reminiscences of Brigham Young, in *JD* 9:294, 18:242 (1852, 1874); and John Taylor in *JD* 6:165 (1858).

34. Levi Hancock, in Mosiah Hancock, "The Prophet Joseph—Some of His Sayings." Brigham Young's statement is in *JD* 9:294 (1862).

35. Orson Hyde, in *JD* 2:83 (1854). Also see Erastus Snow in *JD* 23:295–96 (1883); and the comments of Leonard Arrington and Davis Bitton, *The Mormon Experience: A History of the Latter-day Saints* (New York: Alfred A. Knopf, 1979), 197.

36. Joseph Smith, in *HC* 4:570, 5:19–21, 140, 285–86, 6:58, 410.

37. Udney Hay Jacob, *An Extract from a Manuscript Entitled "The Peacemaker"; or, The Doctrines of the Millennium* . . . (Nauvoo: J. Smith, Printer, 1842). For analysis of the document, see Lawrence Foster, "A Little-Known Defense of Polygamy from the Mormon Press in 1842," *Dialogue* 9 (Winter 1974): 21–34.

38. Joseph Smith, in *HC* 4:445, 5:140, 181. And see the reference in a poem by Eliza R. Snow, one of Smith's plural wives, to the "corroding wrongs" of "tradition's haughty mood." Maureen Ursenbach Beecher, ed., "Eliza R. Snow's Nauvoo Journal," *BYU Studies* 15 (Summer 1975): 400.

39. On the role played by Joseph's sexual and marital ideas in precipitating the collapse of church rule in Nauvoo, see above, in chap. 1, 8–12. Also see affidavits and commentary connecting polygamy with lying in Shook, *True Origin of Mormon Polygamy*, 124–29 passim.

40. Joseph Smith, in *HC* 6:442.

41. Emma Smith, in William Clayton's Nauvoo Journal, 15 Aug. 1844; and the allegations of secrecy mentioned at the trial of Sidney Rigdon in *Times and Seasons* 5 (1 Oct. 1844): 664.

42. Richard E. Bennett, *Mormons at the Missouri, 1846–1852: "And Should We Die . . ."* (Norman: University of Oklahoma Press, 1987), 186–90, 195–98.

43. John Taylor, in *Public Discussion between Revds. C. W. Cleeve, James Robertson, and Philip Cater and Elder John Taylor, of the Church of Jesus Christ of Latter-day Saints, at Boulogne-sur-Mer, France . . .* (Liverpool: John Taylor, 1850), 8. Also see the account by his grandson, Samuel W. Taylor, *The Kingdom or Nothing*, 151.

44. See, e.g., Orson Pratt's concealment of Mormon revelation on polygamy prior to 1843, in *Seer* 1 (Feb. 1853): 30.

45. Charles William Penrose Diaries, 10 Jan. 1897, Charles William Penrose Collection, UHi.

46. Brigham Young, as quoted in Kenney, *Wilford Woodruff's Journal*, 4:12, 4 Feb. 1851.

47. "Adam, Our Father and God," *Mill. Star* 15 (26 Nov. 1853): 770; Brigham Young at the trial of Sidney Rigdon, *Times and Seasons* 5 (1 Oct. 1844): 667; *JD* 8:58, 208 (Brigham Young/1860); *JD* 10:59 (George A. Smith/1862); A. Miner, "How to Obtain the Blessings," *Mill. Star* 29 (27 April 1867): 257–59.

48. Charles Kelly, ed., *Journals of John D. Lee, 1846–47 and 1859* (Salt Lake City: University of Utah Press, 1984), 227, 23 July 1859.

49. Richard Burton, *The City of the Saints and across the Rocky Mountains to California*, ed. Fawn Brodie (1861; New York: Alfred A. Knopf, 1963), 454.

50. *JD* 2:216–17 (George A. Smith/1855); *JD* 6:165 (John Taylor/1858); Jaques, "Polygamy . . . ," 161–65.

51. John D. Hicks, "The Constitutions of the Northwest States," *University Studies Published by the University of Nebraska* 23 (Jan.-April 1923): 138–39.

52. See above, 50, 371.

53. Charles W. Penrose to President John Taylor, 16 Feb. 1887, John Taylor Letter File, typewritten transcriptions by Raymond Taylor, University of Utah Library, Salt Lake City.

54. These issues are discussed in a series of letters written by Richards to the church's First Presidency during the late winter and early spring of 1888. Franklin S. Richards to presidents Wilford Woodruff and George Q. Cannon,

28 Feb. 1888, to George Q. Cannon, 20 March 1888, to presidents Wilford Woodruff and George Q. Cannon, 22 March 1888, and to Brother Mack [Joseph F. Smith], 1 May 1888, photo and typewritten copies, Franklin S. Richards Correspondence, 1886–90, UHi.

55. For Caine's remarks, see *Cong. Rec.*, 50th Cong., 1st sess., 1888, 19, pt. 18:7950–7953. For both Richards and Caine, see *The Admission of Utah: Arguments in Favor of the Admission of Utah as a State* . . . (Washington, D.C.: GPO, 1888), 14–18, 68–69; and *Hearings before the Committee on Territories in Regard to the Admission of Utah as a State* (Washington, D.C.: GPO, 1889), 6–8.

56. Richards to George Q. Cannon, 20 March and 22 March 1888, Franklin S. Richards Correspondence.

57. John W. Taylor, quoted in untitled, *Nephi Ensign*, 22 Feb. 1889.

58. Samuel W. Taylor, "Interviews with Nettie [Janet] M. Taylor," p. 20, July 1947, BYU Library.

59. William Henry Gibbs, Sr., Diary, 9 April 1889, Church Archives.

60. Franklin S. Richards, quoted in Carlos Ashby Badger Diaries, 21 Dec. 1904, Church Archives.

61. Wiley Nebeker to Apostle John Henry Smith, 27 May 1903, John Henry Smith Letters, George A. Smith Family Papers, University of Utah Library.

62. John Henry Smith to Wiley Nebeker, 3 June 1903, John Henry Smith Letterbooks, Church Archives.

63. Katherine Cannon Thomas, interviewed by Leonard R. Grover, 25 March 1980, pp. 3–4, 11, POHP.

64. The instance recalled by Heber Grant Ivins is reported in Heber Grant Ivins, interviewed by Justin Stewart, 27 June 1971, pp. 29–30, box 1, fd. 5, Heber Grant Ivins Collection, UHi. The episode involving the remark that so disturbed Apostle Anthony W. Ivins is told in Florence Ivins Hyde, interviewed by Victor W. Jorgensen, 18 August 1972, transcript in private possession.

65. Carlos Ashby Badger Diaries, 9 Dec. 1905, Church Archives.

66. Rudger Clawson Diaries, 5 Oct. 1904, University of Utah Library.

67. Esmé Cecil Wingfield-Stratford, *Truth in Masquerade: A Study of Fashions in Fact* (London: Williams & Norgate, 1951), 120, 135.

68. George Q. Cannon, quoted in Richard W. Young memorandum, 7 Feb. 1892, John Henry Smith Letters, George A. Smith Family Papers.

69. *Trials*.

70. Matthias F. Cowley, in ibid.

71. Brooks Adams, *The Emancipation of Massachusetts* (Boston: Houghton, Mifflin, 1887), 134; and the comment of Franklin D. Daines, "Separatism in Utah, 1847–1870," *Annual Report of the American Historical Association for the Year 1917* (Washington, D.C., 1920), 334. Two examples of the speed with which Mormon leaders could interpret disagreement as evidence of sinister, other-worldly design are found in Kenney, *Wilford Woodruff's Journal* 4:500, 6 Dec. 1856; and Daniel McArthur's story in *Diary of Charles Lowell Walker*, ed.

A. Karl Larson and Katherine Miles Larson, 2 vols. (Logan: Utah State University Press, 1980), 2:531, 6 Feb. 1881.

72. "Rebellion against Legitimate Authority," *Mill. Star* 18 (12 April 1856): 227; *JD* 12:245 (Brigham Young/1868); "Minutes of a Special Conference of Elders of the Church of Jesus Christ of Latter-day Saints, Assembled in the Tabernacle, Great Salt Lake City, Aug. 28, 1852," *Mill. Star* 15 (Supplement 1853): 3.

73. "Report of the Governor of Utah" [1889], *Report of the Secretary of the Interior . . .* , 5 vols. (Washington, D.C.: GPO, 1890), 3:495.

74. E.g., *JD* 12:164 (Brigham Young/1867); and John Phillips Meakin, *Leaves of Truth: Utah and the Mormons* (Salt Lake City: n.p., 1909), 43.

75. Brigham Young, as reported in Larson and Larson, *Diary of Charles Lowell Walker* 1:25–26, 21 March 1858. The number of such remarks by church leaders, especially during the nineteenth century, is quite large. See, as but a representative sampling, "History of Brigham Young," *Mill. Star* 26 (14 May 1864): 311; Kenney, *Wilford Woodruff's Journal*, 2:331, 10 Dec. 1843; *JD* 3:110 (Heber C. Kimball/1854); *JD* 5:83 (Wilford Woodruff/1857); *JD* 12:105, 126 (Brigham Young/1867, 1867); James G. Bleak, "Annals of the Southern Utah Mission," Vol. 1, book B, pt. 1:176 [Erastus Snow in 1873], typewritten copy, Washington County Library, St. George, Utah; and comments by the non-Mormon Orlando W. Powers in *Proceedings* 1:813–14.

76. Joseph Smith, in *HC* 5:135.

77. Jules Remy, *A Journey to Great-Salt-Lake City . . .* , 2 vols. (London: W. Jeffs, 1861), 2:230; Julian Ralph, "A Week with the Mormons," *Harper's* 37 (8 April 1893): 330; *Proceedings* 1:461; W. M. Raine and A. W. Dunn, "Mormon or Patriot: The Church, Its People and Their Life," *Leslie's Monthly Magazine* 59 (March 1905): 539; J. Bonner Ritchie, "How Strait the Gate, How Narrow the Way? The Institutional Church and the Individual . . . ," *Sunstone* 6 (May-June 1981): 28–35; Dawn Tracy, "LDS and RLDS Churches' Structure Cannot Accept Dissent, Speaker Claims," *SLT*, 30 Aug. 1986.

78. Earl Okelberry, interviewed by Jessie L. Embry, 6 Nov. 1979, p. 10, POHP. Also see Abraham L. Stout, interviewed by Tillman S. Boxell, 5 Sept. 1978, p. 11, POHP.

79. John Taylor, in *JD* 20:353 (John Taylor/1880).

80. Richard W. Young, in *Proceedings* 2:966, 987.

81. Angus Cannon, in *Proceedings* 1:790. Theodore Schroeder, referring to Mormons who repudiated their pledges in connection with polygamy, said they defended themselves by saying that such promises "were improperly exacted under conditions amounting practically to duress." A. Theodore Schroeder, "Polygamy and the Constitution," *Arena* 36 (Nov. 1906): 496.

82. Henry S. Tanner, quoted in Richard Barry, "The Mormon Evasion of Anti-Polygamy Laws," *Pearson's Magazine* 24 (Oct. 1910): 451.

83. 1 Nephi 4:1–18.

84. Heber J. Grant, as quoted by Judd and reported in Carlos Ashby Badger Diaries, 16 Jan. 1904.

85. John Henry Smith, as quoted first in "'Manifesto Only Trick to Beat Devil at Own Game,'" *SLT,* 16 Jan. 1906; then in *Proceedings* 4:13. But see John Henry Smith to T. D. Ehle, undated, John Henry Smith Letterbooks, George A. Smith Family Papers; and denials in *Proceedings* 4:367–68, 405–6.

86. Moojan Momen, *An Introduction to Shi'i Islam: The History and Doctrines of Twelver Shi'ism* (New Haven: Yale University Press, 1985), 183. A disturbing parallel is provided in the recent justification given by a Mormon general authority, Elder Paul Dunn, who said he saw no moral wrong in altering historical truth for the purpose of reinforcing Mormon precepts. "LDS Speaker Admits Spicing Up Stories," *SLT,* 16 Feb. 1991; "Dunn Story Proves Costly for Veteran Journalist," ibid., 21 Feb., 1991; and "Popular LDS Speaker Dunn 'Embellished' Anecdotes," *Ogden Standard,* 16 Feb. 1991.

87. Genesis 20:2.

88. Heber Bennion to Heber J. Grant, 9 July 1929, fd. entitled "Polygamy," in Brigham H. Roberts letterbox 7, Church Archives.

89. H. Grant Ivins, "Polygamy in Mexico as Practiced by the Mormon Church, 1895–1905," 5, 6, typewritten manuscript, University of Utah Library.

90. Stenhouse, *The Rocky Mountain Saints,* 192.

91. Michel de Montaigne, *Essais* 2:18.

92. Thomas Hutchinson, *The History of the Colony and Province of Massachusetts-Bay,* ed. Lawrence Shaw Mayo, 3 vols. (Cambridge, Mass.: Harvard University Press, 1936), 3:162.

93. George E. Hancey, interviewed by Michael H. Schaub, 17 Feb. 1979, p. 3, POHP.

94. Carl A. Badger to "My Dear Charlie," 22 June 1906, Carlos Ashby Badger Collection, Church Archives.

95. George D. Kirby, "Hypocrisy," *Improvement Era* 14 (Nov. 1910): 43.

96. Joseph Bailey, in *Proceedings* 1:332.

97. Richard Barry, "The Mormon Evasion of Anti-Polygamy Laws," 445. Also see the comments of Edward B. Critchlow, in *Proceedings* 1:669–70; and Burton J. Hendrick, "The Mormon Revival of Polygamy," *McClure's Magazine* 36 (Jan. 1911): 461–62.

98. Juab (A High Private in Israel), "To the Methodist Ministers," *Kinsman* 1 (13 Nov. 1897): 2–3.

99. A. Theodore Schroeder, "Polygamy and Inspired Lies," *Kinsman* 1 (Jan.-Feb. 1898): pts. 1–5.

100. "May Lie for Roberts," *SLT,* 9 Jan. 1899.

101. "Polygamist and Liar," *SLT,* 2 Aug. 1910.

102. See, e.g., the First Presidency's "Address," 26 March 1907, *Messages* 4:145–46; the remarks of President Joseph F. Smith as published in "True to God, His People, and the World in Every Promise," *Improvement Era* 14 (Nov. 1910): 71–72; and John Henry Smith, "The Habit of Drifting," ibid., 14 (Dec. 1910): 169.

103. Many of these devices were discussed above in connection with

the post-Manifesto marriages of apostles and First Presidency members in chap. 6.

104. Guy C. Wilson, Jr., *Memories of a Venerable Father and Other Reminiscences* (Fullerton: California State University, Oral History Program, 1988), 129.

105. Fred C. Collier, comp., *Unpublished Revelations of the Prophets and Presidents of the Church of Jesus Christ of Latter-day Saints*, Vol. 1 (Salt Lake City: Collier's Publishing, 1981), pt. 1:145–46.

106. Recent accounts that review claims concerning these events are J. Max Anderson's anti-fundamentalist *Polygamy Story: Fiction and Fact* (Salt Lake City: Publisher's Press, 1979), 63–76; Fred C. Collier's rebuttal, in "Re-Examining the Lorin Woolley Story," *Doctrine of the Priesthood* 1 (Feb. 1981): 1–17; and the very readable description in Van Wagoner, *Mormon Polygamy*, 128–29, 190–91.

107. For fundamentalist discussion and affirmation of this tradition, see "Our Position," *Truth* 10 (March 1945): 269; "Prosecution Won't Stop Us, Polygamists' Leader Says," *Ogden Standard Examiner*, 10 Sept. 1944; Joseph Leslie Broadbent, *Celestial Marriage?* (Salt Lake City: n.p., 1927), 23–24; Joseph W. Musser, *Celestial or Plural Marriage: A Digest of the Mormon Marriage System as Established by God through the Prophet Joseph Smith* (Salt Lake City: Truth Publishing, 1944, 1970), 148; Lynn L. Bishop and Steven L. Bishop, *The Keys of the Priesthood Illustrated* (Draper, Utah: Review and Preview Publishers, 1971), 76–77, 117, 172–74, 192–97, 226–40; [Gilbert Fulton and Rulon Allred], *The Most Holy Principle*, 4 vols. (Murray, Utah: Gems Publishing, 1970–75), 4:20, 68, 164–67, 213; Dennis R. Short, *Questions on Plural Marriage with a Selected Bibliography and 1600 References* (Salt Lake City: privately published, 1975), 9, 10, 18–21, 36, 37, 42, 43, 44. For examples of fundamentalist pragmatics in dealing with the law, see Anderson, *The Polygamy Story*, 87, 88.

108. Dorothy Allred Solomon, *In My Father's House: An Autobiography by Dorothy Allred Solomon* (New York: Franklin Watts, 1984), 31, 42–43, 110–11 passim.

109. While the distinction between church and priesthood is referred to in most Mormon fundamentalist writings, perhaps the two most extensive and carefully developed expositions of the argument are to be found in Bishop and Bishop, *Keys of the Priesthood*, 3–75, 201–3 passim; and all of Gilbert A. Fulton, *That Manifesto* (Kearns, Utah: Deseret Publishing, 1974).

110. See above in chap. 2, 55; and the instructions given by church leaders to territorial delegate John T. Caine, as described in Edward Leo Lyman, *Political Deliverance: The Mormon Quest for Utah Statehood* (Urbana: University of Illinois Press, 1986), 60.

111. "Discourse by President John Taylor," *DN*, 2 June 1880. Also see reference to Taylor's dispersion of authority for performing plural marriages, above, 52–53.

112. Herbert L. James to John M. Cannon, 10 June 1902, original in private possession.

113. Badger Diaries, 22 Dec. 1904 and 12 Feb. 1905.

114. John Taylor, in *Trials*.

115. "A Biographical Sketch of the Life of Mary Evelyn Clark Allred," *Star of Truth* 2 (Nov. 1954): 301; Samuel W. Taylor, *Rocky Mountain Empire: The Latter-day Saints Today* (New York: Macmillan, 1978), 21, 81–97; and idem, *The Kingdom or Nothing,* 301–2, 309–10.

116. Some, like Byron Harvey Allred, believed the process to have been well advanced before the time of Heber J. Grant. He saw the Quorum of Twelve Apostles, with deeds like the expulsion from their number of Matthias F. Cowley and John W. Taylor, as especially culpable. See the entirety of Allred's *A Leaf in Review of the Words and Acts of God and Men Relative to the Fullness of the Gospel* (Caldwell, Idaho: Caxton, 1933). For contentions that, with Heber J. Grant, the church took especially long steps toward compromise with the world, see Bishop and Bishop, *Keys of the Priesthood,* 241–62ff.; and Short, *Questions on Plural Marriage,* 5. Modern church authorities have never rejected the distinction between church and priesthood, albeit the difference sometimes seems vague. See John A. Widtsoe, *Evidences and Reconciliations: Aids to Faith in a Modern Day* (Salt Lake City: Murray & Gee, 1943), 177–78; and Gordon B. Hinckley, "Priesthood Restoration," *Ensign* 18 (Oct. 1988): 72.

117. See the remarks of Lionel Caplan in the introduction to *Studies in Religious Fundamentalism,* ed. Lionel Caplan (Albany: State University of New York Press, 1987), 5–22. The following also provide comparative insight into the Mormon fundamentalist experience: Ernest R. Sandeen, *The Roots of Fundamentalism: British and American Millenarianism, 1800–1930* (Chicago: University of Chicago Press, 1970); George M. Marsden, *Fundamentalism and American Culture: The Shaping of Twentieth-Century Evangelicalism, 1870–1925* (New York: Oxford University Press, 1980); James Barr, *Fundamentalism* (Philadelphia: Westminster, 1977); William R. Hutchison, *The Modernist Impulse in American Protestantism* (Cambridge, Mass.: Harvard University Press, 1976); Rodney Stark, ed., *Religious Movements: Genesis, Exodus and Numbers* (New York: Paragon House, 1985).

Appendix II

Mormon Polygamous Marriages after the 1890 Manifesto through 1910: A Tentative List

Partisans of the church stated, both during the Smoot proceedings and on other occasions, that those who entered plural unions after the Manifesto were only "sporadic" in number, that Mormon church authorities bowed in "respectful submission" to the laws forbidding polygamy, and that those who did not were but "a few over-zealous individuals" who refused obedience to their leaders.[1] The question as to how many individuals joined in such marriages is, therefore, significant because its answer reflects on the veracity of church leaders at a time when they claimed to be doing everything possible to prohibit such unions. That a "sporadic" few would resist conformity is to be expected. If a considerable number were involved, including high church authorities themselves, other conclusions must be inferred.[2] This study has alleged repeatedly that a sizable number of church members were given permission to enter polygamous unions after 1890. It is a claim supporting the book's argument for the special regard in which the principle was held.

While estimates of the numbers involved in post-Manifesto plural marriage ranged from twenty to two thousand, the Smoot investigating committee seems to have been the first to attempt an actual naming of participants.[3] Eighteen persons were identified in the committee's majority report, issued in 1906.[4] This was a conservative calculation and did not contain at least three individuals examined by the committee who could have been included—Loren H. Harmer, David Eccles, and Brigham H. Roberts. Two congressmen, however, speaking in Smoot's behalf, admitted to evidence for twenty cases.[5]

The next project of this kind appeared in two articles published in the *Salt Lake Tribune* in the autumn of 1909.[6] Because some of the twenty-one named by the paper were not included among those identified by the Smoot committee, a list was clearly in the making. The *Tribune* continued the search, adding to the total at every opportunity. Information came from a variety of sources. Between 13 November 1909 and 18 January 1911 no less than 119 articles on post-Manifesto polygamy were published by the *Tribune,* most of which contributed new names to the rapidly growing list. Along the way some persons were added who were later inadvertently left out. Others were named more than once, usually because of misspellings or variable spellings of the first name. Eventually, the *Tribune* compiled a total of 239 men who had taken plural wives since the Manifesto. An investigation of those named by the *Tribune,* for the purpose of confirming the paper's accuracy, produced the tabulations given in Table 1.

Table 1

Duplicate Entry	6
Insufficient Data for Making Judgment	63
Not Authorized	1
Not Polygamous	2
Pre-Manifesto	9
Verified Polygamous	158
Total	239

The church itself, while never publicly acknowledging that such late marriages were approved or precisely describing their extent, did give some indication of the proportions of polygamous family life over a period of nearly two decades after the Manifesto. It was officially stated that in 1890 there were 2,451 Mormon plural families in the United States. By 1899 this number, said the church, had declined to 1,543. By 1903 it further dwindled to 897. By 1905 the number was said to be only 500. And Senator Smoot said in 1908 that he was "positive" there were no more than 400 polygamous families in the church.[7] Except for Senator Smoot's figure of 400 in 1908, these calculations seem to have applied only to the United States, excluding pluralists living in Mexico and Canada. They clearly indicate a steady and precipitous fall in the overall number of Mormons living the principle. Given the apparent extent of post-Manifesto plural marriage, it seems unlikely that Senator Smoot's 1908 statement was accurate. If true, the number of those marrying into polygamy after 1890 would have represented the overwhelming majority of all Mormon polygamous households.

In 1910 Apostle John Henry Smith asked a kinsman from Rexburg,

Idaho, for information regarding the number of polygamists living in his stake. Apostle Smith was told that of ten known polygamists, three were of "more recent" origin.[8] While it is a rough approximation only, if the three-to-ten ratio reported to Apostle Smith is extrapolated to all existing plural marriages in the church, about one-third would have been of "more recent" origin. Considering the number of post-1890 pluralists listed below, the extent of plurality in the church around 1910 was certainly greater than that stated by Smoot.

There were also private efforts at enumeration, like that of Stanley Ivins in his list of polygamous contractions solemnized by his father and others in Mexico. But none seemed prepared to publicly put forth an independent compilation of their own. Then, in 1983 Kenneth L. Cannon II indicated in graph form that he had found a total of 156 instances of Mormon plural marriage occurring between 1890 and President Joseph F. Smith's 1904 "Official Statement."[9] Even before the Cannon article, however, Professor D. Michael Quinn of Brigham Young University stated in a lecture that he had evidence for more than 250 approved polygamous marriages throughout the church in the years after the Manifesto and before 1904. This was followed by Quinn's long and impressive 1985 article in *Dialogue*. It is clear from his research that, while not specifically identified in his study, the figure of 250 could easily be surpassed. And this did not count those given permission by church authorities to enter the practice after 1904.[10]

The present work would be incomplete without a similar attempt. The chief source for the compilation here, extensively based on research by Victor W. Jorgensen and generously shared with the author, was family group sheets located in the church's Family History Library in Salt Lake City, Utah. Family group sheets, however, sometimes contain errors. As throughout the study, efforts have been made to compensate for problems of this kind by providing multiple references to support the information given. This includes using secondary sources such as Quinn's remarkable 1985 study on post-Manifesto polygamy noted above. Some of the materials cited, along with other comments, are identified in the "Remarks" column of the listing. A glance at this column should in most cases give a reader some sense of why a particular individual was believed to have taken a polygamous wife, or wives, after the Woodruff declaration. The total of 262 post-Manifesto plural marriages found and described in the list makes it clear that a strong commitment to the doctrine continued past the turn of the century. Finally, as already mentioned in the discussion of plural marriages during the administration of President Joseph F.

Smith, no new cases are cited after 1910. Although it is possible, even likely, that contractions were approved after that time, not only was available evidence insufficient to justify counting such individuals but, to a degree greater than ever before, the church began taking a firmer and more consistent stand against plural contractions.

Because of difficulties associated with the accessibility of relevant archival records, in some instances less evidence was available than one would like. For this reason, the compilation will unquestionably be revised. But because an effort was made to select prudently, rejecting scores of names about which there was question, the author is confident such revisions will result in a net augmentation, rather than reduction, of the number provided here. For example, as shown in Table 1, sixty-three of the names tallied by the *Tribune* were rejected for want of sufficient information. Undoubtedly, several in this group took plural wives, as the *Tribune* alleged, but because of inadequate or questionable information, they were not included in the category of "verified" polygamists. The precise number authorized to enter polygamy after 1890, however, is less significant than the general magnitude of such activity. Whether it amounted to two hundred or four hundred cases, either figure is substantial. Both constitute more than a "sporadic" number. Both clearly infer that church authorities and many members alike were dedicated to the principle and its *practice,* whatever the cost should discovery occur.

It is also clear that those who undertook such relationships were neither mavericks nor inveterate dissenters—men and women likely to be found at the edge of Mormon orthodoxy in any case. Rather, they were in most instances stalwarts of the faith. The succeeding count shows that more than half served their church as missionaries, had been called as branch presidents, bishops, stake presidents, or other high officers. It was Mormonism's elite that was mostly involved. This is further evidence not only of the dearness of the principle but that permission for its continued practice emanated from the highest councils of the church.

NOTES

1. In addition to testimony given at the time of the Smoot hearings, cited above, 255, see "An Address," 26 March 1907, *Messages* 5:151–52; and "Spry Misrepresentation," *SLT,* 3 Jan. 1910.

2. A similar point was made by counsel for the complainants in the Smoot

hearings when discussing the number of children polygamously fathered by President Joseph F. Smith after the Manifesto. *Proceedings* 1:132–33.

3. Eugene Young, in his 1899 article, said he had located twenty individuals involved in such activities. "Revival of the Mormon Problem," *North American Review* 168 (April 1899): 476–89. Frank Cannon said that the *Salt Lake Tribune*'s list of two hundred or so was probably only one tenth of the actual number. Frank J. Cannon and Harvey J. O'Higgins, *Under the Prophet in Utah: The National Menace of a Political Priestcraft* (Boston: C. M. Clark, 1911), 351–52.

4. *Proceedings* 4:477–78.

5. Albert Jarvis Hopkins and George Sutherland, in *Cong. Rec.*, 59th Cong., 2d sess., Jan. 11 and 28, 1907, 41:943, 1495, respectively.

6. "Some New Polygamists" and "Always More to Add," *SLT*, 13 and 14 Nov. 1909, respectively.

7. "An Address," 26 March 1907, *Messages* 4:152; and Reed Smoot, "The Passing of Polygamy," *North American Review* 187 (Jan. 1908): 120–21.

8. Silas S. Smith, [Jr.], to John Henry Smith, 26 Dec. 1910, John Henry Smith Letterbook, George A. Smith Family Papers, University of Utah Library.

9. Kenneth L. Cannon II, "After the Manifesto: Mormon Polygamy, 1890–1906," *Sunstone* 8 (Jan.-April 1983): 27–35.

10. D. Michael Quinn, "LDS Church Authority and New Plural Marriages, 1890–1904," *Dialogue* 18 (Spring 1985): 9–105. The lecture mentioned was delivered at BYU before the BYU Student History Association in the autumn of 1981.

POST-MANIFESTO POLYGAMOUS MARRIAGES
A TENTATIVE LIST WITH REMARKS

*=DISTG. CHURCH SERVICE	NAME OF HUSBAND / NAMES OF WIVES	NUMBER POST-1890 PL. MARRS.	BORN-DIED	MARRIAGE DATE	YEAR FIRST CHILD	YEAR LAST CHILD	REMARKS
1	ALLREDGE, JR., ISAAC	(1)	1870-1964				MARRIAGE TO MARIA PERFORMED IN MEXICO. FGS.
	1) WESTERN, SARAH ANNIE		1871-	24 OCT 1888			
	2) VAN LEUVEN, MARIA D.		1882-	16 AUG 1902	1903	1918	
*2	ALLEN, HEBER S.	(1)	1864-1944				MARRIAGE TO ELIZABETH PERFORMED BY JOHN W. TAYLOR IN CARDSTON, CANADA. AMY A. PULSIPHER INTERVIEW, POHP, p.6. D. MICHAEL QUINN, "LDS CHURCH AUTHORITY AND NEW PLURAL MARRIAGES, 1890-1904," DIALOGUE 18 (SPRING 1985):94 STATES JOHN A. WOOLF OFFICIATED.
	1) LEONARD, AMY L.		1865-1936	2 APR 1889	1890	1903	
	2) HARDY, ELIZABETH		1884-1952	19 SEP 1903	1913	1924	
*3	ALLRED, JR., BYRON HARVEY	(1)	1870-1937				MARRIAGE TO MARY PERFORMED BY ANTHONY W. IVINS. IVINS R OF M.
	1) PEAD, CHARLOTTE		1870-1908	3 OCT 1888	1889	1908	
	2) CLARK, MARY EVELYN		1884-1954	15 JUL 1903	1904	1924	
*4	ALLRED, BYRON HARVEY	(1)	1847-1912				QUINN, 60, STATES MARRIAGE TO MARY RECORDED IN ALEXANDER F. MACDONALD MARRIAGE BOOK.
	1) COOK, PHOEBE IRENE		1852-1913	5 OCT 1867	1870	1872	
	2) ROLPH, ALTA MATILDA		1855-1948	30 MAY 1875	1876	1884	
	3) TRACY, MARY ELIZA		1874-1949	21 NOV 1890	1895	1904	
5	ALLRED, CALVERT LORENZO	(1)	1864-1932				MARRIAGE TO ANDREA TOOK PLACE IN COLONIA DIAZ. FGS. LETTER OF LORNA ALLRED TO NELLE HATCH (n.d.) SAYS MARRIAGE OFFICIATED BY ALEXANDER F. MACDONALD.
	1) JENSEN, GERTRUDE M.		1870-1913	31 MAY 1888	1889	1912	
	2) JENSEN, ANDREA		1872-1951	25 OCT 1890	1891	1904	
*6	BADGER, RODNEY CARLOS	(1)	1848-1923				FGS FOR ELIZABETH STATES: "COUPLE MARRIED APPROXIMATELY 1895 NO MARRIAGE RECORD AVAILABLE. CONSIDERED A SECRET BY WIFE."
	1) TAYLOR, HARRIET ANN		1847-1908	7 DEC 1871	1872	1891	
	2) NOBLE, LOUISA A.		1849-1943	27 DEC 1877	1878	1889	
	3) HARRISON, ELIZABETH		1865-1932	1895			
7	BAGLEY, JOHN ALLEN	(2)	1862-1941				MARRIAGE, APPARENTLY TO LINDA, IN MAY 1893. QUINN, 77.
	1) LAWSON, SARAH ELLEN		1863-1905	15 AUG 1888	1889	1905	
	2) FURROW, NINA VALVE		-1898	MAY 1893			
	3) AUSTIN, LINDA ELLEN						
	4) PETERSON, MARY M.		1876-1918	1903	1904	1915	

#	Name	Birth–Death	Marriage Date			Notes
*8	BALL, SAMUEL FREDERICK (1)	1849-1923	23 MAR 1873	1873	1896	MARRIAGE TO MARGARET BROWN PERFORMED BY ANTHONY W. IVINS. IVINS R OF M.
	1) POINEY, MARGARET	1851-1954	16 FEB 1882	1883	1900	
	2) POWELL, ELLEN MARIA	1859-1935	16 SEP 1897			
	3) BROWN, MARGARET	1867-				
9	BARLOW, III, ISRAEL (1)	1864-1945	21 SEP 1892	1910		REED SMOOT DIARIES, 28 SEP 1910, BYU LIBRARY, SAYS "ISRAEL BARLOW JR. WAS SUMMONED BEFORE THE QUORUM TO ANSWER THE CHARGES AGAINST HIM OF MARRY-ING MISS WELLING WITHIN THE LAST FEW YEARS." SLT 4 OCT 1910, SAYS JUDSON TOLMAN OFFICIATED.
	1) HJORTH, JOAN VILATE	1886-1952	3 JUN 1909	1910	1930	
	2) WELLING, ALICE BELVA					
10	BARNETT, JOHN WILLIAM (1)	1861-1930	8 MAR 1883	1883	1906	POLYGAMOUS MARRIAGE TO HATTIE PERFORMED BY MARRINER W. MERRILL IN LOGAN TEMPLE. QUINN, 77.
	1) THOMSON, ALICE JANET	1864-1936	16 JUL 1894	1895	1897	
	2) MERRILL, HATTIE L.	1873-				
11	BARNEY, ORIN ELBRIDGE (1)	1868-1952	3 AUG 1892	1893	1914	MORELOS ROM, 1900-1909.
	1) FENN, ANNIE MATILDA	1875-1918	16 AUG 1902	1903	1909	
	2) FENN, SARAH ELIZA	1883-1940				
12	BARRELL, CHARLES (1)		POST-MANIFESTO			CHARLES, A HIGH PRIEST IN SALT LAKE CITY, ENTERED INTO A SPECIAL AGREEMENT OF SOME KIND WITH A NEW WIFE ABOUT 1892. QUINN, 55.
	1) NAME UNAVAILABLE					
13	BECK, ERASTUS (2)	1853-1914	1879			DIAZ ROM, 1886-1907, AND KIMBALL YOUNG COLLECTION, BOX 1, FOLDER 12, GARRETT EVANGELICAL THEOLOGICAL LIBRARY, EVANSTON, ILLINOIS. FGS SAYS MARRIAGE TO NANCY PERFORMED BY ALEXANDER F. MACDONALD IN COLONIA DIAZ.
	1) YOUNG, LEAH JANE	-1898	25 OCT 1890	1893	1911	
	2) ACCORD, NANCY ELIZ.	1869-1935	1902			
	3) WHITING, PEARL	1876-1902				
14	BEECROFT, JOHN C. (1)	1871-1848	11 MAY 1897	1898	1925	MARRIAGE TO LETTIE PERFORMED BY ALEXANDER F. MACDONALD IN MEXICO. FGS.
	1) FARNSWORTH, ELVA A.	1881-1955	23 FEB 1903	1904	1926	
	2) FARNSWORTH, LETTIE A.	1886-1962				
15	BEESLEY, FREDERICK (1)	1864-1940	23 OCT 1885	1886	1903	FIRST WIFE YET LIVING WITH HUSBAND IN THE 26TH WARD OF SALT LAKE STAKE. 1914 CHURCH CENSUS. FGS.
	1) SOLOMON, ELIZABETH	1864-1957	21 APR 1905			
	2) RAWLINGS, KATE					
*16	BENNION, EDWIN TURPIN (2)	1868-1930	12 OCT 1892	1893	1913	THEODORE C. BENNION INTERVIEW, POHP, p.2. ALSO SEE FGS FOR ROBERT LANG CAMPBELL
	1) LINDSAY, MARY ELIZ.	1870-	20 SEP 1903	1906	1929	
	2) CLARK, MARY MINERVA	1883-	SEP 1903			
	3) CAMPBELL, AGNES S.	1860-1942				

*=DISTG. CHURCH SERVICE	NAME OF HUSBAND / NAMES OF WIVES	NUMBER POST-1890 PL. MARRS.	BORN-DIED	MARRIAGE DATE	YEAR FIRST CHILD	YEAR LAST CHILD	REMARKS
*17	BENNION, HEBER	(2)					MARY BENNION MUHS INTERVIEW WITH V. W. JORGENSEN, CSUF ORAL HISTORY PROGRAM, 23. 1930 CHURCH CENSUS, UNDER BENNION, MARY BRINGHURST. TRIALS.
	1) WINTERS, SUSAN M.		1858-1932	11 SEP 1885			
	2) WEBSTER, EMMA JANE		1859-1936	1900	1886	1900	
	3) BRINGHURST, MARY		1881-	DEC 1902	1903	1910	
*18	BENTLEY, JOSEPH CHARLES	(2)	1859-1942				WIFE MARY SUBMITTED HER OWN FGS, AND ON THE BACK IT STATES: "....MARRIED 23 SEP 1901 IN COLONIA JUAREZ, CHIH, MXC, BY APOSTLE MATHIAS F. COWLEY, BUT WAS NEVER OFFICIALLY RECORDED." MARRIAGE TO GLADYS BY GEORGE TEASDALE. SEE CHAPTER 5, ABOVE.
	1) IVINS, MARGARET M.		1868-1928	30 JUN 1886	1887	1908	
	2) WOODMANSEE, GLADYS E.		1865-1906	1894	1895	1906	
	3) TAYLOR, MAUD MARY		1885-1976	23 SEP 1901	1903	1923	
19	BINGHAM, PARLEY PRATT	(1)	1859-1933				MARRIAGE TO ISABEL PERFORMED BY GEORGE TEASDALE IN COLONIA JUAREZ. FGS.
	1) MC FARLAND, MARGARET		1860-1930	8 MAY 1879	1880	1899	
	2) MC FARLAND, ISABEL		1872-1951	15 APR 1886	1897	1920	
20	BLACK, DAVID PATTEN	(1)	1874-1958				MARRIAGE TOOK PLACE IN COLONIA PACHECO, MEXICO. FGS.
	1) KARTCHNER, THEDA		1875-1962	10 DEC 1892	1894	1917	
	2) KARTCHNER, ALZADA		1885-1957	25 NOV 1900	1903	1925	
21	BLACK, MORLEY LARSEN	(1)	1875-1951				MARRIAGE TO RACHEL TOOK PLACE IN COLONIA JUAREZ. FGS.
	1) PORTER, LYDIA ELLEN		1879-1939	6 APR 1896	1897	1922	
	2) LUNT, RACHEL ANN		1883-	21 NOV 1901	1903	1927	
*22	BOWMAN, HENRY EYRING	(1)	1859-1933				MARRIAGE TO WILHELMINA PERFORMED BY ANTHONY W. IVINS. IVINS R OF M.
	1) GUBLER, MARY		1863-1937	3 SEP 1885	1886	1904	
	2) WALSER, WILHELMINA		1880-	27 NOV 1902			
*23	BRAMWELL, FRANKLIN S.	(1)	1859-1926				MARRIAGE TO MARY ANN PERFORMED BY BRIGHAM YOUNG JR. IN MEXICO, MAY-JUNE 1894. QUINN, 62. SEE JOHN MARTIN FGS FOR MARY ANN'S BIRTH DATE.
	1) EGGINSON, EMILY		1866-1952	10 JUN 1892	1899	1909	
	2) HINCKLEY, MARTHA A.		1867-1948	1894	1902		
	3) MARTIN, MARY ANN						
*24	BRANDLEY, THEODORE	(2)	1851-1928				EMMA BIEFER BECAME HOUSEKEEPER AFTER DEATH OF MARY IN 1892. ELIZA WENT TO CANADA AS HOUSEKEEPER IN 1899, AND MARRIAGE TO THEODORE PERFORMED THERE BY JOHN W. TAYLOR. LOUIS BRANDLEY INTERVIEW, p.14,
	1) NAEGLE, MARY ELIZ.		-1892	8 JUL 1872	1874	1887	
	2) KEELER, MARGARET		1863-1910	10 APR 1882	1883	1899	
	3) BIEFER, EMMA M.			11 AUG 1893			

#	Name		Birth–Death	1901	1902	1912	Notes
	4) ZAUGG, ROSINA(ELIZA)		1863-1951	1901	1902	1912	POHP. AND LOUIS BRANDLEY, "FAMILY LIFE OF A POLYGAMIST," BYU LIBRARY, pp.1-2. FGS FOR ELIZABETH AT BACK OF LOUIS BRANDLEY INTERVIEW. SEE ALSO STERLING, CANADA ROM, 1899-1931.
*25	BREINHOLT, JENS CHRISTIAN	(1)	1841-1914				
	1) HANSEN, JOHANNA		1843-1920	13 FEB 1866	1867	1886	MARRIAGE TO MARGRETHE PERFORMED BY ANTHONY W. IVINS. IVINS R OF M. CHRISTIANA LISTED AS LIVING WITH HUSBAND IN COLONIA JUAREZ, ROM, 1906-1916.
	2) LARSEN, CHRISTINE			7 MAR 1870			
	3) HANSEN, CHRISTIANA		1856-1914	30 MAR 1874	1878	1897	
	4) HANSEN, MARGRETHE L.		1859-	20 JAN 1903			
*26	BRIMHALL, GEORGE HENRY	(1)	1852-1932				FAWN BRODIE IN 31 DEC 1943 LETTER TO CLAIRE NOALL SAYS SHE LEARNED IN 1942 THAT HER GRANDFATHER BRIMHALL HAD THREE WIVES, NOT TWO AS BEFORE BELIEVED. UNIV. OF UTAH, MS 188, BX 2, FD 2. FAWN'S SISTER FLORA IN 1988 INTERVIEW WITH NEWELL BRINGHURST STATED THIRD WIFE WAS ALICE REYNOLDS. LETTER 5 DEC 1988, BRINGHURST TO CARMON HARDY. NEITHER GORGE NOR ALICE WERE EMPLOYED AT BYU UNTIL AFTER THE MANIFESTO, AT WHICH PLACE THEY PRESUMABLY MET.
	1) WILKINS, ALSINA E.		1856-1926	28 DEC 1874	1875	1883	
	2) ROBERTSON, FLORA		1865-1950	11 SEP 1885	1886	1909	
	3) REYNOLDS, ALICE						
*27	BROWN, BENJAMIN B.	(1)	1866-1947				MARRIAGE TO MARY PERFORMED BY ANTHONY W. IVINS. IVINS R OF M. DUBLAN ROM, EARLY TO 1912.
	1) PEARSON, MARTHA		1865-1946	24 SEP 1890	1892	1910	
	2) HANSEN, MARY VILATE		1872-1941	26 AUG 1903	1905	1912	
28	BROWN, GEORGE MORTIMER	(1)	1842-1894				MARRIAGE TOOK PLACE AT COLONIA DIAZ. FGS. SEE ALSO DIAZ ROM, 1886-1907.
	1) OLSEN, ELIZABETH				1880	1894	
	2) WILSON, PEARL M.		1871-1907	1892	1893	1894	
*29	BROWN, ORSON PRATT	(3)	1863-1946				MARRIAGE TO ELIZA PERFORMED BY ANTHONY W. IVINS. IVINS R OF M. MARRIAGE TO ELIZABETH PERFORMED BY HER FATHER, ALEXANDER F. MACDONALD. ORSON PRATT BROWN JOURNAL, p.47, UHi. SEE ALSO DUBLAN ROM, EARLY TO 1912.
	1) ROMNEY, MARTHA D.		1870-1943	10 OCT 1887	1888	1908	
	2) GALBRAITH, JANE		1879-	1897	1888	1900	
	3) MACDONALD, ELIZABETH		1874-1904	15 JAN 1901	1902	1904	
	4) SKOUSEN, ELIZA		1882-1958	7 SEP 1902	1903	1914	
*30	BROWN, JR., RICHARD DANIEL	(1)	1846-1923				SEE ROM, HARRISVILLE, EARLY TO 1905 FOR DATA ON BETSY FISH. SECOND WIFE, MARY E. OLMSTEAD BROWN, MOVED FROM HARRISVILLE TO OGDEN 4TH WARD WHERE SHE REMAINED. OGDEN 4TH WARD ROM, 1900-1918. BROWN MARRIED EMILY IN LAYTON, UTAH.
	1) ENSLOW, LUCY ANN		1849-1882	5 DEC 1870	1872	1880	
	2) OLMSTEAD, MARY E.		1861-1914	15 JUL 1885			
	3) FISH, BETSY		1862-1890	29 JUL 1889			
	4) SCHOFIELD, EMILY		1882-1937	20 MAY 1904			

*=DISTG. CHURCH SERVICE	NAME OF HUSBAND / NAMES OF WIVES	NUMBER POST-1890 PL. MARRS.	BORN-DIED	MARRIAGE DATE	YEAR FIRST CHILD	YEAR LAST CHILD	REMARKS
*31	BUDD, GEORGE HENRY	(1)	1877-1946				MARRIAGE TO MARY JANE PERFORMED IN RAYMOND, ALBERTA, CANADA. FGS. EDITH'S FGS STATES SHE WAS LIVING AT RAYMOND 1904-1909.
	1) FARNES, EDITH		1875-	27 SEP 1899	1900	1918	
	2) DUKE, MARY JANE		1884-	26 SEP 1904			
32	BUNKER, FRANCIS NEIL	(1)	1873-1949				MARRIAGE TO EVELYN PERFORMED IN BISBEE, ARIZONA TERRITORY. FGS.
	1) COX, ROSANNAH		1872-1933	1 NOV 1893	1894	1907	
	2) COX, EVELYN RACHEL		1884-	29 OCT 1907	1907	1927	
33	BURTON, JOHN FIELDING	(1)	1872-1959				FGS FOR WILLIAM WALTON BURTON AND CHAUNCEY U. PORTER. PLURAL MARRIAGE TO FLORENCE PERFORMED BY MATTHIAS F. COWLEY IN UTAH. TRIALS. QUINN, 91. BURTON FGS SAYS "#5 (JOHN F) AND MUSETTA PORTER--NO ISSUE SO SHE ASKED HIM TO MARRY HER SISTER SO THEY COULD HAVE CHILDREN."
	1) PORTER, MUZETTA		1874-1950	8 APR 1897	1901	1916	
	2) PORTER, FLORENCE		1876-1947	15 NOV 1901			
*34	CALL, ANSON BOWEN	(3)	1863-1958				MARRIAGE TO DORA PERFORMED BY JOHN W. TAYLOR IN COLONIA JUAREZ. JOHN HENRY SMITH DIARIES, 11 MAR 1898. ALL THREE PLURAL MARRIAGES WERE IN MEXICO. MILDRED CALL HURST, DAUGHTER OF FIRST WIFE, SAID IN INTERVIEW THAT ALEXANDER F. MACDONALD MARRIED HARRIET TO CALL IN COLONIA JUAREZ.
	1) THOMPSON, MARY T.		1868-1957	4 NOV 1885	1886	1905	
	2) CAZIER, HARRIET			11 DEC 1890			
	3) PRATT, DORA		1878-1904	11 MAR 1898	1899	1904	
	4) ABEGG, JULIA SARAH		1885-1937	21 JAN 1903	1906	1929	
35	CALL, WILLARD	(1)	1866-1945				FGS SAYS ANTHONY W. IVINS PERFORMED MARRIAGE TO LEAH IN COLONIA JUAREZ.
	1) WHITE ADELAIDE		1868-1957	1 APR 1886	1886	1904	
	2) PRATT, LEAH		1880-1953	18 AUG 1902	1904	1925	
*36	CANNON, ABRAHAM H.	(1)	1859-1896				WILHELMINA TESTIFIED IN SMOOT HEARINGS THAT ABRAHAM LEFT WITH LILIAN HAMLIN IN JUNE 1896 FOR CALIFORNIA TO BE MARRIED, AND UPON RETURN ASKED HER (WILHELMINA'S) FORGIVENESS FOR HAVING MARRIED LILIAN. PROCEEDINGS 2: 142-146.
	1) JENKINS, SARAH ANN		1860-1940	16 OCT 1878	1879	1888	
	2) CANNON, WILHELMINA M.		1859-1941	15 OCT 1879	1883	1895	
	3) CROXALL, MARY ELIZA		1866-1955	11 JAN 1887	1887	1894	
	4) HAMLIN, LILIAN		1870-1920	JUN 1896	1897		
*37	CANNON, GEORGE MOUSLEY	(2)	1861-1937				ELLEN'S 28 DEC 1953 LETTER TO KATHERINE THOMAS, DAUGHTER OF THIRD WIFE, SAYS MOTHER (KATHERINE), WAS
	1) MORRIS, MARIAN A.		1861-1933	25 DEC 1884	1886	1902	

#	Name	Years	Marriage Date			Notes
	2) STEFFENSEN, ELLEN	1877-1963	17 JUN 1901	1902	1921	MARRIED BY MATTHIAS F. COWLEY IN SALT LAKE CITY. ELLEN, IN SAME LETTER, SAID SHE (ELLEN) WAS ALSO MARRIED IN SALT LAKE CITY. COPY OF LETTER IN POSSESSION OF AUTHOR. ALSO SEE QUINN, 85.
	3) MORRIS, KATHERINE V.	1876-1930	7 AUG 1901			
*38	CANNON, HUGH JENNE (1)	1870-1931				
	1) WILCKEN, MARY	1870-	1 OCT 1890	1891	1905	MATTHIAS F. COWLEY ADMITTED PERFORMING MARRIAGE. TRIALS, AND QUINN, 81,87.
	2) PEART, VILATE	1871-1909	18 JUL 1900			
*39	CANNON, JOHN MOUSLEY (2)	1865-1917				
	1) BENNION, ZINA	1873-1954	18 JUL 1893	1894	1916	FGS FOR AMOS H. NEFF AND JACOB H. PEART. MATTHIAS F. COWLEY PERFORMED BOTH PLURAL MARRIAGES. TRIALS; AND JOHN BENNION CANNON INTERVIEW, pp.3-4, POHP.
	2) PEART, MARGARET	1869-1944	18 JUL 1900			
	3) NEFF, HARRIET	1865-1928	3 NOV 1900			
*40	CANNON, LEWIS MOUSLEY (1)	1866-1924				
	1) CANNON, MARY ALICE	1867-1908	1 OCT 1890	1892	1907	LILIAN WAS MARRIED TO ABRAHAM CANNON UNTIL HIS DEATH IN 1896. SHE THEN MOVED TO PENNSYLVANIA & ILLINOIS UNTIL JUNE 1898. SLT, 7 FEB 1899. SHE THEN RESIDED IN PROVO 5TH WARD UNTIL 15 JUN 1902 WHEN SHE MOVED TO CANNON WARD IN SALT LAKE CITY WHERE LEWIS CANNON WAS BISHOP. SEE CANNON WARD ROM AND CHURCH CENSUS 1910-1930.
	2) HAMLIN, LILIAN	1870-1920	1902	1903	1911	
41	CARDON, LOUIS PAUL (2)	1868-1947				
	1) SANDERS, ELLEN C.	1874-	9 OCT 1895	1896	1901	FGS SAYS MARRIAGE TO EDITH WAS IN COLONIA JUAREZ. MARRIAGE TO MARY WAS PERFORMED BY ABRAHAM O. WOODRUFF AND RECORDED IN IVINS R OF M.
	2) DONE, EDITH JAMIMA	1879-1962	23 FEB 1901	1901	1919	
	3) PRATT, MARY IRENE	1882-1948	11 NOV 1903	1904	1922	
*42	CARROLL, JAMES FRANKLIN (1)	1870-1959				
	1) BLACK, MARY BELL	1875-1955	23 JAN 1894	1894	1916	MARRIAGE TO ANNIE PERFORMED BY ANTHONY W. IVINS. IVINS R OF M.
	2) BURRELL, ANNIE ELIZA	1880-	19 JAN 1903	1904	1919	
43	CARROLL, THOMAS MOULTON (1)	1874-1954				
	1) BLACK, AMY J.	1877-	27 JUN 1894			MARRIAGE TO EFFIE IN FGS FOR WILLARD CARROLL. HUSBAND LIVING WITH AMY AFTER MARRIAGE TO EFFIE. BLANDING ROM, 1909-1918, AND 1914 CHURCH CENSUS.
	2) PORTER, EFFIE VILATE		1902			
44	CARROLL, WILLARD (1)	1848-1906				
	1) MOULTON, CHARLOTTE	1851-1940	16 MAR 1869	1870	1895	MARRIAGE TO ELIZABETH PERFORMED BY GEORGE TEASDALE. GEORGE W. MC CONKIE AND JEFFERSON SLADE FGS.
	2) SLADE, ELIZABETH E.	1871-	21 AUG 1893			

*=DISTG. CHURCH SERVICE	NAME OF HUSBAND / NAMES OF WIVES	NUMBER POST-1890 PL. MARRS.	BORN-DIED	MARRIAGE DATE	YEAR FIRST CHILD	YEAR LAST CHILD	REMARKS
*45	CAZIER, DAVID	(1)	1834-1929				DAVID CAZIER AUTOBIOGRAPHY, 13, BYU LIBRARY SAYS: "I TOOK MY CASE BEFORE THE HIGH COUNCIL IN REGARDS TO GIVING ELIZA A SHAM DIVORCE AND MARRYING SARAH ANN AND THEY GAVE THERE [SIC] CONSENT." DAVID DESCRIBED ELIZA AS A "FITTY WIFE" AND WOULD HAVE DIVORCED HER, BUT COULDNT DO "SUCH A DISHONOR-ABLE THING." p.12.
	1) MANGUM, SARAH F.		1838-1889	7 JUN 1857	1858	1865	
	2) NAYLOR, ELIZA ANN		1841-1893	2 JUL 1864			
	3) ANDREWS, SARAH ANN			30 NOV 1892			
*46	CHAMBERLAIN, II, THOMAS	(1)	1854-1918				FRANCIS AND ANNIE ESPLIN, "ONE HUNDRED YEARS OF CHAMBERLAINS, 1854-1954." MATTHIAS F. COWLEY PERFORMED PLURAL MARRIAGE FOR CHAMBERLAIN IN SALT LAKE CITY. TRIALS. DAUGHTER OF FIRST WIFE SUB-STANTIATED THIS, BX.1, FD.30, KIMBALL YOUNG COLLECTION.
	1) HOYT, ELINOR		1856-1927	3 NOV 1873	1874	1897	
	2) FACKERELL, LAURA		1856-1936	3 NOV 1873	1874	1896	
	3) CARLING, ANN		1859-1894	1 FEB 1875	1877	1883	
	4) CARLING, ELLEN A.		1863-1951	13 NOV 1878	1881	1903	
	5) COVINGTON, CHASTIE E.		1883-1942	25 OCT 1883	1886	1910	
	6) WOOLLEY, MARY ELIZ.		1870-1953	6 AUG 1900	1902	1905	
*47	CHAMBERLAIN, III, THOMAS	(1)	1876-1942				SEE CACHE CO. MARRIAGE BK.6, p.95, LOGAN, UTAH, FOR MARRIAGE TO CHRISTINA. APOSTLE MARRINER W. MERRILL ALLEGEDLY COUNSELED CHAMBERLAIN TO MARRY NEW WIFE IN CIVIL CEREMONY WHILE ESTRANGED WIFE WAS IN IDAHO, AND THEN TAKE PLURAL TO CANADA. QUINN, 54.
	1) EMETT, EMMA JANE		1874-1939	27 OCT 1893	1895	1897	
	2) LARSEN, CHRISTINA		1882-	12 MAR 1902			
48	CHLARSON, HEBER OTTO	(1)	1862-1938				FGS SAYS MARRIAGE TO IDA WILSON TOOK PLACE IN SALT LAKE CITY. SEE ALSO COLONIA CHUICHUPA ROM, 1900-1913.
	1) NORTON, IDA ISABELLE		1869-1946	25 DEC 1888	1889	1910	
	2) WILSON, IDA		1878-1926	18 SEP 1907	1908	1913	
49	CLARK, ARTHUR BENJAMIN	(2)	1854-1917				ALL FOUR WIVES LISTED IN DUBLAN ROM, EARLY TO 1912. MARRIAGE TO ETHEL PERFORMED BY ANTHONY W. IVINS. IVINS R OF M.
	1) ROSS, HELEN M.		1854-	7 DEC 1874	1888	1890	
	2) RASMUSSEN, MARY C.		1864-1938	12 SEP 1878	1906	1912	
	3) GRIFFETH, MARINDA E.		1857-	MAR 1903			
	4) SHIRLEY, ETHEL A.		1876-1964	29 SEP 1903	1904	1914	
50	CLAWSON, JOSEPH INKLEY	(1)	1856-1924				FGS FOR CELESTIA SAYS "PARENTS WERE SEALED IN MEX-ICO BY VISITING APOSTLE." ENTRY IN SEYMOUR B. YOUNG DIARY FOR 9 AUG 1900 INDICATES HE PERFORMED CEREMONY. QUINN, 87.
	1) CARDON, MARY		1861-	27 OCT 1877			
	2) DURFEE, CELESTIA		1878-1960	9 AUG 1900	1901	1918	

No.	Name	Birth–Death	Marriage Date	Year	Year	Notes
*51	CLAWSON, RUDGER (1)	1857-1943				FLORENCE DIVORCED RUDGER AND MARRIED R.P. MORRIS IN 1897. SEE CHAP. 6 FOR DISCUSSION OF THIS CASE.
	1) DINWOODEY, FLORENCE	1864-1947	10 AUG 1882	1884		
	2) SPENCER, LYDIA	1860-1941	29 MAR 1883	1886		
	3) UDALL, PEARL	1880-1950	3 AUG 1904		1903	
52	CLAYSON, NATHAN (1)	1847-1932				SLT, 26 JUL 1910 SAID CLAYSON MARRIED A WIDOW, AGE 56. IN TRIAL FOR PLURAL MARRIAGE, MILES A. ROMNEY WAS ASKED IF MARRIAGE WAS "BEFORE THE ACTION TAKEN IN NATHAN CLAYSON'S CASE, OR AFTER." ROMNEY SAID IT WAS ABOUT THE SAME TIME. HIST REC JUAREZ STAKE HIGH COUNCIL, 1908-11, 29 JAN 1910, CHURCH ARCHIVES. APOSTLE MATTHIAS F. COWLEY DENIED INVOLVEMENT, STATING: "I DID NOT MARRY CLAYSON." TRIALS.
	1) BUTLER, ANNIE	1848-1936	24 FEB 1868	1868		
	2) BURRIS, RHODA	1854-1910	1 FEB 1883	1884	1889	
	3) SHEFFIELD, SARAH	1858-	1889		1888	
	4) MILLS, AVALINE	1860-1920	1904			
*53	CLUFF, JR., BENJAMIN (1)	1858-1948				SEE GEORGE REYNOLDS FGS FOR DATA ON FLORENCE. ALSO HIS JOURNAL, 1881-1906. CHURCH ARCHIVES. ENTRIES FOR 31 MAY 1901 AND 13 OCT 1904 SPEAK OF RECENT BIRTHS TO FLORENCE. DIAZ ROM, 1886-1907. SEE QUINN, pp.87-8, FOR SEYMOUR B. YOUNG OFFICIATING.
	1) JOHN, MARY JANE	1862-1934	16 AUG 1883	1884	1903	
	2) CULLIMORE, HARRIET	1888-1954	17 DEC 1886	1892	1909	
	3) REYNOLDS, FLORENCE M.	1874-1932	7 AUG 1900	1901	1904	
54	CLUFF, HEBER MANASSAH (1)	1863-1913				MARRIAGE TO SUSAN PERFORMED BY ANTHONY W. IVINS. IVINS R OF M.
	1) WEECH, SARAH ANN	1867-1947	4 JUL 1885	1886		
	2) SIMS, SUSAN CAROLYN	1874-	30 OCT 1898		1906	
*55	CLUFF, HYRUM ALBERT (1)	1866-1913				CHARLES GRAY HUMPHREY FGS. ALSO SEE COLONIA GARCIA ROM, EARLY TO 1912.
	1) HAWS, RHODA MATILDA	1870-1951	6 SEP 1886	1889		
	2) HUMPHREY, DELILAH F.	1885-	8 FEB 1903		1912	
*56	COWLEY, MATTHIAS FOSS (2)	1858-1940				MATTHIAS F. COWLEY STATED: "I MARRIED MY LAST WIFE (LENORA) IN CANADA IN THE SUMMER OF 1905, SISTER HARKER (HATTIE) IN 1899...TRIALS. SEE ERNEST L. TAYLOR FGS FOR LENORA MARRIAGE DATE. JOHN A. WOOLF PERFORMED MARRIAGE IN CANADA.
	1) HYDE, ABBIE	1863-1931	21 MAY 1884	1885	1901	
	2) PARKINSON, LUELLA S.	1870-1962	22 SEP 1889	1893	1916	
	3) BENNION, HARRIET	1858-1923	1899	1902		
	4) TAYLOR, LENORA	1885-	16 SEP 1905			
57	COX, AMOS (1)	1856-1937				BOTH WIVES LISTED WITH HUSBAND IN CHUICHUPA ROM, 1900-1913.
	1) PALMER, SARAH A.	1859-	10 JUL 1876	1896		
	2) CHESTNUT, GRACE E.	1872-1943	4 JUN 1894		1916	

*=DISTG. CHURCH SERVICE	NAME OF HUSBAND / NAMES OF WIVES	NUMBER POST-1890 PL. MARRS.	BORN-DIED	MARRIAGE DATE	YEAR FIRST CHILD	YEAR LAST CHILD	REMARKS
*58	CROSBY, JR., JESSE W.	(1)	1848-1915				JESSE W. CROSBY, JR. FGS.
	1) CLARK, SARAH PAULINE		1848-1893	4 OCT 1867	1868	1888	
	2) JACOBS, SARAH F.		1857-1946	7 JUN 1878	1880	1897	
	3) MEEKS, SARAH ANN			21 JUN 1894			
59	CUMMINGS, WILLIAM DAVIS	(1)	1862-1911				SEE NEPHI THAYNE FGS FOR ZINA MARRIAGE DATE; ALSO DUBLAN ROM, EARLY TO 1912.
	1) OLIVER, BEATRICE F.		1871-1946	16 SEP 1887	1887	1912	
	2) THAYNE, ZINA		1886-	MAR 1904			
*60	CUTLER, ALLEN RILEY	(1)	1862-1921				NO MARRIAGE DATE AVAILABLE FOR MALINDA, BUT SHE WAS ONLY FIVE YEARS OLD WHEN MANIFESTO WAS ISSUED, STRONGLY SUGGESTING MARRIAGE WAS POLYGAMOUS.
	1) HARDY, LUCY MAY		1874-1919	28 MAY 1890	1891	1912	
	2) SKIDMORE, MALINDA R.		1885-	POST-MANIFESTO	1910	1919	
*61	DEAN, JOSEPH HENRY	(1)	1855-1947				MARRIAGE TO AMANDA PERFORMED BY ANTHONY W. IVINS, ACCORDING TO 10 MAY 1898 ENTRY IN JOSEPH H. DEAN DIARY. CHURCH ARCHIVES. SEE ALSO QUINN, 80.
	1) ARNOLD, SARAH ALLEN		1854-1932	11 OCT 1876	1877	1898	
	2) RIDGES, FLORENCE		1866-1942	11 JUN 1885	1886	1910	
	3) PETTERSON, AMANDA W.			10 MAY 1898			
*62	DONE, ABRAHAM	(2)	1853-1937				FGS SAYS ANTHONY W. IVINS PERFORMED MARRIAGE TO ELLEN IN COLONIA JUAREZ. ABRAHAM MOVED TO MEXICO TO MARRY LOUISA IN POLYGAMY, AND LOUISA LIVED WITH FIRST WIFE AFTER MARRIAGE, SAID ABRAHAM IN 1935 INTERVIEW WITH FAYE OLLERTON. BX.1, FD.41, KIMBALL YOUNG COLLECTION.
	1) ROBINSON, ELIZABETH		1857-1938	22 JUN 1875	1876	1898	
	2) HAAG, LOUISA M.		1868-1965	18 NOV 1900	1901	1911	
	3) MOFFETT, ELLEN P.		1883-	5 JUN 1903	1904	1924	
63	DROUBAY, PIERRE A.	(1)	1855-1914				FGS ALSO LISTS HUSBAND AS PETER. FGS SAYS MARRIAGE TO MARTHA WAS IN MEXICO CITY.
	1) GOLLAHER, HANNAH B.		1859-1905	20 FEB 1877	1877	1898	
	2) DUNN, MARTHA JANE		1872-1934	JAN 1899	1899	1910	
*64	DUFFIN, JAMES GLEDHILL	(1)	1863-1932				MARRIAGE TO AMELIA WAS 1903 IN MEXICO. FGS. MATTHIAS F. COWLEY OFFICIATED. TRIALS. SEE QUINN, 83, FOR 27 JULY 1903 DATE.
	1) GRAINGER, MARY JANE			19 JAN 1881	1882	1903	
	2) CARLING, AMELIA			27 JUL 1903			
65	DURFEE, JABEZ ERASTUS	(2)	1854-1925				DUBLAN ROM, EARLY TO 1912, LISTS WIVES SARAH, ELLA, AND MARY WITH HUSBAND JABEZ. ELLA LISTED AS ELLA
	1) KENDALL, SARAH E.		1855-1929	26 JAN 1874	1874	1899	

#		Name / Wives	Years	Marriage Date		
		2) MC CLEVE, ISABELL W.	1843-1918	24 JUN 1880	1881	1883
		3) MOTT, JUDITHA ANN	1867-1889	4 JUN 1883	1885	1887
		4) MURPHY, ELLA	1867-	POST-MANIFESTO		
		5) ADAMS, MARY FRANCES	1863-1939	AUG 1902	1903	1907
66	(2)	EAGAR, JOEL SIXTUS	1858-1947			
		1) DE WITT, LUCY JANE	1861-1922	11 FEB 1879	1880	1880
		2) STANWORTH, NANCY A.	1865-1950	3 JUL 1894	1895	1905
		3) LEE, EMILY JANE	1874-1911	16 AUG 1902	1903	1910
67	(1)	ECCLES, DAVID	1849-1912			
		1) JENSEN, BERTHA MARIE	1857-1935	27 DEC 1875	1877	1901
		2) STODDARD, ELLEN	1867-	2 JAN 1885	1890	1909
		3) GEDDES, MARGARET	1865-1954	AUG 1898	1899	
68	(1)	ECHOLS, JOHN	1860-1951			
		1) DRUMMOND, MARGARET		1883		
		2) ANGLE, KATHERINE I.	1870-1935	15 FEB 1894	1896	1907
		3) ANGLE, SARAH ELIZ.	1880-1955	8 NOV 1900	1901	1916
*69	(1)	ELDREDGE, JAMES A.	1857-1940			
		1) JENNINGS, JANE	1856-1926	23 JUN 1879	1892	
		2) NAME UNAVAILABLE		POST-MANIFESTO		
70	(2)	EVANS, EDWIN	1860-1946			
		1) LEWIS, CATHERINE	1859-1933	15 JAN 1880	1881	1898
		2) CLARK, MINERVA A.	1881-1950	6 JUN 1908	1909	1912
		3) CLARK, LOUISA A.	1881-1961	5 JUN 1909	1910	
71	(1)	EVANS, JOHN REESE	1878-1943			
		1) HEDER, MINNIE MAY	1883-1952	25 DEC 1902	1904	1929
		2) DURFEE, CATHERINE E.	1887-	8 OCT 1907	1909	1928

Notes:

HUMPHREYS DURFEE, DAUGHTER OF JAMES MURPHY, INDICATING PRIOR MARRIAGE TO HUMPHREYS. JAMES DANIEL MURPHY FGS SHOWS SHE MARRIED RICHARD M. HUMPHREY IN 1875. JUAREZ STAKE EARLY PIONEER CENSUS, 1898, COLONIA JUAREZ, CHURCH ARCHIVES, GIVES ELLA HUMPHREY 20 DEC 1897 ARRIVAL DATE IN COLONIES, AND YOUNGEST HUMPHREY CHILD BORN ABOUT 1875. DATA PLACE MARRIAGE BETWEEN 1897 AND 1912. SLT, 1 SEP. 1910.

FGS FOR EMILY SAYS SHE WAS MARRIED IN COLONIA JUAREZ "BY AN APOSTLE." EMILY'S SISTER ABIGAIL WAS MARRIED TO CHARLES W. LILLYWHITE BY MATTHIAS F. COWLEY ON SAME DAY, SAME PLACE, SO IT WAS CLEARLY COWLEY WHO OFFICIATED FOR EMILY. WOODRUFF WARD ROM, 1891-1896, p.136, INCLUDES NOTE TO JOEL'S RECORD: "...SEPARATED FROM HIS WIFE [LUCY] AND MOVED AWAY ALONE, TAKING HIS RECOMMEND. OCT. 4, 1893."

CLEO G. GEDDES, HISTORY PLAN B PAPER, "THE ECCLES CASE." UTAH STATE UNIVERSITY. LOGAN, UTAH. SEE ACCOUNT PROVIDED ABOVE IN CHAP. 5.

FGS FOR CALEB ANGLE GIVES SARAH'S MARRIAGE DATE. JUAREZ ROM, 1889-1904.

JUDSON TOLMAN CONFESSED TO QUORUM OF TWELVE APOSTLES THAT HE MARRIED PLURAL WIFE TO JAMES A. ELDREDGE. REED SMOOT DIARIES, 1 OCT 1910.

FIRST WIFE LISTED WITH HUSBAND IN 1914 CHURCH CENSUS. ALSO SLT, 15 JAN 1910.

SLT, 28 OCT 1910, "POINTS ON SPORATICISM," SAYS PLURAL MARRIAGE OCCURRED IN SALT LAKE TEMPLE.

* = DISTG. CHURCH SERVICE	NAME OF HUSBAND / NAMES OF WIVES	NUMBER POST-1890 PL. MARRS.	BORN-DIED	MARRIAGE DATE	YEAR FIRST CHILD	YEAR LAST CHILD	REMARKS
*72	EYRING, EDWARD CHRISTIAN	(1)	1868-1957				MARRIAGE TO EMMA PERFORMED BY ANTHONY W. IVINS. IVINS R OF M.
	1) ROMNEY, CAROLINE C.		1874-1954	11 OCT 1893	1894	1912	
	2) ROMNEY, EMMA		1884-1957	3 NOV 1903	1904	1922	
*73	FARR, HEBER ERASTUS	(1)	1875-1965				MARRIAGE TO RANGMILDA (HILDA) PERFORMED BY ANTHONY W. IVINS. IVINS R OF M. DUBLAN ROM, EARLY TO 1912. ALSO HILDA'S ORAL HISTORY INTERVIEW WITH V. W. JORGENSEN, CSUF ORAL HIST. PROGRAM, pp.1-5.
	2) WILLIAMS, AMANDA E.		1877-1964	25 DEC 1893	1895	1915	
	3) BLUTH, RANGMILDA		1883-	25 MAR 1904	1906	1923	
*74	FARR, LORIN	(1)	1820-1908				FGS GIVES 8 MAR 1901 DATE AND SALT LAKE TEMPLE FOR MARRIAGE TO CLARA. SEE ALSO QUINN, 53.
	1) CHASE, NANCY BAILEY		1823-1892	1 JAN 1845	1845	1863	
	2) GILES, SARAH		1831-1892	26 JUL 1851	1852	1870	
	3) JONES OLIVE ANN		1829-1914	28 FEB 1852	1953	1866	
	4) BINGHAM, MARY		1820-1893	2 DEC 1854	1856	1860	
	5) ERICKSON, NICHOLINE		1837-1915	29 JAN 1857	1858	1870	
	6) BATES, CLARA JANE			8 MAR 1901			
*75	FARR, JR., WINSLOW	(1)	1837-1913				MARRIAGE TO SARAH PERFORMED BY ANTHONY W. IVINS. IVINS R OF M. IN HILDA FARR INTERVIEW WITH V. W. JORGENSEN, CITED ABOVE, pp.10-11, HILDA STATED LOCAL GOSSIP CRITICIZED HER FATHER-IN-LAW WINSLOW FARR FOR WALKING TO CHURCH WITH SARAH INSTEAD OF EARLIER WIFE MATILDA [TILLIE].
	1) COVINSTON, EMILY J.		1856-1903	17 OCT 1858			
	2) BINGHAM, SUSAN M.		1851-	5 MAY 1873	1875	1886	
	3) HALVORSON, MATILDA			11 DEC 1879			
	4) MITCHELL, SARAH			10 JAN 1899			
*76	FELT, DAVID PILE	(1)	1860-1937				DN, 10 AUG 1909, SAID DAVID EXCOMMUNICATED FOR "ILLICIT RELATIONS WITH A WIDOW." SLT, 11 AUG 1909 SAID FRIENDS THOUGHT POLYGAMY. SLT, 22 AUG 1909 QUOTED SON SAYING SLT, NOT DN, ACCURATE, AND FATHER WAS "LIVING HIS RELIGION AS HE UNDERSTOOD IT." FELT'S BISHOP, GEORGE R. JONES, LIKELY IMPLICATED, RESIGNED WITH ALMOST NO NOTICE ON 8 AUG. 1909. 23RD WARD ROM AND SALT LAKE STAKE HISTORICAL RECORD BOOK, 1906-1909, CHURCH ARCHIVES.
	1) SPEIRS, ADELINE		1861-1931	2 NOV 1882	1884	1897	
	2) NAME UNAVAILABLE			POST-MANIFESTO			
77	FILLERUP, CHARLES R.	(1)	1873-1936				FGS FOR MARY SAYS SHE AND HUSBAND WERE "SEALED BY AN APOSTLE SENT TO MEXICO..." AND MARRIAGE TOOK PLACE IN COLONIA DIAZ.
	1) JOHNSON, MONETA		1882-1963	1 JUN 1898	1900	1922	
	2) JOHNSON, MARY E		1883-	19 NOV 1901	1905	1912	

#	Name / Spouses	Dates	Marriage Date			Notes
78	GARDNER, CHARLES FREDRICK (1)	1858-1926				MARRIAGE TO SARAH PERFORMED BY ANTHONY W. IVINS. IVINS R OF M.
	1) ANDERSEN, AMELIA	1863-1954	10 NOV 1880	1882	1903	
	2) COX, SARAH ELLEN	1885-1953	9 MAR 1902	1904	1925	
*79	GRACE, ISAAC HENRY (1)	1857-1951				FIRST WIFE LISTED WITH ISAAC ON 1920 CHURCH CENSUS. SEE ALSO ROM, NEPHI 2ND WARD, EARLY TO 1906.
	1) HUDSON, HELEN	1850-1934	19 JAN 1882	1884		
	2) SORENSEN, KATHRYN	1870-1911	1902	1904		
*80	GRANT, JOSEPH HYRUM (1)	1853-1917				SEE FGS FOR LOUISA'S EARLIER HUSBAND, ETHER COLTRIN, WHO DIED 13 OCT 1892. THE 27 MAY 1903 LETTER OF WILEY NEBEKER TO JOHN HENRY SMITH MENTIONS HER BEING MARRIED TO GRANT, SO HER MARRIAGE DATE TO GRANT MUST FALL BETWEEN THE TWO JUST CITED. JOHN HENRY SMITH LETTERS, GEORGE A. SMITH FAMILY PAPERS, UNIVERSITY OF UTAH LIBRARY.
	1) ELDREDGE, ALICE E.	1855-1911	18 OCT 1875	1876	1895	
	2) WINEGAR, LOUISA	1851-1920	POST-MANIFESTO			
81	GUYMAN, WILLARD RICHARD (1)	1864-1958				FGS FOR ELLEN SAYS MARRIAGE WAS IN COLONIA JUAREZ. SLT, 24 MAY 1910, AND 1 AUG 1910, SAYS ALEXANDER F. MACDONALD PERFORMED MARRIAGE.
	1) ROWLEY, MARY	1871-1965	1 OCT 1886	1890	1912	
	2) BLACK, HARRIET	1880-1945	25 SEP 1889	1901	1909	
	3) LUNT, ELLEN		10 NOV 1900			
82	HARDY, ABEL WOODRUFF (1)	1877-1957				WARRINER AHAZ PORTER FGS.
	1) COOLEY, MARIA	1881-1963	20 DEC 1896	NO CHILDREN		
	2) PORTER, CYNTHIA JANE	1885-1929	9 NOV 1901			
*83	HARDY, GEORGE WILLIAM (2)	1863-1921				HATCH AND HARDY, STALWARTS SOUTH OF THE BORDER, (ANAHEIM, CAL., PRIVATELY PRINTED, 1985), 215-218. JUAREZ ROM, 1906-1916. JOHN W. TAYLOR PERFORMED MARRIAGE TO EMMA. JOHN HENRY SMITH DIARIES, GEORGE A. SMITH FAMILY PAPERS, UNIVERSITY OF UTAH LIBRARY, 8 MAR 1898.
	1) ROGERS, JULIA ANN	1860-1935	2 DEC 1885	1886	1898	
	2) ROWLEY, EMMA S.	1878-1963	8 MAR 1898	1899	1918	
	3) BUTLER, BETSY ANN	1881-	1902	1905		
*84	HARMER, LOREN HANNIBAL (1)	1854-1926				REP. GEORGE SUTHERLAND TOLD SUB COMMITTEE ON JUDICIARY HE PERSONALLY KNEW OF HARMER CASE, AND THAT MARRIAGE TO MARY WAS IN MEXICO. GEORGE SUTHERLAND PAPERS, BOX 8, LIBRARY OF CONGRESS.
	1) TEW, ELLEN AMELIA	1856-1932	27 SEP 1875	1877	1897	
	2) WILLIAMS, IDA ALICE	1859-1931	8 SEP 1881	1882	1902	
	3) ANDERSON, MARY ELLEN	1874-1959	19 NOV 1897	1898	1916	

*=DISTG. CHURCH SERVICE	NAME OF HUSBAND / NAMES OF WIVES	NUMBER POST-1890 PL. MARRS.	BORN-DIED	MARRIAGE DATE	YEAR FIRST CHILD	YEAR LAST CHILD	REMARKS
*85	HART, ARTHUR WILLIAM	(1)	1869-1949				MATTHIAS F. COWLEY PERFORMED PLURAL MARRIAGE. TRIALS. EVADYNA FGS SAYS IT WAS IN SALT LAKE CITY. ELNA HART PALMER INTERVIEW, p.16, POHP.
	1) LOWE, ADA D.		1881-	22 AUG 1900	1901	1925	
	2) HENDERSON, EVADYNA		1886-	21 AUG 1903	1905	1929	
*86	HAWS, GEORGE MARTIN	(1)	1858-1936				MARTHA'S FGS SAYS MARRIAGE PERFORMED BY ALEXANDER F. MACDONALD IN COLONIA JUAREZ.
	1) CLUFF, REBECCA J.		1858-1945	23 NOV 1877	1878	1900	
	2) CLUFF, SUSAN ANN		1871-1947	27 OCT 1886	1888	1910	
	3) WALL, MARTHA H.		1878-1957	15 NOV 1900	1901	1920	
*87	HAYMORE, FRANKLIN D.	(1)	1849-1931				PEARL'S MARRIAGE DATE IN DAVID JOHNSON WILSON FGS.
	1) TAYLOR, LUCINDA A.		1850-1897	2 MAY 1869	1870	1888	
	2) LANT, ELIZABETH ANN		1870-1898	22 MAR 1888	1889	1894	
	3) WILSON, PEARL M.		1871-1907	9 AUG 1897	1899	1907	
*88	HEGSTED, VICTOR C.	(1)	1865-1941				HANNAH'S FGS SAYS MARRIAGE IN SALT LAKER CITY SEE ALSO SALEM (IDAHO) WARD ROM, 1901-1906, p.9.
	1) LEE, LAVINA N.		-1886	5 FEB 1885			
	2) MARTIN, ADA		1871-1912	17 DEC 1890	1891	1910	
	3) GROVER, HANNAH		1870-1945	1 MAY 1904	1905	1915	
89	HENDERSON, WILLIAM	(1)	1851-1933				SEE FGS FOR JOHN EASTHOPE AND LEVI W. TIPPETS REGARDING ELIZA. FGS SAYS FIRST TWO WIVES RECEIVED TEMPLE DIVORCES FROM WILLIAM IN DECEMBER 1899.
	1) PEARSON, MARTHA G.		1853-1934	8 JAN 1872	1873	1885	
	2) CAPPELL, KEZIAH JANE		1860-1948	27 JUL 1882	1883	1896	
	3) EASTHOPE, ELIZA H.		1869-1935	23 JUL 1899			
*90	HENDRICKS, WILLIAM D.	(1)	1829-1909				ELEANOR MARRIED BY ANTHONY W. IVINS. IVINS R OF M.
	1) ANDRUS, MARY JANE		1833-1914	12 MAR 1851	1852	1875	
	2) SMITH, ALVIRA LAVONA		1831-1921	4 AUG 1851	1852	1875	
	3) DAVENPORT, ALMIRA		1847-1928	14 JUN 1865	1866	1880	
	4) OLSEN, CHRISTINE		1862-1923	4 MAR 1885	1888	1900	
	5) MAYBINE, ELEANOR A.		1869-	3 DEC 1897			
91	HICKMAN, GEORGE FRANCIS	(1)	1869-1958				SLT ARTICLES FOR 8 MAY 1910 AND 13 MAY 1910 LINK CHLOE PALMER TO HICKMAN. CHLOE WAS TWELVE AT MANIFESTO, SO MARRIAGE BETWEEN THEN AND 1910. SEE CASTLEDALE WARD ROM, 1900-1919; 1914 CHURCH CENSUS; AND ZEMIRA PALMER FGS.
	1) DOUGLASS, HARRIET		1869-1949				
	2) PALMER, CHLOE		1878-1916	27 MAR 1892 POST-MANIFESTO	1892	1910	

No.	Name	Lifespan	Marriage Date			Notes
*92	HICKMAN, JOSIAH EDWIN (1)	1862-1937				MATTHIAS F. COWLEY PERFORMED MARRIAGE AFTER MANIFESTO TO HICKMAN. TRIALS. 1890 MARRIAGE PERFORMED BY ALEXANDER F. MACDONALD. PROCEEDINGS, 2: 95-96. Cf. HICKMAN FGS.
	1) ROGERS, MARTHA ELLA	1866-1900	18 FEB 1885	1886	1900	
	2) LAWISCH, MARTHA A.	1870-1945	7 JUN 1890	1891	1913	
	3) HANSEN, HELEN J.		JAN 1902			
*93	HIGGS, ALPHA JEDDE (1)	1864-1952				RODNEY CARLOS BADGER FGS. SLT ARTICLES 27 JUL 1909 AND 8 SEP 1910 DESCRIBE HIGGS ELOPING TO CANADA WITH ELIZABETH, LEAVING FIRST WIFE AND FIVE CHILDREN IN SALT LAKE CITY. SLT, 7 SEP 1910 SAYS HE WAS ONLY DISFELLOWSHIPPED. SEE ALSO 1935 CHURCH CENSUS FOR HIGGS.
	1) HILLAM, MARY ANN		7 SEP 1887			
	2) BADGER, ELIZABETH A.	1883-1945	1 FEB 1909	1911	1926	
*94	HILTON, THOMAS HEDDOCK (1)	1870-1915				SEE FGS FOR JOSEPH MC MURRIN, FATHER OF BOTH WIVES.
	1) MC MURRIN, SARAH	1871-1947	4 DEC 1889	1891	1911	
	2) MC MURRIN, JOSEPHINE	1886-1936	1902			
*95	HINTZE, FERDINAND FRIIS (1)	1854-1928				"A HINTZE COMPILATION BEGUN AUG 27 1983 AT THE ANNUAL FAMILY REUNION," COPY IN POSSESSION OF AUTHOR, CONTAINS NORA FGS WHICH STATES THEY "WERE MARRIED 'ON A FERRY BOAT BETWEEN U.S. AND CANADA BY ANTHON H. LUND.' NORA TOLD HER CHILDREN THEY WERE SWORN TO SECRECY." HINTZE DIARY, CHURCH ARCHIVES.
	1) MADSEN, RASMINE	1860-1950	31 JAN 1876	1876		
	2) WALL, AUGUSTA M.	1857-1940	22 AUG 1878	1880		
	3) JENSEN, MARIA SOPHIA	1864-1923	16 OCT 1882	1884		
	4) MIKKELSEN, NORA	1872-1959	1 JAN 1898			
96	HOOD, JAMES (1)	1862-1950				JAMINA MARRIED BY ANTHONY W. IVINS. IVINS R OF M.
	1) RUSSELL, ELIZABETH J.	1867-1930	4 OCT 1883	1884		
	2) RUSSELL, JAMINA J.	1871-	10 AUG 1898	1903		
97	HUBER, JOHN JACOB (1)	1871-1951				PERCIS' FGS SAYS THEY "WERE SEALED IN COLONIA JUAREZ, CHIHUAHUA, MEXICO BY AN APOSTLE." APOSTLE COWLEY IS KNOWN TO HAVE PERFORMED TWO OTHER PLURAL MARRIAGES THAT DATE IN COLONIA JUAREZ, SO HE IS LIKELY TO HAVE PERFORMED THIS MARRIAGE AS WELL.
	1) HUISH, ETTA M.	1872-1939	13 JAN 1892	1895	1908	
	2) MAXHAM, PERCIS LULU	1880-1959	16 AUG 1902	1904	1924	
98	HUNSAKER, SIMEON ATWOOD (1)	1869-1902				MATHILDE'S FGS SAYS MARRIAGE PERFORMED IN SALT LAKE CITY. FOR DATA ON FIRST WIFE, SEE MORELOS ROM, 1900-1909. ADVISED TO STAY OUT OF THE WAY OF CIVIL AUTHORITIES BY APOSTLE RUDGER CLAWSON. CLAWSON DIARIES, 23 NOV 1899. UNIVERSITY OF UTAH LIBRARY.
	1) GREEN, MARY ADA	1876-	29 DEC 1893	1897	1902	
	2) TEUBER, MATHILDE C.	1873-1904	6 JAN 1897	1897	1902	

*=DISTG. CHURCH SERVICE	NAME OF HUSBAND / NAMES OF WIVES	NUMBER POST-1890 PL. MARRS.	BORN-DIED	MARRIAGE DATE	YEAR FIRST CHILD	YEAR LAST CHILD	REMARKS
*99	HURST, PHILIP	(1)	1836-1901				DUBLAN ROM, EARLY TO 1912.
	1) GUYMON, LUCINDA H.			1 JAN 1857	1860	1867	
	2) WILCOX, ELIZABETH		1851-1942	19 SEP 1868	1869	1893	
	3) SANDERSON, REBECCA A.		1858-	9 OCT 1873	1884	1896	
	4) GIBSON, EMMA			30 APR 1892			
*100	HURST, PHILIP HARRISON	(1)	1860-1929				GEORGEANNA FGS SAYS MARRIAGE PERFORMED IN COLONIA DUBLAN. SEE ALSO DUBLAN ROM, EARLY TO 1912.
	1) WILSON, ELLEN ADELIA		1861-1930	10 OCT 1879	1881	1902	
	2) WILSON, MARY M.		1869-1958	9 APR 1889	1891	1912	
	3) JONES, GEORGEANNA		1878-1963	24 DEC 1902	1903	1918	
*101	JACKSON, JOSEPH	(1)	1852-1935				FGS FOR MARY ANN SAYS MARRIAGE PERFORMED IN COLONIA JUAREZ. SEE ALSO DUBLAN ROM, EARLY TO 1912.
	1) PHILLIPS, PRUDENCE			7 JUL 1873			
	2) STOWELL, MARY ANN		1866-1943	22 NOV 1887	1889	1905	
	3) JONES, MARIA		1872-1929	2 DEC 1902	1904	1906	
*102	JAMESON, JR., ALEXANDER	(1)	1859-1943				DUBLAN ROM, EARLY TO 1912.
	1) HATFIELD, MILLICENT		1862-1952	29 DEC 1881	1882	1905	
	2) LARSEN, MARY AMELIA		1869-1924	24 MAY 1901	1904	1915	
103	JARMAN, CHARLES GILL	(1)	1867-1949				FGS FOR EMMA GIVES 12 SEP 1912 DIVORCE DATE OF FIRST WIFE TO CHARLES.
	1) LARSEN, KIRSTEN M.		1863-1948	5 JAN 1889	1889	1905	
	2) COLLIS, EMMA BESSIE		1873-1919	4 JUL 1909	1910	1913	
104	JARVIS, SAMUEL WALTER	(1)	1855-1923				MARRIAGE TO PEARLEY PERFORMED BY ANTHONY W. IVINS. IVINS R OF M.
	1) DE FRIES, FRANCES G.		1859-1933	4 DEC 1877	1879	1902	
	2) TAYLOR, PEARLEY		1881-1919	28 OCT 1902	1903	1919	
*105	JENSEN, DAVID	(1)	1835-1909				DAVID WAS RELEASED AS ALTERNATE HIGH COUNCILMAN IN 1898 BECAUSE OF HIS "RECENT MARRIAGE WITH ANOTHER WIFE." ONEIDA STAKE HIGH COUNCIL MINUTES, 31 MAR 1898, QUOTED IN QUINN, 53. DAVID SAYS IN HIS AUTOBIOGRAPHY HE AND JULIA NOT LIVING TOGETHER. CHURCH ARCHIVES.
	1) PETERSEN, BERTHA S.		1841-1884	20 AUG 1859	1860	1882	
	2) PETERSEN, JULIA K.		1851-1920	18 NOV 1868	1870	1892	
	3) ARNESON, LEONORE A.		1864-1903	2 NOV 1897			

No.	Name		Dates	Marriage			Notes
106	JOHNSON, ABIA EZELIEL		1865-1932				FGS FOR VIVIAN SAYS MARRIAGE TOOK PLACE AT COLONIA DIAZ.
	1) BEVAN, VIOLET JANE		1872-1933	1 OCT 1891	1892	1914	
	2) LEMMON, VIVIAN		1883-	19 NOV 1901	1906	1925	
*107	JOHNSON, JAMES FRANCIS	(1)	1856-1916				MARRIAGE TO CLARA PERFORMED BY BRIGHAM YOUNG, JR. AT COLONIA JUAREZ. PROCEEDINGS, 1: 388-408.
	1) RICHMOND, ROZINA		1862-1949	3 APR 1876	1877	1904	
	2) BARBER, CLARA		1877-	19 MAY 1894	1895	1897	
*108	JOLLEY, HASKELL S.	(1)	1861-1930				MARRIAGE TO ELLEN PERFORMED BY ANTHONY W. IVINS. IVINS R OF M.
	1) LIETHEAD, EFFIE S.		1864-1918	19 OCT 1881	1994	1906	
	2) HARRISON, ELLEN E.		1871-1949	1 JUN 1898	1899	1916	
*109	JONES, DANIEL BROOKS	(1)	1857-1916				SARAH LISTED AS LIVING WITH HUSBAND IN 1914 CHURCH CENSUS. MARRIAGE TO RHODA PERFORMED BY ANTHONY W. IVINS. IVINS R OF M.
	1) WHEELER, SARAH ELLEN		1860-1943	13 MAY 1880	1881	1886	
	2) MERRILL, RHODA ANN		1883-1958	10 MAR 1903	1906	1916	
*110	JONES, JR., FREDRICK W.	(1)	1874-1926				MARRIAGE TO LAURA PERFORMED BY ANTHONY W. IVINS. IVINS R OF M.
	1) LAKE, PHILOMELIA		1874-1898	3 SEP 1892	1893	1897	
	2) PAYNE, ELNORA		1881-	23 DEC 1900	1902	1924	
	3) MOFFETT, LAURA ANN		1885-1940	1 MAR 1904	1904	1912	
*111	JONES, TIMOTHY	(1)	1849-1922				MARY SAID IN INTERVIEW THAT MARRIAGE TO ELIZABETH WAS IN 1894, IN MEXICO. BX.2, FD.35, KIMBALL YOUNG COLLECTION. JOHN DONE FGS.
	1) DONE, MARY JANE		1859-1945	1 JUN 1877	1878	1903	
	2) DONE, ELIZABETH ANN		1854-1920	1894			
112	JORGENSEN, JORGEN S.	(1)	1884-1925				JORGEN LEFT FREDERIKKE IN EPHRAIM, UTAH WHERE SHE DIED ON 24 MAY 1904. EPHRAIM NORTH ROM, 1908-1912, ENTRY 837. SLT, 21 AUG 1910. MARRIAGE TO JOHANNA PERFORMED BY ANTHONY W. IVINS. IVINS R OF M.
	1) HANSEN, HANNAH C.		1849-1883	17 NOV 1872	1875	1882	
	2) JACOBSEN, FREDERIKKE		-1904	25 NOV 1903			
	3) IBORG, JOHANNA L.		1866-				
*113	KELSCH, LOUIS A.	(1)	1856-1917				MATTHIAS F. COWLEY PERFORMED A PLURAL MARRIAGE FOR KELSCH ABOUT 1898. TRIALS. MARY'S ANCESTRAL FILE SAYS MARRIAGE AT SALT LAKE CITY, ABOUT 1898, FHL. SEE WATERLOO ROM, EARLY TO 1937. FHL FILM 889,386. ROSALIA LISTED IN 1920-1930 CHURCH CENSUS AS WIDOW.
	1) ATWOOD, ROSALIA ESTER		1858-	25 OCT 1878	1905	1909	
	2) LYYERLA, MARY LUCRETIA		1872-1944	1898			
*114	LARSEN, RASMUS	(1)	1839-1928				RASMUS GRANTED REQUEST TO TAKE PLURAL WIFE. QUINN, 76. HE AND ANNIE ARRIVED IN MEXICO 10 AUG 1892. JUAREZ STAKE PIONEER REC, 1898, AND COLONIA DIAZ ROM, 1907-1912. ASSUMED MARRIAGE IN 1892, BASED ON RASMUS RECEIVING PERMISSION FOR POLYGAMY AND HIS ARRIVAL IN MEXICO SHORTLY THEREAFTER.
	1) PETERSEN, MAREN C.		1841-	12 DEC 1865	1866	1897	
	2) CHRISTENSEN, ANNIE SOPHIA		1857-1918	1892	1894		

*=DISTG. CHURCH SERVICE	NAME OF HUSBAND / NAMES OF WIVES	NUMBER POST-1890 PL. MARRS.	BORN-DIED	MARRIAGE DATE	YEAR FIRST CHILD	YEAR LAST CHILD	REMARKS
115	LE BARON, DON MORONI		1858-1941				CHURCH CENSUS, 1914-1935, AND DUBLAN ROM, EARLY TO 1912. SEE QUINN, 55 FOR DETAILS OF MARY'S MARRIAGE.
	1) JOHNSON, JULIA ANN	(1)	1860-1959	28 AUG 1878	1879	1903	
	2) JOHNSON, VILATE E.		1859-1939	2 NOV 1882	1883	1901	
	3) PEARCE, MARY JANE		1876-	14 NOV 1904	1905	1907	
*116	LEAVITT, FRANKLIN DEWEY		1870-1959				FGS SAYS MARRIAGE TO JANE AT CARDSTON, CANADA. JOHN W. TAYLOR AUTHORIZED JOHN A. WOOLF TO PERFORM MARRIAGE. TRIALS.
	1) DOWDLE, ELIZAA RUTH	(1)	1869-1904	26 FEB 1890	1891	1904	
	2) GLENN, JANE		1883-1972	11 SEP 1903	1904	1925	
117	LEWIS, WALTER BEERS		1866-1953				MARRIAGE TO ESTHER PERFORMED BY ANTHONY W. IVINS. THE FIRST WIFE IS RECORDED AS THE WITNESS. IVINS R OF M.
	1) HAWLEY, FANNIE BALL	(1)	1871-1924	24 OCT 1894	1895	1909	
	2) WILSON, ESTHER D.		1878-	17 MAY 1902	1904	1920	
*118	LILLYWHITE, CHARLES W.		1874-1947				FGS SAYS MARRIAGE TO ABIGAIL PERFORMED IN COLONIA JUAREZ BY MATTHIAS F. COWLEY.
	1) COPLAN, MARGARET	(1)	1875-1960	5 OCT 1893	1894	1915	
	2) LEE, ABIGAIL E.		1877-1915	16 AUG 1902	1903	1908	
*119	LONGHURST, WARREN		1863-1951				MARRIAGE TO HELEN PERFORMED BY ANTHONY W IVINS. IVINS R OF M. SLT, 25 APR 1910, SAYS LATEST MARRIAGE TOOK PLACE IN SALT LAKE TEMPLE. EVA'S FGS SAYS ONLY THAT SHE WAS MARRIED IN SALT LAKE CITY. SEE ALSO DUBLAN ROM, EARLY TO 1912.
	1) ALLRED, MYRA IRENE	(2)	1872-1912	2 OCT 1889	NO CHILDREN		
	2) CLARK, HELEN M.		1880-	15 JUL 1903			
	3) ALLRED, EVA		1888-1918	17 NOV 1909	1911	1918	
*120	LYMAN, WALTER CLISBEE		1863-1943				FGS SAYS "HUSBAND WALTER, AND WIFE LUCY, MARRIED IN CANADA IN SEP 1904: BUT DAY OF MONTH, PLACE, AND PERSON OFFICIATING NEVER DISCLOSED."
	1) LOVELL, SYLVIA ANN	(1)	1867-1889	4 OCT 1883	1884	1889	
	2) FINLINSON, ELIZABETH		1867-1916	16 DEC 1891	1893	1914	
	3) HALLS, LUCY		1879-1922	SEP 1904	1906	1919	
121	MAXUM, HEBER KIMBALL		1849-1927				CHURCH CENSUS FOR 1914 SHOWS HUSBAND LIVING WITH CAROLINE BUTTERFIELD. SEE ALSO SLT, 25 DEC 1910, FOR THEIR VERSION OF THE PLURAL MARRIAGE. SEE ALSO MORELOS ROM, 1900-1912.
	1) BUTTERFIELD, CAROLINE	(1)	1851-1943	17 APR 1870	1872	1880	
	2) JOHNSON, CAROLINE D.		1874-	NOV 1899			
122	MC CALL, ROBERT LINDSAY		1869-1952				BOTH WIVES LISTED WITH HUSBAND IN MORELOS ROM, 1909-1912.
	1) SMITH, CHRISTINA	(1)	1861-1939	10 OCT 1888	1893	1895	
	2) SUNTHEIMER, CHRISTIN		1875-	12 OCT 1899			

No.	Name	Dates	Dates	Year	Year	Notes
123	MC CLELLAN, GEORGE ALMA (1)	1872-1963			1917	MARRIAGE TO NELLIE PERFORMED BY ALEXANDER F. MACDONALD IN COLONIA JUAREZ. FGS.
	1) WRIGHT, MARY A.	1876-1957	18 SEP 1893	1895		
	2) ALLAN, NELLIE	1881-1962	16 MAY 1901	1903	1921	
124	MC CUNE, HENRY MATTHEW (1)	1862-1945			1903	MC CUNE MARRIED MARTHA JANE SUTTON 18 FEB 1897 IN LOGAN, UTAH WHILE STILL MARRIED AND LIVING WITH ESTHER. 1ST DISTRICT COURT, CACHE COUNTY, LOGAN, UTAH, NO. 17. MC CUNE SENTENCED ONE YEAR 20 APR 1897. CHARLES M. OWEN COLLECTION, FD. 6, CHURCH ARCHIVES. SEE ALSO JAMES W. PAXTON DIARY NO.3, JAN 1898, BYU LIBRARY; AND FGS FOR HENRY F. MC CUNE AND ALLAN S. MC CUNE.
	1) PAXMAN, ESTHER ELIZ.	1865-	9 APR 1885	1892		
	2) SUTTON, MARTHA JANE	1874-	18 FEB 1897	1902		
*125	MC GREGOR, DONALD ALPINE (1)	1876-1938			1913	DONALD ALPINE MC GREGOR FGS.
	1) WATSON, ALMA G.	1874-1969	21 NOV 1895	1896		
	2) WATSON, BERTHA P.		5 JUNE 1909			
*126	MC KEAN, JR., THEODORE (1)	1855-1934			1901	CHURCH CENSUS FOR 1914 LISTS SOPHIA AND FIVE CHILDREN LIVING WITH MC KEAN IN THE SALT LAKE 29TH WARD. THEODORE MC KEAN, JR. FGS.
	1) ALLEN, LUCY ADELIA	1864-1942	28 JUN 1878	1884		
	2) LANE, SOPHIA JANE		7 FEB 1884			
	3) BAGGARLEY, MAUD E.		1908			
127	MC LAWS, JOHN WILLIAMS (1)	1876-			1914	BOTH WIVES LISTED WITH HUSBAND IN JUAREZ ROM, 1906-1916, AND MORELOS ROM, 1909-1912.
	1) BRADSHAW, ELLEN E.	1882-	7 MAR 1900	1901		
	2) BRADSHAW, EMMA	1889-	4 OCT 1906	1907		
128	MECHAM, LUCIAN MORMON (1)	1862-1922			1897	TWO WIVES WERE SISTERS. SEE JOSIAH G. HARDY FGS. MARRIAGE TO MARY PERFORMED BY JOHN W. TAYLOR. JOHN HENRY SMITH DIARIES, 9 MAR 1898. BOTH WIVES LISTED IN 1920 CHURCH CENSUS WITH LUCIAN, AND IN 1925 AS WIDOWS.
	1) HARDY, LAURA ANN	1865-1933	30 MAY 1889	1887		
	2) HARDY, MARY ANN	1862-1941	9 MAR 1898			
129	MEMMOTT, JAMES WILSON (1)	1841-1919			1890	FGS SAYS MARRIAGE TO MARY ANN PERFORMED IN COLONIA JUAREZ. SEE ALSO DUBLAN ROM, EARLY TO 1912.
	1) HOPKINS, ELIZABETH	1855-1898	24 MAR 1861	1872		
	2) MATHEWSON, JANE	1864-1935	15 MAY 1871	1895	1905	
	3) MELLOR, MARY ANN		14 JUN 1894			
130	MERRILL, "MR" (1)		POST-MANIFESTO			JUDSON TOLMAN ADMITTED PERFORMING A PLURAL MARRIAGE TO A MR. MERRILL. REED SMOOT DIARIES, 1 OCT 1910. IT IS PRESUMED THAT THIS MERRILL IS NOT ONE OF THE OTHER THREE ON THIS LIST, AS THEY WERE NOT PERFORMED BY JUDSON TOLMAN.
	1) NAME UNAVAILABLE					

*=DISTG. CHURCH SERVICE	NAME OF HUSBAND / NAMES OF WIVES	NUMBER POST-1890 PL. MARRS.	BORN-DIED	MARRIAGE DATE	YEAR FIRST CHILD	YEAR LAST CHILD	REMARKS
131	MERRILL, CHARLES EDWARD	(1)	1866-1931				PROCEEDINGS, 1: 408-18, 2: 414. FGS.
	1) HENDRICKS, ORTENCIA		1868-1889	30 MAR 1887	1888		
	2) HENDRICKS, CHLOE		1873-1950	14 MAR 1891	1892	1910	
	3) STODDARD, ANNA V.		1869-1938	22 MAR 1893	1896	1909	
*132	MERRILL, MARRINER WOOD	(1)	1832-1906				SEE PETER ERICKSON FGS FOR DATA ON HILDA. SLT FOR 11 FEB 1906 DESCRIBES FUNERAL OF MARRINER, ADDING THAT ALL EIGHT WIVES WERE PRESENT. MATTHIAS F. COWLEY SAID HE PERFORMED MARRIAGE TO HILDA, ABOUT 1903. TRIALS. ACTUAL DATE WAS PRESUMABLY 7 APR 1901, AS CITED IN QUINN, 72.
	1) ATKINSON, SARAH ANN		1834-1916	11 NOV 1853	1854	1875	
	2) STANDLEY, CYRENE		1840-1917	5 JUL 1856	1857	1876	
	3) BAINBRIDGE, ALMIRA		1849-1906	1 APR 1865	1866	1886	
	4) KINGSBURY, MARIA L.		1852-1925	4 OCT 1867	1868	1892	
	5) JONSSON, ELNA			11 FEB 1885			
	6) JACOBSON, JENNIE			1886			
	7) ANGUM, ANNA SOPHIA			18 JUL 1889			
	8) ERICKSON, HILDA M.		1869-1954	7 APR 1901	1902		
*133	MERRILL, OLONZO DAVID	(1)	1867-1939				FGS FOR MARY STATES "POLOGAMY [SIC] MARRIAGE PREFORMED [SIC] IN PRESTON [IDAHO] BY APOSTLE COWLEY GIVING THE TMPL SEALING CEROMONY [SIC] 'WITH ANGELS AS OUR WITNESSES.'"
	1) WHITTLE, MARTHA L.		1868-	13 DEC 1888	1901	1902	
	2) HANSEN, MARY LAURA		1881-1963	23 FEB 1904	1904	1920	
*134	MICKELSEN, MORRIS	(1)	1866-1951				BOTH WIVES AND FAMILIES LISTED WITH HUSBAND IN DUBLAN ROM, EARLY TO 1912. SEE HATCH AND HARDY, STALWARTS SOUTH OF THE BORDER, 487-488.
	1) JENSEN, MINNIE		1868-1931		1887	1907	
	2) SORENSEN, MATHILDA		1878-1933	OCT 1903	1904	1911	
*135	MILLER, JR., REUBEN G.	(1)	1861-1912				MARTHA'S FGS SAYS MARRIAGE WAS AT PRESTON, IDAHO. MATTHIAS F. COWLEY PERFORMED PLURAL MARRIAGE. TRIALS. 1920 CHURCH CENSUS LISTS ANNA WITH HUSBAND.
	1) WINDER, ANNA JANE		1860-	10 DEC 1884			
	2) NELSON, MARTHA		1870-1912	25 JUN 1903	1904		
*136	MORRELL, JOSEPH	(1)	1856-1906				MARY'S FGS SAYS MARRIAGE WAS AT LOGAN, UTAH. MATTHIAS F. COWLEY PERFORMED MARRIAGE. TRIALS. MARGARET "WIDOW" IN 1920 CHURCH CENSUS.
	1) ROWLAND, MARGARET		1858-1937	20 FEB 1879	1879	1893	
	2) DAINES, MARY ANN		1868-1952	23 OCT 1898	1900	1904	
*137	MORRIS, ROBERT	(1)	1843-1913				JOSEPHINE MEYER MORRIS AND SARAH DUNCAN WERE BOTH LISTED AS "WIDOW" ON 1914 CHURCH CENSUS. MARY MONSON MORRIS WAS LISTED "WIDOW" ON THE 1930 CHURCH CENSUS. SEE ALSO QUINN, 53.
	1) WATSON, JANET		1842-1898	21 DEC 1867	1868	1880	
	2) MEYER, JOSEPHINE H.		1856-1923	14 OCT 1878	1879	1889	
	3) MONSON, MARY		1850-	16 JUL 1884			
	4) DUNCAN, SARAH ELLEN		1868-	18 JUL 1900	1902	1904	

No.	Name / Wives	Birth–Death	Marriage Date			Notes
138	(1) MORTON, WILLIAM ALBERT	1866-				DATA OBTAINED FROM 1914 AND 1920 CHURCH CENSUS, WHERE ANNIE IS LISTED WITH HUSBAND, AND IVINS R OF M FOR JOSEPHINE.
	1) ALLEN, ANNIE H.	1867-		1889		
	2) ERICKSON, JOSEPHINE	1872-	13 JUN 1903		1906	
*139	(1) MUIR, DAN	1866-1939				GEORGENIA'S FGS SAYS MARRIAGE IN SALT LAKE CITY. LILLY LISTED WITH DAN ON 1914 CHURCH CENSUS. JUDSON TOLMAN ADMITTED PERFORMING PLURAL MARRIAGE. REED SMOOT DIARIES, 1 OCT 1910.
	1) FISHER, LILLY MAY	1866-	15 APR 1888	1894	1902	
	2) BARLOW, GEORGENIA	1877-1937	14 JUN 1906	1907	1914	
*140	(2) MUSSER, JOSEPH WHITE	1872-1954				MATTHIAS F. COWLEY PERFORMED PLURAL MARRIAGE FOR MARY AND JOSEPH. TRIALS. BOTH PLURAL MARRIAGES WERE IN SALT LAKE CITY.
	1) BORGQUIST, ROSE S.	1872-1954	29 JUN 1892	1893	1907	
	2) HILL, MARY CAROLINE	1874-1930	13 MAR 1902	1903	1915	
	3). SHIPP, ELLIS R.	1879-1966	24 JUL 1907	1908	1919	
*141	(3) NAEGLE, GEORGE CONRAD	1860-1935				MAGGIE MARRIED BY ANTHONY W. IVINS, AND LAST TWO SAME DAY BY ABRAHAM O. WOODRUFF, ALL THREE RECORDED IN IVINS R OF M. MARRIAGE TO MAGGIE WAS POLYGAMOUS, AS SABIA WAS WITH HUSBAND. SEE THOMAS ROMNEY, _LIFE STORY OF MILES PARK ROMNEY_, (INDEP.,MO.:ZIONS, 1948), 322, 363; AND HATCH AND HARDY, STALWARTS SOUTH OF THE BORDER, 499-502.
	1) HIGBEE, SABIA	1857-	18 FEB 1880	1894		
	2) FAUST, ANNA	-1902	JUL 1886			
	3) ROMNEY, MAGGIE	1880-1902	23 JUL 1899	1900	1902	
	4) JAMESON, JENNIE D.	1886-	18 NOV 1903	1905	1924	
	5) KEELER, PHILINDA	1878-	18 NOV 1903	1905	1922	
142	(1) NAEGLE, JR., JOHN CONRAD	1864-1928				MARRIAGE TO MILLICENT WAS IN COLONIA JUAREZ. FGS.
	1) BRINGHURST, ANNA A.	1870-1948	30 MAR 1887	1888	1904	
	2) JAMESON, MILLICENT	1884-1936	31 AUG 1903	1904	1912	
143	(1) NEWTON, SAM SMITH	1858-1954				MARRIAGE LICENSE ISSUED TO SAM AND AMY IN WYOMING ON CITED DATE, PER UINTAH COUNTY MARRIAGE BOOK C, p. 542. THESE TWO THEN WENT TO CANADA, LEAVING FIRST WIFE AND SEVEN CHILDREN IN SALT LAKE CITY.
	1) PARKER, SARAH E.	1861-1905	21 APR 1881	1882	1902	
	2) JOHNSON, AMY SUSAN	1869-1963	22 JAN 1901	1901	1914	
144	(1) NIELSEN, CARL EMIL	1860-1935				EMMA'S FGS SAYS MARRIAGE WAS IN COLONIA JUAREZ.
	1) MOLLER, ULRIKKA B.	1867-1951	4 SEP 1884	1885	1907	
	2) JENSEN, SINE OLINE	1865-1942	7 JUN 1890	1891		
	3) KJAR, ANNA JOHANNA	1867-1954	1 JAN 1895			
	4) STEVENS, EMMA JANE					

*=DISTG. CHURCH SERVICE	NAME OF HUSBAND / NAMES OF WIVES	NUMBER POST-1890 PL. MARRS.	BORN-DIED	MARRIAGE DATE	YEAR FIRST CHILD	YEAR LAST CHILD	REMARKS
145	NORBERG, HYRUM	(1)	1859-1929				HUSBAND'S NAME CHANGED FROM ANDRES HERMAN NORDBERG. JANE'S FGS SAYS MARRIAGE IN SALT LAKE CITY.
	1) JOHNSON, WILHELMINA		1864-1939	24 JAN 1884	1884	1905	
	2) SHEPHERD, JANE		1870-1918	2 JAN 1901	1901	1911	
146	OCKEY, WILLIAM COLE	(1)	1850-1925				SEE FGS FOR JOSEPH WHITE SIMPSON AND HANS CARL L JORGENSEN. MARRIAGE TO OVENA PERFORMED BY ANTHONY W. IVINS. IVINS R OF M. LIZZETTA LISTED AS LIVING WITH HUSBAND IN 1920 CHURCH CENSUS.
	1) WEBB, SARAH ANN		1851-1887		1883		
	2) SIMPSON, LIZZETTA		1868-1943	21 JUL 1898			
	3) JORGENSEN, OVENA		1874-1963	14 SEP 1898	1905	1910	
147	OLSEN, CHRISTIAN F.	(1)	1858-1940				ALEXANDER F. MACDONALD MARRIAGE RECORD, 17 OCT 1890, AS CITED IN QUINN, 60. SEE ALSO JAMES UNSWORTH FGS, AND HYRUM ROM, EARLY TO 1901, WHERE BOTH WIVES ARE LISTED WITH HUSBAND.
	1) ANDERSON, EMMERETT		1884-	7 NOV 1882	1884		
	2) UNSWORTH, MARY ANN		1867-1894	17 OCT 1890	1891	1884	
*148	PARKINSON, GEORGE C.	(1)	1857-1920				MATTHIAS F. COWLEY PERFORMED THE PLURAL MARRIAGE. TRIALS. FANNIE'S FGS SAYS THE MARRIAGE WAS IN COLORADO SPRINGS, COLORADO.
	1) DONEY, LUCY MARIA		1861-1931	14 APR 1881	1884	1899	
	2) WOOLLEY, FANNIE		1864-1946	17 JAN 1902	1903		
149	PAYNE, EDWARD WILLIAM	(2)	1867-1945				LUCY'S FGS SAYS MARRIAGE IN COLONIA JUAREZ, AND THAT CEREMONY PERFORMED BY "APOSTLE OWEN WOODRUFF IN PRESENCE OF ANTHONY W. IVINS." A SIMILAR SEALING TOOK PLACE FOR THE SECOND [PLURAL] MARRIAGE. MARRIAGE TO ROSALIA PERFORMED BY ANTHONY W. IVINS. IVINS R OF M. SEE DUBLAN ROM, AND BX.3, FD.23, KIMBALL YOUNG COLLECTION.
	1) BEAN, EMILY		1869-				
	2) FARR, LUCY ALICE		1880-1951	26 NOV 1899	1900	1919	
	3) TENNY, ROSALIA		1884-	1 MAR 1903	1903	1913	
*150	PIERCE, BRIGHAM HORACE	(1)	1864-1944				BOTH MARY AND SARAH LISTED WITH HUSBAND IN JUAREZ ROM, 1906-1916. SARAH MARRIED BY ANTHONY W. IVINS. IVINS R OF M.
	1) HARRIS, MARY E.		1864-				
	2) THORNTON, MARTHA A.		1871-1892	26 SEP 1889	1890	1892	
	3) HARRIS, SARAH ELLEN		1881-	11 MAR 1904			

No.	Name / Wives		Born–Died	Marriage			Notes
151	PRATT, MATHONI W.	(1)	1856-1937				JUDSON TOLMAN ADMITTED PERFORMING A PLURAL MARRIAGE TO A MR. PRATT. REED SMOOT DIARIES, 1 OCT 1910. AGNES' FGS SAYS MARRIAGE IN SALT LAKE CITY.
	1) SHEETS, ELIZABETH		1862-1918	17 NOV 1880	1882	1906	
	2) URE, AGNES JONES		1870-1949	25 JUN 1903	1905	1910	
*152	PRATT, HELAMAN	(1)	1846-1909				MARRIAGE TO BERTHA PERFORMED BY ANTHONY W. IVINS. IVINS R OF M. SEE ALSO DUBLAN ROM, EARLY TO 1912.
	1) BILLINGSLY, EMELINE		1852-1910	25 JUL 1868	1870	1895	
	2) WILCKEN, ANNA J.		1854-1929	20 APR 1874	1876	1896	
	3) WILCKEN, BERTHA C.		1863-1947	14 JUL 1898	1899	1905	
153	RAINEY, DAVID WILLIAM	(1)	1858-1934				JANET'S FGS SAYS THEY WERE MARRIED BY PRESIDENT CHARLES O. CARD IN CANADA.
	1) OLSEN, MARY MARIA		1859-1903	24 MAR 1880	1881	1902	
	2) HANSON, JANET		1870-1945	3 AUG 1892	1893	1903	
*154	REDD, LEMUEL HARDISON	(1)	1836-1910				NORA REDD PERDUE INTERVIEW, p.9. POHP, SAID WHEN HER GRANDFATHER TOOK THIRD WIFE, HE WAS EXCOMMUNICATED, AND "IT NEARLY KILLED HIM." SHE ADDED THAT SHORTLY BEFORE HE DIED IN 1910, HE WAS REBAPTIZED. ALSO SAID HER GRANDMOTHER WAS UNHAPPY WITH NEW WIFE, AS SHE WAS "COMPLETELY INCOMPATIBLE WITH REST OF FAMILY." REDD WAS MADE PATRIARCH IN 1895.
	1) BUTLER, KEZIAH JANE		1836-1895	2 JAN 1856	1856	1879	
	2) CHAMBERLAIN, SARIAH L.		1849-1908	18 OCT 1866	1890	1895	
	3) HOLT, MARY MARIA			POST-MANIFESTO			
*155	RICH, BENJAMIN ERASTUS	(2)	1855-1913				MATTHIAS F. COWLEY PERFORMED PLURAL MARRIAGE TO LAURA. TRIALS. DATE FROM COWLEY'S MARRIAGE RECORD, AS CITED IN QUINN, 80. MARRIAGE DATE FOR ALICE FROM WILLIAM MC LACHLAN FGS. SEE ALSO 1920 AND 1925 CHURCH CENSUS.
	1) FARR, DIANA		1858-1933	27 DEC 1877	1878		
	2) BOWRING, LAURA		1858-	13 APR 1898	1905	1896	
	3) JENSEN, ANDREA						
	4) MC LACHLAN, ALICE C.		1869-1942	4 OCT 1899	1903		
*156	RICHARDSON, CHARLES EDMUND	(1)	1858-1925				MARRIAGE TO DAISIE PERFORMED BY ANTHONY W. IVINS. IVINS R OF M. SEE ALSO DIAZ ROM, 1886-1907, AND JUAREZ ROM, 1906-1916.
	1) ADAMS, SARAH LOUISA		1867-1942	27 JAN 1882	1883	1905	
	2) ROGERS, SARAH M.			17 MAY 1887			
	3) JACOBSON, CAROLINE R.		1872-1945	19 JAN 1889	1889	1918	
	4) STOUT, DAISIE		1884-1953	13 MAR 1904	1906	1918	
157	RICHINS, ORSON ORIEL	(1)	1862-1926				SARAH'S FGS SAYS MARRIAGE WAS IN COLONIA DIAZ.
	1) HENEFER, RACHEL		1861-1946	25 MAY 1881	1882	1906	
	2) FAWCETT, CAROLINE		1862-1892	20 OCT 1881	1883	1890	
	3) SHURTLIFF, SARAH A.		1865-1947	23 FEB 1895	1895	1911	
158	RILEY, ARTHUR	(1)	1852-1930				MARRIAGE TO SARAH DAVIS PERFORMED BY ANTHONY W. IVINS. IVINS R OF M.
	1) GOODFELLOW, SARAH		1858-1929	10 JUN 1876	1877	1905	
	2) DAVIS, SARAH LYDIA		1864-1938	16 SEP 1897	1898	1905	

*=DISTG. CHURCH SERVICE	NAME OF HUSBAND / NAMES OF WIVES	NUMBER POST-1890 PL. MARRS.	BORN-DIED	MARRIAGE DATE	YEAR FIRST CHILD	YEAR LAST CHILD	REMARKS
*159	ROBERTS, BRIGHAM HENRY	(1)	1857-1933				APOSTLE REED SMOOT SAID HE "HAS IT FROM AN HONEST SOURCE THAT MRS DR. SHIPP STAYED WITH HER FORMER HUSBAND IN SPRINGVILLE AT THE HOUSE OF THE INFORMANT IN 1892." CARL A. BADGER DIARIES, 3 MAR 1906, CHURCH ARCHIVES. CHARLES M. OWEN STATED THAT AN ANALYSIS OF MAGGIE'S RESIDENCES SHOWED CONCLUSIVELY SHE WAS LIVING WITH SHIPP AS LATE AS 1892. FD.12, p.111, OWEN LETTERBOOK, CHURCH ARCHIVES. OWEN LETTERBOOK, p.191, SAYS MAGGIE ASSUMED NAME AND STYLE OF MRS. ROBERTS IN APRIL 1897, BUT HE BELIEVED THEY WERE MARRIED IN 1894. ONE LADY TOLD DAUGHTER IN 1923 THAT WHEN ROBERTS' FIRST WIFE DIED, MAGGIE BECAME LEGAL WIFE INSTEAD OF CELIA, AS DICTATED BY CUSTOM. CIVIL MARRIAGE WAS IN CHICAGO. SUSA DUNFORD LETTER TO LEAH WIDTSOE, COPY IN POSSESSION OF VICTOR W. JORGENSEN, LOGAN, UTAH.
	1) SMITH, LOUISA						
	2) DIBBLE, CELIA ANN		1864-1936	2 OCT 1884	1885	1902	
	3) SHIPP, MARGARET		1849-1926	ABOUT 1894			
*160	ROBINSON, JOSEPH E.	(2)	1867-1941				MATTHIAS F. COWLEY PERFORMED PLURAL MARRIAGE FOR ROBINSON. TRIALS. COWLEY MARRIAGE RECORD GIVES 7 APR 1901 DATE IN SALT LAKE CITY, QUINN, 81; 3 OCT 1901 DATE IN SALT LAKE CITY FOR OTHER WIFE, QUINN, 90.
	1) KNELL, MINNIE ANN		1869-1953	21 DEC 1891	1892	1903	
	2) BROWN, WILLMIA		1877-	7 APR 1901	1902	1921	
	3) SPENCER, HARRIET		1877-1965	3 OCT 1901	1903	1917	
*161	ROBINSON, SAMUEL JOHN	(2)	1863-1948				JOHN W. HEDER FGS. ANNIE'S FGS SAYS MARRIAGE PERFORMED BY GEORGE TEASDALE IN COLONIA JUAREZ. JOHN LOST BISHOPRIC OVER 1907 MARRIAGE. JUAREZ HIGH COUNCIL MINUTES, 1904-1908, 30 NOV 1907, CHURCH ARCHIVES. H. GRANT IVINS IN "POLYGAMY IN MEXICO AS PRACTICED BY THE MORMON CHURCH, 1895-1905," UNIVERSITY OF UTAH LIBRARY, IDENTIFIES MAUD HEDER AS WOMAN ROBINSON MARRIED IN 1907. SAYS IT WAS SOLEMNIZED IN MANTI TEMPLE BY "AN OLD MAN."
	1) STARK, MINNIE AMELIA		1869-1934	28 JUL 1886	1887	1914	
	2) WALSER, ANNIE E.		1870-1903	1 APR 1891	1895	1903	
	3) HEDER, MAUD ELIZ.		1887-	SUMMER 1907			
*162	ROMNEY, MILES ARCHIBALD	(3)	1869-1939				MARRIAGE TO LILLY PERFORMED BY ANTHONY W. IVINS. IVINS R OF M. ELIZABETH'S FGS SAYS MARRIAGE IN COLONIA JUAREZ. MARRIAGE TO EMILY WAS IN THE MANTI TEMPLE. SEE MANTI MESSENGER, 13 MAY 1910.
	1) TURLEY, FRANCES		1873-1953	15 SEP 1889	1890	1913	
	2) BURRELL, LILLY		1877-	23 OCT 1898	1900		
	3) BURRELL, ELIZABETH		1881-	13 SEP 1902	1904	1924	

No.	Name		Dates	Marriage			Notes
	4) BURRELL, EMILY		1878-	2 NOV 1909	1910	1923	
*163	ROMNEY, MILES PARK	(1)	1843-1904				SEE THOMAS ROMNEY, LIFE STORY OF MILES PARK ROMNEY, (INDEP.,MO.: ZION'S, 1948), pp. 282-3, 363-5. MILLIE SNOW WAS A WIDOW OF ERASTUS SNOW, HAD CONSIDERABLE MONEY, AND WAS RESENTED BY FIRST FOUR WIVES BECAUSE OF HUSBAND'S ATTENTIONS TO HER. SEE JAMES HULETT 12 MAR 1937 INTERVIEW OF THOMAS C. ROMNEY, BX.3, FD.39, KIMBALL YOUNG COLLECTION.
	1) HILL, HANNAH HOOD		1842-1929	10 MAY 1862	1863	1887	
	2) LAMBOURNE, CAROLINE		1846-1879	23 MAR 1867	1868	1870	
	3) COTTAM, CATHERINE		1855-1918	15 SEP 1873	1874	1896	
	4) WOODBURY, ANNIE		1858-1930	1 AUG 1877	1879	1897	
	5) SNOW, MILLIE EYRING			FEB 1897			
164	SANDERS, MOSES MARTIN	(1)	1853-1926				FGS SAYS LORA STARR DIVORCED 1 SEP 1920. LILLIAN'S FGS SAYS MARRIAGE WAS IN COLONIA JUAREZ.
	1) CHENEY, ELIZABETH E.		1857-1940	23 NOV 1872	1874	1897	
	2) STARR, LORA ANN		1858-1924	25 MAR 1879	1858	1897	
	3) JACKSON, LILLIAN MAY		1878-1942	21 FEB 1901	1902	1915	
*165	SEARS, WILLIAM GAILEY	(1)	1873-1943				JOSEPH W. SUMMERHAYS ADMITTED PERFORMING PLURAL MARRIAGE TO ATHELIA CALL IN 1906 UNDER DIRECTION OF JOSEPH F. SMITH. REED SMOOT DIARIES, 12 OCT 1910.
	1) MC MURRIN, AGNES M.		1873-	8 APR 1897	NO CHILDREN		
	2) CALL, ATHELIA VIOLA		1888-	21 FEB 1906	1907	1929	
*166	SESSIONS, BYRON	(1)	1851-1928				JANET'S FGS SAYS MARRIAGE AT BYRON, WYOMING. MATTHIAS F. COWLEY PERFORMED PLURAL MARRIAGE FOR SESSIONS ABOUT 1902. TRIALS. QUINN, 94, SAYS DATE WAS 14 SEP 1903.
	1) TWOMBLY, IDELLA WINN		1856-1923	31 OCT 1870	1871	1894	
	2) EASTON, JANET		1883-1966	14 AUG 1903	1905	1906	
*167	SHERWOOD, ROBERT	(1)	1858-1942				ALICE'S FGS SAYS MARRIAGE IN SALT LAKE CITY. ELIZABETH LISTED WITH HUSBAND IN SALT LAKE 32ND WARD ROM, 1905-1930.
	1) SHAW, ELIZABETH		1849-	19 APR 1883	1890		
	2) SHAW, HARRIET			26 OCT 1888	1902	1916	
	3) SCHOENFELD, ALICE T.		1874-1960	28 AUG 1901			
168	SILVER, JOHN ASKIE	(1)	1855-1916				MARRIAGE TO NELL PERFORMED BY ANTHONY W IVINS. IVINS R OF M.
	1) PRATT, ORTHENA		1863-1936	25 NOV 1880	1882	1900	
	2) CLAWSON, NELL YOUNG		1872-1937	31 JAN 1904	1905	1910	
169	SILVER, JOSEPH ASKIE	(1)	1857-1930				MARRIAGE TO ELIZABETH PERFORMED BY ANTHONY W. IVINS. IVINS R OF M.
	1) WATSON, MARY E.		1856-1941	18 MAR 1880	1881	1904	
	2) FARNES, ELIZABETH		1870-1925	24 JAN 1898	1899	1912	
*170	SKOUSEN, DANIEL	(1)	1865-1940				SARAH'S FGS SAYS MARRIAGE WAS PERFORMED BY MATTHIAS F. COWLEY IN EL PASO, TEXAS.
	1) GREER, MELVINA CLAY		1867-1934	9 DEC 1885	1886	1909	
	2) SPILSBURY, SARAH ANN		1883-1968	24 SEP 1901	1902	1924	

*=DISTG. CHURCH SERVICE	NAME OF HUSBAND / NAMES OF WIVES	NUMBER POST-1890 PL. MARRS.	BORN-DIED	MARRIAGE DATE	YEAR FIRST CHILD	YEAR LAST CHILD	REMARKS
171	SKOUSEN, JR., JAMES NIELS 1) WALSER, IDA 2) MORTENSEN, EMMA F.	(1)	1872-1957 1879- 1877-	30 SEP 1896 9 NOV 1901	1897 1902	1916 1921	EMMA'S FGS SAYS MARRIAGE PERFORMED BY ALEXANDER F. MACDONALD IN COLONIA JUAREZ.
*172	SMART, WILLIAM HENRY 1) HAINES, ANNA 2) WALLACE, MARY ELIZ.	(1)	1862-1937 1867-1938 1857-1920	3 OCT 1888 1902	1889	1909	MATTHIAS F. COWLEY PERFORMED PLUAL MARRIAGE FOR "BROTHER SMART" IN SALT LAKE CITY. TRIALS. IN 13 SEP. 1980 INTERVIEW WITH V. W. JORGENSEN, WILLIAM B. SMART SAID GRANDFATHER MARRIED PLURAL IN 1902 OR 1903. DAUGHTER TO PLURAL WAS RETARDED, AND GRANDFATHER THOUGHT IT WAS GOD'S REBUKE FOR POLYGAMY. SEE GEORGE B. WALLACE FGS, AND WILLIAM B. SMART DIARY, 4,8,21,23 APR 1920, CHURCH ARCHIVES.
173	SMELLIE, JOHN TAYLOR 1) RICKS, MARIA LOADER 2) KIRKHAM, ESTHER RUTH	(1)	1863-1933 1868-1951 1885-1919	9 OCT 1885 3 AUG 1905	1886 1907	1906 1919	ESTHER'S FGS SAYS MARRIAGE WAS IN FRANKLIN, IDAHO.
*174	SMITH, ISAAC 1) ENSIGN, HARRIET C. 2) CARLISLE, ANNA E. 3) FUHRIMAN, ELIZABETH	(1)	1857-1914 1859-1930 1871-1944	28 DEC 1877 12 NOV 1885 2 JUN 1894	1878 1895	1905 1913	ELIZABETH'S FGS SAYS MARRIAGE WAS IN CARDSTON, CANADA.
175	SMITH, JESSE MORONI 1) SMITH, HARRIET EMILY 2) SMITH, PRISCILLA	(1)	1858-1937 1877-1954	5 JAN 1904	1904	1918	MATTHIAS F. COWLEY ADMITTED MARRYING PLURAL WIFE TO SMITH. TRIALS. PRISCILLA MARRIED BY COWLEY IN SALT LAKE CITY. OLIVER SMITH AND DOROTHY WILLIAMS, THE FAMILY OF JESSE NATHANIEL SMITH, 1834-1906, (SNOWFLAKE, AZ., n.d.), 146,152.
*176	SNARR, DANIEL HANMER 1) THOMPSON, ALICE 2) MC CARROLL, PHOEBUS	(1)	1860-1927 1861-1951 1874-1959	16 FEB 1882 27 FEB 1897	1882 1897	1903 1919	IVINS R OF M GIVES MARRIAGE DATE OF 22 JUN 1897, WHICH CONTRADICTS FGS, AS CITED HERE.
*177	STEED, WALTER WILLIAM 1) WILCOX, JULIA MARIA 2) CLARK, ALICE BELLE	(1)	1858-1940 1861-1931 1869-1961	16 SEP 1880 22 JUN 1897	1881 1899	1906 1915	MARRIAGE TO ALICE PERFORMED BY ANTHONY W IVINS. IVINS R OF M.

No.		Name / Wives	Life	Marriage			Notes
178	(1)	STEELE, JR., MAHONRI M.	1870-1937				MATTHIAS F. COWLEY PERFORMED PLURAL MARRIAGE. TRIALS. WIVES WERE HALF-SISTERS. SEE WILLIAM LE FEVRE FGS.
		1) LE FEVRE, CHARLOTTE	1873-1941	2 OCT 1889	1880	1911	
		2) LE FEVRE, MARTHA J.	1872-2933	1 NOV 1901			
179	(1)	STEVENS, DAVID ALMA	1859-1947				MARRIAGE TO MARY PERFORMED AT MANTI, UTAH. FGS.
		1) JOHNSON, AGNES S.	1863-1945	10 NOV 1881	1883	1903	
		2) BOICE, MARY ELMIRA	1875-1951	29 JUN 1896	1905	1911	
180	(1)	STEVENS, WALTER JOSHUA	1856-1912				FGS SAYS MARRIAGE TO SARAH PERFORMED IN COLONIA GARCIA.
		1) KENNEY, ELIZABETH	1863-1948	25 SEP 1879	1881	1907	
		2) HAWLEY, SARAH ELLIS		30 NOV 1900			
181	(1)	STOWELL, BRIGHAM	1854-1943				JOHN W. TAYLOR PERFORMED CEREMONY FOR MARRIAGE TO ELLA IN COLONIA GARCIA. JOHN HENRY SMITH DIARIES 10 MAR 1898.
		1) BYBEE, MARY OLIVE	1862-1941	1 MAY 1879	1880	1905	
		2) BYBEE, RHODA MARIA	1868-1935	26 MAR 1886	1889	1911	
		3) SKOUSEN, ELLA MARIA	1841-1943	10 MAR 1898	1899	1909	
182	(1)	STRINGHAM, JR., BRYANT	1852-1927				MARRIAGE TO SABRINA PERFORMED BY ANTHONY W IVINS. IVINS R OF M.
		1) ELDREDGE, JESSE	1857-1940	6 JUN 1878	NO CHILDREN		
		2) SMITH, SABRINA	1874-1940	22 JUN 1897	1898	1912	
*183	(1)	STUCKI, JOHN ULRICH	1837-1918				ANNA SPORI'S FGS SAYS MARRIAGE IN LOGAN TEMPLE. SEE CHARLES M. OWEN LETTER TO J. ELLEN FOSTER, 26 OCT 1904, OWEN COLLECTION, CHURCH ARCHIVES.
		1) HUBER, MARGARETA	1851-1933	19 AUG 1859	1872	1894	
		2) BUTLER, JANE	1859-1947	1 FEB 1870	1893	1895	
		3) SPORI, ANNA CLARA		23 SEP 1891			
*184	(1)	SUMMERHAYS, JOSEPH W.	1849-1929				JOSEPH SUMMONED BEFORE APOSTLES TO ANSWER CHARGE OF MARRYING AFTER MANIFESTO, WAS DETERMINED GUILTY OF OFFENSE, AND DROPPED FROM CHURCH POSITIONS. SUMMERHAYS SAID JOSEPH F. SMITH APPROVED PLURAL MARRIAGE IN 1898. REED SMOOT DIARIES, 12 OCT 1910.
		1) PARKER, MELISSA	1852-	27 JUN 1870	1885	1893	
		2) BISHOP, MARY	1852-	19 JUN 1882	1883	1892	
		3) BARRETT, SARAH	1863-	5 JUN 1884	1893	1905	
		4) JONSON, HILDA	1870-	18 NOV 1888	1889	1911	
		5) NAME UNAVAILABLE		1898			
*185	(4)	TANNER, HENRY SMITH	1869-1935				LAST FOUR WIVES MARRIED IN SALT LAKE CITY. FGS. MATTHIAS F. COWLEY PERFORMED MARRIGE TO CLARICE THATCHER AND MARY RICHARDS. TRIALS.
		1) WOODLAND, LAURA L.	1867-1958	5 MAR 1890	1891	1908	
		2) RICHARDS, MARY I.	1878-	6 JAN 1901	1902	1913	
		3) THATCHER, CLARICE	1879-1960	19 DEC 1901	1902	1918	
		4) BROWN, LOUETTA	1884-	16 JAN 1904			
		5) RICHARDS, COLUMBIA	1887-	1 FEB 1909	1909	1931	

*=DISTG. CHURCH SERVICE	NAME OF HUSBAND / NAMES OF WIVES	NUMBER POST-1890 PL. MARRS.	BORN-DIED	MARRIAGE DATE	YEAR FIRST CHILD	YEAR LAST CHILD	REMARKS
*186	TANNER, JOSEPH MARION	(3)	1859-1927				JOSEPH HAD SIX WIVES, THREE MARRIED SINCE MANIFESTO. ANNIE CLARK TANNER, A MORMON MOTHER, (SALT LAKE CITY, 1973), 154,172,314. SEE MARGERY W. WARD, A LIFE DIVIDED (SALT LAKE CITY, 1980) FOR ALL WIVES BUT SARAH. MATTHIAS F. COWLEY "MARRIED J. M. TANNER TO MRS. EVANS." TRIALS. CHARLES M. OWEN SAID TANNER TOOK WIDOW OF PRIME EVANS FOR PLURAL. FD.14, p.207, CHARLES M. OWEN COLLECTION, CHURCH ARCHIVES. EVANS MARRIED SARAH TAYLOR 27 APR 1887. CACHE CO. MARRIAGE BK.B, p.10. PRIME EVANS DIED 8 JUL 1901. LEHI ROM, BK.B, p.18. SEE 1900 U.S. CENSUS FOR SARAH. SHE MOVED TO OGDEN 11 OCT 1903, AND TAUGHT AT WEBER ACADEMY UNTIL DEATH ON 15 JAN 1908. OGDEN 4TH ROM, 1908-1918, AND OGDEN STANDARD EXAMINER, 18 JAN 1908.
	1) HARRINGTON, JENNIE		1857-1916	15 NOV 1878	1891		
	2) CLARK, ANNIE		1864-1942	27 DEC 1883	1888	1904	
	3) SNOW, JOSEPHINE		1859-1940	25 JUN 1884	1888	1902	
	4) PETERSON, CARRIE		1870-1956	1900	1903		
	5) EVANS, SARAH TAYLOR		1859-	1903			
	6) HOLMGREN, LYDIA		1875-1952	1904	1907	1910	
*187	TAYLOR, ALONZO LEANDER	(1)	1878-1938				KATIE'S FGS SAYS MARRIAGE WAS IN COLONIA DUBLAN. PERFORMED BY MATTHIAS F. COWLEY. HATCH AND HARDY, STALWARTS SOUTH OF THE BORDER, 659-665.
	1) EYRING, ANNA		1877-	4 AUG 1897	1901	1912	
	2) SPILSBURY, KATIE P.		1881-1953	1 JAN 1906	1907	1916	
188	TAYLOR, ERNEST GUY	(2)	1872-1963				SEE JAMES HENRY MARTINEAU FGS; ROM, JUAREZ, 1906-1916, AND 1925 CHURCH CENSUS. LILLY'S FGS SAYS MARRIAGE AT CARDSTON, CANADA. ERNEST'S HALF-SISTER LENORAH WAS MARRIED SAME PLACE AND DATE BY JOHN A. WOOLF, SO HE LIKELY DID THIS ONE TOO.
	1) CARDON, SELENA V.		1875-1962	20 NOV 1893	1895	1912	
	2) MARTINEAU, GERTRUDE		1870-1927	23 MAR 1901			
	3) HICKS, LILLY S.		1880-1929	16 SEP 1905	1906	1920	
*189	TAYLOR, ERNEST LEANDER	(1)	1852-1917				AT HIS TRIAL BEFORE THE HIGH COUNCIL, TAYLOR ADMITTED MARRYING HIS PLURAL WIFE 13 APRIL 1910 IN THE LOGAN TEMPLE. HISTORICAL RECORD, HIGH COUNCIL MINUTES, JUAREZ STAKE, BOOK D, 1908-1911, 98, ENTRY DATED 19 NOV 1910, CHURCH ARCHIVES.
	1) HOLLADAY, LENORAH			11 DEC 1871			
	2) ARNESEN, MARY M		1861-1928	25 DEC 1876	1878	1901	
	3) SKOUSEN, HANNAH M.		1862-1912	21 NOV 1877	1885	1892	
	4) ALEXANDER, ROSALIE		1870-	13 APR 1910			
*190	TAYLOR, FRANK YOUNG	(2)	1861-1953				MATTHIAS F. COWLEY ADMITTED PERFORMING TWO PLURAL MARRIAGES TO TAYLOR. TRIALS. ELIZABETH'S FGS SAYS HER SISTER ANNIE WAS THIRD WIFE, BUT NO DETAILS. SEE ROBERT LANG CAMPBELL FGS.
	1) CAMPBELL, ELIZABETH		1858-1923	21 MAY 1884	1885	1898	
	2) NEFF, ALICE MAY		1877-1964	3 NOV 1900	1902	1919	
	3) CAMPBELL, ANNIE S.		1860-	POST-MANIFESTO			

*191 — TAYLOR, JOHN WHITAKER (4)

Name	Lifespan	Marriage Date		
TAYLOR, JOHN WHITAKER	1858-1916			
1) RICH, MAY LEONA	1869-1945	19 OCT 1882	1889	1907
2) TODD, NELLIE EVA	1870-1956	25 SEP 1888	1893	1910
3) WOOLEY, JANET MARIA	1880-1962	10 OCT 1890	1902	1913
4) WELLING, ELIZA ROXIE	1880-	29 AUG 1901	1903	1911
5) WELLING, RHODA	1886-1935	29 AUG 1901	1910	1916
6) SANDBERG, ELLEN G.		23 JUN 1909		

THIRD WIFE JANET (NETTIE) GAVE MARRIAGE DATE TO SON SAMUEL. "INTERVIEWS WITH NETTIE M. TAYLOR," JULY, 1947, p.8, BYU LIBRARY. SHE ALSO STATED THAT MATTHIAS F. COWLEY OFFICIATED MARRIAGE TO ELLEN SANDBERG. IBID, p.25. CEREMONY TO WELLING HALF-SISTERS IN FARMINGTON, UTAH, BOTH BY COWLEY. TRIALS, AND RAYMOND TAYLOR TO DELBERT STAPLEY, 26 MAR 1966, JOHN W. TAYLOR CORRESPONDENCE, BX.22, FD.2, JOHN TAYLOR PAPERS, U. OF U. LIBRARY.

*192 — TEASDALE, GEORGE (1)

Name	Lifespan	Marriage Date		
TEASDALE, GEORGE	1831-1907			
1) BROWN, EMMA EMILY	1831-1874	25 AUG 1853	1854	1867
2) HOOK, LILLIAS	1840-1921	14 OCT 1875	1896	
3) PICTON, MATHILDA E.	1858-1893		1880	1882
4) PICTON, MARY L.	1863-1895		1886	1895
5) SCOLES, MARION E.	1865-1898	25 OCT 1898	1898	
6) THOMAS, LETITA	1876-1932	17 MAY 1900		

SEE FGS FOR JAMES PICTON AND PRESTON THOMAS. WHEN TEASDALE MARRIED MARION SCOLES, ALL WIVES WERE DEAD EXCEPT LILLIAS. WHEN HE MARRIED LETITIA THOMAS, ALL WERE DEAD EXCEPT LILLIAS WHOM HE DIVORCED IN 1899. MARRIAGE TO MARION PERFORMED BY ANTHON LUND "ON THE HIGH SEAS." SEE ABOVE, IN CHAP. 6.

*193 — THOMAS, JOSEPH FRANCIS (1)

Name	Lifespan	Marriage Date		
THOMAS, JOSEPH FRANCIS	1858-1934			
1) JACK, MARY JANE	1863-1939	25 JUL 1881	1882	1907
2) MICKELSEN, ETHEL G.	1884-1961	22 JUL 1903	1904	1925

ETHEL'S FGS SAYS MARRIAGE IN SALT LAKE CITY.

*194 — THOMPSON, JAMES (1)

Name	Lifespan	Marriage Date		
THOMPSON, JAMES	1848-1915			
1) PETERSEN, KAREN C.	1848-1926	9 MAY 1868	1869	1891
2) SORENSEN, ANNIE S.	1834-1932	10 APR 1871	1870	1878
3) CHRISTIANSEN, CHR.				
4) NIELSEN, BERTHA J.	1880-	3 MAR 1904	1905	1907

MARRIAGE TO BERTHA BY ANTHONY W. IVINS. IVINS R OF M. JAMES LEFT THREE WIVES IN BRIGHAM, AND TOOK BERTHA TO MEXICO. SEE OLEEN N. STOHL 6 NOV 1905 LETTER TO GEORGE F. GIBBS, GIBBS LETTER BOX CHURCH ARCHIVES. SEE BRIGHAM 3RD ROM, EARLY TO 1932; LIBERTY ROM 1927-1947; DUBLAN ROM, EARLY TO 1912.

*195 — THURBER, ALBERT DANIEL (1)

Name	Lifespan	Marriage Date		
THURBER, ALBERT DANIEL	1854-1931			
1) SHIMMONS, ELEANOR	1853-1883	12 DEC 1876	1878	1883
2) BEAN, SARA ELLA	1865-	24 DEC 1884	1889	
3) GARDNER, AGNES	1865-	18 APR 1896	1897	1913

ROM FOR DUBLAN, EARLY TO 1912, LISTS SARA BEAN WITH HUSBAND UNTIL SHE MOVED 2 DEC 1910. SEE ALSO HATCH AND HARDY, STALWARTS SOUTH OF THE BORDER, 703.

*=DISTG. CHURCH SERVICE	NAME OF HUSBAND / NAMES OF WIVES	NUMBER POST-1890 PL MARRS.	BORN-DIED	MARRIAGE DATE	YEAR FIRST CHILD	YEAR LAST CHILD	REMARKS
*196	TODD, DOUGLAS MC CLAIN	(1)					MARRIAGE OF HANNAH PERFORMED BY MATTHIAS F. COWLEY IN SALT LAKE CITY, SAYS FUNDAMENTALIST WORK, [GILBERT FULTON AND RULON ALLRED], MOST HOLY PRINCIPLE, (MURRAY, UT.:GEMS, 1970-1975),4:94.
	1) DRIGGS, FLORENCE		1860-1935	19 JUL 1887	1888	1889	
	2) LUFKIN, MARION D		1869-1889	10 DEC 1890	1892	1908	
	3) MC MURRAY, HANNAH		1869-1920	22 MAY 1899			
197	TOLMAN, JAREN	(1)	1853-1912				FOR DATA ON MARY BYBEE, SEE FGS FOR FIRST HUSBAND, JOHN FIFE PATTERSON. SEE ROM, BOUNTIFUL 1ST WARD, 1905-1935. IN 1925 CENSUS, SARAH JANE TOLMAN IS LISTED AS WIDOW.
	1) BRIGGS, EMMA		1856-1895	1 JUN 1874	1875	1887	
	2) BRIGGS, MARY ANN		1861-1894	26 DEC 1878	1881	1892	
	3) BURNINGHAM, SARAH JANE		1860-1926	26 MAR 1885	1886	1898	
	4) BYBEE, MARY ALICE		1863-1949	15 JUN 1899	1900	1904	
*198	TOLMAN, JUDSON	(1)					MARY REEVES DIVORCED 1857, AND SOPHIA MERRELL DIVORCED 1869. NO EXACT DATE FOR MARRIAGE TO ELEANOR, BUT FGS SAYS HER FIVE CHILDREN WERE SEALED TO TOLMAN 19 NOV 1908 IN SALT LAKE TEMPLE. TOLMAN WAS EXCOMMUNICATED 3 OCT 1910, IN PART FOR MARRYING ELEANOR ODD.
	1) HOLBROOK, SARAH L.		1826-1916	12 JAN 1846	1847	1863	
	2) REEVES, MARY		1832-1869	20 DEC 1852			
	3) MERRELL, SOPHIA			5 FEB 1856			
	4) STOKER, ZIBIAH J.			5 APR 1869			
	5) ODD, ELEANOR			1908			
*199	TRIPP, ENOCH B.	(1)					ENOCH, SENIOR PRESIDENT OF STAKE SEVENTYS QUORUM, ENTERED INTO A SPECIAL AGREEMENT OF SOME KIND WITH PLURAL ABOUT 1897. SEE QUINN, 55.
	1) NAME UNAVAILABLE			POST-MANIFESTO			
*200	TURLEY, EDWARD FRANKLIN	(1)	1869-1940				ANNIE'S FGS SAYS HER MARRIAGE WAS IN COLONIA JUAREZ. SEE JUAREZ ROM, 1906-1916.
	1) EYRING, IDA ELIZ.		1874-1952	11 OCT 1883	1894	1911	
	2) MARTINEAU, ANNIE S.		1875-1963	6 JAN 1901	1901	1911	
*201	UDALL, DAVID KING	(1)					MATTHIAS F. COWLEY PERFORMED A PLURAL MARRIAGE FOR UDALL, THE LAST OF A NUMBER COWLEY PERFORMED DURING PERIOD 1898-1903. TRIALS.
	1) STEWART, ELIZA L.		1851-1938	1 FEB 1875	1878	1897	
	2) HUNT, IDA FRANCES		1855-1937	25 MAY 1882	1885	1897	
	3) MORGAN, MARY		1858-1915	1903			
*202	WALSER, II, JOHN JACOB	(1)	1849-1937				MARRIAGE TO ELIZABETH PERFORMED BY ANTHONY W. IVINS, IVINS R OF M. DAUGHTER OF FIRST WIFE IN 1937 INTERVIEW TOLD OF REGRET AND RESERVATION HELD
	1) SCHERRER, ANNA E.		1851-1932	4 JAN 1870	1870	1891	
	2) FRISCHKNECHT, MARY		1850-1939	11 SEP 1876	1877	1892	

No.	Name	Birth–Death	Date			Notes
	3) BRAITHWAITE, ELIZ.	1858-1939	19 JAN 1903			BY FIRST TWO WIVES WHEN HUSBAND MARRIED A THIRD. MAY 1937 INTERVIEW WITH MINA WALSER BOWMAN, BX.1, FD.11, AND J. J. WALSER INTERVIEW, BX.4, FD.11, KIMBALL YOUNG COLLECTION.
203	WALSER, III, JOHN JACOB (1)	1872-1962				MAE'S FGS SAYS MARRIAGE PERFORMED IN COLONIA JUAREZ.
	1) WHIPPLE, IDA R.	1876-1943	29 MAR 1894	1885	1917	
	2) ROBINSON, MAE	1879-1902	29 DEC 1901	1902		
*204	WHETTEN, JOHN AMASA (1)	1879-1961				MARTHA'S FGS SAYS SHE WAS MARRIED IN COLONIA GARCIA BY ALEXANDER F. MACDONALD.
	1) JESPERSON, IDA E.	1881-1953	7 MAR 1900	1901	1922	
	2) CARLING, MARTHA E.	1885-1925	23 FEB 1903	1904	1925	
*205	WHETTEN, JOHN THOMAS (2)	1862-1932				JOSEPH LEHI FOUTZ FGS. MARRIAGE OCT. 1900 PERFORMED BY ALEXANDER F. MACDONALD IN COLONIA GARCIA, SAYS MACDONALD MARRIAGE RECORD. QUINN, 88. LUDIE'S FGS SAYS SHE WAS MARRIED BY ALEXANDER F. MACDONALD IN COLONIA JUAREZ.
	1) SAVAGE, AGNES B.	1861-1939	10 DEC 1878	1879	1903	
	2) NIELSEN, EMMA J.	1864-1904	18 DEC 1885	1888	1904	
	3) NELSON, LORANIA	1859-1947	18 OCT 1900	1903	1912	
	4) ELLIS, LUDIE	1875-1946	6 MAR 1903			
*206	WHIPPLE, CHARLES (1)	1863-1919				MARY'S FGS SAYS MARRIAGE PERFORMED BY JOHN W. TAYLOR IN COLONIA JUAREZ. THIS DATE CONFIRMED IN JOHN HENRY SMITH DIARIES, 6 MAR 1898.
	1) HANSEN, ANNIE C.	1871-1962	12 OCT 1886	1890	1911	
	2) WALSER, MARY LOUISE	1877-1918	22 FEB 1898	1899	1917	
*207	WILLEY, DAVID ORSON (1)	1849-1929				CHURCH CENSUS FOR 1914 AND 1925 LISTS FIRST WIFE WITH HUSBAND IN BOUNTIFUL UTAH FIRST WARD, AND THE SECOND WIFE IN THE BOUNTIFUL UTAH SECOND WARD.
	1) BARLOW, MARY A.	1851-1936	7 DEC 1868	1869	1893	
	2) COWLEY, ANN ELIZ.	1864-1930	1900	1901	1904	
208	WILLIS, GEORGE WILLIAM (1)	1853-1940				SEE SALT LAKE 19TH WARD ROM, 1887-1908. FIRST WIFE DIED. SECOND WIFE SAID SHE WANTED TO LIVE IN NEPHI WITH FEEBLE MOTHER, AND WAS WILLING FOR LOUISA TO MARRY GEORGE AS LEGAL WIFE. WAS DONE WITHOUT CHURCH SANCTION AND GEORGE WAS DISFELLOWSHIPPED, SALT LAKE STAKE HISTORICAL RECORD, 1910-1912, 17 AUG 1910, pp.92-104.
	1) HAWKINS, ELIZA P.	1855-1905	8 MAY 1879	1880	1896	
	2) HAWKINS, LOUISE J.	1861-1919	24 AUG 1888	1889	1900	
	3) PATTERSON, LOUISA M.		JUN 1910			
209	WILSON, DAVID JOHNSON (1)	1843-1912				MIRIAM'S FGS SAYS BRIGHAM YOUNG JR. PERFORMED MARRIAGE NEAR LAS PALOMAS, MEXICO. BOTH WIVES ARE LISTED WITH HUSBAND IN MORELOS ROM, 1900-1909.
	1) JOHNSON, JULIA D.	1845-1918	26 JUL 1867	1868	1890	
	2) COX, MIRIAM ADELIA	1878-	1 JUL 1895	1896	1912	

*=DISTG. CHURCH SERVICE	NAME OF HUSBAND / NAMES OF WIVES	NUMBER POST-1890 PL. MARRS.	BORN-DIED	MARRIAGE DATE	YEAR FIRST CHILD	YEAR LAST CHILD	REMARKS
*210	WILSON, GUY CARLTON	(2)	1864-1942				ANTHONY W. IVINS PERFORMED MARRIAGES TO AGNES AND ANNA. IVINS R OF M. SEE 1925 CHURCH CENSUS FOR ELVIRA ELIZABETH HARTZBURG; AND HATCH AND HARDY, STALWARTS SOUTH OF THE BORDER, 781-788.
	1) HARTZBURG, ELVIRA E.		1864-1951	25 SEP 1885	NO CHILDREN		
	2) STEVENS, AGNES M.		1883-1965	13 MAR 1902	1902	1905	
	3) IVINS, ANNA LOWRIE		1882-1967	13 MAY 1903	1904	1921	
*211	WILSON, LYCURGUS ARNOLD	(1)	1856-1940				FGS FOR LYCURGUS WILSON, 1828-1911. THE 1920 CHURCH CENSUS RECORDS ZINA LYON WILSON AS WIDOW, WITH COMMENT "FROM FOREST DALE WARD- IS TEMPLE WORKER." 1935 CENSUS LISTS JULIA ANN GLINES.
	1) TUCKER, ALICE MARIE		1865-1907	9 OCT 1876	1879		
	2) PATTEN, MELISSA		1851-	23 DEC 1885	1886	1907	
	3) LYONS, ZINA		1866-	5 JAN 1890			
	4) GLINES, JULIA ANN			15 APR 1907			
*212	WOOD, EDWARD JAMES	(1)	1866-1956				SEE ALFRED SOLOMON FGS FOR 1 FEB 1904 MARRIAGE DATE.
	1) SOLOMON, MARY ANN		1868-1962	28 SEP 1892	1893	1911	
	2) SOLOMON, ADELAIDE		1871-1961	1 FEB 1904	1905	1909	
*213	WOODRUFF, ABRAHAM OWEN	(1)	1872-1904				MATTHIAS F. COWLEY ADMITTED MARRYING AVERY CLARK TO WOODRUFF. TRIALS. FOR JAN. 1901 DATE, SEE ELIZA AVERY CLARK PAPERS, pp.32,42,43. CHURCH ARCHIVES.
	1) WINTERS, HELEN MAY		1873-1904	30 JUN 1897	1899	1903	
	2) CLARK, ELIZA AVERY		1882-1953	JAN 1901	1904		
*214	WOODRUFF, WILFORD	(1)	1807-1898				MATTHIAS F. COWLEY STATED IN HIS HEARING BEFORE THE TWELVE THAT HE BELIEVED WOODRUFF MARRIED AGAIN THE YEAR BEFORE HE DIED. TRIALS. COWLEY, WHOSE MATER-NAL GRANDMOTHER WAS SISTER TO WOODRUFF'S FIRST WIFE, WAS APPARENTLY CONSIDERED "FAMILY." COWLEY BECAME APOSTLE IN OCT. 1897, SAME AS WILFORD'S OWN SON, ABRAHAM O. WOODRUFF. APOSTOLIC APPOINTMENTS DURING THAT PERIOD WERE OFTEN RESERVED FOR SONS AND FAMILY OF PREVAILING PROPHET. COWLEY ALSO LATER WROTE BOOK ON WOODRUFF. ALSO, FUNDAMENTALISTS LATER CLAIMED WOODRUFF MARRIED MOUNTFORD AFTER THE MANIFESTO. SEE ABOVE, CHAP. 6. QUINN, 63-5.
	1) CARTER, PHOEBE W.		1807-1885	13 APR 1837	1838	1853	
	2) JACKSON, MARY ANN		1818-1894	15 APR 1846	1847		
	3) SMITH, EMMA		1831-1912	13 MAR 1853	1857	1879	
	4) BROWN, SARAH		1834-1909	13 MAR 1853	1854	1873	
	5) STOCKING, SARAH		1838-1907	31 JUL 1857	1861	1878	
	6) MOUNTFORD, LYDIA		1848-1917	SEP 1897			

No.	Name	Dates	Marriage date	Year	Year	(1)	Notes
215	WOOLF, JOHN WILLIAM	1869-1950				(1)	MATTHIAS F. COWLEY PERFORMED A PLURAL MARRIAGE FOR WOOLF ABOUT 1899-1901. <u>TRIALS.</u>
	1) LAYNE, LUCINDA M.	1870-1913	27 JUN 1889	1890			
	2) NAME UNAVAILABLE		POST-MANIFESTO				
216	WOOLFENDEN, CHARLES	1863-1924				(1)	MARION'S FGS SAYS HER MARRIAGE WAS IN SALT LAKE CITY. LAURA'S FGS SAYS SHE WAS DIVORCED FROM CHARLES IN 1910.
	1) BIRD, LAURA	1862-1937	1891	1892	1901		
	2) REYNOLDS, MARION G.	1876-1952	31 DEC 1904	1910	1919		
*217	WRATHALL, JAMES L.	1860-1932				(1)	CHARLOTTE'S FGS SAYS HER MARRIAGE WAS PERFORMED IN THE SALT LAKE TEMPLE.
	1) HUNTER, PENINAH S.	1862-1937	2 FEB 1882	1883	1905		
	2) ROWBERRY, CHARLOTTE	1873-1934	23 AUG 1900	1902	1916		
218	WYNDER, HENRY ERNEST	1852-1934				(1)	LOUISA'S FGS SAYS MAUD MARRIED IN SALT LAKE TEMPLE. CHURCH CENSUS FOR 1914 LISTS LOUISA MARRIED TO WYNDER IN CARDSTON, CANADA.
	1) PARKER, LOUISA	1855-1932	17 AUG 1874	1875	1896		
	2) SKINNER, MAUD ELLEN		4 AUG 1903				
*219	YOUNG, JR., BRIGHAM	1836-1903				(1)	MARRIAGE DATE AND BIRTH FOR HELEN ARMSTRONG IN EPHRAIM ROM, BOOK C, EARLY TO 1923. MATTHIAS F. COWLEY PERFORMED A PLURAL MARRIAGE FOR YOUNG ABOUT 1902. <u>TRIALS.</u> QUINN SETS THE DATE IN AUG 1901. QUINN, 72. NAME OF THIS WIFE UNAVAILABLE.
	1) SPENCER, CATHERINE		1856				
	2) CARRINGTON, JANE M.		15 MAR 1857				
	3) FENTON, MARY ELIZ.		7 MAR 1868				
	4) PERKINS, RHODA E.						
	5) STEVENS, ABBIE	1870-1954	1 OCT 1887	1888	1902		
	6) ARMSTRONG, HELEN E.	1856-	7 JUN 1890				
	7) NAME UNAVAILABLE		AUG 1901				
*220	YOUNG, NEWEL KNIGHT	1877-1956				(1)	GENEVA'S FGS SAYS MARRIAGE WAS IN COLONIA JUAREZ. THE MARRIAGE WAS PERFORMED BY ALEXANDER F. MACDONALD. ALSO SEE V. W. JORGENSEN INTERVIEW WITH H. GRANT IVINS, 18 JUL 1972, CSUF ORAL HIST. COLLEC.
	1) BUCHANAN, CASTINA	1876-1944	13 JUL 1898	1899	1922		
	2) COOLEY, GENEVA	1883-	19 NOV 1900	1902	1923		

*131/220 = 59.55%
SERVED ON MISSION, AS
BRANCH PRESIDENT,
BISHOP, STAKE PRESIDENT,
OR APOSTLE.

262 PLURAL MARRIAGES
BETWEEN OCT. 1890 AND DEC. 1910,
INVOLVING 220 DIFFERENT MEN.

Name Index

Throughout this index, the abbreviation *pl.m.* is used in place of the term *plural marriage.*

Abraham (of Old Testament): and Mormon pl.m., 5, 10; law of, and household model, 97–101, 336, 351; and deception, 375
Adams, Brooks, 373
Adams, William, 54
Alcott, William, 86
Alexander, Thomas Glen, xxi, 150, 298, 300, 328
Allen, Alice, 236
Allen, David O., 85
Allen, George, 236
Allen, George Vivian, 226
Allen, James, 286
Allred, Byron Harvey, Jr., 318
Allred, Eva, 314
Allred, Myra Irene, 314
Anderson, Amanda, 171
Anderson, Ellen, 184
Anderson, James Henry, 220
Anderson, Lewis, 323, 324
Anderson, Nephi, 210
Anderson, Stephen Pearl, 85–86
Arrington, Leonard James, xx, 58
Austin, Elna Cowley, 266

Badger, Carlos Ashby: and Abraham H. Cannon, 220; and Brigham H. Roberts, 247; on pl.m., 286, 315–16, 319, 379; lament of, concerning dishonesty, 376; on redeeming reputation of church, 262; and Smoot investigation, 256; and testimony of Joseph F. Smith, 252. *See also* Reed Smoot investigation
Bailey, Joseph Weldon, Sr., 147, 376
Baker, Ray Stannard, 251
Ball, Samuel Frederick, 169
Bancroft, Hubert Howe, 42
Barnett, John W., 208
Barry, Richard, 289, 297
Bartch, George W., and Lorenzo Snow statement on pl.m., 203n.108
Bateman, Samuel, 137
Bates, Irene May, 8
Beadle, John Hanson, 15
Beecher, Henry Ward, 227
Benedict, Amzi, 103
Bennett, John Cook, 8, 365
Bennion, Harriet, 209
Bennion, Heber: and Mormon deception, 375; oath to perpetuate pl.m., 316; permission for pl.m., 327; proposals to women, 169, 216, 320
Bennion, Lowell "Ben," xx
Bentley, Joseph Charles, 170, 171, 216, 319
Berry, James Henderson, 268
Bierbower, Victor, 50
Bodell, James, 93–94
Bowles, Samuel, 40
Bradley, Martha Sontag, 343

Subject Index

Throughout this index, the abbreviation *pl.m.* is used in place of the term *plural marriage*.

abolitionists, and sexual concerns, 61n.6, 88

Abrahamic law, 97

adultery: in early church, 5–6; in California, 221; in Mexico, 174; Mormon pl.m. and crime of, 44, 46, 182, 184, 245, 324–25

affective reward, and the modern family, 351

Alberta, Canada, Mormon settlements in, 178

American Female Guardian Society, 248

American flag, charge of Mormon disrespect for, 46

American home: endangered by Mormonism, 41–43, 248–49, 287, 289, 296; similarity to Mormon home, 339

American Indians, Mormon intermarriage with, 5, 16

American party, 287

American Social Hygiene Association, 285

amnesty petitions, and 1890 Manifesto, 139, 144, 145, 149–50, 161n.104

antinomianism, and early Mormonism, 3

anti-polygamy crusades: and delay in demise of pl.m., 72n.76; legislation during, in U.S. and Mexico, 43–44, 46–47, 49, 174; Mormon strategies for,

48–50, 52–55; political interpretation of, 56–60; and Reed Smoot, 292–95; by *Salt Lake Tribune*, 288–90; violence during, 48, 49–50. *See also* Canada, deception

Anti-Polygamy Standard, 47

apostasy: and female domination, 99; and pl.m. in antiquity, 100

archival records, unavailability of, 328, 392

Articles of Faith, church approval of, 135

asceticism, in Mormonism, 92

Asian societies, and pl.m., 42, 100

bigamy, laws on, 44, 173, 179–82. *See also* plural marriage

birth control, 286, 294

blacks, compared to Mormons, 41

Book of Mormon, 142; on pl.m., 5, 236n.46

"Brighamites," 256, 348. *See also* Reorganized Church of Jesus Christ of Latter Day Saints; Smoot investigation

British North American Act (Canada, 1867), 179

Burlington, Wyoming, 311

California, legality of pl.m. in, 221

Canada: anti-polygamy laws in, 130, 179, 181; colonization policies of, 179; friction in, between Reorganized Church of Jesus Christ of Latter Day

threat of, during Smoot investigation, 261

disorder in early American life, 4, 7–8

divorce: bogus, 226–27; of George Teasdale, 225–26

Doctrine and Covenants: revelation on pl.m. in, 9–10, 16; and 1890 Manifesto, 150, 297

economic despoilation, Mormon charges of, 57–58

Edmunds Act (1882), 140; and amnesty, 144; and Canadian law, 181, 199–200n.76; effects on Mormons, 46, 48; and 1892 Utah law, 152; and Mormon migration to Mexico, 167; provisions of, 46, 84

Edmunds-Tucker Act (1887): and escheatment proceedings, 143; and Mormon millenarianism, 56; provisions of, 49

"Elder Freeman," and Mormon patriarchy, 98

enclosure, social, 365–66

Endowment House, 45, 53, 129, 139–40

England, persecution of Mormons in, 289

Episcopal Women's Home Mission Society, 59

escheatment proceedings, 143–44

eugenics: and intermarriage with Indians, 5; and Mormon society, 102–3, 189, 298–99; 345

Eugenics Education Society, 299

Everybody's, 288, 289, 290

excommunication: instances of, 8, 266, 292, 313, 320, 325, 326, 328; and post-Manifesto pl.m., 292, 294; to protect church, 313

"exiles," the, 258

family, social history of, 65n.31

family life: and anti-polygamy crusade, 41–42, 56–60; and contemporary Mormonism, 349–50; pattern of, 336; self-reliance in, 287, 301

Farmington, Utah, 207

Female Relief Society, 8–9, 313, 366

female suffrage, 49

film industry, and Mormonism, 289, 290

First Presidency: and Cullom Struble

bill, 129; and state criminal code, 245; statements on pl.m., 55, 78n.121, 89, 147, 170, 290, 292–93, 297, 342; on truth-telling and deceit, 363, 364

friendship, in early church, 365–66

Garrett Evangelical Theological Library, xx

Gentiles, avarice of, 57–58; political gains of, 127

Georgia (state), and Rudger Clawson, 210

Grand Junction, Colorado, 211

Granite Stake, 292

Great Basin, Mormon trek to, 12–13

Harper's, 208

heaven, in Mormon thought, 6, 349–51

History of Human Marriage (Edward Westermarck, 1922), and origin of polygamy, 112n.56

honesty, Mormon reputation for, 363–64. *See also* deception

hypocrisy: attacks on Victorian, 285, 286; charged by Mormons, 47, 89; charged against Mormons, 376–77

Idaho: 1889 constitution of, 127; election in, 298; Mormon dissimulation in, 368; test oath of, 130

Immigration and Naturalization Service, 296

India, polygamous converts in, 348

"inner circle," rumor of, 312–13

Isn't One Wife Enough? (Kimball Young, 1954), xix–xx, xxi, 47, 221

Israelites: and the levirate, 213–14; Mormons compared to, 50; and pl.m., 100

Jeffries-Johnson prize fight, 289

Jesus, and pl.m., 97, 100. *See also* apostacy; Second Coming of Jesus

"Josephites." *See* Reorganized Church of Jesus Christ of Latter Day Saints

Journal History of the Church, deceptive entries in, 223–24

"Juab, a High Private in Israel," satirical comments of, 376–77

Juarez Stake High Council: and Samuel J. Robinson, 315; and Miles A.

A Note on the Author

B. CARMON HARDY, professor of history at California State University, Fullerton, is the author of numbers of studies in ancient history, religious history, Mormon history, and American constitutional history.